AF774573

Knowledge Management: Theory and Practice

Knowledge Management: Theory and Practice

Edited by Douglas Schwartz

Clanrye International
www.clanryeinternational.com

Clanrye International,
750 Third Avenue, 9th Floor,
New York, NY 10017, USA

Copyright © 2019 Clanrye International

This book contains information obtained from authentic and highly regarded sources. Copyright for all individual chapters remain with the respective authors as indicated. All chapters are published with permission under the Creative Commons Attribution License or equivalent. A wide variety of references are listed. Permission and sources are indicated; for detailed attributions, please refer to the permissions page and list of contributors. Reasonable efforts have been made to publish reliable data and information, but the authors, editors and publisher cannot assume any responsibility for the validity of all materials or the consequences of their use.

Trademark Notice: Registered trademark of products or corporate names are used only for explanation and identification without intent to infringe.

ISBN: 978-1-63240-782-5

Cataloging-in-Publication Data

Knowledge management : theory and practice / edited by Douglas Schwartz.
p. cm.
Includes bibliographical references and index.
ISBN 978-1-63240-782-5
1. Knowledge management. 2. Management. I. Schwartz, Douglas.
HD30.2 .K56 2019
658.403 8--dc23

For information on all Clanrye International publications
visit our website at www.clanryeinternational.com

CLANRYE INTERNATIONAL

Printed in China.

Contents

Preface

The world is advancing at a fast pace like never before. Therefore, the need is to keep up with the latest developments. This book was an idea that came to fruition when the specialists in the area realized the need to coordinate together and document essential themes in the subject. That's when I was requested to be the editor. Editing this book has been an honour as it brings together diverse authors researching on different streams of the field. The book collates essential materials contributed by veterans in the area which can be utilized by students and researchers alike.

Knowledge management is the process of realizing organizational goals by sharing, managing and creating information of an organization. It is a multidisciplinary field with applications in the areas of computer science, business administration, library and information science, etc. Knowledge management strives to facilitate organizational objectives like innovation, knowledge sharing, improved performance, etc. This book is a compilation of chapters that discuss the most vital concepts and emerging trends in this field while also understanding changes that have occurred owing to technological advancement in the last few decades. It also elucidates new techniques and their applications related to the field of knowledge management in a multidisciplinary manner. Those who are looking to gain deeper insights into the subject will be greatly assisted by this book.

Each chapter is a sole-standing publication that reflects each author´s interpretation. Thus, the book displays a multi-facetted picture of our current understanding of application, resources and aspects of the field. I would like to thank the contributors of this book and my family for their endless support.

Editor

Convergence of functional areas in information operations

Author:
Brett van Niekerk[1]

Affiliation:
[1]School of Management, IT and Governance, University of KwaZulu-Natal, South Africa

Correspondence to:
Brett van Niekerk

Email:
brettvn@gmail.com

Postal address:
Private Bag X54001, Durban 4000, South Africa

Background: Contemporary technology and its rapid rise to a ubiquitous nature are affecting the way in which technology is used. This holds implications for military information operations and information warfare concepts as the previously separate functional areas are increasingly overlapping due to the increased convergence of information technology. Objective: The aim of the article is to illustrate the convergence of the functional areas of information operations through the use of reported examples and descriptive models.

Methods: A qualitative review and analysis of practitioner documents, academic publications, and other reports is conducted. The diverse views of this phenomenon are contrasted and discussed. The possible implications of the convergence and possible management techniques are proposed and discussed.

Results: There is strong opinion that the domains are not converging, however practice shows that there is an increasing overlap of operational considerations and organisational structure.

Conclusion: It is concluded that the domains are not converging, but the operations and management of the information operations functional areas may converge, and this has an impact across all functional areas that needs to be taken into consideration.

Introduction

Contemporary technology such as social media, the rapidly growing prevalence of wireless networking technology and the expanding capabilities of smart mobile devices result in what is termed as digital convergence. This has an impact on the military use of information technology, namely information operations (IO) and information warfare (IW), as the technology upon which the different functional areas are based converge and evolve. Through the use of examples and descriptive models, the convergence of the functional areas of information warfare and information operations is discussed.

An overview of information operations, information warfare and their constituent functional areas is provided, after which the existing relationship amongst the main functional areas is described through the use of generally accepted models of information technology and reviews of existing debates on the topic. The convergence through the prevalence of contemporary information technology is illustrated through the use of reported examples, and the implications of the convergence and management thereof are discussed.

Methodology

The convergence of information operations, in particular between electronic warfare and computer network operations, is being debated, mostly in practitioner forums. There is limited academic contribution to these debates, but it has been indicated that there is a need for academic models for information operations (Armistead 2010:108). This article aims to fill the gap by providing an academic perspective on the debate and by proposing an alternative model to those discussed previously.

The research takes an interpretivist stance in that the analysed documents that consider convergence in information operations are often authored by practitioners whose reasoning is not only intended to understand the concept but to actively participate in defining it. The approach taken is inductive, seeking to develop theory on the convergence amongst the functional areas in information operations. A qualitative document analysis of reports and examples, combined with logical argument, is used to derive on-going convergence and the potential impact thereof. Rouse and Dick (1994:51) illustrate the importance of qualitative research for information systems '... to capture holistic real-world answers to real-world problems in a way that is not possible in a quantitative context'. Publication databases and search engines were used to identify academic and practitioner publications and documents which consider the topics of interest. Search engines were used to identify relevant news reports that illustrate the existence of the concepts under discussion. A total of 11 academic or practitioner publications and 18 news reports were identified. All of these are considered in the article.

Functional areas in information operations

This section describes the various functional areas of information operations. The definition of IO and IW varies by country and organisation. Usually this reflects the specific strategy or focus that is employed. For this paper, two definitions will be considered. Denning (1999) defines IW as the following:

> … offensive and defensive operations against information resources of a 'win-lose' nature. It is conducted because information resources have value to people. Offensive operations aim to increase this value for the offence while decreasing it for the defence. Defensive operations seek to counter potential losses in value. (p. 21)

Brazzoli (2007) considers IW to be as follows:

> All actions taken to defend the military's information-based processes, information systems and communications networks and to destroy, neutralise or exploit the enemy's similar capabilities within the physical, information and cognitive domains. (p. 219)

These definitions highlight the value of information and that certain activities seek to change or maintain the current value or status of the information through activities relating to information assets and related infrastructure and systems. The notion of different domains is also raised: people or psychological, virtual and physical aspects of information. Whilst the military aspect is emphasised, Cronin and Crawford (1999) indicate that information operations can be applied to non-military situations, supporting the views considering information operations as an extension of IW to non-conflict scenarios (such as peacetime and periods of increased competition).

Computer network operations (also known as cyber-warfare) focus on computer networks and the Internet. It comprises of computer network exploitation (intelligence gathering), computer network attack, computer network defence and computer network support. In some instances, this is extended to include the protection of critical infrastructure from attacks through computer networks (Brazzoli 2007:221; Van Niekerk 2011:39–40). This functional area is the newest functional area and is yet to be fully established.

Electronic warfare (EW) focuses on the electromagnetic spectrum, comprising of electronic protection, electronic support and electronic attack. This most commonly includes the jamming, detection and interception of signals (Joint Chiefs of Staff 1998:II–5).

Psychological operations (PSYOP) are actions taken to influence a population's perceptions, attitudes and behaviour (Brazzoli 2007:221). PSYOP can be considered to be limited to military operational areas whereas strategic communication and propaganda can be considered to be of a larger scale, aimed at national or international audiences ranging from competition to conflict scenarios.

Other notable areas deal with intelligence gathering, command and control and the network support to operations and decision-making. It also includes data and audio and imagery communication via wired and wireless networks and infrastructure (Brazzoli 2007:221). This results in a shift from the traditional platform-centric operations and command and control to the network-centric form where information can be shared amongst platforms so that everyone has access to the same information. The intelligence process of gathering, analysing and disseminating data and information to support the decision-making process (command and control) is therefore key. Offensive operations attempt to disrupt these capabilities of the adversary, and defensive operations seek to maintain these capabilities in allied and own forces (Brazzoli 2007:221).

Porche *et al.* (2013:25–28) indicate that there are problems with the current definition and construction of IO: There is a lack of common vision ranging from too focussed to too broad. Many functional areas are treated as compartmentalised (Porche *et al.* 2013:24), and there is no explanation as to how it will act as a co-ordinating function or as to the relationships amongst the different functional areas. The next section describes the relationships between different functional areas of IO through the use of examples and positions advocated in documents.

Relationships amongst functional areas

There has been much debate regarding the relationship between EW, cyber-warfare and computer network operations and the implications of the various forms of terminology. Smith and Knight (2005:53) apply EW concepts to network security. This indicates a number of parallels between EW and cyber-warfare such as jamming and denial-of-service (DoS) or flares and honeypots.

A report by the US Government Accountability Office indicates that the two domains should be considered as separate (Chabrow 2012). Knowles (2013:48) proposes that cyber-space is a man-made physical environment, including telecommunication, data, networks and processors. In contrast, the electromagnetic spectrum is natural. Wireless communication is seen as the human exploitation of an existing natural space whereas cyber-space is a purely man-made construct. However, it can be argued that the physical components of the telecommunication and data networks that form cyber-space are based upon guided or radiated electromagnetic signals and therefore part of the electromagnetic spectrum (Clifford 2011:41; Hahn 2010: 44–46). Clifford (2011:41) argues that it is incorrect to say that cyber-space and the electromagnetic spectrum are equivalent due to the fact that they are based on similar physics. Some of the discussion revolves around terminology: Borque (2008:30–40) discusses whether cyber-operations are a combination of EW and computer network operations and concludes that EW and cyber-operations are separate. Cloud (2007:10–12) takes the contradictory view that cyber-operations entail a broader domain and include the electromagnetic spectrum, indicating that EW is a subset of cyber-operations.

The use of the psychological and cyber-domains is also related. The concept of hacktivism can be considered a combination of two areas: Activism can be seen as a form of psychological operation, and hactivism combines it with cyber-warfare concepts. Therefore website defacement can be described as cyber-enabled PSYOP. In some instances, the cyber-attack is meant to create the psychological impact such as the tactics used by the group Anonymous. The attack on the website of the South African Police Service was a cyber-attack with the intent to cause a psychological impact. It is reported that sensitive information on whistle-blowers was publicly released and that the attackers claimed that it was in retaliation for slow investigations in the Marikana mine shooting (Tubbs 2013). Anonymous Africa targeted a number of websites in Zimbabwe and South Africa with DoS attacks in protest against the Zimbabwean Government (Alfreds 2013; Daily News Correspondent 2013). There are reports of Israel hacking into phone voicemail systems to leave messages (StrategyPage.com 2009). This can be seen as an example of cyber-delivered PSYOP. There is also a possible relationship with EW and PSYOP in that radio or television broadcasts could be jammed to prevent them from being used to incite violence as happened in Rwanda (Van Niekerk & Maharaj 2009:6).

A number of espionage operations have been conducted over the Internet. These are cyber-attacks based on malicious, code-infecting targeted systems which then copy files onto a server from where the attackers can retrieve them. Major attacks of this type are the GhostNet cyber-espionage in 2009 and Red October, discovered in 2013 after an estimated five years of operation (Higgins 2013; Information Warfare Monitor 2009). In 2013, details surfaced of data-collection activities by US intelligence agencies that were monitoring telecommunications meta-data and online communications (Greenwald & MacAskill 2013). However the most recognised case is that of Wikileaks, a website which posts information from whistle-blowers online. The major releases which created both support and condemnation of the website internationally were the series of releases of US military information

BOX 1: Relationship of IW Areas to the OSI Model and IP Layers

OSI Layers	IP Layers	Functional Area
Application	Application	PSYOPs, C2W
Presentation		Network Warfare
Session		
Transport	Transport	
Network	Network	
Data-link	Data-link	Electronic Warfare
Physical	Physical	

TABLE 1: Proposed Layer Model for IW.

Layer	Functional area
Utility	C2W, PSYOPs
Grey area	
Connection	Network warfare
Grey area	
Access (wired and wireless)	Electronic warfare

Source: Maasdorp, F. & Du Plessis, W., 2012, 'Using a layered model to place EW in context within the informationsphere', *Proceedings of the 4th Workshop on ICT Uses in Warfare and the Safeguarding of Peace 2012 (IWSP 2012)*, 16 August 2012, Sandton, pp. 29–33.

and diplomatic cables (Gragido & Pirc 2011:193–195; Van Niekerk & Maharaj 2011:7–8). These incidents indicate a strong relationship between intelligence, counter-intelligence and cyber-space.

As EW targets primarily radiate the use of the EMS (but can conceivably have an effect on guided transmissions as directed-energy) and are concerned with the modulation and frequency of these transmissions, it is applicable to the physical layer of the OSI model and may extend to the data-link layer. As cyber-space is the interconnection of systems and networking, it can be considered to extend from the data-link layer to the presentation layer, and in some cases, it overlaps with the application layer. Other areas, such as PSYOP and command and control, occur at the application layer, as these are ultimately end-user functions where the key aspect is their presentation of information. The functional areas can similarly be mapped to the Internet Protocol (IP) layers as illustrated in Box 1.

Maasdorp and du Plessis (2012:29–33) propose another layered model to describe the relationship amongst the various aspects of IW and IO. This is shown in Table 1. Three layers are proposed: the utility layer, which is what humans will work with and consciously use; the connection layer, which is the logical connections of a network; and the access layer, which is the electromagnetic transport of analogue or digital bits. Overlap between the layers and their corresponding IW functional areas are allowed through the grey areas (Maasdorp & du Plessis 2012:29–33).

The convergence of functional areas through contemporary information technology

Contemporary technology such as the ubiquitous nature of mobile and wireless technology and social media are increasing the overlap amongst the domains and may therefore result in the convergence of IW functional areas.

The most discussed area for potential convergence is cyber-operations and EW, largely due to the evolution of wireless and mobile technology. Retired General Cartwright expressed views regarding the links between EW and cyber-operations (Freedberg 2013b), which are corroborated by reports that the development of new EW technology for the US Army is being complicated by the role of cyber-warfare and new attack methods. Chabrow (2012) also indicates that the management of EW is being complicated by the role and synergies with computer network operations. In conjunction with the development of the new EW systems, a new doctrine for cyber-electromagnetic operations is being developed (Freedberg 2013a), and a new training centre for the US Army is to incorporate aspects of cyber-operations, EW and other communications-related actions (Gould 2013). This culminated in a US Army doctrine for cyber-electromagnetic activities where such operations are seen as the overlap amongst cyber-space operations, electronic warfare and spectrum management operations (Department of the Army 2014:1–2). Similarly, the US Air Force is developing systems for 'spectrum warfare' which will cover EW, cyber-operations and other aspects. Some of the associated programs include research into 'net-enabled electronic warfare technologies' (Keller 2013). This indicates that the electromagnetic spectrum, traditionally the focus of EW, is now being related to computer networks. Another project is aimed at detecting cyber-attacks through the use of radio-frequency measurement and signals intelligence (Prince 2012). This can be seen as an intersection of intelligence, EW and cyber-operations.

Mobile technology, in particular smartphones and tablets, has integrated a number of forms of technology, which would previously have been separate tools for conducting espionage. They have integrated navigation, camera and video capture and the ability to transmit these wirelessly. They support Web browsing, have integrated social media connectivity and can function as a basic telephone in addition to having a variety of other applications. These include a hacking tool and a method for PSYOP message delivery (Van Niekerk & Maharaj 2012:4–7).

The mobile-phone infrastructure is different from traditional fixed-line communications where the data and voice channels are separate. With mobile phones, it is feasible that data-based attacks can impact the voice channels (Amoroso 2013:102). In addition, by targeting the wireless transmission using EW, both voice and data can be simultaneously disrupted or compromised. The introduction of voice over IP (VOIP) allows voice to be carried over the data networks. Many instant-messaging applications provide support for text, voice, video or a combination of these, which are transmitted over data networks. These forms of communication are susceptible to standard network attacks. Examples may include disruption by DoS and possible interception of and eavesdropping on communication.

TABLE 2: Mentions of areas converging.

Cyber-EW	Cyber-intelligence	Cyber-PSYOP	EW-PSYOP
12	4	7	1

TABLE 3: Sentiment regarding convergence.

Pro-convergence	Anti-convergence
6	4

Social media is a useful tool for PSYOP, and as it is cyber-based, it can be seen as a combination of these two as cyber-security concerns to protect the accounts used in such operations will also be relevant. The open nature of social media enables operators to gather intelligence on targeted individuals or groups to enable them conduct PSYOP on these targets (Van Niekerk 2012). Social media can be used on a large-scale in what can be called social IW by allowing groups to protest online with global support and organise and guide physical protests. Examples of this are the Arab Spring demonstrations and the related Occupy movement (Kamzi 2011; Madrigal 2011).

A number of cases discussed in this section will commonly be called convergence. However, Knowles (2013:48) suggests that convergence as a term is over-used and often misused and that sharing is a more appropriate term when discussing this phenomenon. The motivations for separate domains discussed in this section are largely limited to the domains. It is possible that the domains themselves remain separate, but the operations and management related to those domains converge. Therefore, the functional areas of IO can converge. Maasdorp and du Plessis (2012:32–33) support this view to an extent, indicating that there should at least be interaction between researchers and operators in the various fields to increase the efficiency and effectiveness of efforts. The increase in combined training for electronic warfare and cyber-operations indicates that there is a strong view that operations, or the management thereof, in these domains can be combined or integrated from a practical perspective.

Summary of convergence concepts regarding information operations

This section summarises the prior discussions regarding convergence. Table 2 illustrates the number of discussions related to the convergence between specific functional areas. As is evident, the focus is on cyber-operations and the electromagnetic spectrum. There is also some focus on the psychological aspects of cyber-operations, probably due to the number of hacktivist or propaganda-motivated cyber-attacks. The weakest overlap is between EW and PSYOP. Whilst there is some possible overlap between this two, the scope is very limited.

Table 3 illustrates the sentiment regarding convergence: Documents that take a pro-convergence perspective slightly outnumber those that take an anti-convergence perspective.

Implications of the convergence of functional areas in information operations

This section discusses the implications of the convergence of the functional areas of IO. These affects could be ethical, legal and operational and could affect the structuring of units or organisations and require specific management techniques.

The disruptive nature of networked communications

Whilst cyber-operations are still emerging and not yet fully established, they are having disruptive effects on previously established functional areas. The result of the shift to network-centric operations is a primary driver of convergence. This results in an upheaval of previously established functional areas. As was described above, computer network operations are complicating the management of EW, and this may also be the case for other functional areas such as PSYOPs. In addition to the other implications discussed below, specialists in many functional areas are required to adjust their thinking, and many may be dissatisfied with or resistant to some of the implications of convergence.

Legal and ethical considerations

The availability of information due to networked communication has increased drastically, and the open nature of social media has hastened this. A legal issue with conducting PYSOP on social media is that it may be difficult to restrict the operation to a specific target population due to its global availability. Therefore, it is highly likely that unintended audiences could access the content. This becomes problematic when there are legal restrictions on the population that is to be targeted. In addition, whilst a specific website may be for a specific nationality, it may be hosted in a different country that is off-limits. Therefore, targeting the audience of the webpage may fall into a grey area, legally speaking. The implications of this are that, when conducting cyber-enabled PSYOP, very careful legal analyses should be conducted to ensure that some legal boundary is not inadvertently crossed, which could result in severe embarrassment should a public outcry result.

The use of social media for mass influence or mass surveillance has additional ethical and legal concerns, particularly surrounding the misuse of these capabilities. An example is the use of social media by Pakistanis to threaten Indian citizens living in a particular area (Abbas 2012). These citizens then left the area in panic, causing a humanitarian crisis. Social media can be used to frame or misrepresent people as fake profiles can be created under names or legitimate profiles can be compromised with the specific goal of using these profiles to conduct misbehaviour for which the real person will then be blamed. Mass surveillance, legitimate or otherwise, has the real possibility of infringing on personal rights, particularly on privacy. The revelations that the US intelligence agencies were accessing a variety of communications resulted in a massive international outcry (Leyden 2013; Vijayan 2013). The very revelations of the communication intercepts and the information released by Bradley Manning and Wikileaks (Gragido & Pirc 2011:192–195) fall within an ethical grey area. Their actions can be seen as a severe breach of security and irresponsible behaviour. However, their claimed motives and the views of their supporters are that this information is of public interest and illustrate governments' misuse of power. The releases were a form of IO in that the perpetrators were aiming to alter perceptions against the various governments and agencies. However, there seems to be an attitude that mass surveillance and cyber-espionage are allowable as long as you do not get caught: The US often complained about apparent Chinese incursion into their networks, and then the intercept revelations were made (Leyden 2013). French authorities are also showing anger. However, there are reports that they are involved in similar activities (Crowley 2013:12; Leyden 2013; Vijayan 2013). Many nations conduct espionage on competitors and allies alike (Crowley 2013:12), and the vast array of interconnected digital and telecommunications networks makes it easier to intercept or steal that information.

Legal jurisdiction over data and signals may become problematic. Data may cross multiple national boundaries between the sender and receiver, and with cloud computing, data may permanently reside outside of the owner's national borders. Likewise, radiated electromagnetic signals may cross national borders. These signals or data transfers may then be subjected to a wide variety of data or communication laws. If psychological or data attacks transit via a third nation, can this nation consider itself as under attack (when the attack is not aimed at it)? If this question can be answered, it still needs to be proved who the actual perpetrator is, as one of the problematic aspects of cyber-warfare is the difficulty of attribution (Liff 2012:412). This indicates that other attacks delivered through cyber-warfare tactics will probably be difficult to attribute. This perceived difficulty in attributing attacks may provide a feeling of invisibility and encourage activity which borders or crosses the line into being unethical whilst the perpetrators make the assumption that they will not be discovered.

Another issue with the difficulty of attribution is retaliation against an innocent party. This becomes more likely with the attacker actively framing a third party, hoping that the latter will get the blame. Should the retaliation against an attack be destructive in nature, it is imperative that the attribution information is accurate as this may inadvertently target innocent civilians whose system had been compromised by the attacker.

Organisational restructuring

In a business environment, Dennis and Durcikova (2012:109, 452) indicate that technological convergence of voice, video and data results in the audiovisual, IT and telecommunication departments of organisations merging to cope with the integrated technology. In a similar way, military units for PSYOP, EW, communication and cyber-warfare may find themselves strongly supporting each other, and joint-functionality IO cells may be formed for operations.

In a corporate setting, the corporate-communication and public-relations functions need to be concerned with the cyber-dimension in a more dynamic fashion. Not only do they need to run email communications to stakeholders and maintain traditional webpages, but they need to protect the organisation's image on social media. This entails an element of business intelligence where corporate-communication departments need to monitor the social media profiles run by them for negative comments. They also need to have intelligence on other potentially 'hostile' websites and profiles where disgruntled clients or employees could complain or behave in a manner damaging to the corporate image.

From an operational perspective, there is now a broader range of technology that need to be managed, integrated into operations and secured. Due to overlaps in domains and technology, the impact of operations may be broader than expected, and it may become difficult to contain operational effects. This then calls for improved business and competitive intelligence, particularly in the areas of assessing operational impacts. New committees may be required, or existing committees may need additional members with more or different specialities.

IO units or cells could therefore be comprised of a number of specialists working together, each of whom are experts in a specific area. Each specialist provides in-depth knowledge of their individual area. However, their expertise in other areas may be limited, and different views may cause conflict. An alternative is that the IO unit or cell is comprised of generalists who have grounding in multiple (or all) areas but are not necessarily experts in any. The generalists may be able to work together better due to common training and expertise. However, they may not have the depth of understanding that specialists would, potentially resulting in mistakes.

Porche *et al.* (2013) suggest separating the technical and psychological components in IO, and making commanders responsible for the integration of these when required. These authors indicate that the convergence of electronic warfare and cyber-operations requires personnel to have new specialities, pointing to a tendency to having generalists in technical areas (Porche *et al.* 2013:25). This will then effectively require two sets of specialists: those who deal with the technical aspects (cyber and EW) and those who deal with the psychological aspects (PSYOPs, strategic communications and public affairs). As the commanders are expected to be responsible for integration, they could then be considered as generalists.

Management techniques

The convergence of IO functional areas provides those with hostile intent with a variety of 'payloads' and delivery methods. At a strategic level, this may be managed to a certain degree by international policies and agreements. Operations including cyber and psychological aspects should be clarified in international law, particularly as it relates to armed conflict.

At the operational and tactical levels, the use of management information systems for command and control of cyber-operations and EW, such as the proposed systems described by Keller (2013) and the integrated cyber and electronic warfare system (Hatamoto 2013), will increase the efficiency of these operations by providing commanders with decision-support tools. These support systems can be utilised for both technical (EW and cyber) and psychologically based (including strategic communication) operations. These systems will necessitate efficient knowledge management and intelligence, which can be supported by the operations themselves (cyber-espionage and electronic intelligence) for data acquisition.

Training will need to be adjusted to cater for the converging operations. Those with technical skills will need to learn both EW and cyber-warfare concepts, as well as some of the psychological aspects of IO. The psychological operators will need to have combined training for PSYOP and more common public affairs practices with an introduction to the technical aspects, particularly the limitations regarding their use. The extent to which the cross-training is implemented will be determined by the structure of IO units and the extent to which they comprise of specialists or generalists as discussed above. Commanders, who will need to co-ordinate and ensure the integration of operations, will need to have extensive cross-training.

To ensure that operations do not cross any legal or ethical boundaries, legal advisors should be attached to IO cells or should advise commanders overseeing the activities.

Conclusion

IO consists of various functional areas, and a number of operational relationships exist amongst them. The overlaps are becoming larger due to the rapid uptake of wireless technology and social media. The article presented a qualitative document analysis to determine the nature of the convergence and the views thereof. There are many views on the convergence of functional areas in IO. Some strongly advocate that the cyber and electromagnetic domains should be kept separate. This article motivates that the domains can remain separate, but the operations and management thereof must be converging. This has management implications such as legal and ethical considerations for operations, organisational structure and training.

Acknowledgements

Competing interests

The authors declare that they have no financial or personal relationships which may have inappropriately influenced them in writing this article.

References

Abbas, M., 2012, 'Web 2.0: Pakistan's new weapon?', CIOL.com, 21 August, viewed 23 August 2012, from http://www.ciol.com/ciol/news/108402/web-pakistans-weapon

Alfreds, D., 2013, 'ANC admits website hack attack', News24, 14 June, viewed 17 June 2013, from http://www.news24.com/Technology/News/ANC-admits-website-hack-attack-20130614

Amoroso, E.G., 2013, *Cyber attacks: Protecting national infrastructure*, Elsevier, Waltham, M.A.

Armistead, L., 2010, *Information operations matters*, Potomac Books, Washington, D.C.

Borque, J., 2008, 'A (pragmatic) future for joint electronic warfare: Does EW + CNO = Cyber?', *Journal of Electronic Defence* 31(9), 30–40.

Brazzoli, M.S., 2007, 'Future prospects of information warfare and particularly psychological operations', in L. le Roux (ed.), *South African army vision 2020*, pp. 217–232, Institute for Security Studies, Pretoria.

Chabrow, E., 2012, 'Aligning electronic and cyber warfare', viewed 11 July 2012, from http://www.govinfosecurity.com/aligning-electronic-cyber-warfare-a-4930

Clifford, J., 2011, 'What electronic warriors should know about physics, language and concepts', *Journal of Electronic Defense* 34(3), 40–47.

Cloud, D.W., 2007, 'Integrated cyber defenses: Towards cyber defense doctrine', Master's dissertation, Naval Postgraduate School.

Cronin, B. & Crawford, H., 1999, 'Information warfare: Its application in military and civilian contexts', *The Information Society* 15(4), 257–263. http://dx.doi.org/10.1080/019722499128420

Crowley, M., 2013, 'Spy vs. spy', *Time Magazine*, 11 November, p. 12.

Daily News Correspondent, 2013, 'Hackers target Zimbabwe government', *Independent Online*, 14 June, viewed 14 June 2013, from http://www.iol.co.za/dailynews/news/hackers-target-zimbabwe-government-1.1532349#.UbtKl1EaKM8

Denning, D.E., 1999, *Information warfare and security*, Addison-Wesely, Boston.

Dennis, A. & Durcikova, A., 2012, *Fundamentals of business data communications*, 11th edn., Wiley, New York.

Department of the Army, 2014, *Field Manual 3–38: Cyber electromagnetic activities*, US Department of Defence, Washington, D.C.

Freedberg, S., 2013a, 'Army electronic warfare goes on the offensive: New tech awaits approval', 29 January, viewed 01 April 2013, from http://defense.aol.com/2013/01/29/army-electronic-warfare-new-tech/

Freedberg, S., 2013b, 'Gen. Hoss Cartwright talks immigration, cyber, China & Afghans with iPhones', 25 March, viewed 27 March 2013, from http://defense.aol.com/2013/03/25/gen-hoss-cartwright-talks-immigration-cyber-china-and-afghans-w/

Gould, J., 2013, 'New center, school to bring signals, cyber, EW together', *Army Times*, 25 June, viewed 07 September 2013, from http://www.armytimes.com/article/20130625/CAREERS/306250002/New-center-school-bring-signals-cyber-EW-together

Gragido, W. & Pirc, J., 2011, *Cybercrime and espionage*, Elsevier, Burlington.

Greenwald, G. & MacAskill, E., 2013, 'NSA Prism program taps in to user data of Apple, Google and others', *The Guardian*, 7 June, viewed 09 June 2013, from http://www.guardian.co.uk/world/2013/jun/06/us-tech-giants-nsa-data

Hahn, R., 2010, 'Physics of the cyber-EMS problem: Why we have the language wrong', *Journal of Electronic Defence* 33(11), 44–46.

Hatamoto, M., 2013, 'U.S. Army developing cyber, electronic war arsenal', *Daily Tech*, 31 October, viewed 13 November 2012, from http://www.dailytech.com/US+Army+Developing+Cyber+Electronic+War+Arsenal/article33660.htm

Higgins, K.J., 2013, '"Red October" attacks: The new face of cyberespionage', *Dark Reading*, viewed 17 January 2013, from http://www.darkreading.com/attacks-breaches/red-october-attacks-the-new-face-of-cybe/240146237

Information Warfare Monitor, 2009, 'Tracking GhostNet: Investigating a Cyber Espionage Network', viewed 01 September 2009, from http://128.100.171.10/modules.php?op=modload&name=News&file=article&sid=2386

Joint Chiefs of Staff, 1998, *Joint publication 3–13: Information operations*, 09 October, US Department of Defence, Washington, D.C.

Kamzi, A., 2011, 'How anonymous emerged to occupy Wall Street', *The Guardian*, 27 September, viewed 06 October 2013, from http://www.guardian.co.uk/commentisfree/cifamerica/2011/sep/27/occupy-wall-street-anonymous

Keller, J., 2013, 'Industry: Get ready for spectrum warfare program to cover EW, optics, GPS, and cyber operations', *Military and Aerospace Electronics*, viewed 18 July 2013, from http://www.militaryaerospace.com/articles/2013/07/usaf-answer-presolicitation.html

Knowles, J., 2013, 'Why two domains are better than one', *Journal of Electronic Defence* 36(5), 48–50.

Leyden, J., 2013, 'A post-Snowden US had better not squeal about Chinese cyber-spying', *The Register*, viewed 02 November 2013, from http://www.theregister.co.uk/2013/11/01/snowden_effect_us_china_cyberespionage/

Liff, A.P., 2012, 'Cyberwar: A new "absolute weapon"?: The proliferation of cyberwarfare capabilities and interstate war', *Journal of Strategic Studies* 35(3), 401–428. http://dx.doi.org/10.1080/01402390.2012.663252

Maasdorp, F. & Du Plessis, W., 2012, 'Using a layered model to place EW in context within the informationsphere', *Proceedings of the 4th Workshop on ICT Uses in Warfare and the Safeguarding of Peace 2012 (IWSP 2012)*, 16 August 2012, Sandton, pp. 29–33.

Madrigal, A., 2011, 'The inside story of how Facebook responded to Tunisian hacks', *The Atlantic*, viewed 06 October 2013, from http://www.theatlantic.com/technology/archive/2011/01/the-inside-story-of-how-facebook-responded-to-tunisian-hacks/70044/#

Porche, I.R., Paul, C., York, M., Serena, C.C., Sollinger, J.M., Axelband, E. *et al.* 2013, *Redefining information warfare boundaries for an army in a wireless world*, RAND Institute, Santa Monica.

Prince, B., 2012, 'Project aims to detect cyber attacks using radio frequency', *Security Week*, viewed 21 November 2012, from http://www.securityweek.com/project-aims-detect-cyber-attacks-using-radio-frequency

Rouse, A. & Dick, M., 1994, 'The use of NUDIST, a computerized analytical tool, to support qualitative information systems research', *Information Technology & People* 7(3), 50–62.

Smith, R. & Knight, S., 2005, 'Applying electronic warfare solutions to network security', *Canadian Military Journal* 6(3), 49–58.

StrategyPage.com., 2009, 'Gaza cell phones targeted', 02 January, viewed 27 July 2009, from http://www.strategypage.com/htmw/htiw/articles/20090102.aspx

Tubbs, B., 2013, 'SAPS hack spells negligence', viewed 22 May, from http://www.itweb.co.za/index.php?option=com_content&view=article&id=64268:SAPS-hack-spells-negligence&catid=265

Van Niekerk, B., 2011, 'Vulnerability analysis of modern ICT infrastructure from an information warfare perspective', PhD thesis, University of KwaZulu-Natal.

Van Niekerk, B., 2012, 'Tools for conducting operations on social media', South African National Defence Force Psychological Operations Expertise Register Workshop, 12 October, Pretoria.

Van Niekerk, B. & Maharaj, M.S., 2009, 'The future roles of electronic warfare in the information warfare spectrum', *Journal of Information Warfare* 8(3), 1–13.

Van Niekerk, B. & Maharaj, M.S., 2011, 'The information warfare life cycle model', *South African Journal of Information Management* 13(1), 1–9. http://dx.doi.org/10.4102/sajim.v13i1.476

Van Niekerk, B. & Maharaj, M.S., 2012, 'Mobile devices and the military: Useful tool or significant threat?', *Journal of Information Warfare* 11(2), 1–11.

Vijayan, J., 2013, 'Is French outrage against U.S. spying misplaced?', Computer World, viewed 25 October 2013, from http://www.computerworld.com/s/article/9243414/Is_French_outrage_against_U.S._spying_misplaced

Knowledge management a competitive edge for law firms in Botswana in the changing business environment

Author:
Madeleine Fombad[1]

Affiliation:
[1]Department of Information Science, University of South Africa, South Africa

Correspondence to:
Madeleine Fombad

Email:
fombamc@unisa.ac.za

Postal address:
798 Thomas Avenue, Eastwood, Arcadia 0083, South Africa

Background: Law firms in Botswana offer a particularly interesting context to explore the effects of transition in the knowledge economy. Acquiring and leveraging knowledge effectively in law firms through knowledge management can result in competitive advantage; yet the adoption of this approach remains in its infancy.

Objectives: This article investigates the factors that will motivate the adoption of knowledge management in law firms in Botswana, and creates an awareness of the potential benefits of knowledge management in these firms.

Method: The article uses both quantitative and qualitative research methods and the survey research design. A survey was performed on all 115 registered law firms and 217 lawyers in Botswana. Interviews were conducted with selected lawyers for more insight.

Results: Several changes in the legal environment have motivated law firms to adopt knowledge management. Furthermore, lawyers appreciate the potential benefits of knowledge management.

Conclusion: With the rise of the knowledge-based economy, coupled with the pressures faced by the legal industry in recent years, law firms in Botswana can no longer afford to rely on the traditional methods of managing knowledge. Knowledge management will, therefore, enhance the cost effectiveness of these firms. Strategic knowledge management certainly helps to prepare law firms in Botswana to be alive to the fact that the systematic harnessing of legal knowledge is no longer a luxury, but an absolute necessity in the knowledge economy. It will also provide an enabling business environment for private sector development and growth and, therefore, facilitate Botswana's drive towards the knowledge-based economy.

Introduction

During the last decade of the 20th century, the global economy witnessed an increasing transition from the traditional resources of land, labour, and capital to the knowledge economy, whereby knowledge is considered as a prime input to production, innovation and economic benefits. Botswana is taking positive strides towards becoming a knowledge-based economy (Bwalya 2010; World Bank 2012). Botswana's drive towards transformation to a knowledge-based economy is envisaged in its 'National Vision 2016' (Presidential Task Group 1997), and the President of Botswana's inaugural speech (Office of the President 2010). One of the seven thematic areas of the 'National Vision 2016' envisages that as an educated and informed nation after 50 years of independence, the knowledge-based economy will contribute to an overall objective of transforming the country into a knowledge society, with research and innovation as the cornerstones of development. In this regard, the government has made sustainable investments in physical and technical infrastructure, businesses, education, research and development to facilitate a knowledge intensive economy. The public and private sectors are making concerted efforts to enhance the drive towards the knowledge economy. Law firms in Botswana, therefore, provide an important context in the private sector to explore the effects of transition into the knowledge economy. In the knowledge economy the production and services are based on knowledge-intensive activities that contribute to accelerating the pace of technical and scientific advancement (Powell & Snellman 2004). Law firms are knowledge-intensive firms, the competitive advantage of which is built on knowledge and how it is used to help clients. A law firm can be described as a business entity that is formed by one or more lawyers to engage in the practice of law and in rendering effective and efficient legal services to clients. Law firms in Botswana are small and they are either sole proprietors or limited liability partnerships. Although the size of these law firms have increased from one to ten lawyers (Fombad 2010; Fombad, Boon & Bothma 2009) to 21 lawyers from 2014 (Harris 2014), the firm size is considered as small. Concerning the size of firms, Mayer-Schoenberger (1995) observes the following:

> [S]izes of law firms range widely from sole practitioners [*lawyers practising alone*] to small firms consisting of two to 50 lawyers to midsize firms of 50 to 200 lawyers and to very large professional firms having more than 1000 lawyers. (n.p.)

Lawyers possess professional skills such as legal research, judicial problem-solving and analysis, application of the law to relevant facts, negotiation, drafting, advocacy, interviewing and other general skills such as business management, communication, teamwork, and client relations (Collins 1994; Tjaden 2001).

Although knowledge management has increasingly become a topic of discussion in many competitive law firms (Curve Consulting 2003; Kofoed 2002; Leibowitz 2002; Parson 2002; Rusanow 2003), the empirical studies on the potential benefits and strategic use of knowledge management, amidst the changing legal environment, remain unsung in these firms (Dykema 2014). The studies of Du Plessis (2004, 2011) and Du Plessis and Du Toit (2005) on knowledge management in law firms focused on information and knowledge management in support of legal research in a digital environment. Bopape (2010) examines information technology to support knowledge management and Fombad (2010) suggests strategies for knowledge management in law firms in Botswana; whilst Fombad (2014) examines some lessons for knowledge management in small law firms in Botswana. The findings of this article are based on an update of the author's thesis on knowledge management in law firms in Botswana.

Problem statement

It is becoming apparent that the pressures of the knowledge economy and the changing business environment are compelling law firms to rethink their structures, roles, mission and the manner in which they conduct their business by adopting knowledge management. Nonetheless, strategic knowledge management in law firms in Botswana remains in its initial stages (Fombad 2010, 2014; Fombad *et al.* 2009). This article identifies factors that will motivate the adoption of knowledge management and the potential benefits for law firms, and will also provide guidelines for strategic knowledge management.

Research objective

The article seeks to answer the following questions:

- How is the legal information environment changing?
- What factors are motivating the adoption of knowledge management in law firms in Botswana?
- What are the potential benefits of knowledge management in these firms?

Literature review

This section presents an overview of the concept of knowledge economy, the changes in the legal environment, knowledge management, and the potential benefits of knowledge management to law firms.

The knowledge economy

There is no universal definition of the knowledge economy. Interrelated concepts such as knowledge society, modern society and network capitalism have been used to describe the term. An understanding of the concept of the information economy is important to appreciate its meaning. The information economy is the period after the industrial age during which economic development depended largely on information and the exploitation thereof, an increase in the use of computers, telecommunication, e-governance, e-commerce, online education and universal access to telephones (Martin 1995). The information economy era was characterised by information-intensive organisations, a significant information sector, the social use of information and learning society (Moore 1999). On the other hand, the term 'knowledge economy' was coined from the report of Organisation for Economic Cooperation and Development (OECD) entitled 'The Knowledge-Based Economy' (1996). According to this report, it is an economy characterised by a hierarchy of networks that is fuelled by the rapid rate of change in all aspects of life, including learning. As a consequence, the OECD obliged all sectors of the economy to respond to the demands of this economy by equipping people with the knowledge and necessary skills to survive in this milieu. Pink (2005) observes that the knowledge economy is built on logical, linear, computer-like capabilities of the information economy where information means wealth and power to an economy in which wealth and power are gained by those who have the cognitive and creative capabilities to reframe information into useful knowledge, although information is freely available. Britz *et al.* (2006) summarise the distinct characteristics of a knowledge society as:

> access to modern ICTs and the use thereof, the number of scientists in a country, the amount spent on research and development as a percentage of the gross domestic product (GDP), the ability to produce and export, high technology, the number of patents filed in a country, and the number of articles published in highly ranked scholarly journals. (n.p.)

Handzic and Zhou (2005) list the characteristics of a knowledge economy as one that is knowledge centric with visible network effects, rapid and unpredicted changes and innovation. The World Bank identifies the four pillars of development in the knowledge economy as education and training, information infrastructure, economic incentive, an institutional regime, and innovative systems (Chen & Dahlman 2005).

Knowledge economy, therefore, may be referred to as a dematerialised and conceptualised economy driven by affluence and characterised by the use of the following:

- information
- knowledge
- ICTs and distinctive know-how for competitive advantage
- innovation
- learning
- change
- long-term economic growth.

Changes in the legal information environment

Traditionally, the practice of law has been built around law books and print technology. Legal research facilities were centred on the paper-based law library, the precedent bank and the collection of press cuttings (Berring 1997; Suender 2013; Wales Library Resources for Lawyers Project Africa 2001). The situation started changing, albeit gradually with the development of online computer-based research systems like LexisNexis and Weslaw in the 1970s (Katsh 1995). Then, the Internet moved the use of ICTs in law firms beyond the automation of existing practices to innovative concepts and applications such as the intranet, Internet deal rooms, extranet, document and content management, online depositions, real time chat, portals, groupware, expert systems and knowledge management systems (Hopkins & Reynolds 2003; Reach 2006). Nye (1999) predicted that by the year 2025, the Internet would change everything about the practice of law.

As a result of the Internet, the globalisation of business practices has broken down geographical boundaries, leading to an increase in an international collaborative legal practice worldwide (Gottschalk 2014; Wall 1998). Furthermore, there has been an exponential growth in the size of law firms around the world, for example in Botswana the maximum number of lawyers per firm has increased from 11 in 2010 to 21 in 2014. The continuous increase in the number of lawyers and law firms has put pressure on law firms to maintain a competitive edge against one another as far as partners, clients and law graduates are concerned.

The above changes in the legal industry had several consequences, for example information overload has been aggravated. Parson (2002) noted that in the knowledge economy, the explosion of content and the increasing demands for speed in the provision of legal services have ironically led to information anxiety and attention deficit amongst lawyers. Furthermore, clients are becoming computer literate and sophisticated consumers of legal services who expect lawyers to have technologies in place that may enhance their effectiveness (Dubin 2005). In addition, the disintermediation process in law firms has been accelerated (Bradlow 1988; Nye 1999; Susskind 2001). Disintermediation is any activity that does away with an intermediary when rendering services or concluding transactions (Drucker 2000; ESQlawtech 2002). This has given clients the feeling that they are paying for the management skills of lawyers rather than their legal knowledge.

Finally, the competitive business environment has revolutionised the mobility of lawyers. Some are opting for changes to improve on their curriculum vitae and others are in search of greener pastures (Hunter, Beaumont & Lee 2002). There is, therefore, a growing awareness that if measures are not taken, a vast quantity of vital knowledge and expertise would walk out of the door.

Knowledge and knowledge management

Knowledge can take on many different forms and has different meanings to each individual organisation. Closely related concepts such as data and information can easily approximate some form of knowledge. Nonaka and Takeuchi (1995) consider knowledge as a true and justified personal belief that increases an individual's capacity to take action. According to Fahey and Prusak (1998), knowledge is what the knower knows that does not exist independently of a knower, but is rather shaped by one's needs and one's initial stock of knowledge. In this article, knowledge is considered as information combined with experience, context, interpretation, reflection, intuition, creativity plus the ability to use the information to act or innovate. It includes truths, beliefs, perspectives, concepts, judgement, expectations, methodologies and the know-how.

Similar to knowledge, there is still no universally accepted definition of knowledge management. From an information technology perspective Platt (2003) defines knowledge management as accessing, evaluating, managing, organising, filtering and distributing information in a manner that would be useful to end users through a technological platform. From an intellectual capital perspective, Smith (2001) considers knowledge management as an on-going procedural 'bottom-up' process that develops and exploits the tangible assets and intangible knowledge resources of the organisation and shares it across boundaries in the organisation. From a process perspective knowledge management involves activities such as creation, acquisition, identification, storage, sharing and application of knowledge (Gottschalk 2014).

In this article, strategic knowledge management refers to a set of systematic and disciplined actions an organisation can take to obtain the greatest value from the knowledge available. It is the development of an organisational-wide knowledge management capability designed to provide sustainable competitive advantage (Inelcom & K-net 2015). It entails establishing a framework that defines the key elements of knowledge management and their interaction with business strategy, organisational design and the business practice (Gottschalk 2014).

Perceived benefits of knowledge management in law firms

Perceptions of the benefits of knowledge management vary from individual to individual and organisation to organisation. Law firms in Canada, the United States, the United Kingdom and Australia are considering knowledge management as a necessity for meeting emerging client demand for efficiency, accountability, and controlled legal costs (Chester 2002; Nathanson & Levison 2002). Leading United Kingdom law firms have well-developed precedents and know how systems maintained by fulltime professional support lawyers who are senior lawyers and experts in their field (Kay 2002). Several legal researchers (Becerra-Fernandez 1999; Curve Consulting 2003; Gottschalk 2014;

TABLE 1: What would motivate the adoption of knowledge management in your firm? (*N* = 140).

Variable	1 Strongly agree in %	2 Agree in %	3 Neutral in %	4 Disagree in %	5 Strongly disagree in %
Advanced information communication technologies	74.3	23.6	2.1	-	-
The shift from paper-based to electronic sources of information	67.9	26.4	5.7	-	-
The Internet	65.7[a]	30.0[a]	3.6[a]	0.7[a]	-
Electronic publishing	67.1	27.9	-	-	-
Globalisation of legal services	37.1[a]	28.6[a]	19.3[a]	6.4[a]	3.6[a]
Competition amongst firms	33.6	36.4	25.7	4.3	-
Pressure from clients	20.7	34.3	29.3	15.7	-
Information overload	17.9[a]	23.6[a]	32.9[a]	15.7[a]	-
Loss of key personnel and their knowledge	21.4	32.9	15.7	17.9	12.1
The use of knowledge management tools and practices by other competitors	36.4	52.1	3.6	7.9	-
An increase in the mobility of lawyers	20.7	25.7	26.4	13.6	13.6
The need to identify and to protect strategic knowledge in the firm	50.0	33.6	8.6	6.4	1.4
The desire to promote professional satisfaction	65.0	29.3	5.7	-	-
The desire to support and to encourage a learning culture	63.6	31.4	5.0	-	-
The desire to promote teamwork	65.0	25.7	9.3	-	-
The desire to meet the information and knowledge needs of the lawyer	65.7	30.0	4.3	-	-
Pressure from other professional service firms	25.7	27.9	27.1	14. 3	5.0

[a], Percentages that do not add up as a result of non-response.

Kay 2002; Leibowitz 2004; Opp 2004; Whitfield-Jones 1999) have noted that the successful implementation of knowledge management strategy in law firms may result in the following benefits:

- Innovation is sustained and the free flow of ideas is encouraged.
- Learning is enhanced as well as the ability to stay ahead of competition and changes in the legal information environment.
- The quality of knowledge work is improved.
- Individual and group competencies are enhanced.
- It provides opportunities for more effective networking and collaboration.
- Customer service is maintained by streamlining response times.
- Revenue is boosted with the faster arrival of products and services to market.
- Redundancy is eliminated and employee retention rates are enhanced by recognising the value of employees' knowledge and rewarding them for it.
- Operations are streamlined and costs reduced by eliminating redundant or unnecessary processes.

Research methodology

A qualitative and quantitative research method was adopted and open and closed-ended questionnaires and semi-structured interviews were used as instruments. A survey research design was used. The target population was the sampling frame requested and obtained from the Botswana Law Society which consists of a list of registered private law firms; these firms comprised 115 registered law firms in Botswana and a total of 217 lawyers. A census of the total population of 217 was adopted for the questionnaire survey. Interviews were held to complement the census. The researcher adopted the purposive sampling technique and limited the interviews to law firms in Gaborone. Gaborone was deliberately chosen to administer the interviews, because of its accessibility and proximity and the majority of the lawyers are based in Gaborone. In order to validate the instrument, preliminary interviews were conducted with lawyers. The questionnaire was then critically reviewed to ensure that there is some similarity between the interview questions and those in the questionnaire. The questionnaire was modified and the feedback and suggestions from the promoter taking into account, and the opinions of experts in knowledge management research were sought to evaluate the instrument with regard to comments on language and structure. The Statistical Package for Social Scientists (SPSS) version 15.0 was used for the analysis of the data collected from the close-ended questionnaires. On the other hand, qualitative data were derived from the open-ended questions and the interviews conducted, with 15 lawyers who had been selected from different law firms in Gaborone, were coded using thematic content analyses. About 140 completed questionnaires were returned, which translated to a return rate of 64.5%. The participants were asked to rate the questions on a five point scale of 'strongly agree', 'agree', 'neutral', 'disagree' and 'strongly disagree'.

Data analysis and findings

The frequency distribution of participants, concerning their level of education, revealed that a majority, 116 (83%) have bachelor's degrees and 24 (17.1%) have Master's degrees. Furthermore, amongst other qualifications were executive masters in sports organisations, a post graduate diploma in international law, and a diploma in trial advocacy. With regard to longevity of practice, the length of practice of participants ranges from 1–33 years. The mean number of years of practice is 6 years. With regard to organisational characteristics the following demographics are found:

- 55 participants (39.3%) are sole proprietors
- 49 (35.0%) have 2 lawyers
- 23 (16.4%) have 3 lawyers
- 11 (7.9%) have 4 lawyers
- 1 (0.7%) has 5 lawyers
- 1 (0.7%) has nine lawyers.

TABLE 2: The perceived benefits of knowledge management in law firms in Botswana (N = 140).

Variable	1 Strongly agree in %	2 Agree in %	3 Neutral in %	4 Disagree in %	5 Strongly disagree in %
Improve knowledge sharing	60.7	39.3	-	-	-
Improve lawyers efficiency and productivity	63.6	31.4	5.0	-	-
Improve lawyers' relationship vis-à-vis clients and customers	57.1	27.9	15.0	-	-
Prevent duplication in research	60.0	31.4	8.6	-	-
Increase flexibility amongst lawyers	51.4	35.7	7.1	5.7	-
Increase flexibility amongst lawyers	51.4	35.7	7.1	5.7	-
Protect the firm's loss of knowledge	70.0	22.9	7.1	-	-
Result in competitive advantage	52.9	26.4	20.7	-	-
Integrate knowledge within the firm	60.7	31.4	6.4	-	1.4
Improve retention rate of lawyers in the firm	46.4	28.6	20.	50	-
Improve the sharing and transfer of knowledge with partners and strategic alliances	58.6	31.4	10.0	-	-
Enhance economic profitability	60.7	29.3	10.0	-	-

It also emerged from the interviews that the law firms in Botswana remain small with an average of two partners due to the fact that every lawyer wants to become a partner rather than just working as a professional assistant, because partners receive a share of the profit. As a result lawyers constantly leave law firms to start off as sole proprietors or to form small partnerships.

Factors that motivate the adoption of knowledge management in a law firms

Against the background of some of the changes in the legal information environment, this question listed the possible factors that may motivate a firm to adopt knowledge management (Table 1).

In general the responses show that lawyers acknowledged the need for knowledge management in their firms. They acknowledged that the following have triggered the adoption of knowledge management:

- advances in information communication technology (97.9%)
- the Internet (95.7%)
- electronic publishing (95.0%)
- the shift from paper-based to electronic sources (94.3%).

The following are some responses from interviewees about the reasons for adopting knowledge management:

- Lawyers do not stay in one firm; they are moving from firm to firm.
- Lawyers are constantly splitting up in the law firms to start off as sole proprietors or to form partnerships.
- We are under pressure to attract new clientele.
- It will be good to network with other lawyers.
- If only knowledge can be standardised.
- There is a lot of competition out there as to who owns the best knowledge.
- We have to keep up with the changes around us in the international law firms.
- The Internet, computers, observation from other lawyers and networking with other lawyers are a challenge to our firm.

The perceived benefits of knowledge management for the law firms

Various items on perceived benefits of knowledge management are presented in Table 2.

The findings revealed that participants generally recognised the potential benefits of knowledge management. They all agreed (100%) that a good knowledge management attitude would improve knowledge sharing in the firm. Knowledge management attitude is generally reflected in the way a firm accesses and shares its knowledge communication style, trust and teamwork (Forstenlechner 2006; Lambe 2003; Rusanow 2007). These findings contradict the general notion that law firms are noted for their expertise, and secretive, individualistic culture (Lambe 2003; Maiden 2002; Terrett 1998:68). Lawyers further acknowledged that knowledge management would prevent duplication in research, of whom 91.4% agreed. The participants agreed that knowledge management would protect law firms from losing knowledge (92.9%), it would improve the retention rate of lawyers (75.0%) and integrate knowledge within the firm (92.1%). Many lawyers recognised that knowledge management would improve lawyers' relationships with their clients (85.0%). It, therefore, seems that lawyers appreciate the benefits of improving their relationship with their clients (Lim & Klobas 2000). The participants also acknowledged that knowledge management would improve the lawyer's efficiency, productivity (95.0%), and flexibility (87.1%). It is likely that improvement in efficiency and productivity will enhance a lawyer's flexibility, thus resulting in professional satisfaction. These findings confirm the research that knowledge management would expose lawyers with special experience and expertise to work on projects in their area to such an extent that they attain professional excellence, equip themselves with advanced skills and provide exceptional services to clients (Chester 2002; Rodriguez, Garcia & Pizarro 2002; Rusanow 2003, 2007; Wesemann 2006). Timely billing, the ability to respond to the unexpected, the ability to create innovative solutions for blue sky thinking, and the ability to curb legal costs are likely to benefit the client. Law firms in Canada, the United States, the United Kingdom and Australia are considering knowledge management as a necessity for meeting emerging client demand for efficiency, accountability, and controlled legal cost (Chester 2002; Nathanson & Levison 2002; Rusanow 2007; Wesemann 2006).

Most of the participants agreed that knowledge management would enhance economic profitability (90.0%). As a result of the delivery of high quality legal services to satisfied clients, more business will be generated which will result in better economic performance and knowledge management results in the fast delivery of high quality services.

Respondents also agreed that knowledge management will improve the retention rate (75%). Knowledge management initiatives enable firms to attract and retain talented lawyers and also their clients. In situations where lawyers decide to leave the firm, knowledge management provides for a continuity of knowledge. It also helps to capture and effortlessly share senior lawyers' knowledge in the firm. Responses from the 'other' category and the interviews indicated that the perceived benefits of knowledge management in law firms would result in general efficiency, improvement of quality of output, and improvement of the quality of the clients. The following are notable responses from the interviews in this study, with regard to the perceived benefits of knowledge management in law firms in Botswana:

- It is encouraging to know that I can always get what I need within the time frame available for it because currently I spend a lot of time sort of reinventing the wheel.
- It seems to be the trend and an essential function in today's law firm environment.
- As a fairly young legal practitioner, it is heartening to know that with knowledge management in place, there will be somewhere to inquire information about what you do not know because it is presently difficult working without any prior experience and with no one willing to assist you.
- I appreciate its potential to improve the overall efficiency of the firm.
- The thought that it will make my work easy.
- It will improve the quality of clients.
- It will provide the ability to network with other lawyers within and out of the country.

Although lawyers seemingly recognise the potential benefits of knowledge management, these promised benefits remain around the corner because the adoption of knowledge management still remains in its infancy.

Limitations

A major limitation of this paper is that the findings specifically apply to law firms and, therefore, insights into other branches of the legal profession may be lacking that fall under the Judicial Service Commission (e.g. judges, magistrates and court registrars), legal practitioners in the Attorney General's Chambers and, legal academics. Furthermore, it does not examine other professional service firms that render professional services. Although it is believed that these findings could apply to other branches and professional service firms. Future studies should investigate knowledge management as a competitive edge in the legal profession and in other firms in Botswana that render professional services.

Conclusion and recommendations

This article paints a picture of a profession that is aware of the enormous potential benefits of knowledge management amidst the changes in the legal environment, although the adoption of knowledge management is still in its infancy. In order for law firms in Botswana to sharpen their competitiveness, broaden their influence, and survive in a legal environment characterised by aggressive changes, the approach to knowledge management should be strategically thought out. Centaur Media (2014) posits that knowledge management discourse in law firms has moved from creating and managing internal documents to creating value for the client. On the other hand Winston (2014) argues that knowledge management in law firms has shifted beyond the provision of legal services, to supporting and integrating expanding law firms to cope with information overload, and is now focused on helping attorneys do more with less. It, therefore, stands to reason that strategic knowledge management will entail that law firms in Botswana leverage their knowledge for competitive advantage, build up market trends, and develop business strategies directed at meeting the needs of clients and other lawyers. In rethinking the knowledge management approach in these firms, an understanding and sensitivity to the size, ideals and characteristics of these firms is crucial given that they are predominantly small firms (Fombad 2014). Knowledge management in these firms should be simple and implemented at a rate which is commensurate with their level of resources. Also, issues of cultural resistance are critical (Zeide & Liebowitz 2012). To this end, law firms should create an environment where knowledge, creativity and innovation are valued by facilitating communication amongst people in different locations and from different departments. Law firms should encourage ideas, rewards and success, whilst allowing people to fail and learn from their failures.

Therefore, with the rise of the knowledge-based economy, coupled with the pressures faced by the legal industry in recent years, law firms in Botswana can no longer afford to rely on the traditional methods of managing knowledge, because they need the 'best minds' and the best knowledge in their area of practice. Knowledge management will, therefore, enhance the cost effectiveness of these firms. Although knowledge management is not a quick fix or ready-made panacea, it will certainly help prepare law firms in Botswana to be alive to the fact that the systematic harnessing of legal knowledge is no longer a luxury, but an absolute necessity in the knowledge economy above all, it will provide an enabling business environment to private sector development and growth and, therefore, facilitate

Botswana's drive towards the knowledge-based economy as envisaged in its National Vision 2016.

Acknowledgements

Competing interests

The author declares that she has no financial or personal relationships which may have inappropriately influenced her in writing this article.

References

Becerra-Fernandez, I., 1999, 'Knowledge management today: Changing the corporate culture', in *Proceedings of the 5th International Conference of Decision Science Institute*, July 4–7.

Berring, R., 1997, 'Chaos, cyberspace and tradition: Legal information transmogrified', viewed 04 May 2014, from http://www.law.berkly/edu/journals

Bopape, S., 2010, 'Utilisation of information technology to support information and Knowledge management by lawyers in Polokwane City', *South African Journal of Library and Information Services* 76(2), 129–140.

Bradlow, D., 1988, 'The changing legal environment 1980s and beyond', *ABA Journal* 1, 72–76.

Britz, J., Lor, P., Coetzee, I. & Bester, B., 2006, 'Africa as a knowledge society: A reality check', *The International Information & Library Review* 38, 25–40. http://dx.doi.org/10.1016/j.iilr.2005.12.001

Bwalya, K.J., 2010, 'Botswana's novel approaches for knowledge-based economy facilitation: Issues, policies and contextual framework', *International Journal of Information Communication Technologies and Human Development* 2(1), 59–74. http://dx.doi.org/10.4018/jicthd.2010010104

Centaur Media, 2014, 'How helpful is your KM?', *Lawyer* (*Online Edition*) 9(25).

Chen, D.C. & Dahlman, C.J., 2005, 'The knowledge economy, the KAM methodology and World Bank operations', viewed 17 February 2014, from http://siteresources.worldbank.org

Chester, S., 2002, 'Knowledge management in Canadian law firms', Pacific Legal Technology Conference Vancouver Trade and Technology Centre', viewed 07 June 2014, from www.lawsociety.bc.ca

Collins, H., 1994, 'The place of computer in legal education', *Law Technology Journal* 3(3), viewed 08 August 2014, from http://www.law.warwick.ac

Curve Consulting, 2003, 'Global law firm knowledge management survey report', viewed 09 February 2012, from http://www.curveconsulting.com/pages/

Drucker, P., 2000. 'The new economy and the virtual law firm of the future', viewed 25 August 2012, from http://www.digitallawyer.com/virtual2.html

Du Plessis, T., 2004, 'Information and knowledge management in support of legal research in a digital environment', PhD thesis, Faculty of Arts, University of Rand Afrikaans.

Du Plessis, T., 2011, 'Information and knowledge management at South African law firms', *Potchefstroom Electronic Law Journal* 14(4), 233–258. http://dx.doi.org/10.4314/pelj.v14i4.8

Dubin, M., 2005, 'Creating an environment in the law firms where knowledge management will work', viewed 12 January 2013, from http://www.searchwarp.com

Du Plessis, T. & du Toit, A., 2005, 'Survey of information and knowledge management in South African law firms', *South African Journal of Information Management* 7(1). http://dx.doi.org/10.4102/sajim.v7i1.252

Dykema, E., 2014, 'Knowledge management: Law firm reluctant to reap the rewards', viewed 10 February 2015, from https://caserails.com/blog/knowledge-management-law-firms-reluctant-reap-rewards

ESQlawtech, Ltd., 2002, 'Law office technology transforming the legal profession. The Esqlawtech weekly', viewed 09 June 2012, from http://www.mylawtips.com/officetechnology.html

Fahey, L. & Prusak, L., 1998, 'The Eleven deadliest sins of knowledge management', *California Management Review* 40(3), 265–276. http://dx.doi.org/10.2307/41165954

Fombad, M., 2010, 'Strategies for knowledge management in law firms in Botswana', Ph.D., Dept. of Information Science, University of Pretoria, Pretoria.

Fombad, M., 2014, 'Knowledge management in law firms in Botswana: Some lessons for small law firms', *Journal of Librarianship and Information Science*, viewed 30 May 2014, from http://lis.sagepub.com/content/early/2014/05/28/09610006145364

Fombad, M., Boon, J.A. & Bothma, T.J.D., 2009, 'Strategy for knowledge management in law firms in Botswana', *South African Journal of Information Management* 11(2). http://dx.doi.org/10.4102/sajim.v11i2.405

Forstenlechner, I., 2006, 'Impact of knowledge management on law firm performance: An investigation of causality across cultures', PhD Thesis, School of Industrial and Manufacturing Science, Cranfield University.

Gottschalk, P., 2014, 'Knowledge management strategy in professional service firms', *Advances in Management* 7(3), 16–22.

Handzic, M. & Zhou, A.Z., 2005, 'Knowledge management: An integrative approach', Chandos Publishing, Oxford. http://dx.doi.org/10.1142/5639

Harris, J., 2014, 'Neighbourhood watch', *Lawyer* 28, 14(3), 16–16

Hopkins, R. & Reynolds, P., 2003, 'Redefining privacy and security in the electronic communication age: A lawyers ethical duties in the virtual world of the internet', *The Georgetown Journal of Legal Ethics* 16(4), 675–684.

Hunter, L., Beaumont, P. & Lee, M., 2002, 'Knowledge management practice in Scottish law firms', *Human Resource Management Journal* 12(2), 4–21. http://dx.doi.org/10.1111/j.1748-8583.2002.tb00061.x

Inelcom & K-net, 2015, 'Strategic knowledge management & knowledge', viewed 08 February 2015, from http://www.kbos.net/default.aspx?articleID=10315

Katsh, M., 1995, 'Law in the digital world', viewed 08 May 2013, from http://www.umassp.edu/legal/dw control.html

Kay, S., 2002, 'Benchmarking knowledge management in U.S. and U.K law firms', viewed 11 October 2012, from http://www.llrx.com/features/bench markingkm.html

Kofoed, K., 2002, 'Knowledge management in law firms', MBA Cambridge Business School, University of Cambridge, Cambridge.

Lambe, P., 2003, 'What does knowledge management mean for the law firms', viewed 11 September 2014, from http://www.greenchameleon.com

Leibowitz, W., 2002, 'Knowledge management in the law firm. Wendy Tech Articles', viewed 09 September 2013, from http://www.WendyTech.com

Leibowitz, W., 2004, 'Knowledge management in the law firm. Wendy Tech Articles', viewed 09 September 2013, from http://www.WendyTech.com

Lim, D. & Klobas, J., 2000, 'Knowledge management in small enterprises', *The Electronic Library* 18(6), 420–433. http://dx.doi.org/10.1108/02640470010361178

Maiden, C., 2002, 'The secret life if lawyers reinventing law', viewed 15 January 2013, from http:// www.ask.bm

Moore, N.I., 1999, 'Partners in the information Society', *Library Association Record,* 101(12), 702–703.

Martin, W.J., 1995, *The Global Information Society*, Aslib Gower.

Mayer-Schoenberger, V., 1995, 'Lawyering on the Infohbahn: The European perspective', *Law Technology Journal June* 4(1), 5–95.

Nathanson, A. & Levison, A., 2002, 'Differentiate your firm with knowledge management', *Legal Information Technology*, viewed 5 November 2012, from http://www.brco.com/downloads/articles/

Nonaka, I. & Takeuchi, H., 1995, *The knowledge creating company*, University Press, Oxford.

Nye, A., 1999, 'The lawyer of the future', *Maine Lawyer's Review* 7(12).

Organisation for Economic Cooperation and Development (OECD), 1996, 'The Knowledge-Based Economy', viewed 20 February 2014, from http://www.oecd.org/sti/sci-tech/1913021.pdf

Office of the President, 2010, 'Report on public service customer satisfaction and staff perception surveys', prepared by Economic and Management Consultants. Unpublished.

Opp, K., 2004, 'Commentary: The importance of knowledge management to a firm', viewed 05 May 2013, from http://www.accessmylibrary.com

Parson, M., 2002, 'Uncommon knowledge: The Knowledge management questions for service firms', *Professional Review* 11, 2–3.

Pink, D.H., 2005, 'A whole new mind: moving from the information age to the conceptual age', Penguin, New York.

Platt, N., 2003, 'Knowledge is power: knowledge management remains vital to the firm's success AALL Spectrum', viewed 05 August 2013 from, http://www.llrxcom/features/kmpower.html

Powell, W. & Snellman, K., 2004, 'Thee knowledge economy', *Annual Review of Sociology* 30, 199–220. http://dx.doi.org/10.1146/annurev.soc.29.010202.100037

Presidential Task Group, 1997, *Long-term Vision for Botswana: Towards Prosperity for All,* Government Printer, Gaborone.

Reach, C., 2006, Positioning for power: Technology and the law firm librarian, American Bar Association, viewed 11 June 2012, from http://www.abanet.orgpower.html

Rodriquez, C., Garcia, J. & Pizarro, J., 2002, 'Knowledge management in law firm', *Upgrade* 3(1), 51–54.

Rusanow, G., 2003, Knowledge management is a business imperative, viewed 03 August 2013, from http://www.llrx.com

Rusanow, G., 2007, 'Combining business and practice knowledge management and the law', *Knowledge Management World* 16(1), 12–15.

Smith, E., 2001, 'The role of tacit and explicit knowledge in the workplace', *Journal of Knowledge Management* 5(4), 311–321. http://dx.doi.org/10.1108/13673270110411733

Suender, M., 2013, 'Alternatives to the partnership track', *Law Practice: The Business of Practicing Law* 39(3), 40–43.

Susskind, R., 2001, 'The changing face of private law practice: Part 111. Working notes on deliberations of the committee on research about the future of the legal profession on the current status of the legal profession', viewed 10 September 2012, from http://www.abanet.org

Terret, A., 1998, 'Knowledge management and the law firm', *Journal of Knowledge Management* 2(1), 67–76. http://dx.doi.org/10.1108/EUM0000000004608

Tjaden, T., 2001, *Legal research and writing: Law in a nutshell*, Irwin Law, Toronto.

Wales Library Resources for Lawyers Project Africa, 2001, 'The Bar Human Rights Committee of England and Wales and-The British Council', viewed 10 February 2015, from www.barhumanrights.org.uk/sites/default/files/.../uganda_report.do

Wall, D., 1998, 'Information technology and the shaping of legal practice in the UK', paper presented at the 13th BILETA conference, 27–28 March, viewed 16 December 2012, from http://www.bileta.ac.uk

Wesemann, P., 2006, 'Knowledge management: Is the emperor wearing clothes. Edge International', viewed December 2013, from http://www.edge.ai/Edge International.

Whitfield-Jones, C., 1999, *Business as usual or the end of as we know it*, Managing Partner, London.

Winston, A.M., 2014, 'Law firm knowledge management: A selected annotated bibliography', *Law Library Journal* 2(10), 106.

World Bank, 2012, 'Knowledge economy index, moving towards the knowledge economy', viewed 12 February 2015, from http://botswana.opendataforafrica.org/WBKEI2013/knowledge-economy-index-world-bank-2012

Zeide, E. & Liebowitz, J., 2012, 'Knowledge management in law: A look at cultural resistance', *Legal Information Management* 12(1), 34–38. http://dx.doi.org/10.1017/S1472669612000126

3

Knowledge-management practices at selected banks in South Africa

Authors:
Joel Chigada[1]
Patrick Ngulube[2]

Affiliations:
[1]Department of Information Science, University of South Africa, South Africa

[2]School of Interdisciplinary Research and Postgraduate Studies, University of South Africa, South Africa

Correspondence to:
Patrick Ngulube

Email:
ngulup@unisa.ac.za

Postal address:
PO Box 392, Pretoria 0003, South Africa

Background: Effective knowledge organisations (EKO) create dynamic capabilities through the acquisition, creation, sharing and retention of knowledge. These EKOs are designed to enable an organisation to improve best practices in business. As knowledge is different from other organisational resources, decision-makers ought to understand the importance of knowledge to an organisation. In order to fully utilise knowledge-management (KM) practices and to enhance efficiency, management should appreciate and understand the importance of KM. A proper understanding of KM will add value to organisational knowledge.

Objective: This study focused on investigating the knowledge-management practices at selected banks in South Africa. The objective was to establish the extent to which selected banks had implemented knowledge-management practices such as the acquisition, sharing and retention of knowledge.

Method: Quantitative and qualitative data for this study were collected through the use of a multi-methods approach. Data were collected from middle and senior managers through the use of questionnaires and an interview protocol. All usable quantitative data were analysed using Survey Monkey and Microsoft Excel 2010 whilst thematic analysis was used to extract detailed, rich and complex data accounts from interviews.

Results: Though the study revealed the presence of KM practices at selected banks, KM concepts were not universally understood, thus impeding the organisation-wide implementation of KM practices. Knowledge-management practices were only discussed as a footnote because no formal policies existed to add value to KM initiatives.

Conclusion: The study concludes that organisations such as banks should perform a knowledge inventory. Knowledge inventories will become handy during the process of developing KM policies and practices for integrating work processes, collaborating and sharing (including the efficient use of knowledge technology platforms) and developing an enabling institutional culture.

Introduction and background to the study

As pointed out by (Gaffoor & Cloete 2010:1), 'Knowledge management (KM) has become a focal point for debates on mechanisms to assist firms in acquiring a greater competitive edge in the emerging global information economy'. This means that organisations – big and small, global and domestic – are channelling their focus on knowledge assets as strategies for competitive advantage. Knowledge tools and systems are being developed to give an organisation a competitive edge. Fowler and Pryke (2003) defines KM as follows:

> … an established management approach that is successfully applied across corporate sectors by methodically creating, sharing, preserving and optimally applying the extensive knowledge present in the organisation, to better achieve organisational objectives. (p. 254)

The above definition captures fundamental issues that are used in discussing KM practices in this study. In this regard, Cong and Pandya (2003) suggest the following:

> … any given control mechanism has the capacity to affect both the nature and flow of knowledge in a firm by the manner in which the firm processes particular attributes of knowledge. (p. 27)

The South African banking environment is characterised by intense competition, thus compelling the players to use strategies and create knowledge assets that are difficult to imitate. For an institution to remain competitive and relevant in a knowledge environment, there are opportunities to create, own, protect and use commercial and industrial knowledge assets which are difficult to copy. The South African banking industry comprises four commercial banks, namely ABSA, FNB, Nedbank and Standard Bank whilst the other banks focus on unsecured lending (personal loans). FNB and Nedbank were selected for this study for the following reasons:

- FNB was chosen because it is the second largest South African commercial bank (after ABSA) in terms of staff complement, assets and branch network (Moneyweb 2012).
- Nedbank was selected because the first author was formerly employed by the bank. This means that permission to conduct a study on Nedbank was already granted, and recruiting participants for the study was relatively easy.

Selecting one bank would have sufficed, but because a comparative approach is utilised in this study, it is of paramount importance to extrapolate different research issues. If two or more cases show to be supporting the same theory, replication can be claimed, and the greater the number of case studies that show replication, the greater the rigour with which theory has been established (Rowley 2002).

The banking customers' ever-changing tastes and preferences require banks to proactively improvise products, exit projects and product lines that can drag down the business and engage in others that maximise the growth potential as radical market shifts threaten to put the bank's business with the wrong product. By rapidly exploiting and applying fragmented internal and external knowledge, a bank can reliably detect emerging windows of opportunity before competition takes the market by surprise. This study investigated the extent to which selected banks in South Africa have implemented KM practices such as the acquisition, sharing and retention of knowledge.

Literature review

The literature review was used to establish how other scholars investigated the same problem. The purpose of reviewing a variety of scholarly thinking was to look at what other scholars have done in areas that are similar or have a relationship to this study (Leedy & Omrod 2005:64). To gain a better understanding of KM practices, it is important to define the area of interest. In Sarrafzadeh, Martin and Hazeri (2006), KM practices are defined '... as the way ideas are translated into action in the process accomplishing specific goals'. Branin (2003:25) opines that 'KM practices include the understanding of KM, knowledge generation, acquisition, organisation, storage, transfer, sharing and retention'. However, Singh (2007) argues as follows:

> Information professionals need to develop the capabilities to survive in knowledge based society, there is need for organisations such as banks to invest in information and knowledge architectures to produce more knowledge. Investments can be in the form of databases systems, patents and tacit knowledge which when fully utilised in the organisation can produce streamlined processes and high quality services and products. (pp. 177–178)

These outputs from a knowledge-based organisation should add value to the organisation as well as provide value for customers.

Knowledge acquisition

Pacharapha and Ractham (2012) define knowledge acquisition as the process of the development and creation of insight, skill and relationships. For knowledge to be acquired, '... there should be willingness and ability of a recipient to acquire and use knowledge are crucial elements' (Gupta & Govindarajan 2000; Ragsdell 2009). During the process of knowledge acquisition, it is important that both source and recipient should be willing to share. There are three motivational drivers that should be taken into consideration: '... attitude towards knowledge sharing, cost and benefit, subjective norms and organisational climate and perceived value of knowledge' (Ford & Staples 2006:14). Knowledge acquisition envisages learning from others through interaction between recipient and source. Nonaka and Takeuchi (1995) opine that the SECI (socialisation, externalisation, combination, and internalisation) and *ba* models play important roles in knowledge acquisition through interaction and collaboration with other individual systems. In knowledge-intensive institutions such as banks, enabling environments are envisaged that allow different departments or individuals to acquire insight, skill and relationships. Management should counter the silo mentality and allow departments to share information, notwithstanding the privacy and secrecy policies of banks. Training and development programmes inherent in banks should pave ways for knowledge acquisition, which is consistent with the SECI and *ba* models.

Knowledge sharing

KM practices help organisations to refocus on using knowledge that exists already by '... creating an environment for innovation rather than limiting themselves to best practice solutions only' (Laudon & Laudon 2012:245). Turban, Mclean and Wetherbe (2004) define knowledge sharing:

> ... as the wilful application and transfer of one or more person's ideas, insights, solutions and knowledge to another person(s), either directly or via an intermediary, such as a computer-based system. (p. 412)

The definition by Turban *et al.* (2004) illustrates that organisations should have systems in place that help the process of knowledge sharing. A good example of such systems would be computer-based systems because of its speed, ability to store large volumes of information and retrieval capabilities. Knowledge sharing enables organisations such as banks to converge towards '... knowledge portals rather than separate silos of knowledge' (Moneyweb 2013). Knowledge sharing occurs during induction (of new employees) or when employees quit the organisation. Knowledgeable and experienced employees who possess knowledge should be willing to share it. Knowledge shared by individuals and by a community of practice becomes organisational knowledge.

Knowledge may be shared during seminars, conferences, team-building exercises, written reports, performance appraisals and conventional programmes where employees make suggestions. Discussion fora give people opportunities to share personal experiences about a particular event. Seminars and conferences are ideal platforms for 'shy' or 'less vocal' employees to talk freely and openly with their colleagues. Platforms for knowledge sharing should make the communication process easier for different categories of employees. Sentiments or opinions expressed during seminars or conferences should not be used as personal attacks, and managers should not use these events to settle personal scores. Knowledge sharing can encounter challenges such as a lack of time, a lack of experience and a lack of visible rewards for sharing knowledge.

Knowledge retention

Kim (2005:37) defines knowledge retention '… as all systems and activities that capture and preserve knowledge and allow it to remain in the organisational system once introduced'. Management needs to put in place strategies for retaining organisational knowledge before it is lost. The knowledge and expertise of employees should be retained before they leave the organisation. In the absence of knowledge retention strategies, organisations lose tacit knowledge when employees leave for other organisations or due to other forms of attrition. Nonaka and Takeuchi (1995) state that 80% of knowledge lies in the brains of people who possess know-how, secrets and personal skill that will never be shared if no one works on it. This is consistent with Polanyi's (1962) view that '… we know more than we can tell'. In Polanyi's (1962) view, one person may have much knowledge but may not be able to say much about that knowledge. There are employees who carry large volumes of knowledge (tacit knowledge) in their heads, but they may not be prepared to or the environment may limit them from saying much. Tiwana (2008:103) suggests that, in order to make better use of tacit knowledge, a way must be found for it to be transferred directly to one another, making it explicit so that it can be shared throughout the organisation. Individuals who are rich in tacit knowledge (experienced employees, retirees and other talented experts) constitute a wealth of intangible assets for the organisation (Nonaka & Takeuchi 1995).

Wamundila and Ngulube (2011) and Levy (2011) established that knowledge retention could be achieved through documentation and integrating knowledge back into the organisation with special emphasis on retaining best practices. To safeguard against a loss of knowledge, organisations need to devise ways of retaining employees' know-how and best practices so that knowledge can be passed on to future workers, and replacements who should regain the on-the-job knowledge that ex-employees spent years accumulating (Thilmany 2008). Wamundila and Ngulube (2011) posit that knowledge can be retained in an organisation through various strategies that may involve education, training, establishing communities of practice and professional networks, documenting the processes and using advanced technology to capture work processes. This knowledge has to be captured and stored in databases, documents, software and processes, products and services. The human-resources management function of the banks plays a significant role to coordinate planning programmes for training and development as well as induction and succession. For these elements to work together, the prevailing organisational culture, 'as enabler' of KM, helps to facilitate synergy between the KM practices. There are barriers to implementing KM practices. These include a lack of employee interaction, the salience of value, a lack of KM policies, a lack of structural ties and the absence of KM enablers. These barriers require attention should an organisation plan to implement KM practices. Failure to pay attention can result in the failure of KM initiatives as evidenced by the low level of KM practices at selected banks.

Methodology

We used multiple methods in the study to improve the reliability and validity of the data collected, culminating in the collection of a rich set of data (triangulation). Multi-methods research was designed to guarantee the reliability and validity of quantitative measures (Romm & Ngulube in press). An embedded case-study design offered the opportunity to explore in depth the extent to which banks have implemented KM practices such as the acquisition, sharing and retention of knowledge. Embedded case studies are studies in which different levels or sources of data are collected (Yin 2003). According to Powell (1997:66), the population should be selected with great care, bearing in mind the selection criteria, the desired size and the parameters of the survey. In light of the above, We selected two commercial banks from the four commercial banks in South Africa (population) but then targeted middle managers and purposively selected senior-level managers from the population. The population of a study is the group about whom one wants to draw conclusions. In this case, it was all middle-level managers and purposively selected executive managers (Babbie 2010:111). The whole population (190) of middle-level managers was considered in the study whilst four senior executives were purposively selected to participate in face-to-face interviews. These were selected from the already-delineated sample perceived by the researchers to be key individuals who would give invaluable insight and more detailed answers to the research questions on KM policies.

Questionnaires were used to collect data from geographically dispersed participants whilst interview protocol and document analyses were ideal for collecting qualitative data. Questionnaires were distributed and received through Survey Monkey©, an online survey platform. A total of 190 questionnaires were distributed to middle-level managers at the selected banks. The questionnaire comprised open-ended questions that allowed the participants to give as much feedback as possible. A set of pre-designed, open-ended questions were used during the interview process to ask participants questions on KM policy issues that were not addressed in the survey.

All quantitative data were analysed using Survey Monkey© and Microsoft Excel© 2010 whilst thematic analysis was used to analyse qualitative data. Using the constant comparative method of analysis (Leedy & Ormrod 2010:145), we looked for emerging themes and recurring events and categorised them. The themes and patterns emerging from interviews and surveys were grouped together, making it easier to analyse the data. Braun and Clarke (2006:77) argue in this regard that '... thematic analysis can act as a core analytical method because of its flexibility with both interpretive and constructivist paradigms'.

Major findings and discussions

Of the 190 questionnaires distributed, 101 (53.15%) responses were received, which is consistent with the findings of Greenlaw and Brown-Wetty (2009). They (Greenlaw & Brown-Wetty 2009:467) established that '... a response rate of 51.58% from a web-based survey tool was higher than many responses rates of that type of survey as reported in literature'. This study achieved a response rate that was 1.57% rate higher than that of Greenlaw and Brown-Wetty. Of the 101 respondents who participated in the study, 58 (57.43%) were from Nedbank and 43 (42.57%) were from FNB. The gender characteristics of respondents were as follows: 39 (38.61%) male managers from Nedbank compared to 27 (26.73%) male managers from FNB, 19 (18.82%) female managers from Nedbank compared to 16 (15.84%) female managers from FNB. It was established that, in all gender categories, more respondents were from Nedbank. The findings of the study are presented in two sections, namely quantitative and qualitative.

Quantitative findings

Respondents were asked to indicate KM practices and to what extent their bank had implemented KM practices. All study participants indicated that the acquisition, sharing and retention of knowledge are practiced at their bank. The study established that selected banks use different KM practice though a few of these KM practices were indeed found to be similar. The study identified the following KM practices.

Departmental meetings and team-building sessions

The data in Table 1 show that 18.84% of the respondents believed that departmental meetings and team-building sessions were the most widely used KM practices at the selected banks. The study revealed that, during departmental meetings, employees were exposed to information pertaining to global trends in the banking industry such as credit-card fraud, systems to combat cyber-crime and rules from MasterCard and Visa International. Departmental meetings were used as platforms for discussing and highlighting challenges and opportunities in the South African banking industry. It was established that team-building sessions were platforms for fostering awareness of the team spirit and to reinforce commitment to the team's shared goals and objectives' (Jain 2011:6). The study established that team-building sessions were designed to encourage individual team members to cooperate in the team's work environment, interacting and integrating skills into a united effort so that each individual's goal achievement is connected to the greater overall team's goal achievement. This thinking is consistent with the views of Jain (2011), namely that tacit knowledge can be achieved through face-to-face meetings and electronic discussions. Nonaka and Takeuchi (1995) posit that tacit knowledge can be transmitted through social interactions between individuals.

Succession planning

Eleven (10.89%) of the respondents believed that succession plans enable selected banks to retain organisational knowledge. The study established that succession planning is designed to ensure the continued effective performance of selected banks by providing for the deployment and replacement of key people over time. Participants indicated that lateral transfer and redeployment are a common practice at selected banks. Though redeployment and lateral transfer are common, this study could not establish if the motive was in line with KM initiatives. 'Effective succession or talent-pool management concerns itself with building a series of feeder groups up and down the entire leadership pipeline or progression' (Noe *et al.* 2010:447). There is no guarantee that experienced employees will retire or spend the rest of their working life in one organisation. Hence, organisations engage in succession planning programmes to ensure that businesses survive into the future in the event of a loss in tacit knowledge. With the changing demographics of the global village, organisations lose key staff to competitors due to working conditions or opportunities presented by competitors (Hill 2010:276). When key staff resigns or retires, it becomes a challenge to replace the key staff if the organisation does not have contingency measures in place.

Internet and intranet

Respondents indicated that the intranet and Internet play a key role as evidenced by a response rate of 14.85%. Technology facilitates communication between management and employees as well as quick access to, the search for and the retrieval of information. Dewah (2011:106) posits that '... technology comprising collaborative computing tools, knowledge servers, enterprise knowledge portals, electronic document management systems, knowledge harvesting tools and search engines' are critical enablers of knowledge-management. This information-communication technology plays an important role in how banking processes and transactions are conducted. Jain (2011) opines that effective knowledge-management practices could be achieved by utilising the latest IT tools in order to capture, create, store, transfer, share, retrieve, maintain and update knowledge. The study established that employees at selected banks have email addresses and a laptop or a personal computer, justifying their arguments that information and knowledge was created and shared through the Internet and intranet.

Road shows

As shown in Table 1, 3.96% of the respondents stated that road shows were common at Nedbank. Kotler and Keller (2013) define a road show as follows:

> ... a program comprising a series of marketing events that companies organise at multiple locations to generate interest

TABLE 1 Knowledge-management practices at selected banks.

Knowledge-management practices at selected banks	Nedbank (%)	FNB (%)	Total number of respondents (%)
Departmental meetings and team-building sessions	12 (11.89)	6 (5.95)	18 (18.84)
Succession planning	7 (6.93)	4 (3.96)	11 (10.89)
Use of the intranet and Internet	9 (8.91)	6 (5.94)	15 (14.85)
Road shows	4 (3.96)	-	4 (3.96)
Tea or lunch breaks	5 (4.95)	-	5 (4.95)
Seminars	3 (2.97)	-	3 (2.97)
Facebook, Wikis, Blogs and Twitter	6 (5.94)	2 (1.98)	8 (7.92)
Staff promotions/secondment	3 (2.97)	-	3 (2.97)
Mentorship	4 (3.96)	-	4 (3.96)
Project teams	5 (4.95)	3 (2.97)	8 (7.92)
Innovators campaign	-	7 (6.93)	7 (6.93)
Training centre	-	5 (4.95)	5 (4.95)
Extension of retirement age	-	3 (2.97)	3 (2.97)
Knowledge portals	-	3 (2.97)	3 (2.97)
Suggestion boxes	-	4 (3.96)	4 (3.96)
TOTAL	**58 (57.43)**	**43 (42.57)**	**101 (100)**

regarding a subject that they want to promote. It could about new products/services targeted at customers, new investment offerings targeted at investors, new social initiatives targeted at the community and so on. (p. 476)

These marketing events are usually conducted by the chief executive officer or managing executive of the bank in the case of Nedbank. They use the executive to add dignity and credibility to the roadshow as well as to attract high-profile individuals in society. The study revealed that road shows were conducted at Nedbank's regional head offices in Sandton, Pretoria, Polokwane, Cape Town and Durban, thus isolating other towns or cities.

Tea and lunch breaks

Tea and lunch breaks are platforms used to discuss social issues as evidenced by 4.95% of the respondents from Nedbank. Knowledge sharing platforms during tea or lunch breaks are not used at FNB as indicated in Table 1. During tea or lunch breaks, employees sometimes talk about work-related challenges and political and economic matters. These platforms enable employees to create and share knowledge and information. Social issues dominate tea and lunch breaks as friends want to 'catch-up' with weekend events.

Seminars

Nedbank respondents (2.97%) stated that seminars are environments where participants socialise and create and share knowledge with their colleagues. This finding is consistent with Nonaka and Konno (1998) who state that knowledge is shared within a contextualised space, called *ba*, which is a Japanese word roughly meaning 'place'. This designates a specific time and place where interactions between individuals take place. Employees should be given platforms to interact face-to-face, such as conferences meetings, so as to share a common understanding through shared language and narratives across networks. Trust also increases the incentive to exchange knowledge, and norms of reciprocity facilitate the transfer of novel information and tacit knowledge (Sheriff & Sheriff 2008).

Interactive communication channels

Interactive communication channels are tools such as emails, short message services, Facebook, WhatsApp, Twitter, Blogs, Wikis and BlackBerry messaging that handle, store, locate, distribute, receive and communicate tacit and explicit knowledge through social networks amongst people in possession of knowledge. Eight (7.92%) respondents confirmed the use of interactive communication channels at selected banks. Dewah (2011) posits that the adaptive-structuration theory draws some links between individuals and organisational learning due to the key concepts that address aspects of group interaction with technology. Organisational learning is regarded as a continuous phenomenon emerging from the social interactions and practices of individuals (Ryu, Kim & Chaudhury 2005). With the advent of interactive communication technology such as wikis, blogs, Facebook and Twitter, to name but a few, individuals are exposed to new information and knowledge.

Staff promotions and secondment

The study established that knowledge retention is achieved through the use of staff promotions and secondment as evidenced by 2.97% of respondents from Nedbank. Participants from FNB did not indicate the use of staff promotions and secondment as a knowledge retention practice. The study established that staff were promoted on the basis of years of experience, opportunities that arose due staff attrition and as part of Nedbank's succession planning policy. However, it was not clear if staff promotions were in any way aligned to knowledge-management initiatives.

Mentorship

The subject expert or experienced employee transfers tacit knowledge to the inexperienced employee (Nonaka 1995). Mentorship entails the pairing of an experienced member of staff with an inexperienced or new employee in order to assist the new employee in acquiring new knowledge

(Beazley, Boenisch & Harden 2002). During mentoring and apprenticeship training, senior or experienced managers transfer their knowledge, wisdom, specific insights and skills to their juniors within a short space of time so that, when the experienced employees leave the organisation, the organisation's practices, knowledge, history, stories and culture are preserved. The evidence (3.96%) shown in Table 1 indicates that mentorship programmes are used as a practice for the creation, sharing and retention of knowledge at Nedbank.

Project teams

The study found that selected banks have assembled groups of individuals to perform activities that contribute toward achieving a common task-related goal. The study established that product development, systems development, marketing campaigns and training and development projects are managed by project teams consisting of skilled workers from the same or different function areas. Eight (7.92%) of the respondents indicated that assignments or tasks at the selected banks are managed by retirees or experienced employees. They provide critical skills and experience to mentor junior and less-experienced employees, thus allowing senior employees to share knowledge and experiences during project management.

Innovators campaign

Seven (6.93%) of the respondents (from FNB) stated that the innovators campaign is a great success story for knowledge-creation and sharing because FNB's success is attributable to rewards and incentives awarded for innovation. The website Moneyweb (2012) reports on this matter as follows:

> First National Bank awarded R4 million in 2009 to winning ideas through its FNB Innovators initiative, in a bid to improve its service delivery and at the same time motivate staff to higher levels of excellence.
>
> The initiative identifies and rewards staff who display creative thinking and come up with innovations to ensure more efficient and effective systems and procedures. (n.p.)

In addition, the Steve campaign, eBucks and eWallet exemplify innovation initiatives at FNB, and individuals who came up with those concepts were rewarded for creative thinking. The study recorded that the innovators campaign is an important KM practice at FNB. This practice was not found at Nedbank.

Training centre

Results shown in Table 1 show that FNB has put in place KM practices such as training centres as indicated by 4.95% of the respondents. The study established that the FNB training centre is situated in the Sandton Business district, comprising 16 versatile conference venues, 3 boardrooms and a 140-seater auditorium and several breakaway rooms (First National Bank [FNB] 2011/12). The training centre is equipped with state of the art technology and facilities, and it offers an enabling environment for knowledge-creation and sharing (Nonaka & Takeuchi 1995).

Extension of retirement age

The risk of losing critical knowledge has a negative operational impact for organisations. This could be reduced by knowledge retention through capturing the organisations' individual tacit knowledge and subsequently transforming it into organisational knowledge and document processes. Critical knowledge in some of the banks' departments largely rests with people rather than in processes. When such people leave the bank, they take with them that critical knowledge. If the expertise of these senior or experienced people is not shared or transferred to the next employees, the potential to innovate is eroded, and the risk of unavoidable mistakes increases as these become a regular occurrence. It was established that the retirement age at FNB is not fixed to give both the employer and employee room for negotiation. Three (2.97%) respondents indicated that a policy on extending the retirement age exists at FNB whilst such a practice does not exist at Nedbank.

Other practices

The study recorded that knowledge portals (2.97%) and suggestion boxes (3.96%) are used for knowledge sharing at FNB, but there are no knowledge portals at Nedbank. Knowledge portals provide the infrastructure and enabling technology to support the creation, production, acquisition, aggregation, filtering, organisation, transmission, dissemination, usage and/or retention of knowledge. If the computer of today is a network, the desktop of today is a portal (FNB 2011/12). As suggested by Dewah (2011), organisations require ICTs that enable the acquisition, sharing, storage, retention and retrieval of organisational memory for future reuse. Knowledge portals become effective KM enablers if the systems are aligned to organisational KM policies. The study established that FNB's IT department is tasked to manage knowledge-related issues to reduce the cost of information publishing and distribution; to increase compliance with corporate standards, rules and processes for information storage and dissemination; to automate business processes such as price-quote generation or lead and forecast sharing and to preserve and leverage prior investments in back-end document management, enterprise resource planning (ERP) and data-warehousing systems (Moneyweb 2013). This study found that managers tend to conflate IT and KM, and this probably explains why the IT department was given these tasks. Both online and physical suggestion boxes are used as platforms for collecting and sharing information with customers and employees. Loyal customers send feedback on the quality of services delivered. The results are shown in Table 1.

The study noted that there are times when knowledge is relevant, and there are times when knowledge is not relevant. The point is that organisations need to use knowledge as soon as it becomes readily available. It was established that information use leads to knowledge-creation, which is possible if an organisation's management creates an enabling knowledge sharing culture. An environment that promotes knowledge acquisition is an environment where employees are provided with '... spaces for emerging relationships, which might be physical, virtual, or mental, providing a platform for advancing individual and/or collective knowledge' (Nonaka & Takeuchi 1995).

Qualitative findings

The knowledge assets of selected banks were found in places like databases, filing cabinets, Internet, intranet, extranets, annual reports and people's heads. The use of the intranet exposes staff to readily available information in order to acquire as much new knowledge as possible. Consequently, some relevant knowledge is acquired through bulletins posted on the intranet, but the veracity or relevance of the knowledge needs to be questioned. It was not clear whether management at selected banks are formally accepting and adopting knowledge as a strategic organisational asset. The banks' reports did not feature the KM practices in their mission statements or core philosophies. However, the FNB self-study of 2011 reveals that KM principles are in fact resident within the Information Technology Department. This finding is also complemented by Nedbank's self-study of 2011, which states that the Group Technology Shared Services (GTSS) is the custodian of knowledge practices. From this information, it is clear that banks misconstrue IT to be knowledge.

Patrick and Dotsika (2007) view knowledge sharing as the social interaction that involves the sharing of both the goal and the favourable outcome centred on problem solving. Platforms for knowledge sharing should then create opportunities for social interaction. The selected banks demonstrated a global presence on iTunes, U Blogs and social networking with the use of Facebook, Twitter, YouTube, WhatsApp and Blackberry Messaging (BBM). One observation from the study is that information-flow and Web 2.0 technology are used in banks as knowledge sharing tools. In addition, podcasts are included in iTunes to reach as many banking clients as possible. However, an interesting revelation was that the technology was created for customers, but employees have limited access to the use of such (Moneyweb 2012). In view of the selective use of Web 2.0 technology, employees felt marginalised in the process of knowledge sharing.

The process of keeping useful knowledge inside the banks and building organisational memory (OM) is documented in the selected banks' reports. This knowledge is preserved and kept in very safe places to ensure knowledge retention. It was established that KM awareness is limited as reflected in the following statement:

> ... there did not appear to be a documented inventory of the banks' skills base, or evident records of succession planning, even if the banks' annual reports suggested that there were career development practices. (FNB 2011/12; Nedbank Group South Africa 2012)

The absence of documents to indicate the progress on implementing KM practices could possibly explain why the cultures prevailing at the selected banks were not in favour of knowledge retention. In the event of the loss of key staff in these banks, management would have to revert to contingency measures to mitigate the loss in tacit knowledge.

This study noted that knowledge acquisition is a sub-set of knowledge capture because the knowledge acquired at the selected banks came from such sources as individuals and their colleagues as well as the intranet, Internet, documents and databases (Mavodza & Ngulube 2011). One observation was that expert systems are used by organisations to acquire knowledge from experienced individuals before the expiry of that knowledge. Though the selected banks have platforms for the acquisition, creation, sharing and retention of knowledge, it was noted that some of the KM practices do not provide employees with opportunities for asking questions or making suggestions as pointed out by one survey respondent. It seems clear that each KM practice has strengths and weaknesses. Therefore, the use of complimentary practices would be ideal to compensate the weaknesses of some practices.

The data for this study was both quantitative and qualitative in nature. Therefore, I needed to combine the data (triangulation) to provide answers to the research questions. The depth, clarity, reliability, transferability and truthfulness of the research findings are enhanced when two sets of data are put together. It should be noted that quantitative data are represented in numerical and graphical format whilst qualitative data are more descriptive. It was important to combine quantitative and qualitative data to ensure that relevant data was collected to address the KM practices that were investigated in this study. When multiple research methodologies are used, challenges abound when one tries to combine divergent paradigms. The challenges include the following: It is possible to end up by not doing either type of research well, especially as this research was done by an individual (Fidel 2008). Both quantitative and qualitative findings show that the IT departments of the selected banks are mandated to run all KM initiatives, a notion whereby many people conflate IT into KM or whereby all KM practices are part of IT. Findings from both sets of data indicate that ICTs are paramount in the acquisition, sharing and retention of KM practices.

Organisational knowledge conversion theory (SECI Model)

The study noted that KM practices at selected banks are based on the organisational knowledge conversion theory, that is, the SECI model. The conversion of organisational knowledge rests on the premise that knowledge is converted from one state to another (Nonaka &Takeuchi 1995). In this way, critical knowledge can be retained in the organisation by either sharing it or preserving it in the archives, thus forming part of the organisational memory. Nonaka and Takeuchi (1995) opine that organisational knowledge conversion deals with the conversion of knowledge from tacit to tacit (socialisation), from tacit to explicit (externalisation), from explicit to tacit (internalisation) and from explicit to explicit (combination) knowledge.

Socialisation: This entails the process of sharing knowledge between experts, mentors and retirees from whom juniors and new entrants at work can learn and in the process create tacit knowledge such as technical skills that may be obtained through observation, imitation and practice (Nonaka & Takeuchi 1995). In the selected banks, socialisation (originating *ba*) occurred when banking employees had direct, physical, face-to-face experiences with banking clients. Much of the interaction was in the banking halls, specifically with tellers and enquiries counters. The selected banks also used different ICTs in their operations. This means that employees are provided with laptops, and personal computers are made available in the banking halls for customers with online access. The banks also provide guidance on the effective use of technological resources. The latter could be viewed as the starting-point of the knowledge-creation process. The use of PCs in the banking halls is designed for customer convenience and easy access to the Internet. This is a simple way of capturing customer knowledge.

The sharing of tacit knowledge also manifested itself in the card and IT divisions of the selected banks. The study also established that tacit knowledge is transferred to fellow employees in the card division regarding trends in the credit-card payment industry, asset finance and personal loans. Through emails, intranet, electronic bulletin boards, training and brainstorming activities, tacit knowledge is transferred from one employee to other employees. Computer technology makes it possible for the organisational knowledge to be spread across the entire organisation (Nemani 2010).

Externalisation: It refers to the process of articulating tacit knowledge in the form of explicit concepts such as metaphors and analogies (Nonaka & Takeuchi 1995). The study established that selected banks use automated processes as well as manual systems to externalise tacit knowledge into paper records (organisational memory and archival repositories) that are accessed by the employees for use (codification). Externalisation (interacting *ba*) in the selected banks is expressed through the building and management of a collection of knowledge that comes in a variety of formats and their associated technology (Nemani 2010). In the case of FNB, innovative teams excel in bringing new services or products on board whilst, at Nedbank, externalisation is triggered by dialogue, regular formal meetings and brainstorming sessions (*dashikai*).

Combination: This is the process of combining bodies of explicit knowledge. In the process of combination, explicit knowledge is systemised and refined by, for example, utilising information and communication technology and databases (Lwoga, Ngulube & Stilwell 2010; Nonaka & Takeuchi 1995). In the selected banks, explicit knowledge is transferred through emails, documents, meetings and conversations, and such knowledge leads to the generation of new knowledge (Nonaka & Takeuchi 1995). Because of strict security policies, employees in selected banks share their explicit knowledge with fellow professionals during departmental and general meetings, through business cell phones and via emails.

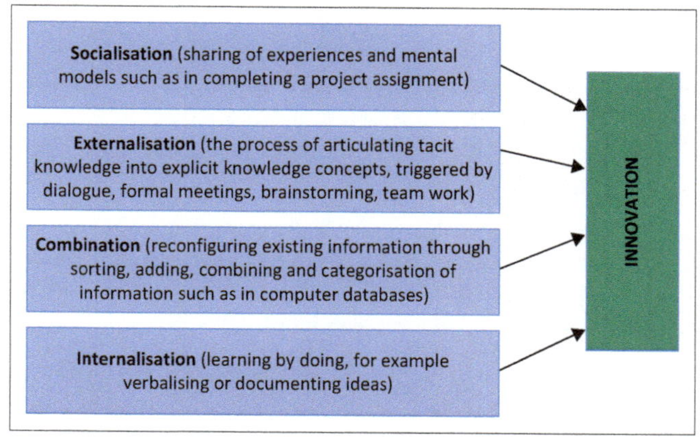

Source: Daud, S., Rahim, R.E.A. & Alimun, R., 2008, 'Knowledge creation and innovation in the classroom', *International Journal of Social Sciences* 3(1), 76.

FIGURE 1: SECI Model: Innovation in selected banks.

Internalisation: It is the process of converting explicit knowledge to tacit knowledge and is closely related to learning by doing (Nonaka & Takeuchi 1995). In this study, archives and procedure manuals were identified as sources of technical knowledge that were acquired by employees and then used to solve some work-related problems. The card divisions of selected banks refer to merchant profiles to determine the levels of fraudulent transactions, merchant transactions and other queries. Innovation by bank staff who work in a modern information environment is subsequently reflected in the enhanced quality of service and innovative products provided. The SECI processes are depicted in Figure 1.

The study established that a culture that promotes the creation of new knowledge in the organisation is vital because this allows organisations to create new knowledge from shared and existing knowledge repositories. The new knowledge must be preserved and retained as knowledge assets in appropriate media. Albers (2009) states that an ideal knowledge-management culture is characterised by trust, openness, teamwork, collaboration, risk taking, common language, courage and learning. Stankosky (2005) states that people are rewarded and recognised for individual achievements, sharing knowledge and contributing to teamwork. This is possible in an environment where the culture of knowledge sharing is a common practice. The implication of a lack of open-mindedness concerning KM practices is that any attempt by the banks to encourage these KM features would be fruitless if they are not a part of the banks' knowledge sharing culture. It would not even matter if there were no proper IT platform to share information. It was established that reward systems could be used to create re-usable knowledge resources. Contributing towards a collection of re-usable knowledge resources, knowledge capture could, if put in place, start happening in a formal way (Dewah 2011).

It was noted that a lack of knowledge-management practices leads to high costs due to a loss of institutional memory, knowledge gaps and uninformed decisions. Managing knowledge in a bank can leverage efficiency across all of its services to customers through accessing the right information for making informed decisions and eliminating duplication of efforts. Baskerville and Dulipovici (2006; see Jain 2007) mention the following:

> ... one of the characteristics of the economic school of KM as incorporating the ability to be a learning organisation that enables creativity and in the process increases the value generation capacity of an organisation. (n.p.)

The study established that knowledge enhances organisational performance as shown by 21.78% of the surveys though the point was raised by 17.83% of the respondents that a combination of knowledge and business strategies enhances organisation performance. Surveys and interviews concurred that, in the knowledge economy, organisations leverage efficiency across departments, thus improving service delivery and processes. This was evidenced by 13.86% of the respondents who viewed KM as a solution to business problems whilst 11.88% of the respondents felt that KM enhances customer relationships. Building relationships with customers or suppliers is regarded as a competitive strategy (Kotler & Keller 2010, 2013).

Building long-term relationships with suppliers and customers will enable the selected banks to leverage such relationships for growth. Nine (8.91%) of the respondents stated that knowledge-management improves work processes whilst 6.93% of the respondents stated that KM improves product and services development – an important factor required to address the ever-changing tastes and needs of customers. An organisation that has technology and processes that produce products and services within a shorter space of time than competitors usually satisfies customers (Kotler & Keller 2010, 2013) – resulting in knowledge work.

Conclusions

KM practices in the banking situation should be actions aimed at improving the internal flow and use of information and knowledge, and banks can be a major participant in these activities. Examples of such practices include the creation of 'best practices', databases, regular training and development programmes as well as the encouragement and promotion of employee interaction within departments and between individual staff and departments (Nonaka & Takeuchi 1995). One issue that was observed was that departments operated in knowledge silos. In this regard, Nonaka and Takeuchi (1995) advocate for interaction between individuals or departments to share knowledge and information. KM practices need not be based on the preconception that an organisation can mandate people to share their knowledge. It is likely that individuals would be willing to share their knowledge because they want to, not because they have been told or coerced to do so. It was established that there are no stipulated practices at selected banks for the acquisition, creation, sharing or retention of knowledge. However, the efforts that are made included staff meetings, team-building sessions, the use of Internet and intranets, succession planning, innovation campaigns, knowledge portals and project management teams.

The study established that knowledge at selected banks is not properly managed to facilitate the implementation of competitive KM practices for surviving in the knowledge economy. Being a dynamic competitive and information-intensive industry, bankers should possess skills that include the identification of knowledge needs, distinguishing knowledge-management from information management which can facilitate a broader and more inclusive KM initiative. This could result in the development of a KM framework for sharing institutional practices that include all employees – an important component of a KM strategy. From the findings presented in this study, it is recommended that the low level of KM practices at selected banks would be mitigated if there were clear KM policies and plans in place. From a structural perspective, it is recommended that the position of chief knowledge officer be established to formulate KM policies and drive all KM initiatives.

Acknowledgements

Competing interests

The authors declare that they have no financial or personal relationships which may have inappropriately influenced them in writing this article.

Authors' contributions

Both J.C. (University of South Africa) and P.N. (University of South Africa) conceptualised the study and then the first author did the research as part of his PhD study. Both authors were involved in writing up of the article and dealing with comments from the reviewers and the Editorial Board.

References

Albers, J.A., 2009, 'A practical approach to implementing knowledge management', *Journal of Knowledge Management Practice* 10(1), 1–8.

Babbie, E., 2010, *The practice of social research*, 12th edn., Wadsworth/Thompson, Southbank.

Baskerville, R. & Dulipovici, A., 2006, 'The theoretical foundations of knowledge management', *Knowledge Management Research and Practice* 4(2), 83–105. http://dx.doi.org/10.1057/palgrave.kmrp.8500090

Beazley, H., Boenisch, J. & Harden, D., 2002, *Continuity management: Preserving corporate knowledge and productivity when employees leave*, John Wiley and Sons, Hoboken.

Branin, J.J., 2003, 'Knowledge management in academic libraries: Building the knowledge bank at the Ohio State University', *Journal of Library Administration* 39(4), 1–56. http://dx.doi.org/10.1300/J111v39n04_05

Braun, V. & Clarke, V., 2006, 'Teaching thematic analysis: Overcoming challenges and developing strategies for effective learning', *The Psychologist* 26(2), 120–123.

Cong, X. & Pandya, K., 2003, 'Issues of KM in the public sector', *Electronic Journal of Knowledge Management* 1(2), 25–33.

Dewah, P., 2011, *Knowledge retention strategies in selected southern African public broadcasting corporations*, University of Fort Hare, East London.

Daud, S., Rahim, R.E.A. & Alimun, R., 2008, 'Knowledge creation and innovation in the classroom', *International Journal of Social Sciences* 3(1), 76.

Fidel, R., 2008, 'Are we there yet? Mixed methods research in library and information science', *Library and Information Science Research* 30, 265–272.

First National Bank, 2011/12, *Annual reports*, viewed 20 May 2013, from http://www.fnb.co.za/htm.pdf

Ford, D.P. & Staples, D.S., 2006, 'Perceived value of knowledge: The potential informer's perception', *Knowledge Management Research and Practice* 4, 3–16. http://dx.doi.org/10.1057/palgrave.kmrp.8500079

Fowler, A. & Pryke, J., 2003, 'KM in public service provision: the child support agency', *International Journal of Service Industry Management* 14(3), 254–28. http://dx.doi.org/10.1108/09564230310478828

Gaffoor, S. & Cloete, F., 2010, 'Knowledge management in local government: The case of Stellenbosch Municipality', *South African Journal of Information Management* 12(1).

Greenlaw, C. & Brown-Wetty, S., 2009, 'A comparison of web-based and paper-based survey methods: Testing assumptions of survey mode and response cost', *Evaluation Review* 33(5), 464–480. http://dx.doi.org/10.1177/0193841X09340214

Gupta, A.K. & Govindarajan, V., 2000, 'Knowledge flows within multinational corporations', *Strategic Management Journal* 1(21), 473–96. http://dx.doi.org/10.1002/(SICI)1097-0266(200004)21:4%3C473::AID-SMJ84%3E3.0.CO;2-I

Hill, C.W.L., 2010, *International business: Competing in the global marketplace,* 7th edn., McGraw Hill/Irwin, New York.

Jain, P., 2007, 'Knowledge management in e-government', *Journal of Knowledge Management Practice* 10(4), 1–10.

Jain, P., 2011, 'Personal knowledge management: The foundation of organisational knowledge management', *South African Journal of Libraries and Information Science* 77(1), 1–14. http://dx.doi.org/10.7553/77-1-62

Kim, M.P., 2005, *Knowledge retention enhances performance-based management*, viewed 28 February 2012, from http://www.dcma.mil/htm.pdf

Kotler, P. & Keller, K.L., 2010, *Marketing management*, 12th edn., Pearson Education Limited, Edinburgh Gate, Harlow, Essex.

Kotler, P. & Keller, K.L., 2013, *Marketing management*, 14th edn., Pearson Education Limited, Edinburgh Gate, Harlow, Essex.

Laudon, K.C. & Laudon, J.P., 2012, *Management information systems: Managing the digital firm*, 11th edn., Prentice Hall, Pearson Education, Upper Saddle River, New Jersey.

Leedy, P.D. & Omrod, J.E., 2005, *Practical research, planning and design*, 8th edn., Pearson Education International, Upper Saddle River, New Jersey.

Leedy, P.D. & Ormrod, J.E., 2010, *Practical research: Planning and design,* 9th edn., Pearson, Upper Saddle River.

Levy, M., 2011, 'Knowledge retention: Minimizing organizational business loss', *Journal of Knowledge Management* 15(4), 582–600. http://dx.doi.org/10.1108/13673271111151974

Lwoga, E.T., Ngulube, P. & Stilwell, C., 2010, 'Understanding indigenous knowledge: Bridging the knowledge gap through a knowledge creation model for agricultural development', *South African Journal of Information Management* 12(1), 436–438.

Moneyweb, 2012, *Information communication technologies in the banking industry in South Africa*, viewed 13 January 2014, from http://www.moneyweb.co.za/html

Moneyweb, 2013, *Modern banking*, viewed 11 February 2014, from http://www.moneyweb.co.za/html

Mavodza, J. & Ngulube, P., 2011, 'Exploring the use of knowledge management practices in an academic library in a changing information environment', *South African Journal of Libraries and Information Science* 77(1), 15–25. http://dx.doi.org/10.7553/77-1-63

Nedbank Group South Africa, 2012, *Annual report*, viewed 19 November 2012, from http://www.nedgroup.co.za/reports/html

Nemani, R.R., 2010, 'The role of computer technologies in knowledge acquisition', *Journal of Knowledge Management Practice* 11(3), 1–11.

Noe, R.A., Hollenbeck, J.R., Gerhart, B. & Wright, P.M., 2010, *Human resource management: Gaining a competitive advantage*, 8th edn., McGraw-Hill Irwin, New York.

Nonaka, I., 1995, 'A dynamic theory of organizational knowledge creation', *Journal of Organization Science* 5(1), 14–37. http://dx.doi.org/10.1287/orsc.5.1.14

Nonaka, I. & Konno, N., 1998, 'The concept of "Ba", building a foundation for knowledge creation', *California Management Review* 4(3), 40–54. http://dx.doi.org/10.2307/41165942

Nonaka, I. & Takeuchi, H., 1995, *The knowledge creating company: How Japanese companies create the dynamics of innovation,* Oxford Press, New York.

Pacharapha, T. & Ractham, V.V., 2012, 'Knowledge acquisition: The roles of perceived value of knowledge content and source', *Journal of Knowledge Management* 16(5), 724–739. http://dx.doi.org/10.1108/13673271211262772

Patrick, K. & Dotsika, F., 2007, 'Knowledge sharing: Developing from within', *The Learning Organisation* 14(5), 395–406, viewed 22 October 2013, from http://www.emeraldinsight.com/0969-6474.htm/

Polanyi, M., 1962, *Personal knowledge: Towards a post-critical philosophy,* University of Chicago Press, Chicago.

Powell, R., 1997, *Basic research for librarians*, 3rd edn., Ablex Publishing Corporation, London.

Ragsdell, G., 2009, 'Inhibitors and enhancers to knowledge sharing: Lessons from the voluntary sector', *Journal of Knowledge Management Practice* 10(1), 1–9.

Rowley, J., 2002, 'Using case studies in research', *Management Research News* 25(1), 16–27. http://dx.doi.org/10.1108/01409170210782990

Romm, N. & Ngulube, P. (in press), 'Mixed methods research', in E.R. Mathipa & G.T. Gumbo (eds.), *Addressing research challenges: Making headway for emerging researchers.*

Ryu, C., Kim, Y.J. & Chaudhury, A., 2005, 'Knowledge acquisition via three learning processes in enterprise information portals: Learning-by-investment, learning-by-doing, learning-from-others', *Management Information Systems Quarterly* 29(2), 245–278.

Sarrafzadeh, M., Martin, B. & Hazeri, A., 2006, 'Library information systems professionals and knowledge management: Some recent perspectives', *Journal of Library Management* 27(9), 621–635. http://dx.doi.org/10.1108/01435120610715527

Sheriff, K. & Sheriff, A.S., 2008, 'The social capital before you think knowledge transfer', in E.M. Jennex (ed.), *Current issues in knowledge management*, pp. 53–56, Hershey, New York. http://dx.doi.org/10.4018/978-1-59904-916-8.ch005

Singh, S.P., 2007, 'What are we managing: Knowledge or information?', *VINE: The Journal of Information and Knowledge Management Systems* 37(2), 169–179. http://dx.doi.org/10.1108/03055720710759946

Stankosky, M.A., 2005, 'Advances in knowledge management: University research toward an academic discipline', in M. Stankosky (ed.), *Creating the discipline of knowledge management: The latest in university research*, pp. 1–14, Butterworth-Heinemann, Burlington. http://dx.doi.org/10.1016/B978-0-7506-7878-0.50005-3

Thilmany, J., 2008, 'Passing on know-how: Knowledge retention strategies can keep employees workplace-acquired wisdom from walking out the door when they retire', *HR Magazine*, June, viewed 16 February 2013, from http://www.knowledgeharvesting.com/documents/HRM%20%20Passing%20n%20know-How.pdf/htm

Tiwana, A., 2008, *The knowledge management toolkit: Orchestrating IT, strategy and knowledge platforms*, 2nd edn., Prentice Hall, Upper Saddle River.

Turban, E., McLean, E. & Wetherbe, J., 2004, *Information technology for management: Transforming organizations in the digital economy*, 6th edn., John Wiley and Sons, New York.

Wamundila, S. & Ngulube, P., 2011, 'Enhancing knowledge retention in higher education: A case of the University of Zambia', *South African Journal of Information Management* 13(1), 439–448. http://dx.doi.org/10.4102/sajim.v13i1.439

Yin, R.K., 2003, *Case study research: Design and methods'*, Sage, Thousand Oaks, California.

Young, R., 2010, *Knowledge management and innovation in a global knowledge economy. KM Egypt 2010, April 20–21,* Knowledge Associates International, London.

4

Measuring the success of business-intelligence systems in South Africa: An empirical investigation applying the DeLone and McLean Model

Authors:
Taurayi Mudzana[1]
Manoj Maharaj[1]

Affiliation:
[1]School of Management, IT and Governance, University of KwaZulu-Natal, South Africa

Correspondence to:
Taurayi Mudzana

Email:
mudzana@yahoo.com

Postal address:
Private Bag X54001, Durban 4000, South Africa

Background: Business intelligence systems (BIS) hold promise for improving organisational decision-making in South Africa. Yet, the use of BIS has been associated with a number of challenges.

Objectives: The aim of the study was to identify post implementation factors that contribute to the success of BIS in South African organisations.

Method: This study draws on the DeLone and McLean Model of Information Systems success and recent literature on business-intelligence (BI) to develop and test a BIS success model. A quantitative study was conducted in the form of a survey of 102 BI users to validate the BIS success model.

Results: Five interrelated factors of BIS success were confirmed. The study found that the quality of information has a strong influence on system use and user satisfaction. It was found that system quality is positively associated with user satisfaction. The results also indicated that service quality is negatively related to user satisfaction. The study also found that user satisfaction is positively associated with nett benefits of a BI system.

Conclusion: The study provides insights for both managers and practitioners on the factors to focus on when implementing BIS thereby minimising the adoption risks associated with BI failures.

Introduction

Business-intelligence systems (BIS) have a potential to provide many benefits to an organisation. Business intelligence (BI) has been identified as a significant growth area due to its valuable functionality and its ability to add value (Woodside 2011). Furthermore, Gartner (2011) reports that worldwide expenditure in BIS was more than USD 10 billion in 2010 and was expected to continue to grow at a rate of approximately 8.1% annually. However, implementing new BIS is often a challenge (Benard & Atir 1993; Clavier, Lotriet & Van Loggerenberg 2012; Olbrich, Poppelbuß & Niehaves 2012). Hence, understanding the drivers of and barriers to BIS success is very important. The success of BIS has not been fully investigated (Chaveesuk 2010; Yeoh & Koronios 2010). A search in the main electronic databases for journals, such as EbscoHost, Emerald, Google Scholar, Proquest and ScienceDirect, suggests that no academic research has validated the DeLone and McLean (2003) model of information-systems (IS) success in the context of BI in South Africa. This study seeks to address this gap. It is important to study the South African context because most reports on IS success are drawn from settings in industrialised countries and are focused on e-government and enterprise resource planning ERP system success (Heeks 2010). Furthermore, the results of these reports cannot easily be translated to the South-Africa context because South Africa is a developing economy. In most developing countries, a shortage of expertise, staff turnover and limitations in financial resources are cited as challenges to the implementation and utilisation of IS (Avgerou 2008).

This paper is organised as follows. The next section briefly reviews the existing literature on BI. Then the information-systems success model used in the study is highlighted. The model chosen for this study is the DeLone and McLean (2003) model. Next, the proposed BIS success model is presented, and the research methodology is discussed. The results of the study are then presented, followed by the discussion section. The conclusion is presented in the final section of the article.

Business intelligence

BI is defined as a collection of technology and applications used to enhance decision-making (Wixom & Watson 2010). Turban *et al.* (2011:12) classify a BI system into four main components: (1) a data-warehouse (DW) environment, (2) business analytics, (3) business performance management (BPM) and (4) a user interface such as a dashboard. BI offers many benefits to the adopting organisation, for example increasing sales, reducing costs and providing new products and services (Hwang & Xu 2007). BI enables organisations to make well-informed business decisions and can thus be a source of competitive advantage (Ranjan 2009). Similarly, Vitt, Luckevich and Misner (2010) argue that the primary goal of BI is to help people make better decisions that improve a company's performance and promote its competitive advantage in the marketplace. Ranjan (2009) asserts that BI reveals the following:

(1) the position of the firm in comparison to its competitors
(2) changes in customer behaviour and spending patterns
(3) the capabilities of the firm
(4) market conditions, future trends, demographic and economic information
(5) the social, regulatory, and political environment
(6) what the other firms in the market are doing. (p. 63)

Hwang and Xu (2007) further point out that return on investment in BI could be as high as 400%. However, international evidence suggests that BIS are expensive and have generally not been a success (Beal 2005; Legodi & Barry 2010). Some explanations for the low levels of success include the following: system quality; information quality; service quality; user satisfaction (Shin 2003), support for end users; accuracy, format and preciseness; fulfilment of end users' needs; reduced effort by developers to produce information; user ability to produce information and better decision-making (Wixom & Watson 2010). BI is clearly very important to an organisation, but it is evident that a number of issues may limit its use and adoption. It is important therefore that we improve our understanding of the key factors that influence the success of BIS in South Africa. The next section of this paper describes the DeLone and McLean (2003) model of IS success, which is the foundational model chosen for this study.

DeLone and McLean information-systems success model

The theoretical underpinning chosen for this study is the updated DeLone and McLean (2003) model of IS success. The DeLone and McLean (1992) model propose six major factors of IS success: (1) system quality, (2) information quality, (3) use, (4) user satisfaction, (5) individual impact and (6) organisational impact. Pitt, Watson and Kavan (1995) propose a modification of the DeLone and McLean (1992) model to include service quality. Seddon (1997) challenges the combination of a process and variance model. He (Seddon 1997:23) argues that the DeLone and McLean (1992) model is 'confusing and mis-specified'. The DeLone and McLean (2003) information-systems success model address

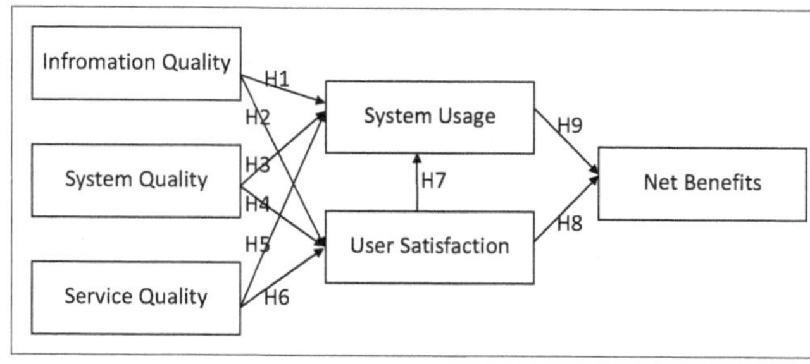

FIGURE 1: Research model.

the weaknesses of the original model. The model consists of the following six factors: system quality, information quality, service quality, use or intention to use, user satisfaction and nett benefit. For the purposes of this study, we have chosen to assess BIS success using the updated DeLone and McLean (2003) model. One of the reasons for this choice was because it was identified as the single most cited IS success model in IS literature (Lowry, Karunga & Richardson 2007). Furthermore, the DeLone and McLean (2003) model framework has been used extensively in various empirical works on IS success. Empirical work has drawn on the updated DeLone and McLean (2003) model to examine the success of a student information system using student users (Rai, Lang & Welker 2002), tourism websites (Stockdale & Borovicka 2006; Wang & Liao 2008), knowledge-management systems (Wu & Wang 2006), e-government systems (Hussein, Abdul Karim & Selamat 2007), online learning systems (Lin 2007) and e-commerce systems (Wang & Liao 2008). Prior studies confirm the model's usefulness in assessing different IS applications. However, in the South African BI context, the researchers found no study that has utilised the updated DeLone and McLean (2003) model to assess the success of local BI systems. The research model and the hypotheses are discussed next.

Research model and hypotheses

Figure 1 illustrates the research model developed for the study. The research model attempts to explain BIS success in a South African context. The research model posits that BIS success is represented by six factors, and each factor is in turn measured, using multiple variables adapted from current literature and input from BI experts.

Information quality

Information quality focuses on the characteristics of the information that is produced by the BIS (Petter, Delone & McLean 2008). This information is mainly in the form of reports. High-quality information is expected to lead to use and user satisfaction of the BIS. There is solid support for the association between information quality and system use and between information quality and user satisfaction (Halawi, McCarthy & Aronson 2007; Kositanurit, Ngwenyama & Osei-Bryson Kweku 2006; Livari 2005; Rai *et al.* 2002). Therefore, in this study, we propose the following hypotheses:

H_{10}: Information quality is not related to system use in a business-intelligence system.

H_{1A}: Information quality is related to system use in a business-intelligence system.

H_{20}: Information quality is not related to user satisfaction in a business-intelligence system.

H_{2A}: Information quality is related to user satisfaction in a business-intelligence system.

System quality

Petter *et al.* (2008) define system quality as follows:

> ... the desirable characteristics of an information system. For example: ease of use, system flexibility, system reliability, and ease of learning, as well as system features of intuitiveness, sophistication, flexibility, and response times. (p. 239)

Previous studies on the success of information systems have demonstrated the positive impact of system quality on user satisfaction and system use (DeLone & McLean 2003; Rai *et al.* 2002; Seddon 1997). Therefore, we propose the following hypotheses:

H_{30}: System quality is not related to system use in a business-intelligence system.

H_{3A}: System quality is related to system use in a business-intelligence system.

H_{40}: System quality is not related to user satisfaction in a business-intelligence system.

H_{4A}: System quality is related to user satisfaction in a business-intelligence system.

Service quality

Service quality focuses on the level of support that BI users receive. Service quality is measured, based on responsiveness, accuracy, reliability, technical competence and empathy of the personnel (Petter *et al.* 2008). Like most studies on IS success, quality service is expected to have a positive influence on user satisfaction and system use (DeLone & McLean 2003; Rai *et al.* 2002). Therefore, we propose the following hypotheses:

H_{50}: Service quality is not related to system use in a business-intelligence system.

H_{5A}: Service quality is related to system use in a business-intelligence system.

H_{60}: Service quality is not related to user satisfaction in a business-intelligence system.

H_{6A}: Service quality is related to user satisfaction in a business-intelligence system.

System use

System use focuses on the utilisation of the BIS by the users. System use is defined as follows:

> ... the degree and manner in which staff and customers utilise the capabilities of an information system. For example: amount of use, frequency of use, nature of use, appropriateness of use, extent of use, and purpose of use. (Petter *et al.* 2008:239)

Previous studies on the success of IS have demonstrated the positive impact of system use on user satisfaction and nett benefits (DeLone & McLean 2003; Rai *et al.* 2002). Therefore, we propose the following hypotheses:

H_{90}: System use is not related to nett benefits in a business-intelligence system.

H_{9A}: System use is related to nett benefits in a business-intelligence system.

User satisfaction

Seddon (1997) defines user satisfaction as follows:

> ... the net feeling of pleasure or displeasure resulting from aggregating all the benefits that a person hopes to receive from interaction with the information system. Each user has a set of expected benefits or aspirations for the information system. To the extent that the system meets or fails to meet each of these aspirations, the user is more or less satisfied. (p. 246)

Previous studies on the success of IS have demonstrated the positive impact of user satisfaction on net benefits (DeLone & McLean 2003; Rai *et al.* 2002; Wang, Fan & Xu 2012). Therefore, we propose the following hypotheses:

H_{70}: User satisfaction is not related to system use in a business-intelligence system.

H_{7A}: User satisfaction is related to system use in a business-intelligence system.

H_{80}: User satisfaction is not related to nett benefits in a business-intelligence system.

H_{8A}: User satisfaction is related to nett benefits in a business-intelligence system.

Research methodology

In order to validate the research model, data were collected by means of an online questionnaire. The online questionnaire consisted of two main parts. The first part included demographic questions such as age, gender and industry. The second part consisted of 35 five-point Likert-scale questions aiming to assess the six factors of the proposed research model. The five-point Likert scale ranged from strongly agree to strongly disagree. The online questionnaire was developed from prior studies and adapted to suit the BI context. Table 1 below shows the items for each construct in the second section of the questionnaire.

Before the major study, the instrument was pilot tested by six professionals to ensure that the wording was understandable and that its length was appropriate. The final instrument was administered over a four-week period. Ethical clearance was obtained before conducting this study. The results of the data analysis used to test the hypotheses will be presented in the next section.

Results

A total of 102 conveniently selected professionals responded to the survey. Most of the responding professionals were

TABLE 1: Survey instrument constructs.

Construct	Description	Adapted from
System quality	Availability	DeLone and McLean (1992); Doll and Torkzadeh (1988); DeLone and McLean (2003)
	Ease of use	-
	Accessibility	-
	Usefulness	-
	Stability	-
Information quality	Content	Doll and Torkzadeh (1988)
	Availability	-
	Accuracy	-
	Timelines	-
	Conciseness	-
System use	I frequently use the system.	Seddon (1997)
	I depend upon the system.	-
	I only use the system when it is absolutely necessary for learning.	-
User satisfaction	Meets information needs.	Rai *et al.* (2002)
	I think the system is very helpful.	-
	Overall, I am satisfied with the system.	-
Nett benefits	The system has a positive impact on my work.	DeLone and Mclean (1992); DeLone and Mclean (2003)
	Overall, the performance of the system is good.	-
	Overall, the system is successful.	-
	The system is an important and valuable aid to me in the performance of my work.	-
Service quality	Assurance	DeLone and Mclean (2003)
	Empathy	-
	Responsiveness	-
	Knowledge	-

TABLE 2: Reliability tests.

Factor	Items	Cronbach alpha
System quality	8	0.77
Information quality	10	0.75
User satisfaction	3	0.86
System usage	3	0.79
Net benefits	6	0.74
Service quality	5	0.85

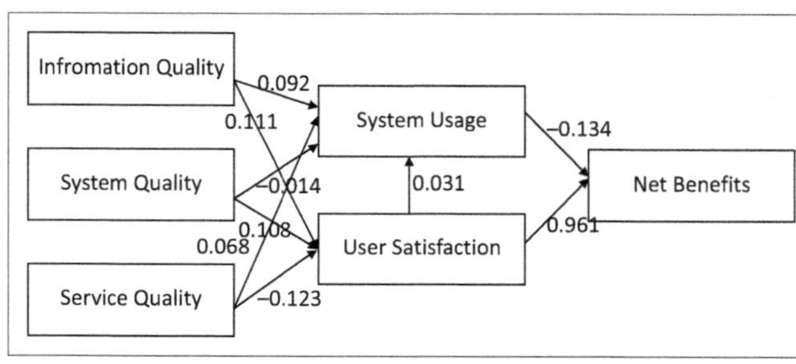

FIGURE 2: Structural model test results.

male (52%), roughly 60% of respondents were between 31 and 40 years of age, and 20% of respondents were between 41 and 50 years old. Over half of the respondents (55%) reported having more than five years of experience in their current role whilst 45% reported less than five years of experience. Approximately two thirds of the responding professionals reported that they use BIS for ad-hoc reporting. All participants participated voluntarily in this study.

Measurement model

The results of the reliability tests are shown in Table 2. The results show that the value of Cronbach's alpha for all constructs is higher than 0.7. This suggests that the questionnaire and its constructs are suited for the study (Hair *et al.* 2006).

Convergent validity was established by examining the average variance extracted (AVE) scores. These were all well above the recommended 0.50 (Fornell & Larcker 1981), confirming that constructs explained above 50% of the variance in their underlying items.

Structural model

After validating the measurement model, the hypotheses were tested by examining the structural model. Figure 2 shows the path coefficients, which indicate the strengths of the relationships between the independent and dependent variables.

The results indicate that information quality is positively related to both system use and user satisfaction. The null hypotheses (H_{10}, H_{20}) were thus rejected. Therefore, the alternative hypotheses (H_{1A}, H_{2A}) stand (0.092 and 0.011, respectively). The path coefficient between system quality and system use is –0.014 with a *p*-value of 0.624. The Kendall correlation coefficient between system use and system quality is 0.046 with a *p*-value of 0.568. System quality is thus not related to system use. Therefore, the null hypothesis cannot be rejected (H_{30}). Considering user satisfaction, however, the results indicate that system quality is positively related to user satisfaction. In this case, the null hypothesis was rejected. Therefore, the alternative hypothesis (H_{4A}) stands (0.108). The path coefficient between system use and service quality is 0.068 with a p-value of 0.188. The Kendall correlation coefficient between system use and service quality is 0.049 with a p-value of 0.574. Therefore, the null hypothesis cannot be rejected. Service quality, in turn, is not related to system use. For the sixth hypothesis, the path coefficient is −0.123 with a p-value of 0.051. The Kendall correlation coefficient between user satisfaction and service quality is −0.200 with a p-value of 0.019. Therefore, the null hypothesis can be rejected. User satisfaction is negatively related to service quality. The results indicate that, as service quality increases, user satisfaction decreases. The path coefficient between system use and nett benefits is −0.134 with a p-value of 0.495. The Kendall correlation coefficient between system usage and nett benefits is −0.028 with a p-value of 0.733. System use is not related to nett benefits. Therefore, the null hypothesis cannot be rejected. The results indicate that the path coefficient between user satisfaction and a nett benefit is 0.961 with a p-value of 0.000. The Kendall correlation coefficient between user satisfaction and nett benefits is 0.314 with a p- value of 0.000. Therefore, the null hypothesis can be rejected. User satisfaction is positively related to nett benefits. Overall, information quality exhibited a stronger effect than system quality and service quality in influencing system use and user satisfaction, respectively.

Discussion and implications

This study formulated and verified a BIS success model. Using the updated DeLone and McLean model as a theoretical framework, we constructed ten measures in information quality, eight measures in system quality, five measures in service quality, three measures in user satisfaction, three measures in system use and six measures in nett benefits. To our knowledge, this is the first study that extends the DeLone and McLean Model (2003) to a BI context in South Africa. Consistent with previous studies (DeLone & McLean 2003; Kositanurit *et al.* 2006; Halawi *et al.* 2007; Holsapple & Lee-Post 2006; Rai *et al.* 2002), our findings indicate that information quality is positively linked to system use and user satisfaction. The results are less clear with respect to the influence of system quality on system use and user satisfaction. System quality was not found to be related to system use. This finding is unexpected and inconsistent with previous studies where system quality is reported to have a significantly positive influence on system use (DeLone & McLean 2003; Fitzgerald & Russo 2005). The different types of applications investigated and the different contexts can explain differences amongst the findings of this study and the research in previous studies. Thus, whilst the present study examined BIS in South Africa, the DeLone and McLean (2003) study examined e-commerce in Western countries. Whilst the DeLone and McLean model is intended to be valid for all IS in general (DeLone & McLean 2003), they recommended that researchers should adapt the research model for specific domains to better address the characteristics of the latter (Dinter, Schieder & Gluchowski 2011). In this study, the success factors where adapted to suit the BI context. The results of the test of the effect of system quality on user satisfaction found that system quality is positively related to user satisfaction. As the quality of the system increases so does the user-satisfaction levels. The results of this study agree with the findings of previous studies (DeLone & McLean 2003; Halawi *et al.* 2007; Holsapple & Lee-Post 2006). The implication for management is that system quality plays an important role in the success of BI projects. Managers could make an effort to address system quality to increase the chances of success of the BIS as users are bound to be satisfied by a high-quality system. The empirical results of the study indicate that there is no significant relationship between service quality and system use. This finding suggests that the quality of service does not influence the use of the system. This is inconsistent with previous studies where service quality is reported to have a significant influence on system use (Caldeira & Ward 2002; Fitzgerald & Russo 2005).

A possible explanation for this is that service quality is outsourced to BI vendors who manage the service, and consequently, BI users do not view it as an integral part of the organisation and tend to take the availability of this service for granted. The results of this study indicate that service quality influences user satisfaction negatively, results which are inconsistent with the information-systems model of DeLone and McLean (2003). DeLone and McLean's work suggest that service quality is positively related to user satisfaction. The different types of systems investigated and their different needs for respective contexts can explain differences amongst the findings of this study and DeLone and McLean's. Hypothesis 7 investigated the relationship between user satisfaction and system use. The empirical results of the study indicate that user satisfaction does not influence system use. This is unexpected, given that one would have expected the levels of system use to increase as the levels of user satisfaction increase. A plausible explanation is that the model used in the present study did not include the intention-to-use factor, and it also did not include system-use and user-satisfaction association. However, this research is not alone in providing evidence of a non-significant relationship between user satisfaction and system use. Some previous studies (Ang & Soh 1997; Vlahos & Ferratt 1995) also found that user satisfaction did not directly influence system use. The influence of system use on the nett benefits of business-intelligence systems in South Africa was examined by hypotheses eight. The empirical results of the study indicate that there is no significant relationship between system use and nett benefits. These results were inconsistent with the theoretical arguments based on DeLone and McLean (2003). The results of this study also do not agree with the findings of other previous studies (Devaraj & Kohli 2003; Leclercq 2007; Zhu & Kraemer 2005). However, a study by Gelderman (1998) did not find a significant positive correlation between system and nett benefit. A plausible explanation for this difference is that the model for the present study focused only on system use and not on the intention to use a system. Furthermore, the model used in this study does not include the nett benefits to the system-use relationship but rather focuses on the relationship between system use and nett benefits. It was found that user satisfaction positively influences nett benefits, results that are consistent with the information-systems model of DeLone & McLean (2003) which suggested that user satisfaction is positively related to nett benefits. The results imply that, as levels of satisfaction increase, so do the nett benefits of the system. In this regard, the results of this study agree with the findings of other previous studies (Gelderman 1998; Law & Ngai 2007).

Implications

The study is one of only a few to formulate and test a BIS success model based on the DeLone and McLean's (2003) IS success model in a South African context. Therefore, this study contributes knowledge to information-systems literature in general and BI in particular. As a result, by using the DeLone and McLean's (2003) model as its basis, this study adds to the area of information-systems success by supporting the DeLone and McLean's (2003) model and by refining it to be more suited to BI success, specifically in the context of South Africa. Some of the factors identified through this study as important to BIS success corroborate previous literature. The different types of applications investigated and the different contexts can explain differences amongst the findings of this study and previous research. Thus, whilst the present study examined BIS in South Africa, the DeLone and McLean's (2003) IS success model examined e-commerce in Western countries. Whilst the DeLone and McLean's (2003) model is intended to be valid for all information systems in general, they recommend that researchers should adapt the research model for specific domains to better address the characteristics of the latter (Dinter *et al.* 2011). In this study, the success factors where adapted to suit the BI context. The model of BI-system success formulated and tested in this study will be of interest to organisations wishing to adopt BI systems. Two groups of people who could possibly be drawn from this study. Firstly, BI developers and BI Managers who will develop and implement a BIS would benefit. Secondly, the BI vendor industry would benefit from this study. The main practical implication of this study for BI developers and managers is that it would make them more aware of the factors that influence the success of the BIS they develop. With these factors in mind, they would then be able to incorporate into their development such factors as the ease of use, ease of learning, stability and security of their system. This research enables people in the BI vendor industry to understand the pitfalls of BI adoption and the reasons why adoption can be problematic. It could allow them to take a more proactive approach when new versions of solutions are been developed.

Limitations

There are some limitations to this study. The first limitation of the study is that context in which the study was set was limited to organisations operating in South Africa. Consequently, caution needs to be taken when generalising the results of this study. A second limitation was that we tested only part of the updated DeLone and McLean (2003) model. Further research could consider incorporating and validating the entire updated DeLone and McLean (2003) model.

Conclusion

The objective of this study was to identify key factors influencing BIS success in South Africa and to test those factors using data from BIS users. We developed a conceptual model for BIS success in South Africa, based on the updated DeLone and McLean (2003) model. Survey data from 102 BI users in South Africa were used to test the BIS success model. This study reached several conclusions based on the empirical findings. Firstly, the results of the empirical analysis indicate that the quality of information has a strong influence on system use and user satisfaction. Secondly, the results indicate that system quality is positively associated with user satisfaction. Thirdly, service quality is negatively related to user satisfaction. Fourthly, nett benefits are positively associated with user satisfaction. Overall, the empirical results of the study provide moderate support for the proposed research model. Of the nine relationships tested, five were significant. In summary, this research sheds light on the key factors to be considered by organisations that are considering implementing or which have already adopted a BI system. Therefore, this study has improved our understanding of the factors influencing the success of BIS in South Africa. The findings also contribute to the growing body of literature on the measurement of the success of information systems in general. Future research should aim to confirm the specific findings of this study and further to investigate the interdependency of the success factors.

Acknowledgements

Competing interests

The authors declare that they have no financial or personal relationships that may have inappropriately influenced them in writing this article.

Authors' contributions

T.M. (University of KwaZulu-Natal) and M.M. (University of KwaZulu-Natal) contributed equally to the writing of this article.

References

Ang, S. & Soh, C., 1997, 'User information satisfaction, job satisfaction, and computer background: An exploratory study', *Information & Management* 32(5), 255–266. http://dx.doi.org/10.1016/S0378-7206(97)00030-X

Avgerou, C., 2008, 'Information systems in developing countries: A critical research review', *Journal of Information Technology* 23(3), 133–146. http://dx.doi.org/10.1057/palgrave.jit.2000136

Beal, B., 2005, *Half of data warehouse projects to fail,* viewed 22 May 2014, from http://searchcrm.techtarget.com/news/1066086/Report-Half-of-data-warehouse-projects-to-fail

Benard, R. & Atir, A.S., 1993, 'User satisfaction with EISs: Meeting the needs of executive users', *Information Systems Management* 10(4), 21–29. http://dx.doi.org/10.1080/10580539308906953

Caldeira, M.M. & Ward, J.M., 2002, 'Understanding the successful adoption and use of IS/IT in SMEs: An explanation from Portuguese manufacturing industries', *Information Systems Journal* 12(2), 121–152. http://dx.doi.org/10.1046/j.1365-2575.2002.00119.x

Chaveesuk, S., 2010, 'The determinants of the adoption and application of business intelligence: An ERP perspective', PhD thesis, Victoria University.

Clavier, P.R., Lotriet, H.H. & Van Loggerenberg, J.J., 2012, 'Business intelligence challenges in the context of goods and service-dominant logic', *proceedings of the 45th Hawaii International Conference,* Hawaii, pp. 4138–4147. http://dx.doi.org/10.1109/hicss.2012.138

DeLone, W.H. & McLean, E.R., 1992, 'Information systems success: The quest for the dependent variable', *Information Systems Research* 3(1), 60–95. http://dx.doi.org/10.1287/isre.3.1.60

DeLone, W.H. & McLean, E.R., 2003, 'The DeLone and McLean model of information systems success: A ten-year update', *Journal of Management Information Systems* 19(4), 9–30.

Devaraj, S. & Kohli, R., 2003, 'Performance impacts of information technology: Is actual usage the missing link?', *Management Science* 49(3), 273–289. http://dx.doi.org/10.1287/mnsc.49.3.273.12736

Dinter, B., Schieder, C. & Gluchowski, P., 2011, 'Towards a life cycle oriented business intelligence success model', *proceedings of the Americas Conference of Information Systems* 361.

Fitzgerald, G. & Russo, N.L., 2005, 'The turnaround of the London ambulance service computer-aided dispatch system (LASCAD)', *European Journal of Information Systems* 14(3), 244–257. http://dx.doi.org/10.1057/palgrave.ejis.3000541

Fornell, C. & Larcker, D.F., 1981, 'Evaluating structural equation models with unobservable variables and measurement error', *Journal of of Marketing Research* 18(1), 39–50. http://dx.doi.org/10.2307/3151312

Gartner, 2011, 'Gartner says worldwide business intelligence, CPM and analytic applications/performance management software market grew seven percent in 2012', viewed 01 January 2013, from http://www.gartner.com/newsroom/id/2507915

Gelderman, M., 1998, 'The relation between user satisfaction, usage of information systems and performance', *Information & Management* 34(1), 11–18. http://dx.doi.org/10.1016/S0378-7206(98)00044-5

Heeks, R., 2010, 'Real money from virtual worlds', *Scientific American* 302, 68–73. http://dx.doi.org/10.1038/scientificamerican0110-68

Hair, J.F., Black, W.C., Babin, B.J., Anderson, R.E. & Tatham, R.L., 2006, *Multivariate data analysis,* 6th edn., Pearson Prentice Hall, New Jersey.

Halawi, L.A., McCarthy, R.V. & Aronson, J.E., 2007, 'An empirical investigation of knowledge management systems' success', *Journal of Computer Information Systems* 48(2), 121–135.

Holsapple, C.W. & Lee-Post, A., 2006, 'Defining, assessing, and promoting elearning success: An information systems perspective', *Decision Sciences Journal of Innovative Education* 4(1), 67–85. http://dx.doi.org/10.1111/j.1540-4609.2006.00102.x

Hussein, R., Abdul Karim, N. & Selamat, M., 2007, 'The impact of technological factors on information systems success in the electronic-government context', *Business Process Management Journal* 13(5), 613–627. http://dx.doi.org/10.1108/14637150710823110

Hwang, M.I. & Xu, H., 2007, 'The effect of implementation factors on data warehousing success: An exploratory study', *Journal of Information, Information Technology, and Organizations* 2(1), 1–16.

Kositanurit, B., Ngwenyama, O. & Osei-Bryson Kweku, K., 2006, 'An exploration of factors that impact individual performance in an ERP environment: An analysis using multiple analytical techniques', *European Journal of Information Systems* 15(6), 556–568. http://dx.doi.org/10.1057/palgrave.ejis.3000654

Law, C.C. & Ngai, E.W., 2007, 'ERP systems adoption: An exploratory study of the organizational factors and impacts of ERP success', *Information & Management* 44(4), 418–432. http://dx.doi.org/10.1016/j.im.2007.03.004

Leclercq, A., 2007, 'The perceptual evaluation of information systems using the construct of user satisfaction: Case study of a large French group', *The Database for Advances in Information Systems* 38(2), 27–60. http://dx.doi.org/10.1145/1240616.1240621

Legodi, I. & Barry, M.L., 2010, *The current challenges and status of risk management in enterprise data warehouse projects in South Africa,* PICMET, Phuket.

Lin, H.F., 2007, 'Measuring online learning systems success: Applying the updated DeLone and McLean mode', *CyberPsychology & Behavior* 10(6), 817–820. http://dx.doi.org/10.1089/cpb.2007.9948

Livari, J., 2005, 'An empirical test of the Delone-McLean model of information system success', *The Data Base for Advances in Information Systems* 36(2), 8–27. http://dx.doi.org/10.1145/1066149.1066152

Lowry, P.B., Karunga, G.G. & Richardson, V.J., 2007, 'Assessing leading institutions, faculty, and articles in premier information systems research journals', *Communications of the Associations of Information Systems* 20(16), 142–203.

Olbrich, S., Poppelbuß, J. & Niehaves, B., 2012, 'Critical contextual success factors for business intelligence: A Delphi study on their relevance, variability, and controllability', *proceedings of the 45th Hawaii International Conference*, Hawaii, pp. 4148–4157. http://dx.doi.org/10.1109/hicss.2012.187

Petter, S., DeLone, W. & McLean, E., 2008, 'Measuring information systems success: Models, dimensions, measures, and interrelationships', *European Journal of Information Systems* 17(3), 236–263. http://dx.doi.org/10.1057/ejis.2008.15

Pitt, L., Watson, R. & Kavan, C., 1995, 'Service quality: A measure of information systems effectiveness', *Management Information Systems Quarterly* 19(2), 173–185. http://dx.doi.org/10.2307/249687

Rai, A., Lang, S.S. & Welker, R.B., 2002, 'Assessing the validity of IS success models: An empirical test and theoretical analysis', *Information Systems Research* 13(1), 50–69. http://dx.doi.org/10.1287/isre.13.1.50.96

Ranjan, J., 2009, 'Business intelligence: Concepts, components,techniques and benefits', *Journal of Theoretical and Applied Information Technology* 9(1), 60–70.

Seddon, P.B., 1997, 'A respecification and extension of the DeLone and McLean model of IS success', *Information Systems Research* 8(3), 240–253. http://dx.doi.org/10.1287/isre.8.3.240

Shin, B., 2003, 'An exploratory investigation of system success factors in data warehousing', *Journal of the Association for Information Systems* 4(1), 141–170.

Stockdale, R. & Borovicka, M., 2006, 'Developing an online business community: A travel industry case study', *proceedings of the 39th Annual Hawaii International Conference,* Hawaii, 134. http://dx.doi.org/10.1109/hicss.2006.123

Turban, E., Sharda, R., Dursun, D. & King, D., 2011, *Business intelligence*, 9th edn., Prentice Hall, New York.

Vitt, E., Luckevich, M. & Misner, S., 2010, *Business intelligence,* O'Reilly Media.

Vlahos, G.E. & Ferratt, T.W., 1995, 'Information technology use by managers in Greece to support decision making: Amount, perceived value, and satisfaction', *Information and Management* 29(6), 305–315. http://dx.doi.org/10.1016/0378-7206(95)00037-1

Wang, J.-b., Fan, C.-j. & Xu, Q.-l., 2012, 'Empirical research on business intelligence system architecture', *International Journal of Applied Science and Technology* 2(7), 257–260. http://dx.doi.org/10.1016/j.giq.2007.06.002

Wang, Y.S. & Liao, Y.W., 2008, 'Assessing eGovernment systems success: A validation of the DeLone and McLean model of information systems success', *Government Information Quarterly* 25(4) 717–733.

Wixom, B. & Watson, H., 2010, 'The BI-based organization', *International Journal of Business Intelligence Research* 1(1), 13–28.

Woodside, J., 2011, Business intelligence best practices for success', *proceedings of the European Conference on Information Management*, Toronto.

Wu, J.H. & Wang, Y.M., 2006, 'Measuring KMS success: A respecification of the DeLone and McLean model', *Information and Management* 43(6), 728–739. http://dx.doi.org/10.1016/j.im.2006.05.002

Yeoh, W. & Koronios, A., 2010, 'Critical success factors for business intelligence systems', *Journal of Computer Information Systems* 50(3), 23–132.

Zhu, K. & Kraemer, K.L., 2005, 'Post-adoption variations in usage and value of e-business by organizations: Cross-country evidence from the retail industry', *Information Systems Research* 16(1), 61–84. http://dx.doi.org/10.1287/isre.1050.0045

5

Factors influencing access to agricultural knowledge: The case of smallholder rice farmers in the Kilombero district of Tanzania

Authors:
Wulystan P. Mtega[1]
Mpho Ngoepe[2]
Luyanda Dube[2]

Affiliations:
[1]Sokoine University of Agriculture, Morogoro, Tanzania

[2]Department of Information Sciences, University of South Africa, South Africa

Corresponding author:
Mpho Ngoepe,
ngoepms@unisa.ac.za

Background: Access to agricultural knowledge is important in transforming livelihoods of those relying on agriculture for a living and in enhancing food security. This access to agricultural knowledge is influenced by infrastructure needed for information dissemination. However, information infrastructure is not uniformly distributed within and between countries. It is because of this that some of the farming communities are information rich while others are information poor. In Tanzania, the agricultural sector is characterised by poor research-extension-farmers linkage and inaccessibility of agricultural knowledge at farm level

Objective: The study investigated the factors influencing access to agricultural knowledge among smallholder rice farmers in the Kilombero district of Tanzania. Specifically, the study identified categories of agricultural knowledge needed by farmers, determined how farmers access agricultural knowledge, and assessed the factors limiting the accessibility of agricultural knowledge among rice farmers in the Kilombero district.

Method: Quantitative data were collected via semi-structured questionnaires administered face-to-face with rice farmers, community leaders, and agricultural agents in four villages at the Kilombero district of the Morogoro region in Tanzania.

Results: The key finding indicates that farmers accessed and used agricultural knowledge in undertaking agricultural activities. It was further revealed that the level of acquisition of agricultural knowledge increased with an increase in age. Farmers needed agricultural knowledge on land preparation, seed selection, and rice planting, while few acquired knowledge on agricultural markets. Among the agricultural knowledge sources used, demonstration plots and agricultural extension agents were found to be used by the majority of the farmers. It was also found that a limited number of demonstration plots, late delivery of information services, a limited number of agricultural extension agents, and poor information and communication technologies infrastructure hindered access to agricultural knowledge among rice farmers in the district.

Conclusion: A strong public–private partnership is needed to enhance access to agricultural knowledge in rural areas. In this regard, the government should set up policies and strategies that motivate private sector investment and involvement in provision of agricultural knowledge in rural areas. The private sector should extend their agricultural-related activities to most rural areas so that more people can have access to agricultural knowledge.

Introduction

Access to agricultural knowledge is important in transforming livelihoods of those relying on agriculture for a living and in enhancing food security (Lwoga 2011). Access to agricultural knowledge is associated with acquiring skills and techniques for improving farming practices, sustaining the environment, and optimising production within a given farm size. For this to take place, a strong link between agricultural research and farmers is required. Agricultural research institutions come up with new technologies and developments which must reach farmers' farms and homes through effective extension and mass media channels, so that they can adopt new technologies and put them into use (Nazari, Bin & Hassan 2011). If agricultural technologies and developments do not reach farmers, transforming agriculture and farmers' livelihoods remains impossible. Thus, access to agricultural knowledge is a factor for change and progress in the agricultural sector.

Information is linked to knowledge through the data–information–knowledge hierarchy (Frické 2009) and knowledge is filtered from information. Therefore, access to agricultural knowledge is influenced by the information infrastructure needed for information dissemination.

The information infrastructure is composed of information and communication systems that process and transport data inside and outside national boundaries (Bowker *et al.* 2010). The information infrastructure is not uniformly distributed within and between countries. It is because of this that some of the farming communities are knowledge rich while others are knowledge poor. According to Kagan (1999), knowledge rich and knowledge poor are described by the gap between the elite and the disadvantaged within countries, and the accessibility versus the inaccessibility to knowledge among people. Because knowledge is a factor for change, progress, and development, those with better access to knowledge are more likely to be better off compared to those who do not.

Access to agricultural knowledge among farmers in most developing countries has been a challenge for many years (Eenhoorn & Becx 2009). Despite the contribution of the agricultural sector in Tanzania, scholars (Lwoga, Ngulube & Stilwell 2011) found that limited access to agricultural knowledge has been mentioned as one of the factors limiting agricultural productivity in Tanzania (Lwoga *et al.* 2011). With climate change the need for agricultural knowledge has become more urgent as agricultural researchers have been working hard to adapt and mitigate the impacts. In Tanzania, Lema and Majule (2009) found that climate change has brought about reduced productivity in Tanzania. To mitigate climate change impacts, farmers need to rely on a rapidly expanding base of biological and agronomic knowledge that is often specific to certain agro-ecosystems, regions, soil types, and slopes (Tilman *et al.* 2002). According to Lobell and Gourdji (2012), climate change has affected crop productivity because rains have been reduced and drought periods prolonged. This has made it important for agricultural research institutions to come up with new technologies and developments to combat the impacts. In order to limit the impacts of climate change, making the right decisions at farm level in terms of input-use efficiency, human health, and resource protection is becoming an increasingly knowledge-intensive task (Tilman *et al.* 2002).

For enhancing access to agricultural knowledge, agricultural extension agents from the public and private sector, access to radio and TV networks, and print resources are important (Shetto 2008). In Tanzania, both governmental and non-governmental organisations are involved in the provision of agricultural knowledge (Rutatora & Mattee 2001). According to Lema and Kapange (2006), agricultural knowledge has been shared through farmers' associations and groups. Moreover, as agro-dealers sell inputs they teach farmers how to use them (Temu *et al.* 2005). Despite the involvement of many stakeholders in provision of agricultural knowledge to farmers, the level of access to agricultural knowledge among farmers in Tanzania is still low (Lwoga 2010). The agricultural sector in Tanzania is characterised by poor research-extension-farmers linkage and inaccessibility of agricultural knowledge at farm level (United Republic of Tanzania 2013). Thus, the current study intends to investigate the factors influencing access to agricultural knowledge among smallholder farmers (smallholder farmers in Tanzania own farms ranging in size from 0.2 – 2 hectares) in Kilombero district of Tanzania. Specifically, the study identified categories of agricultural knowledge needed by farmers, determined how farmers access agricultural knowledge, and assessed the factors limiting the accessibility of agricultural knowledge among rice farmers in the Kilombero district.

Problem statement

Despite the importance of the agriculture sector to the economy and the livelihood of the majority of Tanzanians, the sector has been performing poorly (United Republic of Tanzania 2013). In the Kilombero district, limited access to agricultural knowledge has resulted in irrational decisions on agricultural production and related activities thus dwarfing the sector (Benard, Dulle & Ngalapa 2014; Siyao 2012). At farm level most farmers have inadequate access to and usage of the most important agricultural information services needed for production and post-harvest activities leading to dismal growth of the agricultural sector and prevalence of poverty among households whose livelihoods rely solely on agriculture (Benard *et al.* 2014; Lwoga 2010; Mtega & Benard 2013; Shetto 2008; Siyao 2012; United Republic of Tanzania 2011). Inadequate access to agricultural knowledge limits farmers from making rational decisions regarding agricultural production, pre- and post-harvest handling of agricultural produce which in turn affects the level of income from agricultural activities and livelihood of farmers (Lwoga 2010).

Purpose and objectives of the study

The purpose of this study was to investigate factors influencing access to agricultural knowledge by smallholder rice farmers in the Kilombero district of Tanzania. The specific objectives were to:

- Determine agricultural knowledge needs, acquisition, and usage patterns among rice farmers in the Kilombero district.
- Examine sources of agricultural knowledge used by farmers in the Kilombero district.
- Determine factors limiting access to agricultural knowledge among rice farmers in the Kilombero district.

Literature review

Farmers have been using skills and expertise in agricultural activities; Lwoga (2010) categorises knowledge used by farmers in agriculture into either indigenous or exogenous knowledge. Indigenous knowledge is the basis for agriculture and natural resource management (Lwoga 2010) because new agricultural knowledge is built from what is known. Indigenous knowledge is local knowledge, it is built from and based on thousands of years of experience and passed from one generation to the next (Ajibade 2003). Indigenous knowledge is predominantly tacit; it is traditional and is passed from a generation to the other through word of mouth (Movarej *et al.* 2012). The other type of knowledge is exogenous knowledge; this is a broad base of non-traditional knowledge that local people draw from their interaction with non-local people and institutions; television, and other media; formal education; and adoption of western scientific thinking, values, and philosophies (Karlsson 1995). To attain the competitive edge in their agricultural undertakings, farmers need both indigenous and exogenous knowledge. These two types of agricultural knowledge are needed for improving farmers' farming skills and helping farmers acquire new techniques for agricultural activities.

Agricultural knowledge needs among farmers

The agricultural knowledge value chain is made up of those who generate and use knowledge. According to Nonaka *et al.* (2000), knowledge is created through experience and when people socialise. Once knowledge is created, people acquire it to meet their personal and organisational knowledge needs. However, the various processes constituting agricultural knowledge management involve many actors along the value chain (Lee & Yang 2000). Each category of actors in the value chain has a task in agricultural knowledge management. However, farmers play a central role in agricultural knowledge management as knowledge created aims to help farmers increase agricultural productivity. Therefore, it is important to enhance access to agricultural knowledge among farmers.

Farmers have different agricultural knowledge needs which are relevant to their day-to-day involvement. Farmers need to know what to grow, when to grow it, how to grow more, how to store and preserve their produce, when to sell, where to sell and at what price to sell, and specific agronomic management skills (Abdon & Raab 2005). Farmers must know the optimum usage of agricultural inputs for optimal production. The need for agricultural knowledge is increasing because most activities, including agriculture, are being shifted from being labour-based to knowledge-based.

Scholars (Czapiewski, Floriańczyk & Janc 2010) pointed out that there is a strong link between access to agricultural knowledge and agricultural development. As stated by Dodsworth *et al.* (2003), agricultural development requires creation and use of new knowledge; it is attained through transforming knowledge into actions. However, knowledge can only be transformed into actions if it is acquired from its sources by those who need it.

Acquisition of agricultural knowledge among farmers

Acquisition of knowledge involves the importation of substantial amounts of knowledge from internal and external sources of the organisation (Lwoga, Ngulube & Stilwell 2010). Modes of acquiring indigenous agricultural knowledge may be different from those used in acquiring exogenous knowledge (Yli-Renko, Autio & Sapienza 2001). Moreover, the way in which tacit knowledge is shared is always different from how explicit knowledge is shared. Tacit knowledge is not easily codifiable and recognisable (Movarej *et al.* 2012), which ensures that it is shared most effectively through observation and individual experience. Indigenous knowledge is passed from one person to the other through word of mouth (Lwoga 2010) because it is managed by individuals and stored in the minds of individual owners of knowledge. Indigenous knowledge can be documented and repackaged and shared through several channels (Lwoga 2010). Information and communication technologies (ICT), including radio and television sets, internet, computers, and mobile phones, can be used to acquire documented indigenous knowledge.

Explicit knowledge – the know-how that is described in formal language, print, or electronic media, often based on established work processes, uses a people-to-documents approach (Smith 2001). Acquiring this type of knowledge is quite simple; those who need to acquire it must be able to use explicit knowledge carriers and have a reasonable level of literacy. The explicit nature of exogenous knowledge has made its storage and sharing extremely easy, and its popularisation overwhelming (Ocholla 2007). The way in which explicit knowledge is documented makes it easily shared and acquired. Acquiring explicit knowledge needs one to know where knowledge is managed and how it can be acquired.

Exogenous knowledge is acquired from external organisations and communities. People acquire exogenous knowledge through interactions with non-local people and institutions, media, and formal education (Lwoga 2010). People can also acquire exogenous knowledge from people who interact with people coming from the external environment.

Generally, knowledge is acquired to meet knowledge needs expressed by seekers. To enhance easy access of knowledge, codification of tacit knowledge is important. Moreover, having access to both indigenous and exogenous knowledge is important because the two types of knowledge complement each other. For knowledge to be accessed it has to be created or acquired and shared; these processes involve several actors who usually act dependently.

Actors in enhancing access to agricultural knowledge

An agricultural knowledge value chain is important for enhancing access to agricultural knowledge. The knowledge value chain is simply the application of the value chain model to knowledge development and usage (Powell 2008). The agricultural knowledge value chain involves knowledge acquisition, knowledge innovation, knowledge protection, knowledge integration (intelligence), knowledge dissemination, and knowledge action (Wong 2004). Actors in the agricultural knowledge value chain include those who generate new agricultural knowledge through research and those disseminating the knowledge to those using it for increasing value of the produce or products. Actors in the agricultural sector have to perform all knowledge management processes (creation, storage, sharing, using knowledge) in the agricultural knowledge value chain. A formal agricultural knowledge value chain consists of three functions: research, education and extension, and advisory service (Islam 2010; Nemes & High 2013). Farmers are found at the centre of all agricultural knowledge management activities, because what is being implemented is aimed at increasing agricultural production. However, farmers play a knowledge-creation role just like agricultural research institutions. Farmers generate indigenous knowledge (Lwoga 2010) through experience over a long time and involvement in agricultural activities.

Because of the increasing number of actors in the agricultural knowledge value chain, governments play coordinating roles; thus whatever is being done has a strong positive impact on farmers and other beneficiaries. Kapange (2004) pointed out that governments make sure that agricultural research institutions, universities, extension and advisory services, farmers, and other stakeholders involved in agricultural related activities are effectively involved in agricultural knowledge management processes. Likewise, governments have to invest in knowledge infrastructure in both rural and urban areas; rural knowledge infrastructure is instrumental in boosting the rural development initiatives in villages (Das & Dutta 2004). Thus, for effective agricultural knowledge management, all the actors must act together to enhance access to and usage of agricultural knowledge.

Research methodology

In order to investigate the above research objectives, this quantitative study relied on both secondary and primary data. An extensive literature review was undertaken which helped in framing questions for the primary data collection. Quantitative data were collected via semi-structured questionnaires administered face-to-face with rice farmers, community leaders, and agricultural agents in four villages at the Kilombero district of the Morogoro region in Tanzania. According to National Bureau of Statistics (2012), Kilombero district has a population of 407 880 people and about 75% of them are farmers. Among the 305 910 farmers 152 955 (50%) of them grow rice and 94% (143 778 farmers) of them are smallholder farmers (Rural Livelihood Development Company (RLDC) 2009). Because of a lack of a sampling frame, a purposive sample of 120 smallholder rice farmers, community leaders, and agricultural agents was chosen from four villages within Kilombero district. Each village was represented by one agricultural agent who was purposely included in the sample; a village executive secretary because he or she was concerned with day to day activities of the village; and 28 smallholder rice farmers, chosen using a snowball technique, because they were homogeneous and their responses could generalise views of others in the village. This made a total of 30 respondents from each village.

Even though this type of non-probability sampling does not allow representativeness, the sample was easily accessible and organised. Collected data were analysed using the Statistical Package for Social Sciences where both descriptive and inferential statistics were used in data analysis. Tables, figures, and descriptions were used in presenting the study findings.

Findings and discussion

Analysed data were presented in tables and descriptions as shown. The results are presented as per the objectives of the study.

Demographic characteristics of respondents

The study involved 53 female and 67 male respondents. Among them, 4 males had informal education, 109 (51 females and 58 males) had primary education, and seven (2 females and 5 males) had secondary education and higher. Respondents' ages ranged from 21 to 80 years with the majority of the respondents being between 31 and 40 years of age.

Agricultural knowledge needs, acquisition, and usage among rice farmers in the Kilombero district

Respondents were asked if they have needed and used knowledge for conducting agricultural activities. Findings indicated that more than 93% of respondents mentioned that they needed knowledge for performing agricultural activities. Findings indicated that all females involved in the study mentioned that they needed agricultural knowledge for performing agricultural activities (Table 1).

The findings in Table 1 indicated that, regardless of their level of education, all respondents mentioned that they needed knowledge while conducting agricultural activities. Moreover, the need for agricultural knowledge slightly increased with age.

Respondents were further asked about the types of agricultural knowledge they acquired and used. The findings indicated that farmers acquired and used different types of agricultural knowledge. It was found that farmers acquired knowledge related to land preparation, seed selection, rice planting, and fertiliser application. They also mentioned that they needed knowledge related to how to weed their farms, pre-harvest and post-harvest handling, and agricultural marketing.

TABLE 1: Usage of agricultural knowledge in performing agricultural activities.

Variable	Category	Uses agricultural knowledge	
		f	%
Sex	Female	53	100
	Male	62	93
Education	Informal	4	100
	Primary	105	96
	Secondary and above	6	86
Age	21–30	15	94
	31–40	46	92
	41–50	35	100
	51–60	6	100
	61–70	8	100
	71–80	5	100

Source: The data was obtained from a questionnaire

f, frequency.

The findings in Table 2 indicated that all famers, regardless of their sex, mentioned to have been acquiring and using agricultural knowledge. Findings indicated that more female respondents mentioned that they have acquired and used agricultural knowledge related to seed selection and rice planting as more than 96% of female farmers reported to have acquired and used such knowledge (Table 3). Because of rice farming division of labour, female farmers are more involved in some of the rice farming activities than male farmers (Rugumamu 2014). Likely, there are some activities which involve more male farmers than female farmers. Fertiliser application and weeding using herbicides, which involves spraying, is mostly done by male farmers. The findings in Table 2 indicated that 85.1% of male farmers and 77.4% female farmers acquired and used knowledge on fertiliser application. Also, 88.1% of male farmers and 75.5% of female farmers reported to have acquired and used agricultural knowledge related to using herbicides for weeding. Moreover, male smallholder rice farmers are more involved in pre-harvest or post-harvest handling and marketing of rice (59.7% and 58.2%, respectively). This is explained by the fact that in Tanzania husbands in most cases control the household income. These findings align with those of Rugumamu (2014) who also found that more male farmers involve themselves in marketing agricultural produce.

It was found that the level of acquisition of agricultural knowledge was slightly influenced by the level of education. The findings in Table 2 indicated that, regardless of the level of education, most farmers involved in the study mentioned that they have acquired and used agricultural knowledge related to land preparation, seed selection, and rice sowing. The findings in Table 2 indicated that as a general trend, the level of acquisition of agricultural knowledge among farmers in the Kilombero district decreased with an increase in level of education. This could be explained by the fact that those with higher education might have already accumulated some knowledge needed for performing agricultural activities.

The findings in Table 2 indicated that, regardless of the level of education, more than 88% of farmers involved in the study acquired knowledge related to land preparation, seed selection, and seed sowing whereas less than 67% of farmers involved in the study mentioned that they have acquired knowledge on pre- and post-harvest handling procedures (Table 2). Likely, the need for knowledge related to rice markets increased with an increase in age. It was found that approximately 68% respondents between 31 and 50 years mentioned that they have acquired and used knowledge related to rice marketing; however, the need and the level of acquisition of knowledge related to agricultural marketing increased with an increase in age (Table 2).

Generally, almost all farmers involved in the study needed and acquired agricultural knowledge related to different agricultural activities. They needed knowledge for adding

TABLE 2: Agricultural knowledge acquired by rice farmers.

Variable	Category	Knowledge on land preparation (%)	Knowledge on seed selection (%)	Knowledge on rice planting (%)	Knowledge on fertiliser application (%)	Knowledge on how to weed (%)	Knowledge on pre-harvest and post-harvest handling (%)	Knowledge on agricultural marketing (%)
Sex	Female	47 (88.7)	53 (100.0)	51 (96.2)	41 (77.4)	40 (75.5)	27 (50.9)	26 (49.0)
	Male	61 (91.0)	62 (92.5)	62 (92.5)	57 (85.1)	59 (88.1)	40 (59.7)	39 (58.2)
Education	Informal	4 (100.0)	4 (100.0)	4 (100.0)	4 (100.0)	0 (0.0)	4 (100.0)	0 (0.0)
	Primary	98 (89.9)	105 (96.3)	103 (94.5)	88 (80.7)	20 (18.3)	60 (55.0)	72 (66.1)
	Secondary and above	6 (85.7)	6 (85.7)	6 (85.7)	6 (85.7)	1 (14.3)	3 (42.9)	3 (42.9)
Age	21 – 30	15 (93.8)	15 (93.8)	15 (93.8)	10 (62.5)	9 (56.3)	6 (37.5)	4 (25.0)
	31 – 40	44 (88.0)	46 (92.0)	44 (88.0)	42 (84.0)	42 (84.0)	26 (52.0)	34 (68.0)
	41 – 50	31 (88.6)	35 (100.0)	35 (100.0)	29 (82.9)	29 (82.9)	23 (65.7)	23 (65.7)
	51 – 60	6 (100.00)	6 (100.0)	6 (100.0)	4 (66.7)	6 (100.0)	4 (66.7)	4 (66.7)
	61 – 70	8 (100.0)	8 (100.0)	8 (100.0)	8 (100.0)	8 (100.0)	4 (50.0)	6 (75.0)
	71 – 80	4 (80.0)	5 (100.0)	5 (100.0)	5 (100.0)	5 (100.0)	4 (80.0)	4 (80.0)

Source: The data was obtained from a questionnaire

TABLE 3: Preference of sources of agricultural knowledge by demographic characteristics.

Variables	Category	Village leader (%)	Demons-tration plot (%)	Mobile phones (%)	Farmers' associations (%)	TV (%)	Print resources (%)	Radio (%)	Fellow farmers (%)	Agricultural extension agent (%)
Sex	Female	16 (30.2)	35 (66.0)	16 (30.2)	17 (32.1)	3 (5.7)	17 (32.1)	20 (37.7)	10 (18.9)	35 (66.0)
	Male	25 (37.3)	49 (73,1)	32 (47.8)	35 (52.2)	16 (23.9)	29 (43.3)	33 (49.3)	21 (31.3)	35 (52.2)
Education	Informal	0 (0.0)	0 (0.0)	0 (0.0)	0 (0.0)	0 (0.0)	0 (0.0)	0 (0.0)	0 (0.0)	4 (100.0)
	Primary	41 (37.6)	78 (71.6)	45 (41.3)	46 (42.2)	19 (17.4)	40 (36.7)	50 (45.9)	28 (25.7)	63 (57.8)
	Secondary and above	0 (0.0)	6 (85.7)	3 (42.9)	6 (85.7)	0 (0.0)	6 (85.7)	3 (42.9)	3 (42.9)	3 (42.9)
Age	21 – 30	7 (43.8)	10 (62.5)	3 (18.8)	2 (12.5)	0 (0.0)	3 (18.8)	9 (56.3)	4 (25.0)	5 (31.3)
	31 – 40	16 (32.0)	37 (74.0)	25 (50.0)	27 (54.0)	6 (12.0)	23 (46.0)	22 (44.0)	13 (26.0)	33 (66.0)
	41 – 50	15 (42.9)	24 (68.6)	10 (28.6)	17 (48.6)	6 (17.1)	10 (28.6)	10 (28.6)	8 (22.9)	21 (60.0)
	51 – 60	2 (33.3)	4 (66.7)	3 (50.0)	1 (16.7)	0 (0.0)	3 (50.0)	3 (50.0)	1 (16.7)	6 (100.0)
	61 – 70	0 (0.0)	4 (50.0)	2 (25.0)	2 (25.0)	4 (50.0)	4 (50.0)	6 (75.0)	0 (0.0)	0 (0.0)
	71 – 80	1 (20.0)	5 (100.0)	5 (100.0)	3 (60.0)	3 (60.0)	3 (60.0)	3 (60.0)	5 (100.0)	5 (100.0)

Source: The data was obtained from a questionnaire

value to agricultural undertakings they are involved in. Most farmers appreciated the fact that the usage of agricultural knowledge increased agricultural production and income from agriculture, which in turn increased their livelihood.

Sources of agricultural knowledge used by farmers in the Kilombero district

Farmers involved in the study were asked about the sources from which they acquired agricultural knowledge. It was found that farmers acquired agricultural knowledge from village leaders, demonstration plots, mobile phones, farmers' associations, TV sets, print resources, radio sets, fellow farmers, and agricultural extension agents (Table 3). Among the knowledge sources mentioned by more respondents were demonstration plots; findings in Table 3 indicate that more respondents preferred this source of agricultural knowledge because farmers had opportunities to observe and adopted what has been practiced to their farms. Moreover, more male farmers had more access to these sources of agricultural knowledge because they spent their leisure time after farm activities accessing different knowledge sources, whereas females spent such time for preparing meals.

The findings in Table 2 indicated that more male than female farmers acquired agricultural knowledge for their agricultural activities; likewise, the findings in Table 3 indicated that more male farmers used agricultural knowledge sources for accessing agricultural knowledge. The findings in Table 3 showed that more male farmers (73.1%) reported to use demonstration plots as a source of agricultural knowledge.

Preference of agricultural knowledge was influenced by farmers' level of education. Findings indicated that all farmers with informal education mentioned to have been using agricultural extension agents as their source of agricultural knowledge; most of those with primary level of education (71.6%) mentioned to have been using demonstration plots. Those with secondary levels of education and higher (85.7%) mentioned that they preferred to use demonstration plots, farmers' associations, and print resources as sources of agricultural knowledge (Table 3). With respect to ICT-based sources, more respondents reported to have been using radio sets (45.9%), followed by mobile phones. The findings in Table 3 indicated that the level of usage of these ICTs as sources of agricultural knowledge increased with an increase in the level of education. This shows that literacy plays an important role in the choice of agricultural knowledge sources. The same trend applies to the usage of print resources as sources of agricultural knowledge as none of those with informal education used print resources, whereas 85.7% of those with a secondary level of education and higher used print resources for accessing agricultural knowledge.

Findings in Table 3 indicate that all of the oldest farmers (71–80 years of age) involved in the study said that they have used demonstration plots, mobile phones, fellow farmers, and agricultural extension agents for accessing agricultural

TABLE 4: Sharing of agricultural knowledge by demographic characteristics.

Variable	Category	*f* (%)
Sex	Female	37 (69.8)
	Male	51 (76.1)
Education	Informal	0 (0.0)
	Primary	82 (75.2)
	Secondary	6 (85.7)
Age	21–30	8 (50.0)
	31–40	39 (78.0)
	41–50	26 (74.3)
	51–60	4 (66.7)
	61–70	8 (100.0)
	71–80	3 (60.0)

Source: The data was obtained from a questionnaire

knowledge. Findings indicate further that 60% of respondents within the same age category mentioned that they used farmers' associations, TV sets, print resources, and radio sets for accessing agricultural knowledge. Regardless of age, demonstration plots and agricultural extension agents were the most used sources of agricultural knowledge. This is explained by the fact that these sources were close to where farmers live. Moreover, regardless of age, TV sets were the least used sources of agricultural knowledge among farmers involved in the study. This is explained by the limited TV infrastructure in most rural areas.

Farmers involved in the study were asked if they shared acquired knowledge. It was found that farmers involved in the study used to share knowledge among themselves. The findings indicated that more male farmers (76.1%) shared acquired agricultural knowledge than female farmers (69.8%). Moreover, it can be seen from Table 4 that the level of sharing agricultural knowledge increases with the level of education; none of those with informal education said that they have shared acquired knowledge whereas more than 75% of those with a primary level of education and higher said that they have shared acquired agricultural knowledge.

The findings indicated that sharing agricultural knowledge was the lowest among the youngest farmers involved in the study as only 50% of them said that they have shared agricultural knowledge. Between the two groups with many respondents, it was found that 78% of those between 31 and 40 years of age and 74.3% of those between 41 and 50 years of age said that they have shared acquired agricultural knowledge. Lwoga (2010) mentioned that sharing agricultural knowledge among rural farmers is important because of the limited number of agricultural knowledge sources.

Factors limiting access to agricultural knowledge among rice farmers in the Kilombero district

The study aimed at identifying factors that influence accessibility of agricultural knowledge among farmers. Farmers identified a number of factors that limited access to agricultural knowledge. Table 5 shows that 58% said that they did not get agricultural trainings. Findings indicate that more males included in the study found this to be hindering access to agricultural knowledge (Table 5).

TABLE 5: Factors influencing access to agricultural knowledge.

Factors	*f*		
	Male (%)	Female (%)	Total (%)
Few farmers have been given agricultural training	48 (72)	22 (42)	70 (58)
Few demonstration plots in the village	44 (66)	43 (81)	87 (73)
Unaffordable information services	34 (51)	48 (91)	82 (68)
No exchange visits among farmers	27 (40)	28 (53)	55 (46)
Demonstration plots are not established on time	42 (63)	50 (94)	92 (77)
Limited agricultural campaigns	39 (58)	36 (68)	75 (63)
Information services not delivered on time	52 (78)	37 (70)	89 (74)
Few agricultural extension agents	59 (88)	43 (81)	102 (85)
Few agro-dealers	25 (37)	6 (11)	31 (26)
Limited ICT infrastructure	65 (97)	52 (98)	117 (98)
Illiteracy among farmers	42 (63)	28 (53)	70 (58)

Source: The data was obtained from a questionnaire
ICT, information and communication technologies.

The findings in Table 5 further indicated that other factors limiting access to agricultural knowledge among rice farmers in the Kilombero district included: limited exchange visits among farmers (46%); few demonstration plots established in the village (73%); most demonstration plots found in villages have not been established on time (77%); and the high cost of some of the information services (68%). Despite being mentioned by most respondents to influence access to agricultural knowledge, it was found that more females included in the study mentioned those factors to limit access to agricultural knowledge.

Other factors included a limited number of agricultural campaigns (63%); a delay in most information services (74%); a limited number of agricultural extension agents (85%); few agro-dealers (26%); illiteracy among farmers (58%); and limited ICT infrastructure (98%). As indicated in Table 5, more male respondents included in the study mentioned limited agricultural campaigns; delay in most information services; limited number of agricultural extension agents and agro-dealers; and high illiteracy level hindered access to agricultural knowledge among farmers. Table 5 shows further that both male and female respondents believed that limited ICT infrastructure hindered access to agricultural knowledge.

From Table 3, demonstration plots and agricultural extension agents were mentioned as the most used sources of agricultural knowledge. Despite the fact that they were really useful and that most farmers depended on them, such sources were not adequate. Only a few demonstration plots were established and most of them were not established on time. If enough demonstration plots were established, and those few available could be established on time then their impact on adoption could be higher than it was. According to Shetto and Owenya (2007), most demonstration plots are established by private agricultural service providers including non-governmental organisations. Despite being helpful, private service providers do not provide service in all rural areas or to all institutes and farmers. ICTs could have been used to break the gap; however, findings from this study and other studies (Lwoga 2010; Mtega 2012; Sife, Kiondo & Lyimo-Macha 2010; Shetto 2008) showed that most rural areas have very limited ICT infrastructure.

It could be found that some of the factors limiting access to agricultural knowledge are caused by individual farmers, while others are institutional. Factors relating to individual farmers could include illiteracy and low income, which would limit some farmers from accessing agricultural knowledge. The rest of the factors are institutional factors and in one way or the other, they may be solved through a strong public-private partnership as the public or private sector alone cannot eradicate them. Thus, access to agricultural knowledge depends on the involvement of farmers, and the private and the public sector.

Conclusion and recommendations

The study investigated the factors influencing access to agricultural knowledge among smallholder farmers in the Kilombero district of Tanzania. Key findings indicated that all farmers have been accessing and using agricultural knowledge in undertaking agricultural activities. It was found that the level of acquisition of agricultural knowledge increased with an increase in age and that more farmers needed agricultural knowledge on land preparation, seed selection, and rice planting. It was also found that other farmers needed knowledge on agricultural markets and that demonstration plots and agricultural extension agents were the agricultural knowledge sources consulted by most farmers. Despite the need for agricultural knowledge among farmers in the district, a limited number of demonstration plots, late delivery of information services, a limited number of agricultural extension agents, and limited ICT infrastructure hindered access to agricultural knowledge among rice farmers in Kilombero. A strong public-private partnership is needed to enhance access to agricultural knowledge in rural areas. The government should set up policies and strategies that motivate private sector investment and involvement in the provision of agricultural information in rural areas. The private sector should extend their agriculture-related activities to rural areas so that more people can have access to agricultural knowledge.

Acknowledgements

Competing interests

The authors declare that they have no financial or personal relationships which may have inappropriately influenced them in writing this article.

Authors' contributions

M.N. was the project supervisor and L.D. was the co-supervisor. W.P.M. conceptualised the work, and collected and interpreted the data.

References

Abdon, B. & Raab, R., 2005, 'Knowledge sharing and distance learning for sustainable agriculture in the Asia-Pacific region: The role of the Internet', *Plant Production Science* 8(3), 298–307. http://dx.doi.org/10.1626/pps.8.298

Ajibade, L.T., 2003, 'Knowing the unknown through the known: The case for indigenous knowledge in sustainable development', viewed 14 January 2015, from http://afrrevjo.net/journals/multidiscipline/Vol_2_num_2_art_14_Ajibade.pdf

Benard, R., Dulle, F. & Ngalapa, H., 2014, 'Assessment of information needs of rice farmers in Tanzania; A case study of Kilombero District, Morogoro', *Library Philosophy and Practice (e-journal)*, 1–34, viewed 30 January 2015, from http://digitalcommons.unl.edu/cgi/viewcontent.cgi?article=2666&context=libphilprac

Bowker, G.C., Baker, K.S., Millerand, F. & Ribes, D., 2010, 'Towards information infrastructure studies: Ways of knowing in a networked environment', in J.D. Hunsinger, M. Allen & L. Klastrup (eds.), *International handbook of internet research*, Springer, New York.

Czapiewski, K., Floriańczyk, Z. & Janc, K., 2010, 'Agricultural knowledge and rural economy – analysis on micro and macro scales', viewed 14 January 2015, from http://eprints.rclis.org/bitstream/10760/7210/1/Das_Dutta_XXI_IASLIC_Seminar_2004.pdf

Das, A.K. & Dutta, C., 2004, 'Strengthening Rural Information Infrastructure through E-Choupals', viewed 25 January 2015, from http://eprints.rclis.org/7210/1/Das_Dutta_XXI_IASLIC_Seminar_2004.pdf

Dodsworth, E., Smith, S., Biswas-Benbow, I., Lloyd-Laney, M., Young, J. & Winder, D., 2003, 'New DFID research strategy communications theme-final report', viewed 10 February 2015, from http://www.cimrc.info/pdf/news/CommsStrategy.pdf

Eenhoorn, H. & Becx, G., 2009, 'Constrain constraints: A study into real and perceived constraints and opportunities for the development of smallholder farmers in Sub-Saharan Africa', viewed 12 January 2015, from http://www.resilience-foundation.nl/docs/eenhoornandbecx2009.pdf

Frické, M., 2009, 'The knowledge pyramid: A critique of the DIKW hierarchy', *Journal of InformationScience*35(2),131–142.http://dx.doi.org/10.1177/0165551508094050

Islam, F., 2010, 'Institutionalization of agricultural knowledge management system for digital marginalized brural farming community', viewed 12 January 2015, from https://hal.archives-ouvertes.fr/hal-00516458/document

Kagan, A., 1999, 'The growing gap between the information rich and the information poor both within countries and between countries: A composite policy paper', *IFLA Journal* 26(1), 28–33. http://dx.doi.org/10.1177/034003520002600105

Kapange, B., 2004, 'ICTs and National Agricultural Research Systems: The case of Tanzania', viewed 24 January 2015, from http://www.tzonline.org/pdf/ictsandnationalagriculturalresearchsystems.pdf

Karlsson, J., 1995, 'Methods of information provision to rural communities in South Africa', in E. Johansson (ed.), *Seminar on information provision to rural communities in Africa: Proceedings of the seminar,* pp. 47–57, Gaborone.

Lee, C.C. & Yang, J., 2000, 'Knowledge-value chain', *Journal of Management Development* 19, 783–793. http://dx.doi.org/10.1108/02621710010378228

Lema, M.A. & Majule, A.E., 2009, 'Impacts of climate change, variability and adaptation strategies on agriculture in semi-arid areas of Tanzania: The case of Manyoni District in Singida Region, Tanzania', *African Journal of Environmental Science and Technology* 3(8), 206–218.

Lema, N.M. & Kapange, B.W., 2006, 'Farmers' organizations and agricultural innovation in Tanzania: The sector policy for real farmer empowerment', viewed 25 January 2015, from http://www.kit.nl/sed/wp-content/uploads/publications/912_Case%20Study%20Tanzania.pdf

Lobell, D.B. & Gourdji, S.M., 2012, 'The influence of climate change on global crop productivity', *Plant Physiology* 160(4), 1686–1697.

Lwoga, E.T., 2010, 'Bridging the agricultural knowledge and information divide: The case of selected telecenters and rural radio in Tanzania', *Electronic Journal on Information Systems in Developing Countries* 43(6), 1–14.

Lwoga, E.T., 2011, 'Knowledge management approaches in managing agricultural indigenous and exogenous knowledge in Tanzania', *Journal of Documentation* 67(3), 113–122.

Lwoga, E.T., Ngulube, P. & Stilwell, C., 2010, 'Managing indigenous knowledge for sustainable agricultural development in developing countries: Knowledge management approaches in the social context', *The International Information & Library Review* 42(3), 174–175. http://dx.doi.org/10.1080/10572317.2010.10762862

Lwoga, E.T., Ngulube, P. & Stilwell, C., 2011, 'Information Needs and Information Seeking Behaviour of Small-Scale Farmers in Tanzania', *Innovation: Journal of Appropriate Librarianship and Information Work in Southern Africa* 40 (2010).

Movarej, M., Hashemi, S.M.K., Hosseini, S.M. & Rezvanfar, A., 2012, 'Facilitating sustainable agriculture: Integrating indigenous knowledge in current agricultural knowledge and information systems', *Cercetări Agronomice în Moldova* XLV(1), viewed 14 January 2015, from http://www.uaiasi.ro/CERCET_AGROMOLD/CA1-12-10.pdf

Mtega, W.P., 2012, 'Access to and usage of information among rural communities: A case study of Kilosa District Morogoro Region in Tanzania', *Partnership: The Canadian Journal of Library and Information Practice and Research* 7(1). http://dx.doi.org/10.21083/partnership.v7i1.1646

Mtega, W.P. & Benard, R., 2013, 'The state of rural information and communication services in Tanzania: A meta-analysis', *International Journal of Information and Communication Technology Research* 3(2), 64–73.

National Bureau of Statistics, 2012, 'Population and housing census: Morogoro region population', viewed 15 January 2015, from http://www.nbs.go.tz/sensa/popu2.php

Nazari, M.R., Bin, H.J. & Hassan, S., 2011, 'The role of television in the enhancement of farmers' agricultural knowledge', *African Journal of Agricultural Research* 6(4), 931–936.

Nemes, G. & High, C., 2013, 'Old institutions, new challenges: The agricultural knowledge system in Hungary', *Studies in Agricultural Economics* 115(2), 76–84. http://dx.doi.org/10.7896/j.1303

Nonaka, I., Toyama, R. & Konno, N. 2000, 'SECI, ba and leadership: A unified model of dynamic knowledge creation', *Long Range Planning* 33, 5–34.

Ocholla, D., 2007, 'Marginalized knowledge: An agenda for indigenous knowledge development and integration with other forms of knowledge', *International Review of Information Ethics*, 7, 237–243.

Powell, T., 2008, 'The knowledge value chain (KVC): How to fix it when it breaks', viewed 20 October 2015, from http://www.knowledgeagency.com/sites/knowledgeagency.com/files/KVC%20How%20to%20Fix%20It%20080501.pdf

Rugumamu, C.P., 2014, 'Empowering smallholder rice farmers in Tanzania to increase productivity for promoting food security in eastern and southern Africa', *Agriculture & Food Security* 3(7), viewed 20 January 2015, from http://www.agricultureandfoodsecurity.com/content/3/1/7

Rural Livelihood Development Company (RLDP), 2009, 'Improving rice profitability through increased productivity and better marketing focusing on Tanzania's central Corridor', viewed 20 October 2015, from http://www.rldp.org/downloads/rice_strategy.pdf

Rutatora, D.F. & Mattee, A.Z., 2001, 'Major agricultural extension providers in Tanzania', *African Study Monographs* 22(4), 55–173.

Shetto, M.C., 2008, 'Assessment of agricultural information needs in African, Caribbean and Pacific (ACP) States Eastern Africa Country study: Tanzania', *Final Report, viewed 10 January 2015, from* http://www.researchintouse.com/resources/ext/cta08tz-agriinfoneed-rpt.pdf

Shetto, R., & Owenya, M., 2007, *Conservation agriculture as practiced in Tanzania: three case studies,* African Conservation Tillage Network, Nairobi, viewed n.d., from http://www.fao.org/ag/ca/doc/tanzania_casestudy.pdf

Sife, A.S., Kiondo, E. & Lyimo-Macha, J.G., 2010, 'Contribution of mobile phones to rural livelihoods and poverty reduction in Morogoro region, Tanzania', *Electronic Journal of Information Systems in Developing Countries* 42(3), 1–15.

Siyao, P.O., 2012, 'Barriers in accessing agricultural information in Tanzania with a Gender perspective: The case study of small-scale sugar cane growers in Kilombero district', *Electronic Journal of Information Systems in Developing Countries* 51(6), 1–19.

Smith, E.A., 2001, 'The role of tacit and explicit knowledge in the workplace', *Journal of Knowledge Management* 5(4), 311–321. http://dx.doi.org/10.1108/13673270110411733

Temu, A.E., Nyange, D., Mattee, A.Z. & Kashasha, L.K., 2005, 'Assessing rural services, infrastructure and their impact on agricultural production, marketing and food security in Tanzania', viewed 14 January 2015, from http://www.tanzaniagateway.org/docs/AssessingRuralServiceslandInfrastructureonAgriculturalProduction_Tanzania.pdf

Tilman, D., Cassman, K.G., Matson, P.A., Naylor, R. & Polasky, S., 2002, 'Agricultural sustainability and intensive production practices', *Nature* 418, 671–677. http://dx.doi.org/10.1038/nature01014

United Republic of Tanzania, 2011, *Tanzania Agriculture and Food Security Investment Plan 2011/12 to 2020/21*, Government Printers, Dar es Salaam.

United Republic of Tanzania, 2013, *National agriculture policy,* Government Printers, Dar es Salaam, Tanzania.

Wong, H.K., 2004, 'Knowledge value chain: Implementation of new product development system in a winery', *The Electronic Journal of Knowledge Management* 2(1), 77–90.

Yli-Renko, H., Autio, E. & Sapienza, H.J., 2001, 'Social capital, knowledge acquisition, and knowledge exploitation in young technology-based firms', *Strategic Management Journal* 22, 587–613. http://dx.doi.org/10.1002/smj.183

Leveraging management information in improving call centre productivity

Authors:
Manthisana Mosese[1]
Martie Mearns[2]

Affiliations:
[1]Centre for Information and Knowledge Management, University of Johannesburg, South Africa

[2]Department of Information and Knowledge Management, University of Johannesburg, South Africa

Corresponding author:
Martie Mearns,
mearnsm@uj.ac.za

Background: The availability and efficient use of management information is one of the key strategic levers in driving growth and competitiveness for companies. Management information facilitates vital decision making that assists organisations in improving their competitiveness. For call centre operations, competitiveness entails improving productivity and customer service, and management information is essential in this endeavour.

Objectives: This research explored the use of management information and its impact on two fundamental functions namely, improving productivity without compromising the quality of service, in the call centre of a well-known South African fashion retailer, Edcon. Following the implementation of the call centre technology project the research set out to determine how Edcon can transform their call centre to improve productivity and customer service through effective utilisation of their management information.

Method: Internal documents and reports were analysed to provide the basis of evaluation between the measures of productivity prior to and post the implementation of a technology project at Edcon's call centre. Semi-structured in-depth and group interviews were conducted to establish the importance and use of management information in improving productivity and customer service.

Results: The results indicated that the availability of management information has indeed contributed to improved efficiency at the Edcon call centre. Although literature claims that there is a correlation between a call centre technology upgrade and improvement in performance, evident in the return on investment being realised within a year or two of implementation, it fell beyond the scope of this study to investigate the return on investment for Edcon's call centre.

Conclusion: Although Edcon has begun realising benefits in improved productivity in their call centre from their available management information, information will continue to play a crucial role in supporting management with informed decisions that will improve the call centre operations.

Introduction

The impetus for improving the performance of a company is motivated by the highly competitive and globalized industry in which the company operates. For many organisations, it has become increasingly challenging to stay competitive merely from products and conventional face-to-face services (Du Preez 2008:1). The provision of additional facilities and functional areas that supplement products and services have thus become important competitive differentiators for companies. Call centres are one of the facilities deemed crucial to competitive differentiation (Barnett 2006) and they are the subject of this article.

Call centres have developed into effective means of improving service quality, promoting product offerings, and communicating with current and prospective customers (Du Preez 2008:2; Banks & Roodt 2011:1; Barnett 2006). Consequently, call centres have become a vehicle for improving the performance of organisations. They serve a critical role as they may function as the primary, and possibly the only point of contact between an organisation and its customers (Aksin, Armony & Mehrotra 2007:665). A call centre is defined as a 'place where most crucial customer interactions take place' (Reynolds 2010:3). Rademeyer (2012:7) supplements the above definition by referring to a call centre as a 'one stop shop for sales or for product information and services or for customer service'.

As with many other business processes and functions, call centre operations have become computerised and are often considered a source of testing new information technologies (IT)

(Rowe, Marciniak & Clergeau 2010:337). Call centre IT and systems have evolved into sophisticated devices offering features such as predictive dialling, and intelligent, dynamic routing of calls based on agent skills and knowledge (Robinson & Morley 2006:28). These mechanisations have enabled effortless access to information collected through the interaction with customers and with other systems. Despite the mentioned technological edge, the ability on the part of many enterprises to fully exploit information is still developing (Brooke 2002:393). In his 2003 study, Sharp (2003) reported that workforce management systems (WFM) as one of call centre management information systems (MIS) are used in only 10% of call centres. A more recent study, as found in a 2011 report by DMG Consulting, indicates an improvement in the use of call centre MIS, however, 'the adoption rate of WFM is still surprisingly low' (DMG Consulting 2011:1) for larger call centres. Optimal usage of existing information within the MIS to improve productivity and customer service still remains a challenge for many organisations (Prunty & Pritchard 2006:3) and Edcon was one such enterprise.

Edcon is the largest clothing, footwear, and textiles retailer in Southern Africa with approximately 20 000 employees and more than 1400 stores in South Africa, Botswana, Namibia, Swaziland, Lesotho, Mozambique, Ghana, and Zambia. The Edcon call centre is part of the Edcon Credit and Financial Services (CFS) Division. Edcon is a registered financial services provider and acquired this status in 2007. The call centre was, however, established in 1997 and at the time the focus of the call centre was on credit collections and customer services only. In 2008 its services expanded to offering full-fledged financial services in the form of banking, insurance services and other value-adding services such as the ability to pay for services using the Edcon private label store card. The Edcon call centre employs approximately 1,100 employees and is comprised of outbound and inbound operations. The outbound operations manage collections and on occasion, new business in the form of new accounts, whilst the inbound operations involve customer service and also new business.

In order to improve efficiency amidst the highly competitive and volatile retail industry, the Edcon CFS was compelled to consolidate their different call centre environments, whilst investigating means of acquiring and effectively using management information (MI) to optimise their operations (Edcon RFP 2011). It was through the implementation of a technology project, the CC Project, that new technology in the form of WFM, integrated Interactive Voice Recorder (IVR), Credit Management System (CMS), and comprehensive quality management that enabled the call centre to acquire new MI and enhance their measures of customer service and productivity. For Edcon, productivity is expressed through the number of calls the agents handle per day based on the number of hours worked, call abandon rates, service levels, and talk time. For collections, it is also based on the number and the value of local currency (ZAR for South Africa, Pula for Botswana etc.) collected per agent. The number of calls has to be delicately balanced against effectiveness as agents can handle many short calls without resolving customer's queries or collecting revenue.

With this background in mind, this article argues that through availability and effective use of information, Edcon was able to transform their call centre by improving productivity and customer service. This claim is informed by the research, which aimed to satisfy the following research question:

> Following the implementation of the call centre technology project (CC project), how can Edcon transform their call centre to improve productivity and customer service through effective utilisation of their management information?

Although the subject of call centres has been extensively studied, the focus has generally been on the performance of call centres and the issues relating to improving the performance of call centre agents. Limited research has specifically studied and linked MI to improved productivity and customer services although Belfiore, Chatterley and Petouhoff (2012:7) have found evidence that advanced call centre technology improves call centre performance and customer service. Edcon defines customer service through the following important measures: the speed of answer, first time resolution, call abandon rates, and customer satisfaction. Although first time resolution is an important measure, there is no scientific tool to measure this as it is subjective and the views of the agent and the customer may differ. Edcon does, however, use these predefined statistics to measure customer service:

- 70% of applications completed in 60 minutes
- 95% of applications completed in 24 hours
- 97% of applications completed within 10 business days
- 75% of calls answered within 20 seconds
- 3% abandon rate
- Complaints
  - 70% (responded in 48 hours)
  - 95% (responded in 5 business days)

Rowe *et al.* (2010:337), however, validate the view that there is a lack of association between IT and call centre productivity. This article therefore seeks to demonstrate that the use of MI contributes to improving call centre performance.

The article firstly examines the subject of MI within a call centre environment, and reviews perspectives and principles relating to the concepts of customer service and productivity in general, and within the Edcon call centre.

The management information concept

The meaning of MI can be inferred from defining and understanding the concepts of information and MIS.

Information is said to be one of the strategic and critical assets of any organisation (Higson & Waltho 2010:2). As Adeoti-Adekeye (1997:318) highlights, information is power and whoever possesses information possesses power. In the information and knowledge management sphere, information forms the building blocks to informed decision making and it is defined as data made meaningful and used for decision making. Citing a 1985 Davis and Olson definition of information, Zins (2007:480) defines this term as 'data that has been processed into a form that is meaningful to the recipient'. It is a result of organising data to respond to the questions of what, who, when, and where. Another interesting interpretation of this term as per Zins (2007:483) is that information is data that is meaningful, communicated, has objectives and consequences, and allows coherent decisions.

Given the significance of information in companies, the management of information likewise becomes a vital function that ensures that the right information is available at the right time for use in decision making (Adeoti-Adekeye 1997:320). In this regard, technology has played a valuable enabler with the development of information systems. An information system is a computer system wherein data is recorded and processed to produce information (Giao, Borini & De Miranda Oliveira 2010:336). A MIS is thus an information system that supplies management – at different managerial levels – in an organisation with relevant information required for informed decision making (Mahesh 2010:11).

Having defined the concepts of information and MIS, MI can thus be surmised as information that is derived from MIS, and that is disseminated to managers at different managerial levels to assist them in decision making. According to McCrae *et al.* (2012:27), MI includes financial, operational, performance, productivity and risks information, which is refined through continuous use and will often inspire insight and questions into the performance of an organisation. As an instrument for informed decision making, MI has been used by management in companies for many years to make critical decisions that benefit their organisations (Barzegar, Araghieh & Asgarani 2012:192). It is one of the indispensable tools used for effective decision making. MI provides a holistic view of all information and is thus an essential requirement in meeting the goals of improving customer service and increasing productivity. Dimension Data's 2013–2014 global contact centre benchmarking report affirms that MI has assisted call centre executives and provides evidence (in the form of transformations in performance) that the implementation, upgrade, or transformation of their company call centre has yielded benefits (Dimension Data 2014).

Management information in a call centre

In a call centre, MI can be extracted from a number of MIS including but not limited to the following aspects:

- *Workforce Management* (*WFM*) is a system that uses historical data to forecast the number of calls that can be expected in the future, and thus enables call centre management to schedule agents accordingly. Information relating to schedule efficiency, staff occupancy, and adherence to schedule are available to management for quick and effective decision making (Reynolds 2010:5). Without WFM, call centre managers are confronted with having to balance the right amount of staff, with the right skills for the workload expected, whilst delivering on improved productivity and quality service.
- *Interactive Voice Recorder* (*IVR*) is a tool that provides automatic menus to call centre customers. It is used to encourage customer self-service or to direct the call to the correct agent as directed by the menu options. Information available from the IVR includes the use of menus and the exit points (Reynolds 2010:5).
- *Customer communications recording* allows for all calls entering the call centre to be recorded. The recordings are used to drive the improvement and quality of service provided by the call centre. Typically, a random number of calls are selected for auditing, and decisions on the improvement of service made (Reynolds 2010:5).
- *Customer relationship management* (*CRM*) is regarded as a crucial instrument in improving customer service management. According to Holman, Batt and Holgrewe (2007:31), skills-based routing is thought to be effective relationship management in a call centre. This is debatable as the same authors also indicate that call centre employees need to be well trained and skilled in order to provide quality customer service (Holman *et al.* 2007:31). It is important to have a CRM strategy along with well-skilled employees to increase call centre productivity (Holman *et al. 2007:31).*
- *Credit and Management System* (*CMS*) is a system in which customer information such as credit history, buying patterns, payment records and a wide variety of customer demographic and behavioural information are stored and used to draw insight into customer buying patterns, preferences, payment methods, and the store they visit mostly (Holman *et al.* 2007:31).

The above provide a view of a few of the information systems available in a typical call centre. According to Barzegar *et al.* (2012:191), productivity and customer service are closely linked with access to relevant information and the efficient use of that information. As such, the right information at the right time plays a significant role in improving productivity and customer service.

Call centre productivity concept and measures

Call centres usually measure customer service and productivity by using predefined statistical modelling. This is done through operational data in inputs such as service durations, abandon rates, call arrival rates, and many others (Belfiore *et al.* 2012:7; Marr & Neely 2004:5; Shen & Huang 2008:252). A survey conducted by Knowlagent Productivity Plus (2011), illustrates that increasing productivity was ranked as a priority challenge for call centre executives.

Productivity is defined as the 'measurement of the amount of work accomplished during a specified time frame'; in a call centre environment it would be reflective of the number of customers that can be serviced over a specific time (OECD, n.d.). Rowe *et al.* (2010:341) refer to productivity as a quantitative aspect of a call centre, which deals with measures such as, but not limited to:

- the number of calls waiting versus the proportion of calls answered
- the average call duration
- the customer waiting time
- the number of agents on a call at a given period
- abandonment rate (outbound calls).

Gupta *et al.* (2008:2) suggest that it is necessary to include other factors to improve productivity over and above quantifiable measures. These factors should include: a full picture of information pertaining to customers' profiles, a process that will exploit this customer information, and information on call centre agents' skills required to perform at an optimal level. Marr and Neely (2004:5) endorse this statement by alleging that the employee characteristics that create value for companies and their customers have been largely ignored in favour of quantitative statistics that measure productivity. They argue that quantitative productivity measures alone have shown to be counterproductive to achieving customer satisfaction and that the performance of the call centre as a whole is integral to improved customer service.

Call centre customer service concept and measures

Customer service is the total value of what an organisation does to meet and sometime exceed customer's expectations (Edwards 2009:13). Customer service measures typically revolve around the duration the customer must wait to receive value or quality service from their interaction with the service provider (Aksin *et al.* 2007:666). Customer service measures typically include:

- average speed of answer
- first time resolution
- abandonment rate (inbound calls)
- average talk time
- adherence to schedule.

First time resolution is recognised as the most important customer service measure in a call centre, however, it is found to be the most challenging to measure as it involves customer's perspectives and expectations (Stringham & Cotter 2012:2). Customer satisfaction surveys can be used to offset the challenges of measuring first time resolution and are recorded in Marr and Neely's (2004) study as a key objective of a call centre. There seems to be consensus on the importance of surveys among researchers, however, the response rate is typically very low. This is according to an article by Vocal Laboratories (2014), which also reports the response rate of surveys as varying between just under 1% to over 60%.

The measures of productivity and customer service are the basis of vital information that enables appropriate management of operations for call centre management. Based on the information these measures provide, a view of possible deviations and potential contrasts with global norms can be corrected. Important and informed decisions that may change the course of a call centre operation can thus be made.

Research methods

A combination of both qualitative and quantitative methods was used for the research.

Sampling method

Purposive sampling technique was utilised to select the sample for this research. This type of sampling was particularly suited for this research as the sample was small, limited to Edcon's CFS operation, and the researcher was deliberate in selecting the individuals to interview. These individuals were selected based on their seniority, knowledge, and the insights they possess necessary for this study. As Edcon's CFS call centre is divided into Collections and Services departments, the researcher took care to ensure representation from both operations. The sample was thus made up of the following:

- the executive of the CFS operations
- the head of collections department
- the head of services department
- two managers who oversee the collections and services operations
- eight call centre agents from both departments.

The sample was deliberately mixed as described to allow for balance and impartiality. The total sample for this research was 16 individuals and all relevant ethical clearances were negotiated with the research subjects and organisation.

Data collection and processing methods

The instruments used for collecting data for this research were both qualitative and quantitative. The qualitative data collections method was in the form of semi-structured face-to-face interviews for the individuals in management. The interviews were designed to capture the views and insights of the 16 interviewees pertaining to the current use of MI, the measures of customer service and productivity, and the opportunities and barriers to information access. Different interview questions, targeting the different levels of management were compiled. These questions were used to structure the interviews and to ensure that the scope of the interviews was adhered to, whilst allowing for flexibility to probe and vary the questions based on the direction the interview took. For call centre representatives, group interviews were conducted. The group interviews were also semi-structured and sought to gather different perspectives and views from employees at lower levels. With the permission of the interviewees, the interviews were audio recorded, and then transcribed before the process of analysis began.

A portion of this research involved collecting and analysing historical data, which comprised data prior to the implementation of the CC project. This formed the quantitative portion of the data collected and productivity statistics were analysed from historical documentation over a certain period and then compared with data that was collected post the implementation of the CC project.

Data analysis

As a large amount of textual data was amassed from the semi-structured interviews, Atlas.ti, a computer-assisted qualitative data analysis software tool was utilised to analyse the interviews. For the quantitative data collected from historical information, Microsoft Excel was used to analyse and compare historical information and statistical norms gathered from the MIS that formed part of the call centre department, against the collected information following the implementation of phase one of the CC project.

Research findings and discussion

The findings and results of the research are presented below.

Internal historical information findings

The implementation of the CC project delivered additional MIS and thus the availability and accessibility of new and pertinent MI. Phase one of the CC project included, among others, the implementation of WFM, CRM, CMS integration, improved IVR, and quality assurance solutions. This phase covered the outbound collections department and was implemented in November 2013.

Productivity data on a month to month basis was plotted to show the differences in the measures prior and subsequent the implementation of the CC project. The statistics are comparable data for a period of 6 months in 2013–2014 with the same number of agents. The statistics relate to the collections department, and for the purpose of the article, only a sample of three measures are reported on.

Figure 1 presents a comparison in the number of accounts dialled prior and post the implementation of the CC project.

Figure 1 displays a significant increase in the number of calls being dialled post the implementation of the CC project for the same period. This signifies an increase in the number of successful connections the dialler made. Successful connections equates to improved productivity. The diagram shows tapering and then stability in the number of accounts dialled. This has been attributed to the dialler algorithms aligning to patterns and trends on the best time to call a customer and thus being successful in dialling the right numbers at the right time. The productivity of the agents is also improved as they are speaking to the right people at the right time, consequently increasing their promise-to-pay (PTP) rate.

Figure 2 presents statistics on the average number of dropped calls.

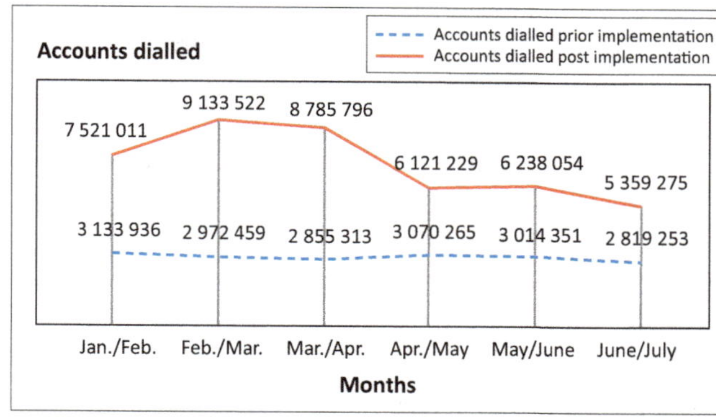

FIGURE 1: Number of accounts dialled.

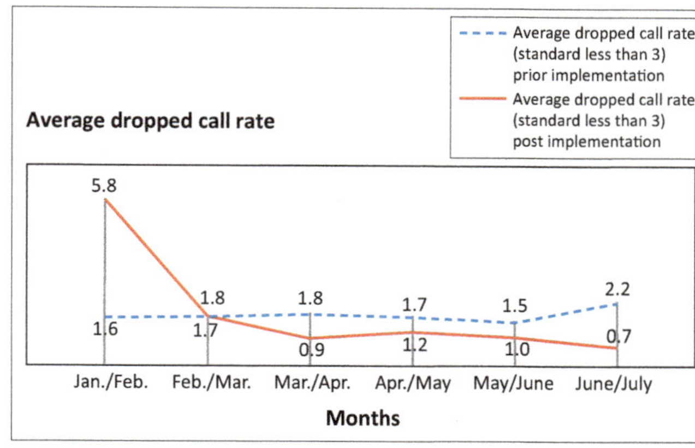

FIGURE 2: Average dropped call rate.

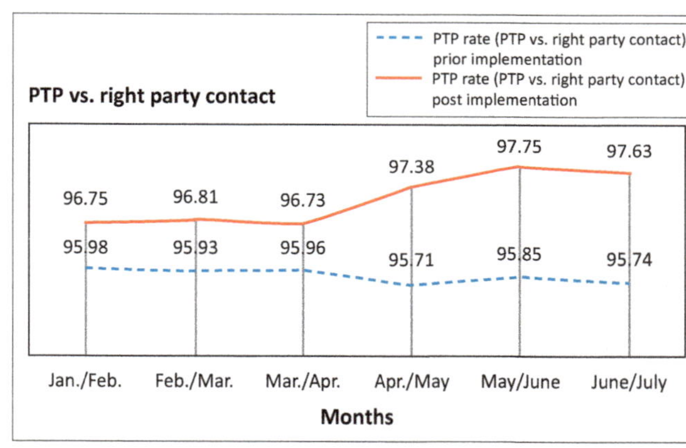

FIGURE 3: PTP versus account-holder contact.

From Figure 2, Edcon has had a steady and acceptable rate of abandoned calls, even prior to the implementation of the CC project. Post the implementation, the number of dropped calls was high and then decreased sharply in subsequent months. A low dropped call rate directly correlates to less calls being abandoned and the predictive dialler accurately connecting to the right customer at the right time. Best practice for the rate of dropped calls should be between 3% and 8% (International Finance Corporation 2015:3). At less than 1%, the CFS is managing this measure exceptionally.

Figure 3 presents measurements on the number of PTPs against the actual account-holder.

The number of PTPs has also increased post the implementation of the CC project as depicted in Figure 3.

Again, this can be credited to the efficiency of the predictive dialler in reaching the right account-holder. This is a clear measure of increased productivity for both the collections department and the agents.

In summary, from the above graphical comparisons of the productivity measures, the difference in productivity improvement for comparable months is distinctive. This is significant for Edcon as it shows that the implementation of the CC project is showing dividends. The agents are doing more work and they are producing results that are beneficial to, both themselves and to Edcon as a company. The new MI associated with the CC project will enable the management of the call centre plan better for the future.

Group and in-depth interviews findings

The transcribed interviews were coded and major themes comprising management information; measures; and challenges and opportunities were identified.

Management information

A number of questions relating to the role of MI in improving customer service and productivity and the effective use of MI for decision making were posed. Confidentiality is maintained using codes such as L1, L2 etc. for the participants of the interviews. For the CFS executive (L1), the role that MI plays in the CFS is crucial as it is an indicator of whether the call centre is living up to the service standards established. To L1, the call centre would not function without the necessary MI that they have daily to make decisions. This view matches the heads of services and collections departments (L2 and L3 respectively). For them MI is also crucial in identifying issues and then working towards a root cause. For lower level managers, phrases such as 'measurement of performance', 'drivers of performance', and 'assistance with staffing requirements' were referenced as crucial to them carrying out their daily tasks. There was consensus regarding the effective use of MI and all managers agreed this could improve.

The implementation of the CC project, and therefore the rollout of WFM and other MIS incited excitement and optimism among the entire management team. New information relating to volume forecasting, automatic scheduling and adherence to schedule seemed to have been much anticipated. The management all reported the cost and time savings, and the improvement in decision making the call centre has achieved (in collections) and will achieve (in services). According to L1, agent's adherence to schedule, as one of the customer service measures, improved from below 80% to 95% in collections since implementation. The International Finance Corporation's (IFC) global best practice guide lists the global metric at 95%, bringing the collections department on par with global norms.

The management team reported that the priority for the CFS was to complete the implementation of the CC project to start realising the same benefits that collection is experiencing in services. They reported an expectation that the benefits the CFS has been able to realise so far will enable the growth of the operation. As a result, the management team have begun applying the MI they are receiving from the WFM in collections. They all understand that the ultimate goal for the call centre is to increase efficiencies and regain lost market share through creative offerings that the call centre can introduce. Increasing the IVR menu options were listed as a definite opportunity that is already underway.

The agents reported that availability and access to information improved their productivity. For them, the availability of their schedules online through WFM has been invaluable when they missed work for some reason or arrived late. This conveyed that this information is, and has been of great support to improving their performance.

Productivity and customer service measures

Questions were aimed at establishing what the interviewees viewed as important measures of good customer service and productivity and how this information is used to improve productivity and customer service.

Almost all the management interviewees responded by referring to the current measures of customer service and productivity, with an exception of L1, whose interest in customer service revolved around service quality. He immediately pointed out that the challenge with measuring service is around ensuring systematic and consistent measurement of quality. The measures mostly quoted by the interviewees include 'first time resolution', 'speed of answer', 'abandon rates', 'call audits', and 'customer satisfaction'. The group services manager (L2) did, however, caution that something like customer satisfaction is also hard to determine because of low survey response rates. This is confirmed by the Vocal Laboratories internet article which reports customer survey response rates at less than 1%. The level of knowledge in the product and service offerings was also noted as what makes customer service outstanding.

It was interesting to note that the first response from the agents on this question was also 'first time resolution'. This is consistent with research as first time resolution is agreed to be the most important customer service measure. One agent also specifically mentioned good customer service goes hand in hand with the right tools for the job which is the right information. For him, without relevant information, he has no knowledge and thus no confidence in his products and services, thus validating the views of management. Supporting this view, Marr and Neely (2004:7) report that researchers from the Netherlands have found that customers expect a level of 'self-efficacy' (among other traits), which is translated to a belief that agents are competent in their duties.

On productivity, measures such as 'minimum amount of handle time' came out prominently for management. Other measures include 'income collected per agent', 'income collected per hour', and 'PTP rate'. For the services department, however, L2 indicated that productivity measures do not matter as much as customer service, given the priorities of that department. L2 further argued that it is imprudent to put a number on customer service. For his department, 75% of the calls must be answered within 20 seconds, 75% of the time. The global benchmark on this, according to IFC's benchmarking report, is at 80% of calls answered within 20 seconds. Marr and Neely (2004:5) argue a similar point, relating that quantitative statistics that measure productivity have largely been favoured over employee characteristics that create value for companies and their customers.

The agent's response to productivity was different and this was made obvious by their priorities and goals. Their measure of productivity included reaching their daily targets of PTP, sales, and the number of multimedia statements (MMS) sent (the agents are goaled on how many customers they convince to take up MMS or email for statements instead of normal post). All agents agreed to these measures, however, their responses were varied on whether they were seeing an improvement in achieving these goals since the implementation of the CC project.

Challenges and opportunities

Information dissemination and communications were disclosed as major challenges still plaguing the call centre for lower level managers and agents. A tight-fisted approach on certain relevant information was stated as hampering decision making and productivity at these lower levels. The agents described cases where a customer will call querying a status on their account that they do not have access to, resulting in the customer waiting on the call while the information is sought, and thus increasing the call duration. An opportunity for the agents in this regards was listed as disseminating information via the Edcon intranet. Access to relevant information will enable them to perform their tasks in the best way and increase their individual productivity, they stated.

Interestingly, skills-based routing became a follow-up question in the interviews with the management of the call centre. There were conflicting views on the usefulness of this from the different managers. Where L1 felt that this is one of the technologies they could certainly look at, L2 preferred multiskilling as an approach.

Communication, particularly in relation to the dissemination of information, emerged as a common thread among agents as one of the major challenges from these interviews. It was interesting to note that L1, being the executive in the call centre, did not believe communications to be a challenge though. This may allude to disconnects and communication breakdowns between the top level management and the agents on what is sufficient and relevant communication.

Discussion

Customer service is one of the pillars of the Edcon's CFS and as a result, major efforts are constantly put in place to ensure its improvement. Even though there are standard indicators of good customer service, such as first time resolution, it transpired from the interviews that measuring customer service is challenging. This is because good customer service may be subjective and it may depend on one brilliant service from one call or one appalling service from another call. What is clear from the interview with L1 is that quality is an imperative for his operation. As referenced in Marr and Neely (2004:8), the benefits of quality in customer service will improve the ability to attract new customers and retain current customers. It is thus apparent why this will rank higher in L1's view. The implementation of WFM in the collections department showed a dramatic improvement in adherence to schedule, bringing this measure in line with global benchmarks and thereby improving one of the measures of customer service.

The Edcon CFS is not unlike many call centres as some of their productivity measures compare with those described in literature. Many of the measures for outbound collections agents are thus centred on the number and the value of income collected per agent as well as PTP rates. This cements the view that there is a divergence of responsibilities and focus for call centre managers who have to intricately balance customer service, with cost reduction and income generation (Robinson & Morley 2006:3). Belfiore *et al.* (2012:10) and Du Preez (2008:10) aptly refer to this as the 'call centre management balancing act'.

It is understandable that there would be a difference in productivity priorities between management and agents. The agents' view pertained to their daily goals whereas management regarded productivity holistically. Another interesting distinction was the difference in approach towards productivity between the collections and the services departments. Again, this is understandable as the collections teams are incentivised on their productivity goals whereas the services teams are not. Notwithstanding, productivity has certainly improved since the implementation of the CC project as demonstrated in the projected statistics above.

The role that MI plays in a call centre environment is vital. Researchers such as Barzegar *et al.* (2012:191) indicate that MIS provides call centres the potential to improve their operations. This is recognised by the management of Edcon's CFS and through implementations of new MIS, they are expecting to get more information that they can use to improve their call centre. The performance of the departments, teams, and individuals, augmented by the implementation of new MIS in CRM and WFM, and the new information insights expected from this implementation, is touted to further improve customer service as it has productivity in the collections department.

In summary, the CFS previously collected appropriate, albeit insufficient, information in the measures of their call centre because of the absence of suitable MIS. This information was being used in the daily operations of the call centre and was imperative in decision making. The CC project, however, addressed the lack of new MI through the implementation of WFM, CRM, and the CMS integration. All indications are that the CFS is moving in the right direction concerning the ideas and strategies they are looking to implement in the near future, based on the efficiencies they have realised in collections. Although there are still areas of improvement in the use of MI, such as considering skills-based routing, the CFS will continue to optimise the use of MI from the MIS they have acquired. Continuing on the vein of improving the functions and the operations of the call centre and using the available MI successfully will surely lead to further improvements in productivity and in working towards delighting their customers continuously and consistently.

Suggested future study for consideration for Edcon would be the measurement of the return on investment (ROI) on the CC project. In their study, Belfiore *et al.* (2012:7) found that there is a correlation between a call centre technology upgrade and improvement in performance, and that ROI is usually realised within a year or two of implementation. However, these researchers' study only focused on 143 call centres and they report this is still insufficient representation.

Conclusion

Increasing competitiveness is at the core of many profit companies. For a call centre, improving competitiveness translates to an increase in the number of calls that can be serviced in a time period, without sacrificing the quality of service to the customer. Call centres have been a subject of study for many researchers since the phenomenon of serving customers over the telephone became popular. The interest in call centres has primarily focused on the profiles and the performance of call centre agents, and what could be measured in a call centre to make it efficient. There have also been arguments and counter arguments, as seen in Marr and Neely's (2004) research report for Fujitsu, on what the appropriate measures should be.

This article, considered a different area that is an important aspect in improving the performance of a call centre, which is MI. The article reasoned that through effective use of MI, Edcon's CFS has been able to see an improvement in the existing productivity measures in their collections division. The effective use of MI was shown to be an important aspect in the decision making process and in actually influencing the improvements in productivity and customer service.

The research showed limitations on the part of Edcon in leveraging some of the important MI available such as customer insights and skills-based routing. Despite these limitations, the findings from the semi-structured, in-depth interviews showed that there is considerable appetite on the part of the CFS executive in finding the best solutions to maintain the call centre profitability. The implementation and availability of newly acquired MIS included in the implementation of the CC project will support this endeavour. Considerations for future research could therefore include exploring the benefits of these new MIS and their contribution to the advancement of Edcon's CFS. The article further recommends an investigation on the ROI of the CC project as advocated by Belfiore *et al.* (2012:7).

In the words of Victor Kiam, the CEO of Remington 'information is a negotiator's greatest weapon' (Sudor 2009:94). MI should thus be a vital consideration for call centre operations and its management. Utilising strategies to optimise this information as opposed to simply reporting on the information is not only prudent on the part of the company, but it will also safeguard their competitiveness in the long-term.

Acknowledgements

Competing interests

The authors declare that they have no financial or personal relationships which may have inappropriately influenced them in writing this article.

Authors' contributions

M.M.[1] (University of Johannesburg) and M.M.[2] (University of Johannesburg) contributed equally to the writing of this article.

References

Adeoti-Adekeye, W.B., 1997, 'The importance of management information systems', *Library Review* 46(5), 318–327.

Aksin, Z., Armony, M. & Mehrotra, V., 2007, 'The modern call centre: A multi-disciplinary perspective on operations management research', *Production and Operations Management Society* 16(6), 665–668.

Banks, D. & Roodt, G., 2011, 'The Efficiency and quality dilemma: What drives South African call centre management performance indicators?', *SA Journal of Human Resource Management* 9(1), 1–17.

Barnett, G., 2006, 'The contact centre industry: Where we've been and where we're going next', viewed 29 April 2015, from http://www.tmcnet.com/call-center/0606/cis-contact-center-technology-0606.htm

Barzegar, N., Araghieh, A. & Asgarani, M., 2012, 'The role of management information systems (MIS) to increase productivity in the workforce (case study of Iran)', *Journal of Educational and Management Studies* 3(3), 191–194.

Belfiore, B.L., Chatterley, J. & Petouhoff, N., 2012, 'The impact of technology on contact centre performance', viewed 29 April 2015, from http://www.cisco.com/c/dam/en/us/products/collateral/customer-collaboration/unified-contact-center-enterprise/technology_contact_center_performance_research_report.pdf

Brooke, C., 2002, 'Information systems at call centre', *International Journal of Information Management* 22(2002), 389–401.

Dimension Data, 2014, 'Global contact centre benchmarking, Top 5 series', viewed 29 April 2015, from http://www.dimensiondata.com/Global/Downloadable%20Documents/Top%205%20Series%20-%205%20Steps%20to%20Clearer%20Performance%20Management%20Information.pdf

DMG Consulting, 2011, 'Making WFM work: best practices and ROI model', viewed 29 April 2015, from http://www.neccf.org/whitepapers/Making_Workforce_Management_Work.pdf

Du Preez, J.J., 2008, 'Call centre design, operation and optimisation – A structured and scientific based approach', Master's dissertation, University of Stellenbosch, Stellenbosch.

Edcon RFP, 2011, 'Request for proposal for a migration strategy for the contact centre infrastructure at the Regional Credit Offices as well as an enterprise wide unified communication strategy', viewed 29 April 2015, from http://intranet/default.aspx

Edwards, S., 2009, Best practice guide for customer service professionals, Customer 1st International, UK, viewed 29 April 2015, from http://www.customerserviceglobal.com/files/customer_service_1st_sample_bpgcsp_ebook.pdf

Giao, P.R., Borini, F.M. & De Miranda Oliveira Jr., M., 2010, 'The influence of technology on the performance of Brazilian call centres', *Journal of Information Systems and Technology Management* 7(2), 335–352.

Gupta, A., McMahon, S., Jain, A. & Kanagasabai, K., 2008, 'Redefining the mission for banks; call centres: Cut costs, grow sales or both?', viewed 29 April 2015, from http://www.booz.com/media/uploads/Redefining_Mission_for_Banks_Call_Centers.pdf

Higson, C. & Waltho, D., 2010, 'Valuing information as an asset', SAS White paper, viewed 29 April 2015, from http://www.eurim.org.uk/activities/ig/InformationAsset.pdf

Holman, D., Batt, R. & Holtgrewe, U., 2007, 'The global call centre report: International perspectives on management and employment', viewed 29 April 2015, from http://www.globalcallcentre.org

International Finance Corporation, 2015, 'Measuring call centre performance, Global best practices', viewed 29 April 2015, from http://www.ifc.org/wps/wcm/connect/ifc_ext_design/ifc+search/search/searchresultlandingpage?cx=009183910618791464029%3Aik2jtgcdpms&cof=FORID%3A11&ie=&q=call+centre

Knowlagent Productivity Plus, 2011, 'Knowledge surveys on contact centre productivity', viewed 29 April 2015, from http://info.knowlagent.com/fastfacts.html

Mahesh, S.N., 2010, 'A study on effectiveness of MIS in organised retail stores in Vijayawada (with reference to BIG BAZAR)', viewed 29 April 2015, from http://www.scribd.com/doc/44758500/RETAIL-STORES-MIS-BY-S-MAHESH-GUMMADIDURRU-9248528762-k-l-university#

Marr, B. & Neely, A., 2004, 'Managing and measuring for value: The case of call centre performance', Cranfield University School of Management, viewed 29 April 2015 from http://www.uk.fijutsi.com

McCrae, J., Stephen, J., Mehta, R. & Guermellou, T., 2012, 'Improving decision making in Whitehall: Effective use of management information', viewed 29 April 2015, from http://www.instituteforgovernment.org.uk/sites/default/files/publications/Improving%20decision%20making%20in%20Whitehall.pdf

OECD, n.d., 'Measuring productivity', viewed 29 April 2015, from http://www.oecd.org/std/productivity-stats/2352458.pdf

Prunty, M. & Pritchard, A., 2006, 'White paper on: The customer focused contact centre', viewed 29 April 2015, from http://www-935.ibm.com/services/us/gbs/bus/pdf/the-customer-focused-contact-center.pdf

Rademeyer, D., 2012, 'A benefits model for the call centre strategy', Master's dissertation, University of Johannesburg, Johannesburg.

Reynolds, P., 2010, 'Call centre metrics: Best practices in performance measurement and management to maximise quiltline efficiency and quality', viewed 29 April 2015, from http://cymcdn.com/sites/www.naquitline.org/resource/resmgr/issue_papers/callcentermetricspaperbestpr.pdf

Robinson, G. & Morley, C., 2006, 'Call centre management: responsibilities and performance', *International Journal of Service Industry Management* 17(3), 284–300.

Rowe, F., Marciniak, R. & Clergeau, C., 2010, 'The contribution of information technology to call centre productivity', *Journal of Information Technology and People* 24(4), 336–361.

Sharp, D., 2003, 'Call Centre operation: Design, operation and maintenance', Elsevier, Amsterdam.

Shen, H. & Huang, J.Z., 2008, 'Interday forecasting and intraday updating of call centre arrivals', *Manufacturing and Service Operations Management* 10(3), 391–410.

Stringham, R. & Cotter, M., 2012 'Best practices for improving first-contact resolution in the contact centre', viewed 29 April 2015, from http://www.oracle.com

Sudor, G., 2009, *International business*, SAGE, London.

Vocal Laboratories, 2014, 'Improving survey response rates', viewed 29 April 2015, from http://www.vocalabs.com/newsletter/improving-survey-response-rates

Zins, C., 2007, 'Conceptual approaches for defining data, information and knowledge', *Journal of the American Society for Information Science and Technology* 58(4), 479–493.

7

Safeguarding information as an asset: Do we need a redefinition in the knowledge economy and beyond?

Authors:
Adeniji K. Adesemowo[1]
Rossouw von Solms[2]
Reinhardt A. Botha[1]

Affiliations:
[1]School of ICT, Nelson Mandela Metropolitan University, South Africa

[2]Centre for Research in Information and Cyber Security, Nelson Mandela Metropolitan University, South Africa

Corresponding author:
Adeniji Adesemowo,
kayode.adesemowo@nmmu.ac.za

Background: With the evolution of data, via information into knowledge and beyond, intangible information assets (seen as an integral part of IT assets in this article) increasingly come to fore. A contemporary issue facing organisations in the knowledge economy and beyond is how best to safeguard and derive optimum value from their evolving information assets. A well-known fact is that risk exists because there is the possibility of threats to an asset. Likewise, no assets equals no risk. Although a large body of work is addressing threat models, the nature of the assets of the knowledge economy and beyond has not been well researched.

Objectives: To investigate the definition of information assets across a number of financial, risk and information technology standards, frameworks and regulations, in order to ascertain whether a coherent definition exists across the board. If there is none (or limited), then propose a workable definition that is apt for the knowledge economy and beyond.

Method: Qualitative thematic content analysis and a comparative study based on four main themes (Assets, Types of Asset, Information, and Information Assets). This then serves as a basis for argumentation schemes that lead to a proposed re-definition. The qualitative research approach assists us to address the concern of the incoherent definition of information and information assets across the board.

Results: Contrary to expectations, the research study found the current definition to be incoherent. When the asset to be controlled is not properly defined and understood, it stands the risk of not being identified properly. This implies that the effectiveness, efficiency, reliability of internal control, and compliance with the applicable legislation and regulations would not be appropriate. This article highlights the need for a fundamental shift in how information assets (valuable, but unvalued organisational intangible assets) are being viewed and treated, especially with regard to information risk and internal controls.

Conclusion: This article has identified a major defect in most standards, frameworks, and regulations dealing with regard to the safeguarding and management of information assets (and IT assets). It has established from the review carried out that information assets have not been properly defined across the board. Beyond this significant finding, it was further shown that the principle of risk (assessment) across the board requires the identification of the asset that needs to be controlled. A starting point, then, is a coherent definition (as proposed) for the information asset in itself. Therefore, proper definition across the board might assists in proper identification that could result in appropriate control and graceful handling of the end-of-life disposal.

Introduction

Information has not only permeated the knowledge economy and beyond (Buera & Kaboski 2009:2540; Goede 2011:36), but it has become a critical business asset without which an organisation's competitive advantage would be eroded (Ahmad, Bosua & Scheepers 2014:28; Evans & Price 2014:113; Laney 2014; Laskowski 2014; Naidoo & Van Niekerk 2014:33, 36–37).

This is much in line with Leavitt and Whisler's (1958:41) projection of information having strategic importance (at middle and top management levels), when the technology that processes, transmits, and stores information was rightly termed Information Technology (IT) in their business review paper 'Management in the 1980s'. The permeation of information and its strategic importance resonates well with Moody and Walsh's (1999:2) notion that information is a strategic business asset, which is indeed a 'valuable, but [*largely*] unvalued asset'.

The importance of information can be seen in its strategic relevance across middle- and top-management levels (ISACA 2012; King 2009; Leavitt & Whisler 1958). The use of information (whether by individuals in an organisation and/or by a group of people at middle, top management and board level, or usage across the whole organisation) has a far-reaching, enterprise-wide impact. Information is a strategic intangible asset, and therefore requires that commensurate internal control(s) be applied to it and the management thereof.

This is much in line with the application of internal controls on any other corporate asset, as stipulated by the Committee of Sponsoring Organisations of the Treadway Commission – COSO (2013), which advises that the safeguarding of assets is of cardinal importance. COSO's internal control requirement mandates a careful balance between effective and efficient safeguarding.

This article posits that information assets, being intangible assets, cannot have internal control(s) applied to them *per se*; but rather control(s) should be applied to the process and/or the container or processor (being the related IT asset). Drawing upon the fundamental issue of internal control, control(s) to be applied to an IT asset must be commensurate with the carrying (information) value of the underlying information asset. However, from an IT/information risk viewpoint, the value can only be determined if the information asset is understood, known, clearly defined (Haider, Koronios & Quirchmayr 2006:288), identified, and appraised appropriately; because any associated risk must be taken into consideration as well (ISO/IEC 2014:14–15).

A challenge arose in this instance when the net value of the information asset (benefit to the organisation) and risk (liability) are not used to determine the level of appropriate control(s) required. The authors are of the view that the inability to apply a commensurate level of control seems to be a factor of not properly understanding 'the information asset' in itself. Knowing 'the information asset' is directly linked to the definition of the 'information asset'. To find answers to these challenges, this article reviews information assets and reputation loss, which then leads into the need to ascertain which definition(s) exists for information assets in the form of standards, frameworks, and regulations.

The ascertaining of information assets' definitions across the board was carried out by using qualitative-content analysis and a comparative review of a number of standards, frameworks, and regulations across financial, asset management, service management, and IT. Next, the findings on the lack of definition, or an inadequate definition thereof, was presented and discussed; and a definition was proposed. The article concludes with the five P-factors of unrelenting reputation loss, as a result of the lack of sufficient internal control over IT assets (container of information asset).

Review: Information asset and reputation loss

Data, information, and knowledge (all integral dimensions of information assets) are terms that are loosely used interchangeably. Yet, they differ from one another. A contextualisation of their meaning could assist us to look at the information component of information assets from a resource angle. As a resource, information gives the strategic competitive advantage (Ahmad *et al.* 2014:28; Moody & Walsh 1999:2); and when it is not safeguarded, as it ought to be, reputation loss, amongst others, can arise.

Data, information and information assets

Taken from the Oxford Dictionary (http://www.oxforddictionaries.com/definition/english/data), data (the plural of datum) is defined as facts and statistics collected together for reference or analysis. Data can also be known as the quantities, characters, or symbols on which operations are performed on by a computer, which may be stored and transmitted in the form of electrical signals and recorded on magnetic, optical, or mechanical recording media. Data can even comprise that which is stated in human discourse (Gates & Matthews 2014:107). In Moody and Walsh (1999:2), data are the raw materials for information.

Information, on the other hand, is defined as the facts provided or learned about something or someone. It could otherwise be defined as computing the data that were or are being processed, stored, or transmitted by a computer.

We shall look at the definition of information in King III and COBIT 5 later in this article as part of the finding.

Furthermore, to properly contextualise information and understand its meaning accurately, this article views information in two main lines of personal information and corporate information. Defined in the US Privacy Law, in the EU Directive, in the *Australian Privacy Act*, and in the South African Protection of Personal Information (POPI) Act, personal information is the personally identifiable information (Gates & Matthews 2014:106) that can be used on its own, or with other information to uniquely identify, contact, or locate a single person, or to identify an individual in context (Australian Parliament 1988; California Senate 2002; European Parliament 1995; Parliament of the Republic of South Africa 2013). This is the realm of identity theft (when personal information has been breached, and/or results in a loss of personal reputation).

On the other hand, corporate information is the information that uniquely identifies an organisation (public) or information that is used or processed internally (private), which might not have been made public (concept seen in insider trading, internal control procedures, and intellectual properties). Corporates' 'private' information (business information assets), the focus of this article, are processed and used internally, in order to gain a competitive advantage, to add to, and/or to derive economic values (information management). Furthermore, they are strategically controlled (information governance) to derive optimal investment value (Evans & Price 2014:115). However, when improperly safeguarded or controlled, business information assets could become a liability (e.g. reputation loss).

Information assets and reputation loss

A number of security breaches, some highlighted in Figure 1, arose from improper safeguarding of information assets. These security breaches against business information assets have resulted in reputation issues – and for some, reputation loss to the organisation (Arlitsch & Edelman 2014:49; Jones 2009:3; Silva 2012; Warner 2011:737)

It can be seen that, on the one front, information assets continually remain a target with success; while on the other hand, IT assets that contain the information assets are getting to the 'wild' – with or without control(s) in place. This loss keeps occurring, in spite of the vast array of technologies available, which have been put in place to safeguard IT assets. Additionally, standards, best practices, and guidelines also abound to ensure that (business) information assets are cared for; and that the regulatory laws mandating protection are enforced (Burdon 2010:64–65). Okere, Van Niekerk and Carroll (2012:1) highlighted the human factor, generally dubbed as the 'weakest link', which can possibly be overcome by strengthening the associated information security culture. Hence, it can safely be said that technology, or know-how, or regulations, are not the only key factors in the ongoing security breaches; although they do contribute. There is yet another contributory factor!

Control inefficiency over information assets

Do we then say that these technical and process controls, enabled by hi-tech security technologies, are not effective, or are being misapplied? Or rather, should we say that these multifaceted standards, best-practices, and guidelines are not appropriate enough to ensure a secure environment; or are they just impossible to implement? Perhaps, regulatory deterrents are ineffective in terms of the penalties and enforcement, so that organisations take them with a pinch of salt? This is a point of view taken by Burdon (2010:64), when stating that the general levels of corporate information security practices are inadequate, hence the emergence of data-breach notification laws. All these technical and process controls have their place; and are somewhat effective - to the extent for which they were intended.

Xtra! Xtra! - Read 'bout it!	
2015 Jan:	Anthem BlueCross BlueShield Cyber-attack on IT system Target: members' private information Dedicated site Anthemfacts.com dealing with reputation loss
2014 Jan:	Theft of unencrypted laptops behind Coca-Cola breach impacting 74,000# (Identity Protection estimated at US$11m per year)
2014 Jan:	Michaels Store (NYSE:MIK) attack (25th) (Lawsuit already instituted - databreaches.net)
2014 Jan:	Neiman Marcus (NYSE:NMG) attack cautionary (10th) As at Feb. 14, 157-pages analysis, 350,000 customer cards (US$1.1m)
2013 Dec:	Targets Corp (NYSE:TGT) Security Breach 40m cards, 70m Personal Info, forecast > 30m direct/indirect cost
2007:	BlueCross BlueShield Tennessee (BCBST) 57 Hard drives HIPAA/HITECH fine US$1.5m; reputation, legal cost over US$17m
2007:	UK HM Revenue and Customs: Lost two discs, 25m accounts
2007:	TJX (NYSE: TJX) loss of 40 million customer account records
2007:	U.S. Department of Veterans Affairs (VA) loss of information on more than half a million people (initially reported 48000)

Source: Collation of authors' knowledge of the events listed herein and the study of papers listed in the section-(Information Assets and Reputation Loss)

FIGURE 1: Some of the security breaches discussed in this paper sourced from author's collation of breaches in the media and literature.

Research domain: Problem and methodology

Surely, the fundamental of risk remains the possibility of a threat to an asset (ISO/IEC 2014, sec. 2.68); and that of accounting is equity, which is the differential sum of asset and liability (IASB 2010, sec. 4.4). If controls are available, and the means to safeguard assets are advanced and sophisticated nowadays, as seen from the review above, yet security breaches continue to be relatively unabated, then, there is a need to look again at the internal controls and the IT risk chain, with a focus on information risk.

Poller, Türpe and Kinder-Kurlanda (2014) have advocated the strong need to factor stakeholders directly into the risk-analysis equations. The concept of stakeholders used in business impact analysis exercises would then be carried over to risk-analysis exercises as well. Their approach is laudable as it would bring the Responsible, Accountable, Consulted, Informed model to the fore. An interesting space to watch!

Nonetheless, a possible rationale that can be attributed to the risk challenge might be how we value our assets (in this instance, IT assets, which are primary containers for information assets). This shifts us from 'the control' (minimising possibility of threat) to 'what is being controlled' (preservation, maximising, and growing value).

It therefore implies that what is being controlled (IT assets and underlying information assets), requires insightful understanding of its attributes in order to be better understood and identified. Hence, there is a need for a rethink of an IT asset value, especially for risk purposes. In order to do this, there is a need to look deeper into what the real target is in security breaches – which is the underlying information asset. It is the information asset that is not properly defined and understood, as it ought to be.

To the best of the authors' knowledge, as highlighted in the methodology, there has been no literature or white paper that has carried out a comprehensive comparative study on the definition of information assets or IT assets across financial, risk, or IT standards, framework and regulations. Yet, this is critical in gaining insight into what information assets are. The importance of such a comparative study is that it could provide a lens to understudy the missing link that possibly lies in the inherent attribute of an IT asset in itself (its hybrid physical tangible asset and intangible information asset).

Research problem domain

Given that an information asset is the main target in a number of security breaches, because of the value it holds; and noting that the intangible information asset is processed, transmitted and stored in a container (the IT asset), and used within and/or across a process, then internal control(s) ought to be applied on the information asset via the container and/or the process. These controls are applied on the basis of standards, frameworks, best and good practices, strategic imperatives, regulatory requirements, and stakeholders' expectations. Controls are applied to what is known and/or can be known, and/or to the extent it is known. Therefore, commensurate controls are applied on the basis of the value of what needs to be controlled (information asset) and what is known.

However, is there a coherent definition across the board for an information asset in itself (and its derivatives)?

This is a primary question one needs to ask. Furthermore, one then seeks to find out if the incoherent definition has a bearing on the incommensurate internal controls being applied, and hence on the possible loss of the information asset itself.

This assertion of a lack of coherent definition for an information asset, being a basis for the improper understanding of information assets (which is the inherent underlying carrying value of an IT asset), would hold true by reason of argumentation, if it can be shown that there (truly) exist such incoherent definitions of IT assets, their inherent information assets, and the underlying information. Procedural argumentation (Walton 2013:3, 15), which need not be proved in the absolute, would assist and suffice in this regard.

Thus, procedural argumentation, starting with the underlying information requires a practical reasoning on the lack of, or an incoherent definition of information asset, in order to conclude that it is the basis for the hitherto unknown contributory factor to the lack of commensurate safeguarding of IT assets. If an incoherent definition can be shown to exist, then an improper understanding of information asset would exist. When the assertion holds true, then a redefinition (of information asset) is required to assist with identification of the asset to be safeguarded.

Research methodology

In order to prove the above argumentation schemes (Walton 2013:6), we will now take a qualitative research approach, premised on a thematic content analysis and a comparative study.

The qualitative research approach (Babbie 2012:24) assists us to address the concern of the incoherent definition of information and information assets across the board. This was carried out by a blend of comparative study (Rajasekar, Philominathan & Chinnathambi 2013:10) of standards and frameworks (Susanto, Almunawar & Tuan 2011:24, 25), and content analysis (Krippendorff 2012:1, 4) of the definitions of information and information assets, as well as the context thereof (Krippendorff 2012:24).

The thematic content analysis was based on four main themes (Assets, Types of Asset, Information, and Information Assets). This analysis was done comparatively across a number of financial and information system standards, frameworks, and regulations, as outlined in Figure 2. Logical discussion of the findings would then form a basis for a redefinition.

Although, the standards, frameworks, and regulations were purposively selected, based on their universal adoption or oversight in their fields, others were based on discussion in literatures in this article, notably those in Naidoo and Van Niekerk (2014:35, 38).

Findings and discussion

International Organisation for Standardisation (ISO) standards typically have a part and/or section for definitions and concepts explanation. Other standards and frameworks would have a definition section and/or a glossary. It is naturally expected that assets, types of assets, information, and information assets would be defined in the standards, frameworks, and regulations dealing with them.

In this section, the findings of the four themes (assets, types of asset, information, and information asset) across standards, frameworks, and regulations (listed earlier in the methodology) are presented. The birds-eye view of the research finding is shown in Figure 3.

In the interests of space, the detailed findings for the four themes are only summarised in this article. It is intriguing to note that whereas assets are not defined across the board in the standards, frameworks, and regulations, types of assets, on the other hand, are listed and/or implied across a number of them.

Research findings: Asset definition

In order to look at information assets, a natural starting point would be information and assets. We look at the definition of assets across financial, information security and other standards, frameworks, and regulations.

The findings outlined in Table 1, indicate a dearth of definitions across the board.

Asset definition trending the line of financial international accounting standards board or international financial reporting standards

It was noted that a common trend across financial standards, frameworks, and regulations is the reliance on the International Accounting Standards Board/International Financial Reporting Standards (IASB/IFRS) definition of an asset. The financial IASB conceptual framework defines an asset as a *resource controlled by the entity, as a result of past events, and from which future economic benefits are expected to flow to the entity*.

Information Technology Infrastructure Library's asset definition linking financial and information technology

In Information Technology Infrastructure Library 2011 (ITIL2011) (in its service strategy), an asset is seen as any

FINANCIAL:	
IFRS38 (IAS38)	**Asset Definition, Intangible Asset Recognition**
IFRS 3	**Business Combination Reporting, Intangible Asset**
King III	**Governance, Control over Asset**
GRAP 31 (ASB South Africa)	**Intangible**
STANDARDS:	
ISO55001 (PAS55)	**Enterprise Asset Mgt, Deriving Value**
ISO27001	**Information Asset, Asset Register, Risk Assessment**
ISO38500	**IT Governance, Strategy**
COBIT	**IT Acquisition, Control, Mamgement**
ISO 20000 (ITIL)	**IT Service Management, CMDB, CI**
REGULATIONS:	
Sarbanes Oxley	**Mandatory Control over Financial ⇔ Software Licensing**
Software Alliance	**Software licensing Piracy – www.bsa.org**
POPI (SA)/DPA (UK)/US Privacy	**Personal Info, Mandatory Disclosure**

*ISO27001 is classify as *required,* as it is neither *mandatory* nor *statutory*, though highly regarded.
In some sectors, such as banking in Nigeria, it is mandated by the Central Bank.

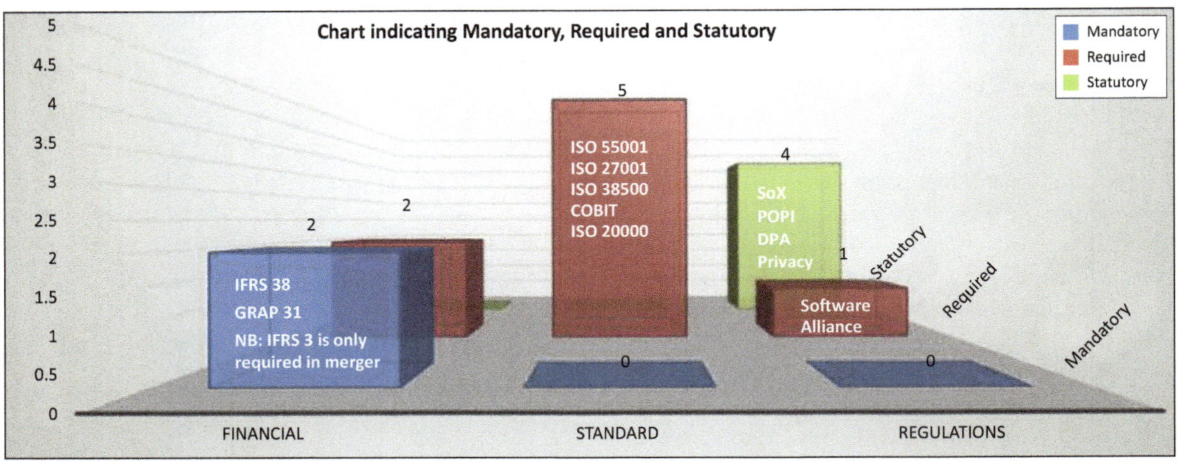

Source: Authors' careful analysis of the listed standards and regulations

FIGURE 2: Comparative study asset definition across financial, standards and regulations.

resource or capability. A service provider's assets include anything that could contribute to the delivery of a service (AXELOS 2011:5). Although this might initially be viewed to be at variance with the financial world that stipulates specific criteria for asset recognition (uniquely identified material over one financial year), it nonetheless tallies with the IFRS/IASB *resource* view of asset. Although missing in the current standard, in ISO27001:2009, asset was seen as anything that is of value to an organisation (asset 2.3). This resonates well with the financial IASB view of an asset as a resource. Therefore, one can deduce that ITIL's view of an asset is the link between the financial and IT worlds. An asset, as envisaged by ITIL2011, need not necessarily be included on a balanced sheet, or have a book value. However, the asset needs to be safeguarded in order not to have unintended incident.

Research findings: Types of assets

An asset is not defined across the board in the standards, frameworks, and regulations; on the other hand, types of assets are listed and/or implied across a number of them, according to the summary in Table 2.

Distinct categorisation of assets

The major focus of ISO55000 is on the traditional physical property, plant and equipment (PPE); whereas information assets and intangible assets are clearly indicated not to be the main focus of the standard, as discussed below. The focus naturally shifts to financial assets, especially IASB (to which other financial related standards and frameworks refer, or imply), ISO27000 and Software Asset's ISO19770. In the case of IASB, the various types of assets are delineated in three main categories: physical, monetary, and intangible.

Much attention is paid to the recognition of assets in section 4.44 of the IASB, with a particular emphasis on physical (PPE) and monetary aspects. Intangibles are rather treated under notes or auxiliary standards, such as IAS38, IFRS3 and in South Africa, in the Generally Recognised Accounting Practice (GRAP 31). An intangible asset as a type of asset is defined in GRAP31, as an identifiable non-monetary asset without physical substance. One category of intangible asset that has gained prominence (notably after the Enron's saga, and hence the introduction of Sarbanes–Oxley Act 2002) is software. The ISO19770 that focuses on software asset management provides further insight into this type of asset (whether executable or non-executable software). ISO19770's software and record type of assets map well with ITIL2011 (and ISO20000) types of configuration items.

Legend: ● Defined ≈ Implied o In context ○ Not Defined

Asset Definition and Classification Across Standards, Frameworks and Regulations	Asset Definition	Types of Area	Information Define	Information Asset	Asset Identification
ISO2700x - Information Security	○	≈	○	○	●
COSO - Internal Control	○	○	○	≈	●
IFRS/IAS - Accounting	●	●	≈	≈	●
GRAP 31 (102) - Intangible Asset South Africa	IFRS/ IAS	≈	≈	≈	●
King III/ISO38500 - Governance	IFRS/ IAS	●	●	≈	IFRS/ IAS
ISO5500x - Asset Management	●	●	o	○	●
ISO2000x/ITIL2011 - Service Management	≈ refer CI	≈ per CI	≈	o (Service)	●
COBIT5 - IT Controls, Risks, Values and Governance	≈ info	○	●	≈ info/IT	●
POPI - Protection of Personal Information South Africa	○	○	o electronic	o personal info	o for use
ISO19770 - Software Asset Management	IFRS/ IAS	IFRS/ IAS	IFRS/ IAS	o related	●
Sarbanes Oxley 2002	○	IFRS/ IAS	○	≈ (software)	IFRS/ IAS

Source: Authors' viewpoint and collation of the findings across the different standards, frameworks and regulations

FIGURE 3: Summary of information asset definition findings across board based on authors' thematic content analysis and comparative study.

Intangible information assets remain tangible particular emphasis on physical assets still

With the value attributed to software (chiefly that of its licensing), financial IASB, SOX, and ISO19770 have found a way to 'tangibilise' the intangible software. When the real value of software is considered, it can be seen that its real value is in its function, that of the processing of information within an IT asset (Moody & Walsh 1999:10). Yet, assets even in the knowledge economy, are still defined largely from the financial PPE point of view. Has ISO5500x, just like ISO19770, missed a golden opportunity to cater for the asset of the future?

Research findings: Information

Information assets have been affirmed to be a type of asset; nonetheless, the challenge faced is in quantifying it, along with the rest of tangible and intangible assets. Underpinning information assets is information. The efficient flow and use of information are of strategic importance to an organisation's well-being.

King III (2009) and the ISO38500 IT Governance standard (2009) have taken cognisance of this. Indeed, King III para 36: 'information management' indicates that information records

TABLE 1: Comparative study of asset definition across financial, standards and regulations, based on the authors' content analysis of asset definition.

Standard/framework/regulation	Asset definition	Comment
ISO/IEC 27000:2012(E)	**Define**	Sec 2.4 any item that has value to the organization
ISO/IEC 27000:2014(E)	Not defined	Asset: not defined
COSO (integrated framework)	Not defined	Asset: not defined (seems to rely on SEC financial reporting, hence IASB)
IASB/IFRS	**Define**	Asset: IASB conceptual framework 2010 (4.4a, 4.8)
GRAP 31	Implied	(South Africa ASB – intangible asset) asset: refer to IFRS/IAS
ISO5500x	**Define**	Asset: define (physical intended)
ISO19770	Implied	(Software asset management) asset: financial definition (IFRS/IAS implied). Closely related IAITAM's Best Practice library (IBPL) 12 KPAs indicate that IBPL (like ISO5500x and ISO19770) is focused on physical IT assets, its components (ITIL's CIs) and software licenses
SOX (US Sarbanes-Oxley 2002)	In context	Asset: no (financial IFRS/IAS implied)
King III/ISO38500	Implied	Asset: implied IFRS/IAS (King III para 14.1, 35)
ISO2000x/ITIL2011	Implied	Asset: Implied (reference to configuration Item (CI) – uniquely identified, traceable, auditable)
COBIT5	Implied	Asset: implied (Information)
POPI	Not defined	(South Africa Protection of Personal Information) Asset: Not define

TABLE 2: Comparative study of types of assets across financial, standards and regulations.

Types of asset	Standard/framework/regulation	Comment
Physical (tangible)	IASB, ISO55000, ITAM	PPE: Property, plant, equipment. See IASB section 4.44
	ITIL/ISO2000	In ITAM, IT asset is seen mainly from physical point of view while information, records et al are seen as supporting more from an information system point of view
Intangible	IASB, ISO17990, GRAP31	Largely software. IAS38 (IASB) and South Africa's GRAP31 focus mainly on intangible asset. OECD is assisting with classification of intangibles
	ISO27000	Primarily information asset. OECD sees information as an increasingly asset of importance in the (and beyond the) knowledge economy
Information asset (Intangible)	ISO27001, King III, Cobit5	Recognised as asset that is information in nature. A key driver and strategic asset of an organisation. In South Africa's POPI, it is seen from a personal information point of view

are the most important information assets, as they are evidence of business activities. Apart from King III, only COBIT®5 has a definition for information amongst the standards, frameworks, and regulations that were reviewed as summarised in Table 3.

What is remarkable is that ISO27000:2014, a standard for information security, does not have any definition for information. Considering that no definition for assets exists in ISO27000:2014, there is a concern that a standard that stipulates the safeguarding of information assets and provides a control mechanism has neither information nor assets defined! Typically, ISO standards use conjugations to define compound terms. For example, if an asset is defined as anything that has value, then an information asset would be an asset of the type of information that has value. Nonetheless, ISO27000:2014 was explicit that all types of information assets, including financial information, intellectual property, and employee details, or information entrusted to the care of an organisation by their customers or third parties, must be safeguarded (ISO 27000:2014 2014:0.1 Overview).

Research findings: Information assets

The ISO2000x standard and ITIL® framework both recognised the importance of service management as a capability platform in the knowledge economy and beyond. Service, innovation, and wisdom are products in these economies. We note that intangibles, and notably information assets, are key assets of this economy and beyond.

A definition for information assets resides in the past only

Though King III and ISO38500 implied a definition for assets from the financial world (IASB/IFRS implied), it was observed that IT assets, information assets, and private information (privacy) are explicitly recognised as types of assets. A number of other standards, frameworks, and regulations, as shown in Table 4, implied information assets as forms of intangible assets or simply 'financial record'. In fact, in earlier editions of ISO27000:2009, information asset (2.18) was explicitly defined as knowledge or data that has value to the organisation. What then is intriguing is *the omission of any definition for assets, information, and information assets*, in the current ISO2700x family of standards.

We assumed that the IT Security Techniques standardisation subcommittee (SC27) of the ISO/IEC Joint Technical Committee is possibly aware of the IASB ongoing redefinition effort of its 2010 Conceptual Framework (IASB 2010), to redefine an asset and a liability as a 'resource'. It is noted though that IASB's asset definition might change, when the ongoing review of IASB 2010 Concept Framework is completed. The OECD, likewise, is facing challenges in its ongoing task of classifying intangible assets of which an information asset is a part (OECD 2011).

TABLE 3: Comparative study of information definition across financial, standards and regulations.

Standard/framework/regulation	Information definition	Comment
ISO/IEC 27000:2012(E)	Implied	Section 0.1 Overview and section 2.4 Asset
ISO/IEC 27000:2014(E)	Not defined	Section 0.1 Overview
COSO (integrated framework)	Not defined	Rely on SEC financial reporting, hence IASB
IASB/IFRS	Implied	Financial reporting implied
GRAP 31	Implied	Financial reporting, intellectual property (as a form of intangibles)
ISO5500x	Not defined	Information for the asset management system!
ISO19770	Implied	Records, information for management system
SOX (US Sarbanes-Oxley 2002)	In context	Financial reporting (IFRS/IASB implied)
King III/ISO38500	**Define**	Glossary of Terms
ISO2000x/ITIL2011	Implied	ISO20000-1: 3.8 document – information and its supporting medium (ISO9000:2005)
COBIT5	**Define**	Oral, paper or electronic business intangible asset
POPI	Implied	Electronic communication, record

TABLE 4: Comparative study of information assets across financial, standards and regulations.

Standard/framework/regulation	Information asset	Comment
ISO/IEC 27000:2012(E)	Implied	Last defined in ISO27000:2009
ISO/IEC 27000:2014(E)	Not defined	Sections 3.1, 3.2.1, 3.2.5, 3.2.3/3.5.5 (identified information assets!), 3.2.4 (organization's information assets), 3.4/2.68 (associated risks), 3.6 (protect information assets), 0.1 (security of information assets)
COSO (integrated framework)	Implied	SEC financial reporting, hence IASB
IASB/IFRS	Implied	Intangibles (IAS38, IFRS3)
GRAP 31	Implied	Intangibles (IP, software)
ISO5500x	In context	Intangibles explicitly out of scope
ISO19770	**Define**	Records, software related assets (media, documents, data)
SOX (US Sarbanes-Oxley 2002)	Implied	Software (SEC, IFRS/IASB)
King III/ISO38500	Implied	King III Principle 5.6, paragraph 36
ISO2000x/ITIL2011	In context	CI relating to service, security and other documentations
COBIT5	Implied	Information and/or IT assets
POPI	In context	Personal information, public records, special personal information

ISO, International Organisation for Standardisation.

Nonetheless, an organisation must implement a framework for managing the security of their information assets (ISO/IEC 2014, sec. 0.1 Overview and sec 2.68 Risk – Note 6). The starting point for this is the identification for the assets. We posit that the effectiveness of the identification process is premised on proper understanding of the assets to be identified.

Research findings: Birds-eye view of information assets definition across board

Contrary to expectations, the findings (summarised in Figure 3), present a rather worrisome picture.

It was found that only King III and COBIT®5 have definitions for information amongst the standards, frameworks, and regulations that were reviewed. In line with literatures, King III and COBIT®5 both defined information as an asset that is essential to an enterprise's business. On the flip side, ISO27000:2014, a standard for information security, does not have any definition for information. It nonetheless define information asset as knowledge or data that has value to the organisation.

Information and information assets were found not defined; or at best, they were simply implied in a number of standards, frameworks, and regulations. However, across all of them, they all required assets (in this instance intangible information assets) to be identified and safeguarded.

The question remains: *How then can risks to assets' value be safeguarded when the asset is not well defined?*

Research discussion: Implications of incoherent definition across the board

The significant findings in this research have confirmed that there is an incoherent definition across the standards, frameworks, and regulations reviewed. The implication of this is that it can then be shown that our earlier assertion of a lack of coherent definitions for information assets holds true.

Given that the hitherto unknown contributory factor to the lack of commensurate safeguarding of IT assets has been premised on: (1) The lack of understanding of the hybrid nature of an IT asset, and hence its value; and (2) an improper understanding of its information asset, which is the inherent underlying carrying value of an IT asset; it can then be said that the lack of, or the incoherent definition, of an information asset could result in information assets not being identified and adequately valued. Although there are other contributory factors, as alluded to under the review section, that result in the lack of adequate safeguarding, the lack of coherent definition has unfortunately been grossly overlooked.

What could then be said to be the implications of these findings?

Property, plant, and equipment assets that have formed the bulk of critical assets to most organisations might provide some clarity in this regard. It is a known fact that PPE assets have been well defined, identified, managed, and safeguarded. To a large extent, IT assets and investments in IT (Kim, Poon & Young 2011:2) have traditionally been treated along the lines of PPE. Hence, the book value recorded in balance sheets (when done at all) and the asset value considered in risk analysis, have typically been based on IT assets' tangible value. In most cases, there is a variance occasioned by the approaches of practitioners who rely on subjective determination!

However, in the knowledge economy and beyond, information assets (and the containing IT assets) are increasingly becoming important and critical to the sustenance of organisations. The purchase of WhatsApp by Facebook Inc. (reported by the Times as US$22 billion in cash and stock) is a case in point. Likewise, the demise of DigiNotar (Charette 2011) in 2011 is another! What we have at the moment, and which is not appropriate for the knowledge economy and beyond, is that the traditional PPE and evolving intangible approach has not yet taken into due consideration, nor has it addressed the intrinsic nature of information assets and the hybrid nature of the container (IT assets). We therefore posit that the challenge faced in defining – and the difficulty in the safeguarding of information- related assets – is because information assets are not well understood, as they ought to be.

Without a definitive definition for an information asset, or any explicit reference to its inherent and intrinsic nature (attributes), the safeguarding of information-related assets could be subjective. The logical implication of this would then be that the containing IT assets would not be valued properly. This would then result in a possible mismatch between the value of the IT asset and the safeguarding controls being applied to the IT asset.

Research discussion: Information assets' identification and safeguarding

With information assets not being adequately defined, which has been linked to it being not properly understood, the identification and safeguarding thereof can only be in danger. Consequently, effective and efficient safeguarding of (information) assets, which refers to protecting such assets against the unauthorised and wilful acquisition, use, or disposal of (information) assets, cannot be achieved as it ought to be.

The COSO framework is primarily used along with others, by practitioners, for enterprise-risk management and internal controls. As indicated in the earlier discussion relating to ISO2700x, risk assessment (and by inference risk management) cannot be as effective as it ought to be when the 'item' to which risk refers to is not properly understood and/or identified. The accurate identification of an asset is a critical requirement in IASB (section 4.44: recognition of assets), ISO27000 (3.2.3/3.5.5: identified information assets), and ISO27005 (Risk Management). COSO (2013:3, 4), with its focus on controls, expectantly takes risk assessment seriously, as part of the components of internal control: 'Risk assessment forms the basis for determining how risks will be managed'.

Rethinking information assets definition

In this section, before concluding this article, a definition for information assets will be proposed and the essence of a redefinition discussed.

In order to be able to look at the appropriateness of control(s) over information assets, and to determine whether assets are well defined, it is imperative to look at the internal control requirements of an asset. This we will do, from an audit assertion viewpoint, which also provides a basis for redefinition.

Audit assertion over information assets

The key components of audit assertion: classification, completeness, valuation, and allocation, are also viewed as: completeness, existence, and accuracy (Srivastava & Kogan 2010).

Classification is referred to as ensuring that transactions and events have been recorded in the related accounts properly (Srivastava & Kogan 2010:269). For information assets, we are of the view that a definition should include events having material impact on the carrying information value of the information asset, and by inference its' containing IT asset. Therefore, a definition for information assets and IT assets must consider their inherent attributes.

Completeness is the state of ascertaining that all the assets, interests, and obligations of an entity requiring recording, have been recorded in the financial statements. When information assets are not fully understood, we assert that they cannot be identified and recorded properly.

Valuation and allocation According to Srivastava and Kogan (2010:269), all the assets, obligations, and equity interests have to be valued appropriately; and if any allocation was needed, then it has to be done on the basis of the identification and valuation having been already done. Applying this to information assets, we maintain that if information assets are not properly identified, they cannot be properly valued; and the commensurate control cannot be applied. Furthermore, the best value cannot be derived from them.

The audit assertion of classification, completeness, and valuation has further affirmed that appropriateness of control over information assets can only be ascertained if information assets are well defined and understood. Otherwise, safeguarding of information assets (and their containing IT assets) would be an exercise in futility. The vast array of internal controls technologies/mechanisms and regulations would continue to inappropriately safeguard information assets; as is currently being evidenced.

The need for a rethink of a definition for Information assets

So far, the research study presented here has shown that contrary to 'expectations', information assets (the core of IT assets) are not well defined in standards, frameworks, and regulations. Furthermore, it has been suggested that misunderstanding can be attributed to the lack of an exact or coherent definition. Conversely, this poor definition is a result of, and leads to misunderstanding of the information asset.

To further the thematic content analysis and comparative study across a number of standards, frameworks, and regulations, a look at audit assertion (Srivastava & Kogan 2010:269) shows that a good understanding assists with definition of information assets, and how these assets should be safeguarded.

Information: A redefinition for corporate information

King III (2009, sec. Glossary) defines information as:

> The raw data that [*have*] been verified to be accurate and timely; [*and that are*] specific and organised for a purpose, [and are] presented within a context that gives meaning and relevance, and which leads to [*an*] increase in understanding and [*a*] decrease in uncertainty.

Information is defined in COBIT®5, as an asset that, like other important business assets, is essential to an enterprise's business; and it can exist in many forms: printed or written on paper, stored electronically, transmitted by post or electronically, shown on films, or spoken in conversation (ISACA 2012, sec. COBIT5 Glossary).

In this article, from the transposition of King III, COBIT®5 and ISO27000, information can then be defined as:

> A critical corporate asset produced by processing raw data (whether printed or written on a medium, stored electronically, transmitted by post or electronically, or spoken in conversation), accurately, timeously, and organised for a specific organisational purpose, which is presented within a context that gives it meaning and direct relevance, and leads to an increase in understanding and a decrease in uncertainty, thereby assisting in gaining competitive advantage.

This proposed definition of (corporate) information is apt for a key driver, enabler, and definer of the knowledge economy and beyond. It further differentiates between personal/private information (discussed earlier) and corporate information (that is being redefined here).

Information assets redefined

In the previous section, information was redefined; and information assets were shown to be: (1) critical business information assets; (2) identified and valued properly; and (3) an organisational resource that needs to be safeguarded appropriately.

The redefinition of information and information assets' characteristics have provided a platform to now redefine *information assets* as:

> Intangible assets consisting of information having no physical form that could be identified singly or collectively, which when arranged systematically or logically could, give an organisation a competitive advantage and the necessary leeway to innovate.

It can then be reasonably assumed that an IT asset as a container of information assets, can be said to be a resource (of the type of hardware, software, data, or derivatives) with definable cost or value within the information channel, which is used to process, transmit, or store information; or a resource having the capability of performing, or which performs an IT function, that has the potential to bring economic benefit to an organisation.

It is hoped that the redefinition would provide further clarity on information assets and IT assets.

Essence of information assets redefinition

It has been shown that an IT asset is a container of physical IT devices, and also a processor/storer of information to which internal control mechanisms can be applied, in order to safeguard both the tangible physical assets and the intangible information assets of which it consists. As a processor, control(s) can be applied to the process. For internal control purposes, the control(s) to be applied are expected to be commensurate with the value of the asset being safeguarded (Poller *et al.* 2014:71).

With the proposed redefinition, we reasonably expect a better understanding of the asset of the knowledge economy and beyond. This we can see on two fronts. Information assets are identifiable singly or collectively; although they are abstract in nature. Secondly, IT assets are resources that consist of tangible and intangible parts. This then implies that the nature of information assets and IT assets could be far better understood, and their attributes could be outlined.

The redefinition as proposed also provides fresh view to the already held notion of information assets simply being data, information, and knowledge that are inputs to a production system. It also contextualises the classes of information assets considered to be databases, documents, published contents, uncaptured, tacit expertise, and experience resident in individual workers (Evans & Price 2014:114; Ladley 2010:397, 456).

Conclusion

The assertion of Haider *et al.* (2006:288) that one cannot manage what one cannot measure readily comes to mind. Organisations would continue to 'fire-brigade' this evolving asset of the knowledge economy bringing forth contemporary issues to management and the board, and finding it difficult to address stakeholders' concerns.

This article has identified a major defect in most standards, frameworks, and regulations dealing with the safeguarding and management of information assets (and IT assets). It has established from the review carried out that information assets have not been properly defined across the board. Beyond this significant finding, it was further shown that the principle of risk (assessment) across the board requires the identification of the asset that needs to be controlled.

However, an often overlooked aspect in the information risk quagmire is the *lack of proper understanding of the very (information) asset to be identified and safeguarded*. Hence, it was *argued* and *deduced* in this article that the effectiveness, efficiency, and reliability of internal control and compliance with applicable laws/regulations would not be appropriate if the (information) assets to be controlled are not:

- properly understood
- properly defined
- properly identified
- properly controlled
- properly retired.

In effect, when the very foundation is shaky, the structure is inevitably defective. Poller *et al.* (2014:70) refer to this as *purely patching a concept that is fundamentally flawed*. Information assets and the associated containing IT assets will continue to be undercontrolled (per internal control), undervalued or overvalued, disposed or retired improperly and finding their way to the wild (unintended public space) until they are understood. A challenge with understanding is that what is not understood might not be defined properly; and conversely, what is not defined properly, might not be understood properly. With a proposed redefinition and the possible applicability to internal control and risk scenarios, further empirical research could assist in defining valuation metrics for information assets, and thereby reduce the over-reliance on subjective valuation.

Although we have not focused on defining information in its entirety across financial, economics, information science, information technology, and the related fields, we have contributed to the body of knowledge with our comparative content analysis study of information assets across a number of frontline standards, frameworks, and regulations that have evidenced incoherent definition. The missing link of incoherent definition of an information asset, misunderstanding of an information asset, and its containing IT asset (frequently overlooked) when applying control over IT assets has been highlighted in this research. We posit that this missing link can possibly lie in the inherent attribute of an IT asset in itself (its hybrid physical tangible asset and intangible information asset).

In the knowledge economy and beyond, information assets will increasingly become distinct and prominent! The inability to properly understand its intrinsic nature and/or to isolate this physical IT asset from its inherent intangible information asset could result in undervaluing both the information asset and IT asset's financial value, and lead to the underallocation of information security controls to be safeguarded. This intrinsic nature requires further research in order to explicitly classify these attributes.

Gazing into our crystal ball, we postulate that it is a matter of time (6–10 years) before firms will be required to disclose more precise information and/or additional specific disclosure and recognition of separately identified intangible assets (information asset being chief). Already, there is an increasing demand for corporate governance's sustainability reporting that addresses the integrity, reliability, and relevance of financial reporting.

By looking beyond the immediate financial gain, a company protects its reputation – its most significant asset powered by information – and builds trust. Even so, with the advent of sustainable governance and holistic financial reporting that takes social and environmental issues into due consideration (King 2009, sec. 17).

The International Association of IT Asset Managers (IAITAM) has gained prominence in IT assets management. It is recommended that IAITAM's Best Practice Library (IBPL), as well as Asset Disposal and Information Security Alliance's IT asset disposal standard be included in future definitions comparative studies. This could lead to more insights into the challenging terrain of IT assets' dynamic-changing characteristics across the asset's lifecycle: Acquisition, Identification, Provision, Managing, Compliance, and Disposal.

Another further research that might arise from the limitation of this article is the acknowledgment that definition alone (by itself) cannot solve the subjective challenges faced in risk management, and to some extent, in internal control. What has been shown in this research is an aspect of the uncertainty that has to do with the asset leg of risk (comprising the possibility of threats to assets). It has been affirmed that a relook, a rethink, and a redefinition for the information assets (and IT assets) of the future is required. More work in this area would bring to the fore, the very dual contrasting nature of these assets of the future: what threats they would be faced with; how to model these threats; and possibly devise the necessary countermeasures.

Acknowledgements

Competing interests

The authors declare that they have no financial or personal relationships which may have inappropriately influenced them in writing this article.

Authors' contributions

A.K.A. an information security specialist, IT auditor, and lecturer, carried out the underlying research arising from industry observation and primary research for his PhD IT. R.v.S. was the project leader, and along with R.A.B. gave conceptual contributions and research validity of the article. In addition to their research prowness, R.V.S. brought his vast information risk experience to reshape the article and R.A.B., an I.T.I.L. expert, critically reviewed the process flow and ITIL alignment.

References

Ahmad, A., Bosua, R. & Scheepers, R., 2014, 'Protecting organizational competitive advantage: A knowledge leakage perspective', *Computers & Security* 42, 27–39. http://dx.doi.org/10.1016/j.cose.2014.01.001

Arlitsch, K. & Edelman, A., 2014, 'Staying safe: Cyber security for people and organizations', *Journal of Library Administration* 54(1), 46–56. http://dx.doi.org/10.1080/01930826.2014.893116

Australian Parliament, 1988, *Privacy Act 1988*, Australian Parliament, California, Australia, viewed 3 June 2014, from http://www.austlii.edu.au/au/legis/cth/consol_act/pa1988108/s6.html

AXELOS, 2011, 'ITIL ® glossary and abbreviations', in A. Hanna (ed.), pp. 1–93, AXELOS Limited, viewed 3 August 2013, from http://www.itil-officialsite.com/InternationalActivities/ITILGlossaries_2.aspx

Babbie, E., 2012, *The practice of social research*, 13th edn., Cengage Learning, Belmont, CA, viewed 24 January 2014, from http://books.google.com/books?id=-YoJAAAAQBAJ&pgis=1

Buera, F.J. & Kaboski, J.P., 2009, 'The rise of the service economy', *American Economic Review* 102(6), 2540–2569. http://dx.doi.org/10.1257/aer.102.6.2540

Burdon, M., 2010, 'Contextualizing the tensions and weaknesses of information privacy and data breach notification laws', *Santa Clara Computer & High Technology Law Journal* 27(1), 63–129, viewed 4 June 2014, from http://digitalcommons.law.scu.edu/chtlj/vol27/iss1/3/

California Senate, 2002, *California Senate Bill SB 1386 ref paragraph SEC. 2 1798.29. (e)*, California Senate, CA, viewed 3 June 2014, from http://www.leginfo.ca.gov/pub/01-02/bill/sen/sb_1351-1400/sb_1386_bill_20020926_chaptered.html

Charette, R., 2011, 'DigiNotar certificate authority breach crashes e-Government in the Netherlands', *IEEE Spectrum*, viewed 13 March 2014, from http://spectrum.ieee.org/riskfactor/telecom/security/diginotar-certificate-authority-breach-crashes-egovernment-in-the-netherlands

COSO, 2013, *Internal control–integrated framework (framework)*, in Committee of Sponsoring Organizations of the Treadway Commission (ed.), American Institute of Certified Public Accountants, viewed 3 November 2013, from http://www.coso.org/documents/coso2013icfrexecutive_summary.pdf

European Parliament, 1995, *Protection of personal data – Directive 95/46/EC*, EU: Ec.europa.eu, viewed 3 June 2014, from http://ec.europa.eu/justice_home/fsj/privacy/index_en.htm

Evans, N. & Price, J., 2014, 'Responsibility and accountability for Information Asset Management (IAM) in organisations', *Electronic Journal Information Systems Evaluation* 17(1), 113–121, viewed 25 November 2015, from http://www.ejise.com/issue/download.html?idArticle=943

Gates, C. & Matthews, P., 2014, 'Data is the new currency', in *Proceedings of the 2014 Workshop on New Security Paradigms Workshop – NSPW*, ACM Press, Victoria, BC, Canada, pp. 105–116. http://dx.doi.org/10.1145/2683467.2683477

Goede, M., 2011, 'The wise society: Beyond the knowledge economy', *Foresight* 13(1), 36–45. http://dx.doi.org/10.1108/14636681111109688

Haider, A., Koronios, A. & Quirchmayr, G., 2006, 'You cannot manage what you cannot measure: An information systems based asset management perspective', in J. Mathew *et al.* (eds.), *Engineering Asset Management*, pp. 288–300, Springer, London. http://dx.doi.org/10.1007/978-1-84628-814-2

IASB, 2010, *The conceptual framework for financial reporting*, International Accounting Standards Board: IFRS Foundation Publications Department, viewed 18 August 2013, from http://eifrs.ifrs.org/eifrs/bnstandards/en/2012/framework.pdf

ISACA, 2012, *COBIT 5: A business framework for the governance and management of enterprise IT*, ISACA, Rolling Meadows, IL, viewed 17 April 2014, from http://books.google.com/books?hl=en&lr=&id=1iLKVlOlg9EC&pgis=1

ISO/IEC, 2009, *SANS 38500:2009 South African National Standard Corporate governance of information technology*, 1st edn., SANS 38500:2009, ISO/IEC, Pretoria, South Africa.

ISO/IEC, 2014, *ISO/IEC 27000:2014(E) Information technology — Security techniques — Information security management systems — Overview and vocabulary*, 3rd edn., ISO/IEC 27000:2014(E), ISO/IEC, Geneva, Switzerland.

Jones, A., 2009, 'Lessons not learned on data disposal', *Digital Investigation* 6(1–2), 3–7. http://dx.doi.org/10.1016/j.diin.2009.06.017

Kim, S., Poon, S. & Young, R., 2011, 'Issues around firm level classification of IT investment', in P. Seltsikas et al. (eds.), *Proceedings of the 22nd Australiasian Conference on Information Systems ACIS 2011*, pp. 81, Australasian Conference on Information Systems, Sydney, Australia, viewed 15 September 2014, from http://aisel.aisnet.org/acis2011/81

King, M.E., 2009, *King Report on Governance for South Africa 2009*, Institute of Directors, Johannesburg, South Africa, viewed 14 April 2014, from http://african.ipapercms.dk/IOD/KINGIII/kingiiireport/?Purge=true

Krippendorff, K., 2012, 'Content analysis: An introduction to its methodology', in A. Virding (ed.), *Language arts & disciplines*, 3rd edn., Sage, Thousand Oaks, CA, viewed 03 April 2014, from http://www.abebooks.com/book-search/isbn/0761915451/

Ladley, J., 2010, *Making Enterprise Information Management (EIM) work for business: A guide to understanding information as an asset*, Morgan Kaufmann, viewed 25 November 2015, from https://books.google.com/books?hl=en&lr=&id=ck4BVZuw_jcC&pgis=1

Laney, D., 2014, *The hidden shareholder boost from information assets, technology*, Forbes, viewed 17 March 2015, from http://www.forbes.com/sites/gartnergroup/2014/07/21/the-hidden-shareholder-boost-from-information-assets/

Laskowski, N., 2014, *Infonomics treats data as a business asset, CIO decisions: The new infonomics reality – Determining the value of data*, TechTarget, viewed 17 March 2015, from http://searchcio.techtarget.com/feature/Infonomics-treats-data-as-a-business-asset.

Leavitt, H.J. & Whisler, T.L., 1958, 'Management in the 1980's', *Harvard Business Review* 36(6), 41–48, viewed 17 April 2014, from http://hbr.org/1958/11/management-in-the-1980s/ar/1

Moody, D. & Walsh, P., 1999, 'Measuring the value of information: An asset valuation approach', in *7th European Conference on Information Systems (ECIS'99)*, 7th edn., pp. 1–17, ECIS, Copenhagen. PMID:9316228.

Naidoo, V. & Van Niekerk, B., 2014, 'Strategic information security management as a key tool in enhancing competitive advantage in South Africa', *Journal of Contemporary Management* 11, 33–46, viewed 17 April 2014, from http://hdl.handle.net/10520/EJC148885

OECD, 2011, 'New sources of growth: Intangible assets', in OECD (ed.), *OECD project report 2011*, OECD, viewed 03 July 2014, from http://www.oecd.org/science/inno/48918196.pdf

Okere, I., van Niekerk, J. & Carroll, M., 2012, 'Assessing information security culture: A critical analysis of current approaches', in H.S Venter, M. Loock, & M. Coetzee (eds.), *Information Security for South Africa (ISSA), 2012*, pp. 1–8, IEEE, Johannesburg, South Africa. http://dx.doi.org/10.1109/ISSA.2012.6320442

Parliament of the Republic of South Africa, 2013, *Protection of Personal Information Act, 2013, National Gazettes, No 37067*, Government Gazette of the Republic of South Africa, Cape Town, South Africa, viewed 3 November 2014, from http://www.gov.za/documents/download.php?f=204368

Poller, A., Türpe, S. & Kinder-Kurlanda, K., 2014, 'An asset to security modeling? Analyzing stakeholder collaborations instead of threats to assets', in *Proceedings of the 2014 Workshop on New Security Paradigms Workshop – NSPW*, pp. 69–82, ACM Press, Victoria, BC, Canada. http://dx.doi.org/10.1145/2683467.2683474

Rajasekar, S., Philominathan, P. & Chinnathambi, V., 2013, 'Research methodology', *Physics education*, arXiv:phys, p. 23, viewed 04 June 2014, from http://arxiv.org/abs/physics/0601009

Silva, C., 2012, 'Blue Cross Tenn. pays $1.5 million for HIPAA violation', *Nashville Business Journal*, viewed 13 August 2014, from http://www.bizjournals.com/nashville/news/2012/03/13/blue-cross-tenn-pays-15-million-for.html

Srivastava, R.P. & Kogan, A., 2010, 'Assurance on XBRL instance document: A conceptual framework of assertions', *International Journal of Accounting Information Systems* 11(3), 261–273. http://dx.doi.org/10.1016/j.accinf.2010.07.019

Susanto, H., Almunawar, M.N. & Tuan, Y.C., 2011, 'Information Security Management System standards: A comparative study of the big five', *International Journal of Electrical & Computer Sciences* 11(5), 21–27, viewed 8 August 2014, from http://www.ijens.org/IJECS Vol 11 Issue 05.html

Walton, D., 2013, *Methods of argumentation*, 1st edn., newbooks-services.de, Cambridge University Press, New York, viewed 17 September 2014, from http://dx.doi.org/www.cambridge.org/9781107677333

Warner, J., 2011, 'Understanding cyber-crime in Ghana: A view from below', *The International Journal of Cyber Criminology* 5, 736–749, viewed from http://www.cybercrimejournal.com/warner2011ijcc.pdf

8

Competitive intelligence practice in the South African property sector

Author:
Tshilidzi E. Nenzhelele[1]

Affiliation:
[1]Department of Business Management, University of South Africa, South Africa

Corresponding author:
Tshilidzi Nenzhelele,
eric@zds.co.za

Background: The South African property sector contributes highly to creating jobs, skills development, poverty reduction and economic growth. Although South Africa dropped in the global competitiveness ranking, the property sector of South Africa remains very competitive. To survive in a competitive sector, firms around the world practice competitive intelligence (CI). Although the use of CI has been examined in other sectors in South Africa, no study on CI practice has been conducted in the property sector.

Objectives: The objective of this research was to establish the extent to which the property sector of South Africa practices CI.

Method: This research was quantitative in nature and a web-based questionnaire was used to collect data from estate agencies in the South African property sector.

Results: The results indicate that the South African property sector is very competitive and estate agencies practice CI to gain competitive advantage and make quality decisions. Moreover, the results reveal that the property sector practice CI legally and ethically. The results indicate that the majority of estate agencies are very small employing at most five employees and make at most 5 million Rands annual turnover.

Conclusion: The South African property sector ethically and legally practices CI to gain competitive advantage and to aid in making quality decisions.

Introduction

Competitive intelligence (CI) is a critical success factor for for-profit and non-profit, large and small, public and private firms (Pellissier & Nenzhelele 2013a). CI improves product or service quality, quality of decisions and quality of life (Du Toit & Sewdass 2014; Maune 2014). CI gives competitive advantage to firms that operate in a competitive business environment (Barnea 2014). The South African property sector is very competitive, and it continues to thrive despite being negatively affected by the recession (Estate Agency Affairs Board [EAAB] Annual Report 2013/2014). According to the Estate Agency Affairs Board (EAAB) Annual Report (2013/2014), the South African property sector contributes highly to job creation, wealth creation, skills development, poverty reduction and economic growth. It contributes R191.4 billion to the South African economy (EAAB, 2014). The South African property sector remains competitive in spite of South Africa having dropped in ranking on the Global Competitiveness Report (EAAB Annual Report 2013/2014; The Global Competitiveness Report 2014–2015). To survive in a competitive business sector, firms seek tools that offer competitive advantage and help in decision-making (Bartes 2014a). CI is widely accepted as offering competitive advantage and help in decision-making (Weiss & Naylor 2010). Though research about CI practice has been conducted in other sectors in South Africa, no such research has been conducted in the property sector. There is a cry to conduct research on CI practice in all sectors of South Africa (Sewdass 2012). The purpose of this research is to establish the practice of CI in the South African property sector.

Definition of competitive intelligence

Many definitions of CI exist in the literature (Weiss & Naylor 2010). Some scholars define CI as a product and some as a process (Brody 2008). Roitner (2008) concludes that CI is both a product and a process. Most of these definitions differ because of a change of words, the use of synonyms and emphasis (Brody 2008). CI practitioners are so busy that they do not have time to define CI (Fleisher & Wright 2009). The existence of so many definitions in the field of CI creates confusion among scholars and practitioners (Colakoglu 2011). Also, it makes CI to be a practice with unstable borders (Haddadi, Dousset & Berrada 2010). Because of a lack of agreement on the definition of

CI, it has been confused with industrial espionage (Colakoglu 2011). However, CI is different from industrial espionage because CI is legal and ethical (Haliso & Aina 2012). Having realised the problem of endless definitions, Pellisier and Nenzhelele (2013a) analysed 50 CI definitions to establish commonality and differences in order to propose a comprehensive and universally acceptable definition. Pellissier and Nenzhelele (2013b) define CI as 'a process or practice that produces and disseminates actionable intelligence by planning, ethically and legally collecting, processing and analysing information from and about the internal and external or competitive environment in order to help decision-makers in decision-making and to provide a competitive advantage to the enterprise'. This definition will be used for the purpose of this study.

Competitive intelligence needs

Managers are paying more attention to CI and as a result there is a growing desire to fulfil CI needs (Barnea 2014; Lin & Yan-Zhang 2015). The end product of CI must satisfy the needs of decision-makers and trigger new intelligence needs (Bartes 2014a; Pinto 2014). In order to have clear, unambiguous and easy-to-understand intelligence needs, there needs to be two-way communication between the CI unit and the decision-makers (Du Toit & Sewdass 2014; Nasri & Zarai 2013). Formal meetings must be organised for CI practitioners and decision-makers to discuss the intelligence needs (Bartes 2014b). Decision-makers have plenty of intelligence needs and these needs must be differentiated from information needs, prioritised and translated into key intelligence topics (KITs) (Bartes 2014b; Degaut 2015; Nasri 2011; Prescott 1999). KITs are those decision-based, strategic issues about which managers must be regularly informed to set and implement strategy (Herring 1999). CI is aimed at answering KITs (Bartes 2014b). According to Herring (1999), only intelligence needs that are of highest priority and key to the success of the organisation must be fulfilled with the scarce resources (Prescott 1999). KITs are established and clearly defined during the planning phase of the CI process (Bulley, Baku & Allan 2014; Yassine 2014). KITs can come from different levels of management such as strategic, functional and tactical (McGonagle & Vella 2012). Quality CI depends on clearly defined and unambiguous KITs (Bartes 2014b; Nasri 2011).

According to Barnea (2014), KITs must cover world competition, tactical and strategic issues instead of just local competition and tactical issues. To gain competitive advantage from CI, KITs must be clearly defined (Barnea 2014). According to Herring (1999), there are three categories of KITs, namely strategic decisions and actions, topics requiring early warning and profiles, and characteristics and descriptions of the key players. Strategic decision and actions include the development of strategic plans and strategies. Early-warning topics include competitor initiatives, technological surprise and government actions. Descriptions of key players include competitors, customers, suppliers, regulators and potential partners.

Evolution of competitive intelligence

CI evolves from economics, marketing, military theory, information science and library and strategic management (Deng & Luo 2010; Juhari & Stephens 2006). Governments of countries rely on intelligence for the protection of their citizens (Deng & Luo 2010). Marketing departments of firms all over the world rely on intelligence for marketing, pricing and promotion of their products or services (Nasri & Zarai 2013). Libraries rely on intelligence for quality sources of information for scholars (Fleisher 2004). Strategists rely on intelligence to anticipate and prepare for future competition (Barrett 2010).

CI has been around for longer than the first time it was officially practised in business and recorded in the literature (Juhari & Stephens 2006). Since its inception, CI has been practised by public, private, for-profit, non-profit, large and small organisations. While CI is a relatively new business discipline, CI is evolving in complexity and importance to keep pace with rapid business development (Heppes & Du Toit 2009). Because of its benefits, more organisations are practising CI either formally or informally (Nenzhelele 2012).

Post-apartheid, South African firms have been exposed to global competition (Pellissier & Nenzhelele 2013b). To survive in the midst of global competition, South African firms are practising CI (Du Toit & Sewdass 2014). This is confirmed by Muller (2006) who points out that CI took root in South Africa in the mid-1990s and early-2000s. CI in South Africa emerged from the business sector (Heppes & Du Toit 2009). Although South African firms have been inward-looking, they are starting to realise the importance of CI from year to year (Adidam, Gajre & Kejriwal 2009). De Pelsmacker *et al.* (2005) point out that enterprises that formally practise CI are growing in numbers and that CI is especially strong in the banking sector, the information technology sector, the telecommunications sector and the electric supply sector. Although CI practice has been widely reported for large organisations, Nenzhelele (2012) establishes that smaller enterprises in South Africa are also practising CI. Although CI practice has been widely reported in South Africa for for-profit organisations, there is lack of report of CI practice on non-profit organisations (Sewdass & Du Toit 2014).

Competitive intelligence process

CI is a process or practice, which follows predetermined phases (Du Toit & Sewdass 2014). CI process has been portrayed as a circle to indicate that it is continuous and that the end product of one phase is the input of the next phase (Calof & Skinner 1998). There are influential factors that play a role during the CI process (Bartes 2014a). The CI process is made up of the following steps, which are depicted in Figure 1 (Pellissier & Nenzhelele 2013a).

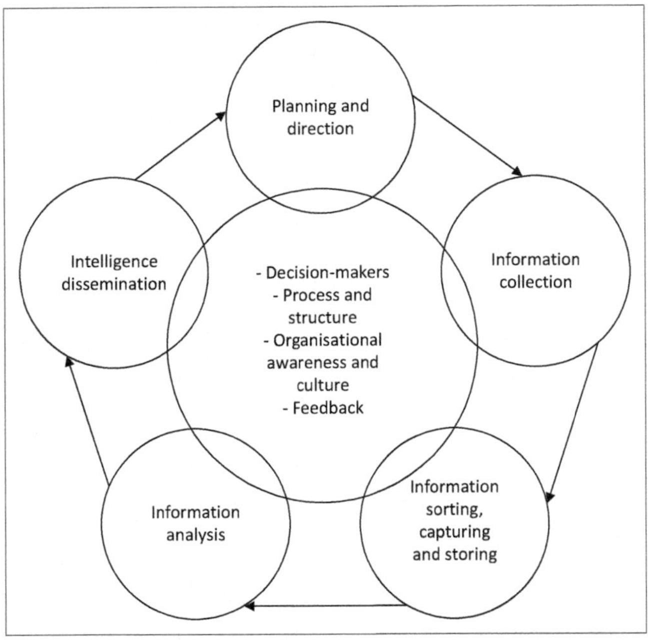

Source: Pellissier, R. & Nenzhelele, T.E., 2013a, 'Towards a universal competitive intelligence process model', *South African Journal of Information Management* 15(2), Art. #567, 7 pages. http://dx.doi.org/10.4102/sajim.v15i2.567

FIGURE 1: Competitive intelligence process.

Planning and direction

The intelligence requirements of the decision-makers are defined in this phase. The intelligence requirements are narrowed down into KITs. KITs are topics that are significant to the organisation's decision-makers and give directions to CI operations. The KITs must be clear and easy to understand. The KITs must be converted into information requirements and the source of information be clearly outlined. The purpose for conducting CI is defined in this phase. The participants, resources required and recipients of the actionable CI are clearly identified in this phase.

Information collection

Quality information is collected during this phase. Information must be collected legally and ethically. The information collectors must comply with the CI code of ethics. Efforts must be exercised to collect information from public sources. Information collected must meet the KITs. Information can be collected from internal or external sources.

Information sorting, capturing and storing

Collected information must be sorted, captured and stored. Related information must be sorted and captured together. Information must be stored in files that are easily accessible by all permitted users. The information must be stored in secured storage media.

Information analysis

This is the most important phase of the CI process and can be challenging. Information analysis should be conducted by an experienced CI practitioner. That way the outcome of this phase will be quality, actionable intelligence. The CI practitioner must, during this phase, be in constant communication with the decision-makers to ensure that their intelligence requirements are met. Different analysis techniques should be considered and those that are relevant must be used to produce intelligence that meet the KITs.

Intelligence dissemination

Quality actionable CI is communicated to the decision-makers during this phase. Care must be given to ensure that safe and secure means of communication are used. CI must be communicated to the correct users of it, and on time, or else it is no longer intelligence. There are different methods of communicating CI. These methods must be considered and the best method is selected and used.

Decision-makers

Decision-makers are the users of actionable CI. They are the initiators of the CI process. Decision-makers are responsible for coming up with intelligence requirements. Decision-makers have an important influence over the CI process. They, therefore, should be consulted throughout the CI process in order to establish whether their intelligence needs have changed during the CI process. If the intelligence needs have changed, adjustments must be made and relevant information must be sourced to produce relevant intelligence.

Process and structure

The CI process is influenced by policies, procedures, code of ethics and structures within the organisation. The CI practitioners must ensure that they comply with policies, procedures and code of ethics while conducting CI. Failure by CI practitioners to comply may put the organisation in disrepute. It may also lead to legal consequences. Therefore, organisations that practise CI must include the CI code of ethics in their policies and code of ethics. A formal CI function and process will ensure that CI is of quality.

Organisational awareness and culture

A culture of CI awareness and competitiveness will ensure that CI is performed optimally. It will also lead to production of quality CI. Organisations must raise CI awareness with all employees. Employees who are aware of CI will not give information to competitors cheaply. Moreover, employees who are aware of CI will help in the CI process. Organisations must train and educate employees on CI and its benefits to the organisation. This will reduce the CI challenges and help in the smooth development of CI.

Feedback

This is an influential factor in the CI process. There should be continuous feedback throughout the CI process. CI practitioners must communicate with the decision-makers to ensure that relevant and actionable CI is produced. Constant feedback ensures timely adjustments to KIT. Constant feedback throughout the CI process will help to produce quality CI.

The property sector of South Africa

The property sector of South Africa is an economic enabler and allows upward economic mobility for future generations (EAAB Annual Report 2013/2014). It contributes to job creation, wealth creation, poverty reduction, skills development and quality of life. It is attractive for investors, facilitates inheritance, creates wealth and alleviates poverty (EAAB Annual Report 2012/2013). According to the EAAB Annual Report (2013/2014), the property sector fulfils the constitutional rights of South Africans. The property sector gives South Africans an opportunity to own a home. Moreover, property ownership enables access to capital, creates income streams and a sense of security.

However, since the 2008/2009 economic meltdown, the property sector has been striving to recover (EAAB Annual Report 2010/2011). Many estate agencies have been shut down because of lack of funds to sustain them. Many estate agencies owned by people from disadvantaged backgrounds struggle to survive under these economic conditions (EAAB Annual Report 2013/2014). The *National Credit Act* has contributed to the slow growth of the property sector due to strict measures to protect consumers from sinking into debt (EAAB Annual Report 2008/2009).

Despite the stringent economic conditions, principal and non-principal agents, firms and attorneys registered with the EAAB have increased leading to a very competitive property sector (EAAB Annual Report 2010/2011; EAAB Annual Report 2013/2014). To remain competitive, more and more property practitioners are listing property on the internet, making it easily accessible and viewable by consumers. There are many websites in South Africa dedicated to listing properties and reporting of property sector trends. Potential consumers login to these websites searching for properties to buy or to let. These websites also allow individuals to list their properties for sale or to let, making them accessible for buyers, lessees or estate agents.

The South African property sector is regulated and controlled by the EAAB (*Estate Agency Affairs Act 112* of 1976). The EAAB was established in 1976 in terms of the *Estate Agency Affairs Act 112* of 1976. Since 17 May 2012, the EAAB has been relocated from the Department of Trade and Industry to the Department of Human Settlement (EAAB Annual Report 2013/2014). The core mandate of the EAAB remains the following five key regulatory pillars, namely Registration, Education, Inspections and Investigation, Disciplinary and Claims and its industry supervisory role in terms of the *Financial Intelligence Centre Act* (EAAB Annual Report 2009/2010). According to the EAAB Annual Report 2013/2014, the EAAB regulates and controls activities of estate agents in the public interest. Moreover, the EAAB ensures that all estate agents that service the public are registered. The report indicates that each registered estate agency is issued with a fidelity fund certificate, which is renewable every year and serves as registration evidence. The fidelity fund certificate also confirms that the estate agency is legally entitled to carry out the activities of an estate agency. The EAAB is also mandated to train and educate estate agents. It does so by introducing improved education and training standards and the setting of practical experience requirements (EAAB Annual Report 2013/2014).

The EAAB has started an alliance with other organisations to fulfil its mandates and protect consumers from unscrupulous estate agencies (EAAB Annual Report 2013/2014). According to the EAAB Annual Report 2013/2014, the EAAB works together with the following organisations: Independent Regulatory Board for Auditors, South Africa Institute of Charted Accountants, National Consumer Commission, Financial Services Board, Banking Association of South Africa, Service Sector Education and Training Authority, Black Conveyancers Association and the Financial Intelligence Centre. The EAAB is also a member of the Association of Real Estate Licence Law Officials (ARELLO) and the international organisation of real estate regulators. As a result, the EAAB is able to contribute to the international real estate sector. Its membership to ARELLO makes the EAAB remain in the forefront of the international property sector. Therefore, the EAAB is aware of best practices and puts the South African property sector in a better position in the world property sector. This makes the South African property sector attractive, competitive, secure and safe for international investors (EAAB Annual Report 2013/2014).

According to the EAAB 2008/2009 Annual Report, estate agents perform the following activities or functions:

- selling, purchasing or publicly exhibiting for sale immovable property or any business undertaking or negotiating in connection therewith, or canvassing or undertaking or offering to canvass a seller or purchaser thereof; or
- letting or hiring, or publicly exhibiting for hire immovable property or any business undertaking, or negotiating in connection therewith or canvassing or undertaking or offering to canvass a lessee or lessor thereof; or
- collecting or receiving any monies payable on account of a lease of immovable property or any business undertaking; or
- collecting or receiving money payable by any person to or on behalf of a developer or a body corporate in terms of the *Sectional Titles Act* in respect of a unit or a proposed unit. Estate agents have to comply with the EAAB code of conduct for estate agents. Failure by estate agents to comply with this code of conduct for estate agents may lead to a fine, withdrawal of their fidelity fund certificate or prosecution.

Research methodology

The research was quantitative in nature, and a web-based questionnaire was used to collect data from the estate agencies. The questionnaire was validated by a group of academics knowledgeable in the field of CI. A 5-point Likert scale was used to establish the level of agreement to statements about competitiveness and CI awareness. The scales ranged from strongly disagree to strongly agree. Contact details of 3878 estate agencies were sourced from one of South Africa's most popular property websites. Of these estate agencies, 350 were randomly sampled for the purpose of this research. The names of the estate agencies were arranged in a table in Microsoft Word, printed and cut into pieces, which were placed in a basket for a lottery draw. The contact details of the sampled estate agencies were then sourced from the original database. An e-mail was sent to the sampled estate agencies with the link to the web-based questionnaire. By completing the questionnaire, the property practitioners gave consent that their responses may be used for the purpose of the research. For every e-mail that sent back a delivery failure, a new estate agency was sampled to replace it. A total of 242 responses were received, yielding a response rate of 69.14%. Only 239 questionnaires completed were usable. Reminder e-mails were sent to sampled estate agencies in order to increase the response rate. Data were collected over a period of 1 month. The web-based questionnaire was exported to a spreadsheet for analysis. The internal data reliability was calculated to be 0.9129 (Cronbach's Alpha).

Research results

Demographics

According to Neuman (2006), there are four forms of enterprises in South Africa, namely company, close corporation (CC), partnership and proprietorship. They are defined as follows:

- Proprietorship is an enterprise that has one owner, and there is no distinction between the personal estate of the owner and the business estate.
- Partnership is an enterprise formed when a minimum of two and a maximum of 20 people conclude an agreement to do business with a partnership.
- A CC is a separate legal entity and is regulated in terms of the *South African Close Corporation Act 69* of 1994. The CC must be registered in term of this act in order to attain separate legal entity status. A CC must have at least one member and not more than 10 members.
- A company is an association of people incorporated in terms of the *Companies Act 61* of 1973. A company can have share capital or can be incorporated not for gain, in which case it will not have share capital.

Firms that participated in this research were companies (42.86%), CCs (29.06%), sole proprietorships (23.65%) and partnerships (4.43%). Table 1 indicates the percentage response and frequency of forms of business.

South Africa consists of nine provinces. The majority of the estate agencies operate their business in Gauteng (40.39%) and the Western Cape (28.57%). The other provinces were represented as follows: KwaZulu-Natal (8.87%), Free State (7.39%), Eastern Cape (3.45%), Mpumalanga (3.45%), Limpopo (2.96%), NorthWest (2.96%) and Northern Cape (1.97%). Table 2 indicates the percentage response and frequency of provinces.

Their focus areas were property rentals, sales, management and development (68.47%), sales only (28.57%) and rentals (2.96%). Table 3 indicates the percentage response and frequency of business focus area.

The majority of estate agencies were very small with one to five employees (45.32%). The rest of the estate agencies had 6 to 10 employees (29.56%), 11 to 20 employees (15.27%), 21 to 50 employees (5.42%), 20 to 200 employees (2.96%) and 201 or more employees (1.48%). Table 4 indicates the percentage response and frequency of the number of employees.

Financially, the majority of the estate agencies (36.95%) were making a total annual turnover of R1m to R5m. However, 32.51% were making a total annual turnover of less than R1m. A reasonable percentage of estate agencies (12.32%) were making a total annual turnover of more than R64m. Other estate agencies were making R6m to R10m (9.36%), R21m to R30m (5.91%), R31m to R50m (1.48%) and R51m to

TABLE 1: Percentage response and frequency of forms of enterprise (N = 203).

Business enterprise	Response (%)	Frequency
Sole proprietorship	23.65	48
Partnership	4.43	9
Close corporation	29.06	59
Company	42.86	87

TABLE 2: Percentage response and frequency of provinces (N = 203).

South African province operates from	Response (%)	Frequency
Eastern Cape	3.45	7
Free State	7.39	15
Gauteng	40.39	82
KwaZulu-Natal	8.87	18
Limpopo	2.96	6
Mpumalanga	3.45	7
Northern Cape	1.97	4
North West	2.96	6
Western Cape	28.57	58

TABLE 3: Percentage response and frequency of business focus area (N = 203).

Focus area of business	Response (%)	Frequency
Property rentals, sales, management and development	68.47	139
Rentals only	2.96	6
Sales only	28.57	58
Development only	0	0
Management only	0	0

TABLE 4: Percentage response and frequency of number of employees (N = 203).

Number of employees in organisation	Response (%)	Frequency
1 to 5	45.32	92
6 to10	29.56	60
11 to 20	15.27	31
21 to 50	5.42	11
51 to 200	2.95	6
201 or more	1.48	3

R64m (1.48%). Table 5 indicates the percentage response and frequency of number of total annual turnover.

The majority of the estate agencies have been operating their business for 6 years or more (60.59%). The other estate agencies had been in operation for 3–5 years (25.12%), 1–3 years (10.34%) and less than 1 year (3.94%). Table 6 indicates the percentage response and frequency of number of years of business operation.

The majority of the respondents were owners/managers of the estate agencies (82.18%). The other respondents were property practitioners (10.40%), sales/marketing managers (6.93%) and CI professionals (0.50%). Table 7 indicates the percentage response and frequency of number of positions held in the organisation.

Competition in the property sector

With regard to competition within the property sector of South Africa, the majority (50.63%) of estate agencies indicated that competition is too high in the property sector. Only 20.92% of the estate agencies disagreed that competition is too high in the property sector, while 28.45% neither agreed nor disagreed. Therefore, a mean value of 3.42 indicates that the majority of estate agencies agree that competition is too high in the property sector. A standard deviation of 1.07 indicates that there was a wide spread of responses to this variable. Table 8 indicates the frequency of responses of the level of competition in the property sector.

TABLE 5: Percentage response and frequency of total annual turnover (*N* = 203).

Organisation's total annual turnover (sales)	Response (%)	Frequency
Less than R1m	32.51	66
R1m to R5m	36.95	75
R6m to R10m	9.36	19
R21m to R30m	5.91	12
R31m to R50m	1.48	3
R51m to R64m	1.48	3
More than R64m	12.32	25

TABLE 6: Percentage response and frequency of years of business operation (*N* = 203).

Business operating years	Response (%)	Frequency
Less than 1 year	3.94	8
1 to 2 years	10.34	21
3 to 5 years	25.12	51
6 or more years	60.59	123

TABLE 7: Percentage response and frequency of positions held in the organisation (*N* = 202).

Position in the organisation	Response (%)	Frequency
Owner or manager	82.18	166
Sales or marketing manager	6.93	14
Property practitioner	10.40	21
Competitive intelligence professional	0.50	1

Competitive intelligence practice

Regarding CI practice within estate agencies, the majority (86.19%) indicated that they practise CI in their firm. Only 5.44% of the estate agencies indicated that they do not practise CI within their firm and the remaining 8.37% neither agreed nor disagreed. A mean value of 4.10 indicates that the majority of the estate agencies agreed that they practise CI within their firm. A standard deviation of 0.80 indicates that there was a smaller spread of responses to the CI practice variable. When asked how long they have been practising CI, the majority (47.16%) of the estate agencies indicated that they have been practising CI for 6 or more years. The rest had been practising CI for 3–5 years (27.95%), 1–2 years (13.10%) and less than a year (11.79%). Table 9 indicates the frequency of responses of CI practice in the property sector.

Purpose of competitive intelligence

With regard to the purpose for practising CI, the majority (75.32%) of the estate agencies indicated that they practise CI to aid with decision-making. Only 10.46% of the estate agencies indicated that they do not practise CI for decision-making and the remaining 14.23% neither agreed nor disagreed. Therefore, a mean value of 3.83 indicates that the majority of estate agencies agree that they practise CI to aid with decision-making. A standard deviation of 0.97 indicates that there was a smaller spread of responses in the practice of CI to aid with the decision-making variable.

Regarding the practising of CI to gain competitive advantage, the majority (71.97%) of estate agencies indicated that they practice CI to gain competitive advantage over their competitors. Only 7.12% of the estate agencies disagreed that they practise CI to gain competitive advantage over their rivals and the remaining 20.92% neither agreed nor disagreed. Therefore, a mean value of 3.88 indicates that the majority of estate agencies agree that CI provide them with competitive advantage over their rivals. A standard deviation of 0.89 indicates that there was less spread of responses to this variable.

TABLE 8: Frequency of responses to level of competition in the property sector (*N* = 239).

Response	Strongly disagree	Disagree	Neither agree nor disagree	Agree	Strongly agree
Competition is too high in our business sector	9	41	67	82	38

TABLE 9: Frequency of responses to competitive intelligence practice in the property sector (*N* = 239).

Response	Strongly disagree	Disagree	Neither agree nor disagree	Agree	Strongly agree
We practice competitive intelligence in our business	2	11	20	131	71

Table 10 indicates the frequency of responses of purpose of CI practice in the property sector.

Competitive intelligence ethics

With regard to ethicality and legality of CI, the majority (84.94%) of the estate agencies indicated that they practise CI legally and ethically. Only 2.93% of the estate agencies disagreed that they practise CI legally and ethically while 12.13% neither agreed nor disagreed. Therefore, a mean value of 4.26 indicates that the majority of estate agencies agree that they practise CI legally and ethically. A standard deviation of 0.80 indicates that there was less spread of responses to this variable. Table 11 indicates the frequency of responses of legal and ethical CI practice in the property sector.

Competitive intelligence activities

Concerning CI activities, the majority (68.62%) of the estate agencies indicated that they collect information about their competitors and analyse it. The remaining 14.22% disagreed that they collect information about their competitor and analyse it, and 17.15% neither agreed nor disagreed. Therefore, a mean value of 3.73 indicates that the majority of the estate agencies agreed that they collect information about their competitors and analyse it. A standard deviation of 0.98 indicates that there was less spread of responses to this variable.

The majority (86.61%) of the estate agencies indicated that they were collecting information about pricing of real estate and related services of competitors. Only 3.77% of estate agencies disagreed that they collected information about pricing by competitors and 9.62% neither agreed nor disagreed. Therefore, a mean value of 4.16 indicates that the majority of the estate agencies agreed that they collect information about the pricing of real estate and related services by competitors. A standard deviation of 0.80 indicates that there was a smaller spread of responses to this variable.

The majority (69.04) of estate agencies indicated that they know who their competitors' customers are. Only 11.72% of the estate agencies disagreed that they know their competitors' customers and the remaining 19.25% neither agreed nor disagreed. Therefore, a mean value of 3.83 indicates that the majority of estate agencies agree that they know their competitors' customers. A standard deviation of 1.04 indicates that there was a wide spread of responses to this variable.

Regarding the competitors' strengths and weaknesses, the majority (69.04%) of the estate agencies indicated that they collect information about the competitors' strengths and weaknesses. Only 7.12% of the estate agencies disagreed that they collect information about their competitors' strengths and weaknesses and the remaining 23.85% neither agreed nor disagreed. Therefore, a mean value of 3.81 indicates that the majority of estate agencies agree that they collect information about the strengths and weaknesses of their competitors. A standard deviation of 0.85 indicates that there was less spread of responses to this variable.

Concerning competitors' suppliers, the majority (43.51%) of the estate agencies indicated that they knew the suppliers of their competitors. A large number of estate agencies (34.31%) neither agreed nor disagreed and the remaining 22.18% disagreed that they knew their competitors' suppliers. Therefore, a mean value of 3.28 indicates that the majority of the estate agencies agreed that they knew their competitors' suppliers. A standard deviation of 1.00 indicates that there was a wide spread of responses to this variable.

Regarding processing and storing collected information for CI, the majority (52.30%) of the estate agencies indicated that they process and store information collected for CI. Only 21.76% of the estate agencies disagreed that they process and store collected information for CI, while 25.94% neither agreed nor disagreed. Therefore, a mean value of 3.42 indicates that the majority of estate agencies agree that they process and store information collected for CI. A standard deviation of 1.10 indicates that there was a wide spread of responses to this variable. Table 12 indicates the frequency of responses of CI practice activities in the property sector.

Collected and stored information is analysed to produce actionable CI. Different analysis techniques are used by estate agencies. The majority of the estate agencies use teamwork and brainstorming, SWOT analysis and valuation techniques. Table 13 indicates the percentage response and frequency of CI practice analytical tools in the property sector.

TABLE 10: Frequency of responses to purpose of competitive intelligence practice in the property sector (*N* = 239).

Response	Strongly disagree	Disagree	Neither agree nor disagree	Agree	Strongly agree
We gather competitive intelligence for decision-making	9	16	34	126	50
Competitive intelligence provides us with competitive advantage over our rivals	3	14	50	113	57

TABLE 11: Frequency of responses to legal and ethical competitive intelligence practice in the property sector (*N* = 239).

Response	Strongly disagree	Disagree	Neither agree nor disagree	Agree	Strongly agree
We practice competitive intelligence legally and ethically	1	6	29	96	104

TABLE 12: Frequency of responses to competitive intelligence practice activities in the property sector (N = 239).

Response	Level of agreement to the following competitive intelligence practice activities				
	Strongly disagree	Disagree	Neither agree nor disagree	Agree	Strongly agree
We collect information about our competitors and analyse it	2	11	20	131	71
We know the prices of our competitors' products or services	3	6	23	123	81
We know who our competitors' customers are	7	21	46	95	67
We know our competitors' strengths and weaknesses	2	15	57	118	44
We know who our competitors' suppliers are	8	45	82	79	24
We process and store information collected for competitive intelligence	12	40	62	85	37

TABLE 13: Percentage response and frequency of competitive intelligence practice analytical tools in the property sector (N = 219).

Analytical tools or methods used by enterprise to generate competitive intelligence	Response (%)	Frequency
Financial ratio	18.72	41
Valuation technique	51.14	112
Political, Economic, Social, Technological and Environmental (PESTE) analysis	6.85	15
Value chain analysis	7.31	16
Statistical programmes	27.85	61
Teamwork and brainstorming	59.82	131
SWOT analysis	57.99	127
Macro-environment analysis	29.68	65

Actionable CI must be disseminated to decision-makers. There are different methods used to disseminate actionable CI. The majority of estate agencies use face-to-face, e-mails, presentation and written reports to disseminate actionable intelligence. Table 14 indicates the percentage response and frequency of CI practice dissemination tools in the property sector.

Management support for competitive intelligence

Regarding the managers' support for CI practice, the majority (84.10%) of estate agencies indicated that their managers support CI practice. Only 3.35% of the estate agencies indicated that their managers do not support CI practice within their firms and the remaining 12.55% neither agreed nor disagreed. Therefore, a mean value of 4.06 indicates that the majority of estate agencies agree that their managers support CI practice. A standard deviation of 0.73 indicates that there was a smaller spread of responses to this variable. Table 15 indicates the frequency of response of management support of CI practice in the property sector.

Outsourcing of competitive intelligence

Regarding the outsourcing of CI, the majority (77.82%) of estate agencies indicated that they do not hire people or other businesses to practise CI on their behalf. Only 10.04% of the estate agencies agreed that they hire people or other organisations to practise CI on their behalf, while 12.13% neither agreed nor disagreed. Therefore, a mean value of 2.03 indicates that the majority of estate agencies disagree that they hire people or other businesses to collect information on their behalf. A standard deviation of 0.96 indicates that there was a smaller spread of responses to this variable. Table 16 indicates the frequency of response of CI outsourcing in the property sector.

TABLE 14: Percentage response and frequency of competitive intelligence practice dissemination tools in the property sector (N = 219).

Dissemination or distribution methods used by enterprise to present competitive intelligence results	Response (%)	Frequency
Briefs	24.20	53
Conferences	15.07	33
E-mails	66.67	146
Face-to-face meetings	80.82	177
Intranet	12.79	28
Presentations	32.42	71
Written reports	31.05	68
Industry audits	7.76	17
Daily flashes	11.87	26
Central database	17.81	39
Newsletters	28.77	63
Seminars	15.07	33

Competitive intelligence performance measurement

Regarding performance measurement of CI, the majority (34.73%) of estate agencies indicated that they measure the impact of CI on profit. The remaining 33.89% of the estate agencies indicated that they do not measure the impact of CI on profit while 31.38% neither agreed nor disagreed. Therefore, a mean value of 3.01 indicates that the majority of estate agencies agree that they measure the impact of CI on profit. A standard deviation of 1.07 indicates that there was a wide spread of responses to this variable. Table 17 indicates the frequency of response of the impact of CI performance measurement on profit in the property sector.

Location of competitive intelligence

Competitive intelligence is placed in the following locations with the estate agency firms: marketing department (41.67%), knowledge management (27.78%), strategy management department (25.93%), and independent department (4.63%). Table 18 indicates the frequency of response of the location of CI in firms in the property sector.

Discussion

Despite South Africa dropping in ranking in the Global Competitiveness Report, the property sector of South Africa remains competitive. This is evident in the majority of estate agencies agreeing that competition is too high in the property sector of South Africa. When competition is high, firms tend to seek tools that help them gain a competitive advantage over their rivals. It is not a surprise that the majority of the estate agencies agreed that they practise CI in their firms.

TABLE 15: Frequency of response to management support of competitive intelligence practice in the property sector (N = 239).

Response	Strongly disagree	Disagree	Neither agree nor disagree	Agree	Strongly agree
Our managers support competitive intelligence practice	1	7	30	139	59

TABLE 16: Frequency of response to competitive intelligence outsourcing in the property sector (N = 239).

Response	Strongly disagree	Disagree	Neither agree nor disagree	Agree	Strongly agree
We hire people or other businesses to collect information on our behalf	75	110	29	20	4

TABLE 17: Frequency of response to the impact of competitive intelligence performance measurement on profit in the property sector (N = 239).

Response	Strongly disagree	Disagree	Neither agree nor disagree	Agree	Strongly agree
We measure the impact of our competitive intelligence performance on profit	18	63	75	64	17

TABLE 18: Frequency of response to the location of competitive intelligence in firms in the property sector (N = 216).

Business competitive intelligence location	Response (%)	Frequency
Independent department	4.63	10
Marketing department	41.67	90
Knowledge management	27.78	60
Strategy management department	25.93	56

Moreover, the majority of these estate agencies have been practising for 6 years or more. Therefore, they are experienced in the practice of CI. A larger number of the estate agencies indicated that they practise CI in order to gain competitive advantage. They also practise CI in order to aid decision-making. The majority of the estate agencies locate their CI in the marketing department. Perhaps this is because of the fact that the majority of the estate agencies are small and cannot afford to have a standalone CI department.

While there are ethical issues in the practice of CI, the majority of estate agencies indicated that they practise CI ethically and legally. That means that they do not buy information from employees of other estate agencies or reconstruct papers found in the bins of their competitors because the property sector of South Africa is guided by law and a code of conduct. It might be because of the education and training programmes offered by the EAAB. It could also be because of the consistent inspection by EAAB, punishment of unethical behaviour, whistle-blowing within the property sector or the ethics hotline.

In the process of practising CI, the majority of the estate agencies collect information about their competitors. Such information includes the pricing of real estate. That means that they know how much different properties cost to sell, to let or develop in different locations. The majority of the estate agencies agreed that they interact with the customers of their competitors. These interactions may help in getting useful information to improve their real estate services. Moreover, the majority of the estate agencies indicated that they collect information about the strengths and weaknesses of their competitors. Information about the weaknesses and strengths of the competitors help in strategic planning.

The majority of the estate agencies indicated that they know who their competitors' suppliers are. This ensures that they get the same or better deal from the same suppliers. They, therefore, will not be spending more than what their competitors are spending for the same supplies. This ensures that resources are saved and invested in strategic areas of business. The majority of the estate agencies collect information from customers, internet and extranet, newspapers and business associates. The customers of estate agencies include buyers, sellers, owners and lessees. All these customers have needs that must be satisfied by estate agencies. It is no surprise that customers are the main source of information for CI. Collected information is then processed and stored for analyses.

The majority of estate agencies agreed that they analyse the information they collected to produce actionable CI. Estate agencies have realised that the analysis phase is the critical success factor of CI and that without the analysis phase, CI does not exist. The majority of estate agencies use teamwork and brainstorming, SWOT analysis and valuation techniques to analyse the collected information. These analysis techniques are widely used in other business sectors. The actionable CI is then disseminated to decision-makers in different levels of the firm. Actionable CI helps in making quality decisions. The majority of estate agencies use face-to-face meeting, e-mails and presentations to disseminate actionable CI.

Although the majority of estate agencies are small and have a low total annual turnover, they have been in operation for many years and have experience in how to survive in a competitive property sector because estate agencies managers support CI practice. Moreover, most estate agencies are managed by owners/managers who are supportive of CI practice. The majority of estate agencies practise CI in-house instead of outsourcing it. Perhaps this is because they are very small and lack the resources to appoint external contractors. It might be that estate agencies do not trust external firms or individuals. It might be that estate agencies want to ensure ethicality and legality in the practice of CI.

Most of the estate agencies have vested interest in the impact of CI on profit. As a result they measure the performance and impact of CI on profit. This helps them decide whether they should continue to invest in CI. Estate agencies are for-profit organisations and, therefore, invest in projects that contribute to profit. Considering that they have been practising CI for many years maybe they have found it to contribute positively towards profit.

Conclusion

Competition is very high in the South African property sector. To survive in this competitive sector, the majority of the estate agencies are practising CI. Regardless of the wide reporting of ethical concerns in CI practice, estate agencies practise CI ethically and legally. They respect the law and code of ethics in practising CI. They are, therefore, able to differentiate between CI and industrial espionage. Estate agencies in South Africa collect information about their competitors such as weaknesses and strength, pricing of real estate, suppliers of competitors and competitors' customers. Customers are their main source of information for CI. Collected information is stored in internal and external hard drives for further analysis. Considering that the analysis phase is the critical success factor of CI, estate agencies analyse collected information to produce actionable CI. Teamwork and brainstorming, SWOT analysis and valuation techniques are widely used by the estate agencies to analyse collected information. Estate agencies disseminate actionable intelligence through face-to-face meetings, e-mails and presentation. Like firms in other sectors, the majority of estate agencies do not outsource CI practice but prefer to do it in-house. Because estate agencies are for-profit firms, they measure the performance of CI and its contribution to profit. Estate agencies continue to see the value of CI and they have been practising CI to a greater extent for over 6 years.

To remain competitive in a highly competitive property sector, estate agencies in South Africa should continue practising CI. Estate agencies should continue to practise CI ethically and legally as this ensures that CI is respected as a profession. The EAAB and other educational institutions should offer educational programmes in CI. Because they are the main source of information for CI, estate agencies should build good relationships with their customers. Estate agencies should continuously measure the performance of CI to determine its contribution to profit.

Future research should be conducted to determine why estate agencies locate the CI in the marketing/sales department. Furthermore, research must be conducted to determine factors that influence estate agencies to practise CI ethically and legally. Research must be conducted to determine why estate agencies do not outsource CI practice. Further research must be conducted to determine how estate agencies measure the performance of CI. Further research must be conducted to determine tools, techniques and software used by firms in the property sector to practice CI.

Acknowledgements

This work is based on the research supported by the National Research Foundation. The authors also acknowledge the University of South Africa (South Africa) for the funding and support without which this research would not have been possible.

Competing interests

The authors declare that they have no financial or personal relationships which may have inappropriately influenced them in writing this article.

References

Adidam, T.J., Gajre, S. & Kejriwal, S., 2009, 'Cross-cultural competitive intelligence strategies', *Marketing Intelligence and Planning* 27(5), 666–680. http://dx.doi.org/10.1108/02634500910977881

Barnea, A., 2014, 'Competitive intelligence in the defense industry: A perspective from Israel – A case study analysis', *Journal of Intelligence Studies in Business* 4(2), 91–111.

Barrett, S.E., 2010, 'Competitive intelligence: Significance in higher education', *World Future Review* 2, 26–30. http://dx.doi.org/10.1177/194675671000200405

Bartes, F., 2014a, 'Defining a basis for the new concept of competitive intelligence', *ACTA Universitatis Agriculturae ET Silviculturae Mendelianae Brunensis* 62(6), 1233–1242. http://dx.doi.org/10.11118/actaun201462061233

Bartes, F., 2014b, 'The objectives of competitive intelligence as a part of corporative development strategy', *ACTA Universitatis Agriculturae ET Silviculturae Mendelianae Brunensis* 62(6), 1243–1250. http://dx.doi.org/10.11118/actaun201462061243

Brody, R., 2008, 'Issues in defining competitive intelligence: An exploration', *Journal of Competitive Intelligence and Management* 4(3), 3–16. http://dx.doi.org/10.1109/emr.2008.4648884

Bulley, C.A., Baku, K.F. & Allan, M.M., 2014, 'Competitive intelligence information: A key business success factor', *Journal of Management and Sustainability* 4(2), 82–91. http://dx.doi.org/10.5539/jms.v4n2p82

Calof, J.L. & Skinner, B., 1998, 'Competitive intelligence for government officers: A brave new world', *Optimum* 28(2), 38–42.

Colakoglu, T., 2011, 'The problematic of competitive intelligence: How to evaluate and develop competitive intelligence', *Procedia – Social and Behavioral Sciences* 24(1), 1615–1623. http://dx.doi.org/10.1016/j.sbspro.2011.09.075

Degaut, M., 2015, 'Spies and policymakers: Intelligence in the information age', *Intelligence and National Security,* 31(4), 509–531. http://dx.doi.org/10.1080/02684527.2015.1017931

Deng, Z. & Luo, L., 2010, 'An exploratory discussion of new ways for competitive intelligence on Web2.0', *International Federation for Information Processing* 252(1), 597–604.

De Pelsmacker, P., Muller, M., Viviers, W., Saayman, A., Cuyvers, L. & Jegers, M., 2005, 'Competitive intelligence practices of South African and Belgian exporters', *Marketing Intelligence and Planning* 23(6), 606–620. http://dx.doi.org/10.1108/02634500510624156

Du Toit, A.S.A. & Sewdass, N., 2014, 'A comparison of competitive intelligence activities in Brazil, Malaysia, Morocco and South Africa', *Acta Commercii* 14(1), Art. #234, 7 pages. http://dx.doi.org/10.4102/ac.v14i1.234

EAAB, 2014, *Property contributes R191.4 billion to the national economy*, viewed 16 July 2015, from http://www.eaab.org.za/property_sector_charter_council

EAAB Annual Report 2008/2009, viewed 16 July 2015, from http://www.eaab.org.za/article/annual_report_2008_/_2009

EAAB Annual Report 2009/2010, viewed 16 July 2015, from http://www.eaab.org.za/article/annual_report_2009_/_2010

EAAB Annual Report 2010/2011, viewed 16 July 2015, from http://www.eaab.org.za/article/annual_report_2010_/_2011

EAAB Annual Report 2012/2013, viewed 16 July 2015, from http://www.eaab.org.za/article/annual_report_2012_2013

EAAB Annual Report 2013/2014, viewed 16 July 2015, from http://www.eaab.org.za/article/annual_report_2013/14

Fleisher, C.S., 2004, 'Competitive intelligence education: Competencies, sources, and trends', *Information Management Journal* 38(2), 56–62. http://dx.doi.org/10.1108/03090560810877196

Fleisher, C.S. & Wright, S., 2009, 'Examining differences in competitive intelligence practice: China, Japan, and the West', *Thunderbird International Business Review* 51(3), 249–261. http://dx.doi.org/10.1002/tie.20263

Haddadi, A.E., Dousset, B. & Berrada, I., 2010, 'XplorEveryWhere – The competitive intelligence system for mobile', viewed 18 August 2015, from http://ieeexplore.ieee.org/stamp/stamp.jsp?tp=andarnumber=5945635

Haliso, H. & Aina, R.F., 2012, 'Quality collection of library resources in meeting users' needs in academic institutions: Competitive intelligence approach', *Global Journal of Human Social Science* 12(12), 25–31.

Heppes, D. & Du Toit, A., 2009, 'Level of maturity of the competitive intelligence function: Case study of a retail bank in South Africa', *Aslib Proceedings: New Information Perspectives* 61(1), 48–66. http://dx.doi.org/10.1108/00012530910932285

Herring, J.P., 1999, 'Key intelligence topics: A process to identify and define intelligence need', *Competitive Intelligence Review* 10(2), 4–14.

Juhari, A.S. & Stephens, D., 2006, 'Tracing the origins of competitive intelligence through history', *Journal of Competitive Intelligence and Management* 3(4), 61–82.

Lin, S. & Yan-Zhang, W., 2015, 'Identifying the core competitive intelligence based on enterprise strategic factors', *Journal of Shanghai Jiaotong University of Science* 20(1), 118–123. http://dx.doi.org/10.1007/s12204-015-1598-7

Maune, A., 2014, 'Competitive intelligence and firm competitiveness: An overview', *Corporate Ownership and Control* 12(1), 29–42.

McGonagle, J.J. & Vella, C.M., 2012, *Proactive intelligence: What is competitive intelligence and why should you care about it?* Springer-Verlag, London.

Muller, M.L., 2006, 'Parts of competitive intelligence: Competitor intelligence', *South African Journal of Information Management* 8(1), from http://www.sajim.co.za/index.php/SAJIM/article/viewFile/209/205

Nasri, W., 2011, 'Investigate competitive intelligence process: An exploratory study in Tunisian Companies', *International Business Research* 4(4), 62–73. http://dx.doi.org/10.5539/ibr.v4n4p62

Nasri, W. & Zarai, M., 2013, 'Key success factors for developing competitive intelligence in organisation', *American Journal of Business and Management* 2(3), 239–244. http://dx.doi.org/10.11634/216796061302397

Nenzhelele, T.E., 2012, 'A study of the awareness and practice of competitive intelligence in SMEs in the City of Tshwane Metropolitan Municipality', Masters dissertation, University of South Africa, South Africa.

Neuman, W.L., 2006, *Social Research Methods: Qualitative and Quantitative Approaches,* Allyn and Bacon, Boston.

Pellissier, R. & Nenzhelele, T.E., 2013a, 'Towards a universal competitive intelligence process model', *South African Journal of Information Management* 15(2), Art. #567, 7 pages. http://dx.doi.org/10.4102/sajim.v15i2.567

Pellissier, R. & Nenzhelele, T.E., 2013b, 'Towards a universal definition of competitive intelligence', *South African Journal of Information Management* 15(2), Art. #559, 7 pages. http://dx.doi.org/10.4102/sajim.v15i2.559

Pinto, V.A., 2014, 'Supporting competitive intelligence with linked enterprise data', Masters dissertation, FUMEC University, Belo Horizonte.

Prescott, J.E., 1999, 'The evolution of competitive intelligence: Designing a process for action', *APMP Spring* 37–52, viewed 19 August 2015, from http://files.paul-medley.webnode.com/200000023-97ce398c7e/Competitive%20Intelligence%20A-Z.pdf

Roitner, A., 2008, 'Competitive intelligence in Austria: An empirical study', Masters dissertation, University of Vienna, Austria.

Sewdass, N., 2012, 'Proposing a competitive intelligence (CI) framework for public service departments to enhance service delivery', *South African Journal of Information Management* 14(1), 1–13.

Sewdass, N. & Du Toit, A., 2014, 'Current state of competitive intelligence in South Africa', *International Journal of Information Management* 34(1), 185–190. http://dx.doi.org/10.1016/j.ijinfomgt.2013.10.006

The Global Competitiveness Report 2014–2015, viewed 16 July 2015, from http://www3.weforum.org/docs/WEF_GlobalCompetitivenessReport_2014-15.pdf

Weiss, A. & Naylor, E., 2010, 'Competitive intelligence: How independent information professionals contributes to organisational success', *American Society for Information Science and Technology* 37(1), 30–34.

Yassine, F.L.Y.A., 2014, 'The level of applying competitive intelligence as perceived by managers at Telecom Company "Zain" in Jordan', *International Journal of Business and Social Science* 5(1), 22–34.

9

The role of user satisfaction in implementing a Business Intelligence System

Author:
Philip A.E. Serumaga-Zake[1]

Affiliation:
[1]School of Business Leadership, University of South Africa, South Africa

Corresponding author:
Philip Serumaga-Zake,
serumpa@unisa.ac.za

Background: Despite increasing importance of the use of Business Intelligence (BI) as a technology-driven process for giving decision support, the success or failure of BI has not been investigated fully in South Africa. BI is not well understood because of an absence of documented proof of its practice.

Objectives: This study was intended to investigate BI and identify the moderating and mediating effects of user satisfaction on the relationship between system quality, information quality and service quality on the one hand and perceived net benefits on the other in South Africa.

Methods: The quantitative methods approach was predominantly used in this study. A total of 211 responses were obtained from a random sample of 250 BI users throughout South Africa. A semi-structured online survey questionnaire was used to collect the data, and correlation and multiple regression analyses were used to analyse it.

Results: It was found that user satisfaction mediates the relationship between perceived net benefits and system quality and service quality. It also moderates the effects of system quality and service quality on perceived net benefits. Information quality is not related with user satisfaction and perceived net benefits.

Conclusion: The implication of the results is that system quality and user satisfaction should be enhanced and maintained to achieve perceived positive net benefits in order to make the BI system more effective and efficient.

Introduction

Business intelligence (BI) systems have become increasingly important over the past few decades and are, today, one of the top spending priority areas of most organisations (Davenport 2010; Foley & Manon 2010; Gartner 2009; Olszak & Batko 2012; Trninic, Durkovic & Rakovic 2011; Turban et al. 2011a) because decision makers need accurate and timely information in order to make effective decisions. For the purpose of this study, BI will be defined as a technology-driven process, which facilitates achievement of organisations' mission objectives through providing required information to the decision makers (Petrini & Pozzebon 2009; Turban et al. 2011b; Wixom & Watson 2001). According to Martin, Maladhy and Venkatesan (2011), a typical BI system consists of a data warehouse (Ponniah 2010); an extraction, transformation and loading tool; and a set of analytical tools.

A lot of research has been done on BI; however, with its rapid development, some researchers (e.g. Cidrin & Adamala 2011; Mohamad & Mohamed 2012; YellowFin 2012) argue that it still warrants further academic scrutiny. One of the reasons for this is that most of the available research does not apply to the developing countries because it has been done in developed countries (which have a different culture) (Avgerou 2008; Murugan, Magid & Uzoamaka 2000) and it focuses on technological and operational features rather than on human, managerial and strategic factors (Chaveesuk 2010). Ponelis and Britz (2011) assert that an absence of documented proof of BI practice in developing countries might imply that it is still at an early stage of adoption.

In South Africa, BI has been widely adopted by many organisations and attempts have been made to explore and examine the success factors of BI systems (Dawson & Van Belle 2013; Nkuna 2011), but these studies have been case studies, thus making the results not capable of being generalised to all business organisations in the country. Indeed, the fact that there have been case studies reporting penetration of BI in South Africa's socio-economic value chains is evident enough to show that something is happening; however, the success or failure of a BI system has not been well articulated in the country (Chaveesuk 2010; Yeoh & Koronios 2010). There is still a limited amount of empirical research that investigates the nature of end-user satisfaction with BI systems (Acheampong & Moyaid 2016; Boonsiritomachai, McGrath & Burgess 2014) and many of the firms in South Africa that have adopted BI are not yet utilising BI to the full potential. Therefore, this study was an attempt to narrow this knowledge gap, aiming at providing insight into those factors that organisations need to address to improve BI projects' chances of success and ensure an effective and efficient initiative. The study focuses on identifying the moderating and mediating effect of user satisfaction on the relationship between system quality, information quality and service quality on the one hand and perceived net benefits on the other in South Africa.

Literature review and theoretical framework

Several authors (e.g. DeLone & McLean 1992, 2003; Hayen, Rutashobya & Vetter 2007; Shin 2003) have found that system quality has an effect on the use of BI system and user satisfaction, and user satisfaction has an influence on individual and organisational impact, which together make up a firm's 'net benefits'. Studies indicate that in general service quality also has a positive influence on user satisfaction (Almutairi & Subramanian 2005; Coombs, Doherty & Loan-Clarke 2001; Gelderman 2002; Halawi, McCarthy & Aronson 2007; Livari 2005; McGill, Hobbs & Klobas 2003; Seddon & Kiew 1996; Wu & Wang 2006) and that when users are satisfied with a BI system it is hoped that they would derive positive benefits from using it (Gelderman 1998; Law & Ngai 2007).

Researchers (e.g. DeLone & McLean 1992; Doll & Torkzadeh 1988), by utilising, for example, the case study design, survey design or Delphi technique method have identified user satisfaction as one of the most extensively used single measure of BI success. Chiu et al. (2005) further explained that the user's level of satisfaction is based on the level to which the application meets the users' expectations. According to Smart (2009), individual impact affects the organisational impact of the BI system and they are both influenced by user satisfaction. This study adopted Seddon's (1997:246) definition of user satisfaction as 'the net feeling of pleasure or displeasure resulting from aggregating all the benefits that a person hopes to receive from interaction with the information system'. Perceived net benefits are the core dimension used to determine the diverse and multifaceted success of BI (Wixom & Watson 2001).

This study was based on three theoretical models, namely, technology acceptance model (TAM) (Davis 1989), task technology fit (TTF) (Goodhue & Thompson 1995) and social cognitive theory (SCT) (Bandura 1986). TAM posits that perceived usefulness of a BI system is directly impacted by perceived ease of its use and they both determine an individual's intention to use it with intention to use serving as a mediator of actual system use. The model assumes that when people form an intention to act, they will be free to act without limitation, and in practice, constraints such as limited ability, time, environmental or organisational limits, and unconscious habits will limit the freedom to act. In this study, this model was extended by introducing six major factors of information systems success, namely: (1) system quality, (2) information quality, (3) use, (4) user satisfaction, (5) individual impact and (6) organisational impact factors from the DeLone and Mclean model (1992). The TTF theory holds that IT affects individual performance if its capabilities match the concerned tasks and quality, compatibility, ease of use/training, systems reliability and relationship with users, etc., and affect the task–technology fit which in turn determines the system's effectiveness (Goodhue & Thompson 1995). SCT identifies human behaviour as an interaction of personal factors, behaviour, and the environment (Bandura 1986) (which involves the influences of a person's thoughts and actions). The second interaction between the person and the environment involves human beliefs and cognitive competencies that are developed and modified by social influences and structures within the environment. The third interaction between the environment and behaviour involves a person's behaviour determining the aspects of their environment (Jones 1989) and in turn their behaviour is modified by that environment.

This study hypothesised that in the BI system, user satisfaction moderates the effects of system quality, information quality and service quality on perceived net benefits and it mediates the relationship between these independent variables and net benefits. System quality as an essential factor in a successful data warehouse implementation (Seddon 1997) comprises five key dimensions: flexibility, reliability, response time, accessibility and integration (Nelson, Todd & Wixom 2005; Petter, DeLone & McLean 2008; Seddon, 1997). Information quality consists of four dimensions: accuracy, completeness, currency and format, which are, by implication, an essential asset for BI success for any organisation (Haley 1997; Hwang & Xu 2008; Nelson et al. 2005; Rudra & Yeo 1999; Shin 2003; Thomann & Wells 1999; Wixom & Watson 2001). Zhu and Kraemer (2005) identified four attributes with respect to information quality as follows: (1) origin has an effect on reliability of the data and the trust one can place in it referring to the origin relationship as data lineage, (2) correctness signifies that the data are free of errors, (3) completeness describes the coverage of the data and (4) objectivity refers to the lack of prejudice in the data. Service quality is defined as the quality of the support that BI system users receive from the IS department and IT support personnel (Pitt, Watson & Kavan 1995; Petter et al. 2008). Grover and Segars (1996), defined service quality based on the degree of disparity between what the customer expects in terms of service standard and perceived service performance (Culiberg & Rojsek, 2010; Parasuraman, Zeithaml & Berry 1988).

The conceptual framework diagram is shown in Figure 1.

Table 1 shows the items or concepts that were measured for a particular construct.

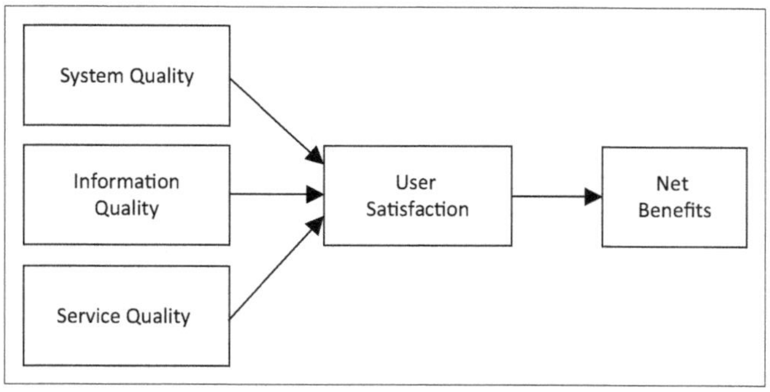

Source: Adapted from Davis 1989 and DeLone and Mclean 1992 models

FIGURE 1: Conceptual framework for successful Business Intelligence System implementation.

TABLE 1: Survey instrument constructs.

Construct	Item	Description
System quality	1	Availability
	2	Ease of use
	3	Accessibility
	4	Usefulness
	5	Stability
Information quality	1	Content
	2	Availability
	3	Accuracy
	4	Timelines
	5	Conciseness
	6	I depend upon the system
	7	I only use the system when it is absolutely necessary for learning
Service quality	1	Assurance
	2	Empathy
	3	Responsiveness
	4	Knowledge
User satisfaction	1	Meets information needs
	2	I think the system is very helpful
	3	Overall, I am satisfied with the system
Net benefits	1	The system has a positive impact on my work
	2	Overall, the performance of the system is good
	3	Overall, the system is successful
	4	The system is an important and valuable aid to me in the Performance of my work

Source: Derived from Davis 1989 and DeLone and Mclean 1992 models

Research design and methodology

Data

A total of 211 businesses (with more than 100 full-time employees) and a maximum response of two BI users (from different departments) were used in this study. An anonymous and confidential online semi-structured questionnaire was used to collect data.

Profile of the participants

The majority (53.08%) of the respondents were aged between 31 and 40 years and most of them were male respondents (57.35%) (Singh 2004) and blacks (47.87%), followed by whites (35.07%). Some of the respondents (35.3%) were from the financial services field and accounting and many were operational staff (76.78%). The highest education level was mostly a bachelor's degree (49.29%), followed by a diploma (37.91%).

Normality of the data

Skewness of the constructs (ranging between -1.216 for system quality and -0.385 for information quality) showed that the data approximately followed a normal distribution (Hair et al. 2007). Kurtosis (ranging from 2.404 for net benefits to 4.283 for user satisfaction) was relatively high. See the relevant histograms in Figure 2.

By looking at the histograms and distribution curves of the constructs, and their skewness and kurtosis, it can be concluded that all constructs except information quality and service quality, were not normally distributed. However, although some of the variables did not appear to be normally distributed, it was not necessary to transform and normalise them for the reason that independent variables did not have to be normally distributed to obtain valid results. The skewness of net benefits of -0.777 and kurtosis of 2.404 indicated that the variable was more or less normally distributed and it did not require any transformation. The desired statistical analyses were applied.

Data analysis

In this study, correlational analysis and multiple regression were used to analyse the data. The dependent variable was perceived net benefits. System quality, information quality and service quality were the independent variables and user satisfaction was treated as a moderating or mediating variable. A moderator is a variable that alters the direction or strength of the relationship between an independent variable and a dependent variable. This implies that the effect of an independent variable on the dependent variable depends on the level of another variable referred to as a moderating variable, just like an interaction effect. A mediator helps to explain a relationship between an independent variable and a dependent variable. The multiple regression model used in this study was:

$$y_i = b_1x_{i1} + b_2x_{i2} + \ldots + b_4x_{i4} + e_i \quad \text{[Eqn 1]}$$

where y_i is the ith observation on the net benefit variable, x^{th} is the ith observation on the jth independent variable, and b_i is the effect of the jth independent variable on net benefit and e_i is the error of the ith observation.

Statistical significance was checked by the *F*-test of the overall model fit and *t* tests of individual parameters. In order to test for the moderation effect of user satisfaction on the effect of the independent variables on the dependent variable, new variables were created by multiplying system quality, information quality and service quality by user satisfaction and including the interaction terms in the regression model. Two regression models were fitted; the first one included only the independent variables and user satisfaction. The second, apart from the independent variables and user satisfaction, also included the newly created interaction variables. Because in multiple regression, interaction variables are often highly correlated with the variables from

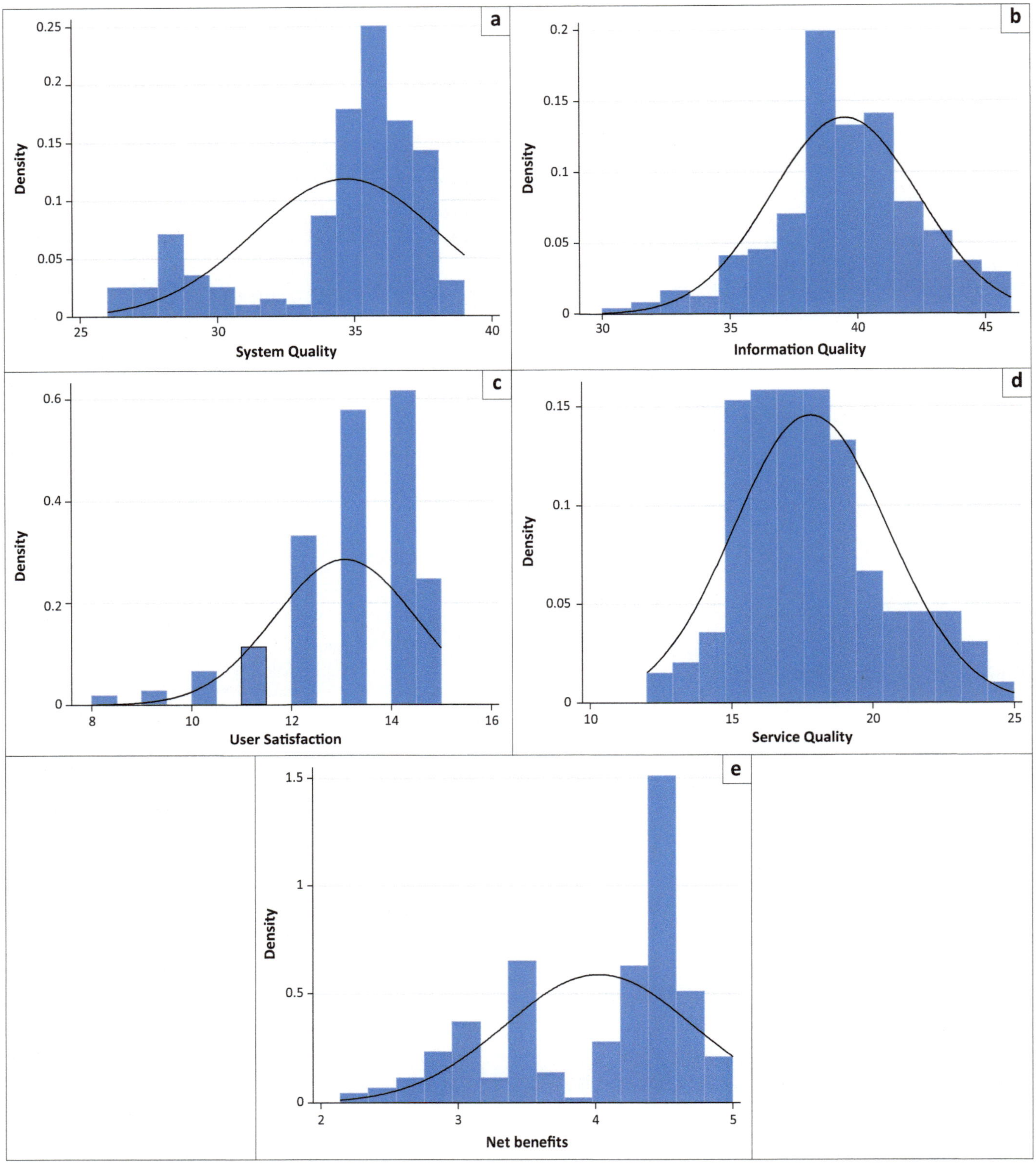

FIGURE 2: Histograms and curves for key study variables: (a) system quality; (b) information quality; (c) user satisfaction; (d) service quality; (e) net benefits.

which they are created, the independent variables and interaction variables were standardised to decrease the correlation.

In order to know whether adding the interactions led to a significant improvement in how well the regression performed, R^2 was examined to find out whether it increased. This increase was tested for significance using the *F*-test.

To test for mediation, again, two models were fitted. The first one was fitted with only system quality, information quality and service quality as independent variables, and the second one, apart from including these variables, also included user satisfaction. The mediation effect of user satisfaction was identified by examining whether the differences between the coefficients of the first model and those of the second model were statistically significant. The Stata Statistical Package was used to analyse the data.

Results

Descriptive analysis

The mean scores of the constructs were 4.34, 3.95, 3.49 and 4.36 for system quality, information quality, service quality and user satisfaction, respectively. This implies that in general, the respondents were satisfied with the BI system.

The Kendall rank correlation coefficient was used to measure the correlations between the constructs as the sample was relatively small (Field, Miles & Field 2012; Yamane 1967). Table 2 shows the results (with probabilities in the brackets).

The results indicate that there is a high positive correlation between system quality and user satisfaction ($r = 0.34$, $p = 0.000 < 0.01$), information quality and user satisfaction ($r = 0.27$, $p = 0.001$), information quality and perceived net benefits ($r = 0.20$, $p = 0.006 < 0.01$) and user satisfaction and perceived net benefits ($r = 0.31$, $p = 0.000 < 0.01$); and there is a high negative correlation between service quality and user satisfaction ($r = -0.20$, $p = 0.019 < 0.05$) and service quality and perceived net benefits ($r = -0.21$, $p = 0.007 < 0.01$). However, these correlations are close to zero, which implies that the relationships are weak.

Inferential analysis

User satisfaction regression model

Table 3 indicates that there is no relationship between information quality and user satisfaction ($t = -0.36$, $p = 0.716 > 0.05$) but there is a negative relationship between user satisfaction and system quality ($t = -3.18$, $p = 0.002 < 0.01$) and service quality ($t = -3.67$, $p = 0.000 < 0.01$).

This implies that when system quality or service quality increases, user satisfaction decreases, holding other variables constant. The reason for this kind of relationship was not investigated in this study.

Moderating effect of user satisfaction

First, only information quality, system quality, service quality and user satisfaction were included in the regression model as independent variables (see Table 4).

The results indicate that all the independent variables except information quality ($t = 0.53$, $p = 0.596 > 0.05$) affect perceived net benefits positively at least at the 10% level of statistical significance. The adjusted R-square is 0.2167, which means that the regression model explains about 22% of the variation in the data. Table 5 shows the regression results when the interaction variables were added to the model.

TABLE 2: Correlation matrix.

Construct	System quality	Information quality	Service quality	User satisfaction	Net benefit
System quality	1	-	-	-	-
Information quality	0.132 (0.072)	1	-	-	-
Service quality	0.084 (0.282)	-0.123 (0.117)	1	-	-
User satisfaction	0.337† (0.000)	0.268† (0.001)	-0.200‡ (0.019)	1	-
Net benefits	0.125 (0.093)	0.205† (0.006)	-0.214† (0.007)	0.314† (0.000)	1

†, Significant at 1% level; ‡, Significant at 5% level.

TABLE 3: Regression model for user satisfaction.

Variable	Coef.	Std. Err.	*T*	Prob.	95% Conf. Interval		Source		
					Minimum	Maximum	SS	*df*	MS
System quality	-0.252	0.079	-3.18	0.002	-0.407	-0.095	-	-	-
Information quality	-0.025	0.067	-0.36	0.716	-0.157	0.108	-	-	-
Service quality	-0.290	0.079	-3.67	0.000	-0.446	-0.134	-	-	-
Constant	5.44e-08	0.067	0.00	1.000	-0.132	0.132	-	-	-
Model	-	-	-	-	-	-	14.788	3	4.929
Residual	-	-	-	-	-	-	195.212	207	0.943
Total	-	-	-	-	-	-	**21.000**	**210**	**1.000**

Coef., coefficient; Std. Err., standard error; *T*, *t*-value; Prob., probability; SS, sum of squares; *df*, degrees of freedom; MS, mean squares.
Note: No. of observations = 211; $F(3, 207) = 5.23$; Prob. > F = 0.002; R-squared = 0.070; Adj. R-squared = 0.057; Root MSE = 0.971.

TABLE 4: Regression model for net benefits (without interaction terms).

Variable	Coef.	Std. Err.	*T*	Prob.	95% Conf. Interval		Source		
					Minimum	Maximum	SS	*df*	MS
User satisfaction	1.731	0.302	5.73	0.000	1.136	2.326	-	-	-
System quality	2.044	0.351	5.82	0.000	1.351	2.737	-	-	-
Information quality	0.155	0.292	0.53	0.596	-0.421	0.731	-	-	-
Service quality	0.595	0.354	1.68	0.095	-0.104	1.294	-	-	-
Constant	28.175	0.290	97.04	0.000	27.603	28.748	-	-	-
Model	-	-	-	-	-	-	1104.494	4	276.124
Residual	-	-	-	-	-	-	3664.018	206	17.786
Total	-	-	-	-	-	-	**4768.512**	**210**	**22.707**

Coef., coefficient; Std. Err., standard error; *T*, *t*-value; Prob., probability; SS, sum of squares; *df*, degrees of freedom; MS, mean squares.
Note: No. of observations = 211; $F(4, 206) = 15.52$; Prob. > F = 0.000; R-squared = 0.232; Adj. R-squared = 0.217; Root MSE = 4.217.

TABLE 5: Regression model for net benefits (with interaction terms).

Variable	Coef.	Std. Err.	*T*	Prob.	95% Conf. Interval		Source		
					Minimum	Maximum	SS	*df*	MS
User satisfaction	1.654	0.306	5.41	0.000	1.051	2.256	-	-	-
System quality	1.591	0.336	4.73	0.000	0.928	2.253	-	-	-
Information quality	0.150	0.272	0.55	0.582	-0.386	0.687	-	-	-
Service quality	0.234	0.342	0.68	0.495	-0.441	0.909	-	-	-
Interaction (system quality and user satisfaction)	0.895	0.396	2.26	0.025	0.114	1.675	-	-	-
Interaction (information quality and user satisfaction)	-0.152	0.309	-0.49	0.623	-0.763	0.458	-	-	-
Interaction (service quality and user satisfaction)	-1.184	0.244	-4.84	0.000	-1.666	-0.702	-	-	-
Model	-	-	-	-	-	-	1641.712	7	234.530
Residual	-	-	-	-	-	-	3126.800	203	15.403
Total	-	-	-	-	-	-	**4768.512**	**210**	**22.707**

Coef., coefficient; Std. Err., standard error; *T*, *t*–value; Prob., probability; SS, sum of squares; *df*, degrees of freedom; MS, mean squares.
Note: No. of observations = 211; *F*(7, 203) = 15.23; Prob. > *F* = 0.000; *R*-squared = 0.344; Adj. *R*-squared = 0.322; Root MSE = 3.925.

TABLE 6: Regression model for net benefits (without user satisfaction).

Variable	Coef.	Std. Err.	*T*	Prob.	95% Conf. Interval		Source		
					Minimum	Maximum	SS	*df*	MS
System quality	1.609	0.369	4.37	0.000	0.883	2.336	-	-	-
Information quality	0.113	0.314	0.36	0.720	-0.506	0.732	-	-	-
Service quality	0.093	0.369	0.25	0.801	-0.634	0.821	-	-	-
Constant	28.175	0.312	90.34	0.000	27.560	28.790	-	-	-
Model	-	-	-	-	-	-	519.739	3	173.246
Residual	-	-	-	-	-	-	4248.773	207	20.525
Total	-	-	-	-	-	-	**4768.512**	**210**	**22.707**

Coef., coefficient; Std. Err., standard error; *T*, *t*–value; Prob., probability; SS, sum of squares; *df*, degrees of freedom; MS, mean squares.
Note: No. of observations = 211; *F*(3, 207) = 8.44; Prob. > *F* = 0.000; *R*-squared = 0.109; Adj. *R*-squared = 0.096; Root MSE = 4.530.

According to the results, it is only the effects of system quality and service quality (on perceived net benefits) that seem to be moderated by user satisfactions because the probability values corresponding to the interaction terms [and *t* values (2.26 and -4.84)] are, respectively, 0.025 (< 0.05) and 0.000 (< 0.01). The coefficient of the service quality interaction term is negative. This implies that the higher the value of the interaction, the lower the score of perceived net benefits will be, provided other factors are held constant. It also implies that the moderating effect of user satisfaction is to suppress or decrease the effect of service quality on perceived net benefits. The interaction between system quality and user satisfaction affects perceived net benefits positively, such that the higher the value of the interaction, the higher the score of perceived net benefits will be. This implies that the moderating effect of user satisfaction is to increase or enhance the effect of system quality on perceived net benefits. In other words, user satisfaction tends to suppress the effect of service quality on perceived net benefits but to enhance the effect of system quality on perceived net benefits.

Applying the *F* formula, we obtain:

$$F_{(f-r,N-f-1)} = \frac{(N-f-1)(R_f^2 - R_r^2)}{(f-r)(1-R_r^2)}$$

$$= \frac{(211-8-1)(.3217-.2167)}{(8-5)(1-.2167)} = \frac{202X.1050}{3X.7833} = \frac{21.21}{2.3499} = 9.0259$$

$$\text{Prob.} > F(3, 202) = 3.782 < 0.01. \qquad \text{[Eqn 2]}$$

The *F* ratio calculated from the change in *R*-square between the first and second model is 9.0259. The corresponding theoretical F ratio (3, 202) (at the 1% level) obtained from the F table is 3.782. This means that the F ratio is statistically significant; so, the null hypothesis that the interaction terms in the model are not significant is rejected, and the alternative hypothesis that at least one interaction term is significant is accepted. Because the interaction terms of system quality and service quality are the only ones that are significant, this implies that user satisfaction moderates the effects of system quality and service quality on perceived net benefits.

Mediation effect of user satisfaction

To test user satisfaction as a mediator between the independent variables and perceived net benefits, at first, the regression model included only the independent variables (i.e., information quality, system quality and service quality). Then, both the independent variables and user satisfaction were included in the same regression model. This was done, as implied above, to find out whether user satisfaction would significantly decrease or increase the relationships between the independent variables and net benefits. When the regression model was fitted without user satisfaction, the results in Table 6 were obtained.

The results show that only system quality ($t = 4.37, p = 0.000 < 0.01$) affects perceived net benefits positively at the 1% level. If the level of system quality increases by one unit, the level of perceived net benefits increases by 1.609 units, holding other factors constant. Adjusted *R*-square is 0.0961, which implies that about 9% of the variation of the perceived net benefits is explained by the model.

Table 7 shows the results when user satisfaction was also included in the model.

TABLE 7: Regression model for net benefits (with user satisfaction).

Variable	Coef.	Std. Err.	*T*	Prob.	95% Conf. Interval		Source		
					Minimum	Maximum	SS	*df*	MS
System quality	2.044	0.351	5.82	0.000	1.351	2.737	-	-	-
Information quality	0.155	0.292	0.53	0.596	-0.421	0.731	-	-	-
Service quality	0.595	0.354	1.68	0.095	-0.104	1.294	-	-	-
User satisfaction	1.731	0.302	5.73	0.000	1.136	2.326	-	-	-
Constant	28.175	0.290	97.04	0.000	27.603	28.748	-	-	-
Model	-	-	-	-	-	-	1104.494	4	276.124
Residual	-	-	-	-	-	-	3664.018	206	17.786
Total	-	-	-	-	-	-	**4768.512**	**210**	**22.707**

Coef., coefficient; Std. Err., standard error; *T*, *t*-value; Prob., probability; SS, sum of squares; *df*, degrees of freedom; MS, mean squares.
Note: No. of observations = 211; $F(4, 206) = 15.52$; Prob. > $F = 0.000$; R-squared = 0.232; Adj. R-squared = 0.217; Root MSE = 4.217.

The regression results in Table 7 show that there is no relationship between information quality and perceived net benefits ($t = 0.53$, $p = 0.596 > 0.05$). In the regression model of Table 6 (before user satisfaction was included in the model), information quality was not significant. Also, when it was included in the model, still it was not significant. This means that inclusion of user satisfaction in the model did not change the coefficient of information quality. Therefore, it can be concluded that user satisfaction does not affect the relationship between information quality and perceived net benefits and is hence not a mediator between them.

According to the results, there is a relationship between system quality and user satisfaction and between service quality and user satisfaction. There is also a relationship between user satisfaction and perceived net benefits ($t = 5.73$, $p = 0.000 < 0.01$). It is interesting to note that inclusion of user satisfaction in the model dramatically changed the coefficients of system quality [from 1.609 ($t = 4.37$, $p = 0.000 < 0.01$) to 2.044 ($t = 5.82$, $p = 0.000 < 0.01$)] and service quality [from 0.093 ($t = 0.25$, $p = 0.801$) to 0.595 ($t = 1.68$, $p = 0.095 < 0.1$)]. System quality is significant in the first regression model and also in the second regression model (but with a bigger *t*-value) at the 1% level. Service quality is not significant in the first regression model, but after including user satisfaction, it became significant in the second regression model (of Table 7) at the 10% level. Therefore, it can be concluded that user satisfaction has a mediation effect on the relationships between system quality and perceived net benefits and between service quality and perceived net benefits.

The regression results in Tables 5 and 7 disqualify the hypothesised BI model in Figure 1 but suggest the BI model shown in Figure 3 as the model applicable in South Africa. It has been found that user satisfaction does not have any moderating or mediating effect on the effect of information quality on perceived net benefits and information quality does not affect perceived net benefits. The only paths left are those shown in Figure 3.

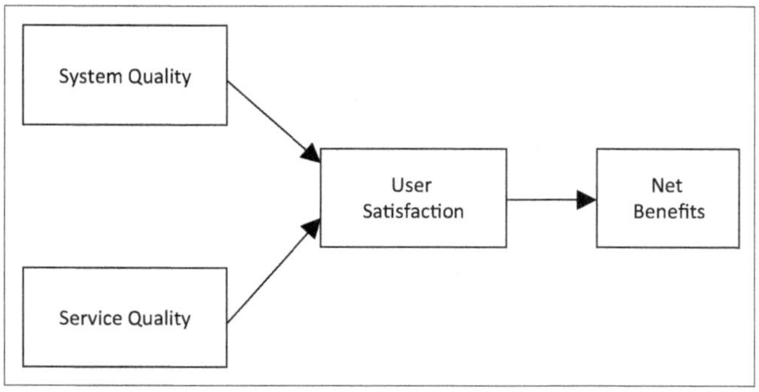

FIGURE 3: Business Intelligence System success model.

Conclusion

It has been found that there is no relationship between information quality and perceived net benefits and user satisfaction in a BI system. System quality and service quality are negatively related to user satisfaction but positively related with perceived net benefits in a BI system. User satisfaction is positively related to perceived net benefits in a BI system. User satisfaction mediates the relationship between perceived net benefits and system quality and service quality and moderates the effect of system quality on perceived net benefits by enhancing it, whereas it moderates the effect of service quality on perceived net benefits by reversing it.

Self-reporting bias may have led the study participants to over-report those factors that seem to be more acceptable and under-rate those that seem to be less acceptable. Some of them may have been unwilling to disclose problems or negative aspects about their systems.

Recommendations

In South Africa, system quality and user satisfaction should be enhanced and maintained in order to achieve perceived positive net benefits and this would make the BI system more effective and efficient. A research study focussing on a specific industry could be very helpful in facilitating a clearer understanding of the relationships among the variables.

Acknowledgements

Competing interests

The author declares that he has no financial or personal relationship(s) that may have inappropriately influenced him in writing this article.

References

Acheampong, O. & Moyaid, S.A., 2016, 'An integrated model for determining business intelligence systems adoption and post-adoption benefits in banking sector', *Journal of Administrative and Business Studies* 2(2), 84–100.

Almutairi, H. & Subramanian, G.H., 2005, 'An empirical application of the DeLone and McLean model in the Kuwaiti private sector', *Journal of Computer Information Systems* 45(3), 113–122.

Avgerou, C., 2008, 'Information systems in developing countries: A critical research review', *Journal of Information Technology* 23, 133–146. https://doi.org/10.1057/palgrave.jit.2000136

Bandura, A., 1986, *Social foundations of thought and action: A social cognitive theory*, Prentice-Hall, Englewood Cliffs, NJ.

Boonsiritomachai, W., McGrath, M. & Burgess, S., 2014, 'A research framework for the adoption of business intelligence by small and medium-sized enterprises', paper presented at the 27th Annual SEAANZ Conference on Enhancing SME success in the digital economy, July, Sydney, Australia.

Chaveesuk, S., 2010, 'The determinants of the adoption and application of business intelligence: An ERP Perspective', s.l. Unpublished.

Chiu, C., Hsu, M., Sun, S., Lin, T. & Sun, P., 2005, 'Usability, quality, value and e-learning continuance decisions', *Computers & Education* 45(4), 399–416. https://doi.org/10.1016/j.compedu.2004.06.001

Cidrin, L. & Adamala, S., 2011, 'Key success factors in business intelligence', *Journal of Intelligence Studies in Business* 1, 107–127.

Coombs, C.R., Doherty, N.F. & Loan-Clarke, J., 2001, 'The importance of user ownership and positive user attitudes in the successful adoption of community information systems', *Journal of End User Computing* 13(4), 5–16. https://doi.org/10.4018/joeuc.2001100101

Culiberg, B. & Rojsek, I., 2010, 'Identifying service quality dimensions as antecedents to customer satisfaction in retail banking', *Economic and Business Review* 12, 151–166.

Davenport, T.H., 2010, 'Business intelligence and organizational decisions', *International Journal of Business Intelligence Research* 1, 1–12. https://doi.org/10.4018/jbir.2010071701

Davis, F.D., 1989, 'Perceived usefulness, perceived ease of use, and user acceptance of information technology', *MIS Quarterly* 13(3), 319–339. https://doi.org/10.2307/249008

Dawson, L. & Van Belle, J.P., 2013, 'Critical success factors for business intelligence in the South African financial services sector', *South African Journal of Information Management* 15(1), 12. https://doi.org/10.4102/sajim.v15i1.545

DeLone, W.H. & McLean, E.R., 1992, 'Information systems success: The quest for the dependent variable', *Information Systems Research* 3, 60–95. https://doi.org/10.1287/isre.3.1.60

DeLone, W.H. & McLean, E.R., 2003, 'The DeLone and McLean model of information systems success: A ten-year update', *Journal of Management Information Systems* 19, 9–30.

Doll, W.J. & Torkzadeh, Z., 1988, 'The measurement of end user computing satisfaction', *MIS Quarterly* 12, 259–274. https://doi.org/10.2307/248851

Field, A., Miles, J. & Field, Z., 2012, *Discovering Statistics Using R.*, Sage, London.

Foley, E. & Manon, G., 2010, 'What is business intelligence?', *International Journal of Business Intelligence Research* 1, 1–28. https://doi.org/10.4018/jbir.2010100101

Gartner, 2009, *Gartner EXP Worldwide Survey of More than 1,500 CIOs Shows IT spending to be flat in 2009*, viewed 01 February 2011, from http://www.gartner.com/it/page.jsp?id=855612

Gelderman, M., 1998, 'The relation between user satisfaction, usage of information systems and performance', *Information & Management* 34(1), 11–18. https://doi.org/10.1016/S0378-7206(98)00044-5

Gelderman, M., 2002, 'Task difficulty, task variability and satisfaction with management support systems', *Information & Management* 39(7), 593–604. https://doi.org/10.1016/S0378-7206(01)00124-0

Goodhue, D.L. & Thompson, R.L., 1995, 'Task-technology fit and individual performance', *MIS Quarterly* 19(2), 213–236. https://doi.org/10.2307/249689

Grover, V.S.R. & Segars, A.H., 1996, 'Information systems effectiveness: The construct space and patterns of application', *Information and Management* 31, 177–191. https://doi.org/10.1016/S0378-7206(96)01079-8

Hair, J.F., Money, A.H., Samouel, P. & Page, M., 2007, *Research methods for business*, Wiley, Chichester.

Halawi, L.A., McCarthy, R.V. & Aronson, J.E., 2007, 'An empirical investigation of knowledge management systems' success', *Journal of Computer Information Systems* 48(2), 121–135.

Haley, B.J., 1997, 'Implementing the decision support infrastructure key success factors in data warehousing', PhD dissertation, University of Georgia, Athens, GA.

Hayen, R.L., Rutashobya, C.D. & Vetter, D.E., 2007, 'An investigation of the factors affecting data warehousing success', *International Association for Computer Information Systems (IACIS)* 8(2), 547–553.

Hwang, M.I. & Xu, H., 2008, 'A structural model of data warehousing success', *Journal of Computer Information Systems* 49(1), 48–56.

Jones, J.W., 1989, 'Personality and epistemology: Cognitive social learning theory as a philosophy of science', *Zygon* 24(1), 23–38. https://doi.org/10.1111/j.1467-9744.1989.tb00974.x

Law, C.C. & Ngai, E.W., 2007, 'ERP systems adoption: An exploratory study of the organizational factors and impacts of ERP success', *Information & Management* 44(4), 418–432. https://doi.org/10.1016/j.im.2007.03.004

Livari, J., 2005, 'An empirical test of the DeLone-McLean Model of information system success', *The DATA BASE for Advances in Information Systems* 36(2), 8–27.

Martin, A., Maladhy, D. & Venkatesan, P.V., 2011, 'A framework for business intelligence application using ontological classification', *International Journal of Engineering Science and Technology* 3, 1213–1221.

McGill, T., Hobbs, V. & Klobas, J., 2003, 'User-developed applications and information system success: A test of DeLone and McLean's Model', *Information Resources Management Journal* 16(1), 24–45. https://doi.org/10.4018/irmj.2003010103

Mohamad, S.E. & Mohamed, I., 2012, *MyBI: A business intelligence application development framework for Malaysian Public Sector*, IEEE, Langkawi, Kedah, Malaysia, pp. 115–118.

Murugan, A., Magid, I. & Uzoamaka, P.A., 2000, 'A perspective from a less developed country', *Information Technology & People* 13, 298–312.

Nelson, R.R., Todd, P.A. & Wixom, B.H., 2005, 'Antecedents of information and system quality: An empirical examination within the context of data warehousing', *Journal of Management Information System* 21(4), 199–235.

Nkuna, D., 2011, 'Business intelligence usage determinants', Master thesis, University of Witwatersrand, Johanesburg.

Olszak, C. & Batko, K., 2012, *The use of business intelligence systems in healthcare organizations in Poland*, IEEE, Wrocław, pp. 969–976.

Parasuraman, A., Zeithaml, V.A. & Berry, L.L., 1988, 'SERVQUAL: A multiitem scale for measuring consumer perceptions of the service quality', *Journal of Retailing* 64, 12–40.

Petter, S., DeLone, W. & McLean, E., 2008, 'Measuring information systems success: Models, dimensions, measures, and interrelationships', *European Journal of Information Systems* 17, 236–263. https://doi.org/10.1057/ejis.2008.15

Petrini, M. & Pozzebon, M., 2009, 'Managing sustainability with the support of business intelligence: Integrating socio-environmental, indicators and organizational context', *Journal of Strategic Information Systems* 18, 178–191. https://doi.org/10.1016/j.jsis.2009.06.001

Pitt, L., Watson, R. & Kavan, C., 1995, 'Service quality: A measure of information systems effectiveness', *MIS Quarterly* 19(2), 173–185. https://doi.org/10.2307/249687

Ponelis, S. & Britz, J., 2011, *An exploratory study of business intelligence in knowledge-based South African SMEs*, viewed 07 October 2015, from www.globdev.org/files/AMCIS%20Proceedings%202011/Paper%201.pdf

Ponniah, P., 2010, *Data warehousing fundamentals for IT professionals*, John Wiley, Hoboken, NJ.

Rudra, A. & Yeo, E., 1999, 'Key issues in achieving data quality and consistency in data warehousing among large organisations in Australia, HICSS-32', paper presented at Hawaii International Conference on System Sciences, January, Maui, Hawaii.

Seddon, P.B., 1997, 'A respecification and extension of the DeLone and McLean model of IS success', *Information Systems Research* 8, 240–253. https://doi.org/10.1287/isre.8.3.240

Seddon, P.B. & Kiew, M.Y., 1996, 'A partial test and development of DeLone and McLean's model of IS success', *Australian Journal of Information Systems* 4(1), 90–109.

Shin, B., 2003, 'An exploratory investigation of system success factors in data warehousing', *Journal of the Association for Information Systems* 4, 141–170.

Smart, W.J., 2009, *Information system success: Evaluation of a carbon accounting and sequestration system*, ePublications@SCU, Lismore.

Thomann, J. & Wells, D., 1999, 'Data warehouse quality management', paper presented at the Data Warehousing Institute's Fourth Annual Implementation Conference, 14–19 February, Anaheim, CA.

Trninic, J., Durkovic, J. & Rakovic, L., 2011, 'Business intelligence as support to knowledge management', *Perspectives of Innovations, Economics and Busines* 8, 35–40.

Turban, E., Sharda, R., Delen, D. & King, D., 2011a, *Business intelligence: A managerial approach*, 2nd edn., Prentice Hall, Upper Saddle River, NJ.

Turban, E., Sharda, R., Dursun, D. & King, D., 2011b, *Business intelligence*, 9th edn., Prentice Hall, New York.

Wixom, B.H. & Watson, H.J., 2001, 'An empirical investigation of the factors affecting data warehousing success', *MIS Quarterly* 25(1), 17–41. https://doi.org/10.2307/3250957

Wu, J.H. & Wang, Y.M., 2006, 'Measuring KMS success: A respecification of the DeLone and McLean model', *Information and Management* 43(6), 728–739. https://doi.org/10.1016/j.im.2006.05.002

Yamane, T., 1967, *Statistics: An introductory analysis*, 2nd edn., Harper and Row, New York.

YellowFin, 2012, *Majority of business intelligence implementations fail*, viewed 28 August 2013, from http://www.yellowfinbi.com/YFCommunityNews-Majority-of-Business-Intelligence-implementations-fail-115614

Yeoh, W. & Koronios, A., 2010, 'Critical success factors for business intelligence systems', *Journal of Computer Information Systems* 50, 23–32.

Zhu, K. & Kraemer, K.L., 2005, 'Post-adoption variations in usage and value of e-business by organizations: Cross-country evidence from the retail industry', *Information Systems Research* 16(1), 61–84. https://doi.org/10.1287/isre.1050.0045

10

Evaluating the influence of information and communications technology on food security

Authors:
Ntabeni J. Jere[1]
Manoj S. Maharaj[1]

Affiliation:
[1]School of Management, IT and Governance, University of KwaZulu-Natal, South Africa

Corresponding author:
Ntabeni Jere,
jeren@ukzn.ac.za

Background: This study integrates the diffusion of innovation, technology acceptance model and Hofstede's cultural dimensions theory to assess the role that information and communications technology (ICT) plays in ensuring food security. A survey of smallholder farmers from the iLembe district municipality of the KwaZulu-Natal Province of South Africa was conducted, and the data were used to test the proposed model.

Objectives: The study evaluates the influence of ICTs in improving food security in KwaZulu-Natal Province. A theoretical framework was developed as the lens through which diffusion and adoption of ICTs can be understood. The theorised model was developed using constructs from the diffusion of innovation (DOI) theory, technology acceptance model (TAM) and Hofstede's cultural dimensions theory.

Method: Survey data from 517 smallholder farmers from the district municipality of iLembe were collected using a questionnaire. A quantitative approach was followed, and the developed theorised model was analysed using structural equation modelling techniques.

Results: This study proposes that ICT influence on food security is associated with culture, perceived usefulness and perceived ease of use. The study further finds that perceived ease of use of ICTs has the most significant effect with regard to ICT adoption and diffusion amongst smallholder farmers in iLembe district municipality. There are, however, no associations found with perceived attributes of innovation and the nature of social systems. The study consisted of a largely homogeneous social system; therefore, the researcher could not make any comparisons.

Conclusion: The proposed framework for evaluating the influence of ICTs on food security put forward in this study highlights a number of issues. Firstly, there is need for further study to be conducted to understand adoption of ICTs specifically for food security. This would help in creating more accurate adoption strategies. Secondly, the study informs ICT innovation developers on the need to prioritise ease of use of ICT-based interventions when developing innovations that focus on smallholder farmers. The study also contributes to policy guidelines and suggests clear guidelines be developed to address cultural aspects such as gender imbalances.

Introduction

The instability, both socially and politically, in North Africa and the Middle East in 2008 and 2011 has, in part, been attributed to poverty, unemployment and other social inequalities. These sparks of unrest also coincided with large peaks in food prices globally (Lagi, Bertrand & Bar-Yam 2011), leading to food insecurity. The population globally is projected to exceed 9 billion by the year 2050 (United Nations 2012); this situation is very concerning, and measures to increase food security are being encouraged. Information and communications technologies (ICTs) that include mobile phones, radio, TV, computers and satellite systems have been identified as a potential contributor to achieving global food security (Bowman, Mensah & Urama 2014).

Food security is a state that exists at household or community level when poverty has been eliminated. The inverse of this state is referred to as food insecurity, and it is closely associated with poverty and lack of access to good nutritious food (Cousins 2010; De Klerk et al. 2004; May & Woolard 2007). Other attributes that are associated with food insecurity are unemployment and illiteracy (Duveskog, Friis-Hansen & Taylor 2011). In South Africa, 40% of its 50 million population live in rural areas (National Planning Commission 2012) and are largely dependent on smallholder farming to provide a means of livelihood, either through employment or through provision of food. As far back as the 1960s, the benefits and potential of smallholder farmers have been argued not only in reducing food insecurity but also in contributing to production (Schultz 1964). These farmers, therefore, need to be supported and developed (Aliber & Hart 2009) as this would directly improve food security at a household level. One of the challenges smallholder farmers face in their practice is the lack of timely and accurate information. These challenges could be addressed through the implementation (and effective utilisation) of suitable ICTs (Davis, Babu & Blom 2014).

Adejo and Haruna (2009) categorise ICTs as conventional (radio, television) and contemporary (telephones, computer or Internet). In South Africa, the Census 2011 Municipal report (StatsSA 2012) shows a decline in the number of households owning radios or landlines and an increase in the number of households owning televisions, computers and mobile phones. Mobile phone penetration has grown by 63.3% between 2001 and 2011. This growth is mirrored by rural populations (Aker & Mbiti 2010). This presents an opportunity for the provision of services through mobile applications in various sectors including agriculture (Somers & Stapleton 2014). ICT application in agriculture has the potential to improve the farmers' work environment, thus increasing profitability, productivity and efficiency. This in turn impacts positively on food security.

ICTs are recognised globally as a key driver of social economic growth (Adu, Adelabu & Adjogri 2014; Chourabi et al. 2012; Musingafi & Zebron 2014) such that the United Nations included ICT use for information dissemination as part of the millennium development goals to be attained by 2015 for all its member states (United Nations 2010). However, this potential has not been realised in the agricultural sector in sub-Saharan Africa (Kelsey 2011; Kiplang'at 1999; Udry 2010).

There is limited research on the adoption and diffusion of ICTs by smallholder farmers in South Africa. In this article, we present a model that will guide the implementation of ICT by smallholder farmers to address the issue of food security. The article presents these findings to the research objective: To explore the adoption of ICTs by smallholder farmers and their role on influencing food security in KwaZulu-Natal.

Theoretical models on information and communications technology adoption and diffusion

This article evaluates the influence of ICTs in improving food security in KwaZulu-Natal Province. A theoretical framework was developed as the lens through which diffusion and adoption of ICTs can be understood. The theorised model was developed using constructs from the diffusion of innovation (DOI) theory, technology acceptance model (TAM) and Hofstede's cultural dimensions theory.

Diffusion of innovation

Rogers' DOI theory is widely used in information systems (IS) research with over 4000 publications on this topic (Rogers 2010). The DOI theory consists of four key components: innovation, communications channels, time and a social system.

Innovation

As defined earlier, an innovation is 'an idea, practice or project that is perceived as new by an individual or other unit of adoption' (Rogers 2003). The innovation release date is not relevant to the adopter of that innovation for as long as they perceive that innovation to be new to them, then they will still consider it an innovation.

Communication channels

Rogers (2003) defines a communication channel as 'a process in which participants create and share information with one another in order to reach a mutual understanding'. A channel is a media type through which a message is transmitted to the designated recipient.

Time

Rogers (2003) identifies the time element in the innovation diffusion process to be an important factor. The adopter classification and the rate of adoption both use the time element. The rate of adoption and the innovation-decision process all make use of the time element.

Social system

Rogers (2003) states a social system as being 'a set of interrelated units engaged in joint problem solving to accomplish a common goal'. Due to the fact that innovation diffusion takes place within a social system, the nature of that social system impacts on individual's innovativeness.

This study used Roger's DOI theory because this theoretical framework has frequently been reviewed to take into account the changing societies we live in including the various cultural differences that exist in them (Rogers 1995, 2003, 2010). This theory is the most established diffusion theory and more encompassing in terms of the variables it addresses unlike most other technology diffusion models (Bagchi & Udo 2007; Venkatesh et al. 2003), thereby providing a more comprehensive understanding of diffusion of technology. It provides an added advantage in that it is widely used in IS research (Kapoor, Dwivedi & Williams 2014). DOI is applicable at both micro level of social systems (individual level) and its relevance at the macro level (organisational level). Sharif, Troshani and Davidson (2014) offer the theory's simplicity as an advantage.

Technology acceptance model

The TAM is also widely employed in IS research and was selected to complement the DOI theory. TAM consists of imbedded aspects of behavioural intentions; this is due to the fact that the TAM theory originates from the theory of reasoned action which was modified in the TAM theory although now specifically towards IS.

It was included in this study to provide insight on how ICT adoption and diffusion amongst smallholder farmers in KwaZulu-Natal may be improved. TAM may also be used to explain an individual's behaviour regarding a wide range of technologies (Davis 1989). TAM is applied at an individual level and is based on the argument that individuals use technology for personal achievements, that is, improving your personal effectiveness, increasing work output by the individual and enhancing the decision-making process.

Hofstede's cultural dimensions

Hofstede (1980) states that 'the collective mental programming of the people in an environment' is referred to as culture. The author goes further to say 'culture refers to the collective mental programming that these people have in common, the programming that is different from other groups'. Hofstede's cultural dimensions are used extensively in studies to determine the influence of culture on values (Hofstede 1980). Hofstede's research on IBM employees from over 70 countries gave rise to his definition of culture being a conditioning of behaviours of a group to be similar with one another but can be differentiated from other groups (Hofstede 2001). Hofstede identifies five cultural dimensions that are discussed subsequently.

Power distance

This refers to the extent to which a society gives credence to the fact that there is an unequal distribution in power within an organisation, that is, the distribution of power between people in authority and their subordinates and also between various organisations (Hofstede 1980).

Uncertainty avoidance

Hofstede (1980) states that uncertainty avoidance refers to the 'extent to which a society feels threatened' by unclear and inexplicit situations.

Individualism versus collectivism

The individualism versus collectivism dimension refers to the extent to which individuals are integrated into a society or an organisation.

Masculinity versus femininity

The masculinity versus femininity dimension focuses on gender and the characteristics that are generally attributed to either masculinity or femininity.

Long-term versus short-term orientation

The long-term versus short-term orientation dimension is an extension to Hofstede's original model and was originally referred to as 'Confucian dynamism'. This dimension refers to individuals and societies focus using the time factor as the main determinant (now or future oriented) of how effort should be applied to tasks and the importance an individual applies towards tradition.

Constructs from DOI and TAM represented technological and social factors, whereas constructs from Hofstede's cultural dimensions represented cultural factors associated with adoption of ICTs amongst smallholder farmers and their relationship with agricultural extension officers.

A criticism of diffusion models such as the DOI and TAM is that they do not take into account external influences such as organisational or environmental factors (Bagchi 2001; Lee & Cheung 2004). Studies have shown the need to understand other factors such as social–cultural and organisational factors together with technological factors (Bakkabulindi, Nkata & Amin 2008; Damanpour & Schneider 2009) in order to more holistically understand innovation diffusion research. This shortcoming was addressed by the inclusion of Hofstede's cultural dimensions theory that provided an added perspective of understanding the influence that culture has on the ICT innovation adoption process by smallholder farmers. Figure 1 illustrates how the constructs of the three theories were used in this study.

Materials and methodology

The study adopted a quantitative approach. The study population was identified through formal structures in the municipality, in particular in conjunction with organisations in the municipality such as Enterprise iLembe and the Economic Development Agency for the iLembe district municipality. A population of 1008 smallholder farmers was identified. Taking into consideration the design effect (Kish 1965) which refers to an approximation of the extent to which this supposition is violated with a contingency of 5%, a sample of 517 smallholder farmers were surveyed.

The survey instrument was developed with insights from IT experts, experts from the School of Agriculture/Food Security Center at the University of KwaZulu-Natal and experts from the government department of agriculture head office in Cedara (strategic support services which is the unit that is involved in training of extension officers and the food security unit in the government department of agriculture). The smallholder questionnaire was translated into IsiZulu,

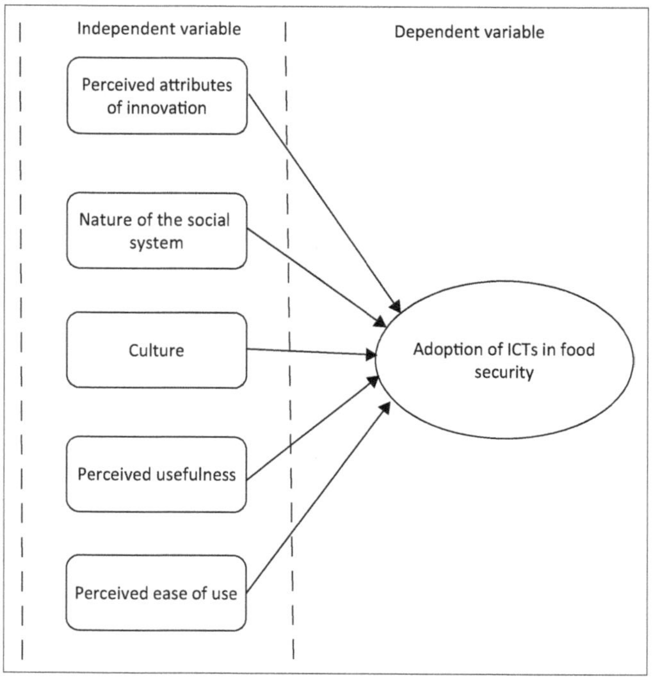

FIGURE 1: Theorised model.

the local language of the research area. Research assistants were trained to administer the questionnaire.

Structural equation modelling (SEM) was the method of analysis employed in this study. This technique is mostly confirmatory by nature rather than being of an exploratory nature (Byrne 2013, 2016; O'Rourke & Hatcher 2013). It is for this reason that the technique was most suitable as it assists to determine the validity of a model rather than the most suitable one. The ability to use multiple measures in association with a single latent construct also made the choice of using the SEM technique attractive in this study.

The results of the Cronbach's alpha reliability (Tavakol & Dennick 2011) are presented in Table 1 which demonstrate good instrument reliability (above the recommended value of 0.7).

Findings and discussions

Based on the quantitative data collected via a survey questionnaire, the validity of the theorised model (Figure 1) was tested using SEM and hence served more as a confirmatory analysis.

The model then required to be interpreted and the impact of each variable analysed using path analysis. The results of each path are then presented graphically and in table format. During the SEM analysis, it was of importance to analyse the 'fit' of the theorised model as this would help provide an understanding of how well it models the data. It is based on this fit that the theorised model will be accepted or rejected.

Chi-square, root mean square error of approximation (RMSEA), relative fit index (RFI) and incremental fit index (IFI) are the various goodness of fit indices that are produced as AMOS outputs (Byrne 2013). The interrelated nature and similarity of conclusion by these various indices relate to goodness of fit of the model to data provided.

The concept of goodness of fit relates to how well the data fits the model. According to Byrne (2013), an indication of good model fit is when the RFI is ≥0.95 and the RMSEA value is below 0.05 with a p-value above 0.05. Lei and Wu (2007) concur with these findings and suggest an RMSEA value of ≤0.06 as an indication of good model fit. IFI is not impacted by sample size and a good fitting model based on IFI indices are values in the range of 0.95 (Byrne 2013; Newsom 2012).

An analysis using SEM revealed that the theorised model did not fit the data well because of a significant chi-square test statistic, that is, $\chi^2 = 524.695$ and $p = 0.000$. Modifications were then made to the theorised model and a revised model (Figure 2) proposed in order to get a good fit to the data. The revised model and its implications to the existing theories are then discussed in relation to the initial proposed model.

TABLE 1: Results of Cronbach's alpha reliability analysis: Farmer questionnaire.

Questions	Similarity of scale	Cronbach's alpha
12, 14, 18, 29, 31, 35 and 37	Very small extent to very large extent	0.764
11, 13, 25–28	Strongly disagree to strongly agree	0.73
21 and 24	More than once per day to never	0.749

The model was analysed in AMOS (version 21) and the results are given in Figure 3.

The variables of culture, perceived usefulness and perceived ease of use were all significant in their influence of the role of ICTs in food security with p-values all less than 0.05 (Table 2).

The initial model produced a chi-square test result of 3.423 and had a p-value of 0.133. These initial results are considered to be non-significant at the 5% level and based on this the SEM indicated that the theorised model does not fit the data well. The revised model, on the contrary, using the SEM technique was considered to have been a good fit for the data (Bollen 2014; Byrne 2013). The produced results for the revised model revealed the following indices: the RFI was 0.971, and the RMSEA was 0.008 with a p-value of 0.899. In addition to this, the IFI result was 0.959. The resulting indices all confirmed a good fit of the revised model to the data.

The results reveal the following

Perceived ease of use has the most significant influence on the role of ICT in food security. The most significant variable

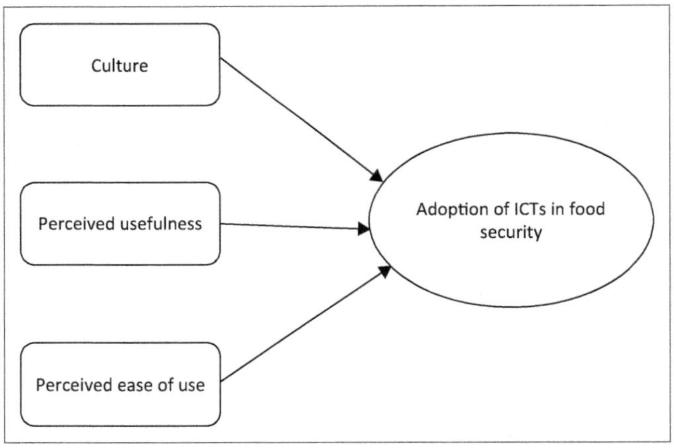

FIGURE 2: Revised model.

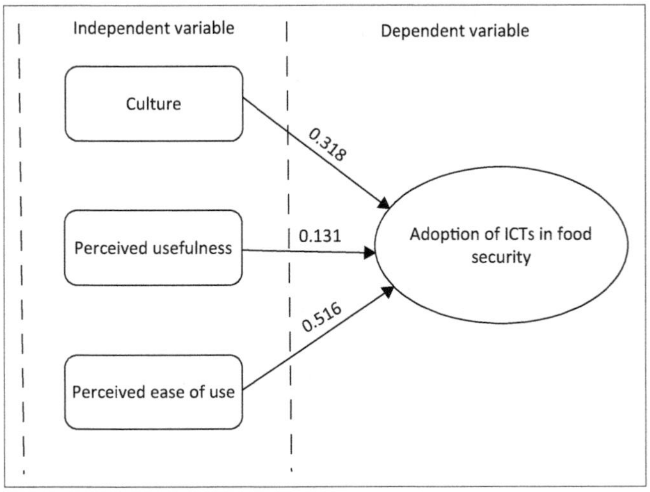

FIGURE 3: Revised model showing weights.

TABLE 2: Regression weights.

Dependent variable	Path	Independent variables	Estimate	S.E.	C.R.	*p*
Role of ICTs	<---	Culture	0.318	0.074	4.310	0.000
Role of ICTs	<---	Perceived usefulness	0.131	0.043	3.060	0.002
Role of ICTs	<---	Perceived ease of use	0.516	0.042	12.405	0.000

S.E., standard error; ICTs, information and communications technologies; C.R., critical ratio.

in the revised model originates from the TAM put forward by Davis (1989). Perceived ease of use is one of two variables (the second being perceived usefulness). The results of the analysis reveal that much as both constructs from TAM are important and significantly impact ICT adoption for food security, perceived ease of use is of more importance. This result is in line with findings in studies such as that of Van Der Heijden (2004). Based on the results, the smallholder farmers might find perceived ease of use, to be the most important construct in ICT adoption for food security due to the tasks that the ICTs are used for (Gefen & Straub 2000). Literacy levels also play a role in creating complexity and hence the easier it is to use an ICT the more useful the farmers will find that technology, this is the position held by authors such as Venkatesh (2000). It is therefore understandable that smallholder farmers might find the aspect of how easy it is to use an ICT of most importance rather than its utility. ICT developers and marketers need to always consider the ease of using the technology when attempting to deploy technology amongst smallholder farmers.

Perceived usefulness also significantly impacts the role of ICT in food security. It is evident that perceived usefulness of ICTs in food security is an important construct in understanding ICT adoption in food security by smallholder farmers. The findings of this study revealed that much as perceived usefulness might have a lesser significance to that of perceived ease of use specifically amongst smallholder farmers, it is the second most significant determinant to ICT adoption in food security amongst farmers. Van Der Heijden (2004) expounds that for utilitarian IS, which is IS that are focused on improving performance, perceived usefulness is the most important construct. The inclusion of ICTs in food security is an attempt at using all available technologies and methods to create food secure communities. It is therefore important to recognise the importance of the perceived usefulness of an ICT innovation. When developing ICT innovations for farmers in food security, these systems should include a strong focus on improving farmer performance, as this is their primary goal in being included in the food security field. It is also important to note that no amount of ease of use of a technology will replace the level of usefulness of that technology (Keil, Beranek & Konsynski 1995).

Culture is one of the important predictors of ICT adoption and diffusion amongst smallholder farmers, and this has a significant positive effect on ICT influence on food security. The results reveal that for technology adoption amongst smallholder farmers to be successful, the construct of culture has to be taken into consideration (Hofstede 1980). As the technology diffusion is amongst people, aspects such as the interactions between smallholder farmers and other stakeholders such as extension officers need to be taken into consideration. The extent to which these various stakeholders assist the smallholder farmers in decision-making for farming processes is also important. It is through understanding these cultural norms and interactions that successful ICT innovation implementation can take place.

The nature of the social system and perceived attributes of innovation have no significant direct impact on ICT influence in food security.

Proposed future work

The proposed theoretical model that was developed based on the literature review that was conducted and later revised based on the findings lends itself to testing in different similar environments (rural communities) and is open to further advancements. Further analysis on the relationships between the measured variables could improve the model and provide insights to the relationships that exist. A suggestion would be to test specific ICTs individually as this may provide a better focus in the survey instrument and the results that follow. Further research is also proposed in shedding more light on the above findings.

Conclusion

With food security having gained global attention and its inclusion as one of the sustainable development goals (SDGs), the idea of harnessing the potential benefits of ICTs in food security is gaining ground. It is thought that farmers in their farming practices can utilise the benefits that ICTs bring to improve their production and distribution processes. Based on the potential benefits of ICTs in food security, it is important to understand ICT adoption and its influence on food security. The broad nature of ICTs is somewhat problematic when it comes to identifying adoption and diffusion variables. Van Der Heijden (2004) addresses this issue by classifying IS as being utilitarian or hedonic in nature to help better understand user adoption of technology. It is found that in hedonic systems, the perceived ease of use is the predominant variable in determining the adoption of a technology unlike in utilitarian systems where perceived usefulness is the predominant variable. Various literatures have identified perceived ease of use and perceived usefulness as being critical variables in understanding user technology adoption.

This study proposes a framework for evaluating the influence of ICTs on food security. The resulting findings in this study support existing literature identifying perceived usefulness and perceived ease of use as key variables in understanding user adoption of technology. General technology adoption literature identifies perceived usefulness as the primary variable used in the understanding of technology adoption and perceived ease of use as the secondary support variable. Despite this general trend, this study finds that perceived ease of use of ICTs has the most important effect with regard to ICT adoption and diffusion amongst smallholder farmers in iLembe district municipality having a weighting of over 50%. In this study, perceived usefulness is the second most important variable in understanding technology adoption amongst smallholder farmers. The study also finds that technology adoption does not just involve the perceptions of the technology but that attention should also be placed on the cultural aspects that exist in that social system and the interactions between the various key role players such as extension officers. The study also showed that perceived attributes of innovation and nature of the social system does not have a significant impact on its influence on ICT adoption and diffusion amongst farmers.

The results of this study call for a number of recommendations. Further study should be done to better understand adoption of specific ICTs for food security. This will avoid generalisation and a more accurate adoption strategy to be created for smallholder farmers. ICT innovation developers should consider the findings of this study and prioritise the ease of use of ICT-based interventions when dealing with smallholder farmers. Clear policy guidelines should also be set out that address cultural aspects such as gender imbalances, reducing bureaucracy to create clear channels of communication between smallholder farmers and other stakeholders.

Acknowledgements

Competing interests

The authors declare that they have no financial or personal relationship(s) that may have inappropriately influenced them in writing this article.

Authors' contributions

N.J.J. was the project leader and M.S.M. was responsible for conceptual contributions and proofing.

References

Adejo, P. & Haruna, U., 2009, 'Access of farmers to ICTs for agricultural development in Bauchi local government area, Bauchi state', in *Proceedings of the 43rd Annual Conference of the Agricultural Society of Nigeria*, Abuja, October 20–23, 2009, pp. 704–707.

Adu, E.O., Adelabu, O. & Adjogri, S.J., 2014, 'Information and Communication Technology (ICT): The implications for sustainable development in Nigeria', in *World Conference on Educational Multimedia, Hypermedia and Telecommunications*, Tampere, Finland, June 23, 2014, pp. 50–58.

Aker, J.C. & Mbiti, I.M., 2010, 'Mobile phones and economic development in Africa', *The Journal of Economic Perspectives* 24, 207–232. https://doi.org/10.1257/jep.24.3.207

Aliber, M. & Hart, T.G., 2009, 'Should subsistence agriculture be supported as a strategy to address rural food insecurity?', *Agrekon* 48, 434–458. https://doi.org/10.1080/03031853.2009.9523835

Bagchi, K., 2001. 'The impact of national culture and other national-level indicators on information technology (IT) diffusion', PhD dissertation, Florida Atlantic University.

Bagchi, K. & Udo, G., 2007, 'Empirically testing factors that drive ICT adoption in Africa and OECD set of nations', *Issues in Information Systems* 8, 45–52.

Bakkabulindi, F., Nkata, J. & Amin, M.E., 2008, 'Organizational characteristics as correlates of ICT adoption in Makerere University', *Kampala International University Research Digest* 1, 124–137.

Bollen, K.A., 2014, *Structural equations with latent variables*, Wiley, Hoboken, NJ.

Bowman, W., Mensah, M. & Urama, K., 2014, 'Information and telecommunication technologies in Africa: A potential Revolution?', *Innovation for Sustainable Development* 6, 45–50.

Byrne, B.M., 2013, *Structural equation modeling with AMOS: Basic concepts, applications, and programming*, Routledge, Abingdon.

Byrne, B.M., 2016, *Structural equation modeling with AMOS: Basic concepts, applications, and programming*, Routledge, Abingdon.

Chourabi, H., Nam, T., Walker, S., Gil-Garcia, J.R., Mellouli, S., Nahon, K., 2012, 'Understanding smart cities: An integrative framework', in *2012 45th Hawaii International Conference on System Science (HICSS)*, Maui, HI, January 4–7, IEEE, pp. 2289–2297.

Cousins, B., 2010, *What is a 'smallholder'?* PLAAS, University of the Western Cape, Cape Town, Working Paper, 16.

Damanpour, F. & Schneider, M., 2009, 'Characteristics of innovation and innovation adoption in public organizations: Assessing the role of managers', *Journal of Public Administration Research and Theory* 19, 495–522.

Davis, K., 1989, 'Perceived usefulness, perceived ease of use and acceptance of information technology', *MIS Quarterly* 13, 319–340.

Davis, K., Babu, S.C. & Blom, S., 2014, *The role of extension and advisory services in building resilience of smallholder farmers*, International Food Policy Research Institute, Washington, DC.

De Klerk, M., Drimie, S., Aliber, M., Mini, S., Mokoena, R., Randela, R., 2004, *Food security in South Africa: Key policy issues for the medium term*, Human Sciences Research Council Integrated Rural and Regional Development Position Paper, Human Sciences Research Council, Pretoria.

Duveskog, D., Friis-Hansen, E. & Taylor, E.W., 2011, 'Farmer field schools in rural Kenya: A transformative learning experience', *The Journal of Development Studies* 47, 1529–1544. https://doi.org/10.1080/00220388.2011.561328

Gefen, D. & Straub, D.W., 2000, 'The relative importance of perceived ease of use in IS adoption: A study of e-commerce adoption', *Journal of the Association for Information Systems* 1, 8.

Hofstede, G. (ed.), 1980, *Culture's consequences*, Sage, Newbury Park, CA.

Hofstede, G., 2001, 'Identifying organizational subcultures: An empirical approach', *Journal of Management Studies* 35, 1–12.

Kapoor, K.K., Dwivedi, Y.K. & Williams, M.D., 2014, 'Rogers' innovation adoption attributes: A systematic review and synthesis of existing research', *Information Systems Management* 31(1), 74–91. https://doi.org/10.1080/10580530.2014.854103

Keil, M., Beranek, P.M. & Konsynski, B.R., 1995, 'Usefulness and ease of use: Field study evidence regarding task considerations', *Decision Support Systems* 13, 75–91. https://doi.org/10.1016/0167-9236(94)E0032-M

Kelsey, J., 2011, *Market inefficiencies and the adoption of agricultural technologies in developing countries*, White Paper, Agricultural Technology Adoption Initiative, Abdul Latif Jameel Poverty Action Lab, MIT, Cambridge, MA.

Kiplang'at, J., 1999, 'An analysis of the opportunities for information technology in improving access, transfer and the use of agricultural information in the rural areas of Kenya', *Library Management* 20, 115–128.

Kish, L., 1965, *Survey sampling*, Wiley, New York.

Lagi, M., Bertrand, K.Z. & Bar-Yam, Y., 2011, 'The food crises and political instability in North Africa and the Middle East', arXiv preprint arXiv:1108.2455.

Lee, S. & Cheung, C., 2004, 'Internet retailing adoption by small-to-medium sized enterprises (SMEs): A multiple-case study', *Information Systems Frontiers* 6, 385–397. https://doi.org/10.1023/B:ISFI.0000046379.58029.54

Lei, P.W. & Wu, Q., 2007, 'Introduction to structural equation modeling: Issues and practical considerations', *Educational Measurement: Issues and Practice* 26, 33–43. https://doi.org/10.1111/j.1745-3992.2007.00099.x

May, J. & Woolard, I., 2007, *Poverty traps and structural poverty in South Africa: Reassessing the evidence from KwaZulu-Natal*, Chronic Poverty Research Centre, Manchester, Working Paper 82.

Musingafi, M.C. & Zebron, S., 2014, 'The role of information and communication technology in rural socio-economic development in Africa', *International Journal of Public Policy and Administration Research* 1, 38–46.

National Planning Commission, 2012, *National Development Plan 2030: Our Future – Make It Work*, Government of South Africa, Pretoria.

Newsom, J., 2012, 'Some clarifications and recommendations on fit indices', *USP* 655, 123–133.

O'rourke, N. & Hatcher, L., 2013, *A step-by-step approach to using SAS for factor analysis and structural equation modeling*, Sas Institute, Cary, NC.

Rogers, E.M., 1995, *Diffusion of innovations*, Collier Macmillan, New York.

Rogers, E.M., 2003, *Diffusion of Innovations*, Free Press, New York.

Rogers, E.M. (ed.), 2010, *Diffusion of innovations*, Simon and Schuster, New York, NY.

Schultz, T.W., 1964, *Transforming traditional agriculture*, Yale University Press, New Haven, CT.

Sharif, M.H.M., Troshani, I. & Davidson, R., 2014, 'Adoption of social media services: The case of local government', in Z. Sun & J. Yearwood (eds.), *Handbook of research on Demand-Driven Web Services: Theory, technologies, and applications*, pp. 287–303, IGI Global, Hershey, PA.

Somers, S. & Stapleton, L., 2014, 'e-Agricultural innovation using a human-centred systems lens, proposed conceptual framework', *AI & Society* 29, 193–202. https://doi.org/10.1007/s00146-013-0475-x

StatsSA, 2012, *Census 2011 Municipal report KwaZulu-Natal*, Statistics South Africa, Pretoria.

Tavakol, M. & Dennick, R., 2011, 'Making sense of Cronbach's alpha', *International Journal of Medical Education* 2, 53. https://doi.org/10.5116/ijme.4dfb.8dfd

Udry, C., 2010, 'The economics of agriculture in Africa: Notes toward a research program', *African Journal of Agricultural and Resource Economics* 5, 284–299.

United Nations, 2010, *We can end poverty 2015 millenium development goals*, viewed 18 July 2014, from http://www.un.org/millenniumgoals/

United Nations, 2012, *World Agriculture towards 2030/2050: The 2012 Revision*, Food and Agriculture Organization of the United Nations, Rome, Italy.

Van Der Heijden, H., 2004, 'User acceptance of hedonic information systems', *MIS Quarterly* 28(4), 695–704.

Venkatesh, V., 2000, 'Determinants of perceived ease of use: Integrating control, intrinsic motivation, and emotion into the technology acceptance model', *Information Systems Research* 11, 342–365. https://doi.org/10.1287/isre.11.4.342.11872

Venkatesh, V., Morris, M., Davis, G. & Davis, F., 2003, 'User acceptance of information technology: Toward a unified view', *MIS Quarterly* 27, 425–478.

11

Information and communication technologies for knowledge management in academic libraries in Nigeria and South Africa

Authors:
Rexwhite T. Enakrire[1]
Dennis N. Ocholla[1]

Affiliations:
[1]Department of Information Studies, University of Zululand, South Africa

Corresponding author:
Rexwhite Enakrire,
enakrire@yahoo.com

Background: Presently, libraries, especially academic libraries, have increasingly used information and communication technologies (ICTs) to automate their core functions in order to implement efficient and effective library operations and services. This now requires library and information professionals as knowledge workers to intensify managing both explicit and tacit knowledge for the organisational growth of the libraries.

Objectives: The objective of this study was to investigate the use of ICT facilities that support knowledge management (KM) in academic libraries in Nigeria and South Africa.

Methods: Both quantitative through survey and structured questionnaires and qualitative by content analysis and interview research methodologies were applied in the initial study. The qualitative approach of content analysis was applied to literature review, and key informants were also interviewed. One hundred and thirty-two professional librarians and six key informants across the sampled academic libraries in the two countries were targeted for information. The study sampled only six academic libraries, three in each country, which renders generalisation difficult. This article largely focuses on quantitative aspects of the study in the reported findings.

Results: Availability and accessibility of ICTs for KM among the sampled libraries were not uniform, even within one country. Infrastructural support has affected some of the university libraries to a great extent. The knowledge and skills for using ICT for KM were largely adequate, but varied within the libraries and librarians as well. The challenges facing the libraries border on inadequate infrastructure and professional staff, but irrespective of the challenges faced, libraries have devised strategies for coping and rendering services. The study has provided new information relating to the use of ICT facilities and services for KM in academic libraries that calls for rigorous continuing education for re-skilling the librarians. The changing user behaviour also calls for major attention. Government support for academic libraries with policy and funding is still crucial.

Conclusion and recommendation: The study concludes that because ICTs have had robust histories as used to support information services, both staff and students' information needs to be met in a variety of ways in academic libraries. This would help to foster and improve the understanding of how librarians manage the organisation in present-day library operations. We recommend that staff development be intensified to enable how librarians could cope with changes and new technologies for modern information services being encouraged and acquired. This article provides a unique long-term survey on the use of ICT facilities and services, strategy and structure in an academic and/or university library services.

Introduction and conceptual background

The purpose of university libraries is to support research, teaching and learning in universities. Information and communication technologies (ICTs) play a crucial role in the development of academic libraries. ICT has been defined as a diverse set of technological tools and resources that can be used to communicate, create, disseminate, store and manage information and knowledge in the global context (Blurton 1999:46). Also, UNESCO (2002) acknowledges that ICTs consist of a range of technologies that are applied in the process of collecting, storing, editing, retrieving and transferring information in various forms. They comprise both old and new technologies such as telecommunication technologies comprising telephony, cable, satellite, television, radio, computer-mediated conferencing and video conferencing; digital technologies such as computers, information networks, Internet, World Wide Web, intranets and extranets; and software applications (Anunobi et al. 2011; Ofori-Dwumfuo & Kommey 2013:92).

Libraries, especially academic libraries, are increasingly using ICTs to access digitalised information. This became feasible through automated core functions of library operations and services. The efficiency and effectiveness of the core functions result in implementation of laid down policy that guides the academic library. Increasingly, library and information professionals are now being referred to as 'knowledge managers' and libraries and information centres as 'knowledge centres' (Rowley 2003) as they handle both explicit and tacit knowledge. Explicit knowledge is the human knowledge that has been captured orally (e.g. in song), in writing (documents or books), and in movies and images, among others (Dalkir 2011:9). This type of knowledge is easy to interpret, represent and share among individuals for effective application (Evangelista et al. 2010). Knowledge that is tied to the senses (e.g. tactile experiences, movement, skills, intuition and unarticulated mental models) or implicit rules of thumb can be defined as 'tacit' knowledge (Nonaka & Krogh 2009). Tacit knowledge is rooted in action, procedures, routines, commitment, ideals, values and emotions (Nonaka, Umemoto & Senoo 1996). Tacit knowledge is difficult to express, represent and communicate. It can be described as personal knowledge that is embedded within the individual, representing his or her experiences and involving intangible factors such as personal beliefs, perspectives, instincts and values (Nonaka 1994; Nonaka, Ichijo & Von Krogh 2004). We assume that when the differences between explicit and tacit knowledge are known, it is possible for an academic library and librarians to strategize its full exploitation. The principal challenge faced in handling tacit knowledge is still that of translating the knowledge into communicable form (Minonne 2007).

Knowledge management (KM) is largely viewed to be the management of explicit and tacit knowledge (Skyrme 1997) whose components include people, processes and technology, all of which occur in the library environment. KM has benefited from ICT application, as libraries have largely managed explicit knowledge for centuries. Despite its historical application in libraries, KM is still viewed to be an emerging discipline drawn from a broad range of established disciplines such as organisational learning, networking, intellectual capital, social construction, communities of practice and social interaction (Beesley & Cooper 2008).

The relevance of ICTs for KM cannot be downplayed in today's knowledge economy. The essence of this assertion is that, prior to the advent of ICTs, the management of knowledge, either the explicit or the tacit, has been hampered by several reasons: (1) the slow nature of the acquisition and processing, (2) storage and retrieval mechanism used, (3) librarians fatigue as a result of many volume of work, and (4) unwillingness or drive because of lack of motivation by the organisation. Therefore, for the utilisation of ICTs for KM to be actualised, strategies of management techniques must be in place in order to foster knowledge creation or acquisition, processing, repackaging, storage, retrieval and dissemination in academic libraries. This would enforce the adoption and application of ICTs used in the library organisation. According to Martin (2015), ICTs improve work performance and foster innovation among employees in organisations. Other reasons for ICTs in libraries, as raised by Bhardwaj and Walia (2012), Online Computer Library Center (2002), Dafiaghor (2012) and Ridwan (2015), include the following:

- Indexed and abstracted sources of information, and theses and dissertations that are available in web portals and institutional repositories can be easily accessed and retrieved via library websites because of ICTs (Bhardwaj & Walia 2012).
- The influx of large volumes of information and knowledge is easily managed in different databases by librarians with ICT tools in libraries (Bhardwaj & Walia 2012).
- Users of libraries can easily access and use library resources with the aid of Online Catalogue of Library of Congress or Online Computer Library Center (OCLC) without necessarily physically visiting the library building (Bhardwaj & Walia 2012; OCLC 2002).
- Generally, library and information operations and services have profoundly improved since the introduction of ICTs in libraries (Dafiaghor 2012).
- Library professionals have changed from custodians of information and knowledge to facilitators of library resources and services through organised workshops, seminars, and current awareness or display activities (Ridwan 2015).
- Librarians have adopted new techniques, knowledge and skills of managing information and knowledge through the use of the latest ICT tools (Ridwan 2015).
- Presently, librarians have improved themselves through training and re-training in different programmes, and research collaboration among colleagues (Ridwan 2015).

The rationale of the study is that current trends of library operations and services require the use of ICTs to facilitate meeting users' information needs. As a result of influx of information and knowledge in diverse context and area of specialisation, ICTs are essential for proper management functions of the organisation. The authors considered the technology acceptance model (TAM) developed by Davis (1989) appropriate for this article for the following reasons: (1) TAM addressed the principles and challenges that relate to the access and the use of ICT; (2) TAM has been validated through several testing of the theory, as it predicts phenomenon (Taiwo & Downe 2013; Venkatesh et al. 2008; Venkatesh, Thong & Xu 2012); (3) TAM accurately predicts users' intentions with regard to the use of technologies (Al-Qeisi 2009:1); (4) TAM was chosen with the intention of the intervening variables of 'use and perceived ease of use' (Davis 1989). The theory was meant to address specifically the factors that affect or influence the acceptance and use of computer technology or ICT facilities in organisations. The TAM theory has two unique variables of usefulness and perceived ease of use which has attracted a lot of attention by both proponents and opponents of the model. The rationale behind adopting this theory in this research article was that it fundamentally looks at how an individual found systems to be useful and perceived ease of use in their operations in the organisations. Many studies use TAM for understanding how ICT is perceived and used. For example, studies by Lee, Kozar and Larsen (2003), Ramayah (2006), Venkatesh and Davis (2000), Venkatesh (2000), Venkatesh et al. (2003), Venkatesh and Bala (2008), Davis, Bagozzi and Warshaw (1989), King and He (2006), just to mention but a few, have demonstrated the relationship of attitude and intention to use and not to use systems. Most of these studies also agree that intervening variables reflect flexible, proven, valid and reliable measures that predict the acceptance to use new technologies by end users in this contemporary knowledge economy. We have found other recent studies (e.g. Fari 2015) that represent arguments by TAM critics quite useful, particularly in confirming that TAM is still useful for application in related studies such as this one.

Purpose of the study

This study's fundamental focus was on how and to what extent ICT facilities support KM in selected university libraries in Nigeria and South Africa. In this article, we focused on the following research questions:

- What are the available ICT facilities used to support KM in academic libraries in Nigeria and South Africa?
- To what extent are librarians utilising ICTs to support KM in academic libraries in Nigeria and South Africa?
- What are the challenges faced in the use of ICTs for the support of KM in academic libraries in Nigeria and South Africa?

Methodology

The quantitative (survey) and qualitative (interpretive and content analysis) research methods were employed in this article. The research design employed for this research article was the survey, interpretive and content analysis. The population largely covered professional librarians across six sampled university libraries in Nigeria and South Africa. The non-probability sampling, specifically purposive sampling, enabled the selection of three university libraries from the southern part of Nigeria, namely the University of Ibadan (UI), Federal University of Technology (FUT) and Delta State University (DSU), and three university libraries from KwaZulu-Natal Province in South Africa: the University of KwaZulu-Natal (UKZN), University of Zululand (UZ) and Durban University of Technology (DUT). In the six sampled university libraries above, 171 professional librarians were targeted for the study. This was done through selection of accidental and purposive sampling. The selection was based on the available librarian working in each of the university chosen for the study. Therefore, 38 were obtained from UI library, 18 were recorded in FUT library, 44 from DSU library, 12 from the UZ library, 33 made up of UKZN library and 26 from DUT. These made up the 171 professional librarians sampled in the six university libraries in both countries. The UI and UKZN libraries were selected based on the fact that they are well established, as well as the oldest universities in the two respective countries. The FUT and DUT libraries were selected because they both are technology-based libraries that are vocational and professional oriented, whereas the DSU and UZ libraries were included in the study because of their rural location and proximity to the researchers.

The structured questionnaires were administered to the professional librarians across the sampled university libraries in Nigeria and South Africa. The administration of the questionnaire to the respondent across the six university libraries was between July and August, 2013, and it lasted for 3–4 weeks. Six key informants working in the university libraries in the two countries were also interviewed. The responses obtained were captured and reported in the findings of this article. Observation was used to gather data regarding the university libraries' environment, physical structure and location, office space (conduciveness), availability and accessibility of computers and other ICT tools, collections (print and electronic resources), shelving space, size and lighting in the office, and attitude of staff towards their work. Of the 171 questionnaires administered, 132 (77.2%) were returned. The 132 (77.2%) returned questionnaires consisted of 77 respondents from university libraries in Nigeria and 55 respondents from university libraries in South Africa. The 132 copies of questionnaires returned were analysed using descriptive statistics. The profiles of the respondents are presented in Table 1.

Results and discussion of findings

The results of this article are presented in the following sections.

What are the available information and communication technology facilities for the support of knowledge management in the selected academic libraries in Nigeria and South Africa?

The question on the available ICT facilities for KM was done in order to obtain clear understanding of each of the item in the variables (availability, with emphasis to accessibility and effectiveness of ICT facilities). Result of the available ICT facilities is represented in Table 2. It was found that ICT tools varied from library to library. The most available ICT tools across the sampled university libraries in the two countries appeared to be computers, CD-ROMs, scanners, projectors, telephones, printers and monitors. It was noted, through inter-country comparison, that the most resourced libraries were FUT Library, Akure (FUTA) and UZ. UI and UKZN were almost equal in the availability of ICT resources or tools. Findings from the interviews and observation concurred with those of the questionnaire, with the addition of ICT tools such as microphones, CCTV and video cameras, Wi-Fi, e-catalogues, databases and telephones. However, these were not mentioned in the questionnaire. It was not possible to ascertain whether all the facilities mentioned and

TABLE 1: The profile of the respondents.

Variables	Demographic data across university libraries (Nigeria and South Africa)													
	UI library		FUT library		DSU library		UZ library		UKZN library		DUT library		Total	
	F	%	*F*	%	*F*	%	*F*	%	*F*	%	*F*	%	*F*	%
Gender														
Male	17	26.2	10	15.4	14	21.5	2	3.1	13	20.0	9	13.8	65	49.2
Female	12	17.9	6	9.0	18	26.9	7	10.4	15	22.4	9	13.4	67	50.8
Total	**29**	**44.1**	**16**	**24.4**	**32**	**58.4**	**9**	**13.5**	**28**	**42.4**	**18**	**37.2**	**132**	**100**
Age														
20–29 years	2	6.9	0	0.0	2	6.3	1	11.1	1	3.6	1	5.6	7	5.3
30–39 years	14	48.3	3	18.8	12	37.5	1	11.1	8	28.6	8	44.4	46	34.8
40–49 years	11	37.9	9	56.3	12	37.5	3	33.3	13	46.4	6	33.3	54	40.9
50–59 years	2	6.9	3	18.8	6	18.8	4	44.4	5	17.9	2	11.1	22	16.7
60 years and above	0	0.0	1	6.3	0	0.0	0	0.0	1	3.6	1	5.6	3	2.3
Total	**29**	**100**	**16**	**100**	**32**	**100**	**9**	**100**	**28**	**100**	**18**	**100**	**132**	**100**
Qualifications														
Bachelor's degree	8	18.2	6	13.6	13	29.5	5	11.4	7	15.9	5	11.4	44	33.3
Honours degree	0	0.0	0	0.0	0	0.0	2	13.3	9	60.0	4	26.7	15	11.4
Master's degree	18	28.1	9	14.1	15	23.4	2	3.1	11	17.2	9	14.1	64	48.5
PhD degree	3	33.3	1	11.1	4	44.4	0	0.0	1	11.1	0	0.0	9	6.8
Total	**29**	**79.6**	**16**	**38.8**	**32**	**97.3**	**9**	**27.8**	**28**	**104**	**18**	**52.2**	**132**	**100**
Position or rank														
University librarian	0	0.0	1	100	0	0.0	0	0.0	0	0.0	0	0.0	1	100
Dep. Uni. librarian	1	50.0	1	50.0	0	0.0	0	0.0	0	0.0	0	0.0	2	100
Principal librarian	3	33.3	2	22.2	1	11.1	0	0.0	3	33.3	0	0.0	9	100
Senior librarian	7	17.5	0	0.0	2	5.0	2	5.0	18	45.0	11	27.5	40	100
Librarian I	2	22.2	3	33.3	3	33.3	0	0.0	0	0.0	1	11.1	9	100
Librarian II	5	26.3	3	15.8	7	36.8	2	10.5	1	5.3	1	5.3	19	100
Assistant librarian	1	9.1	0	0.0	7	63.6	1	9.1	2	18.2	0	0.0	11	100
Chief library officer	0	0.0	1	33.3	1	33.3	0	0.0	0	0.0	1	33.3	3	100
Senior library officer	1	16.7	2	33.3	1	16.7	2	33.3	0	0.0	0	0.0	6	100
Higher library officer	7	46.7	1	6.7	2	13.3	1	6.7	2	13.3	2	13.3	15	100
Chief library assistant	2	18.2	2	18.2	3	27.3	0	0.0	2	18.2	2	18.2	11	100
Principal library officer	0	0.0	0	0.0	0	0.0	0	0.0	0	0.0	0	0.0	0	0.0
Principal library assistant	0	0.0	0	0.0	0	0.0	1	100	0	0.0	0	0.0	1	100
Total	**29**	**-**	**16**	**-**	**32**	**-**	**9**	**-**	**28**	**-**	**18**	**-**	**132**	**100**
Work experience														
1–5 years	11	35.5	1	3.2	4	12.9	4	12.9	5	16.1	6	19.4	31	100
6–10 years	4	10.8	6	16.2	11	29.7	0	0.0	9	24.3	7	18.9	37	100
11–15 years	10	45.5	4	18.2	2	9.1	0	0.0	3	13.6	3	13.6	22	100
16–20 years	2	9.5	2	9.5	9	42.9	1	4.8	6	28.6	1	4.8	21	100
21–25 years	2	18.2	2	18.2	4	36.4	1	9.1	2	18.2	0	0.0	11	100
26 years and above	0	0.0	1	10.0	2	20.0	3	30.0	3	30.0	1	10.0	10	100
Total	**29**	**-**	**16**	**-**	**32**	**-**	**9**	**-**	**28**	**-**	**18**	**-**	**132**	**100**

UI, University of Ibadan; FUT, Federal University of Technology; DSU, Delta State University; UZ, University of Zululand; UKZN, University of KwaZulu-Natal; DUT, Durban University of Technology.

TABLE 2: Availability of information and communication technology tools for the support of knowledge management (%).

Information and communication technology tools	UI	FUT	DSU	UZ	UKZN	DUT	Ave %
Computer	97	100	97	100	100	100	100
CD-ROM	97	100	75	78	93	94	88.3
Multi-media	97	94	56	100	93	100	97.7
Projector	93	100	53	100	82	100	94
Scanner	97	100	84	89	96	100	95
Modem	83	88	75	89	61	61	70.3
Telephones	93	75	75	100	96	94	96.7
Printer	97	100	91	100	96	89	95
Monitor	97	100	94	100	89	100	96.3
Smart board	72	63	38	56	39	44	46.3

UI, University of Ibadan; FUT, Federal University of Technology; DSU, Delta State University; UZ, University of Zululand; UKZN, University of KwaZulu-Natal; DUT, Durban University of Technology; Ave, Average.

observed were in good working order. However, it was noted that the computers that the librarians use, were functioning. Another clear indication of a tool that was working in the libraries was the online public access catalogue (OPAC), which is used to retrieve information resources across all fields of study.

It was noted that some of the computers, microphones and projectors, among other equipment, were not tested in our presence to see whether or not they were functioning. Even if we had to test them, there is no regular electricity supply in Nigeria to regulate the use of these tools. The reverse is true with university libraries in South Africa, where the electricity supply is very regular in the library facilities across the country. The availability of the various ICTs mentioned and observed in South Africa could mean that there are policies guiding their acquisition in the libraries. Adequate funds, trained ICT and KM personnel in the operation of the tools are other major factors to consider in the university libraries.

The study also revealed that ICT tools are largely used on a daily basis in the management of information and knowledge resources and specifically with job execution in the libraries. This reiterates the applicability of the perceived usefulness that is discussed in TAM by Davis (1989). Thus, it can be noted that the willingness and decision of an individual to use available systems depend on a number of factors. One of such factors, for example, is the technical know-how, competence that is required to use the facilities and user friendliness of the technology itself. Limited use of ICTs can also be attributed to lack of ICT knowledge, skills, experience and attitudes that stem from both external and internal influences. We believe that the re-skilling and training of librarians to acquire ICT knowledge and skills is one way that helps improve the usefulness and perceived ease of use of ICTs in libraries.

Accessibility of information and communication technologies for knowledge management

It is common knowledge that a service or product may be available, but not accessible. The accessibility of ICTs for proper KM depends largely on the university libraries for quick and free access. It was revealed that the UI accessibility was far better than those in the sample, followed by the three universities in South Africa. These had a relative mean accessibility rate of 87%. The availability of ICTs for KM operations in UI was lower than that of South African university libraries. This again confirms that the availability of ICT tools does not automatically translate into accessibility. Accessibility was believed to be higher in South Africa than in Nigeria with respect to e-mail, text summarising and OPAC. The support of libraries with functional technological tools has great effect on the information services rendered to users and other management functions. As noted by Chao (2014:43), it enforces and improves productivity of staff during accessibility. Chao (2014:43) and Brown (2008) elaborated on the importance of information technology infrastructure and the proper configuration of the virtual computing environment. He acknowledged the need for outstanding operating systems that could provide a flexible structure for quality service delivery. Therefore, librarians should strive in order to have access to diverse information resources and services through the aid of emerging technologies in their university libraries.

Effectiveness of information and communication technologies for knowledge management

Findings from the questionnaire revealed that the most effective ICTs used for KM differ across all sampled university libraries in the two countries. This includes the Internet, e-mail, file sharing and text summarising. The UI in Nigeria appeared to have the most effective tools, followed by DUT in South African university libraries. It can be noted that the effectiveness of ICTs for KM depends on the knowledge, skills and experience the librarians possess for the services they offer. Recent trends in research and development of library and information services have shown that the effectiveness of technological tools in managing resources and improving staff productivity in organisations is very crucial (Chaubey 2015; Omotayo 2015). According to Chisenga (2006:9), the effectiveness of ICTs for KM has allowed library users to access information resources globally without necessarily visiting the physical library building. It is acknowledged that the Internet and the mobile phone have predominantly contributed to the effectiveness of ICT for KM, and the 'perceived ease of use and usefulness' of the tools, again, play a key role.

To what extent are librarians utilising information and communication technologies to support knowledge management in academic libraries in Nigeria and South Africa?

Result for this research question is presented in Table 3. Findings from the questionnaire revealed that the most frequently used ICT tools consisted mainly of software that performs highly specialised tasks and requires high expertise. Computers, scanners, printers, CD-ROMs, monitors, search engines and information retrieval tools and its peripherals were most commonly used. The simulation tools, artificial intelligence, decision support systems, data mining and

TABLE 3: Extent to which librarian utilise information and communication technologies for the support of knowledge management (%).

Extent of librarian utilisation of information and communication technologies for knowledge management	UI	FUT	DSU	UZ	UKZN	DUT	Ave %
Rendering information and administrative services	86	75	71	94	71	72	79
Support for research and curriculum development process	76	96	90	96	94	78	89
Formulation of policies and strategic planning	66	93	93	89	84	68	80
Teaching and learning processes for newly registered users	91	86	90	82	93	78	84
Problem-solving and decision-making	76	76	87	82	97	77	85
Minutes in staff management meetings	85	75	84	67	82	81	77
In-service development and training for support staff	92	100	86	77	99	92	89
Transferring existing knowledge into other parts of the organisation	99	96	92	82	92	94	89
Generating new knowledge and filtering old knowledge	95	86	99	82	80	92	85
Accessing valuable knowledge from external sources	75	76	86	83	86	66	78
Storing content documents in databases	76	86	93	99	87	72	86

UI, University of Ibadan; FUT, Federal University of Technology; DSU, Delta State University; UZ, University of Zululand; UKZN, University of KwaZulu-Natal; DUT, Durban University of Technology; Ave, Average.

online analytic tools were the least used across the two countries' libraries. At the university libraries' level, the greatest use of ICT tools was at UI, followed by UZ. It was further revealed that the low application of ICT hardware can be attributed to challenges relating to funding, whereas low utilisation of specialised software can be traced back to lack of knowledge of ICT tools. Findings from the interviews revealed that procurement, processing, access, planning, metadata, policy design, community service, abstracting and indexing services, photocopying, scanning and digitisation of documents, networking, preservation, training of staff and users, lending and inter-library loan services, and dissemination of information and knowledge to meet users' needs were feasible through diverse set of the ICT tools. These were extensively used in the library environment on daily basis. The operations or functions that lead to the use of these set of tools can be classified into specific and general work operations.

Ofori-Dwumfuo and Kommey (2013:92) agree that ICTs now include new devices such as cell phones, tape recorders and magnetic devices to improve knowledge collection, storage and exchange on a scale that was not possible in the past. Users now place great emphasis on web 2.0 technologies (e.g. WhatsApp, Facebook, YouTube, Social networking, Wikis, Wikipedia, Twitter, skype, instant messaging, blogs and Myspace) and web-based resources that satisfy their information needs 'at the touch of a button', as also noted by Ward (2001) referring to Internet and www.

Comparing the use of information and communication technologies for knowledge management in academic libraries

The surveyed librarians and interviewed informants revealed that there were lots of differences with the use of ICT tools used to manage knowledge in their various libraries. It was established that the use of ICT for KM at UI was relatively higher than that occurred at UZ, UKZN and DUT that was moderate. DSU library was the lowest followed by FUT. It can be expected that the availability of these services rendered by librarians results in the frequent use of the tools. Notably, the South African university librarians attest to use the tools for KM most when compared with the Nigerian sample. The libraries converged in use of text summarising and text messages. The widest gaps between the samples in the two countries were in file sharing and OPACs. The correlation coefficient of these two variables was weak but significant. File sharing appears to occur between university libraries and persons outside the university as it correlates more with the Internet than with the intranet. Raju (2014) also observed that different ICT tools, in particular social media, mobile devices, tablets and its peripherals, and library virtual space, have influenced the expansion of collections and services rendered to users by Library and Information Science (LIS) professionals. A study by Kalusopa (2005:422) also agrees that the provision of current and precise information that is systematically collected and repackaged opens up new sources and services for users in present-day library operations.

Extent to which librarians utilise information and communication technologies to support knowledge management

The utilisation of the ICT tools cannot be quantified if we have to do so. The essence is that there is no time that its use has not been of immerse value to man and specifically in management function of library operations. The extent to which the ICTs are utilised cut across the followings reasons: (1) rendering information and administrative services to users; (2) support for research and curriculum development processes; (3) formulation of policies and strategic planning; (4) teaching and learning processes; (5) registration of new users; (6) problem-solving and decision-making; (7) in-service development and training; (8) supporting staff in transferring existing knowledge to other parts of the organisation; and (9) generating new knowledge and filtering old ones. The uses occurred in all the sampled libraries with DSU, UZ, UKZN and UI leading the pack.

Information sources that guide librarians in the use of information and communication technologies for knowledge management

The librarians attest to different or multiplicity of sources that support the use of ICTs for KM. The most sourced resources are library catalogues, theses and dissertations, reviews or journal articles and Internet sources. It was further revealed that all the university libraries across the two countries preferred one information source over another based on the information needs of the users and libraries. The choice of particular information or source is influenced by the purpose of searching for such information and on the information needs of the users. Fillip and Foote (2007:v) acknowledge that information access has become more appreciated since the rise of the Internet and digital technologies. This has helped to create and foster the sharing of knowledge with peers in the library environment. Studies by Wachira and Onyancha (2012) and Declan (2011) assert that formal and informal sources of information and human resources are now used to meet diverse users' information needs.

What are the challenges faced in the use of information and communication technologies to support knowledge management in academic libraries in Nigeria and South Africa?

The most voiced challenges highlighted in Table 4 include inadequate funding, lack of motivation and lack of infrastructure. The least cited challenges include moving to other professions, language barriers and the ability to work independently. The challenges were most pronounced at DUT and least pronounced at FUT. It was established that inadequate funding has a negative impact on infrastructural development and capacity building. We note that some of these problems result from context (environment), cultural background, lack of maintenance of available infrastructure and the misplacement of organisational priority.

The results suggested that on average, university libraries in South Africa were experiencing fewer challenges than in

TABLE 4: Challenges faced in the use of information and communication technologies for the support of knowledge management (%).

Challenges faced in the use of information and communication technologies	UI	FUT	DSU	UZ	UKZN	DUT	Ave %
Lack of motivation	90	100	91	89	89	100	93
Lack of trust	86	88	81	89	79	83	84
Inadequate funds	93	100	94	89	96	89	94
Knowledge of subject expert	83	94	75	78	86	83	83
Drift to other professions	72	56	66	67	75	67	67
Lack of infrastructure	93	94	100	89	93	83	92
Lack of organisational growth	79	81	78	89	86	78	82
Lack of self-development	90	94	91	89	82	94	90
Inaccessibility of library resources	86	69	91	100	89	89	87
Inability to cope with changes	93	94	91	89	82	89	90
Insufficient ability to manage knowledge assets	90	69	91	78	82	89	83
Unreliable Internet network	90	88	88	89	82	89	88
Unreliable electricity	90	100	97	89	75	89	90
Insufficient KM sources	90	81	84	78	75	89	83
Lack of current trends	79	75	88	78	82	94	83
Language barrier	79	63	59	78	71	89	73
Poor KM practices	83	81	91	89	82	78	84
Lack of personal computer	83	63	81	89	71	94	80
Costs of hardware and software	97	69	84	89	86	94	87
Lack of policy implementation	86	81	94	100	86	94	90
Lack of adherence to instructions	97	69	72	100	96	89	87
Lack knowledge to use ICTs and web	86	75	91	89	82	94	86
Lack of knowledge of library holdings	79	69	69	89	93	89	81
Inability to understand users' queries	93	75	81	89	93	89	87
Lack of knowledge production	83	81	78	100	89	94	88
Inability to work independently	83	88	63	78	64	83	77

UI, University of Ibadan; FUT, Federal University of Technology; DSU, Delta State University; UZ, University of Zululand; UKZN, University of KwaZulu-Natal; DUT, Durban University of Technology, Ave, Average.

Nigeria. Inadequate funding and infrastructural challenges were more pronounced in Nigeria. Notably, the most critical challenges to address in the use of ICTs for the support of KM include lack of infrastructure, inadequate funds, unreliable electricity and unreliable Internet networks. A study by Ajuwon and Rhine (2008) determined that ICT facilities and the regular training of librarians are essential for the full support of KM in academic libraries.

Interviews with the key informants revealed that the most crucial challenges faced by Nigerian university libraries include inadequate funding, poor or old ICT facilities, and inadequate professional staff. The South African interviewees cited inadequate professional staff, lack of commitment to work and increased user needs. Evidently, inadequate professional staff is a common problem in both countries' libraries. As attested in the interview conducted was the worrisome issue of the ability of the management of libraries to act towards the eradication of these problems. Related studies by Agboh (2015), Fink and Disterer (2006), Jones, Davies and Muir (2003), and Khatibi, Thyagarajan and Seetharaman (2003) also identify the lack of government support systems, complex procedures, managerial leadership, cost benefits and needs analysis, legal issues, turnover, security and lack of human capital, among others, to be the most critical challenges in university libraries.

Conclusion

The utilisation of ICTs for KM in present-day library organisation cannot be undermined. This has brought new paradigm of how information and knowledge are repackaged for decision-making and planning. The authors noted that the availability and accessibility of ICTs for KM among the sampled university libraries were not uniform, even within one country. Infrastructural support has affected some of the university libraries to a great extent. The irregular electricity supply in Nigeria made it difficult to believe that the ICTs were really functional. The knowledge and skills for using ICT for KM were largely adequate, but varied within the libraries and librarians as well. The need for re-skilling of librarians becomes significant as it would help to bridge the gap and reduce knowledge loss in the library organisation. Relative to the Nigerian sample, the South African sampled university libraries were better equipped in using ICTs for KM in terms of availability, accessibility, services and effectiveness. Satgoor's (2015) study confirms that university libraries in South Africa are better equipped and funded for information services. It is, though, not unusual to find that most African university libraries are poorly resourced and funded (Enyia 2013; Okiy 2005; Osagie & Orheruta 2013:195).

The challenges facing the libraries, as reported in Table 2, are numerous, with inadequate professional staff topping the list. However, irrespective of the challenges faced, libraries have devised strategies for coping and rendering services. The re-skilling of librarians through continuous education becomes feasible with the help of government or institutional support through functional policies, and funding should enable the better integration of ICT with KM in the libraries where this has not occurred. Based on the findings, there are sound lessons to be learnt by the university libraries from both countries, and a forum for doing so is urgently needed.

Acknowledgements

This study is extracted and revised from a PhD thesis produced by one of the authors (see http://uzspace.uzulu.ac.za/handle/10530/1470). The University of Zululand and Delta State University are acknowledged for the support provided towards the development and finalisation of this research work. The authors also acknowledge the support they received from reviewers towards the improvement of the quality of the article.

Competing interests

The authors declare that they have no financial or personal relationships that may have inappropriately influenced them in writing this article.

Authors' contributions

R.T.E. is the author of the PhD thesis from which the article was extracted, conceptualised the research idea, executed the study and jointly wrote the article. D.N.O. is the supervisor of the PhD project and with R.T.E. has jointly written the article.

References

Agboh, D.K., 2015, 'Drivers and challenges of ICT adoption by SMES in Accra metropolis, Ghana', *Journal of Technology Research* 6, 1–16, viewed 20 August 2015, from http://www.aabri.com/manuscripts/142044.pdf

Ajuwon, G. & Rhine, L., 2008, 'The level of Internet access and ICT training for health information professionals in Sub-Saharan Africa', *Health Information and Libraries Journal* 25, 175–185. https://doi.org/10.1111/j.1471-1842.2007.00758.x

Al-Qeisi, K.I., 2009, 'Analysing the use of UTAUT model in explaining an online behaviour: Internet banking adoption', PhD thesis, submitted at the Department of Marketing and Branding, Brunel University.

Anunobi, C.V., Anyanwu, O.P., Oga, M. & Benard, I.I., 2011, 'The adoption of ICT for library and information services', *Nigerian Libraries* 44(1), 89–104.

Beesley, L.G.A. & Cooper, G., 2008, 'Defining knowledge management (KM) activities: Towards consensus', *Journal of Knowledge Management* 12(3), 48–62. https://doi.org/10.1108/13673270810875859

Bhardwaj, R.K. & Walia, P.K., 2012, 'Web based information sources and services: A case study of St. Stephen's College, University of Delhi', *Library Philosophy and Practice*, ISSN 1522–0222, viewed 19 January 2015, from http://www.webpages.uidaho.edu/~mbolin/bhardwaj-walia.htm

Blurton, C., 1999, 'New directions of ICT-use in education', viewed 12 July 2012, http://ehlt.flinders.edu.au/education/

Brown, S.A., 2008, 'Household technology adoption, use, and impacts: Past, present, and future', *Information Systems Frontiers* 10(4), 397–402. https://doi.org/10.1007/s10796-008-9098-z

Chao, L., 2014, 'Application of infrastructure as a service in IT education', *American Journal of Information Systems* 2(2), 42–48.

Chaubey, A.K., 2015, 'Skill and competency require in knowledge management in libraries and information centre in current era', *E-Journal of Library and Information Science* 2(4), 184–210.

Chisenga, J., 2006, 'Information and communication technologies: Opportunities and challenges for national and university libraries in Eastern, Central and Southern Africa, 2006', in *Standing Conference of African National and University Libraries of Eastern, Central and Southern Africa*, Dar es Salaam, Tanzania, July 9–10, 2006, viewed 12 July 2012, from http://eprints.rclis.org/bitstream/10760/9579/1/Chisenga_SCANUL_2006.pdf

Dafiaghor, F.K., 2012, 'Problems and prospects of electronic resources usage in Nigerian academic libraries', *Journal of Economics and International Finance* 4(9), 220–225.

Dalkir, K., 2011, *Knowledge management in theory and practice*, MIT, Cambridge, MA.

Davis, F.D., 1989, 'Perceived usefulness, perceived ease of use, and user acceptance of information technology', *MIS Quarterly* 13(3), 319–340. https://doi.org/10.2307/249008

Davis, F.D., Bagozzi, R.P. & Warshaw, P.R., 1989, 'User acceptance of computer technology: A comparison of two theoretical models', *Management Science* 35(8), 982–1003. https://doi.org/10.1287/mnsc.35.8.982

Declan, W., 2011, 'Human resources: Formal vs. informal recruitment', viewed 25 April 2014, from http://www.candidatemanager.net/news/2011/04/formal-informal-recruitment.asp

Enyia, C.O., 2013, 'The management of library development funds in the Nigerian University System', *Journal of Librarianship and Information Science* 34(2), viewed 7 November 2014, from http://lis.sagepub.com/content/34/2/91.abstract

Evangelista, P., Esposito, E., Lauro, V. & Raffa, M., 2010, 'The adoption of knowledge management systems in small firms', *Electronic Journal of Knowledge Management* 8(1), 33–42.

Fari, S.A., 2015, 'Applying social capital theory and the technology acceptance model in information and knowledge sharing research', *Inkanyiso: Journal of Humanities and Social Sciences* 7(1), 19–28.

Fillip, B. & Foote, D., 2007, 'Making the connections scaling telecentres for development', *Information Application Centre*, viewed 12 July 2014, from http://connection.aed.org/pages/makingconnections.pdf

Fink, D. & Disterer, G., 2006, 'International case study: To what extent is ICT infused into the operations of SMEs', *Journal of Enterprise Information Management* 19(6), 608–624. https://doi.org/10.1108/17410390610708490

Jones, P., Davies, P.B. & Muir, E., 2003, 'E-business barriers to growth within the SME sector', *Journal of Systems and Information Technology* 7(1), 1–25. https://doi.org/10.1108/13287260380000771

Kalusopa, T., 2005, 'The challenges of utilizing information communication technologies (ICTs) for the small-scale farmers in Zambia', *Library Hi Tech* 23(3), 414–424. https://doi.org/10.1108/07378830510621810

Khatibi, A., Thyagarajan, V. & Seetharaman, A., 2003, 'E-commerce in Malaysia: Perceived benefits and barriers', viewed 20 June 2015, from www.vikalpa.com/pdf/articles

King, W.R. & He, J., 2006, 'A meta-analysis of the technology acceptance model', *Information and Management* 43, 740–755. http://dx.doi.org/10.1016/j.im.2006.05.003

Lee, Y., Kozar, K.A. & Larsen, K.R.T., 2003, 'The technology acceptance model: Past, present, and future', *Communications of the Association for Information Systems* 12, Article 50, viewed 17 November 2014, from http://aisel.aisnet.org/cais/vol12/iss1/50

Martin, L., 2015, *Innovative work practices, ICT use and employees' motivations*, Luxembourg Institute of Socio-Economic Research (LISER), Luxembourg, viewed 23 November 2014, from http://www.liser.lu

Minonne, C., 2007, 'Towards an integrative-approach for managing implicit and explicit knowledge: An exploratory study in Switzerland', viewed 19 August 2012, from http://ebookbrowse.com/article-clemente-minonne-eckm-2007-v-1-2-pdf-d144113461

Nonaka, I., 1994, 'A dynamic theory of organizational knowledge creation', *Organizational Science* 5(1), 14–37. https://doi.org/10.1287/orsc.5.1.14

Nonaka, I., Ichijo, K. & Von Krogh, G., 2004, *Enabling knowledge creation: How to unlock the mystery of tacit knowledge and release the power of innovation*. Oxford University Press, New York.

Nonaka, I. & Krogh, G.V., 2009, 'Tacit knowledge and knowledge conversion: Controversy and advancement in organizational knowledge creation theory', *Organization Science* 20(3), 635–652, viewed 12 June 2014, from https://ai.wu.ac.at/~kaiser/literatur/nonaka-knowledge-conversion.pdf

Nonaka, I., Umemoto, K. & Senoo, D., 1996, 'From information processing to knowledge creation: A paradigm shift in business management', *Technology in Society* 18(2), 203–218. https://doi.org/10.1016/0160-791X(96)00001-2

Ofori-Dwumfuo, G.O. & Kommey, R.E., 2013, 'Utilization of ICT in knowledge management at the Ghana Volta River Authority', *Current Research Journal of Social Sciences* 5(3), 91–102, viewed 28 May 2013, from http://www.maxwellsci.com/print/crjss/v5-91-102.pdf

Okiy, R.B., 2005, 'Funding Nigerian libraries in the 21st century: Will funding from alternative sources suffice', *The Bottom Line: Managing Library Finances* 18(2), 71–77. https://doi.org/10.1108/08880450510597514

Omotayo, F.O., 2015, 'Knowledge management as an important tool in organisational management: A review of literature', *Library Philosophy and Practice (e-journal)*, Paper 1238, viewed 16 January 2016, from http://digitalcommons.unl.edu/cgi/viewcontent.cgi?article=3330&context=libphilprac

Online Computer Library Center, OCLC, 2002, 'Academic librarians can influence students' web based information choices: OCLC white paper on the information habits of college students', viewed 22 December 2015, from http://www.oclc.org/downloads/community/informationhabits.pdf

Osagie, R. & Orheruata, M.U., 2013, 'Budgeting and funding of the library at the University of Benin, Edo State, Nigeria', *Education* 134(2), Winter 2013, viewed 7 November 2014, from https://www.questia.com/library/journal/1G1-356352098/budgeting-and-funding-of-the-library-at-the-university

Raju, J., 2014, 'Knowledge and skills for the digital era academic library', *The Journal of Academic Librarianship* 40, 163–170. https://doi.org/10.1016/j.acalib.2014.02.007

Ramayah, T., 2006, 'Interface characteristics, perceived ease of use and intention to use an online library in Malaysia', *Information Development* 22(2), 123–133. https://doi.org/10.1177/0266666906065575

Ridwan, S.M., 2015, 'Application of information and communication technology in management of information resources and services in Kaduna State Tertiary Institutions' Libraries, Kaduna-Nigeria', *European Scientific Journal* 1, 25–32. ISSN: 1857–7881.

Rowley, J., 2003, 'Knowledge management – The new librarianship: From custodians of history to gatekeepers to the future', *Library Management* 24(8), 433–440. https://doi.org/10.1108/01435120310501112

Satgoor, U., 2015, 'Celebrating libraries in 20 years of democracy: An overview of library and information services in South Africa', *International Federation of Library Association* 41(2), 97–111. https://doi.org/10.1177/0340035215585100

Skyrme, D., 1997, *Knowledge management: Approaches and policies*, viewed 17 July 2011, from http://www.skyrme.cm/pubs/deedskm.doc

Taiwo, A.A. & Downe, A.G., 2013, 'The theory of user acceptance and use of technology (UTAUT): A meta-analytic review of empirical findings', *Journal of Theoretical and Applied Information Technology* 49(1), 48–58.

UNESCO, 2002, *Information and communication in education: A curriculum for schools and programme of teachers' development*, UNESCO, Paris.

Venkatesh, V., 2000, 'Determinants of perceived ease of use: Integrating control, intrinsic motivation, and emotion into the technology acceptance model', *Information Systems Research* 11, 342–365. https://doi.org/10.1287/isre.11.4.342.11872

Venkatesh, V. & Bala, H., 2008, 'TAM 3: Advancing the technology acceptance model with a focus on interventions', Manuscript in-preparation, viewed 6 August 2014, from http://www.vvenkatesh.com/it/organizations/theoretical_models.asp

Venkatesh, V., Brown, S.A., Maruping, L.M. & Bala, H., 2008, 'Predicting different conceptualizations of system use: The competing roles of behavioural intention, facilitating conditions, and behavioural expectation', *MIS Quarterly* 32(3), 483–502.

Venkatesh, V. & Davis, F.D., 2000, 'A theoretical extension of the technology acceptance model: Four longitudinal field studies', *Management Science* 46(2), 186–204. https://doi.org/10.1287/mnsc.46.2.186.11926

Venkatesh, V., Morris, M., Davis, G. & Davis, F.D., 2003, 'User acceptance of information technology: Toward a unified view', *MIS Quarterly* 27(3), 425–478, viewed 18 October 2014, from http://www.cis.gsu.edu/~ghubona/info790/VenkEtAlMIQ03.pdf

Venkatesh, V., Thong, J.Y.L. & Xu, X., 2012, 'Consumer acceptance and use of information technology: Extending the unified theory of acceptance and use of technology', *MIS Quarterly* 36, 157–178.

Wachira, M.N. & Onyancha, O.B., 2012, 'Serving remote users in selected public university libraries in Kenya: discussions with section heads', Paper presented at the SCECSAL XXth Conference hosted by KLA, the Laico Regency Hotel, Nairobi, Kenya. Published in Pretoria, June 4–8, 2012.

Ward, M., 2001, 'A survey of engineers in their information world', *Journal of Librarianship and Information Science* 33(4), 168–176. https://doi.org/10.1177/096100060103300402

12

Evidence-based case selection: An innovative knowledge management method to cluster public technical and vocational education and training colleges in South Africa

Authors:
Margaretha M. Visser[1]
Judith A. Van Biljon[2]
Marlien Herselman[2,3]

Affiliations:
[1]Education and Skills Development Research Programme, Human Sciences Research Council, South Africa

[2]College of Science, Engineering and Technology, School of Computing, University of South Africa, South Africa

[3]Council for Scientific and Industrial Research, University of South Africa, South Africa

Corresponding author:
Mariette Visser,
mmvisser@hsrc.ac.za

Background: Case studies are core constructs used in information management research. A persistent challenge for business, information management and social science researchers is how to select a representative sample of cases among a population with diverse characteristics when convenient or purposive sampling is not considered rigorous enough. The context of the study is post-school education, and it involves an investigation of quantitative methods of clustering the population of public technical and vocational education and training (TVET) colleges in South Africa into groups with a similar level of maturity in terms of their information systems.

Objectives: The aim of the study was to propose an evidence-based quantitative method for the selection of cases for case study research and to demonstrate the use and usefulness thereof by clustering public TVET colleges.

Method: The clustering method was based on the use of a representative characteristic of the context, as a proxy. In this context of management information systems (MISs), website maturity was used as a proxy and website maturity model theory was used in the development of an evaluation questionnaire. The questionnaire was used for capturing data on website characteristics, which was used to determine website maturity. The websites of the 50 public TVET colleges were evaluated by nine evaluators. Multiple statistical techniques were applied to establish inter-rater reliability and to produce clusters of colleges.

Results: The analyses revealed three clusters of public TVET colleges based on their website maturity levels. The first cluster includes three colleges with no websites or websites at a low maturity level. The second cluster consists of 30 colleges with websites at an average maturity level. The third cluster contains 17 colleges with websites at a high maturity level.

Conclusion: The main contribution to the knowledge domain is an innovative quantitative method employing a characteristic (in this case website maturity) as a proxy for MIS maturity. The method can be applied in quantitative, qualitative and mixed methods research, to group a population and thereby simplify the process of sample selection of cases for further in-depth investigation.

Introduction

'A scientific discipline without a large number of thoroughly executed case studies is a discipline without systematic production of exemplars, and a discipline without exemplars is an ineffective one.' (Flyvbjerg 2006:1)

Case research is a mature methodology in information and knowledge management research, and there is agreement that case selection is critical in ensuring high-quality case research (Benbasat, Goldstein & Mead 1987). Furthermore, the case selection should be based on characteristics of the context in which the phenomenon being investigated is found, because cases cannot be translated from one context to another, for example, from a developed country context to a developing country context (Mudzana & Maharaj 2015). What has received less attention is the development of methods for rigorous selection of case studies when there are a large number of cases from which to select (Seawright & Gerring 2008).

The study contributes to improving information and knowledge management practice, especially if one wants to ensure objectivity in case selection. The purpose of the study is to propose an evidence-based quantitative method for the selection of cases for case study research and to demonstrate this by clustering technical and vocational education and training (TVET) colleges in South Africa into groups with information systems at similar levels of maturity. The research context is public TVET colleges in South Africa. A broad overview of public TVET colleges in South Africa is provided in the next section.

Samples are data sets, taken from a wider data universe using a particular procedure, in order to generalise about the wider universe with a particular level of confidence (Ben-Zvi, Bakker & Makar 2015). To make the selection of a representative sample of public TVET colleges more rigorous, the use of an innovative sampling method was investigated and applied.

It is often not possible or feasible to survey all cases in a context because of cost implications and time constraints. Therefore, sampling is a key factor in making reliable statistical inferences about the universe. It is incumbent on the researcher to clearly define the target population and sample selection approach, but sometimes sampling is an underestimated part of a research study (Field & Hole 2003; StatPac 2014). The sample population is defined in keeping with the objectives of the specific study, and although guidelines are available, the researcher has to rely on logic and judgement to make the appropriate sample selection for the study, the latter being a subjective process. The method described here informs an evidence-based approach to case study selection.

Mouton (2001) identifies the use of biased sampling, because of the use of non-probability sampling techniques, as one of the main errors encountered in selecting data sources. Despite the maturity of this issue, the development of statistical reasoning in terms of samples and sampling in the education community deserves further attention (Ben-Zvi et al. 2015). Popular techniques for sample selection in qualitative research where case study strategies are implemented are convenient or purposive sampling, which only allows the researcher to generalise the research findings to the specific case under investigation. Serious challenges are likely to develop if a very small sample is randomly selected from a large population of cases without any prior stratification being done (Seawright & Gerring 2008; Williamson 2003).

The research question for the study was therefore formulated as follows: *How can an evidence-based quantitative method be used for case selection in information systems research?*

The process that was used to address the problem is based on web maturity models (WMM) theory (Rhoads 2008). An evaluation questionnaire was developed to investigate the level of maturity of websites of the public TVET colleges. The colleges were then clustered by using algorithmic methods and statistical analysis software.

The article is presented in four parts. The first part provides the background to the investigation undertaken into the available literature. The methodological approach is then discussed, followed by the presentation of the findings. The article concludes by discussing the findings, with specific reference to their implications for improving rigor in case selection.

Literature review

The aim of the literature review is to provide background on public TVET colleges and to offer conceptual clarification of the key concepts and theoretical frameworks underpinning the empirical study.

Background on public TVET colleges

The TVET sector is defined by the United Nations Educational, Scientific and Cultural Organisation (UNESCO) as:

> a comprehensive term referring to those aspects of the educational process involving, in addition to general education: the study of technologies and related sciences; as well as the acquisition of practical skills, attitudes, understanding, knowledge relating to occupations in various sectors of economic and social life. (Del Mar 2011:4)

Public TVET colleges in South Africa were formerly known as public further education and training colleges and were renamed in 2014 (Department of Higher Education and Training [DHET] 2013). Public TVET colleges were established and operated under the authority of the Continuing Education and Training Act 16 of 2006, and they are subject to the authority of the DHET (2013).

The college sector is seen as central to the provision of post-school education and training in South Africa, and strengthening and expanding this sector is the DHET's highest priority. A number of areas require strengthening at the colleges, including improving and developing information systems (DHET 2013; Dzvapatsva, Mitrovic & Dietrich 2014; Visser, van Biljon & Herselman 2013). There are 50 registered and accredited public TVET colleges in South Africa; these operate on more than 264 campuses in both rural and urban areas of the country (TVET Colleges South Africa 2015).

Sample selection and types of sampling

Sampling entails the selection of a subset of cases from the population under investigation. It is not always possible or feasible to conduct a census (which is an official count or survey that collects data from the entire population), because of time and cost constraints. A subset of the population under examination, if representative of the population and if large enough, can provide statistically significant results.

Theory on sampling deals with two domains: probability and non-probability sampling. Probability samples contain some type of randomisation and consist of simple, stratified, systematic, cluster, complex multi-stage or sequential sampling types (Oates 2006; Summers 1991). Non-probability samples lack randomisation and consist of the following sample types: convenience or accidental, purposive, quota, accessible, judgement, volunteer or self-selection, snowball and expert. The core distinctions between the two domains are that probability sampling study findings can be generalised to the target population and that it is mainly used in quantitative methods. Non-probability sampling study findings can only be generalised to the institution from which the sample was drawn, and it is primarily implemented when using qualitative research methods (Feild et al. 2006; Oates 2006; Summers 1991). Seddon and Scheepers (2012) emphasise the importance of sample representativeness and the need for researcher judgement when any claim is made about the likely truth of sample-based knowledge claims in other settings.

Seawright and Gerring (2008) emphasise the importance of the selection process when case selection has to be implemented. In most case selection techniques discussed in the literature, in-depth familiarity of each case is needed before a non-probability sample can be drawn.

Case selection in case study research has the same objectives as random sampling, which are: (1) to acquire a representative sample and (2) a useful variation on the dimensions of theoretical interest (Seawright & Gerring 2008). The selection of cases is therefore guided by the position of the case along these two dimensions within the population of interest. Seawright and Gerring (2008) identified the following case selection techniques: typical, diverse, extreme, deviant, influential, most similar and most different cases, and defined these as indicated in Table 1.

Miles, Huberman and Saldana (2014) provide criteria that can be used to evaluate the sample strategy that was used in a research study. The authors suggest that the sample should be relevant to the conceptual frame and research question(s) and that the researcher should make sure that the phenomena under investigation will appear in the sample. The sample plan should be viable in terms of cost, time, access to people and the researcher's own work style. The sampling plan should be ethical in terms of issues such as potential risks and benefits, informed consent and the relationship with informants. The researcher should also evaluate: if the plan will enhance generalisability of findings, either through conceptual power or representativeness; and if the findings will produce believable descriptions and explanations, which would be true in real life.

TABLE 1: Cross-case technique of case selection.

Technique	Definition
Typical	Cases (one or more) are typical examples of some cross-case relationship.
Diverse	Cases (two or more) exemplify diverse values.
Extreme	Cases (one or more) exemplify extreme or unusual values relative to some univariate distribution.
Deviant	Cases (one or more) deviate from some cross-case relationship.
Influential	Cases (one or more) with influential configurations of the independent variables.
Most similar	Cases (two or more) are similar in terms of specified variables.
Most different	Cases (two or more) are different in terms of specified variables.

Source: Seawright, J. & Gerring, J., 2008, 'Case selection techniques in case study research: A menu of qualitative and quantitative options', *Political Research Quarterly* 61(2), 297. http://dx.doi.org/10.1177/1065912907313077

This brief literature review on sampling provides evidence that sampling is essential to the rigor of any research that relies on statistical inference, and also in research where the selection of the case study needs to be justified as non-convenient as often applies to research in information management and educational contexts. Sample selection is critical in ensuring research rigor yet non-trivial and that provides the rationale for this study into innovate, evidence-based sampling methods.

Web maturity models theory

The literature revealed that information and communication technology (ICT) is an essential enabler for economic and social development in an organisation and that it enhances the competitiveness of organisations (UNCTAD & TNSO 2008). ICT, which includes websites and management information systems (MISs), improves communication, operational efficiencies, sales turnover and information quality in organisations (Burgess, Sellitto & Karanasios 2009). Hence, the maturity and sophistication level of an organisation's website is indicative of the level of sophistication of its ICT, including its MISs.

Maturity models reveal the degree of technological sophistication and organisational transformation (Ziemba & Papaj 2013). Organisations also recognise the strategic importance of knowledge management and sharing, and the practise of using platforms such as the World Wide Web for this purpose (Mannie, Van Niekerk & Adendorff 2013).

The term 'maturity' relates to the degree of formality and optimisation of processes. The concept of maturity is fundamental to the evaluation of systems, and maturity models are used in different fields, such as business, education and information systems, to evaluate and monitor progress. The capability maturity model (CMM) identifies different levels of maturity in organisations; for most of the CMMs, the maturity scale structure includes five levels (Esterhuizen, Schutte & du Toit 2012; Paulk et al. 1993; Rhoads 2008). CMMs exist for many applications used in organisations, such as software development; information technology development; management; and project, data, business and knowledge management (Esterhuizen et al. 2012).

The WMM builds on the CMM and can also be used to assess the maturity of an organisation's website (Rhoads 2008).

The European Union eGovernment WMM represents the degree of technological sophistication and organisational transformation in government agencies (Ziemba & Papaj 2013). Fath-Allah et al. (2014) compared 25 eGovernment maturity models and identified *presence, interaction, transaction* and *integration* as the criteria that differentiated the first four maturity levels in most of those websites. The levels of service and complexity are similar to those described for the European Union eGovernment model, but the latter proposes five levels because it distinguishes between one-way interaction and two-way interaction (Ziemba & Papaj 2013). The general website maturity model of the University of British Columbia (UBC) (UBC 2015) identifies *initial, repeatable, defined, managed* and *continual process* improvement as the five stages, and it becomes clear that the stages depend on the context and the purpose of the website.

The design of an evaluation questionnaire for the evaluation of public TVET colleges' websites was modelled on Paulk et al. (1993) and Rhoads (2008), who focused on process control. The levels are as follows:

- level 1 relates to ad hoc business practices with no control at all
- level 2 relates to stable processes with a repeatable level of statistical control
- level 3 relates to defined processes to ensure consistent implementation
- level 4 relates to managed result metrics
- level 5 relates to active optimisation of the processes.

The WMM suggests that a website develops in maturity from level 1 to level 5, as depicted in Figure 1. Websites at level 1 provide basic introductory information about the institution (*presence*). The website evolves to level 2, if it includes text or information about the organisation, graphics, contact details and a feedback mechanism (*interaction*); websites develop to level 3 (*transactional*) if there is a search engine and more detailed information on what is offered by the institution (e.g. courses, training programmes and catalogues); websites develop to level 4 (*integration*) if they have systems such as content and distribution management, and evidence customer relationship management strategies and credit card processing functionality. A website maturity level 5 offers portal capability and personalised capability and contains multimedia content such as videos and multiple language choices.

In addition to evidence of specific components (functionality) on the website, as suggested by the WMM, Remenyi (2002) provides 10 main evaluation criteria for website maturity; each of these includes a number of sub-criteria. The main

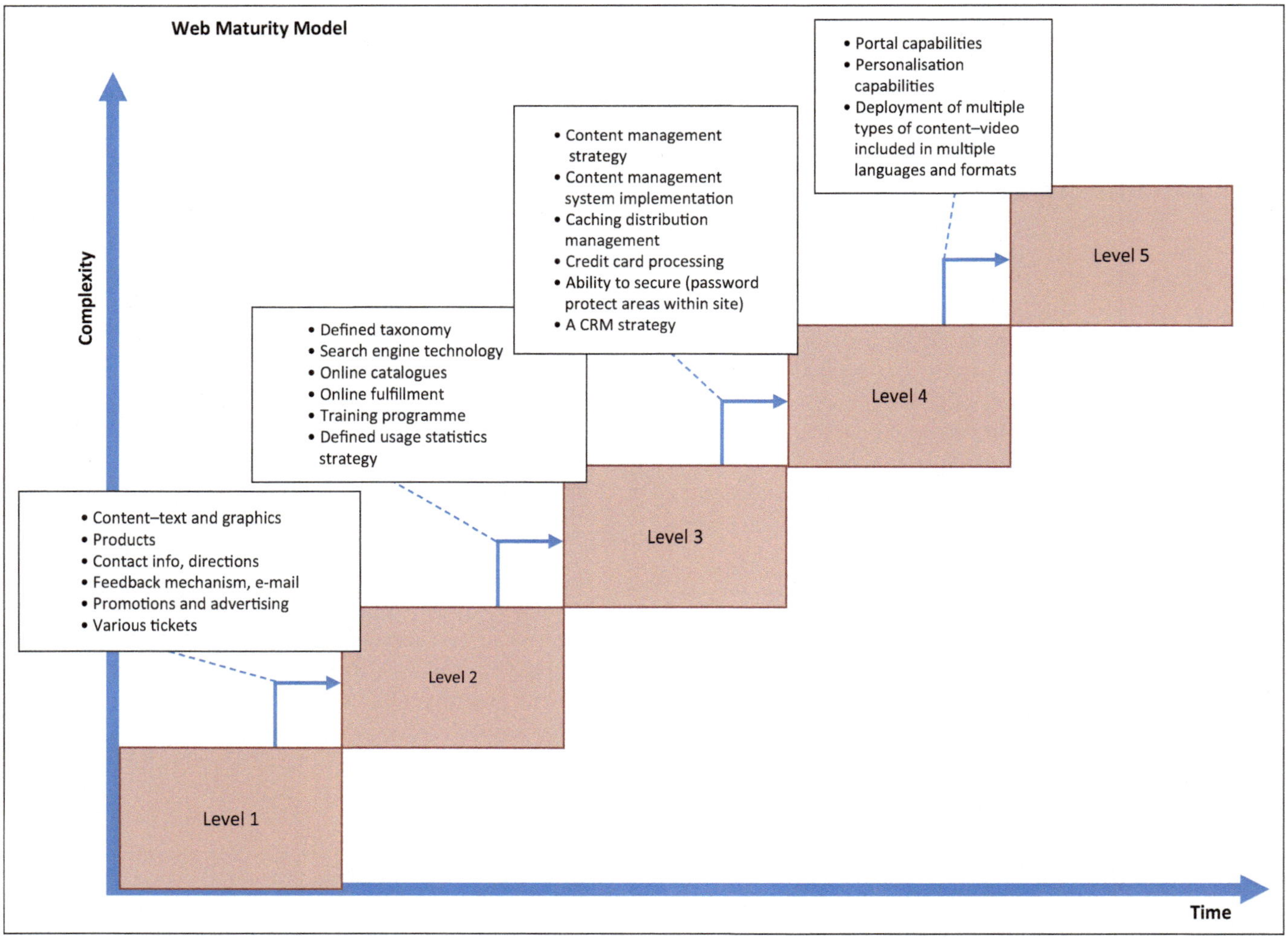

Source: Rhoads, V., 2008, *Web maturity models, business, technology*, viewed 19 March 2015, from http://www.slideshare.net/vtrhoads/web-maturity-models

FIGURE 1: Web maturity model.

evaluation criteria include the following (Remenyi 2002): first impressions, navigation, content, attractors, findability, making contact, browser compatibility, knowledge of users, user satisfaction and other useful information. Most of these criteria relate to *user experience*.

The concepts *website maturity*, *user-centred design* and *usability* are intricately related (Earthy, Jones & Bevan 2001). Tullis and Albert (2013) view *usability* as the ability of the user to use the product to successfully perform a task; this is measured in terms of effectiveness, efficiency and user satisfaction in completing a task. *User experience* takes a broader view of the entire interaction with the product and includes thoughts, feelings and perceptions (Tullis & Albert 2013). This aligns with the view of Rubinoff (2004), who describes *user experience* as consisting of four factors, namely usability, content, branding and functionality. A discussion of *user experience* and *usability* is beyond the scope of this study, but it suffices to say that the study aligns with the view of *user experience* subsuming *usability*, with the focus here being on *usability*, *content* and *functionality*, for purposes of identifying the maturity attributes. Furthermore, *content* is measured in terms of its authority, purpose, usefulness, coverage, currency, objectivity and accuracy (Dalhousie University 2015).

Inter-rater reliability

The reliability of a measure is defined as the ability to produce the same results under the same conditions (Field & Hole 2003). Whenever humans are involved in conducting an evaluation, concerns are raised about the reliability and consistency of the results. Inconsistency in ratings is possible because the evaluators or raters could have been distracted, they become tired of doing repetitive tasks or they could have misinterpreted the evaluation criteria. However, there are ways in which consistency among raters can be determined.

Four general classes of reliability estimates are identified (Trochim 2006). The inter-rater or inter-observer reliability procedure is used to measure the degree to which the same phenomenon receives a consistent score by different raters. In statistics, inter-rater reliability, inter-rater agreement and concordance are described as the extent of agreement among raters. It shows how much homogeneity, or consensus, there is in the ratings. The second class of reliability estimates includes test–retest reliability, which is a procedure used to assess the consistency of a measure from one time to another. A single rater can, for instance, rate a phenomenon twice at different times. The third class includes parallel-forms reliability. This procedure is used to measure consistency in the results of two tests constructed in the same way using the same content domain. The fourth class consists of internal consistency reliability procedures, which assess the consistency of results across items within a test.

The most commonly known procedures that can be used for inter-rater reliability tests are the joint probability of agreement test (Uebersax 1987); Cohen's (1960) Kappa statistics, which works for two raters; and Fleiss' Kappa (Fleiss 1971), which is an improvement on Cohen's Kappa (1960) and which works on any fixed number of raters. Correlation coefficients such as Spearman's ρ (rho) and Pearson's r can also be used to consider pairwise correlation among raters when using a scale that is ordered. Another method by which reliability testing can be performed is intraclass correlation coefficients (ICC); this is done by calculating the proportion of variance of an observation because of between subject variability in the true scores (Field 2006; Landis & Koch 1977; Ludbrook 2010).

Field (2009) notes two common uses of ICC: firstly, comparing paired data on the same measure; and secondly, assessing the consistency between the ratings provided by raters for a set of objects.

Calculation of the ICC depends on whether a measure of consistency (in which the order of scores from a source is considered but not the actual value around which the scores are anchored) or absolute agreement (in which both the order of scores and the relative values are considered), and whether the scores represent averages of many measures or just a single measure, is required (Field 2009).

Cluster analysis

Cluster analysis is a group of multivariate statistical techniques used to group data from a population into groups with similar characteristics. Three types of clustering techniques exist: hierarchical, non-hierarchical and a combination of hierarchical and non-hierarchical clustering techniques (Caccam & Refran 2012).

In hierarchical cluster analysis, the algorithm initially creates a cluster for each record or case in the database and then groups the cases together on the basis of similarities. It is a stepwise procedure that results in the construction of a hierarchy or tree-like structure of clusters (Sadiq 2012; Sarstedt & Mooi 2014). In non-hierarchical clustering analysis, a pre-determined number of categories are created, based on a selected criterion; the cases are then sorted into the categories or clusters based on similarities, using an iterative algorithm that optimises the chosen criterion (Sadiq 2012; Sarstedt & Mooi 2014).

The third technique, in which both hierarchical and non-hierarchical cluster methods are used, is called TwoStep cluster analysis (Elliott & Woodward 2007; Sadiq 2012). This method uses a hierarchical approach first and then a non-hierarchical approach. The hierarchical procedure produces the clusters; the non-hierarchical method then uses the produced clusters and clusters each case again to provide a more accurate cluster membership.

Research design

Data source and sample

An evaluation questionnaire was developed based on WMM theory, which included *user experience* attributes (cf. the section on WMM theory and Appendix 1). The aim of the questionnaire was to gather data on the website characteristics of the total population of 50 public TVET colleges in South Africa. A Microsoft Access form was created to capture the collected data. Nine evaluators scored the different aspects of the college websites and captured their scores on the Microsoft Access form. The Statistical Package for the Social Sciences (IBM SPSS) programme was utilised to calculate the inferential statistics. Inter-rater reliability was established and the collected data on website characteristics were subjected to cluster analysis techniques, in order to present clusters of public TVET colleges with similar website characteristics. TVET colleges' website maturity was used as a proxy for TVET colleges' MIS(s) maturity.

The questionnaire consisted of 17 questions. Fifteen of the seventeen questions queried the websites in terms of the availability of specific components, such as establishment date, contact and direction details, having a feedback mechanism, having search engine technology and having social media links. These components are related to the different maturity levels of websites. The other two questions, together with their sub-questions (question 4 and sub-questions 4a to 4g; question 5 and sub-questions 5a to 5e), required the evaluators to provide a score from 1 (poor) to 5 (excellent) for the appearance, usability and content information presented on the websites.

A sample of nine evaluators from three institutions was selected to conduct the survey – seven female and two male evaluators. One of the evaluators was part of the research team, and the other eight were master's interns (5) and university students (3), who were chosen conveniently. One of the evaluators was a researcher, another was an expert in web design, five were studying in the domain of computer–user interaction and the other two had studied mechanical engineering. The evaluators were trained on how to rate each aspect of the website to ensure that they used the same evaluation criteria. The total population of public TVET college websites was evaluated.

Because the method used to cluster the public TVET colleges relied heavily on the scores given by the evaluators, it was important to check the scores for consistency and reliability. ICC were calculated to determine inter-rater reliability (cf. the section about inter-rater reliability) to establish absolute agreement in the average scores of the nine evaluators on questions 4 and 5.

After inter-rater reliability had been established, TwoStep cluster analysis (cf. the section on cluster analysis) was used to group the colleges, based on website maturity level. The level of maturity of a college's website was used as a proxy for the maturity level of the college's MIS(s).

Data management and analysis for this study were conducted by using IBM SPSS, Microsoft Excel and Microsoft Access. The results and findings are presented in the following section.

Results and findings

About the websites

An analysis of the year of establishment of the websites revealed that most of the websites were established recently. Seventeen (34%) of the websites were less than 2 years old; 10 (20%) were 2 to 3 years old; 4 (8%) were 4 to 5 years old and 4 (8%) were older than 5 years. Two (4%) TVET colleges did not own a website, and the dates of establishment were not displayed on 13 (26%) of the websites (Figure 2).

Table 2 presents the number of websites that contained the listed components. Evidently, most of the 48 college websites contained components associated with the second level of web maturity, such as contact details (98%), directions (96%) and a feedback mechanism (74%). The fact that 77% of the websites had social media links could indicate a high usage of this functionality by stakeholders (students, staff, suppliers, etc.). Just more than half (53%) of the websites made provision for students to download a registration form. The reason for this phenomenon could be related to the illegal practice of downloading and selling registration forms to potential students who are without Internet access (as explained on one of the college websites).

In the light of the current focus on e-learning, the utilisation of social media platforms for improving academic performance of TVET students in the country and the fact

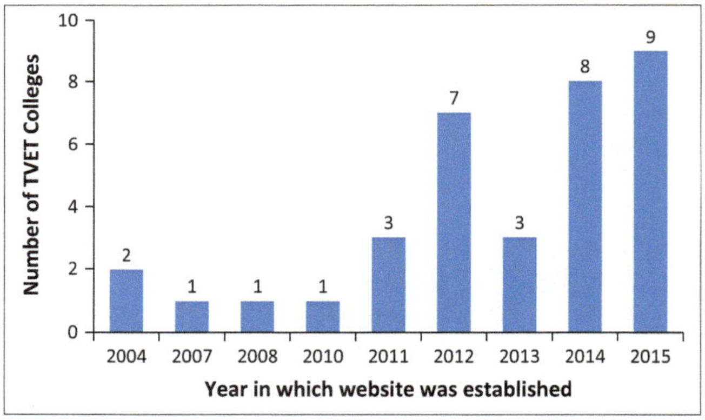

FIGURE 2: Year of establishment of TVET college websites.

TABLE 2: Number of websites by availability of specific components.

Components on website	Websites with capability		Web maturity level
	Number	%	
Contact details	46	98	2
Directions to college	45	96	2
Feedback mechanism	35	74	2
Search engine technology	27	57	3
Social media links	36	77	3
Registration form can be downloaded	25	53	3
Register online	6	12	4
Payment online	1	2	4
Portal capabilities for students	10	21	5
Deploy multiple types of content	7	15	5
Linked to a career portal or partners	17	36	5
Login facilities for staff or suppliers	16	33	5

that one of the biggest challenges identified by public TVET college lecturers was the lack of adequate contact hours for teaching (Dzvapatsva et al. 2014), it is surprising that only one in five websites (10 websites or 21%) had a portal capability for students. More than a third (17 or 36%) of the websites had electronic links to career portals.

The evaluators had to provide a score ranging from 1 (*poor*) to 5 (*excellent*) to questions and sub-questions 4 and 5 in the survey instrument. These questions examined the 'look-and-feel and usability' and 'content and information' of the websites, respectively (cf. Appendix 1). A weighted average index (WAI) was calculated for the scores provided by the evaluators at questions 4 and 5, as presented in Table 3. The WAIs of all evaluators were above the average of 2.5, which indicated that, on average, most of the websites were user-friendly and contained useful information. The minimum and maximum WAI values were (3.2 and 4.1) and (2.8 and 4.0), respectively, for the 'look-and-feel and usability' and value of 'content and information'. This indicates that more attention should be given to the 'content and information' on the websites.

Inter-rater reliability findings

An inter-rater reliability analysis was performed, using the ICC to determine absolute agreement among the average scores of the evaluators at questions 4 and 5 separately. The averages for questions 4a to 4g (variables were named $evalq4^i$ where $i \in \{1,2,3, \ldots 9\}$) and questions 5a to 5e (variables were named $evalq5^i$ where $i \in \{1,2,3, \ldots 9\}$) were calculated for each TVET college per evaluator. These average scores were used in the calculation of the ICC to establish inter-rater reliability.

The ICC were calculated by using a two-way random model, which controlled for evaluator effects and measured absolute agreement in which both the order of scores of evaluators and the relative values were considered. An ICC value of 0.7 and above is generally interpreted as acceptable, 0.8 and above is considered optimal and 0.9 and above is considered excellent (Field 2006, 2009).

Table 4 depicts the results of the ICC for the 'look-and-feel and usability' evaluation of the websites (from $evalq4^i$); Table 5 depicts the results for the 'content and information' evaluation (from $evalq5^i$). The tables include two sets of results: one for single measures and the other for average measures. We are interested in the average measures, which show how consistent the ratings were among all evaluators.

The inter-rater reliability on the scores for 'look-and-feel and usability' (Table 4) was found to be ICC (2,9) = 0.806 ($p < 0.000$), 95% CI (0.697, 0.885). In other words, the ICC value was 0.806, which indicates optimal agreement in the evaluators' scores. The confidence interval (CI) indicates that 95% of the samples of the data can be expected to have an ICC value between 0.697 and 0.885. The data thus seem to be reliable, with little variability between the evaluators.

TABLE 3: Frequencies of website scores provided by evaluators.

Category	Evaluator value	Score					Total	WAI
		Poor-->--Excellent						
		1	2	3	4	5		
Look-and-feel and usability	Evaluator 1	0	4	6	20	17	47	4.1
	Evaluator 2	2	8	21	11	5	47	3.2
	Evaluator 3	0	6	27	10	4	47	3.3
	Evaluator 4	0	9	23	9	6	47	3.3
	Evaluator 5	3	4	15	21	0	43	3.3
	Evaluator 6	1	3	28	11	2	45	3.2
	Evaluator 7	1	1	11	22	10	45	3.9
	Evaluator 8	1	1	12	19	12	45	3.9
	Evaluator 9	5	7	12	13	7	44	3.2
Content and information	Evaluator 1	0	1	13	16	17	47	4.0
	Evaluator 2	0	5	20	13	9	47	3.6
	Evaluator 3	0	11	19	15	2	47	3.2
	Evaluator 4	2	5	19	19	2	47	3.3
	Evaluator 5	6	4	24	10	0	44	2.9
	Evaluator 6	2	2	27	16	0	47	3.2
	Evaluator 7	1	2	8	19	15	45	4.0
	Evaluator 8	2	3	14	19	7	45	3.6
	Evaluator 9	9	10	8	15	2	44	2.8

WAI, weighted average scores.

TABLE 4: Intraclass correlation coefficient of rater scores for websites in terms of look-and-feel and usability.

Measure	Intraclass correlation‡	95% confidence interval		*F*-test with true value 0			
		Lower bound	Upper bound	Value	*df* 1	*df* 2	Sig
Single	0.316a†	0.204	0.460	6.410	40	320	0.000
Average	0.806	0.697	0.885	6.410	40	320	0.000

df, degrees of freedom; Sig, significance.

†, The estimator is the same, whether the interaction effect is present or not; ‡, Type A intraclass correlation coefficients using an absolute agreement definition.

Note: Two-way random effects model where both people effects and measures effects are random.

TABLE 5: Intraclass correlation coefficient of rater scores for websites in terms of content and information.

Measure	Intraclass correlation‡	95% confidence interval		F-test with true value 0			
		Lower bound	Upper bound	Value	*df* 1	*df* 2	Sig
Single	0.223†	0.126	0.359	4.908	40	320	0.000
Average	0.721	0.564	0.835	4.908	40	320	0.000

df, degrees of freedom; sig, significance.
†, The estimator is the same, whether the interaction effect is present or not; ‡, Type A intraclass correlation coefficients using an absolute agreement definition.
Note: Two-way random effects model where both people effects and measures effects are random.

In addition, 80.6% of the variance in the means of the evaluators' scores was real and not because of chance.

The inter-rater reliability for evaluator scores on the 'content and information' (Table 5) was found to be ICC (2,9) = 0.721 ($p < 0.000$), 95% CI (0.564, 0.835). In other words, the ICC value was 0.721, which indicates an acceptable agreement in the evaluators' scores. The CI indicates that 95% of the samples of the data can be expected to have an ICC value between 0.564 and 0.835. The data thus seem to be reliable, with little variability between the evaluators. In addition, 72.1% of the variance in the means of the evaluators' scores was real and not because of chance.

After inter-rater reliability had been established and the data were found to be reliable, cluster analysis was performed on the data.

Cluster analysis findings

A TwoStep cluster analysis, which includes both hierarchical and non-hierarchical cluster methods, was performed on the data to find a suitable model to cluster the colleges. The TwoStep cluster analysis made use of the log-likelihood distance measurement and was based on Schwarz's Bayesian criterion.

Three input variables were used in the clustering analysis, that is, the overall average of all evaluators' scores for question four (variable named *Avgq4*) and for question five (variable named *Avgq5*), and a newly created variable called *Compfinal*. The variable *Compfinal* represented the number of components included on the websites of the colleges; this was generated by calculating the sum of the values for questions 6 and 8 to 17 in the questionnaire for each college. The values for the variable *Compfinal* could, therefore, be any number from 0 to 11 (dichotomous variables: 0 = no or 1 = yes). Descriptive statistics for the variable *Compfinal* were calculated: values ranged from 0 to 7, the mean was $M = 4.08$ and the standard deviation was SD = 1.75.

Figure 3 presents the results of the most suitable model of clusters. The model presents a silhouette measure of cohesion and separation of above 0.5, which indicates cluster quality and a good model fit. Usually, an acceptable ratio of cluster sizes is between 2 and 3 (Sadiq 2012; Sarstedt & Mooi 2014), but because two TVET colleges did not own a website, a separate cluster to contain those colleges and the colleges with websites at a low maturity level made sense, and the cluster ratio size of 10.00 was accepted.

The model presented three clusters: cluster 1 (6% or 3 colleges) represents colleges with no websites or websites at a very low maturity level; cluster 2 (60% or 30 colleges) represents colleges with websites at an average maturity level; cluster 3 (34% or 17 colleges) represents colleges with good quality websites. The technical report in which the outcome of the cluster analysis is presented can be viewed at http://tinyurl.com/zde2fa5.

The results can be summarised as follows:

- *Websites in cluster 1* had, on average, one of the 11 components; were evaluated at 0.55, on average, for 'look-and-feel and usability', were rated, on average, at 0.46 for 'content and information' quality.
- *Websites in cluster 2* had, on average, three of the 11 components; and scored, on average, 3.29 and 3.06 for 'look-and-feel and usability' and 'information and content', respectively.
- *Websites in cluster 3* had, on average, six of the 11 components; and scored, on average, 4.02 and 3.67 for 'look-and-feel and usability' and 'information and content', respectively.

The results are graphically presented in Figure 3, in which it is evident that the input variable *Avgq5* had the highest predictor importance (1.00) and the other two variables – 'mean score of evaluators on question 4' (*Avgq4*) and *Compfinal* – contributed 0.99 and 0.96 to the prediction of the clusters, respectively.

Ethical consideration

Ethical clearance for the research study was granted by the College of Science, Engineering and Technology's (CSET) Research and Ethics Committee, which is part of the University of South Africa (UNISA).

Discussion

This study has implications for methods of selecting cases for qualitative case study research. The study showed how the set of 50 public TVET colleges was grouped into groups with similar website characteristics. An evaluation questionnaire was developed, based on WMM theory. The evaluation questionnaire included user experience attributes and was used by nine evaluators to evaluate the websites of the 50 public TVET colleges in South Africa. Inter-rater reliability of the nine evaluators was established, with the calculation of ICC. Hierarchical and non-hierarchal cluster analysis (TwoStep) was used to cluster the population of public TVET colleges.

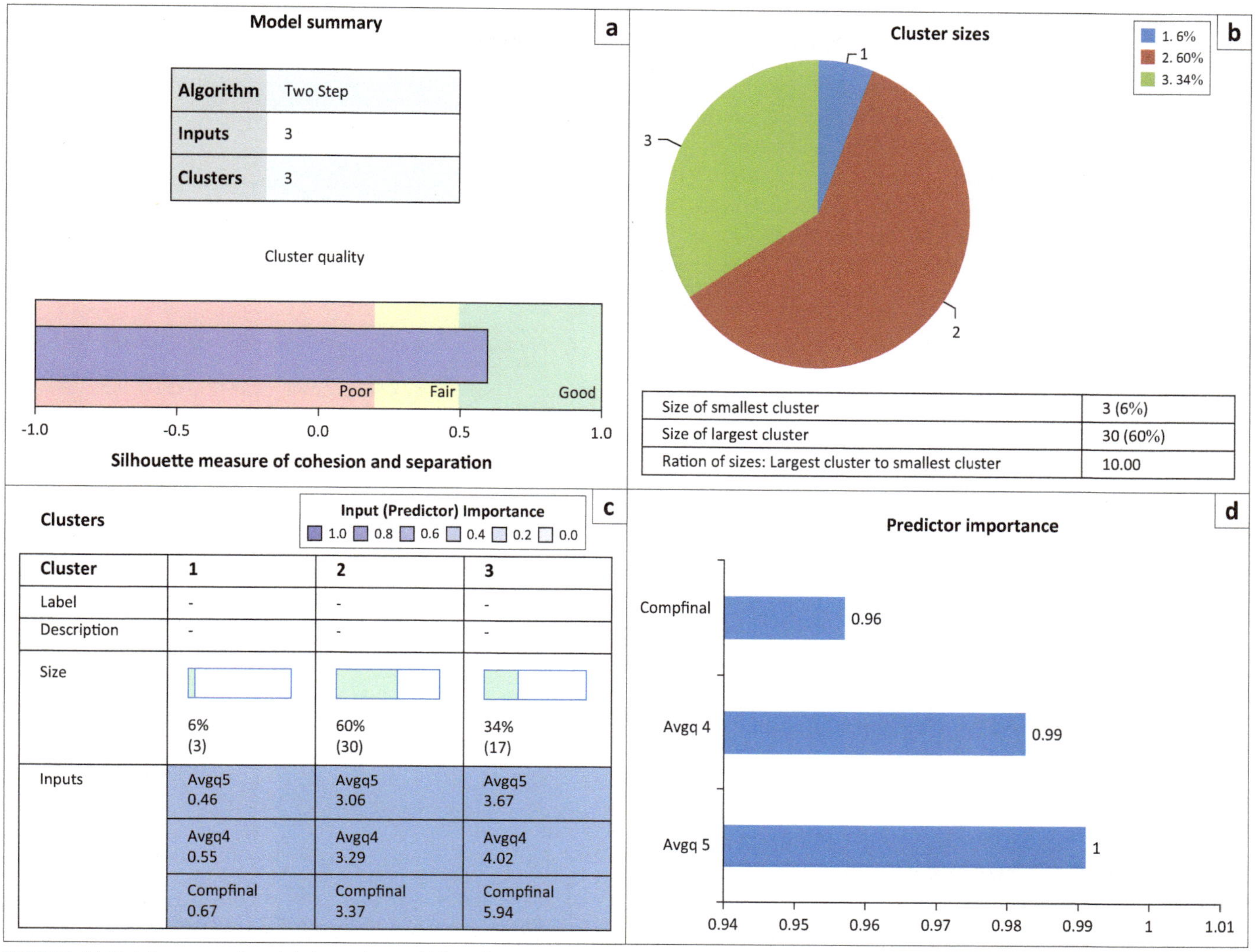

FIGURE 3: (a) Model summary, (b and c) cluster sizes and (d) predictor importance, as calculated using TwoStep cluster analysis.

Three groups emerged from the analysis (cf. Figure 3): colleges without a website or websites at a low maturity level (cluster 1); colleges with websites that achieved an average score for first impression of structure, appearance, navigation, ease of finding specific functionality and the comprehensiveness and usefulness of content and information about programmes offered and how to apply and register at the college (cluster 2); and colleges that met the usability requirements of user experience and satisfaction, information requirements and comprehensive functionality in terms of number of components available (cluster 3).

It is important to keep in mind that the outcome of statistical or technical procedures should (as far as possible) be verified with qualitative empirical evidence (Punj & Stewart 1983). Although we have to reject clusters that do not meet minimum statistical requirements, this does not mean that clusters that are statistically acceptable are the only meaningful clustering outcome (Klastorin 1983). Future studies could investigate other methods to cluster public TVET colleges into groups with similar website or MIS characteristics.

Furthermore, for future research that focuses on websites or MISs at public TVET colleges, researchers could select cases from the three clusters to ensure representation of all categories. One should also take into consideration that college websites and MISs develop and grow in maturity over time, and therefore, it might be necessary to repeat this analysis in future to enable up-to-dating of the categorisation of public TVET colleges in groups with similar website or MIS characteristics.

Conclusion

The aim of the study was to propose an evidence-based quantitative method for the selection of cases for case study research. The method was demonstrated by clustering TVET colleges in South Africa based on website maturity models, as a proxy for information systems maturity.

The method of case selection presented in this article is a more rigorous alternative to convenient or purposive sample selection techniques and was intended to be uncomplicated and replicable by researchers and practitioners with different levels of proficiency in statistical analysis.

Technological developments have provided many tools for new and innovative ways of analysing data. However, to ensure rigor in the selection of cases in qualitative research studies, it is important that researchers also develop innovative methods for sample selection to overcome subjectivity and bias. The evidence-based method, which used quantitative data, is a contribution in terms of basic practice for sample selection. Quantitative data were gathered through an evaluation questionnaire to generate a proxy for the level of IS development of individual public TVET colleges in South Africa. The presented method can be applied by any researcher to ensure that objectivity is ensured when selecting cases and to ensure rigour in the research methodology of a study.

Besides the practical contribution of clustering public TVET colleges, the value of this study resides on the evidence-based method, and the replicative value that it offers researchers and practitioners in any field of study, where cases for in-depth case studies, has to be selected. A summary of the method is provided in Appendix 2. The novelty lies in using a specific characteristic as proxy for clustering the cases, so that at least one case from each cluster can be selected. Clustering of the population in this study was based on the maturity level of the population's websites, but in other populations, other easily accessible and available relevant information could be collected, captured and used in cluster analysis. Future research is needed to triangulate the findings from the quantitative clustering with a qualitative method, for example, clustering by expert review.

Acknowledgements

The authors would like to express their sincere gratitude to the nine evaluators who took the time to evaluate the 50 public TVET college websites. Our appreciation also goes to Dr. Linda Zuze, for comments made on the draft version of this article. The study was partly funded by UNISA and the Human Sciences Research Council (HSRC).

Competing interests

The authors declare that they have no financial or personal relationship that may have influenced them inappropriately in writing this article.

Author's contributions

The study was conducted as part of the doctoral degree requirements of Mariette Visser. Judy van Biljon acted as the supervisor, and Marlien Herselman acted as the joint supervisor for the study.

References

Benbasat, I., Goldstein, D.K. & Mead, M., 1987, 'The case research strategy in studies of information systems', *MIS Quarterly* 11(3), 369–386. https://doi.org/10.2307/248684

Ben-Zvi, D., Bakker, A. & Makar, K., 2015, 'Learning to reason from samples', *Educational Studies in Mathematics* 88, 291–303, viewed 11 April 2015, from http://link.springer.com/article/10.1007/s10649-015-9593-3/fulltext.html

Burgess, S., Sellitto, C. & Karanasios, S., 2009, *Effective web presence solutions for small businesses: Strategies for successful implementation*, IGI Global, Hershey, PA.

Caccam, M. & Refran, J., 2012, *Cluster analysis*, Slideshare, 1–100, viewed 19 March 2015, from http://www.slideshare.net/jewelmrefran/cluster-analysis-15529464

Cohen, J., 1960, 'A coefficient for agreement for nominal scales', *Education and Psychological Measurement* 20, 37–46. https://doi.org/10.1177/001316446002000104

Dalhousie University, 2015, *Criteria for websites. Evaluating web resources*, Dalhousie University, viewed 19 March 2015, from http://libraries.dal.ca/using_the_library/evaluating_web_resources/6_criteria_forwebsites.html

Del Mar, V., 2011, *Introducing UNESCO's Technical Vocational Education and Training (TVET) definition and strategy*, United Nations Educational, Scientific and Cultural Organization (UNESCO), viewed 13 September 2015, from http://www.uis.unesco.org/StatisticalCapacityBuilding/

Department of Higher Education and Training (DHET), 2013, *White paper for post-school education and training: Building an expanded effective and integrated post-school system*, Department of Higher Education and Training (DHET), Pretoria.

Dzvapatsva, G.P., Mitrovic, Z. & Dietrich, A.D., 2014, 'Use of social media platforms for improving academic performance at Further Education and Training colleges', *South African Journal of Information Management* 16(1), Art. #604, 1–7. https://doi.org/10.4102/sajim.v16i1.604

Earthy, J., Jones, B.S. & Bevan, N., 2001, 'The improvement of human-centred processes – Facing the challenge and reaping the benefit of ISO 13407', *International Journal of Human-Computer Studies* 55(4), 553–585, viewed 11 April 2015, from http://www.idealibrary.com

Elliott, A.C. & Woodward, W.A., 2007, *Statistical analysis quick reference guidebook: With SPSS examples*, Sage Publication Ltd., London.

Esterhuizen, D., Schutte, C. & du Toit, A., 2012, 'A knowledge management framework to grow innovation capability maturity', *South African Journal of Information Management* 14(1), Art. #495, 1–10. https://doi.org/10.4102/sajim.v14i1.495

Fath-Allah, A., Cheikhi, L., Al-Qutaish, R.E. & Idri, A., 2014, 'E-government maturity models: A comparative study', *International Journal of Software Engineering & Applications* 5(3), 71–91.

Feild, L., Pruchno, R.A., Bewley, J., Lemay, E.P. & Levinsky, N.G., 2006, 'Using probability vs. nonprobability sampling to identify hard-to-access participants for health-related research: Costs and contrasts', *Journal of Aging and Health* 18(4), 565–583. https://doi.org/10.1177/0898264306291420

Field, A.P., 2006, 'Intraclass correlation', *Encyclopedia of Statistics in Behavioural Science, Volume 2*, pp. 948–954, John Wiley and Sons Ltd., Chichester, UK.

Field, A.P., 2009, *Discovering statistics using SPSS*, 3rd edn., Sage Publication Ltd., London.

Field, A.P. & Hole, G., 2003, *How to design and report experiments*, Sage Publications Ltd. London.

Fleiss, J.L., 1971, 'Measuring nominal scale agreement among many raters', *Psychological Bulletin* 76(5), 378–382.

Flyvbjerg, B., 2006, 'Five misunderstandings about case-study research', *Qualitative Inquiry* 12(2), 219–245, viewed 25 March 2016, from http://qix.sagepub.com/content/12/2/219.abstract

Klastorin, T.D., 1983, 'Cluster analysis results', *Journal of Marketing Research* 20(1), 92–98. https://doi.org/10.2307/3151416

Landis, J.R. & Koch, G.G., 1977, 'The measurement of observer agreement for categorical data', *Biometrics* 33, 159–174. https://doi.org/10.2307/2529310

Ludbrook, J., 2010, 'Confidence in Altman–Bland plots: A critical review of the method of differences', *Clinical and Experimental Pharmacology and Physiology* 37(2), 143–149. https://doi.org/10.1111/j.1440-1681.2009.05288.x

Mannie, A., Van Niekerk, H.J. & Adendorff, C.M., 2013, 'Significant factors for enabling knowledge sharing between government agencies within South Africa', *South African Journal of Information Management* 15(2), Art. #569, 1–8. https://doi.org/10.4102/sajim.v15i2.569

Miles, M.B., Huberman, A.M. & Saldana, J., 2014, *Qualitative data analysis: A methods sourcebook*, Sage Publications, Inc., Thousand Oaks, CA.

Mouton, J., 2001, *How to succeed in your master's and doctoral studies: A South African guide and resource book*, Van Schaik Publishers, Pretoria.

Mudzana, T. & Maharaj, M., 2015, 'Measuring the success of business-intelligence systems in South Africa: An empirical investigation applying the DeLone and McLean Model', *South African Journal of Information Management*, 17(1), Art. #646, 1–7, viewed 21 March 2016, from http://www.sajim.co.za/index.php/SAJIM/article/view/646

Oates, B.J., 2006, *Researching information systems and computing*, Sage Publication Ltd, London.

Paulk, M.C., Weber, C.V., Curtis, B. & Chrissis, M.B., 1993, *Capability maturity model for software (Version 1.1)*, Technical Report, Software Engineering Institute, Carnegie Mellon University, Pittsburgh, PA, CMU/SEI-93-TR-024 ESC-TR-93-177.

Punj, G. & Stewart, D.W., 1983, 'Cluster analysis in marketing research: Review and suggestions for application', *Journal of Marketing Research* 20(2), 134–148. https://doi.org/10.2307/3151680

Remenyi, D., 2002, *Criteria to evaluate a website*, Management Centre International Limited, England, viewed 19 March 2015, from http://www.mcil.co.uk/review/7-10-criteria.htm

Rhoads, V., 2008, *Web maturity models, business, technology*, viewed 19 March 2015, from http://www.slideshare.net/vtrhoads/web-maturity-models

Rubinoff, R., 2004, 'Quantify user experience', *Design & UX*, viewed 12 June 2015, from http://www.sitepoint.com/quantify-user-experience/

Sadiq, M.M., 2012, *Cluster analysis in SPSS (hierarchical, non-hierarchical & two-step)*, viewed 19 March 2015, from https://www.youtube.com/watch?v=eW9KnSRDyTk

Sarstedt, M. & Mooi, E., 2014, *A concise guide to market research: The process, data, and methods using IBM SPSS statistics*, Springer-Verlag, Berlin, viewed 19 March 2015, from http://www.guide-market-research.com/

Seawright, J. & Gerring, J., 2008, 'Case selection techniques in case study research: A menu of qualitative and quantitative options', *Political Research Quarterly* 61(2), 294–308. https://doi.org/10.1177/1065912907313077

Seddon, P. & Scheepers, R., 2012, 'Towards the improved treatment of generalization of knowledge claims in IS research: Drawing general conclusions from samples', *European Journal of Information Systems* 21, 6–21. https://doi.org/10.1057/ejis.2011.9

StatPac., 2014, *Survey sampling methods*, StatPac, viewed 11 April 2015, from https://www.statpac.com/surveys/sampling.htm

Summers, S., 1991, 'Selecting the sample for a research study', *Journal of Post Anesthesia Nursing* 6(5), 355–363, viewed 17 September 2015, from http://www.ncbi.nlm.nih.gov/pubmed/1833537

Trochim, W.M., 2006, *The research methods knowledge base*, 2nd edn., Research Methods: Knowledge Base, viewed 2 April 2015, from http://www.socialresearchmethods.net/kb

Tullis, T. & Albert, W., 2013, *Measuring the user experience – Collecting, analyzing, and presenting usability metrics, 2nd edn.*, Morgan Kauffman, 320 p.

TVET Colleges South Africa, 2015, *Public TVET Colleges: Overview*, The official website for the DHET TVET Colleges, viewed 25 March 2015, from http://www.fetcolleges.co.za/

UBC, 2015, *Web maturity model – Information technology*, University of British Columbia, viewed 5 December 2015, from http://www.it.ubc.ca

Uebersax, J.S., 1987, 'Diversity of decision making models and the measurement of interrater agreement', *Psychological Bulletin* 101, 140–146. https://doi.org/10.1037/0033-2909.101.1.140

UNCTAD & TNSO, 2008, *United Nations Conference on Trade and Development. Measuring the impact of ICT use in business: The case of manufacturing in Thailand. Prepared jointly by the UNCTAD secretariat and the Thailand National Statistical Office (TNSO)*, United Nations, New York, viewed 12 November 2016, from http://unctad.org/en/docs/sdteecb20073_en.pdf

Visser, M.M., van Biljon, J.A. & Herselman, M.E., 2013, 'Evaluation of management information systems: A study at a Further Education and Training college', *South African Journal of Information Management* 15(1), Art. #531, 1–8. https://doi.org/10.4102/sajim.15i1.531

Williamson, G.R., 2003, 'Misrepresenting random sampling? A systematic review of research papers in the Journal of Advanced Nursing', *Journal of Advanced Nursing* 44(3), 278–288. https://doi.org/10.1046/j.1365-2648.2003.02803.x

Ziemba, E. & Papaj, T., 2013, 'A pragmatic approach to the e-government maturity in Poland – Implementation and usage of SEKAP', Academic Conferences International Limited, Varese, Italy, June 2013, pp. 560–570.

Appendix 1

Questionnaire: Evaluation tool

The following three pictures depict the pages in the Microsoft Access tool that was used in the evaluation of the TVET college websites.

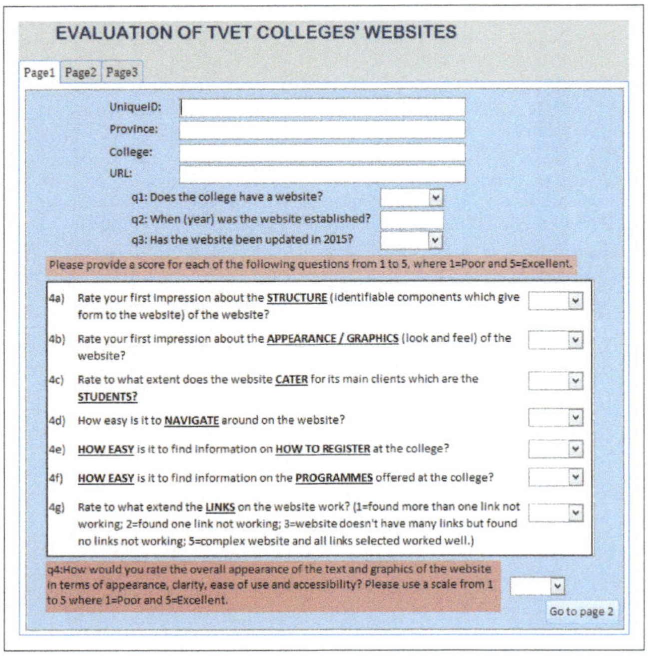

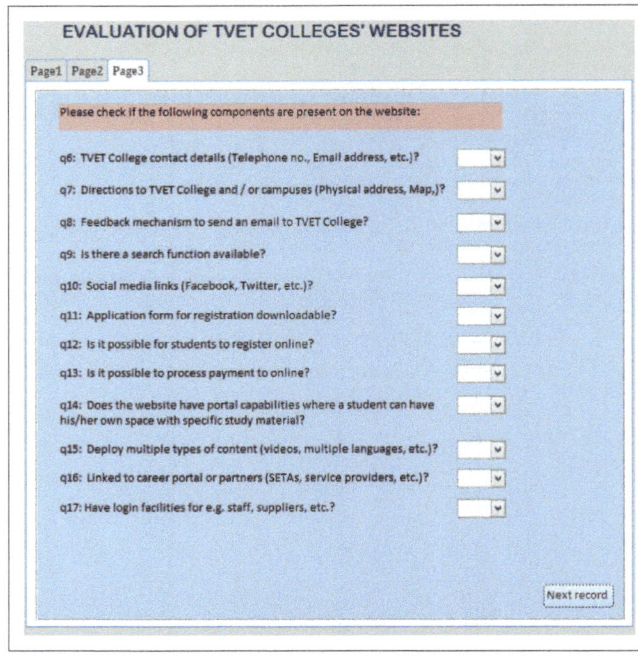

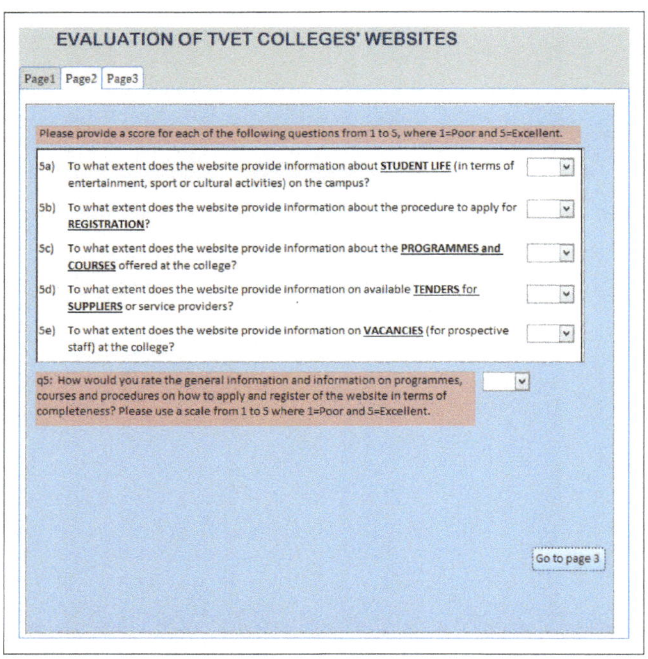

Appendix 2

Steps in the method proposed in this study

Step 1: Decide which characteristics the clusters should be included, based on the research study for which the cases are required.

Step 2: Do a literature study on the characteristics under investigation (in this study, the IS characteristics of public TVET colleges, based on the web maturity level of the websites).

Step 3: Design and develop (based on extant literature) a survey or evaluation questionnaire to capture appropriate quantitative data on the characteristics.

Step 4: Select and brief reviewers or data collectors.

Step 5: Collect the data and compile into an electronic data set.

Step 6: Import the data set into a statistical software package and perform descriptive and inferential statistical procedures to ensure a rigorous outcome.

Step 7: To calculate the ICC, the following steps were followed separately for variables $evalq4^i$ and $evalq5^i$: in IBM SPSS, select 'Analyse', 'Scale', 'Reliability Analysis', then select the appropriate variables (in this study, first $evalq4^i$ and then $evalq5^i$ in the second analysis), then click on 'Statistics'. Make sure that the box next to 'Intraclass Correlation Coefficient' is checked. After the ICC box has been checked, select the 'Two-way Random' (or context applicable) model and the 'Absolute Agreement' type. Then run the analyses.

Step 8: Three variables were created for inclusion in a cluster analysis (*Avgq4*, *Avgq5*, *Compfinal*). The following steps were followed in IBM SPSS: select 'Analyse', 'Classify', 'TwoStep Cluster'. Then select the variables and place them in the applicable variable type box (categorical/ continuous). Change the 'Determine automatically maximum' clusters to the required number (in this study, 4 was chosen). Under 'Output', check 'Create cluster membership variable', to enable the creation of a variable for the classification of the TVET colleges.

Step 9: Select cases from each cluster, as appropriate.

13

Motivational theory and knowledge sharing in the public service

Authors:
Nthabiseng N. Mosala-Bryant[1]
Ruth G. Hoskins[1]

Affiliations:
[1]Department of Information Studies, University of KwaZulu-Natal, South Africa

Corresponding author:
Nthabiseng Mosala-Bryant,
bryantn@unizulu.ac.za

Background: Knowledge sharing has been identified as the core process of knowledge management for institutions which are interested in the retention of knowledge invested in their human capital in the event of their departure from the institutions. To this end, knowledge sharing has been the focus of research institution-wide, and less focus has been paid to communities of practice (CoPs) within the South African public service.

Objectives: This study aimed to explore factors that motivated knowledge sharing practices in a South African public service CoP.

Method: This study used the mixed methods design through the lens of the motivational theory. Primary quantitative data were collected by means of self-administered questionnaires returned by 23 of the 31 KwaZulu-Natal (KZN) Provincial Human Resource Development Forum (PHRDF) members to whom the questionnaires were distributed. In addition, primary qualitative data were collected from the senior managers of Human Resource Development (HRD) units from 10 different KZN Provincial Departments of the 14 managers requested. The quantitative analysis was established using SPSS software, whereas qualitative analysis was established using thematic codes with the NVIVO software.

Results: The findings from the results revealed that PHRDF members were intrinsically motivated to share their knowledge rather than extrinsically motivated.

Conclusion: Although literature confirmed the main barrier to knowledge sharing in organisations as being the unwillingness to share, CoPs were likely to reduce the extent to which knowledge sharing was hindered. Members of a CoP ultimately related to one another as homogeneous groups despite representing different departments. To this end, hedonic intrinsic motivation occurred as members shared knowledge for the good of the whole regardless of the absence of extrinsic motivation. Departmental silos fell away, and there was no anticipation of rewards or incentives for knowledge sharing. It is, therefore, imperative that the South African public service strategically positions CoPs as knowledge sharing platforms to curb the loss of knowledge when employees leave its employ for whatever reason.

Introduction

Knowledge has always been treasured in business as it contributes to the success of any organisation; hence, it is required to successfully accomplish organisational goals. However, if knowledge is retained by a few individuals without sharing with others, there is a risk of losing such knowledge should those individuals leave the organisation. Knowledge management (KM) emerged in the 20th century as one of the business processes used to avoid the loss of knowledge with the aim to capture, store and redistribute organisational knowledge. Notwithstanding the business industry's proactive stance towards realising the importance of managing knowledge produced in organisations, the public sector has finally caught up with making KM one of its management processes. Members of the public increasingly demand that the public sector determine, define and forecast their needs as clients and to develop, modify and adjust services to match these needs (Durrant 2001). KM is one of the tools that could be used to provide solutions to the problems of service delivery which the public experience by applying proven best practice to service delivery challenges and problems.

As KM focused on managing knowledge by sharing such knowledge, and the public service operates according to the mandate of delivering uniform and quality service to every citizen, it is imperative that knowledge sharing amongst public servants be used as a vehicle to accomplish such objectives. KM consists of activities whose purpose is to capture, store and share knowledge in various ways (Majewski, Usor & Khan 2011). The South African public service organisational structure consists of a Human Resource Development (HRD) unit in each government department, which is responsible for equipping public servants with various skills to perform their jobs competently. In the KwaZulu-Natal (KZN) provincial administration, the HRD units are monitored by the Provincial Public Service Training Academy (PPSTA), which is located in the Office of the Premier (OTP). The Department of Public Service and Administration (DPSA) receives KZN departmental HRD reports such as Assessment and Training Reports (ATR) and Workplace Skills Plans (WSPs) sent by the PPSTA. The PPSTA is also responsible for drafting the KZN Provincial Human Resource Development Strategy (PHRDS). The KZN HRD units acknowledge that KM is one of the pillars of organisational development. This article is based on a PhD study, which explored knowledge sharing in the public service. The KZN Provincial Human Resource Development Forum (PHRDF), which is a forum for HRD practitioners, was used as a case study because it comprised a 'group of people who share a concern, a set of problems, or a passion about a topic, and who deepen their knowledge and expertise in this area by interacting on an ongoing basis' (Ntala 2010).

Problem statement

There is ample knowledge created and accumulated by South African public servants in their duties towards fulfilling their service delivery mandates. The knowledge created is enhanced by the amount of training that occurs through the HRD units and also as applied during projects which government undertakes as prompted by the State of the Nation Address (SONA) or State of the Province Address (SOPA) and supported by the annual budget speeches. Whether the knowledge accumulated by South African public servants was shared amongst one another and what motivated the sharing was the subject of the study. Because of the high turnover of employees in the South African public service as a result of resignations, retirements, promotions, sickness or death, sharing the knowledge which has been acquired by these employees through government spending on their training and other capacitating initiatives would be a justifiable exercise. However, there is no available national KM strategy or policy which would enable the management and sharing of knowledge in the South African public service. Notwithstanding attempts that had been made by the DPSA in drafting a National Framework for Knowledge Management, the area of KM has not received the attention it deserves (Mphahlele 2010). According to the Public Service Commission (2011), the movement of senior managers (SMs)[1] through their ranks is prevalent and normal. However, there is no study that shows what motivates public servants to share their knowledge with one another.

1. SMs ranks start from Level 13 to Level 16 and are named Senior Director, Chief Director, Deputy Director-General and Director General at National Government, respectively, and are called Senior Manager, General Manager, Senior General Manager and Head of Department or Director-General in case of the Office of the Premier in Provincial Government.

Purpose of the study

Several studies have been done on KM and how it contributes to service delivery in South Africa (Bhyat, Van der Westhuizen & Blackburn 2005; Chaba 2003; Fraser 2004; Kgarimetsa-Phiri 2009; Radebe 2002; Soko 2005). Some studies were undertaken to explore indigenous knowledge sharing activities in communities (Lwoga, Ngulube & Stilwell 2012; Munyua & Stilwell 2012). A few studies explored knowledge sharing in the South African public service (Mkhize 2015), whereas other studies focussed on KM in the South African public service (Gaffoor & Cloete 2010; Maponya 2005). The above studies did not focus on isolating knowledge sharing in public service CoPs and what motivates group members to share their knowledge with one another. This article aimed at describing knowledge sharing activities in a case study of a CoP within a public service environment and the various factors that motivated knowledge sharing in this environment.

Objectives of the study

The objective of this article is to explore what motivates knowledge sharing practices of the KZN PHRDF so that the findings could be replicated to encourage the use of CoPs in the public service, specifically for knowledge sharing.

Research question

In order to locate the motivating factors behind knowledge sharing by PHRDF members, this article is guided by the following major question: What factors motivated knowledge sharing between PHRDF members?

Theoretical framework

In order to determine why the PHRDF members shared knowledge, this study examined the motivational factors, which drove their knowledge sharing behaviours. Motivation theory suggests that motivation drives human behaviour (Jeon, Young-Gul & Koh 2011). This study adopted Lam and Lambermont-Ford's (2010) model, 'a three-category taxonomy of motivation to examine knowledge sharing behaviour in' an organisation. The three-category taxonomy of motivation consists of the traditional dichotomy of extrinsic and intrinsic motivation and adding hedonic motivation as a way of closing the gap between the two. The gap occurs because 'extrinsic motivation may support the transfer of explicit knowledge, which is measurable but often fails in the case of tacit knowledge' which is intangible (Lam & Lambermont-Ford 2010).

Literature review

Motivational theories are psychological ways of understanding what inspires human beings to extend their abilities and perform according to expectations. There are various motivational theories developed by theorists such as Abraham Maslow, Douglas Mcgregor, Frederick Herzberg and others. Motivation theory suggests that motivation drives human behaviour (Jeon et al. 2011). In order to determine why the PHRDF members share knowledge, this study examined the motivational factors which drive their knowledge sharing behaviours. Although 'knowledge sharing is a key process in translating individual learning into organisational capability', facilitating it is a difficult task (Jeon et al. 2011). According to Lam and Lambermont-Ford's (2010) study, 'a three-category taxonomy of motivation to examine knowledge sharing behaviour' in an organisation was used, which this study adopted. Lindenberg (2001) divided 'intrinsic motivation into normative and hedonic types which interact with each other and with extrinsic motivation'. This division provided a 'more complete match between the individual and organisational environments' for knowledge sharing.

'Normative intrinsic motivation is directed towards the individual's sense of compliance with personal and social norms', and the 'degree to which individuals act or do not act when normatively motivated' (Lam & Lambermont-Ford 2010). This type of motivation 'depends on the importance that they attach to compliance in a given context and also the external reaction to non-compliance' (Lam & Lambermont-Ford 2010). Lindenberg (2001) posited that 'hedonic intrinsic motivation is derived from the engagement in self-determined, competence enhancing and enjoyable activity achieved through physical and social wellbeing and improvement in the individual's condition'. 'This influences the willingness of an individual to share knowledge, depending on the importance that the individual' appropriates to being involved in such an activity. The significance of hedonic motivation includes its ability to stimulate creativity and innovation as it induces knowledge-seeking behaviour and increases cognitive effort (Lam & Lambermont-Ford 2010). The relationship between intrinsic, extrinsic and hedonic motivation maybe the complex interaction effects between them. For example, 'extrinsic rewards may undermine intrinsic motivation for interesting tasks and encourage knowledge hoarding' (Lam & Lambermont-Ford 2010). 'Self-esteem may be lessened when the individual's intrinsic motivation is not acknowledged, implying that their efforts are not appreciated' (Lam & Lambermont-Ford 2010). 'This may occur when incentives are given for specific performances or behaviours, affecting the internally driven behaviours' (Lam & Lambermont-Ford 2010) and causing individuals to prefer reward-driven behaviours.

On the contrary, there are beneficial effects of extrinsic motivators on hedonic and normative motivation, which result from the individual's perception that they are supportive and congruent with the underlying normative and hedonic motivational preferences (Lam & Lambermont-Ford 2010). 'These are extrinsic motivators that provide feedback', recognise and reward as well as confirm or improve competencies leading to increased self-esteem (Lam & Lambermont-Ford 2010). Similar 'extrinsic motivators (such as career progression and increased involvement that aligns with the individual's normative and hedonic motivators) could have a synergistic effect. High personal commitment (normative) and enjoyment (hedonic) of the task at hand can be unaffected by extrinsic motivation' because the activity itself becomes the motivation (Lam & Lambermont-Ford 2010). Extrinsic motivations serve to satisfy indirect or instrumental needs and they can be financial or social rewards, whereas intrinsic motivations are driven by values provided directly within the work itself (Lam & Lambermont-Ford 2010). Amabile (1993) and Huber (2001) argued that 'normative and hedonic motivation are seen to be essential in knowledge sharing and creative activities' and that the 'options for an organisation in terms of motivation are limited by its structure' and the nature of the tasks performed.

Although research on knowledge sharing in the public sector is limited, in the past 20 years there has been 'significant changes of moving from a traditional bureaucratic approach to a more managerial one', so much so that today's public sector organisations are also known as knowledge-based organisations (Amayah 2013). Amayah's (2013) claims depicted that knowledge had become as 'critical a resource in the public sector as it is for private sector firms'. Moreover, public organisations (as with the private sector) 'have to contend with greater competition for resources and competition from alternative services. Improving knowledge sharing processes would help ensure that employees benefit as much as possible from senior employees' knowledge and experience before they retire' (Amayah 2013).

Prior studies of knowledge sharing have focused on similarities and differences between private and public sector organisations, and factors that affect knowledge sharing. For example, Amayah (2013:456) citing Liebowitz and Chen (2003) revealed that 'it is more difficult to share knowledge in public sector organisations because most people associate knowledge with power and their promotion opportunities'. Subsequently, studies were conducted specifically on factors affecting knowledge sharing in the public sector – for instance, Seba, Rowley and Delbridge (2012) discovered that 'organisational structure, leadership, time allocation, and trust could be barriers to knowledge sharing in the Dubai police force'. Chiem (2001) claimed that knowledge sharing in the private sector can always be encouraged and rewarded financially, whereas in the public sector limited resources could hinder that practice. In addition, government workers are often 'bogged down' with completing paperwork for even the most trivial tasks. This contributes to slow productivity, generates frustration and creates a tendency to perform the most minimal tasks. They may therefore 'perceive KM initiatives as extra work and resist efforts to build a culture of knowledge sharing' (Yao, Kam & Chan 2007).

Ardichvili (2008) discovered that the following motivational factors affect individuals' willingness to share knowledge: 'personal benefits, community-related considerations and normative consideration; barriers categorized into interpersonal, procedural, technological, and cultural aspects;

enablers such as supportive corporate culture, trust and tools'. Amongst these processes, knowledge sharing has been determined as the cornerstone of KM. According to Huang, Davison and Gu (2008), 'an anticipated reciprocal relationship does not significantly influence an individual's willingness to share knowledge'. In their study, 'knowledge was shared to make work more effective, not because individuals expected something in return' (Huang et al. 2008). On the contrary, 'social interaction was found to influence significantly the extent to which knowledge sharing occurred' (Huang et al. 2008).

In a study of public sector organisations in Puerto Rico, employees identified 'lack of management commitment, alongside' the organisational environment as well as 'lack of emotional intelligence as significant barriers to knowledge sharing' (Seba et al. 2012). Another 'study of public sector employees in Malaysia concluded that whilst the employees in the public sector understood the importance of knowledge sharing, the fact that the overall knowledge sharing strategy was not clearly explained by their departmental managers affected their willingness to share information' (Seba et al. 2012). In addition, insufficient rewards for knowledge sharing, lack of interaction, lack of time and weak information technology also contributed to poor knowledge sharing. A study of public organisations in 'China also concluded that managerial position and support together with communication between organisational levels and advanced' information technology 'systems were important' to knowledge sharing (Seba et al. 2012).

Methodology and research methods

The case study methodology and the mixed methods design described in this article were used to explore knowledge sharing practices of the KZN PHRDF. According to Creswell (2008:476), 'a case study is an in-depth exploration of a bounded system based on extensive data collection'. Both qualitative and quantitative data were collected simultaneously during a single phase of data collection. The entire population of KZN PHRDF members who represented the 14 KZN Provincial Departments were surveyed using structured questionnaires and semi-structured interviews (Figure 1).

Thirty-one self-administered structured questionnaires were physically and electronically distributed to the PHRDF members who were not part of the SMs category. Of these 31 distributed questionnaires, 23 were returned. Of the 14 requests sent, 10 SMs were interviewed using the semi-structured interview schedule. Combinations of qualitative and quantitative approaches for data analysis were used, NVivo was used for creating themes for the qualitative data analysis and SPSS 18 was used for quantitative analysis of data. In order to fulfil the requirements of the ethics policies, the purpose of this study was explained clearly to the respondents before the start of the face-to-face interview, and informed consent cover letters were attached to the self-administered questionnaire. The respondents were also assured that the information they provided would only be used for academic purposes and that their identities would remain confidential and anonymous.

Validity and reliability

In an attempt to achieve validity in this study, the instruments used to collect data, the self-administered questionnaire and the semi-structure interview schedule had adequate coverage of the research question guiding the study.

The pre-testing of the instruments on the KwaZulu-Natal Records Managers and Deputy Information Officers Forum (KRMDIOF) members was used to ensure reliability of the data. The questionnaire used for respondents consisted of both closed and open-ended questions, and the interview schedule consisted of closed and open-ended questions. After grammatical and editorial errors were corrected in the pre-tested instruments, the same questionnaire was used to collect data from all the respondents and the same semi-structured interview schedule was used to collect information from all the interviewees to obtain consistent results and ensure reliability of the results.

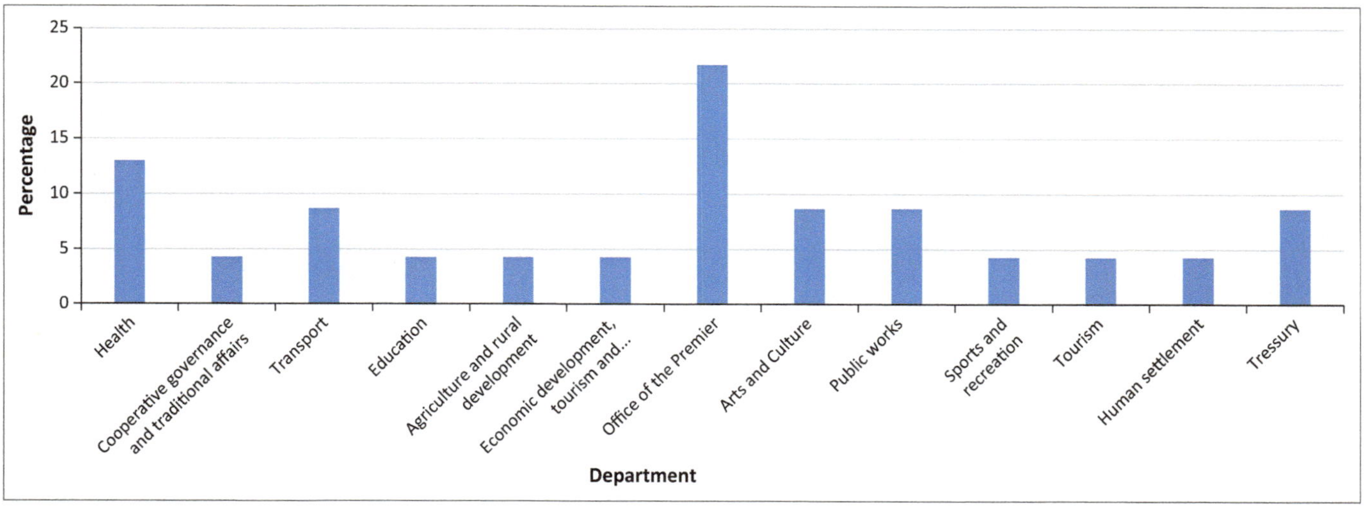

FIGURE 1: Percentage of respondents by department (N = 23).

Ethical consideration

Ethical guidelines were followed as per University of KwaZulu-Natal (UKZN) research ethics and ethical clearance was provided by the UKZN ethics committee.

Major findings and discussion

The results and findings collected from respondents who completed the questionnaires, and interviewees were presented according to the research question. The factors that influenced the members' motivation to share knowledge are discussed in terms of their position held, experience, recognition of expertise and trust (Figure 2).

Position held

This study's findings revealed that the PHRDF consisted of different categories of HRD professionals in terms of position, rank or level and job title, which is often associated with the level of importance depending on the individual's position (high or low) in the organisation's hierarchy (Table 1). According to the findings, the PHRDF members appreciated this diversity within the PHRDF as it was one of the rare occasions where the different categories could mix freely and discuss issues relevant to functions and responsibilities, in this case, HRD.

It emerged from the results that 87% of the respondents felt that the diversity encouraged knowledge sharing across levels and promoted learning from senior to junior members. A few members (13%) believed that learning

TABLE 1: Job titles of respondents (N = 23).

Job title	Frequency	%
HRD	6	26.1
Skills development officer or facilitator or specialist	5	21.7
Practitioner	4	17.4
Deputy manager	3	13.0
Mrs	1	4.3
Trainer	1	4.3
Training advisor	1	4.3
HR policy, systems and HRD	1	4.3
SDF	1	4.3
Manager	1	4.3
Total	**23**	**100.0**

HRD, Human Resource Development; Mrs, Title referring to a married woman; SDF, Skills Development Facilitator.

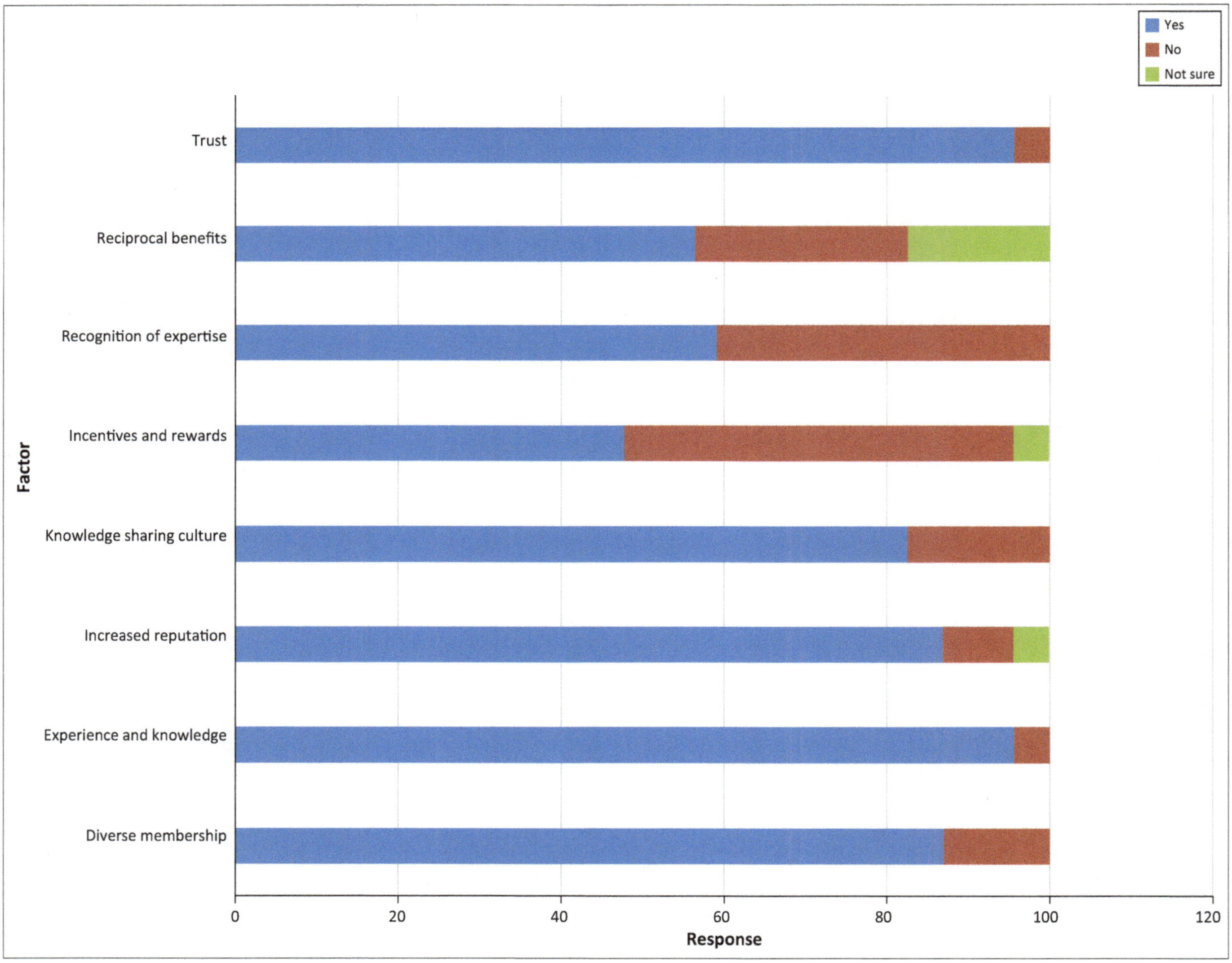

FIGURE 2: Factors which motivated knowledge sharing in the Provincial Human Resource Development Forum.

occurred both ways, from seniors to juniors and vice versa. Diversity of ranks and levels in the PHRDF encouraged knowledge sharing as well as learning. According to Mkhize (2015), knowledge of participants' demographics could help with imitating innovative collaborations where every member of the community could equally contribute.

Experience

The findings revealed that most PHRDF members (95.7%) had experience and knowledge of their field and were therefore motivated to participate in knowledge sharing because of the confidence enhanced by having experience and knowledge. This finding is consistent with the presence of hedonistic intrinsic motivation in this group, which emerged from engagement in competence and self-determined activity. Mannie, Van Niekerk and Adendorff (2013) observed that when an organisation is leaning towards being 'a learning organisation, subject matter experts are more likely to be recognised, empowered and used' for sharing their knowledge. This observation placed the PHRDF as a learning organisation whose members were motivated to share knowledge because they were becoming subject experts. Consistent with normative intrinsic motivation expressed at organisational level, they also attributed their willingness to share knowledge and experience to the fulfilment which they derived from sharing the knowledge that they had gained throughout the period in which they had been in the HRD field.

The findings also revealed that sharing knowledge enhanced reputation and that motivated PHRDF members (86.9%) to share their knowledge even more. This showed that they benefited from sharing knowledge, expressing hedonic and intrinsic motivation to share their knowledge which resulted in the social well-being of the individuals. Personal benefits identified in literature include 'status and career advancement, a better professional reputation, emotional and intellectual benefits' (Amayah 2013). On the contrary, all the SMs interviewed (100%) were motivated to share their knowledge-based on their obligation as managers and leaders to capacitate their staff members. Amayah (2013) referred to this as a 'moral obligation that individuals feel to advance or benefit others in their network'. SMs (50%) were concerned about succession planning, prevention of silos, preservation of institutional memory, encouraging innovation and people development – all of which motivated them to share their knowledge. This sense of obligation also known as 'normative intrinsic motivation' is driven by the individual's sense of compliance with social and personal norms. Enhanced reputation as a result of sharing knowledge was found to be positively related to the repeat of knowledge sharing. However, the absence of mechanisms to recognise the knowledge sharer could result in knowledge hoarding (Akhavan, Rahini & Mehralian 2013).

Recognition of expertise

In terms of the presence of a knowledge sharing culture as a motivator for knowledge sharing, the findings revealed that the majority of PHRDF members (82.6%) agreed that a knowledge sharing culture in the PHRDF was significant. The knowledge sharing culture in the PHRDF was preluded by the high degree of information sharing, which laid a foundation for building a knowledge sharing culture. Findings revealed that there was a high level of knowledge sharing in the PHRDF, hence the members confirming the presence of a knowledge sharing culture. According to Christensen (2005), motivation to share could be affected by both altruistic and intrinsic motivators where both kinds of behaviour could potentially exist in a continuum within a CoP, as illustrated in Figure 3.

The study's findings revealed that there were no incentives for PHRDF members to share their knowledge and that knowledge sharing occurred voluntarily. Half of the members (47.8%) considered the idea of introducing incentives for sharing knowledge to be a positive one, and half (47.8%) were against the idea. Those who favoured incentives regarded these as motivators for knowledge sharing, whereas those who were against the idea raised the point of fearing abuse of the knowledge sharing practice. According to Lam and Lambermont-Ford (2010), the 'exclusive use of extrinsic motivation often places the individual in a transactional rather than a relational stance in respect of the organisation'. In addition, 'extrinsic rewards may undermine intrinsic motivation for interesting tasks and encourage knowledge hoarding' (Lam & Lambermont-Ford 2010).

On the contrary, extrinsic motivators that provide feedback, recognition and reward lead to increased self-esteem. From a management point of view, SMs who were interviewed regarded sending their staff members to courses, workshops and training as an incentive for knowledge sharing as they were required to share lessons learnt from attending these events. Some SMs considered allowing staff members to attend events such as sports days and social functions as creating opportunities and incentives for meeting colleagues and sharing knowledge whilst networking at these events. These means to encourage sharing knowledge are what Jeon et al. (2011) referred to as social rewards where in the context of CoPs they exist as acquisition of opportunities. They observed that 'people pursuing social rewards' tended 'to have a relatively greater interest in the social benefits' derived from 'the acquisition of an opportunity' (Jeon et al. 2011).

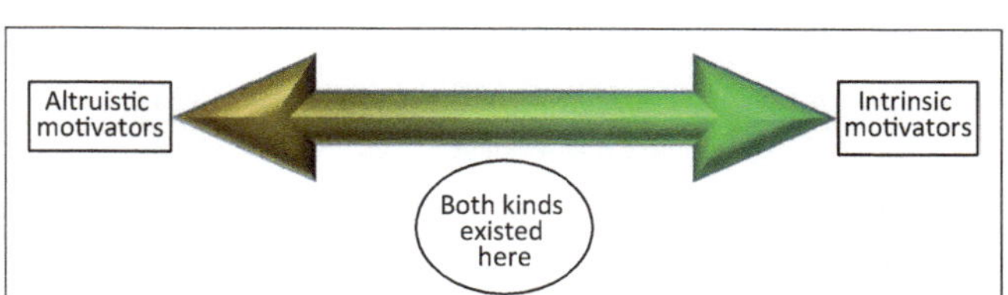

FIGURE 3: Continuum of altruistic and intrinsic motivators.

In terms of recognition of expertise as a motivator for knowledge sharing, the majority of PHRDF (59.1%) agreed that they would be motivated even more to share knowledge if their expertise was recognised. This revealed that most of the respondents were not averse to extrinsic motivation. Extrinsic motivation serves to satisfy indirect or instrumental needs and can also be satisfied by social rewards, especially in a CoP where individuals join the community based on a shared enthusiasm for a common cause rather than as a consequence of anticipating specific economic rewards (Jeon et al. 2011). Those (41.9%) who were not concerned about whether they were recognised or not for sharing knowledge showed that they were motivated to share their knowledge for the sake of goodwill and growth of their colleagues. This finding revealed that there was an element of altruism amongst the members of the PHRDF regarding their motivation to share knowledge, which is closely related to intrinsic motivation. The enjoyment of helpful behaviour is related to altruism as it involves helping others with no expectation of reciprocity (Jeon et al. 2011).

In addition to the above finding, the majority of PHRDF (56.5%) shared knowledge with one another because they expected their colleagues to share knowledge with them should they need it. This motivation to share knowledge is based on reciprocal rewards which are socially extrinsically motivators greatly observed in CoPs (Jeon et al. 2011). The members recognised that as a CoP they would not be able to work in isolation and should they hoard their knowledge, their colleagues would potentially do the same. 'When one member of a CoP shares his knowledge with other CoP members, if reciprocity holds, he/she would anticipate receiving the required knowledge from other CoP members' (Jeon et al. 2011).

The issue of trust

The issue of trust was regarded as a significant factor for PHRDF members' (95.7%) willingness to share their knowledge. Their trust for others' capabilities and competencies, experience and knowledge and the strong relationships formed by their PHRDF members resulted in their willingness to share their knowledge with others at the PHRDF. 'Trust can be widely accepted as being closely linked to organisational culture' (Mannie et al. 2013) which was held in high regard by PHRDF members (65.2%). Venter, Erasmus and Seale (2015) reported that trust was amongst the attributes that promoted the knowledge sharing process in a CoP and was accelerated by the richness and depth of relationships formed during consecutive meetings. If a high level of mutual obligation, expectation and trust exists in a relationship, there will be less risk and uncertainty in future knowledge sharing exchanges (Zhang & Jiang 2015). A high level of trust which led to a high level of knowledge sharing observed in the PHRDF supported the assertion by Maponya (2005) that there must be a certain level of trust to develop and strengthen work relations and social interaction for knowledge sharing. According to Dube and Ngulube (2012), organisations could benefit from strengthening trust as there is a potential for it to lead to openness, honesty, shared goals and outputs.

This high level of a knowledge sharing culture as well as the PHRDF members not being completely enticed or repelled by incentives supported this view that the perceptions run from one end of being enticed to the other end of being repelled by incentives to share knowledge

Recommendations

The recommendations made in the following section relate to motivators for knowledge sharing in the public service utilising CoPs as this article has revealed that there was a large percentage of success in knowledge sharing in the PHRDF. Because of the fact that there were a small percentage of respondents who had reservations regarding the liberty to share knowledge, it is recommended thus:

- *Forums create specific CoPs*: The many forums in the public service should contain aspects of a CoP where meetings are held solely for knowledge sharing targeting technical knowledge rather than information dissemination.
- *Develop a knowledge sharing guidelines*: It is usually difficult to implement any business process without an approved guiding document (such as a strategy or a policy) as most processes in public service are driven by compliance obligations. For KM to succeed, knowledge sharing processes and procedures must be clearly specified in order for these to be properly implemented. From the KM strategy or policy, knowledge sharing guidelines would include motivators for knowledge sharing, and these could be adapted in order to be utilised in other CoPs in the public service.
- *Establishment of a knowledge portal or repository*: Considering that there is a large amount of knowledge sharing during PHRDF meetings, it is recommended that there should be a knowledge reservoir such as a knowledge portal or institutional repository where this knowledge is kept in order to avoid the knowledge gap or 'brain drain' which occurs when some of the members exit the public service. Proven motivators should be used to encourage CoP members to use the knowledge portal or institutional repository to share their knowledge with others.
- *Develop strategies to encourage knowledge sharing:* Although the findings revealed that there was a knowledge sharing culture in the PHRDF and the level of sharing knowledge was high, it is recommended that knowledge sharing be included in performance assessments in order to reward those who share their knowledge because of their altruistic values and to encourage those who might be reluctant to share their knowledge. Motivators such as trust, recognition of expertise, knowledge and experience and the presence of a knowledge sharing culture should be exploited to encourage knowledge sharing as a performance attribute.

Conclusion

This article reveals the PHRDF members were highly motivated to share knowledge during their meetings. The level of knowledge sharing was high, motivated by both intrinsic and extrinsic motivators such as diverse membership, experience and knowledge, increased reputation, the presence of a knowledge sharing culture, incentives and rewards, recognition of expertise, reciprocal benefits and trust. It can be concluded that in a CoP, challenges such as diversity of rank or position, competing for recognition, silo mentality, conflicts because of interdepartmental relations and lack of organisational support were limited as members become unified as they regard knowledge sharing as beneficial in the pursuit of similar goals. In addition, members in a CoP become homogeneous in their pursuit of know-how, and knowledge sharing becomes altruistically and intrinsically motivated to achieve the goal of rendering uniform services across departments. Most forums in the South African public service become CoPs by default because they are established mainly for the purpose of information sharing amongst practitioners of the same occupation. The use of the concept of CoPs in reference to groups meeting for the purpose of sharing knowledge is not prevalent. Encouraging CoPs such as the PHRDF and utilising the above-mentioned motivators for members to share their knowledge with one another could assist the public service in implementing efficient service delivery across departments.

The findings revealed that intrinsic motivation (whether hedonistic or normative) was significant in the PHRDF as a result of collegiality and comradeship created by the meetings. If intrinsic motivators such as trust, experience and knowledge, knowledge sharing culture and altruistic values such as recognition of expertise, increased reputation and reciprocal benefits motivated PHRDF members to share knowledge, it is highly possible that the same motivators would be relevant to other CoPs in the public service. Therefore, it can be said that the same motivators from this study will be relevant across the board in the public service, as the respondents clearly agreed that they are intrinsically motivated to share knowledge because of their shared goals.

Further research could look at the length of time the individuals were in their current position to assess if knowledge sharing at a CoP enhanced their chances of promotion.

Acknowledgements

Competing interests

The authors declare that they have no financial or personal relationships that may have inappropriately influenced them in writing this article.

Authors' contributions

N.M-B. is the original author of this article. R.H. was the supervisor of the research done by N.M-B. on knowledge sharing in the public service for her PhD and also supervised and edited this article.

References

Akhavan, P., Rahini, A. & Mehralian, G., 2013, 'Developing a model for knowledge research centers', *Vine* 43(3), 357–393. https://doi.org/10.1108/VINE-06-2012-0020

Amabile, T., 1993, 'Motivational synergy: Toward new conceptualizations of intrinsic and extrinsic motivation in the workplace', *Human Resource Management Review* 3(3), 185–202. https://doi.org/10.1016/1053-4822(93)90012-S

Amayah, A.I., 2013, 'Determinants of knowledge sharing in public sector organisations', *Journal of Knowledge Management* 17(3), 454–471. https://doi.org/10.1108/JKM-11-2012-0369

Ardichvili, A., 2008, 'Learning and knowledge sharing in virtual communities of practice: Motivators, barriers and enablers', *Advances in Developing Human Resources* 10(4), 541–554. https://doi.org/10.1177/1523422308319536

Bhyat, M., Van der Westhuizen, J. & Blackburn, D., 2005, 'Knowledge management, service delivery, protests and the struggle: Is there a link?' *Convergence* 6(4), 94–97.

Chaba, S., 2003, 'Sharing knowledge is power: Issues', *Service Delivery Review* 2(1), 36–37.

Chiem, P.X., 2001, 'In the public interest: Government employees also need incentives to share what they know', *Knowledge Management Magazine*, August, viewed 12 August 2013, from http://www.destinationcrm.com/articles/default.asp?ArticleID=1843

Christensen, P.H., 2005, *Facilitating knowledge sharing: A conceptual framework*, SMG Working Paper 4, viewed 03 March 2016, from http://openarchive.cbs.dk/bitstream/handle/10398/7486/cbs%20forskningsindberetning%20smg%2024.pdf?sequence=1

Creswell, J.W., 2008, *Educational research: Planning conducting, and evaluating quantitative and qualitative research*, Pearson Education Inc, Hoboken, NJ.

Dube, L. & Ngulube, P., 2012, 'Knowledge sharing in a multicultural environment: Challenges and opportunities', *South African Journal of Libraries and Information Science* 78(1), 68–77. https://doi.org/10.7553/78-1-48

Durrant, F., 2001, *Knowledge management in the context of government. E-government, information and communication technologies in public sector management*, Caribbean Regional Ministerial Consultation & High Level Workshop, 10–14 December 2001, University of West Indies, Jamaica.

Fraser, D., 2004, 'Managing knowledge: Issues', *Service Delivery Review* 3(2), 60–63.

Gaffoor, S. & Cloete, F., 2010, 'Knowledge management in local government: The case of Stellenbosch municipality', *South African Journal of Information Management* 12(1), 1–7. https://doi.org/10.4102/sajim.v12i1.422

Huang, Q., Davison, R.M. & Gu, J., 2008, 'Impact of personal and cultural factors on knowledge sharing China', *Asia Pacific Journal of Management* 25, 451–471. https://doi.org/10.1007/s10490-008-9095-2

Huber, G.P., 2001, 'Transfer of knowledge in knowledge management systems: Unexplored issues and suggested studies', *European Journal of Information Systems* 10(2), 72–79. https://doi.org/10.1057/palgrave.ejis.3000399

Jeon, S., Young-Gul, K. & Koh, J., 2011, 'An integrative model for knowledge sharing in communities of practice', *Journal of Knowledge Management* 15(2), 251–269. https://doi.org/10.1108/13673271111119682

Kgarimetsa-Phiri, M., 2009, 'Applying knowledge management for public sector service delivery: ICT', *Government Digest* 29(5), 28–29.

Lam, A. & Lambermont-Ford, J., 2010, 'Knowledge sharing in organisational contexts: A motivation-based perspective', *Journal of Knowledge Management* 14(1), 51–66. https://doi.org/10.1108/13673271011015561

Liebowitz, J. & Chen, Y., 2003, 'Knowledge sharing proficiencies: The key to knowledge management', in C.W. Holsapple (ed.), *Handbook on knowledge management 1: Knowledge matters*, pp. 409–424, Springer, Berlin.

Lindenberg, S., 2001, 'Intrinsic motivation in a new light', *Kyklos* 54, 317–342. https://doi.org/10.1111/1467-6435.00156

Lwoga, E.T., Ngulube, P. & Stilwell, C., 2012, 'Information and knowledge needs, access and use for small-scale farming in Tanzania', *Innovation: Journal of Appropriate Librarianship and Information Work in Southern Africa* 44, 126–140.

Majewski, G., Usor, A. & Khan, I., 2011, 'Knowledge sharing in immersive virtual communities of practice', *Vine* 41(1), 41–61. https://doi.org/10.1108/03055721111115548

Mannie, A., Van Niekerk, H.J. & Adendorff, C.M., 2013, 'Significant factors for enabling knowledge sharing between government agencies within South Africa', *South African Journal of Information Management* 15(2), 1–8. https://doi.org/10.4102/sajim.v15i2.569

Maponya, P.M., 2005, 'Fostering the culture of knowledge sharing in higher education', *South African Journal of Higher Education* 19(5), 900–911.

Mkhize, P.L., 2015, 'A knowledge sharing framework in the South African public sector', *South African Journal of Information Management* 17(1), 1–10. https://doi.org/10.4102/sajim.v17i1.620

Mphahlele, M.Y., 2010, 'Knowledge management practices in the South African public sector: 2002–2008', M.Phil. thesis, University of Stellenbosch, Stellenbosch.

Munyua, H.M. & Stilwell, C., 2012, 'The applicability of the major social science paradigms to the study of the agricultural knowledge and information systems of small-scale farmers', *Innovation: Journal of Appropriate Librarianship and Information Work in Southern Africa* 44, 10–43.

Ntala, A.M.T., 2010, *Predictors of knowledge sharing among civil service employees in a community of practice*. (3440354 Ph.D.), Southern Illinois University at Carborndale, Carborndale, IL, ProQuest Dissertations and Theses A and I Database, viewed n.d., from http://search.proquest.com/docview/854330529?accountid=11921

Public Service Commission, 2011, *Public Service Commission Fact sheet on the duration of employment per grade of senior management service members*, viewed 03 March 2016, from http://www.psc.gov.za/documents/2012/Approved%20Fact%20Sheet%20March%202012%20%282%29.pdf

Radebe, T., 2002, 'Knowledge management for the public service: Issues', *Service Delivery Review* 1(1), 8–11.

Seba, I., Rowley, J. & Delbridge, R., 2012, 'Social factors of work environment creativity', *Journal of Knowledge Management* 16(1), 114–128. https://doi.org/10.1108/13673271211198972

Soko, S., 2005, 'Getting value from knowledge management: Issues', *Service Delivery Review* 4(1), 50–52.

Venter, K., Erasmus, M. & Seale, I., 2015, 'Knowledge sharing for the development of service learning champions', *Journal for New Generation Sciences* 13(2), 147–163.

Yao, L.J., Kam, T.H.Y. & Chan, S., 2007, 'Knowledge sharing in Asian public administration sector: The case of Hong Kong', *Journal of Enterprise Information Management* 20(1), 51–69. https://doi.org/10.1108/17410390710717138

Zhang, X. & Jiang, J.Y., 2015, 'With whom shall I share my knowledge? A recipient perspective of knowledge sharing', *Journal of Knowledge Management* 19(2), 277–295. https://doi.org/10.1108/JKM-05-2014-0184

14

Data management for early hearing detection and intervention in South Africa

Authors:
Selvarani Moodley[1]
Claudine Storbeck[1]

Affiliations:
[1]Centre for Deaf Studies, University of the Witwatersrand, South Africa

Corresponding author:
Selvarani Moodley,
selvarani.moodley@wits.ac.za

Introduction: Internationally, newborn hearing screening is becoming part of standard neonatal healthcare service guidelines for the implementation of early hearing detection and intervention (EHDI) initiatives, including screening, diagnosis, data management and intervention. Data management includes the processes of data collection and storage thereof, as well as analysis and interpretation of data to guide the future planning, implementation and evaluation of EHDI programmes. There have been limited studies on data management in the South African EHDI context.

Methods: The aim of this study was to determine the type of data management systems in use in South Africa and whether they allow for cross-disciplinary sharing and evaluation of the EHDI processes. A survey instrument on the management of EHDI data was developed and sent to HI HOPES referral agents in both public and private sectors.

Results: A return rate of 80% was achieved, with 19 (59%) public sector and 13 (41%) private sector audiologists participating in the study. The data revealed that there was no uniform data management system in use nationally, and no consistent shared system within the public or private sectors. The majority of respondents (44%) used a paper-based system for data recording. No institutions were using data management systems that enabled sharing of information with other medical professionals.

Conclusion: Data management and tracking of the pathway from screening to diagnosis to intervention is necessary to ensure quality care and outcomes for children identified with hearing loss. International studies reveal the importance of effective implementation of data management systems; however, to date these have focussed on developed country contexts. Data management challenges identified in this study reflect international challenges as well as challenges unique to a developing country context.

Introduction

Internationally, newborn hearing screening is becoming part of standard neonatal healthcare services within developed countries (including the UK, Australia, Canada and some European countries). The importance of early detection of paediatric hearing loss and the benefits of early intervention for these babies have been recognised through extensive international research (Yoshinaga-Itano 2003:252–266, 2014:43; Yoshinaga-Itano et al. 1998:1161–1171). The Joint Committee on Infant Hearing (JCIH) (2007:898–921) has clear guidelines for the implementation of early hearing detection and intervention (EHDI) initiatives, including principles and process guidelines for screening, diagnosis, data management and intervention. These guidelines have come to represent the international gold standard as it serves as a reference document for countries globally, including those that are resource-constrained such as low- and middle-income countries (Olusanya 2015:51–64).

Within the South African context, the Health Professions Council of South Africa (HPCSA) recognised the importance and value of early hearing screening and diagnosis, and commissioned the development of a South African position statement on EHDI programmes. This statement was modelled closely on the JCIH position statement (JCIH, AAP & ASHA, 2000) and includes principles and guidelines for screening, diagnosis and data management with specific adaptations for the South African EHDI contexts. The HPCSA (2007) EHDI position statement therefore recommends screening by 2 months, diagnosis by 4 months and intervention by 8 months of age as opposed to the JCIH which recommends the 1:3:6 timeline for these three phases. In addition to these time-based guidelines, the importance of information systems for data management has been outlined in both the JCIH (2007) and HPCSA (2007) EHDI position statements. Data management refers to the processes of data collection and storage, as well as the analysis and interpretation of the data to guide the future planning, implementation and evaluation of specific EHDI programmes (JCIH 2007).

Data management (from a medical records perspective) involves the keeping of records and logging of data from appointments as a means of supporting patient care (Mann & Williams 2003), and is 'primarily created to provide an account of diagnosis and care' (Parkes 2004:899). Häyrinen, Saranto and Nykänen (2008:291–304) state that medical data can take one of the three formats: (1) a personal health record which is a summary of all health information on an individual and is kept by the individual; (2) an electronic medical record which is an electronic version of paper-based medical records and which is owned by healthcare providers from a single organisation providing medical care; and (3) electronic health records which are healthcare information records containing longitudinal information that has been collected from various sources, the purpose of which is efficient and integrated healthcare. Young and Spencer (2008:648–656) identified a fourth online format of data that would allow for the interface and potential linking of database systems for the improved information flow within and between the different components of the EHDI referral process. The key advantage of such an online data management system would be the immediate access and availability of the complete patient healthcare records to authorised healthcare providers at the point of consultation (Mostert-Phipps, Pottas & Korpela 2012:326–331), which would include doctors, audiologists and interventionists.

Globally such an online central data management system, allowing for interdisciplinary access to the pathway from screening to diagnostic and follow-up appointments, has been shown to be a key component in ensuring the success of a comprehensive hearing screening programme (Finitzo & Grosse 2003:73–78). Within the South African public healthcare context, such a system would be essential to the success of a universal newborn hearing screening (UNHS) programme because of the hierarchical nature (Legodi & Wolvaardt 2015) of our three-tier public health referral system. An online data management system would allow for interdisciplinary tracking along the referral pathway, where paediatric hearing screening occurs at the primary healthcare facility with referral to a secondary or tertiary healthcare facility if advanced diagnostic testing and confirmation of hearing loss is required. This is then followed by the return to the primary healthcare provider for habilitation and/or intervention. It is therefore clear that, to ensure a seamless referral process along the three-tiered health system, online data would need to be as up-to-date, accurate and complete as possible (Alam, Gaffney & Eichwald 2014:220–223).

Since the development of the HPCSA EHDI position statement (2007), which is not a legislated document, some institutions in South Africa have begun implementing screening initiatives. Voluntary screening programmes are offered at private hospitals, and routine high-risk screening occurs at certain government hospitals. Pilot studies reported thus far include a newborn hearing screening programme at one private healthcare hospital in Gauteng (Swanepoel et al. 2007:881–887), infant hearing screening at an immunisation clinic in Gauteng (Swanepoel, Hugo & Louw 2006:1241–1249), the use of nurses as screening personnel in the Western Cape (Friderichs, Swanepoel & Hall 2012:552–559) and screening at Maternity Obstetric Units (MOUs) (de Kock, Swanepoel & Hall 2016:124–131) in the Western Cape. Results from these screening forums indicated that once hearing was screened and a referral result was obtained, parents did not bring the child for the rescreening appointment. A follow-up study was done to gain a South African perspective on why parents were not bringing their children in for rescreening, and the results showed that 24% of caregivers forgot about the appointment with a further 32% believing that the follow-up appointment was not necessary. This loss to follow-up of 56% of families highlights the benefit of a quality data management system for the effective tracking of referred infants, and telephonic reminders by dedicated personnel to improve follow-up compliance. Before such a central system could even be considered, it is important to explore the current status and practice of data management. South Africa does not have standard methods for audiology record keeping.

As stated in a recent review of EHDI in South Africa, limited studies were found on data management (Moodley & Storbeck 2015:1–10), despite the fact that such data management systems have been identified globally as part of the gold standard because of the importance for both patient care and evaluation and quality control (Finitzo & Grosse 2003:73–78).

It is therefore necessary to determine what, if any, data management practices and systems are in use in South Africa and if they allow for cross-disciplinary sharing and evaluation of the EHDI processes employed in the screening, diagnosis and intervention of paediatric hearing loss.

The aims of this study were to:

- identify the data recording and management systems used by South African audiologists in the public and private healthcare sectors
- determine whether these data management systems allow for sharing of information across healthcare professionals
- establish the challenges associated with the use of an online or electronic database system in the South African public and private healthcare systems.

Methods

Study population

This survey on the practice of data management in three provinces of South Africa is part of a larger study, which includes a broader survey on diagnostic audiology practice.

The sample for the survey included audiologists who referred children to the HI HOPES early intervention programme from September 2006 to December 2011, and who are part of a larger research project involving this longitudinal data set on deaf children ($n = 532$) in South Africa (Störbeck & Young 2016:45). The survey was sent to the 40 referral agents, where 21 were from the public and 19 were from the private health sector. Six surveys were not returned, with an additional one private sector audiologist choosing not to participate and a second who did not fully complete the survey. The response rate for the data management component of the survey was thus 32 of the 40 audiologists, making the response rate 80%. Completed surveys were from 19 public sector audiology departments (59%) and 13 from private sector audiologists (41%). In terms of provincial breakdown, 20 (63%) were from Gauteng, 10 (31%) were from Kwazulu-Natal (KZN) and 2 (6%) were from the Western Cape.

Procedures

A survey instrument was developed and included questions on diagnostic audiology practices as well as EHDI data management in South Africa. The survey instrument was developed to be quickly completed and provide information on the aspects of data management that were identified to be important from the literature, i.e. data record systems, sharing of audiology diagnostic information and challenges with the use of database systems. The survey comprised six close-ended questions in a multiple choice format. Options from which respondents could choose were those identified as common to EHDI data management systems and options specific to a developing county context. Respondents were given the option of providing their own responses as well as including further comments.

After the development of the survey instrument, it was piloted on audiologists who were not referral agents to the programme and were thus not eligible to complete the survey. Pilot respondents included an international as well as South African expert in the field of audiology, as well as two audiologists in the public and private health sectors, respectively. The piloting of the questionnaire allowed for checking of the appropriateness of the questionnaire for answering the research questions, as well as detecting any flaws in the questionnaire (Brink, van der Walt & van Rensburg 2006).

Before the survey could be sent to public sector audiology departments, permission was obtained from the government research council for each province (Gauteng, KZN and Western Cape). Permission was then obtained from each individual hospital medical manager for the audiology department to complete the survey. Once written permission was obtained from the hospital medical managers, the audiology departments were contacted telephonically to inform them of the study and to request completion of the survey. Surveys were emailed to the audiology department at those hospitals that agreed to fill in the survey.

Each private audiologist was contacted telephonically to inform them of the study and to invite them to participate in the study. If agreed, the survey was emailed directly to the audiologist.

Data analysis

A data collection sheet was designed specifically for the comprehensive logging of the survey information relating to data management. Data were coded and collated.

The coded data were then transferred to an Excel spreadsheet for systematic analysis. Data were grouped and analysed according to the variables of private versus public sector and the province in which the practices were located to determine the variation in data management with respect to these variables.

Data analysis techniques included basic descriptive statistics such as average values, standard deviation, frequencies and percentages.

Results

Results will be presented in the format of: (1) the data system used for recording of the audiology information, (2) information included in audiology records, (3) data sharing and, (4) challenges encountered by audiologists in the implementation of an electronic or online database system.

Data recording systems

Audiologists were asked to indicate what data system they were using for recording of EHDI data in their audiology department/practice. The majority of respondents (44%; $n = 14$) use only a paper-based system for recording of data. An additional 27% ($n = 9$) of respondents use a paper-based system in addition to a computer-based (Excel or Access) program to generate reports. 25% ($n = 8$) of public sector audiologists use a computer-based programme system only. Two respondents (6%), both in the private healthcare system (one in the province of Gauteng and one in KZN), use a web-based data tracking system in addition to computer- and paper-based systems.

The systems used for recording data are varied, with both the private and public health systems using both paper-based and computer systems for data capture.

Information included in audiology records

The next question in the survey focussed on the information that is included in data records. Multiple choice options included demographic and medical information as well as the capability of the system to allow for generation of reports, account (billing) information and flag for follow-up appointments.

The analysis of information reported to be included in data systems indicates that the majority of data records include medical information (Table 1). A flag for follow-up appointments is available in 16 (47%) institutions (10 in the public sector and 6 in the private sector). Respondents in KZN and Gauteng in both the private and public healthcare sectors have data recording systems that can generate and record reports, with account information being recorded more in the private sector (12; 92%) than the public sector (4; 21%).

Data sharing

The next question in the survey focussed on data sharing amongst professionals within and across hospitals. The Gauteng public sector (70%, *n* = 7), as well as some KZN public sector audiology departments (57%, *n* = 4), uses systems that are available to other medical professionals in the hospital, as well as two (20%) audiology departments in Gauteng having systems that are accessible to professionals in other hospitals. There is no sharing of audiology data across hospitals in the private sector, with only two practices (one in Gauteng and one in KZN) having a system that is accessible to other medical professionals within their hospital.

Implementation of an electronic/online database system

Audiologists were asked to indicate difficulties they would face if they were to implement the use of an electronic database system and online database system in their audiology department/practice. A list of challenges to choose from was provided, as well as providing an option to list additional challenges. The most common difficulty with implementing the use of an electronic/online database system (Table 2) was the lack of time and limited staff for data entry. A limited budget and frequent electricity cuts were identified as difficulties by a few institutions across the public and private healthcare sectors, with one public sector institution identifying limited electricity points as a difficulty. The public sector identified Internet connection as a difficulty with implementing an online database system, with one public sector institution commenting that there is a shortage of computers in the department.

Ethical consideration

According to research protocol at the University of the Witwatersrand, an application is made to the University research committee for ethical clearance relating to each research project. Formal ethics approval is required before data collection can begin. The University of the Witwatersrand Ethical Clearance Medical Board provided ethical clearance (Protocol number: M111144) for a comprehensive survey study of audiologists in the public and private sectors who referred deaf and hard of hearing children to the HI HOPES early intervention programme in the 5-year period between September 2006 and December 2011. This is part of a larger longitudinal study of EHDI data for children receiving comprehensive home-based intervention in the HI HOPES programme during this time period.

Discussion

Through hearing screening programmes being implemented in a number of countries (including South Africa), more hearing loss is being identified early. However, a factor that has been identified as a challenge within the EHDI system is the variability in the level of diagnostic follow-up services.

TABLE 1: Information included in EHDI data management systems.

Data records – information included	Public						Private						Total (*n* = 32)	
	GT (*n* = 10)		KZN (*n* = 7)		WC (*n* = 2)		GT (*n* = 10)		KZN (*n* = 3)		WC (*n* = 0)			
	n	%	*n*	%	*n*	%	*n*	%	*n*	%	*n*	%	*n*	%
Demographic information	10	10	7	100	2	100	8	80	3	100	-	-	30	94
Medical Information	10	10	7	100	0	0	9	90	3	100	-	-	29	91
Generate and record reports	6	60	6	86	0	0	7	70	2	67	-	-	21	66
Account information	2	20	2	29	0	0	8	80	3	100	-	-	15	47
Flag for follow-up appointments	6	60	3	43	1	50	3	30	3	67	-	-	15	47

GT, Gauteng; KZN, Kwazulu-Natal; WC, Western Cape.

TABLE 2: Difficulties implementing an online or electronic database system.

Electronic database implementation – difficulties	Public						Private						Total (*n* = 32)	
	GT (*n* = 10)		KZN (*n* = 7)		WC (*n* = 2)		GT (*n* = 10)		KZN (*n* = 3)		WC (*n* = 0)			
	n	%	*n*	%	*n*	%	*n*	%	*n*	%	*n*	%	*n*	%
Limited electricity points	0	0	1	14	1	50	0	0	0	0	-	-	2	6
Frequent electricity cuts	1	10	3	43	0	0	**1**	**10**	**0**	**0**	-	-	**5**	**16**
	-	-	-	-	-	-	*2*	*20*	-	-	-	-	*6*	*19*
Limited budget	**3**	**30**	**4**	**57**	2	100	**3**	**30**	0	0	-	-	**12**	**38**
	4	*40*	*3*	*43*	-	-	*2*	*20*	-	-	-	-	*11*	*34*
Lack of time for data entry	3	30	3	43	2	100	**6**	**60**	1	33	-	-	**15**	**47**
	-	-	-	-	-	-	*5*	*50*	-	-	-	-	*14*	*44*
Limited staff for data entry	4	40	3	43	2	100	4	40	1	33	-	-	14	44
Internet connection	*8*	*80*	*3*	*43*	*0*	*0*	*0*	*0*	*1*	*33*	-	-	*12*	*38*

GT, Gauteng; KZN, Kwazulu-Natal; WC, Western Cape.
Bold, electronic database system; italics, online database system;
Note: If values were the same it is listed normally.

To ensure quality EHDI programmes and services aligned with evidence-based care, there is a need to continuously monitor access, quality and outcomes of services (Russ, Dougherty & Jagadish 2010:S7–S18).

The monitoring of systems and data are through analysis of details from data records. This allows for identification of factors that will be effective in (as well as prevent effective implementation of) EHDI services across the continuum of screening, diagnosis and intervention.

The majority of respondents using a paper-based system for data recording could pose a difficulty with transfer and access of information when referring between the primary, secondary and tertiary departments of the South African public healthcare system. Mostert-Phipps et al. (2012:326–331) found that referral between healthcare providers using a paper-based record system results in insufficient information being provided in the referral letter as well as the possibility that information may not be provided in time for the primary healthcare providers (as well as at each step of the EHDI pathway) to be informed of all factors for follow-up care. In addition, Shulman et al. found that reporting systems relying on handwritten forms were found to be more prone to errors than those using computer-based systems (Shulman et al. 2010:S19–S27). In South African audiology, it has been found that paper-based audiology records provided by audiologists conducting diagnostic testing, in both the public and private sectors, are varied in terms of format as well as details included in the report (Moodley 2016:1–7).

In this sample of 32 audiologists, the information they state are included in reports indicates that these audiologists may have difficulty with following up on appointments, as few institutions have a flag for follow-up included in their reporting system. This is important as South African research has indicated that following up on appointments for screening is a challenge (de Kock et al. 2016:124–131; Scheepers, Swanepoel de & le Roux 2014:652–658; Swanepoel et al. 2007:881–887). To improve the documented rate of follow-up testing in the USA EHDI programmes, data management systems were amended to include a component for reminding parents of follow-up testing (Williams, Alam & Gaffney 2016). This has been a recommendation from a South African study on parental reasons for not complying with follow-up testing recommendations and appointments (Scheepers et al. 2014:652–658).

The nature of healthcare provision in the public sector relies on referral from primary to secondary to tertiary healthcare for different steps of the EHDI pathway. This means that children will move between various healthcare providers, at the different levels of healthcare, for provision of services.

No institutions in this sample were using systems that enabled sharing of information with other medical professionals. The Gauteng public sector is most likely to use a system that is compatible with systems used by other medical professionals in the same hospital, indicating the ability for development of a system for data sharing. Data sharing within institutions can be achieved through the use of an electronic system accessible by all healthcare providers, while an online database system is necessary for sharing information with medical professionals at other institutions.

The use of an electronic healthcare system has been shown to result in more complete and accurate documentation by EHDI healthcare professionals, as well as being important for health policy planning (Finitzo & Grosse 2003:73–78; Hutt & Rhodes 2008:87–91). An electronic health record system may assist in avoiding double or unnecessary tests as well as providing data for comparison with earlier tests conducted and a reduction of ineffective treatments (Ueckert et al. 2003:99–108). A study on the use of electronic records in South African healthcare concluded that there is an increased need for sharing of information on procedures and tests done, across the different levels of healthcare provision (Mostert-Phipps et al. 2012:326–331), to ensure integrated, quality EHDI services.

Challenges faced in the implementation of an integrated data system in the United States included a lack of funding for: (1) a web-based data system accessible to providers, (2) staff for the development of the system, and (3) provider training on the use of the system (Uhler et al. 2014:34–43). Challenges identified in the current study include those common to the USA, that is, challenges of funding and a lack of staff for data entry. However, South Africa also has additional challenges such as provision of electricity and Internet connection, which are reflective of a developing country.

Conclusion

This study has looked at EHDI data management systems used by public and private sector audiologists in three provinces of South Africa. There was mainly use of a paper-based system, with the majority of records including medical information. While paper-based systems are not easily accessible and could be prone to errors, the inclusion of medical information allows for some holistic evaluation and care. However, systems did not allow sharing of information between different professionals or for following up of appointments. This indicates a lack of integrated care.

An online data system for integrated care and decision support is especially important in South Africa where there is the implementation of pilot screening initiatives. Data can be used to gather information on the cost of screening, determining the best screening forums, and the best screening techniques. Especially since screening is conducted at different forums by different personnel, data management and analysis are important for the evaluation of quality of services provided, and monitoring of accuracy and timeliness of services.

South Africa has the advantage of learning from global studies on the importance of data management, and including this as part of EHDI programmes from the beginning. The identification of challenges in implementing data management systems allows for effective preparation and formulation of ideas for how these challenges can be overcome. From this study, difficulties such as lack of time and staff for data entry reflect the international challenges of having a shortage of audiologists. Difficulties such as electricity access and Internet connection are part of difficulties related to being a developing country.

Acknowledgements

This article is part of S.M.'s PhD study which was funded by the School of Education, University of the Witwatersrand.

Competing interests

The authors declare that they have no financial or personal relationships that may have inappropriately influenced them in writing this article.

Authors' contributions

This article is part of S.M.'s PhD study. C.S. was the study supervisor and assisted with study conceptualisation, drafting and revision of the article.

References

Alam, S., Gaffney, M. & Eichwald, J., 2014, 'Improved newborn hearing screening follow-up results in more infants identified', *Journal of Public Health Management Practice* 20(2), 220–223. https://doi.org/10.1097/PHH.0b013e31829d7b57

Brink, H., Van der Walt, C. & Van Rensburg, G., 2006, *Fundamentals of research methodology for health care professionals*, Juta and Company Ltd., Cape Town

De Kock, T., Swanepoel, D. & Hall, J.W., 2016, 'Newborn hearing screening at a community-based obstetric unit: Screening and diagnostic outcomes', *International Journal of Pediatric Otorhinolaryngology* 84, 124–131. https://doi.org/10.1016/j.ijporl.2016.02.031

Finitzo, T. & Grosse, S., 2003, 'Quality monitoring for early hearing detection and intervention programs to optimise performance', *Mental Retardation and Developmental Disabilities Research Reviews* 9(2), 73–78. https://doi.org/10.1002/mrdd.10062

Friderichs, N., Swanepoel, D.W. & Hall, J., 2012, 'Efficacy of a community based infant hearing screening programme utilising existing clinical personnel in Western Cape, South Africa', *International Journal of Pediatric Otorhinolaryngology* 76(4), 552–559. https://doi.org/10.1016/j.ijporl.2012.01.015

Häyrinen, K., Saranto, K. & Nykänen, P., 2008, 'Definition, structure, content, use and impacts of electronic health records: A review of the research literature', *International Journal of Medical Informatics* 77, 291–304. https://doi.org/10.1016/j.ijmedinf.2007.09.001

Health Professions Council of South Africa (HPCSA), 2007, *Early hearing detection and intervention programmes in South Africa position statement*, Health Professions Council of South Africa, Pretoria, South Africa.

Hutt, N. & Rhodes, C., 2008, 'Post-natal hearing loss in universal neonatal hearing screening communities: Current limitations and future directions', *Journal of Paediatrics and Child Health* 44(3), 87–91. https://doi.org/10.1111/j.1440-1754.2007.01275.x

JCIH, AAP & ASHA., 2000, 'Year 2000 position statement: principles and guidelines for early hearing detection and intervention programs', *Pediatrics* 106(4), 798–817.

Joint Committee on Infant Hearing (JCIH), 2007, 'Year 2007 position statement: Principles and guidelines for early hearing detection and intervention programs', *Pediatrics* 120(4), 898–921.

Legodi, T.L. & Wolvaardt, J.E., 2015, 'A blank page: Feedback from first referral hospitals to primary health care clinics', *South African Family Practice*, 57 (4), 282–285. https://doi.org/10.1080/20786190.2015.1055670

Mann, R. & Williams, J., 2003, 'Standards in medical record keeping', *Clinical Medicine* 3(4), 329–332. https://doi.org/10.7861/clinmedicine.3-4-329

Moodley, S., 2016, 'Paediatric diagnostic audiology testing in South Africa', *International Journal of Pediatric Otorhinolaryngology* 82, 1–7. https://doi.org/10.1016/j.ijporl.2015.12.015

Moodley, S. & Storbeck, C., 2015, 'Narrative review of EHDI in South Africa', *South African Journal of Communication Disorders* 62(1), 1–10.

Mostert-Phipps, N., Pottas, D. & Korpela, M., 2012, 'Improving continuity of care through the use of electronic records: A South African perspective', *South African Family Practice* 54(4), 326–331. https://doi.org/10.1080/20786204.2012.10874244

Olusanya, B.O., 2015, 'Screening for neonatal deafness in resource-poor countries: Challenges and solutions', *Research and Reports in Neonatology* 5, 51–64. https://doi.org/10.2147/RRN.S61862

Parkes, S.E., 2004, 'Legal aspects of records based medical research', *Archives in Disorders of Childhood* 89, 899–901. https://doi.org/10.1136/adc.2003.045666

Russ, S.A., Dougherty, D. & Jagadish, P., 2010, 'Accelerating evidence into practice for the benefit of children with early hearing loss', *Pediatrics* 126(Suppl 1), S7–S18. https://doi.org/10.1542/peds.2010-0354E

Scheepers, L.J., Swanepoel de, W. & le Roux, T., 2014, 'Why parents refuse newborn hearing screening and default on follow-up rescreening – A South African perspective', *International Journal of Pediatric Otorhinolaryngology* 78(4), 652–658. https://doi.org/10.1016/j.ijporl.2014.01.026

Shulman, S., Besculides, M., Saltzman, A., Ireys, H., White, K.R. & Forsman, I., 2010, 'Evaluation of the universal newborn screening and intervention program', *Pediatrics* 126(Suppl 1), S19–S27. https://doi.org/10.1542/peds.2010-0354F

Störbeck, C. & Young, A., 2016, 'The HI HOPES data set of deaf children under the age of 6 in South Africa: Maternal suspicion, age of identification and newborn hearing screening', *BMC Pediatrics* 16(1), 45. https://doi.org/10.1186/s12887-016-0574-1

Swanepoel, D.W., Ebrahim, S., Joseph, A. & Friedland, P., 2007, 'Newborn hearing screening in a South African private health care hospital', *International Journal of Pediatric Otorhinolaryngology* 71(6), 881–887. https://doi.org/10.1016/j.ijporl.2007.02.009

Swanepoel, D.W., Hugo, R. & Louw, B., 2006, 'Infant hearing screening at immunization clinics in South Africa', *International Journal of Pediatric Otorhinolaryngology* 70(7), 1241–1249.

Ueckert, F., Goerz, M., Ataian, M., Tessmann, S. & Prokosch, H.U., 2003, 'Empowerment of patients and communication with health care professionals through an electronic health record', *International Journal of Medical Informatics* 70(2), 99–108. https://doi.org/10.1016/S1386-5056(03)00052-2

Uhler, K., Thomson, V., Cyr, H., Gabbard, S.A. & Yoshinaga-Itano, Y., 2014, 'State and territory EHDI databases: What we do and don't know about the hearing or audiological data from identified children', *American Journal of Audiology* 23(1), 34–43. https://doi.org/10.1044/1059-0889(2013/13-0015)

Williams, T.R., Alam, S. & Gaffney, M., 2016, 'Progress in identifying infants with hearing loss – United States, 2006–2012', *Morbidity and Mortality Weekly Report* 64(13), 351–356.

Yoshinaga-Itano, C., 2003, 'Early intervention after universal neonatal hearing screening: Impact on outcomes', *Mental Retardation and Developmental Disabilities Research Reviews* 9(4), 252–266. https://doi.org/10.1002/mrdd.10088

Yoshinaga-Itano, C., 2014, 'Principles and guidelines for early intervention after confirmation that a child is deaf or hard of hearing', *Journal of Deaf Studies and Deaf Education* 19(2), 143–175. https://doi.org/10.1093/deafed/ent043

Yoshinaga-Itano, C., Sedey, A.L., Coulter, D.K. & Mehl, A.L., 1998, 'Language of early- and later-identified children with hearing loss', *Pediatrics* 102(5), 1161–1171. https://doi.org/10.1542/peds.102.5.1161

Young, S.Y. & Spencer, N.J., 2008, 'A data collection system to audit post-newborn hearing surveillance programme: Problems and possibilities', *Child: Care, Health and Development* 34(5), 648–656. https://doi.org/10.1111/j.1365-2214.2008.00854.x

The linkage of information quality to an executive decision support framework for the financial service sector of a developing economy

Authors:
Visvanathan Naicker[1]
Denisha Jairam-Owthar[2]

Affiliations:
[1]Department of Business Information and Administration, Cape Peninsula University of Technology, South Africa

[2]Graduate School of Business Leadership, University of South Africa, South Africa

Corresponding author:
Visvanathan Naicker,
naickervi@cput.ac.za

Background: Executives are steering organisations in our most turbulent economic times, whereby market disrupters are becoming the norm that are eradicating entire value chains of organisations. It is for this reason that decision support mechanisms for executives have become more critical than ever before. We have seen many leading organisations being reduced to market followers. This leaves many critical questions: What could the executives of those prior leading organisations have done to prevent this? Does the information that is being presented at various senior committees for decisions in an organisation contain information quality and is information quality linked to decisions made by executives?

Objectives: This article presents mathematical evidence that information quality does form part of an executive decision support framework (EDSF) and confirms that information quality should form part of an EDSF.

Method: A mixed method research approach was then followed where semi-structured interviews were held with chief information officers. The semi-structured interviews thereafter informed the survey questionnaires design. The survey questionnaires were statistically analysed using structural equation modelling and the maximum likelihood estimates method, to mathematically prove if information quality does form part of an EDSF.

Results: This research provides evidence that information quality is linked to an EDSF and that information quality should form part of an EDSF.

Conclusion: It is clear, therefore, that information quality is mathematically linked to an EDSF. Although information quality is made up of other latent variables that affect it, there is a strong correlation between information quality and an EDSF.

Introduction

Technological advancements have aided the digital era in generating daily gigabytes of information across various channels such as call centres, online portals, mobile phones, podcasts and branch offices (Hauser & Rouse 2007). However, a major challenge is creating information with quality. Marshall and Harpe (2009) explain that it is only possible to utilise information effectively if the data used to provide the information have quality.

Information quality currently has no industrialised understanding and definitions. Globally different organisations have different understandings and definitions of information quality. However, information quality is critical because information cannot be used if it cannot be trusted. Therefore, information quality is important. The purpose of this research is to ascertain if information quality should form part of executive decision support framework (EDSF) and to prove if information quality is mathematically linked to an EDSF. Other studies have only mentioned that information quality is important with varying classifications of information quality, but none of the previous research studies have incorporated a comprehensive view of various experts to conclude if information quality should form part of EDSF and mathematically endeavours to prove that information quality is linked to an EDSF. This article, therefore, adds value to the body of knowledge by focussing on the above explained aspects.

Literature review

The literature review will be structured to discuss the following with regard to information quality: definition, significance, challenges, solutions to challenges, evidence of information quality's importance according to experts, relevance of information quality to the financial services sector, important components of information quality, EDSFs, limitations, future research and, finally, a summary of the literature review. The current status of the above topics in information quality will be discussed, and thereafter, the limitations and recommendations for future research will be discussed. Reference studies will be mentioned that have made significant reference to information quality in their research. Firstly, however, a brief overview of Company A, which was used as a compelling case for this research study will be provided.

Overview of Company A

The services sector has direct impact on customers where improvements are needed (Tomlinson 2011). Furthermore, the financial services sector was selected as a compelling case because the recent global economic downturn resulted from a myriad of financial services sector failures that affected customers and economies directly (Crotty 2009). Examples of organisations in the financial services sector that failed economically in their lifecycles were the Lehman Brothers, J P Morgan and Chase, Merrill Lynch and Goldman Sachs.

Company A was once a market leader in South Africa in the financial services sector in which it operates. It had merged with a global company thereafter, expanding its services to the rest of Africa. After the merger took place, a restructuring of Company A occurred. During this transition of alignment, Company A had become a market follower, from a technological and customer-centric perspective.

Definition of information quality

According to Somers, Gorla and Wong (2010), information quality refers to the quality of outputs the information system produces which can be in the form of reports or online screens. GARP (2011) refers to information quality as being available and containing integrity. Information quality as explained by Goel, Indushobha and Smith (2010) is a multidimensional concept, which can be classified into five major categories: intrinsic quality, contextual quality, representation, accessibility and completeness. The researchers agree that information quality has several aspects to it. Hamblin and Phoenix's (2013) definition of information quality is congruent with Goel et al.'s (2010) that outlines the characteristics of effective information quality as intrinsic data quality, accessibility, contextual quality and timeliness. From the researchers' view, perhaps the most holistic definition is encompassed by Hauser and Rouse (2007) who defines information quality as a state of completeness, validity, consistent and timely to serve for specific business decisions.

These components of Hauser and Rouse's (2007) definition are further explained:

- *Completeness*: Degree to which values are present in the attributes that require them.
- *Consistency*: The agreement or logical coherence among data that free them from variation of contradiction.
- *Timeliness*: The expectation that a particular data item or multiple items are provided at the time requested or specified.
- *Validity*: Conformance of data values that are edited for acceptability or fall within acceptable ranges of allowable values.

For the purposes of this research, the definition provided by Hauser and Rouse (2007) above will be used, because it provides the most comprehensive coverage of the information quality definition.

Significance of information quality

A survey was conducted by Somers et al. (2010) for improving information quality because it emerged as one of the top five concerns facing executives. Somers et al. iterate that information quality is highly important to organisations to derive value in terms of improved decision-making and providing accurate and timely information. Fulmer (2012) describes that information quality is the new 'black' because it is the new fashion due to it being the only way to ensure profitability going forward. Cunningham (2012) agrees that the need to ensure information is reliable and authentic and has never been higher. Performance monitoring of information quality is important (Delbaere & Ferreira 2007).

The researchers duly note that from these authors, therefore that there is a linking of information quality to profitability and performance of companies. Delbaere and Ferreira (2007) agree that information quality can be measured across multiple dimensions, for example, how well a data element meets a company's information integrity goals and needs. Because information quality is a multidimensional measure, it is important to determine which aspects of information are critical to organisations. Somers et al.'s (2010) research portrays that information quality is directly impacted by the information systems quality. According to Somers et al., excellence in information systems quality involves state-of-the-art technology, following industry's 'best practice' software standards and delivering error-free performance.

The researchers argue that a performance metrics to measure information quality, because it is a multidimensional concept, would be beneficial to an organisation to highlight information quality maturity and to focus on improvements. Allen et al. (2011) assert that a business's information is one of its most important assets. Allen et al.'s extensive research has emphasised the strategic value of information. The strategic value together with the advancement and complexity of networking technologies can create opportunities for attacks and security breaches that can cause great financial loss. The researchers emphasise that the link between losses and information highlights the linkage of information quality and information security.

Wang and Chang (2011) agree with the opinion that information security enhances information quality. They explain that a number of information security breaches can cause economic loss. Ezingeard, McFadzean and Birchall

(2007) support this view by explaining that companies that admit to breaches within their confidential information had a reduction in their stock market price, which can contribute to a financial crisis. Furthermore, Hall, Sarkani and Mazzuchi (2010) found that information security is also significant for information quality.

The researchers agree that information security should form part of information quality as probed by the experts. Hauser and Rouse (2007) are of the opinion that the usual ad hoc information clean-up projects put in place relating to improving quality issues do little to sustain a cultural commitment to information quality across the organisation. The researchers contend that although information security is a key element of information quality, it is not the only element of information quality. The researchers agree as suggested congruently by the authors that there is a need to govern information quality because of its many aspects, through an overarching information policy. The researchers thereby argue that although an information policy and procedure need to be developed within an organisation, effective embedment within the organisation requires an entire culture change throughout the organisation on information itself. A culture change of an organisation as mentioned by Hauser and Rouse requires a holistic strategy, rather than mediocre remediation projects. The researchers highlight that accountability on how information is managed, stored and processed has emerged as a focal area as promulgated by the Protection of Personal Information Act (POPI), soon to be implemented into South African legislation.

Hauser and Rouse (2007) agree the inter-relationship between data, technology, process and people needs to be considered overall for information quality optimisation in an organisation. Hamblin and Phoenix (2013) promulgate that information management goes beyond external stakeholder requirements as there are also a multitude of internal users. From the view of these experts, the researchers assimilate that an overall approach to information quality is encouraged, internally and externally. Ezingeard et al. (2007) agree that although information security is important, information systems specialists lack a common understanding resulting in limited dialogue and inadequate definitions of what comprises successful performance of information quality.

The researchers argue that as a resolution, all definitions should be made clear in the information policy to promote a common understanding, thereafter to allow dialogue towards the performance of successful information quality. Adversities in information quality have negative impact to organisations and users (Cunningham 2012; Iwasaki & Jones 2010). The researchers, therefore, suggest that a hybrid approach involving people, process and technology is vital to migrate towards a successful information quality culture. The starting elements of driving an information quality culture are introducing dialogue.

The researchers use examples from organisations such as Google, Uber and Facebook, whereby the microcosm of their business is information management. These gigantic organisations possess an advanced organisational culture for information and data management, enabling them to be powerful 'mogul' organisations of our decade. The researchers emphasise that confidence suffers and economic functions underperform when there is uncertainty about the integrity of information. According to Cunningham (2012), events in which data were improperly and illegally manipulated have driven the requirements for ensuring information quality. Cunningham asserts that adverse events, such as security beaches and data reconciliations from different systems, have placed a higher burden on organisations to ensure information quality. The researchers agree with the experts whereby there is an increasing high emphasis on information quality in organisations.

Challenges of information quality

Various problems and solutions occur in the information quality sphere as discussed below. Poor information quality could have the following impact on organisations as highlighted by different authors in Tables 1 and 2.

Some solutions which could help resolve some of these issues to aid in database normalisation processes, as mentioned by Iwasaki and Jones (2010), are:

- setting up internal control procedures
- monitoring the implementation of information quality strategy and

TABLE 1: Negative strategic impact of poor information quality.

Number	Negative Impact	Author
1	Incorrect strategic decisions.	Hamblin and Phoenix (2013)
2	Time wasted as data needs to be reconciled and verified to source before presentations at meetings.	Hamblin and Phoenix (2013)
3	Unauthorised access to users on confidential information that could cause material harm to the organisation such as reputation damage.	Cunningham (2012)
4	Slowing the speed of quick decisions that need to be made.	Iwasaki and Jones (2010)
5	Lack of seamless linkage between 'siloed databases' causing duplicates.	Hauser and Rouse (2007)
6	Lack of robustness in estimations for future trending.	Hamblin and Phoenix (2013)
7	Lack of analytical view of figures.	Hamblin and Phoenix (2013)
8	Inadequate audit trail of information.	Hamblin and Phoenix (2013)

Note: Please see the full reference list of the article, Naicker, V. & Jairam, D., 2017, 'The linkage of information quality to an executive decision support framework for the financial service sector of a developing economy', *South African Journal of Information Management* 19(1), a781. https://doi.org/10.4102/sajim.v19i1.781, for more information.

TABLE 2: Negative operational and tactical impact of poor information quality.

Number	Negative impact	Author
1	Inconsistent data field definitions.	Hauser and Rouse (2007)
2	Multiple shadow or customised databases.	Hauser and Rouse (2007)
3	Duplicate customer records.	Hauser and Rouse (2007)
4	Reduction in reputation.	Ezingeard et al. (2007)
5	Poor customer service.	Ezingeard et al. (2007)
6	Inhibits the firm's ability to operate.	Ezingeard et al. (2007)

Note: Please see the full reference list of the article, Naicker, V. & Jairam, D., 2017, 'The linkage of information quality to an executive decision support framework for the financial service sector of a developing economy', *South African Journal of Information Management* 19(1), a781. https://doi.org/10.4102/sajim.v19i1.781, for more information.

- introducing external experts to guide information quality initiatives and projects in the organisation.

Deeper negative underlying items of poor information that culminate holistically into poor information quality are supported by various authors, which are highlighted in Table 2.

Hauser and Rouse (2007) and Fulmer (2012) suggest some solutions for improvement of the operational and tactical items of poor information quality:

- remove redundant information from databases
- reduce processing time of data
- introduce monitoring processes to resolve quality errors
- design and implement a strategy for information quality management
- enhance quality by implementing data quality processes, roles and responsibilities for compliance, fraud prevention and loss control
- develop suitable information quality measures such as of data integrity mandates, standardisation of data and
- introduce reporting and process controls for end to end information quality management.

The researchers agree and acknowledge the negative impact, both directly and indirectly, that poor information quality can have on an organisation. Information quality issues can, therefore, be at strategic, tactical and operational levels in an organisation (Cunningham 2012; Ezingeard et al. 2007; Hamblin & Phoenix 2013; Hauser & Rouse 2007; Iwasaki & Jones 2010) According to Somers et al. (2010), information quality problems can include system problems such as incorrect information because of program or data errors and irrelevant information because of changed user requirements. They explain that although 50 years of software development has come and gone, software quality today is no better than it was decades ago. They further elaborate that software problems, difficult user interfaces and fragmented models are difficult to integrate data for information quality to be achieved. Therefore, data integration from different systems can compromise information quality (Delbaere & Ferreira 2007).

The researchers iterate that in industry, a fundamental challenge exists, whereby ownership of data within the systems requires clear understanding. The researchers are of the view that ownership of data can assist in alleviating information quality issues where controls can be instituted by the data owner to manage data integration, data errors and limit duplications. Delbaere and Ferreira (2007) are of the opinion that data emerging from different source systems in different data formats create information quality challenges.

The researchers highlight some challenges posing integrity issues that include collection, reconciliation and integration of data. Hauser and Rouse (2007) agree that fragmented data decrease information quality. Solutions can be implemented such as improving reconciling data from different sources (Iwasaki & Jones 2010). Achieving the 'one view of the customer' presents a challenge for many financial services industries, as with Company A (i.e. *a huge conglomerate in the banking industry in SA*). This is an integral aspect of achieving competitive success with a customer that transacts using many products housed in one financial services institution. Amalgamating information from different products source systems into one source involves data integration. For successful data integration, controls such as reconciliations should be performed to ensure information quality for trust to be built on the outputs of the processed information, as suggested by Delbaera and Ferreira (2007) and with which the researchers agree. Solutions to some challenges in information quality will be highlighted.

Solutions to challenges

Iwasaki and Jones (2010) propose a solution of using external assurance as one of the ways to enhance credibility to information. They highlighted that the benefit of this is primarily to enhance confidence of information for the benefit of its users who have little control over its production. Ezingeard et al. (2007), however, explains that there is no universally accepted definition on what constitutes 'information assurance'. Nonetheless 'information assurance' is a strategic issue because of the potential impact on the rest of the business, for example, a decrease in stock market price.

The researchers emphasise that trust of presented information to executives needs to be built. One of the methods as part of the journey of building trust of the information is reconciliations as mentioned by Delbaera and Ferreira (2007). The researchers are of the view that reconciliations, therefore, can be automated as a form of 'information assurance'. The researchers argue that although external assurance maybe a solution, the practical feasibility to have external assurers available to check every report that has tight deadlines, to be sent to executive management, may not be possible. However, it may be feasible for external assurers to be used for external reports only, to be provided for external stakeholders of the organisation. The researchers are of the view that external reports being produced for external stakeholders to some extent rely in internal information or reports (e.g.: corporate sustainability projects that the organisation is carrying out for the community where information is found within the organisation to report this to external stakeholders). However, as emphasised prior, external assurance on every report may not always be practically achievable because of costs and timeliness for the organisation.

Evidence of the importance of information quality according to experts

Fulmer (2012) presents an example with evidence on information quality that cost lenders of mortgage loans close to US$2 trillion in direct loses because of foreclosures, settlements with residential mortgage backed securities investors, repurchases and regulatory fines. He explains that the data quality is the foundation that supports sustainable loans. The most important revenue generator in some financial services organisations is obtained from lending products, as with Company A (*for anonymity*).

The researchers argue that achieving information quality would, therefore, serve as a critical success factor for the financial services sector, in support of Fulmer's (2012) view for attaining sustainable income for the organisation. Surveys conducted in Leon et al.'s (2012) research show that most organisations have no formal policies to ensure integrity of information. Leon et al. revealed that companies reported, while informal guidelines were common, formal guidelines existed in only half of the 43 companies in total that were surveyed. The researchers are of the view that the awareness of information quality in companies have increased in 2015. The researchers provide instances of growing increase, whereby the current financial services organisations such as the large banks in South Africa have dedicated business units within the information technology departments whereby information quality is starting to be managed. The Sarbanes-Oxley regulations hold publicly trading companies in the USA accountable for implementing and evaluating controls for reporting to reduce risk. Hauser and Rouse (2007) explain that public companies throughout USA have increasing levels of scrutiny because of the Sarbanes-Oxley regulation where senior executives are required to take a more active interest in the accuracy and timeliness of their data.

The researchers note, however, that the Sarbanes-Oxley regulations are not legislation in developing economies. Carly Fiorina, the former chairperson of Hewlett-Packard, explains that information obtained is meaningful only if it is accurate. In her collective experience, she states that quality of information once reports are compiled in many organisations are below acceptable standards (Mattix & Henning 2010). Hauser and Rouse (2007) confirm via their empirical studies that organisations do not lack information, but they lack high-quality information. These authors continue to suggest that 'siloed data' result in poor-quality information where organisations suffer through decreased customer retention, decreased customer profitability and decreased product market maturity by using cross-sell or up-sell techniques. The researchers agree with the experts on the criticality of information quality within organisations. Information quality which serves as a catalyst for the financial services sector will be elaborated on next.

Relevance of information quality to the financial services sector

The relevancy of information quality in the financial services sector is explained further (Fulmer 2012; Iwasaki & Jones 2010). Fulmer explains that there are inconsistencies in data between information submitted by the borrower of mortgage loans and information obtained from other independent sources such as credit bureaus. Loans with variances must be investigated and corrected before the loan is approved, and lending forms an integral part of generating profits for banks. Therefore, Fulmer claims that data integrity for information quality is imperative for mortgage lenders.

The researchers acknowledge, therefore, that mortgage loan products are, therefore, vital for the banking industry as it generates a substantial amount of profits in the form of interests charged on loans, whereby data integrity is critical. Iwasaki and Jones (2010) iterate that the financial services sector is important to the market economy as even though the overall contribution to the gross domestic product is relatively small; its impact on capital flows is fundamental. When the world-wide economic crisis occurred, the usefulness of auditors in the banking sector were in question. The researchers argue, however, as stated prior that the practicality of using auditors, also classified as external assurers, may not always be possible for all management reports. The components of information quality are discussed in detail below.

Important components of information quality

Somers et al. (2010) explain that information quality has a data quality component because data quality is at the heart of information quality. The authors continue to explain that poor data quality results in poor information quality. The ripple effect being, poor information quality adversely affecting the organisation at all levels. Selection and execution of sound business strategy becomes difficult because of inaccurate or delayed information, causing strategic drift. Delbaere and Ferreira (2007) also link information quality to data integrity. They advocate that data integrity involves maintaining the quality of information throughout the organisation.

Delbaere and Ferreira (2007) elaborate that information quality also includes how effectively data support decisions as highlighted in the proposed research study. They refer to decision support that is needed to meet organisations strategic objectives, for executive and senior management decisions.

The researchers, therefore, argue that at the heart of information quality lies data quality and integrity, whereby information quality is largely dependent on data quality and integrity. Wang and Chang (2011) go further to dissect information security, which forms part of information quality such as confidentiality, integrity and availability. Wang and Chang explain that the confidentiality aspect is information that remains safe from any unauthorised access and has not been subject to modification and forgery.

Wang and Chang (2011) further outline that information availability refers to the extent to which information is readily accessible. The researchers agree, therefore, that information accessibility can also form as part of the information security component of information quality. Li and Chang (2007) explain that organisational culture must be aligned for effective information security in the organisation. Li and Chang's research findings, however, suggest that cooperativeness negatively affects confidentiality. Confidentiality as outlined by Wang and Chang (2011) is crucial for information security. Therefore, enterprises should adopt an integrated strategy combining both information security and organisation culture aspects.

The researchers highlight as prior per above that a people, process and technology integrated approach is important for enhancing information quality in an organisation. Hauser and Rouse (2007) explain that one of the major components for information quality is a centralised source of customer data for the organisation. However, the dreams of a single source of truth have not always been realised because of the variation across source systems (Hauser & Rouse 2007). Hauser and Rouse refer to adversities such as systemic errors that are difficult to eradicate and further investment maybe needed to cleanse data and integrate sources. This supports GARP's (2011) view which states that there are various duplicate sources of information which creates doubt on the correctness of the information presented.

The researchers iterate that this forms part of the data integration problem across different systems for achieving information quality as mentioned prior. There are new proposed solutions to information quality and there are still challenges to be addressed if information quality is to be enhanced by information assurers (Hamblin & Phoenix 2013). Elements of information assurance for managing information quality, according to Hamblin and Phoenix, comprise of standard definitions to be developed, trialled and implemented to ensure a common data language exists through the organisation.

Page (2011) is of the opinion that for data and information quality, the organisation should have a corporate wide agenda for data, a joint effort between business and the information technology unit of the organisation and an evolutionary process throughout the company to support quality. Differences must be identified and the underlying reasons elicited and resolved for an institutional standard for information assurance (i.e. an information policy for information assurance for improving information quality) to be implemented (Hamblin & Phoenix 2013).

The process for information assurance, however, must avoid over checking and substantial costs but provide sufficient frequency for integrity, objectivity and independence with executive management support (Hamblin & Phoenix 2013). Therefore, from the above experts, the researchers argue that a correct balance must be established between costs and information quality through information assurance. In support of this view, Hamblin and Phoenix explain that although this is a new proposed solution of 'information assurance', there are specific challenges that come with this solution such as practical feasibility and costs.

Therefore, information assurance may not provide the solution to compromised information quality. An integrated approach to information across the organisation as mentioned by Page (2011) above presents a more feasible and practical solution. A summary of the literature review on information quality will now be provided.

Executive decision support framework

The literature on EDSFs as compared to developed disciplines such as medicine and engineering which are more than 2000 years old is still to be developed. It is important to note that even in developed disciplines such as engineering and medicine, EDSFs are still recommended for further research within these advanced disciplines although EDSFs may already be in use in these areas.

The young discipline of specifically Executive Decision Support Systems is only 35 years old which provides an opportunity through this research to add to the body of knowledge (Davis, Keenan & Power 2013). Being able to investigate a key component such as information quality and mathematically prove their linkages for an EDSF is therefore a value add to the body of knowledge. EDSF is defined for the purposes of this research as a framework that would support executives in their decision-making.

Summary of information quality literature review

Information quality is made up of several components and is of high relevance to the financial services sector. Information quality is significant for providing trustworthy information to executive and senior management. Although there are challenges to information quality, solutions have been evidenced. From this literature review, it can, therefore, be noted that information quality is a key component of an EDSF. The arrow showing the information transfer control below. Hence, emanating from the above literature reviewed, the following research question was conceptualised.

'Should information quality form part of an executive decision support framework?' and 'Is information quality mathematically linked to an executive decision support framework?'

Research methodology

A research methodology was conducted as per Figure 1 that was used to assess if information quality does indeed form part of an EDSF for decision support for executives.

The research paradigm consisted of a pragmatic approach per the epistemology and ontology because of a mixed methods research methodology. It was conducted using a case study of Company A, which is an organisation in the financial services sector of a developing economy. A deductive research logic because theory was looked at first, as per the theoretical default framework above. The time horizon was cross sectional because of time and resource constraints of the researchers.

The mixed method approach methodology consisted of semi-structured interviews as the qualitative aspect. The reason a mixed method methodology was used was to ensure high validity and high reliability of the conducted research, because quantitative and qualitative research is deals with high validity and high reliability respectively. Semi-Structured interviews were held using a purposive sample with the four chief information officers (CIO's) to obtain depth of knowledge and context, before the survey questionnaires could be designed.

The results of the semi-structured interviews were thereafter used to inform the quantitative aspect per the survey questionnaires. The semi-structured interviews were conducted using a voice recorder and interview notes. The survey questionnaires were then designed and piloted among nine persons across the organisation before the survey questionnaires could be finalised for distribution. This pilot was done to ensure the questionnaires were understood by participants. No major corrections on the survey questionnaires resulted after the pilot was conducted.

The survey questionnaire was in the form of a Likert scale. The population consisted of 706 persons in total because of the total number of senior and executive managers across the organisation. Thereafter proportional sampling techniques were performed to carry out the survey questionnaires to ensure a stratified sample response across the divisions in the organisation.

The results of the semi-structured interviews were analysed and synthesised using themes and counting techniques, to ensure all input was included for consideration into the survey questionnaires. The analysed feedback was then inputted into the formation of the survey questionnaire. The survey questionnaires were handed out manually and sent via email to participants to increase response rates. A reminder for survey responses had to be sent via email to participants to ensure an increased response rate across the divisions, which is summarised in Table 4.

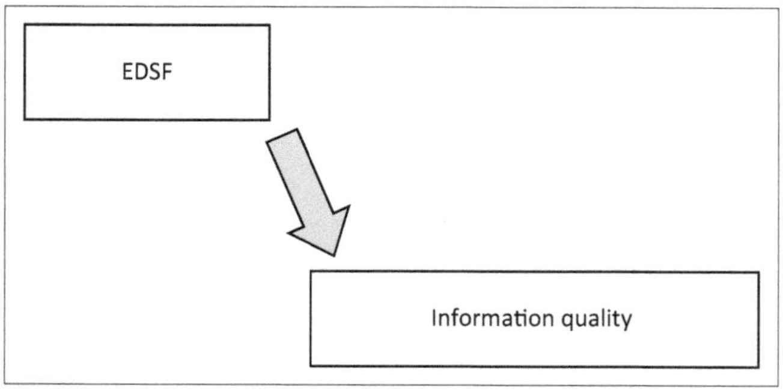

FIGURE 1: Proposed linkage between the two constructs: Information quality and executive decision support framework.

The results of the survey questionnaires after the survey questionnaire was conducted, were inferentially analysed using SPSS and IBM AMOS computer software to identify trends and patterns because the SPSS and IBM AMOS software has more accuracy than manual analysis of trends and patterns. Thereafter descriptive statistics were used to represent the results emerging from the survey questionnaires using bar graphs and/or pie charts.

Triangulation of results took place by the researcher to increase the validity and reliability of the research, through manually comparing the results emanating from the semi-structured interviews to the survey questionnaires. This provided in-depth triangulation outcome results after the comparison of the data was completed. High validity was maintained using the qualitative semi-structured interviews and high reliability was maintained using the quantitative survey questionnaires, therefore, confirming the choice of a mixed method methodology of maintaining high results in both validity and reliability of the research.

Ethics throughout the research process was maintained. For the statistical analysis, structural equation modelling was used for validity and reliability of the research; and the maximum likelihood estimates method were used to show if the constructs were mathematically related.

Results

The semi-structured interviews are summarised in the figures below which highlights the common themes and outlying themes for every construct from the CIOs from each division of Company A.

As from Table 3 a common thread is data accuracy, data governance, differing reports and business being responsible for information. As aligned with the literature review, information quality consists of many elements of which not

TABLE 3: Information quality survey results summarised, September 2015 – A: Information quality.

Theme	Common	Outliers
Accuracy	X	-
Never really understood	-	X
Technically based on business rules	-	X
Accuracy and integrity	X	-
Information quality depends on business requirements	X	-
Business's responsibility	X	-
Business's responsibility: Accepts remediation projects	X	-
Affects clients directly: one view of the client	-	X
Data volumes	X	-
Legacy system integration	-	X
Data governance needs improvement	X	-
Reports differ	X	-
Users have source system access, minimum use of warehouse	-	X
Too many spreadsheets	X	-
Meta data, master data management, data linage, reference data	-	X

all employees in organisations are completely clear on (GARP 2011; Goel et al. 2010; Hamblin & Phoenix 2013; Somers et al. 2010). It is interesting to note that data governance and volumes which lead to a data-driven culture, also came up as common themes. This highlights that a data culture is important to harness as recommended by the experts (Hauser & Rouse 2007).

Geographic and demographics analysis

The respondents to this survey totalled one hundred and seven ($n = 107$) bank officials. Those in the Retail and Business Bank divisions accounted for 43% of respondents, the remainder comprised: Corporate and Investment Banking, 17.8%; Financial Services Insurance 14.0% and Enterprise Support Services 25.2%. Almost all of the respondents are based in South Africa (99.1%) while the remainder (0.9%) are from Barclays Africa (12 countries). The respondents in South Africa amounted to 99.1% (Table 4).

As compared to the initial sample frame of 141 respondents at the onset of the research per the research methodology; there was a 76% response rate. There was no initial sample target set for respondents in South Africa. However, as stated, most respondents were from South Africa, that is, 99.1%. Retail and Business bank had a targeted response rate of 19.7%; the actual response rate achieved was 43%. Corporate and Investment Banking had a targeted response rate of 20%; 17.8% was actually achieved. Financial Services Insurance was initially allocated a 20% response rate target; a 14% actual response rate was achieved. Enterprise Support Services was initially allocated a 20% response rate and achieved a 25.2% response rate. Retail and Business Banking and Enterprise Support Services had an increased response rate of 24% (i.e. 43%–19.7%) and 5.5% (i.e. 25.2%–20%) respectively, based on the initial sample frame. Corporate and Investment Banking and Financial Services Insurances had a decreased response rate of 2.2% (i.e. 20%–17.8%) and 6% (i.e. 20%–14%) respectively. An overall summary of responses will be provided next.

Overall summary of responses

The questionnaire outcomes are summarised in Table 5.

Most of the sample population 'agreed' or 'strongly agreed' with the questions on information management. The questions on information management were positioned from the literature review and the semi-structured interviews, thereby in practice participants have 'agreed' and 'strongly agreed'.

Structural equation modelling for validity and reliability

To evaluate reliability of the measurement items by determining how participants interpreted the questions per category, Cronbach's alpha with an acceptable value of 0.70 as confirmed by Hair et al. (2009) was calculated and confirmed to be greater than the recommended value of 0.70 (Table 6).

Maximum likelihood estimates

Information quality was analysed to ascertain how much it contributes to an EDSF using the statistical method of maximum likelihood estimates. This is summarised in Table 7.

Limitations

A selected case study was used, therefore, it would be irresponsible to generalise outside the financial services sector. Confidentiality was of the selected case had to be maintained because of the high competitive nature of Company A. Although generalizability is not random, the outcomes can be transferable to any other case exhibiting similar characteristics to that of company A.

Feedback for the research methodology was obtained only from senior and executive management because time for the research study did not permit other levels of management such as operational and tactical management to be included. Provided that this is an EDSF, this seems fair.

TABLE 5: Frequency distribution of the overall opinion on information management.

Option	Frequency	%
Disagree	1	0.9
Neutral	4	3.7
Agree	72	67.3
Strongly agree	30	28
Total	**107**	**100**

TABLE 6: Structural equation modeling for validity and reliability.

Construct	Instrument (questionnaire)	Number of items (number of questions)	Cronbach's alpha	Number of valid sample
Information management	A1 – A22	22	0.833	100

TABLE 7: Maximum likelihood estimates results.

Relationship	Estimate	SE	CR	*p*-value	Label
IQ and EDSF	0.108	0.030	3.535	***	c1

IQ, information quality; EDSF, executive decision support framework; SE, standard error; CR, critical ratio.

Note: The asterisks in the *p*-value column of the table, illustrate a strong correlation between these constructs: IQ and EDSF. The model equations in the structural framework are, therefore, as follows: IQ = 0.108 EDSF + $Z1$. IQ is made up of 0.108 of EDSF. $Z1$ represents all other aspects that constitute IM.

TABLE 4: Percentage response from each division of Company A.

Area	Frequency	%	Valid (%)	Cumulative (%)
Retail and Business bank	46	43	43	43
Corporate and investment banking	19	17.8	17.8	60.7
Company A financial services (insurance)	15	14	14	74.8
Enterprise Support Services (IT, risk, compliance, HR, finance)	27	25.2	25.2	100
Total of each area	**107**	**100**	**100**	**Not applicable**

Future research

It is recommended that other sectors of developing economies can conduct this research, such as engineering and the public sector. Future research is also recommended to determine the impact that an EDSF with information quality has on other levels of management such as operational and tactical management. The impact that information quality has on the board of directors of a company can also be researched further. Behavioural changes once information quality is implemented throughout an organisation can also be researched in future.

Conclusion

There have been several challenges with information quality such as incorrect strategic decisions which may result in time wasted on data that needs reconciliation for verification purposes before decisions can be made, lack of trends and estimations that may result and a lack of an audit trail of information. Information quality has several components, which executive and senior management require in order for information to be trusted for decision-making and thereby is of high relevance to the financial services sector. Because IQ is not an industrialised concept as explained in the literature review, the understanding of this construct may not be as advanced in Africa and South Africa.

As per the research questions mentioned above: 'Should information quality form part of an executive decision support framework?' and 'Is information quality mathematically linked to an executive decision support framework?'

From the literature review it can clearly be noted that information quality is critical and should form part of an EDSF, because information that cannot be trusted cannot be used for decisions. This is supported throughout the literature review by various expert views which were also supported by the researcher's views. This research also proves that information quality is mathematically linked to an EDSF via the statistical analysis done with structural equation modelling and maximum likelihood estimates conducted through the mixed method research methodology. No other research proves a mathematical link between these constructs, although much prior research refers to the importance of information quality only, without specificity to an EDSF. The purpose and objective of this research has been met from answering the set questions above.

Acknowledgements

The authors gratefully acknowledge the editor and reviewers' constructive comments on an earlier version of the article.

Competing interests

The authors declare that they have no financial or personal relationships that may have inappropriately influenced them in writing this article.

Authors' contributions

D.J. and V.N. are the project leaders of this study. They made conceptual contributions to this study. Calculations were performed by an independent paid statistician. This article emanated from D.J.'s doctoral thesis.

References

Allen, J.P., Karlsson, F., Kolkowska, E. & Hedstrom, K., 2011, 'Value conflicts for information security management', *Elsevier Journal of Strategic Information Systems* 20, 373–384. https://doi.org/10.1016/j.jsis.2011.06.001

Crotty, J., 2009, 'Structural causes of the global financial crisis: A critical assessment of the new financial architecture', *Cambridge Journal of Economics* 33(4), 562–580.

Cunningham, P., 2012, 'GARP focus', *Information Management Journal* 9(2), 21–22.

Davis, B.G., Keenan, P. & Power, D.J. 2013, 'History of decision support systems', viewed 03 August 2013, from http://dssresources.com/history/dsshistory.html

Delbaere, M. & Ferreira, R., 2007, 'Addressing the data aspects of compliance with industry models', *IBM Systems Journal* 46(2), 319–334. https://doi.org/10.1147/sj.462.0319

Ezingeard, J.N., McFadzean, E. & Birchell, D., 2007, 'Mastering the art of corroboration: A conceptual analysis of information assurance and corporate strategy alignment', *Emerald Journal of Enterprise Information Management* 20(1), 96–118. https://doi.org/10.1108/17410390710717165

Fulmer, A., 2012, 'Is data integrity the new black', *ABI Inform Complete Mortgage Banking* 72(9), 23–25.

Generally Accepted Record Keeping Principles (GARP), ARMA International, 2011, 'Protect and maintain information integrity to decrease business risk', *Information Management Journal* 3, 37–40.

Goel, S., Indushoba, N. & Smith, C., 2010, 'Metrics for characterizing the form of security policies', *Elsevier Journal of Strategic Information Systems* 19, 281–295. https://doi.org/10.1016/j.jsis.2010.10.002

Hair, J.F., Black, C.W., Barry, B.J., Anderson, E. & Tatham, R.L., 2009, Multivariate data analysis: A global perspective, 7th edn., Prentice Hall, Upper Saddle River, NJ.

Hall, J.H., Sarkani, S. & Mazzuchi, T.A., 2010, 'Impacts of organisational capabilities in information security', *Emerald Information Management and Computer Security Journal* 19(3), 155–176. https://doi.org/10.1108/09685221111153546

Hamblin, D.J. & Phoenix, D.A., 2013, 'A model for managing data assurance in higher education', *Journal of Higher Education Policy and Management* 34(4), 421–435. https://doi.org/10.1080/1360080X.2012.689195

Hauser, S.A.M. & Rouse, C., 2007, 'The whole truth and nothing but the truth? The role of data quality today', *Direct Marketing: An International Journal* 1(3), 161–171. https://doi.org/10.1108/17505930710779333

Iwasaki, J. & Jones, M., 2010, 'Governance benefits of new assurance reports', *International Journal of Disclosure and Governance* 8(1), 4–15.

Leon, L., Kalbers, L., Coster, N. & Abraham, D., 2012, 'A spreadsheet life cycle analysis and the impact of Sarbanes-Oxley', *Elsevier Decision Support Systems* 54, 452–460. https://doi.org/10.1016/j.dss.2012.06.006

Li, C.S. & Chang, S.E., 2007, 'Exploring organisational culture for information security management', *Emerald Industrial Management and Data Systems* 107(3), 438–458. https://doi.org/10.1108/02635570710734316

Marshall, L. & Harpe, D.L.R., 2009, *Decision making in the context of business intelligence and data quality*, Cape Peninsula University of Technology, Published by InterWord Communications for the Department of Information and Knowledge Management, University of Johannesburg, Pretoria.

Mattix, M. & Henning, S., 2010, 'Ensuring data integrity', *Claims Magazine*, 02 April, p. 27

Page, J., 2011, 'How to launch data governance initiative', *Business Intelligence Journal* 16(2), 17–25. https://doi.org/10.1016/j.jsis.2010.05.001

Somers, M.T., Gorla, N. & Wong, B., 2010, 'Organisational impact of system quality, information quality and service quality', *Elsevier Journal of Strategic Information Systems* 19, 207–228.

Tomlinson, R.M. 2011. 'Managing the risk in housing delivery: Local Government in South Africa', *Elsevier Habitat International* 35(3), 419–425.

Wang, C.P. & Chang, K.C., 2011. 'Information systems resources and information security', *Information Systems Front, Department of Information Management* 13, 579–593.

16

Knowledge management in small software development organisations: A South African perspective

Author:
Mzwandile M. Shongwe[1,2]

Affiliations:
[1]Department of Information Studies, University of Zululand, South Africa

[2]Department of Information Studies, University of KwaZulu-Natal, South Africa

Corresponding author:
Mzwandile Shongwe,
shongwem@unizulu.ac.za

Background: Software organisations have been experiencing software development failures since the beginning of software development. Globally, latest Standish Group CHAOS reports indicate that only 29% of projects are successful. In South Africa (SA), the ITWeb report (2013) indicates that only 11% of all projects are successful. Intervention strategies such as software process improvement (SPI) frameworks and new software development methodologies such as agile methods have been introduced to address this issue. These intervention strategies do not seem to be effective because software development projects continue to fail. To address this issue, software organisations are turning to knowledge management (KM). This is because software development is a knowledge-intensive task.

Objectives: The study aimed to investigate KM practices in small, medium and micro (SMMEs) software development organisations in SA and to determine if KM has benefited the organisations.

Method: Fifteen software development project managers from 15 software development SMMEs were interviewed. Content analysis was used to analyse the data.

Results: The study found six KM practices in the organisations: knowledge acquisition, creation, storage, sharing, organisation and application. The study found that KM has benefited organisations by making them effective, efficient and productive.

Conclusions: The study concluded that software development organisation have adopted KM, although informally, and that KM practices have improved organisational routines and processes.

Introduction

Globally, software organisations are faced with many challenges. They include, among others, poor software quality, failure to learn from past mistakes, projects exceeding their budget and time, collapse in organisational intelligence and lack of software development skills (Charette 2005; Gruner & van Zyl 2011; Lindvall, Rus & Sinha 2002; Lyytinen & Robey 1999; Tarawneh 2011). The Standish Group CHAOS report (2015) indicates that only 29% of projects are successful, 52% are challenged and 19% fail outright. In South Africa (SA), the ITWeb software development surveys (2011, 2012 and 2013) indicate that 11% of software development projects (in-house or outsourced) are successful. That is, they are delivered on time, on budget and with expected functionalities and quality. The 2013 report further indicates that 2% are a complete disaster and the rest (87%) are challenged. That is, they are late, over-budget and of poor quality. These results paint a grim picture of the software development industry locally and globally.

Software process improvement (SPI) frameworks such as the capability maturity model and capability maturity model integration and new software development methodologies such as agile methods have been introduced in the industry to address software development challenges (Bellini & lo Storto 2006; Lehtinen et al. 2014). These intervention strategies do not seem to have absolutely addressed these problems. This is because organisations either do not know these frameworks or perceive them as expensive, time consuming and difficult to perform (Al Tarawneh, Abdullah & Ali 2009; Richardson & von Wangenheim 2007; Saranya & Kannan 2013).

Consequently, software organisations are turning to knowledge management (KM) strategies in an attempt to address the challenges they face (Lindval et al. 2002; Sholla & Nazari 2011). This is because software development is a knowledge-intensive task that has the potential to benefit from KM principles (Dorairaj, Noble & Malik 2012; Jiang et al. 2009). In the global software industry,

KM has helped to improve the execution and coordination functions across the organisation and increased the speed of the delivery and precision of quality products (Bjornson & Dingsoyr 2008; Chandani, Neeraja & Sreedevi 2007; Kristjansson, Helms & Brinkkemper 2014). According to the FDI Intelligence Report (2012) and the Switzerland Global Enterprise (2014), SA has the biggest information technology (IT) industry in Africa. Software development is one of the major services provided by this industry. Unfortunately, as indicated by the ITWeb survey report (2013), SA software development organisations encounter software development failures just like other organisations around the globe. In developed countries such as Germany, Australia and Ireland – to mention but a few – studies by Aurum, Daneshgar and Ward (2008), Heavin and Adam (2012) and Betz, Oberweis and Stephan (2014) have been conducted to investigate KM practices in software development organisations. Developing countries in the Brazil, Russia, India, China, SA (BRICS) block such as Brazil, China and India have investigated this issue too (Jiang et al. 2009; Neves et al. 2014; Sharma, Singh & Goyal 2012). This does not seem to be the case in SA, yet she is an African IT giant. A review of the SA literature on this subject revealed only three studies by O'Neil (2005), Silverman (2006) and Khoza and Pretorius (2016). This means that such a problematic issue has been ignored by SA researchers, thus denying the industry and the country valuable knowledge about the current KM situation in software development organisations and possible KM-driven solutions to software development problems. This study aimed to fill that gap. Specifically, it aimed to answer the following questions: (1) What KM practices are adopted by small, medium and micro software development organisations in SA? (2) What benefits has KM brought to the organisations? We believe that this investigation will shed light on KM practices and offer practical and theoretical KM solutions to the SA software development industry.

The rest of the paper is structured as follows. A brief overview of the IT industry in SA follows this section, then the theoretical background and brief literature review, research methodology, results and discussion, and lastly conclusions and recommendations.

Software development in South Africa

South Africa has the biggest IT market in Africa. It consists of hardware and software products and services. The software industry deals with software development and packaged software services. It is projected to be worth $3919 billion in 2016. The Gauteng province is the leader in the IT industry with 60% of all projects, followed by the Western Cape (35%) and KwaZulu-Natal (KZN) (5%) (FDI Intelligence 2012; Switzerland Global Enterprise 2014). The Johannesburg Centre for Software Engineering Source Code Report (JCSE) (2012) indicates that there are fewer than 8000 software development organisations in SA. Most of these are SMMEs with fewer than 50 employees. Depending on the sector of the economy, a SMME is an organisation with fewer than 200 full-time paid employees (SA Department of Trade and Industry 2008). The software development industry employs about 180 000 people, of whom 15 000 are software developers (JCSE Source Code Report 2012). Citing a Gartner research report, the Switzerland Global Enterprise (2014) states that SA is one of the top 30 software development destinations in the world.

Theoretical background and literature review

Knowledge management has gained popularity in the software engineering field over the past decade. The growing interest in this field is instigated by the notion that KM plays a vital role in software development because software development is a knowledge-intensive task. It is associated with innovation and efficiency, activities which are vital in software development (Bjornson & Dingsoyr 2008; Chandani et al. 2007; Gendreau & Robillard 2013). Software development methods such as agile methods, strategies such as post-mortem reviews and SPI frameworks are regarded as KM activities (Desouza, Dingsøyr & Awazu 2005; Chouseinoglou et al. 2013).

Knowledge management scholars agree that there is no single definition of KM. Wiig (1993) defines it as approaches and processes aimed at identifying positive and negative uses of knowledge in different organisational operations. Dalkir (2011) synthesises definitions from many scholars and concludes that KM is the planning, organising, motivation and controlling of processes, routines and people within an organisation to ensure that knowledge is accessed by those who need it. Holsapple and Joshi (2003) hold that the goal of KM is to provide the right knowledge at the right time to the right people in the right presentation.

Knowledge management is viewed from several perspectives: personalisation and codification (Hansen, Nohria & Tierney 1999), schools of thought (Earl 2001) and from the lifecycle perspective (Alavi & Leidner 2001; Dalkir 2011; Evans & Ali 2013). The personalisation and codification perspective focuses on the importance of converting tacit knowledge into explicit form (Hansen et al. 1999). This means that organisations should focus on converting knowledge in the minds of people to documented knowledge so that it can be easily accessed and used by everyone within the organisation. The schools of thought perspective views KM from three broad schools: the economic, technocratic and behavioural. The economic school focuses on the economic gains brought by KM, the technocratic school focuses on the use of technology to support KM activities and the behavioural school focuses on KM human activities; that is, how human beings can be proactive in KM activities (Earl 2001). The lifecycle perspective views KM as a series of processes that when used together create a KM strategy. The processes include, among others, knowledge acquisition, creation, storage, transfer, application and learning. There are many KM frameworks that have been created in the KM field to explain this perspective. Examples are Wiig (1993), Alavi and Leidner (2001), Evans and Ali (2013) and Shongwe (2016). This study adopted the KM lifecycle perspective. This perspective was chosen because it shows the various KM activities or processes that organisations adopt and is widely accepted in KM. No particular framework was adopted for this study. Respondents were asked questions constructed from frameworks found in the literature.

The following subsection presents a brief literature review and identifies the literature gap addressed by this study.

Knowledge management practices in software organisations

Studies have been reported in the literature on how software development organisations manage their knowledge assets. The studies have been conducted in small, medium, micro and large organisations. They take several KM perspectives: schools of thought, software development frameworks and methods, KM lifecycle, and KM in terms of the personalisation and codification strategy. For example, Bjornson and Dingsoyr (2008) used Earl's schools of thought to classify KM studies in software engineering into behavioural, economics and technocratic schools. Jelínek (2010), Galvis-Lista and Sánchez-Torres (2013), Lakulu (2010) and Cabral, Ribeiro and Noll (2014) are of the view that software development methodologies such as the waterfall, agile, rational unified process, software process reference models, SPI and open source software development apply KM principles. The study by Abdullah, Eri and Talib (2011) shows the importance of KM and SPI in software organisations. Other studies focus on KM from the KM lifecycle perspective, for example, studies by Aurum et al. (2008) and Heavin and Adam (2012).

Studies investigating KM practices in software organisations have been conducted in many parts of the world. The study by Aurum et al. (2008) in Australia found that Australian organisations use information networks of colleagues to share knowledge and that they store their knowledge in directories, archives and repositories. The study also discovered the following KM activities in software organisations: knowledge creation (sharing ideas with colleagues); acquisition, adaptation and identification (reusing past knowledge to identify current problems); organisation (directories); distribution (sharing knowledge with colleagues); and application (developers reapplying their accumulated knowledge in a range of scenarios). Heavin and Adam (2012) conducted a similar study in Ireland and found that software organisations engage in six KM activities: knowledge creation, transfer, storage, maintenance, codification and acquisition. Pástor, Šipikal and Rehák (2013) found evidence of knowledge creation through innovation and knowledge acquisition from external sources in Slovakian organisations. Neves et al. (2014) investigated the role of KM in mitigating risk in micro and small software organisations in Brazil. Their study found that combination – as explained by Nonaka and Takeuchi (1995) – is mostly used to mitigate risk in software development teams.

In SA, a few studies focusing on the software development industry are found in the literature. Labuschagne, Marnewick and Jakovljevic (2008) investigated IT management maturity in SA and discovered that IT project maturity has improved, but IT projects continue to fail. Similar results are seen in Bogopa (2010) and Pretorius, Steyn and Jordaan (2012). Only three studies focusing on KM were found. Silverman (2006) found that KM practices contributed positively to software development success; O'Neil (2005) found that software organisations found it harder to manage tacit knowledge than explicit knowledge; and Khoza and Pretorius (2016) found factors that influence knowledge sharing to include, among others, job security, poor communication, unrealistic expectations, lack of time and psychological factors.

The literature reveals KM practices in software development organisations in different parts of the world. However, what is noticeable is the lack of such studies in SA. It is not known whether such activities are adopted in SA and whether organisations have benefited from KM. This study aims to fill that literature gap by focusing on SA software development SMMEs.

Research methodology

This is an interpretive, qualitative case study (Olikowski & Baroudi 1991) of KZN. This province was selected because of its accessibility to the researcher and because it has the third largest number of IT projects in SA (FDI Intelligence 2012; Switzerland Global Enterprise 2014). It targeted software development SMMEs. This is because according to the JCSE (2012), most software development organisations in SA are SMMEs. According to this study, software development organisations are organisations whose core business is the development of software products. Software vendors are excluded because they do not develop software, but sell completed software. Fifteen software development organisations were identified on a list provided by the JCSE (2012), using web searches and snowball sampling. The JCSE list was used first to locate the organisations, but it was discovered that most of them had closed down or moved to other locations. Only two organisations from the original list were located. A web search of the SA Yellow Pages and a local portal (Snupit) and snowball sampling were then used to locate the other 13. A pilot study was conducted in a different organisation to test the research instrument (interview schedule), and necessary adjustments were made before the final data were collected. Structured face-to-face interviews were conducted with 15 software development project managers. The interview questions were informed by a hybrid combination of KM processes found in the literature. The interviews were conducted at the organisations' premises and lasted on average 1 h each. A tape recorder was used to record them. Data were analysed by a deductive qualitative content analysis approach. This approach is appropriate in situations where theory exists and data are used to test or advance theory. In this approach, data are grouped into categories and themes (Cho & Lee 2014; Elo & Kyngäs 2008; Mayring 2000). Deductive qualitative content analysis steps proposed by Elo and Kyngäs (2008:110) were adopted in this study. The results are presented in the following section.

Results analysis and discussion

Responses of the 15 software project managers are presented in this section. To ensure confidentiality, pseudonyms are used to indicate participants, with the use of P1–P15.

Knowledge management practices in software organisations

The findings reveal six KM practices in SA software SMMEs: knowledge acquisition, creation, sharing, storage, organisation and application. They are discussed in detail below.

Knowledge acquisition

Software development organisations were asked whether they encounter knowledge gaps and to indicate the knowledge sources they use to fill the knowledge gaps.

All 15 software project managers indicated that their organisations do encounter knowledge gaps at some point in time. It could be knowledge about the industry or technical software development knowledge. When asked if they encounter knowledge gaps, one manager said:

> 'Yes, it happens a lot.' [Male; Manager; P3]

Another said:

> 'Every time! You're trying to write a piece of code, but you have no idea what you're doing.' [Male; Manager; P4]

This was confirmed by another manager who said:

> 'Yes! With software development there are new technologies, and in our case there is hardware we need to support, e.g. a new printer, and you have to find information about it.' [Male; Manager; P5]

Another manager concurred:

> 'Yes, always. As a person you don't always know everything.' [Male; Manager; P6]

They were then asked to identify the knowledge sources they use to fill the knowledge gaps. Their responses indicate that knowledge is acquired from internal and external sources.

Internally, knowledge is acquired from employees and organisational documents. Internal knowledge acquisition happens when employees exchange knowledge among themselves. It could be junior employees helping each other or more experienced seniors helping out juniors. One manager said:

> 'I become the main source of knowledge when new employees are recruited.' [Male; Manager; P11]

This was supported by another manager, who said:

> 'If we have new employees they might struggle to get new information. Obviously, they have to ask senior people in the organisation for assistance.' [Male; Manager; P1]

The managers also confirmed that junior staff members acquire knowledge from each other. One manager said:

> 'The programmers usually help each other when they have information gaps relating to their specific work areas. That is when they ask each other questions.' [Male; Manager; P7]

Another manager who is also a programmer said:

> 'We ask each other questions and explain how to do it so that you can learn.' [Male; Manager; P9]

The study also revealed that various organisational documents are used to acquire knowledge. One manager said:

> 'The best thing is to acquire knowledge from documents and teach yourself.' [Male; Manager; P8]

Another said:

> 'I consult the textbooks if I encounter programming challenges.' [Male; Manager; P4]

Manuals, textbooks, minutes of meetings, programming code samples, notes and emails are documents kept by organisations.

External knowledge sources are the Internet, customers or clients and industry networks. All managers indicated that the Internet is the main source of external knowledge. When asked about the main sources of external knowledge, one manager said:

> 'Google! We do a lot of online research, searching a lot of websites.' [Male; Manager; P11]

Another concurred, saying:

> 'We usually get [development] information from Internet forums such as Google groups and the Microsoft development network.' [Male; Manager; P2]

Two managers indicated that they use video tutorials they download from YouTube; others indicated that they use social networks, blogs and discussion forums, one responded:

> 'We simply go to Google user groups and look at things there, and then you find information.' [Male; Manager; P2]

Another manager wondered:

> 'I don't know how I would perform my duties without Google', [Male; Manager; P10]

Clients or customers are sources of knowledge too. The managers revealed that clients interact with them on a regular basis, thus providing valuable feedback on their products. They use this feedback to improve their processes and products, if necessary. This was confirmed by a manager, who said:

> 'We have software packages that we have developed and enhanced. We do that based on feedback that we get from our clients.' [Male; Manager; P2]

Another said:

> 'You have to extract the knowledge from the customer because that is where it is.' [Male; Manager; P7]

The same sentiments were shared by another manager, who stated that:

> 'You can be short of business knowledge, which means that you have to get close to the clients.' [Male; Manager; P3]

Another manager confirmed:

> 'Client base is a very rich source of information for us.' [Male; Manager; P8]

Networks of peers in the software industry have also been cited as sources of knowledge, especially technical knowledge. These are alliances formed by some of the organisations, specifically to share knowledge. For example, if a member company encounters a problem, the other alliance members help. A manager said:

> 'We get people from our network to help the developers.' [Male; Manager; P2]

Another manager gave an example of a situation whereby his company had no knowledge of Oracle integration. They had to ask industry peers to integrate it for them, he said:

> 'For example, we don't work with Oracle database, so we ask others to help us.' [Male; Manager; P11]

Another indicated that they use developers from other organisations to help them, he said:

> 'We use available resources like Skype and social networks [to communicate].' [Male; Manager; P6]

One manager indicated that they are in partnership with a big, well-known software developer and vendor. The vendor provides them with needed expertise each time they need it:

> 'We are a Microsoft partner and we get most of the information from them. You simply go to their network and look at things there.' [Male; Manager; P2]

The results reveal that organisations encounter knowledge gaps and that they use a number of internal and external sources to fill them. Studies conducted in other parts of the world show similar results. Sharma et al. (2012) found that the Internet is widely used to acquire knowledge. Aurum et al. (2008) found that networks of peers are used as sources of knowledge. Gendreau and Robillard (2013) confirm the importance of peers as sources of knowledge. In the SA case, we see that organisations also use vendors and clients as knowledge sources.

Knowledge creation and sharing

Knowledge creation and sharing are similar activities that could be easily confused. Pentland (1995) and Taskin, Verville and Al-Omari (2011) define knowledge creation as a process of developing new knowledge or content from existing knowledge. Citing Schwartz (2006), Paulin and Suneson (2012:83) define knowledge sharing as 'the exchange of knowledge between and among individuals, and within and among teams, organisational units, and organisations'. In this study, it was discovered that these activities are similar. For example, a training or brainstorming session could be a knowledge creation or sharing activity.

Knowledge creation and sharing activities found in the organisations are meetings, brainstorming sessions, training, conferences and workshops, and reading and acting on information from the Internet and organisational documents. Brainstorming sessions are used for knowledge creation and sharing. These are informal sessions where employees share, refine and adopt ideas. Once adopted, the ideas become organisational knowledge because employees act on them, one manager said:

> 'We come together as a group to brainstorm on what, why and how the project goes.' [Male; Manager; P15]

Another said,

> 'We do a lot of brainstorming on how best we could handle projects.' [Male; Manager; P11]

Managers also indicated that they hold meetings to share ideas about their work:

> 'We do a lot of meetings for our internal processes.' [Male; Manager; P14]

Another one said:

> 'We usually update our staff in meetings.' [Male; Manager; P12]

Formal and informal training is also used for knowledge creation and sharing purposes. When asked if they conduct training sessions, the managers responded as follows:

> 'Look, we are very small; offering [formal] courses internally is not really worthwhile, but we do offer one-on-one training.' [Male; Manager; P2]
>
> 'We occasionally do training, but it has been ten years since I last attended training myself.' [Male; Manager; P9]
>
> 'What happens if we need help, we just call someone to teach us.' [Male; Manager; P6]

Other organisations indicated that they send employees to workshops and conferences to acquire new knowledge. This was confirmed by one manager, who said:

> 'Some of our employees are taken to the US [United States of America] to learn about technologies of the future.' [Male; Manager; P4]

Another said:

> 'They will notify us [and] send us emails, and we'll attend [workshops] if we're interested.' [Male; Manager; P5]

Reading has been found to be an effective way of knowledge creation. As discussed earlier, employees use documents and the Internet to acquire information. When the information from these sources is internalised and acted upon, it becomes valuable organisational knowledge. The Internet plays a huge role in this regard. One manager said:

> 'I think all the knowledge is found on the WWW [World Wide Web].' [Male; Manager; P10]

Another stated:

> 'We download video tutorials about the latest software trends, so we keep updated by watching these tutorials.' [Male; Manager; P6]

This was confirmed by another who said:

> 'We use the Internet a lot, especially for standards and specifications. For example, if you want to design a solar panel [simulator] you look for the specifications on the Internet.' [Male; Manager; P9]

The results indicate that formal training does not seem to be conducted often in most organisations and that the Internet is widely used for knowledge creation and sharing. Apart from not opting for formal training methods, the rest of the results are a confirmation of studies conducted previously. Dorairaj et al. (2012) explain that in software organisations, knowledge is generated by brainstorming, customer collaboration, formal training; communities of practice and self-learning. Boden, Nett and Wulf (2010) state that knowledge is transferred by holding meetings, training sessions and the use of technology (the Internet in this case).

Knowledge storage

All organisations indicated that they do store their knowledge using different storage methods and technologies. They use central storage places such as portals, servers, external hard drives and email systems. When asked where they store their knowledge, one manager said:

> 'Usually in our emails with the boss.' [Male; Manager; P6]

Another said:

> 'We have stored it [knowledge] in the server in product files. We also use DropBox to move it around.' [Male; Manager; P2]

Another manager said:

> 'We have a portal that is a helpdesk. It is where conversations about customer issues are recorded and stored.' [Male; Manager; P3]

Another manager said:

> 'Most of the stuff is with individual hard drives.' [Male; Manager; P7]

Others indicated that they don't store their knowledge in central locations, but in many storage devices within the organisation. One manager stated that:

> 'We don't have a central repository to store organisational knowledge. I encourage the guys to email me whatever they get. If there is one central repository, that could be me'. [Male; Manager; P11]

Another said:

> 'We don't store our knowledge in a central place, but have several repositories using disparate systems, some new, and others with people in spreadsheets and workflow systems.' [Male; Manager; P7]

The results indicate that the organisations use different systems to store their knowledge. Some companies use central storage facilities, and others use different storage locations found all over the organisation. Previous studies indicate that it is a good idea to have one central storage facility for knowledge storage rather than to have it scattered. A central facility allows easy access, organisation and retrieval. Basili, Caldiera and Rombach (1994) suggest an experience factory model for information storage. This is a system in which a central database is created for easy storage, organisation and access to knowledge. Garcia et al. (2011) support the idea and argue that a central database supports easy retrieval and learning in agile teams. This system has effectively been used by the National Aeronautics and Space Administration Agency to store software engineering knowledge (Jansma & Means 2012).

Knowledge organisation

Organisations were also asked to explain how they organise their stock of knowledge. The results reveal that they organise their knowledge resources mostly in their servers, using basic organisation techniques such as folders. One manager said:

> 'We organise it in the server. What we do is that we have folders associated with products'. [Male; Manager; P1]

Another manager from a different organisation said:

> 'Everything is organised in our computers in terms of folders. For example, if it is information pertaining to training, that document goes to the training folder. If it's something to do with programming knowledge, it goes to the folder for that.' [Male; Manager; P6]

Others indicated that they do not organise their knowledge. Knowledge is found in different places in the organisations. This was confirmed by one manager from a different company who said:

> 'What we should do, but usually don't [organise knowledge], is to have a central location database like SharePoint where everyone is depositing data and pulling out when necessary. But we don't do it.' [Male; Manager; P7]

The results indicate that knowledge is organised, but the conclusion is that it is done at a very basic level or not at all. This could be because of two reasons: (1) the organisations are small, so not a lot of information exists and (2) organising could be difficult as it is scattered. Organisations are encouraged to adopt the knowledge organisation framework proposed by Chow and Wong (2011) to cater for multiple facets of knowledge and the tool suggested by Mat and Liu (2011) use to organise knowledge.

Knowledge application

Software organisations were asked to state how they apply the knowledge they have in their tasks. A couple of examples were given by the managers. Two managers gave examples where stored knowledge was used when employees left the organisation. One said:

> 'Unfortunately the lady who developed it left, and we used the documentation in the server.' [Male; Manager; P1]

The other said:

> 'When one of our senior developers died, we used the code samples he developed to finish the project.' [Male; Manager; P6]

Others gave different scenarios in which available knowledge is used in the development process. For example, one said:

> 'We definitely incorporate the knowledge we have into our coding.' [Male; Manager; P15]

Another said:

> 'What we do is look at the actual costs of the project and the time taken to complete that project. We then apply that information to future projects.' [Male; Manager; P7]

This was confirmed by a similar scenario, whose manager stated that:

> In terms of programming, what we do is that we put comments after each programming code. So if we want to use that code in another project, basically what we do is that we copy and paste that code so that we can make it work in another program.' [Male; Manager; P4]

The results reveal that organisations use the knowledge at their disposal in their daily development tasks. In fact, all the managers indicated that knowledge is used in their organisations. Dorairaj et al. (2012) and Chandani et al. (2007) found similar results. They found that software organisations apply the knowledge they have thus learning from it.

Improved software development

After the revelation that knowledge is applied in organisational routines and processes, managers were asked to indicate if KM has improved their processes. All organisations indicated that KM has enabled them to change their behaviour and do things better than they did before. They indicated that KM has made their organisations more accurate, effective, efficient and productive by saving time and preventing the 'reinvention of the wheel'. When asked if KM has changed the way things are done in their respective organisations, one manager said:

> 'Definitely! This stuff we have discovered over the years has made us more efficient and accurate as a company. For example, what took a couple of hours to run previously is run within minutes today.' [Male; Manager; P11]

Another manager said:

> 'Now we have libraries of code which we use in the development environment. That prevents reinvention of the wheel and helps us learn from our past mistakes.' [Male; Manager; P7]

These sentiments were echoed by the manager who said:

> 'Definitely, it [KM] makes us more efficient as a company. If there is a problem and none of us has come across that problem, we basically research and document it. That information is then used in future projects instead of researching the problem again. So it helps us become more efficient and productive as a company.' [Male; Manager; P6]

> 'Let's say one encounters a set of conditions that you struggle with. It's absolutely essential that knowledge be kept somewhere', said another manager.' [Male; Manager; P2]

This statement could be interpreted as meaning that stored knowledge is used to solve problems.

The responses show clear evidence of the importance of KM in software development organisations. Managers indicated that KM practices have one way or the other improved their processes. They concur with Chandani et al. (2007), who state that KM has helped improve the execution and coordination functions across organisations. That assertion is echoed by Sholla and Nazari (2011), who state that the goal of KM in software organisations is to produce software faster, with fewer costs and with higher quality. It is not clear though what exact processes have been improved, but we conclude that KM is benefiting software development organisations.

Summary, conclusions and recommendations

The study found six KM practices in SA software development SMMEs: knowledge acquisition, creation, sharing, storage, organisation and application. Table 1 summarises the results.

The conclusion is that SA software development SMMEs have adopted KM, but we assume that it is informal because there was no mention of KM specialists responsible for driving KM initiatives and policies in the organisations during the interviews. Aurum et al. (2008), and Heavin and Adam (2012) found that KM in SMMEs was applied informally. Apart from the knowledge sources found in the literature, the study discovered that clients and vendors are sources of knowledge in the SA context. Software organisations do not conduct formal training and organise their knowledge resources using basic methods. KM has made them more effective, efficient and productive. We believe that if organisations can formally adopt KM, improvements could be seen in the software development industry.

It is therefore recommended that software development organisations formally adopt KM by: (1) adopting formal

TABLE 1: Summary of knowledge management practices.

KM process	KM activities in software organisation
Acquisition	Internal sources – knowledge exchange between employees and organisational documents (manuals, textbooks, programming code samples, notes, emails and minutes of meetings) External sources – Internet, customers and industry networks
Creation and sharing	Meetings, brainstorming sessions, training, conferences and workshops, reading and organisational documents
Storage	Storing knowledge in servers, portals, external hard drives and email systems
Organisation	Creating folders in storage devices
Application	Organisational routines and processes (software development process)

KM, knowledge management.

training methods to reskill developers; (2) storing their knowledge assets in central databases for easy access, organisation and retrieval; and (3) employing KM specialists and implementing formal KM policies to facilitate the full implementation of KM.

The main limitation of the study is that data were collected in one province only. The study could have carried more weight if all three major software development provinces were included.

A quantitative study to measure the actual KM benefits and their impact on the organisations' performance is recommended. The research could determine how KM has benefited software organisations in terms of reducing or eliminating software development failures.

The contribution of this study to the literature is that it gives a different context of KM adoption. Many studies have been conducted in developed countries in Europe, North America and Australia, but relatively few in developing countries, especially in SA. This study offers a perspective on a developing country with limited knowledge, skills and resources in software development.

Acknowledgements

This project was funded by the University of Zululand.

Competing interests

The author declares that he has no financial or personal relationships that may have inappropriately influenced him in writing this article.

References

Abdullah, R., Eri, Z.D. & Talib, A.M., 2011, 'A model of knowledge management system in managing knowledge of software testing environment', paper read at the 5th Malaysian Conference in Software Engineering (MySEC), Johor Bahru, Malaysia, 13–14th December, pp. 229–233.

Al Tarawneh, M.Y., Abdullah, M.S. & Ali, A.B.M., 2009, 'Software process improvement (SPI) in small software firms', viewed 23 November 2014, from http://www.zuj.edu.jo/conferences/ICIT09/PaperList/Papers/Software%20Engineering/594mejhem.pdf

Alavi, M. & Leidner, D., 2001, 'Review: Knowledge management and knowledge management systems: Conceptual foundations and research issues', *MIS Quarterly* 25(1), 107–136. https://doi.org/10.2307/3250961

Aurum, A., Daneshgar, F. & Ward, J., 2008, 'Investigating knowledge management practices in software development organisations – An Australian experience', *Information and Software Technology* 50, 511–533. https://doi.org/10.1016/j.infsof.2007.05.005

Basili, V.R., Caldiera, G. & Rombach, D.H., 1994, 'The experience factory', in Marciniak J.J. (ed.), *Encyclopedia of software engineering*, vol. 1, pp. 469–476, Jonh Wiley, New York.

Bellini, E. & lo Storto, C., 2006, 'CMM implementation and organizational learning: Findings from a case study analysis', in *Proceedings of the PICMET 2006*, Istanbul, Turkey, 9–13th July, pp. 1256–1271.

Betz, S., Oberweis, A. & Stephan, R., 2014, 'Knowledge transfer in offshore outsourcing software development projects: An analysis of the challenges and solutions from German clients', *Expert Systems* 31(3), 282–297. https://doi.org/10.1111/exsy.12005

Bjornson, F.O. & Dingsoyr, T., 2008, *A study of a mentoring program for knowledge transfer in a small consultancy company*, Lecture notes in Computer Science 3547, Springer Verlag, Heidelberg, pp. 245–256.

Boden, A., Nett, B. & Wulf, V., 2010, 'Operational and strategic learning in global software development', *IEEE Software* 27(6), 58–65. https://doi.org/10.1109/MS.2009.113

Bogopa, M.E., 2010, 'The maturity of IT project management in South Africa', viewed 08 December 2014, from http://www.bogopa.co.za/Research%20For%20IT%20Project%20Management%20Maturity%20Model.pdf

Cabral, A.R.Y., Ribeiro, M.B. & Noll, R.P., 2014, 'Knowledge management in agile software projects: A systematic review', *Journal of Information & Knowledge Management* 13(1).

Chandani, A., Neeraja, B. & Sreedevi, 2007, 'Knowledge management: An overview and its impact on software industry', in *IET-UK International Conference on Information and Communication Technology in Electrical Sciences* (ICTES 2007), pp. 1063–1068, Chennai, India.

Charette, R.N., 2005, 'Why software fails: We waste billions of dollars each year on entirely preventable mistakes', *IEEE Spectrum*, 02 September 2005, 42, 42–49.

Cho, J.Y. & Lee, E.-H., 2014, 'Reducing confusion about grounded theory and qualitative content analysis: Similarities and differences', *The Qualitative Report* 19(64), 1–20.

Chouseinoglou, O., İren, D., Karagöz, N.A. & Bilgen, S., 2013, 'AiOLoS: A model for assessing organizational learning in software development organizations', *Information and Software Technology* 55(11), 1904–1924. https://doi.org/10.1016/j.infsof.2013.05.004

Chow, K.O. & Wong, T.L., 2011, 'A multiplicity approach to organization of knowledge and development of web software', in *Proceedings of the 9th IEEE International Conference on Dependable, Autonomic and Secure Computing*, Sydney, Australia, December 12–14, pp. 1192–1198.

Dalkir, K., 2011, *Knowledge management in theory and practice*, Elsevier, Burlington, MA.

Desouza, K.C., Dingsøyr, T. & Awazu, Y., 2005, 'Experiences with conducting project postmortems: Reports versus stories', *Software Process Improvement and Practice* 10(2), 203–215. https://doi.org/10.1002/spip.224

Dorairaj, S., Noble, J. & Malik, P., 2012, *Technical report 12–08: Knowledge management in distributed agile software development*, viewed 20 July 2014, from http://ecs.victoria.ac.nz/foswiki/pub/Main/TechnicalReportSeries/ECSTR12-08.pdf

Earl, M., 2001, 'Knowledge management strategies: Toward taxonomy', *Journal of Management Information Systems* 18(1), 215–233.

Elo, S. & Kyngäs, H., 2008, 'The qualitative content analysis process', *Journal of Advanced Nursing* 62(1), 107–115. https://doi.org/10.1111/j.1365-2648.2007.04569.x

Evans, M. & Ali, N., 2013, 'Bridging knowledge management life cycle theory and practice', paper read at the International Conference on Intellectual Capital, Tel-Aviv, Israel, November, pp. 156–165.

FDI Intelligence, 2012, *Software & IT services: Sector fact sheet*, viewed 08 September 2014, from http://www.wesgro.co.za/publications/publication/software-and-it-services

Galvis-Lista, E. & Sánchez-Torres, J.M., 2013, 'A critical review of knowledge management in software process reference models', *Journal of Information Systems and Technology* 10(2), 323–338. https://doi.org/10.4301/S1807-17752013000200008

Garcia, J., Amescua, A., Sanchez, M.-I. & Bermon, L., 2011, 'Design guidelines for software processes knowledge repository development', *Information and Software Technology* 53(8), 834–850. https://doi.org/10.1016/j.infsof.2011.03.002

Gendreau, O. & Robillard, P.N., 2013, 'Knowledge acquisition activity in software development', in Rocha Á., Correia A., Wilson T. & Stroetmann K. (eds.), *Advances in information systems and technologies*, vol. 206, pp. 1–10, Springer-Verlag, Berlin.

Gruner, S. & van Zyl, J., 2011, 'Software testing in small IT companies: A (not only) South African problem', *South African Computer Journal* 47, 7–32. https://doi.org/10.18489/sacj.v47i0.9

Hansen, M.T., Nohria, N. & Tierney, T.J., 1999, *What's your strategy for managing knowledge?*, viewed 13 September 2015, from https://hbr.org/1999/03/whats-your-strategy-for-managing-knowledge/ar/1

Heavin, C. & Adam, F., 2012, 'Characterising the knowledge approach of a firm: An investigation of knowledge activities in five software SMEs', *The Electronic Journal of Knowledge Management* 10(1), 48–63.

Holsapple, C.W. & Joshi, K.D., 2003, 'A knowledge management ontology', in C.W. Holsapple (ed.), *Handbook on KM*, vol. 1, pp. 81–124, Springer Verlag, Heidelberg.

ITWeb, 2011, Software Development Survey, viewed 14 November 2016, from http://www.itweb.co.za/index.php?option=com_content&view=article&id=47732&Itemid=2488

ITWeb, 2012, Software Development Survey, viewed 14 November 2016, from http://www.itweb.co.za/index.php?option=com_content&view=article&id=60527&Itemid=2826

ITWeb, 2013, Software Development Survey, viewed 14 July 2016, from http://www.itweb.co.za/index.php?option=com_bfsurvey_pro&view=stats&catid=838&Itemid=2879

Jansma, P.A. & Means, E.R., 2012, 'Developing the NASA systems engineering body of knowledge', in *Aerospace Conference*, Big Sky, MT, March 3–10, pp. 1–17.

Jelínek, B.P., 2010, 'Knowledge management in software development', Unpublished Masters thesis, Faculty of Informatics, Masaryk University, Brno, Czech Republic.

Jiang, M., Jong, C., Poppell, P., Budhathoky, K. & Hu, R., 2009, 'Establishing business oriented system infrastructure development life cycle for enterprise systems', paper read at the International Conference on Computational Intelligence and Software Engineering, Wuhan, China, 11–13th December, pp 1–6.

Johannesburg Centre for Software Engineering Source Code Report, JCSC, 2012, viewed 03 March 2014, from https://www.jcse.org.za/sites/default/files/u12/jcse_FINAL%202012%20-%202013.pdf

Khoza, L.T. & Pretorius, A.B., 2016, 'Knowledge sharing in software development projects', in *Proceedings of the 13th ICICKM*, Ithaca, NY, 14–15th October, pp.143–150.

Kristjansson, B., Helms, R. & Brinkkemper, S., 2014, 'Integration by communication: Knowledge exchange in global outsourcing of product software development', *Expert Systems* 31(3), 267–280. https://doi.org/10.1111/exsy.640

Labuschagne, L., Marnewick, C. & Jakovljevic, M., 2008, 'IT project management maturity: A South African perspective', in *Proceedings of the PMSA Conference: From Strategy to Reality*, Midrand, South Africa, 26–28 May, 2008, pp. 1–12.

Lakulu, M., 2010, 'A framework of collaborative knowledge management system in open source software development environment', *Computer and Information Science* 3(1), 81–90. https://doi.org/10.5539/cis.v3n1p81

Lehtinen, T.O.A., Mäntylä, M.V., Vanhanen, J., Itkonen, J. & Lassenius, K., 2014, 'Perceived causes of software project failures – An analysis of their relationships', *Information and Software Technology* 56, 623–643. https://doi.org/10.1016/j.infsof.2014.01.015

Lindvall, M., Rus, I. & Sinha, S., 2002, *Technology support for knowledge management*, Fraunhofer Center for Experimental Software Engineering, College Park, MD.

Lyytinen, K. & Robey, D., 1999, 'Learning failure in information systems development', *Information Systems Journal* 9, 85–101. https://doi.org/10.1046/j.1365-2575.1999.00051.x

Mat, A.R. & Liu, S., 2011, 'Organizing knowledge to support requirements analysis', paper read at 3rd International Conference on Computer Research and Development, Shanghai, China, 11–13th March.

Mayring, P., 2000, 'Qualitative content analysis', *Forum Qualitative Sozialforschung/ Forum: Qualitative Social Research* 1(2), viewed 25 October 2016, from http://www.qualitative-research.net/index.php/fqs/article/view/1089/2385

Neves, S.M., da Silva, C.E.S., Salomon, V.A.P., da Silva, A.F. & Sotomonte, B.E.P., 2014, 'Risk management in software projects through knowledge management techniques: Cases in Brazilian incubated technology-based firms', *International Journal of Project Management* 32, 125–138. https://doi.org/10.1016/j.ijproman.2013.02.007

Nonaka, I. & Takeuchi, H., 1995, *The knowledge creating company: How Japanese companies create the dynamics of innovation*, Oxford University Press, Oxford.

O'Neil, S., 2005, 'Managing tacit knowledge in a hi-tech learning organisation', Unpublished Masters dissertation, Business Studies Unit, Durban University of Technology.

Olikowski, W.J. & Baroudi, J.J., 1991, 'Studying information technology in organisations: Research approaches and assumptions', *Information Systems Research* 2(1), 1–28. https://doi.org/10.1287/isre.2.1.1

Pástor, R., Šipikal, M. & Rehák, S., 2013, 'Knowledge creation and knowledge acquisition in the software industry in Slovakia: The case study of Košice region', *Regional Science Policy & Practice* 5(4), 401–416. https://doi.org/10.1111/rsp3.12018

Paulin, D. & Suneson, K., 2012, 'Knowledge transfer, knowledge sharing and knowledge barriers – Three blurry terms in knowledge management', *The Electronic Journal of Knowledge Management* 10(1), 81–91, viewed 25 October 2016, from www.ejkm.com

Pentland, B.T., 1995, 'Information systems and organizational learning: The social epistemology of organizational knowledge systems', *Accounting, Management and Information Technologies* 5(1), 1–21. https://doi.org/10.1016/0959-8022(95)90011-X

Pretorius, S., Steyn, H. & Jordaan, J.C., 2012, 'Project management and project management success in the engineering and construction industries in South Africa', *South African Journal of Industrial Engineering* 23(3), 1–12. https://doi.org/10.7166/23-3-507

Richardson, I. & von Wangenheim, C.G., 2007, 'Why are small software organisations different', *IEEE Software* 24(1), 18–22. https://doi.org/10.1109/MS.2007.12

Saranya, A. & Kannan, S., 2013, 'SPI challenges of small and medium sized software companies – Problems and prospects', *International Journal of Engineering Research & Technology* 2(1), 1–5.

Schwartz, D.G., 2006, *Encyclopedia of knowledge management*, Idea Group Publishing, Herschey, PA.

Sharma, N., Singh, K. & Goyal, D.P., 2012, 'Adoption of knowledge management practices in software engineering organizations', in *2012 Second International Conference on Advanced Computing & Communication Technologies*, Rohtak, India, January 7–8, 2012, pp. 24–29.

Sholla, A. & Nazari, E., 2011, 'KM and factors that influence the success of codification strategies in medium-sized companies that develop software: The model, strategies and tools', *Journal of Information Technology and Economic Development* 2(1), 54–63.

Shongwe, M.M., 2016 'An analysis of knowledge management lifecycle frameworks: Towards a unified framework', *The Electronic Journal of Knowledge Management* 14(3), 140–153, viewed 10 November 2016, from www.ejkm.com

Silverman, S., 2006, 'Improving systems development methods by incorporating the principles of knowledge management', Unpublished Masters dissertation, School of Economic and Business Sciences, University of Witwatersrand, South Africa.

Switzerland Global Enterprise, 2014, 'Information & communication technology (ICT) industry – South Africa', viewed 25 October 2016, from http://www.s-ge.com/sites/default/files/private_files/1411_sA_ICT.pdf

Tarawneh, H., 2011, 'A suggested theoretical framework for software project success', *Journal of Software Engineering and Applications* 4, 646–651. https://doi.org/10.4236/jsea.2011.411076

Taskin, N., Verville, J. & Al-Omari, A., 2011, 'A comprehensive framework for knowledge management system lifecycle', *African Journal of Business Management* 7(5), 1285–1295.

The Department of Trade and Industry, Republic of South Africa, 2008, 'Annual review of small businesses in South Africa 2005–2007', viewed 03 March 2014, from http://www.thedti.gov.za/sme_development/docs/smme_report.pdf

The Standish Group, 2015, *CHAOS Manifesto: Think Big, Act Small*, viewed 02 August 2015, from https://www.standishgroup.com/

Wiig, K.M., 1993, *Knowledge management foundations: Thinking about thinking, how people and organisations create, represent, and use knowledge*, Schema Press, Arlington, TX.

17

Small- and medium-sized enterprises' knowledge management systems as edifiers of new value innovations

Authors:
Boniface Okanga[1]

Affiliations:
[1]Department of Business Management, University of Johannesburg, South Africa

Corresponding author:
Boniface Okanga,
boniokanga@gmail.com

Background: New value innovations are organically ingrained and complementary to the process of knowledge management. However, epistemological trends highlight only limited studies to have explored how the effectiveness of knowledge management leverages new value innovations.

Objectives: This research evaluates how the effectiveness of the small- and medium-sized enterprises' (SMEs) knowledge management systems enhance new value innovations so as to identify the major paradoxes and a business model that coherently integrates knowledge management with new value innovations.

Method: Using a qualitative research method, semi-structured interviews were used to explore the opinions of 20 purposively sampled managers from 20 SMEs on how knowledge management edifies new value innovations.

Results: A strong culture of information utilisation was found to enhance relevant analysis and identification of new gaps in the markets that must be filled through new value innovations or modifications of the existing products. However, poor culture of knowledge utilisation, cost of knowledge management and the often poorly functional business information systems were still reiterated as major paradoxes hampering effective knowledge management as one of the determinants of new value innovations.

Conclusion: The study concluded with a model highlighting a continuum of knowledge management–new value innovation pillars like a strong culture of information utilisation, and encouragement of creativity that the executives must consider to create an effective knowledge management foundation that subsequently leverages the overall effectiveness of new value innovations.

Introduction

A new value innovation process that is organically intricate, complementary and inherently ingrained with knowledge management leverages the overall effectiveness of new value innovations (Cohendet & Simon 2015). Effective knowledge management systems enhance thorough analysis and eliciting of sufficient information on the critical unfilled gaps in the markets. This enables the generation of the corresponding array of new ideas on the new product models that must be selected and developed to fill such gaps (Cohendet & Simon 2015; Zhou & Li 2012). As firms become more abreast with the existing unmet customer needs and demands and the prevailing nature of the market and industry trends, effective knowledge management also bolsters the executives' ability to effectively deal with the information paradoxes and puzzles on whether new innovations will perfectly match or even exceed customer expectations and perceptions. It also aids the positioning and re-positioning of new innovations in a way that diffuses immediate threats that may emerge from the competitors' retaliations and reactions (Zhou & Wu 2010).

In other words, a firm's possession of sufficient customer and product information enable necessary reconfigurations and modifications to ensure that the existing product features, attributes and quality are modified to perfectly respond to the changes in customer needs and demands (Zhou & Li 2012). All these render it glaringly evident that the effectiveness of knowledge management spurs new value innovation and subsequently a business' overall sustainability (Zhou & Wu 2010). However, a shortfall arises from the fact that most of the studies on new value innovations have often been approached as if innovations are a unique process that does not, in any way, relate or get edified by the overall effectiveness of an enterprise's knowledge management system (Hernandez et al. 2010; Leal, Salgueiro & Ortega 2013; Yayavaram & Ahuja 2008). Such approach limits the creation of a strong knowledge management culture or the accumulation and management of sufficient information and the tracking of the required unfolding trends to drive the improvement of new value innovations. This study fills this gap by evaluating how the existing small- and medium-sized enterprises' (SMEs) knowledge management systems edify the effectiveness of the process of new value innovations. The motive of the study was to identify the major paradoxes that SMEs face when seeking to utilise their existing knowledge management systems to leverage new value innovations, so as to socially construct a suitable business model that coherently synchronises knowledge management with new value innovations. It is anticipated that the conclusion of this research will motivate most businesses to begin considering the development of an effective knowledge management system as a prerequisite for enhancing the effectiveness of new value innovations.

Literature review

The argument that effective knowledge management drives new value innovations to leverage a firm's sustainable performance in the increasingly discontinuous contemporary business environment is implicitly echoed in most of the theories on knowledge management and new value innovation (Hernandez et al. 2010; Leal et al. 2013; Yayavaram & Ahuja 2008).

Knowledge management

Knowledge management is a strategic process of planning, acquiring, organising and utilising tacit and explicit knowledge and information to create new or modify the existing processes, methods and products. Such initiatives are often undertaken to bolster the improvement of a firm's overall market performance (Nonaka & Takeuchi 1995; Omotayo & Olubunmi 2015). It, therefore, edifies not only the improvement of business processes and operational methods, but also constant reconfiguration and modifications to enhance adaptability to the constantly emerging new changes in the external business environment. Although tacit knowledge is the knowledge and ideas possessed by the individual, explicit knowledge is tacit knowledge codified and translated into documents. Nonaka's knowledge creation model posits the interplay between tacit and explicit knowledge that creates new values to often occur through four main interactive modes encompassing socialisation, externalisation, combination and internalisation (Nonaka & Takeuchi 1995). Socialisation is an interactive process in which the tacit knowledge deeply rooted in the experiences and ideas of different individuals is shared among the participants in a socialisation process (Teo et al. 2011). Although externalisation is the conversion of tacit knowledge into explicit knowledge, combination facilitates the linking and manipulation of different bodies of explicit knowledge to create new knowledge or improve on the existing knowledge. Internalisation is nevertheless the process of generating new tacit knowledge from explicit knowledge (Teng & Song 2011). However, the effectiveness of knowledge management and the attainment of its associated business values are often predicted by certain eight main steps that include setting the knowledge management goals and knowledge identification, acquisition, development, distribution, use, preservation and measurement (Teng & Song 2011).

Setting knowledge management goals is often influenced by the results of environmental analysis and forecasting highlighting the prevailing and the likely foreseeable trends vis-à-vis a business' internal capabilities (Bosua & Venkitachalam 2013). Such analysis highlights the reasons why a particular tacit or explicit knowledge is required to either develop new products or improve the features of the existing products to respond to the unfolding market and industry changes and trends (Bosua & Venkitachalam 2013). The clear delineation of the essence of knowledge generation influences the identification of the tacit and explicit knowledge that must be acquired. Although explicit knowledge and tacit knowledge can be generated using the available human resources and technologies, it may also in certain cases require recruiting new staffs with requisite skills, competencies and experiences (Bosua & Venkitachalam 2013). It may also require undertaking investment in relevant technologies and the establishment of the required structures, such as a department for research and innovation.

The assembling of such key capabilities and competencies enhances the development of knowledge and its translation into new values or products (Wang & Noe 2010). These can contribute enormously to turning around the performance of an organisation. To enable further modifications of the newly developed knowledge, its distribution and sharing through certain defined networks are a prerequisite for it to suit the required needs when it is being used (Wang & Noe 2010). Although knowledge use can be rendered less important with the passage of time, it is often required that it is well preserved to facilitate easier retrieval in case it is required in the future. Such initiatives must also be accompanied by constant knowledge management to assess the compatibility of the culture that has evolved, and its effects on operational efficiency and the improvement of a business' performance. However, in an argument that seems a modification of Nonaka and Takeuchi's (1995) view of knowledge management, Hedlund and Nonaka (1993) pointed that how an organisation manages its knowledge agents such as individuals, groups, the organisation and inter-organisational agents encompassing customers, suppliers, competitors and other stakeholders determines how it is able to effectively create, transfer and exploit its knowledge resources. As Skandia's Model notes, knowledge management streamlines the flow and management of information to provide the intellectual capital that in turn drives the improvement of an organisation's new innovation initiatives.

Value innovation

Value innovation is a strategic process of generating relevant information and ideas that are converted into new products or the initiatives that modify the existing products or service features (Lee, Olson & Trimi 2012). Value innovation does not only entail the innovation and production of new products, but also the modifications of the existing products and services to improve the overall level of differentiation and responsiveness to the changes in customers' demands and preferences (Lee et al. 2012). In the process of the modifications of the existing products or the production of new ones, value innovation also edifies a firm's cost competitiveness. It is through value innovation that firms are able to minimise wastes and optimise the usually limited business resources to produce as maximum output as possible. From this view, effective knowledge management is implicitly the epicentre of new value innovation initiatives.

However, such a strong nexus between effective knowledge management and value innovation has not been widely explored by most of the contemporary studies on new value innovations (Kono & Barnes 2010). Such a view suggests enterprises with underdeveloped knowledge management culture may tend to face challenges as compared to the businesses with entrenched knowledge management culture (Kono & Barnes 2010). A culture of knowledge management edifies the inquisitiveness of the executives and the managers to devise the best way of generating and utilising the obtained information to provide business advantages for the firm (Hernandez et al. 2010). For knowledge management to translate into the values that enhance value innovation, Cohendet and Simon (2015) argue that it must not only be about generating the required insights, but also the management of ideas as a socio-cognitive process that must be organised and managed. In their analysis, Cohendet and Simon (2015) highlight three new perspectives on how to deal with the challenges of creativity and innovation to entail; the management of the ideation process to foster creativity, the tension between the logic of creation and production, and undertaking a disruptive innovation to transform a traditional industry.

In the process of managing ideation to foster creativity, the challenge is often not the creativity to generate as valuable new ideas as possible, but the translation of such ideas into new viable business concepts (Lee & Olson 2010). The conversion of the generated new ideas into new viable business concepts requires investment of the executives' time and resources. It also requires the development of the appropriate facilities to enhance the efficient identification, actualisation and extraction of the potentially viable new business concepts from an array of equally competing new ideas (Lee & Olson 2010). Such a process and capabilities depend on the unique capabilities that each business has. It cannot easily be delegated or replicated by other businesses. Firms that are more proficient at converting ideas into unique business concepts may not only derive unique sources of competitiveness, but also experience consistent superior market performance (Lee & Olson 2010). The effectiveness of such a process of converting new ideas into tangible business concepts is often further determined by two artefacts encompassing codebook and the manifesto that comprise part of a firm's business culture.

Manifesto refers to the general vision and belief on how new ideas must be used to achieve the desired business benefits and values. Just like the manifesto, codebook defines what the business needs to know and do in order to transform the selected idea into a viable business concept that in turn generates other enormous business values once the ideas have been concretised into a new product, service or a process (Boisot 1987). Even if the business manages to extract a lucrative business concept from the generated ideas, a challenge often still arises from the management of the tension between the logic of creation and the logic of production (Zhou & Li 2012). The diffusion of such tension is often accomplished using stage-gate process in which after the irreversible process of idea generation, selection and discarding of the unwanted ideas, the process of innovation tend to flow along six other gates that include conception, prototyping, demonstration, production, marketing and testing (Zhou & Li 2012). It is the complete knowledge of the product in a particular stage that enhances its progress from one stage to the next.

If certain information is not understood or not yet known about a particular product, the product often does not progress to the next stage until all which is required is put in place. An attempt to proceed to the next stage without sufficient information can put the process of innovation and production at a risk of choosing a wrong, yet an irreversible path. The selection of a wrong path can cause waste and costly corrections (Zhou & Li 2012). Considering the constantly changing market trends and industry turbulence, no new innovations are, however, irresistible to the impetus of change. The emergence of new products, better innovations and other threats implies that constant new ideas must be generated and converted to enable the modifications of the existing products to resist and reshape the emerging new volatile trends to a firm's advantages (Hernandez et al. 2010). In other words, the idea that the effectiveness of knowledge management influences acquisition of extensive knowledge that subsequently spawns the improvement of employee creativity is also echoed in Naggar's (2015) argument in the creativity canvass.

It is argued in the creativity canvass that the effectiveness of the process of new value innovations is not only defined by the extent to which they are perfectively responsive to customer needs and demands. Instead, it is bolstered by the modalities adopted for optimising the existing resources and networks of innovation communities to coherently aid in the identification, building and nurturing of the selected ideas and assets into new value creating new business concepts. However, the knowledge management–related challenges that often still affect such a process are linked to the unwillingness to share ideas and knowledge beyond a trusted network or fear of exposure to criticisms and competition (Zhou & Li 2012). Besides the poor motivation of the talented employees to generate and share the required critical knowledge and ideas, the other challenges are also often associated with lack of the required resources and equipment to facilitate the sharing and improvement of the identified new ideas into new viable business concepts (Zhou & Li 2012). In other words, theories imply that in new value innovations, knowledge management systems provide sufficient information that leverages creativity, and the generation and conversion of new ideas into new values or viable business concepts. This creates a strong foundation of knowledge management that influences planning, acquisition, organising and utilisation of tacit and explicit knowledge to create new values or improve the existing processes, methods and products to influence a business' overall effective market performance (Hernandez et al. 2010; Leal et al. 2013; Yayavaram & Ahuja 2008). It enhances ideation, conception, prototyping, demonstration, production, marketing and testing (Cohendet & Simon 2015:3). All these may impact positively on the improvement of a business' sustainability in the increasingly discontinuous business environment (Cunningham 2012; Manzini 2015; Mohsam & Van Brakel 2011).

As much as it is quite certain that knowledge management spawns the eliciting of relevant information for new value innovations, limited research in that area seems to have affected the emergence of the appropriate business model that the SMEs can emulate to develop more effective knowledge management systems as foundations for new value innovations. This affects the extent to which most of the SMEs are able to continuously undertake new innovations to leverage their sustainability in the increasingly discontinuous contemporary global markets. Since Nonaka's knowledge creation model and Naggar's (2015) creativity canvass have been widely replicated by most of the big businesses, they would offer the most suitable models for SMEs to replicate when seeking to synchronise the effectiveness of knowledge management with the critical processes of new value innovations. However, just like Nonaka's knowledge creation model that limits the evaluation of the interplay between tacit and explicit knowledge to create new values, Naggar's (2015) creativity canvass also only emphasises the essence of creativity as a strategy for leveraging ideation during the innovations. This implies, although Nonaka's knowledge creation and Naggar's (2015) creativity canvass have been widely replicated by most of the big businesses, it may still not be easily practicable for SMEs to easily replicate how effective knowledge management flows to influence not only ideations, but also later modifications and reconfigurations of the product after its introduction into the market. In other words, considering the unique conditions and circumstances in which most SMEs operate, it is such a gap that this research fills by exploring a unique business model that the SMEs can use to facilitate the synchronisation of knowledge management with the relevant processes of new value innovations to leverage their sustainability.

Research statement

Poorly developed SMEs' knowledge management systems affect the evolution of a culture of information and knowledge utilisation to edify the generation of adequate information that can be analysed to develop an array of ideas on the probable new product developments or modifications of the existing products that can be undertaken.

Aim of the research

The aim of this research is to evaluate how effectively the existing SMEs' knowledge management systems edify the effectiveness of the process of new value innovations, so as to identify the major inhibitors and a suitable business model that can be extracted to facilitate coherent synchronisation of knowledge management with new value innovations. In a bid to accomplish this, the study was preoccupied with the evaluation of three fundamental questions that included:

- How do the existing SMEs' knowledge management systems edify new value innovations?
- What conditions determine the effectiveness of the SMEs' knowledge management systems as edifiers of new value innovations?
- Which business model can be developed to coherently link and synchronise the process of knowledge management with new value innovations?

Methodology

Research on knowledge management has led to the development of key steps and constructs that measure the effectiveness of knowledge management. Likewise, the key steps that edify the effectiveness of new value innovations are also well-developed as a result of detailed elucidations in the previous studies. However, the analysis of the linkage between the overall effectiveness of knowledge management and new value innovations has not been widely examined either in the previous quantitative or the qualitative studies. Lack of such a theory constraints the initiatives of most of the businesses engaged in new value innovations to effectively utilise their knowledge management systems to leverage effective management of new value innovations. To develop a grounding theory that SMEs can emulate, this research uses an interpretivist-qualitative research approach to critically analyse different knowledge management literature vis-à-vis new value innovation theories to extract the relevant knowledge management theory that effectively links knowledge management to new value innovations (Clark 2010; Morse 2010). The results of such analysis were triangulated with the interview findings from 20 purposively sampled managers from 20 SMEs.

Purposive sampling was used in the period between March and August 2016 to facilitate the identification and selection of only the SMEs with well-developed knowledge management systems and significant development of a culture of innovation. To accomplish this, the four criteria used in the purposive sampling process entailed ensuring that (1) the selected SME was not only based in Gauteng but also operational in at least three of the nine South African provinces; (2) the SME must have had a turnover of at least 5 million rands in the past 5 years; (3) from the available media reports and other studies, the SME must have had some form of industry leadership for better product innovations and better industry practices, and (4) the selected employee to participate in the study must have been either a manager or any key employee well-informed on matters of information technology (IT) applications and knowledge management and its value on new value innovations. Brief analysis of the existing literature and interviews with key employees were conducted with key employees and managers in each of the selected businesses to ensure that the SME to be selected met all these criteria.

The ascertainment of the business' satisfaction of such requirements led to the selection of about 20 SMEs that emerged mainly from the firms in the hospitality, manufacturing, retail, finance and insurance, construction, and logistic handling and distribution industries. Most of the employees that were interviewed were mainly marketing and IT managers due their perceived familiarity with the linkage between IT and new value innovations as compared with the other employees. Interviews were based on semi-structured questionnaires to permit further probing and re-probing to elicit detailed information on how the selected SMEs use the process of knowledge acquisition, storage and management to leverage not only new product innovations, but also improvement of their operational processes and methods.

To accomplish this, one-on-one interviews were used to probe whether companies have effective knowledge management systems in place. If so, how such knowledge management systems have been of value during new value innovations or modifications of the existing products or business concepts? This led to the eliciting of the views of the managers on what they perceive to be the conditions that determine the effectiveness of SMEs' knowledge management systems as edifiers of new value innovations, and the type of the business model that they felt could be developed to coherently link and synchronise the process of knowledge management with new value innovations. The obtained qualitative interview data was thematically analysed and triangulated with the results of the interpretations of the theoretical findings on the linkage between knowledge management and new value innovations. Such analysis enabled the reaching of a logical conclusion on the business model that can be extracted and suggested to coherently link and synchronise the process of knowledge management with new value innovations (see Figure 1). The details of the findings are as presented and discussed in the next sections.

Findings

In line with the research questions for this article, the findings are presented according to the two sub-headings that include:

- SME's knowledge management system as an edifier of new value innovations.
- Determining conditions: SME's knowledge management system as an edifier of new value innovations.

The details are as follows.

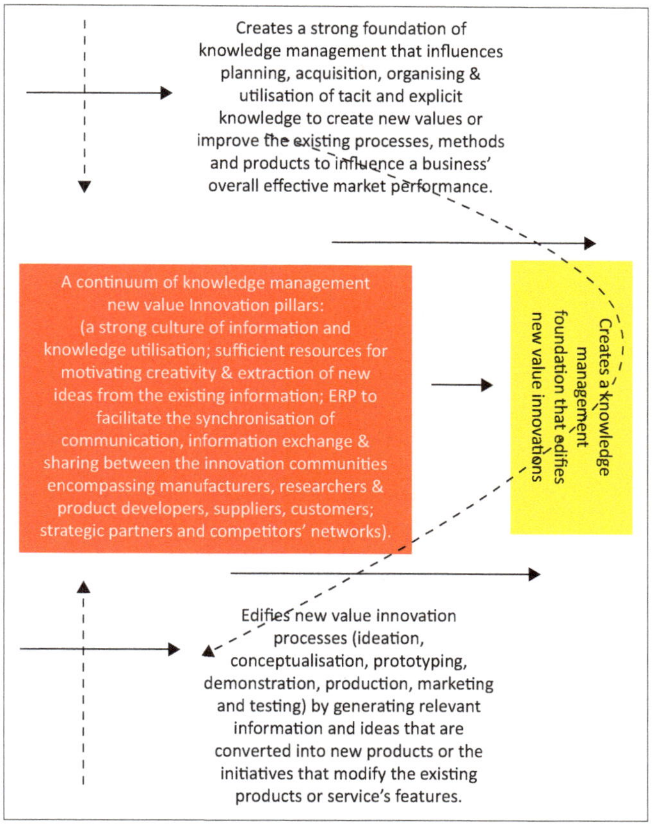

FIGURE 1: A continuum of knowledge management–new value innovation pillars that create an effective knowledge management foundation that edifies the effectiveness of the process of new value innovations.

Small- and medium-sized enterprise's knowledge management system as an edifier of new value innovations

Thematic analysis of the interview findings indicated the overall effectiveness of most of the SMEs' knowledge management system to leverage new value innovations. In this process, it was found that the effectiveness of SMEs' knowledge management systems does not only provide a foundation for ideation and new innovations, but also reconfigurations, modifications or reshaping of new innovations. The details of these key themes are elucidated as follows.

Provides a foundation for ideation and new innovations

It emerged from the analysis of the interview data that an entrenched culture of knowledge management provides the foundation for ideation and new product innovations. It facilitates constant analysis and sensing of the probable changes in the industry and market trends. In such analysis, most of the interviewed managers noted that as a firm becomes increasingly inquisitive to gain information and understand the prevailing trends, the enormous amount of the generated information often provides the advantages for the firm to generate different alternatives that must be pursued. This bolsters the creativity of the personnel and the extent to which they are able to emerge with new ideas about the direction that the business must take. It also easily aids the emergence of new ideas for new products that must be introduced to fill the gaps that are presently not filled by the business or any other industry operators. In the accomplishment of such practices, some of the managers argued that enterprises that cherish and value information generation and management may, therefore, tend to find it easier to develop new ideas to be narrowed down to the kind of a new business or the product that must be developed. Such a view is accentuated in the opinions of one of the interviewed managers working for a firm in the hospitality industry who stated that:

> 'For us in the more competitive hospitality industry, new changes and improvements can only be effected if you understand the needs and demands of the customers. For that reason, whether it is a complaint or compliments from the visitors, we usually maintain accurate information of their perceptions of our services such as meals, beddings, cleanliness, safety of the environment and room services. Quite often, we do this directly by conducting a survey or encouraging all our staffs to maintain friendly relationships and to intensely interact with our customers so as to develop conversations that render it possible for us to elicit critical information on how they feel about our services. This enables us to not only understand their perceptions, but also to understand the suggestions on the innovative improvement measures that must be undertaken.' [Participant 16, female, 33 years, marketing manager]

In other words, when corroborated with the opinions of the other participants, such a findings signifies effectiveness of knowledge management leverages an enterprise's ability to accumulate well documented trends on customer tastes and preferences, the nature of the competition and the degree of industry volatility. It emerged from the interview findings that such analysis also aids the understanding of the supplier and supply chain dynamics and the prediction of the likely dimensions that the existing trends are most likely to undertake in the near future. With such sufficient information, it often turns quite easier for enterprises to narrow down the array of the generated ideas to only a few ideas that are considered to have the potential to turn into viable business ventures or products in the future. In other words, interview findings imply that innovative enterprises with well-developed and functional knowledge management systems also tend to possess sufficient knowledge and information, or well-developed techniques for acquiring and storing information that renders it easier for products to be modified and improved through different developmental gates that often encompass conceptualisation, prototyping, development, testing and production. Such a finding is echoed in the views of one of the managers involved in the development and manufacturing of plastic containers in Midrand, who explained that:

> 'Irrespective of whether we are manufacturing products on orders for certain corporate clients, or we are producing items such as plastic cups, buckets and dishes for the larger markets, my experience indicates that the manufacturing process is a back and forth thing. Initially, research and studies are conducted and the idea that was previously rejected may easily turn useful after the generated prototype has been developed into samples where customers have to provide opinions before undertaking mass production. In that process, you find that although initially what you had imagined and discarded that perhaps the market would not prefer has instead turned into a lucrative item with enormous early trials. That means, you have to go back to the drawing board and redevelop the product to modify the present version to match customer expectations identified during the sale and marketing of the small trial samples. This process goes on like that and of course in our industry, you may develop a particular item and you do not need to develop it again once the market has liked it. However, you still need to expand the product portfolios by conducting new studies as we did recently to venture into the manufacturing of children's plastic toys. That means, you need to logically and systematically keep all the information, product photofits, prototypes and formulas. It saves time for the reason that in case the concept that you previously rejected, turns as the concept that customers prefer, it becomes easier for you to easily retrieve the formulas and information.' [Participant 8, male, 44 years, production manager]

In other words, interview findings signify an effective enterprise knowledge management system that furnishes product developers with enormous critical information that enables them to always make the right decisions. This prevents the likelihood of the process of new product innovations from taking irreversible wrong routes. Sufficient information provided by the enterprise' knowledge management system spawns the improvement of the efficiency of the innovation process. It also aids the elimination of wastes and costly errors that often affect the successful development and launch of new innovations. It is not only during the ideation process that the information generated through an effective knowledge management systems tend to play significant roles, but also after the market launch and introduction of the new product.

Edifies reconfigurations, modifications or reshaping of new innovations

It emerged from the analysis of the interview findings that one of the causes of the failures of new product innovations is often linked to the use of wrong messages targeted to the wrong segments. Or even lack of complete understanding of the market and industry dynamics in terms of the competitors' responses to the promotional messages upon the new innovations' market introduction. This view is substantiated in the explanations of one of the managers working for a firm engaged in the manufacturing of carpets who stated that:

> 'Of course, it is true that keeping essential information is important for improving the effectiveness of the process of innovation. However, in practice, there is usually a tendency for more experienced personnel to bypass consultations and exchange of views with customers. In most of the cases, most of the product developers use sketchy information about customer usage and demand for the product to sense and imagine the kind of the product that the customer would prefer. In most of the cases, they score it right just as well as also wrongly. If the prediction and imaginations are wrong, then you loose as the process must be started all over again. But as the new process is being started all over again, information about the reasons why the previous product failed provides critical data that guides decisions on what needs to be done or not to be done to ensure that the new process leads to the development of a concept that

> perfectly matches customer needs. However, that also still depends on whether all the critical information on the failed product was also well stored, preserved and not discarded.' [Participant 11, male, 47 years, chemical engineer]

As some of the managers pointed out, challenges also tend to arise from the failure to gather sufficient information and interpret the likely retaliations or actions that major rivals are most likely to undertake. With the emergence of well-developed knowledge management systems, most of the participants reiterated that most of the businesses are often able to deal with such circumstances. Well-developed knowledge management systems do not only provide details on the unfolding market trends, but also critical customer touchpoints or triggers of the interest of certain market segments. Upon the introduction of new innovations, such accurate information provides insights on the critical customer touchpoints that the promotional messages of the new innovations must be based. This enables the undertaking of relevant corresponding actions to improve the positioning of new products in the minds of the targeted market segments, and subsequently the extent of the new innovations' successful launch. Such a finding corroborates the opinions of one of the marketing managers in the tin fish production company who stated that:

> 'Whether or not the product is successfully launched, our experience indicates that the information that you have in place may also enhance the constant tracking of customer perceptions about the new innovation's market performance. It facilitates the analysis of whether certain customer disappointments are linked to the quality, attributes and the features of the new products, or the pricing and distribution to improve customers' accessibility to new innovations. These enable the enterprise to re-evaluate and undertake the necessary modifications of the quality, features, attributes and distribution approach of the existing products to ensure that they perfectly match or exceed customer perceptions and expectations.' [Participant 14, female, 28 years, sales representative and marketing manager]

In other words, most of the participants seemed to agree that well-developed enterprise knowledge management system also leverages constant analysis and sensing of the probable competitors' reactions upon the introduction of new innovations into the market. It is the understanding of such likely reactions from the competitors that renders it possible for businesses to undertake proactive and precautionary strategic measures to insulate new innovations from any reactions from rivals. If well-developed, managed and utilised, views from most of the managers indicated that the overall effectiveness of an enterprise's knowledge management system can significantly bolster the attainment and sustenance of a firm's superior market performance. However, further analysis of the interview data and triangulation with relevant theories indicated the extent to which an enterprise's knowledge management system is able to edify new value innovations are often predicted by a combination of certain pre-existing conditions (Cant & Wiid 2013; Olawale & Garwe 2010; Pillay 2016; Ramukumba 2014; Scheers 2011).

Determining conditions: Small- and medium-sized enterprise's knowledge management system as an edifier of new value innovations

Further analysis of the interview themes revealed a combination of the pre-existing conditions that often determine whether the SMEs' knowledge management systems are to edify the effectiveness of the process of new value innovations are often linked to a culture of knowledge management and information utilisation, and the availability of information resources and facilities. The details of these themes are evaluated as follows.

Culture of knowledge and information utilisation

Implicitly, it emerged from the interview data that a culture of knowledge and information utilisation is of significant importance for edifying the effects of knowledge management on new value innovations. A strong culture of knowledge management and information utilisation implies that most of the executives, managers and employees may tend to be motivated to act just on sensing the symptoms of the need to take certain specific actions. It signifies everyone in the organisation must be constantly inquisitive and concerned with how the existing information and new information can be gathered to devise better ways and new unique ideas for improving an enterprise's performance (Naidoo & Urban 2010). Unfortunately, the interview findings revealed that only a few enterprises tend to exhibit such characteristics. Even for the enterprises with well-developed knowledge management systems, there is often still a challenge of the utilisation of the accumulated information and knowledge to conclude certain critical strategic decisions and actions that can turnaround an enterprise's performance. This is reflected in the views of one of the managers working for a firm involved in the manufacturing of gas from petroleum wastes who stated that:

> 'From the experience of working across different industries, I have found that some of the executives and most of the employees are often not very bothered on how the existing information or the new ones can be acquired and utilised to develop new ideas and products that can turnaround an enterprise' performance. Instead, businesses tend to work hard to develop one concept or just a few concepts that they utilise for a long time to recoup as much funds used in the development of such a product as possible. During such a process, all new emerging information tend to be ignored. It costs a lot of funds to develop a product, hence, most of the businesses tend to use the existing templates rather than develop new products until it is established that the product's market performance is no longer impressive. In that process, even the staffs that are charged with the tasks of information gathering and analysis tend to only undertake the process of information gathering and analysis just as a daily formality, unless a serious event occurs to force the executives to recognise the importance to recall, analyse and act on the available information.' [Participant 9, male, 43 years, logistics manager]

Even for the businesses that have ended up with certain vibrant business concepts or new innovations, some of the managers reiterated the process of information gathering and conceptualisation are often merely based on very sketchy information. The participants attributed this to the fact that some of the executives tend to believe that to emerge with vibrant business concepts, it is not mandatory to have too much information that distorts focus, but only key highlights of major trends. Although such a process often only emerges after the concerned personnel have gained the requisite expertise, it still affects the evolution of a culture of intense information analysis and utilisation among the other staffs. This can place the enterprise at risks by ignoring critical relevant details that should have been considered to ensure that the process of innovation takes a right irreversible path. Whereas poor information and knowledge utilisation are often linked to the deliberate executives' actions, some of the participants highlighted the other challenge that also affects information and knowledge utilisation to create new values to be linked to insufficient resources and facilities.

Information resources and facilities

To ensure effective utilisation of the existing information to edify the effectiveness of the process of new value innovations, views from most of the managers in the hospitality as well as financial and insurance industries that significantly rely on information systems indicated that investment in the necessary information resources and facilities is a prerequisite. It may require investment in the necessary information systems such as enterprise resource planning (ERP) system. As it emerged from the evaluations of interview data, the establishment of an effective ERP system leverages the improvement of operational efficiency, information gathering, sharing and exchange among the innovation communities that often constitute of the manufacturers, suppliers, customers and the other partner organisations. This is substantiated in the views of one of the managers working with a firm that specialises in the manufacturing and distribution of industrial protective and safety wear who reiterated that:

> 'Initially, the senior managers ignored the essence for investing in an effective ERP system. However, with time, we found out that giving it a trial would enable us to assess how it would either facilitate or constrain our manufacturing operations. The values turned out to be enormous. Firstly, it facilitated frequent research and analysis to identify areas of safety challenges where we could conduct further research to develop new products to respond to such safety challenges. I mean, there is a lot of information that our research and development departments are able to easily gather not only from interactions with the customers, but also from the other industry players, media houses and suppliers. As the ERP system was developed, it facilitated liaison with the suppliers as well as customers, thereby improving the flow of information along the supply chains. We created a platform and distributed unique identification numbers to all the suppliers and our major customers and distributors. In this process, suppliers just log into our system and assess whether any information has been logged in to suggest that in a week or so we shall run out of the required inputs. Using this information, the suppliers instruct transporters and the logistic service providers to respond by delivering the required materials. As on the other hand, while also using the distributed unique numbers, customers also log in and place the necessary orders that we respond by delivering more effectively. As these services are being used, the query sections tend to provide us with enormous information that we usually analyse to assess how we can not only improve our products or even develop new ones, but also innovate better operational methods and systems.' [Participant 5, female, 26 years, production supervisor]

As ERP system is used to influence the improvement of the efficiency of internal operations as well as acquisitions of more information for further innovations and improvements, some of the managers also reiterated that ERP system is also used to thwart competitive threats in today's volatile competitive landscape. In today's volatile competitive landscape where the use of gaming theory may even entail forging partnerships with some of the rivals in some of the other markets to minimise competition threats, ERP systems are often also extended to create linkages with more friendly competitors or rivals. It is on that basis that ERP improves a firm's rate of the acquisition of new information and the assessment of the probable changes in the market and industry trends. This enables most of the high performing enterprises to identify new trends and respond by either modifying the existing products or developing new products to respond to the unfolding new market needs and demands. As firms enjoy such enormous business values of ERP, it is critical that the executives allocate sufficient resources to ensure that its implementation is a success. Unfortunately, it emerged from the interview data that although most of the enterprises cherish to reap the enormous business values associated with the use of ERP systems, the allocation of the required sufficient financial resources has often been a challenge. Most of the businesses struggle with the issue of sufficient financial resources, with the effect that such a challenge tends to get exacerbated by the hefty costs required for the establishment of an effective ERP system. As for the businesses with sufficient financial resources to establish an effective ERP system, some of the interviewed participants noted that the major constraint has still often arisen from the poor culture of the utilisation of the existing information and new information to develop new products. Such poor culture of information utilisation is often further exacerbated by the inability to read and interpret the accumulated information and knowledge. The inability to read and interpret the accumulated information and knowledge is also in turn affected by insufficient talented staffs to extract new ideas and initiate actions from the information and knowledge that the organisation has at its disposal. This is reflected in the opinions of one of the IT managers working for the manufacturers of industrial chemicals and the other domestic chemicals who stated that:

> 'Of course the development of an ERP system is critical for influencing the effectiveness of innovation. However, there is usually over excitement at the beginning and after the system is developed, frequent failures arising from poor maintenance tend to affect the use of ERP system in research and innovation. This is because from my experience, we tend to use well developed templates during the daily process of product development. As such templates are being used, frequent improvements and modifications are ignored for fear of deviating from the tested and approved product quality and specifications. This implies

that even if an ERP system is not functional at some points, it may not matter until it reaches a point where those authorised with product development have identified the need for product improvement or innovation of new products. It is during that process that significant attention is paid towards the improvement of the functionality of the ERP system so as to enhance the understanding of the views of the customers, suppliers, employees and even competitors. Although such a process is critical for aiding the effectiveness of innovation, it is critical to note that during the periods that the system was not functional, a lot of data could have been lost or even the company could have lost track of certain events which could have been of essence for influencing the overall effectiveness of product innovations.' [Participant 19, male, 36 years, manager]

At the same time, it also emerged from the findings that even if the challenge is not insufficient skills, most of the executives are often still quite slow to sense and initiate their own actions from the existing knowledge and information that they have. In most of the cases, there is a tendency to wait and see until the trends that were identified during market and industry analysis have started unfolding. Although the responses are usually reflected in the introduction of new products or modifications of the existing product features and attributes to respond to such new threats, most of the interviewed participants pointed that the failure to utilise the available information to take early actions often cause circumstances, where actions are only undertaken in haste. This affects the importance of calmness and stability that are often the critical prerequisites for undertaking new products' conceptualisation and development. Lack of sufficient financial resources also affects the building of the necessary networks and the motivation of talented employees to continuously search and identify new ideas that can be converted into new viable business concepts.

Discussion

Survival and sustainability in the increasingly discontinuous business environment require businesses to constantly modify their existing products or develop new products (Cohendet & Simon 2015). Constant modifications and introduction of new products enhance the extent to which a firm is able to effectively thwart new competitive threats or respond to the changes in the market needs and demands (Cohendet & Simon 2015). Constant new product development and modifications are also the critical market consolidation or fortifying strategies that enable a firm consolidate their industry positions and thwart risks of infiltration by rivals. However, for firms with less entrenched culture of knowledge management and information utilisation, constant product modifications or innovations may tend to be a challenge (Hernandez et al. 2010; Leal et al. 2013; Yayavaram & Ahuja 2008). A strong culture of information and knowledge utilisation edifies the accumulation of sufficient information that renders it possible for relevant analysis to be conducted so as to identify new gaps in the markets that must be filled through either new value innovations or modifications of the existing products.

Although this enhances the extent to which the SME's knowledge management system is able to edify new innovation processes, it is also critical that the embracement of a strong culture of information and knowledge utilisation is also accompanied by the dedication of the sufficient financial and non-financial resources (Cant & Wiid 2013; Naidoo & Urban 2010; Olawale & Garwe 2010; Pillay 2016; Ramukumba 2014; Scheers 2011). The allocation of sufficient financial resources can enhance effective use of monetary rewards to motivate talented employees to effectively use the existing information systems to constantly scan the existing information for the unfolding changes and the corresponding new innovations that can be undertaken. This enhances the identification of an array of ideas that can be successfully converted into new viable business concepts or new products. Combined with the establishment of more valuable business information systems such as ERP systems, it is through such approach that the executives can ensure that the improvement in the level of information and knowledge utilisation edify the effectiveness of the entire process of new innovations. In other words, it enhances the improvement of the effectiveness of the process of new innovations that are often linked to ideation, conceptualisation, prototyping, development, market testing, introduction and further modifications to ensure that the new innovations either perfectly match or exceed the customer expectations. However, considering that a culture of information and knowledge utilisation, as well as information resources and facilities were still found to be challenges, it is argued that this research is associated with enormous managerial implications for the contemporary managers.

Managerial implications

It is indicated in Figure 1 that the managerial implications of the findings signify that managers that aim to undertake constant new value innovations as prerequisites for survival and sustainability in the increasingly discontinuous business environment must consider commencing the process by building a strong culture of knowledge management. This must be undertaken in conjunction with the integration of certain pillars that foster a continuum of knowledge management-new value innovation.

These pillars include a strong culture of knowledge management that emphasises effective information and knowledge utilisation, and sufficient resources for motivating creativity and extraction of new ideas from the existing information. The other pillar would require investment in ERP system to facilitate effective integration and synchronisation of communication, information exchange and sharing among the innovative communities encompassing manufacturers, researchers, product developers, suppliers, customers, strategic partners and competitors' networks. Effective establishment of these pillars creates an effective knowledge management foundation that in turn spawns the effectiveness of the process of new value innovations. This implies that with such a strong culture of information and knowledge utilisation, it becomes easier for enterprises to engage in the process of planning, acquiring, organising and utilising tacit and explicit knowledge to create new products or improve the existing processes, methods and products to influence a business' overall effective market performance. It is on that basis that knowledge management also concurrently enhances the generating of relevant information and ideas that are converted into new products or the initiatives that modify the existing products or services' features. In other words, deeper entrenchment of a culture of knowledge management influences the effective accomplishment of critical new value innovation activities that are often linked to ideation, conception, prototyping, demonstration, production, marketing and testing.

Summary and conclusion

Knowledge management systems provide sufficient information that edifies creativity, and the generation and conversion of new ideas into new values or viable business concepts. This creates a strong foundation of knowledge management that in turn influences planning, acquisition, organising and utilisation of tacit and explicit knowledge to create new or improve the existing processes, methods and products. All these may influence a business' overall effective market performance. Well-developed knowledge management systems do not only provide details on the unfolding market trends, but also critical customer touchpoints or triggers of the interest of certain market segments. Upon the introduction of new innovations, such accurate information provides insights on the critical customer touchpoints that the promotional messages of the new innovations must be based. This enables the undertaking of relevant corresponding actions to improve the positioning of new products in the minds of the targeted market segments, and subsequently the extent of the successful launch of new innovations.

However, as contrasted to the logic in Nonaka's knowledge creation model and Naggar's (2015) creativity canvass that only limited the analysis of the effectiveness of knowledge management as an edifier of the effectiveness of ideation, findings signify knowledge management effectiveness spawns not only the effectiveness of ideation. Instead, it also leverages the entire effectiveness of the process of new value innovations that often spans across ideation, conceptualisation, development, market testing and modifications prior to launching the final product. During the ideation process, the effectiveness of knowledge management enhances the generation of an array of alternative ideas that renders it possible for a firm to select the best ideas. As the conceptualisation, development and market testing processes unfold, knowledge management aids further modifications and reconfigurations to improve the extent to which the product is able to perfectly match or even exceed customer expectations. Although this spurs the development and market introduction of the best concept, quite often, that it is often not the end of all the processes of new value innovations.

Constant changes in market and industry trends may require constant review and modifications of the product to enable it remain consistently relevant to the changes in market needs. This implies that even after the launch of the final product, an entrenched culture of information and knowledge utilisation still leverages the accumulation and management of sufficient information that in turn spurs relevant analysis to identify new gaps in the markets that must be filled through improvements or modifications of the existing products. In other words, the maintenance of an efficiently functional knowledge management system facilitates consistent and systematic analysis and generation of critical information for firms to understand the unfolding trends and to modify the already introduced products to match such trends. It facilitates the analysis of whether certain customer disappointments are linked to the quality, attributes and the features of the new products, or the pricing and distribution to improve the customers' accessibility to new innovations. These enable the enterprise to re-evaluate and undertake the necessary modifications of the quality, features, attributes and distribution approach of the existing products to ensure that they perfectly match or exceed customer perceptions and expectations.

As much as such frequent product modifications improve the strategic fitness between the firm and the unfolding industry and market trends, it is often not only product modifications facilitated by effectiveness of knowledge management that improves a strategic fit between the enterprise and such unfolding market and industry trends, but also the extent of a firm's operational efficiency to effectively match their needs and demands. This implies with an entrenched culture of knowledge management, it often turns easier for firms to conduct relevant analysis to identify and correct deviating costly processes that may affect cost and quality management. It is also during such process analysis and evaluation that firms are able to effectively modify and improve their processes, work methods and operational efficiency to meet the emerging changes in market demands and needs. All these enhance the improvement of the survival and sustainability of the business in the increasingly discontinuous business environment. However, it is still often quite critical that the embracement of a strong culture of information and knowledge utilisation is accompanied by the dedication of sufficient financial and non-financial resources towards the development of effective knowledge management systems.

As the effectiveness of knowledge management facilitates the generation of alternative ideas, the availability of the required financial resources and skills titivates the effectiveness of the implementation of new innovations and improvement measures that must be undertaken. Unfortunately, it emerged from the findings that despite a largely infant level of innovation culture among most of the SMEs, the effective utilisation of their knowledge management systems to leverage the effectiveness of new value innovations is still often undermined by poor maintenance of knowledge management systems. Besides lack of a clear business model linking knowledge management to the effectiveness of new value innovations, the other challenges are often linked to inadequate financial resources, skills and facilities. This study attempted to address such challenges by suggesting a continuum of knowledge management-new value innovation pillars (a strong culture of knowledge management that emphasises effective information and knowledge utilisation, and sufficient resources for motivating creativity and extraction of new ideas from the existing information) that the executives must consider to create an effective knowledge management foundation that subsequently edifies the effectiveness of the process of new value innovations. However, future research can still explore how new value innovations can be used as a driver for reshaping the increasingly discontinuous industries and markets.

Acknowledgements

Competing interests

The author declares that he has no financial or personal relationships that may have inappropriately influenced him in writing this article.

References

Boisot, M., 1987, *Information and organisations: The manager as anthropologist*, Fontana-Collins, London.

Bosua, R. & Venkitachalam, K., 2013, 'Aligning strategies and processes in knowledge management', *Journal of Knowledge Management* 17(3), 331–346. https://doi.org/10.1108/JKM-10-2012-0323

Cant, M.C. & Wiid, J.A., 2013, 'Establishing the challenges affecting South African SMEs', *International Business & Economics Research Journal* 12(6), 707–716. https://doi.org/10.19030/iber.v12i6.7869

Clark, V.L., 2010, 'The adoption and practice of mixed methods: US trends in federally funded health-related research', *Qualitative Inquiry* 16(1), 428–440. https://doi.org/10.1177/1077800410364609

Cohendet, P. & Simon, L., 2015, 'Introduction to the special issue on creativity in innovation', *Technology Innovation Management Review* 22(4), 122–204.

Cunningham, S., 2012, *The fundamentals of innovation system promotion for development practitioners*, Mesopartner, Pretoria.

Hedlund, G. & Nonaka, I., 1993, *Models of knowledge management*, Macmillan, London.

Hernandez, M.R., Cepeda, C.G., Cegarra, N.J.G. & Leal, M.A., 2010, 'The role of cultural barriers in the relationship between open-mindedness and organisational innovation', *Journal of Organisational Change Management* 23(4), 360–376. https://doi.org/10.1108/09534811011055377

Kono, P.M. & Barnes, B., 2010, 'The role of finance in the strategic-planning and decision-making process', *Graziadio Business School Review* 12(1), 19–87.

Leal, M.A., Salgueiro, J.L. & Ortega, S., 2013, 'Knowledge management and the effectiveness of innovation outcomes: The role of cultural barriers', *The Electronic Journal of Knowledge Management* 11(1), 62–71.

Lee, S. & Olson, D., 2010, *Convergenomics: Strategic innovation in the convergence era*, Gower Publishing, Surrey.

Lee, S., Olson, D. & Trimi, S., 2012, 'Co-innovation: Convergence, collaboration, and co-creation for organizational values', *Management Decision* 50(5), 817–831. https://doi.org/10.1108/00251741211227528

Manzini, S.T., 2015, 'Measurement of innovation in South Africa: An analysis of survey metrics and recommendations', *South African Journal of Science* 11(12), 1–8. https://doi.org/10.17159/sajs.2015/20140163

Mohsam, F. & Van Brakel, P.A., 2011, 'Information and knowledge sharing trends of small and medium-sized enterprises in the Western Cape, South Africa', *South African Journal of Information Management* 13(1), 1–10. https://doi.org/10.4102/sajim.v13i1.462

Morse, J.M., 2010, 'Simultaneous and sequential qualitative mixed method designs', *Qualitative Inquiry* 16(1), 483–491. https://doi.org/10.1177/1077800410364741

Naggar, R., 2015, 'The creativity canvas: A business model for knowledge and idea management', *Technology Innovation Management Review* 5(7), 50–58.

Naidoo, R. & Urban, B., 2010, 'The relevance of operational skills towards business sustainability: A focus on SME manufacturers in the Vaal Triangle region', *Acta Commercii* 1(1), 234–248.

Nonaka, I. & Takeuchi, K., 1995, *The knowledge creating company: How Japanese companies create the dynamics of innovation?* Oxford University Press, London.

Olawale, F. & Garwe, D., 2010, 'Obstacles to the growth of new SMEs in South Africa: A principal component analysis approach', *African Journal of Business Management* 1(3), 729–738.

Omotayo, F. & Olubunmi, M., 2015, 'Knowledge management as an important tool in organisational management: A review of literature', *Library Philosophy and Practice* 12(8), 1–23.

Pillay, K., 2016, *South Africa manufacturing industry leader*, Deloitte, Johannesburg.

Ramukumba, T., 2014, 'Overcoming SMEs challenges through critical success factors: A case of SMEs in the Western Cape Province, South Africa', *Economic and Business Review* 16(1), 19–38.

Scheers, L.V., 2011, 'SMEs marketing skills challenges in South Africa', *African Journal of Business Management* 4(1), 504–525.

Teng, J.T.C. & Song, S., 2011, 'An exploratory examination of knowledge-sharing behaviours: Solicited and voluntary', *Journal of Knowledge Management* 15(1), 104–117. https://doi.org/10.1108/13673271111108729

Teo, T., Nishant, R., Goh, M. & Agarwal, S., 2011, 'Leveraging collaborative technologies to build a knowledge sharing culture at HP analytics', *MIS Quarterly Executive* 10(1), 1–18.

Wang, S. & Noe, R.A., 2010, 'Knowledge sharing: A review and directions for future research', *Human Resource Management Review* 20(2), 115–131. https://doi.org/10.1016/j.hrmr.2009.10.001

Yayavaram, S. & Ahuja, G., 2008, 'Decomposability in knowledge structures and its impact on the usefulness of inventions and knowledge-based malleability', *Administrative Science Quarterly* 53(2), 333–362. https://doi.org/10.2189/asqu.53.2.333

Zhou, K.Z. & Li, C.B., 2012, 'How knowledge affects radical innovation: Knowledge base, market knowledge acquisition, and internal knowledge sharing', *Strategic Management Journal* 3(1), 219–277. https://doi.org/10.1002/smj.1959

Zhou, K.Z. & Wu, F., 2010, 'Technological capability, strategic flexibility, and product innovation', *Strategic Management Journal* 31(5), 547–561.

18

Between a rock and a hard place: Management and implementation teams' expectations of project managers in an agile information systems delivery environment

Authors:
Songezo Nkukwana[1]
Nicky H.D. Terblanche[1]

Affiliations:
[1]University of Stellenbosch Business School, Stellenbosch University, South Africa

Corresponding author:
Nicky Terblanche,
nicky@flipside.co.za

Background: To address the low success rate in information system (IS) projects, organisations in South Africa are adopting agile implementation methodologies. Agile delivery environments advocate an iterative approach where autonomous, self-organising teams share project management (PM) activities. This encroaches on the traditional project manager role. Are project managers still relevant in agile delivery environments and how should they adapt?

Objectives: This case study investigated how project managers could adapt to agile IS implementation environments to remain relevant. Specifically, the views of their key stakeholders (the management and implementation teams) were elicited to provide insights into what is expected from agile project managers.

Method: A qualitative, inductive content analysis approach using purposive sampling was used to identify 13 participants (comprising management and implementation team members) within a large South African insurance company. Semi-structured interviews were conducted with all participants.

Results: The management and implementation teams agreed that PM remains highly relevant in an agile environment for ensuring project governance including delivery, risk management, reporting and budgeting. There was, however, disagreement between the management and implementation teams on project management interaction with the implementation team. Management preferred a command and control type project manager, while the implementation team favoured a more inclusive, facilitative PM style.

Conclusion: To remain viable in an agile IS project implementation environment within large corporates, project managers need to be aware of what various stakeholders expect of them. They need to retain some of the classic PM functions while adapting to the interpersonal and collaborative requirements of the agile way.

Introduction

Information system (IS) development projects have a reputation for failure in terms of overrun in budget, timeliness and not meeting users' expectations (Karleskey & Voord 2008; Savolainen, Ahonen & Richardson 2012; Yeo 2002). Evidence for this reputation is that only 29% of worldwide IS projects achieved project management (PM) success (The Standish Group International 2015). This failure rate is high when compared with other high-tech projects and is the reason for concern given that IS is increasingly seen as being of critical strategic and operational importance in organisations (Sauer & Reich 2009). Furthermore, within the knowledge economy, software is seen as a source of knowledge and IS development as a source of knowledge creation (Bailin 1997; Shongwe 2015), and creating knowledge affords organisations the opportunity to gain and sustain competitive advantages (Mitchell & Boyle 2010).

In an attempt to address the failure of traditional approaches to IS delivery, organisations are turning to agile methodologies (Dybå & Dingsøyr 2008; Lindvall et al. 2004). Agile software development differs from the traditional waterfall approach in that, in a waterfall approach, a formal, sequential process of planning, analysing, designing, implementing and maintaining is followed. Agile, on the contrary, is characterised by fast and flexible results based on iterative delivery, frequent feedback loops and constant involvement of the customer (Cohn 2004; Rao, Naidu & Chakka 2011; Stettina & Horz 2015). The wide-spread adoption of agile implementation methodologies is attributed to their ability to respond to fast changing business requirements, market conditions and technology innovation (Augustine, Payne, Sencindiver & Woodcock 2005; Stavru et al. 2014).

From a PM perspective, the move to agile implementation has introduced a number of challenges. The project manager can no longer only be concerned with planning, organising and controlling, but instead has to learn to facilitate and coach to encourage collaboration between team members in line with the agile way (Highsmith 2003; Nerur, Mahapatra & Mangalaraj 2005). They also have to play an active role in project knowledge management, which contributes to project success (Srikantaiah, Koenig & Hawamdeh 2010:v). A further complication is that agile software development encourages autonomous, self-organising teams who are meant to share PM tasks and responsibilities such as estimation, planning and progress tracking. This new focus encroaches on the project manager's territory and raises questions about the project manager's role (Hoda & Murugesan 2016).

To complicate matters even more, many, especially large organisations, struggle to make the transition from traditional to agile IS implementation methodologies (Dybå & Dingsøyr 2008; Nerur et al. 2005; Sidky, Arthur & Bohner 2007). In fact, it is more likely that large organisations employ both traditional and agile IS implementation practices in what is termed *an ambidextrous approach* (Vinekar, Slinkman & Nerur 2006), this duality presenting additional complex challenges to the PM role.

Given these team-related and organisational challenges faced by project managers, the question arises: how should project managers adapt to fit into an agile implementation environment within large corporates? This research set out to explore this question by obtaining the perspectives of the following two important project stakeholders: the management team and the implementation team. How do they view the role of a project manager in an agile environment and what do they require from such a role to more successfully complete IS implementation projects? If project managers who operate in implementation environments that are moving into an agile space are aware of the traditional versus agile needs of their key stakeholders, they could adapt their approach to strike a balance between the old and new way of working.

The rest of this article is structured as follows: Firstly, theoretical perspectives on IS projects in agile environments are presented. Next the case study research design used in this research is explained, and finally, the findings, discussion and key guidelines for the adapted role of PM are provided.

Information system implementation and project management challenges

The global business landscape has changed dramatically in the last few decades. Access to data, disruptive technological advances and the speed of innovation are some of the key drivers fuelling this revolution (Barkema, Baum & Mannix 2002). IS development is a crucial part of delivering technology innovation (Schwaber 2004), and as a result, business is both more aware and more critical of the success of IS projects. Business sees IS as being of strategic and operational importance – they want to see a return on their investment in IS and they have become more mature in their understanding of the nature of IS and IS projects (Sauer & Reich 2009).

Despite many efforts for IS implementation to meet customers' value needs in recent years, many software projects still fail to deliver value. They use more resources than planned, deliver less functionality at lower quality than expected and take longer to complete than anticipated (Barros, Werner & Travassos 2004). Some of the reasons offered for these failures include badly defined requirements, unrealistic expectations from business, poor reporting on project status and poor management of risks (Charette 2005). To manage risks, one has to manage knowledge (Neef 2005) and project knowledge is considered as one of the most powerful tools in managing risk (Cooper 2003; Srikantaiah et al. 2010). PM can play a significant role in knowledge management and, therefore, risk management because of the distributed interaction it has with many layers in the organisation (Schiel 2010).

Most IS professionals believe that using IS project methodologies will improve the PM success rate; however, project managers face a number of challenges that limit their success: unrealistic project deadlines, working on multiple projects simultaneously, ineffective use of PM software and lack of knowledge of PM methodologies (Terlizzi, De Souza Meirelles & De Moraes 2016). The nature of IS projects has also changed in recent years with an increase in technical complexity, rate of technology change, importance of security, business change involved in projects, prevalence of virtual teaming, organisational instability and interdependence with other organisations. All of these factors contribute to the fact that information system project management has become increasingly challenging (Sauer & Reich 2009:184).

The move from traditional to agile

Agility in organisations emerged from multiple domains including logistics and manufacturing (Stettina & Horz 2015) and found its way into software development at the end of the 1980s (Nagel & Dove 1991). One of the drivers towards agile methodology involves moving away from the extensive use of planning, codified processes that enforce standardisation, rigorous software reuse, heavy documentation and big upfront design, which traditional software development processes demand (Arikpo & Osofisan 2010; Nerur et al. 2005). In traditional waterfall methods, a sequential process is followed whereby projects force users to describe their needs accurately upfront, to capture as much information as possible, and only to deliver the requested features at the end of the process (Hong et al. 2011; Stoica, Mircea & Ghilic-Micu 2013). This has created a challenge for most organisations, mainly because of the false impression that proper planning and collecting detailed user requirements assist project teams in learning everything that they need to know about user requirements (Goodpasture 2015). The reality is that because of rapidly changing technology, market and social conditions, most real-world development efforts are conducted in more volatile environments (Augustine et al. 2005; Nerur et al. 2005). As a result, system requirements will change fast, often at 'Internet speed' (Baskerville et al. 2003).

Agile development leverages the concept of lean manufacturing that aims at deferring a decision until the reasonable moment, thereby assisting an organisation not to waste time on tasks until the odds of actually doing them are high (Schiel 2010). The agile approach follows four basic principles: individuals and interaction over process and tools, working software over comprehensive documentation, customer collaboration over contract negotiation and responding to chance over following a plan (Fowler & Highsmith 2001).

Agile methodology allows for the prioritisation of functionality, as development teams deliver product features sooner, through iterations. Agile also entails frequent feedback loops and iterative reviews (Stettina & Horz 2015). By using agile methods, customers are constantly involved in the development process by providing input into what should form part of the feature, which gives customers the assurance that the outcomes will be as close as possible to their requirements (Cooke 2014). The role of management in an agile environment is that of facilitating rather than controlling and developers often work collaboratively or in pairs, whereas in the traditional approach they are required to work more individually within teams (Hoda, Noble & Marshall 2008).

Although there is increased awareness of and interest in agile methods, it appears to be more difficult to implement in larger projects (Dybå & Dingsøyr 2008). The speed of change and close customer involvement required by agile is particularly challenging for larger organisations with well-established processes and structures (Stettina & Horz 2015). There currently seems to be no structured approach for the adoption of agile methodology, resulting in organisations asking different questions on the way to proceed when adopting agile practices (Sidky et al. 2007). Agile systems development requires changes to organisational culture (Vinekar et al. 2006), and this may take several years to achieve (Adler & Shenhar 1990), implying that there are varying levels of agile maturity within an organisation. A number of agile maturity frameworks exist, an example being the agile maturity model (AMM) by Patel and Ramachandran (2009). This model lists five stages of agile maturity based on the level of agile process improvement: initial, explored, defined, improved and sustained. Many large organisations claim to follow an agile IS implementation approach, but in reality because of current low levels of agile maturity within large organisations, many employ both traditional and agile implementation approaches (Vinekar et al. 2006). This presents unique challenges to the PM discipline and the role of the project manager in IS implementation projects within large organisations.

The challenges of agile project management

In response to the shift towards agile IS implementation methodologies, the PM discipline has started to reinvent itself in the form of the emerging agile project management (APM) discipline (Lee & Yong 2010; Persson, Mathiassen & Aaen 2012). APM is a conceptual PM framework for undertaking software development projects in which the emphasis is moved from planning to execution (Chin 2004), and encompasses the study of which methods, tools and techniques to employ to improve the performance of the project by promoting agility (Conforto & Amaral 2016). Taking a brief look at APM may assist in a better understanding of the challenges that face traditional PM in agile environments.

According to Augustine et al. (2005), APM lets software project managers and employees adapt to changing circumstances rather than trying to impose rigid formal controls, as in traditional linear development methods and this in itself poses a challenge to traditional PM approaches. Although PM remains an important and necessary part of any software development process in terms of managing the teams, customer relationships, cost reduction, risk management, maintaining project time line and budget, the manner in which it is done in an agile environment has changed (Hoda et al. 2008). Project managers are left in the lurch, since many of the commonly known PM practices and tools are geared towards large and relatively slow-moving projects (Chin 2004).

One such example is the emphasis on documentation in the traditional environment. Because of the fast changing context of the agile space, if a project manager attempts to rigorously document variations on the originally agreed-upon plan, their time will be consumed with tracking, analysing and documenting ever more complex variations, and they risk demoting their position to that of an administrative role (Chin 2004). Roles and responsibilities have also changed. Agile introduced a new set of roles such as product owner and scrum master, which share some of the traditional responsibilities of the project manager, further blurring the line of PM (Hoda et al. 2008).

To manage changes in requirements, an agile environment needs to allow for innovation and creativity, and by applying traditionally heavy PM techniques, the project manager risks stifling innovation. A balance is, therefore, required between too much process and too little process (Chin 2004). The agile manager is, however, responsible for establishing clear roles and responsibilities to ensure proper team alignment and accountability. They also need to be vigilant in identifying practices not being followed, understand the causes of the impediments and endeavour to remove any obstacles (Augustine et al. 2005).

Chin (2004) recommends two strategies that project managers could employ to adapt to agile environments:

- take more of an outward-facing perspective to facilitate the integration of the project and the business

- focus energy on delivering results that solve business needs rather than staying within present project boundaries (Chin 2004).

Augustine et al. (2005) echo this sentiment by stating that project managers should become visionary leaders rather than uninspired taskmasters and embrace the notion of self-directed teams with 'light touch' leadership. Agile project managers must aim to steer and guide the various entities involved in an agile project, and encourage continuous learning and adaptation by acting as facilitators (Augustine et al. 2005; Nerur et al. 2005). Nerur et al. (2005), however, also warn that shifting from authoritative manager to facilitator may not be easy for people who thrive on authority.

Having surveyed the literature, the researchers concluded that prior research into the changing role of the project manager in an agile environment seems to have been limited mostly to theoretical concepts leaving a clear gap for empirical research to be conducted. To provide a novel angle on what is expected from a project manager in an agile environment, perspectives were sought from the people who interact on a daily basis with project managers, namely the management team and the implementation team.

Research design

This research followed a qualitative, case study approach. This design was chosen to obtain descriptions of the phenomena (perceptions held by management and implementation teams) within the relevant context as described by the study participants, based on their experiences (Darke, Shanks & Broadbent 1998). Interpersonal expectations, as explored in this research, are highly complex and the qualitative case study approach allowed the researcher to deal with this complexity by gaining insights into behavioural conditions from the participants' perspectives (Zainal 2007).

Sampling and research setting

Purposive sampling was used (Wilmot 2005) to identify 13 participants working within the IS department of a business unit within a large insurance company in South Africa. Five of the participants belonged to the management team and the remaining eight were part of the IS implementation team. The management team roles consisted of the IT executive, senior IT consultant, project manager head, software methodology head and a program manager. The implementation team roles included project managers, developers, testers, architects and analysts. Members of these teams have been part of both successful and failed agile projects within the organisation.

Participants were included based on their advanced level of experience and knowledge about IS project implementations, with all of them having been involved in IS for at least 10 years. Participants were approached directly by the researcher and all participants signed informed consent forms, where the nature of the research and their rights as participants were explained. The ethics committee of the University of Stellenbosch approved this research.

Data collection and analysis

Semi-structured interviews were conducted with all participants. A basic interview guide was used to elicit deep reflection about the experiences of participants during IS implementation projects (Barriball & While 1994; Merriam & Tisdell 2015). This approach allowed participants to share their understanding of the challenges they faced and specifically the role that project managers played. Interviews were digitally recorded, transcribed and proofread by the researcher.

Data were analysed using an inductive qualitative content analysis approach (Hsieh & Shannon 2005). This analysis method was used because of its ability to extract the meaning of data through a process of coding and to describe theoretical concepts by means of an inductive approach (Cho & Lee 2014). The qualitative data analysis software package ATLAS.ti was used to identify initial categories through line-by-line coding (open coding), followed by category reduction through axial coding (Corbin & Strauss 1990). Initial coding yielded 380 codes, which after axial coding and memo writing (Charmaz 2014) was reduced to a set of 10 main challenges faced during agile implementation projects. This article reports on one of these identified challenges namely what is expected of project managers.

Findings and discussion

The expectations that the management team (hereafter referred to as 'M-1', 'M-2', etc.) and the implementation team (hereafter referred to as 'I-1', 'I-2' etc.) had of the PM role in an agile environment within a large corporate consisted of two main themes namely 'Performing a governance role' and 'Interacting with the implementation team'. The latter theme ('Interacting with the implementation team') had two sub-themes: 'Exerting control' and 'Serving as a coach and facilitator'.

The expectations of both teams with regard to these themes are illustrated in Figure 1. Although project governance expectations are shared, expectations on how to interact with the implementation team differ. The rest of this section discusses these findings.

Performing a project governance role

Traditionally, project governance is a key part of the PM role within IS projects and is used to achieve more predictable rates of PM success (Terlizzi et al. 2016). In an agile environment, where there is supposedly less focus on process and tools and more on individuals and interactions (Fowler & Highsmith 2001), one would assume that expectations from management and implementation teams would have changed. The findings of this research, however, reveal that both the management and implementation teams still value and expect project managers to fulfil a governance role, specifically relating to project delivery, risk management, reporting and budgeting.

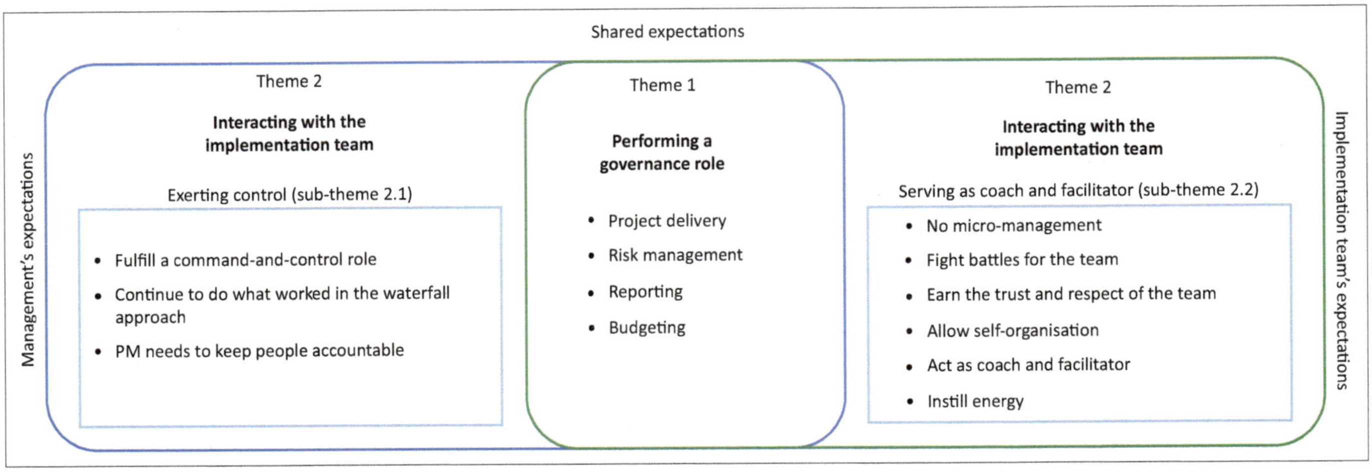

FIGURE 1: Management and implementation teams' expectations from project managers in an agile environment within a large corporate organisation.

In terms of project delivery, both the management and implementation teams agreed that driving a project plan is one of the key roles that remain important for a project manager in an agile environment as illustrated in these comments:

> 'A project manager has to focus on chasing the plan ensuring that people stick to what they promised, according to the plan.' [I-7; male; project manager]
>
> 'A project manager's role is to report progress and risks to the executives.' [M-1; male; IT executive]
>
> 'In our case I don't think you can do without the project manager because there's detail and high level issues that must be dealt with on a daily or weekly basis that impacts your timelines, so you can't do without the project manager role.' [M-3; male; head of PMO]

The traditional PM governance role was seen as critical in an agile environment since there is the perception that pure agile, as opposed to the traditional waterfall approach, does not provide the necessary tools 'to ensure accountability and responsibility on the delivery team members as individuals' (M-1). This finding is contrary to what agile software development advocates. Sprint teams are expected to be autonomous and self-organising and keep themselves accountable by sharing some of the typical PM tasks such as planning and estimation (Hoda & Murugesan 2016). The fact that the perception exists that individuals are not held accountable may point to the fact that there is a low level of agile maturity in this specific environment possibly, because there are no formal agile process improvement initiatives in place (Patel & Ramachandran 2009). According to Goodpasture (2015), self-organisation is often as the result of highly motivated, highly skilled and experienced team members and evolves over time. From a management perspective, this need for control can perhaps be understood in the context of the high rate of IS project implementation failure (Savolainen et al. 2012).

There seems to be an expectation that a project manager should be able to take ultimate responsibility for ensuring that tasks are completed. This is argued by I-6, who cannot imagine a team without a project manager, who takes full responsibility, ensuring that due process is followed. A project manager is someone that takes the responsibility for 'pushing the people when things are falling behind' (I-6). The expectation is more than merely meeting a deadline. I-4's view is that the organisation expects the project manager to be able to connect the original business case with project delivery and also to play a role in ensuring that the desired end result is reached. From a management perspective, there was a concern that in an agile environment, there is the danger that without a project manager there is no one who takes ultimate responsibility for project delivery and above all, project failure (M1). This sentiment is in line with the fact that traditionally project managers have been held responsible for time, cost and quality aspects of IT projects (Sheffield & Lemetayer 2013).

M-3 raised the importance of creating awareness around project risks:

> '...in an Agile world, there are people thinking that you do not need project management roles when using an agile approach, which I think is not correct... you still need to know what the overall milestones are, what the budget is, what the risks are, all arising project issues, managing the stuff that does not change.' [M-3; male; head of PMO]

The implementation team in general affirmed this view by stating that a project manager manages the delivery of the project in terms of time and that a project manager should remain aware of the project scope and overall quality. In addition, governance disciplines ensure proper compliance and conformance to project ceremonies and these are typically a PM role, even in an agile environment (I-5). In implementations of agile such as Scrum, the view is counter to that expressed by the participants: project managers have no project plans or time reporting, but instead rely on the frequent delivery cycle of the agile approach to show results (Schwaber 2004).

There was a clear expectation from management that project managers must take responsibility for executive management reporting on agile projects (M-1; M-3). They were particularly adamant about this given the perception in the organisation that agile projects do not provide clear feedback to management stakeholders:

> 'I think agile hasn't done a lot of work on communicating transparent scope changes and agreements outside the project... because of the daily stand-ups, people know what's going on, its crystal clear to the people around, but in terms of the person outside the project who's giving the money and who wants to know every six months as an investment if their money is safe, how do roles such as Head of Business, CIO, and other senior business representatives get visibility in an agile project?' [M1; male; IT executive]

This perception, however, is contradicted by the nature of feedback in pure agile environments which takes the form of regular, rapid feedback to customers, developers and end-users through frequent releases of the working software (Cohn 2004; Rao et al. 2011). It would appear that at senior management level, the need to be personally present at feedback sessions is a pragmatic obstacle:

> 'They (senior management) don't have time in a day to come look at that level of details as sponsors.' [M1; male; IT executive]

It is clear from these findings that both the management and implementation teams value the governance role that project managers fulfil on agile projects, particularly with regards to project delivery, risk management, reporting and budgeting. This finding points to the dual nature of IS delivery methodologies in large organisations where organisations, while realising the need to embrace agile, still have a need for the structure provided by traditional development approaches (Vinekar et al. 2006). In terms of interacting with project stakeholders, this implies that project managers are challenged to function in both paradigms as revealed in the discussion that follows.

Interacting with the implementation team

A key change in an agile environment as opposed to a traditional IS delivery approach is the way in which the implementation team operates. The agile manifesto prescribes individual interaction over process and tools, collaboration over contracts and being responsive rather than following a rigid plan (Fowler & Highsmith 2001). Agile IS development places a premium on people and their interactions. The emphasis is on teams and on the intense dynamics of team interactions (Vinekar et al. 2006). The findings discussed in this section reveal how the project manager has to renegotiate their role within the implementation team based on the expectations of both management and implementation. The two sub-themes capturing this aspect are 'Exerting control' and 'Serving as a coach and facilitator'.

Exerting control

Some of the management team members expect project managers to take on a command and control role; whereas, the implementation team spoke out against such form of restriction. Three of the management team members (M-1; M-2; M-3) supported the existing culture of control in the organisation and expected project managers to help sustain this approach in an agile environment:

> 'If you've grown up in the waterfall world, you've come up through the ranks there, you know what the issues are, you know that you got to pay attention to this and that, to make this go right.' [M-2; male; IT consultant]

> 'Say you have a team of 10 where eight pull their weight whereas the other two do not, but you as a project manager don't actually take on those two, if the other eight see that they are getting away with it, then the whole team takes a fall.' [M-3; male; head of PMO]

> 'One of the tenets of project management is meant to be a mechanism that identifies the goal and helps the community achieve that goal. So it implies an element of drive to control people by saying yes/no.' [M-1; male; IT executive]

Only one manager [M-4] disagreed by expressing that command and control are not necessary in an agile environment since the team manages itself.

This expectation from management that seems to contradict the agile principles was pointed out by Cockburn and Highsmith (2001) who stated that PM style in a traditional waterfall organisation tends to exert command and control over developers. They further emphasise the importance of collaborative decision-making to improve agility within business. They believe that a command and control approach inhibits agility and ultimately fails the implementation teams in an agile environment (Cockburn & Highsmith 2001). IS professionals and project managers are knowledge workers. They often identify themselves in terms of their area of expertise and not the organisations they work for. Therefore, organisations who apply a 'boss and subordinate' approach to PM may face the risk of losing these professionals (Srikantaiah et al. 2010:4). Augustine et al. (2005) echoes this sentiment by stating that 'skilled professionals don't adapt well to micromanagement'.

Contrary to management's view, the implementation team felt strongly that there is no place for command and control from project managers in the agile space:

> 'Styles like micro management, authoritative, that doesn't work. Being too detail oriented. You can't be too set about what you're actually going to get, you have to be flexible, you have to be able to change.' [I-2; female; business analyst]

> 'The ones that are not succeeding with agile are those that are very commanding and controlling. If you going to have someone that is commanding and controlling, who will end up pushing people to do things, people are going to leave.' [I-3; male; developer]

I-3 argued that a project manager needs to be the person who works for the project team, one who is the eyes and ears of the people in the team and is expected to fight battles for the team, attending meetings with management to ensure they get the 'stuff required to keep the project running'. Styles like micromanagement and being authoritative do not work in agile environments (I-2). I-4 supported this view: in a waterfall project, project managers can be authoritative or dictatorial, but in their experience this does not work in an agile environment since the project structure is less hierarchical, allowing the implementation team members to by-pass the project manager by, for example, speaking directly to business. This is in fact aligned with the notion of self-organising, autonomous teams as advocated in an agile approach (Schiel 2010). Project managers should realise that in an agile environment and specifically where the scrum methodology is used, it is expected of individual team members to be autonomous and self-organising (Augustine et al. 2005). As a result, some of the typical PM tasks are shared by the team members (Hoda & Murugesan 2016), and they should, therefore, become one of the team members instead of elevating themselves above the team. This approach can be achieved by project managers attending daily check-in sessions with the implementation team to show interest and to keep up to date with what is happening in the team (I-4). I-8 felt that project managers have the responsibility to win the trust of the teams so that the team chooses to listen to them:

> 'It is not all about you sitting there and doing the mantra and going on trying to get everyone to listen to you, it is about being able to be bigger than the room, and if you are not, you're going to struggle. Agile works where you have very high trust between the development organisation and the client or the management group.' [I-8; male; developer]

Developing and sustaining a sense of trust has been shown to be at the root of agile success (Schwaber 2004). Furthermore, trust may lead to balanced decision-making that could potentially shift the balance of power from management to the development teams (Nerur et al. 2005). Trust also encourages continuous learning, spontaneity and creativity and working together towards a single goal (Moe, Dingsøyr & Dybå 2009).

I-4 makes a strong case for why command and control by project managers in an agile environment is not a good idea. I-4 believes that each team member has enough authority to make decisions on what should happen in their teams. If the team is unable to think for themselves, it will not be able to 'catch some of the things that the project manager drops', which will ultimately impact the ability of the project manager to deliver on project expectations. Learning and growth is also stunted through command and control management style:

> '...if the team does only what the project manager tells them to do, the role of management or lead can never be any better in such a team.' [I-4; male; test manager]

This sentiment is echoed by Cockburn and Highsmith (2001), who emphasise the importance of collaborative decision-making to affect agility within business, and also speaks to the notion of autonomous, self-management teams (Hoda & Murugesan 2016).

This tension that seems to exist between the view of the management team and that of the implementation team on the level of control that a PM should exert in an agile environment can perhaps be ascribed to the difficulty of letting go of power. Nerur et al. (2005) warn that the shift from authoritative manager would challenge those attitudes and culture of people who enjoy authority, making implementing agile difficult.

If project managers could step back from the command and control paradigm and allow agile teams to self-organise, there could be benefits:

> 'If one allows the team to sort themselves out, they realise that they have to work extra as a team and that they do not need to worry that much, because they do not feel forced to do it, or they do not have to do it all the time.' [M-4; male; methodology lead]

Schiel (2010) and Dybå & Dingsøyr (2008) support this view, stating that self-organising teams are empowered to organise work tasks in a way that give them common ownership. However, Lalsing, Kishnah and Pudaruth (2012) and Goodpasture (2015) highlight the fact that self-organisation is an advanced skill and that it may be difficult to recruit staff capable of forming self-organising teams. In addition, agile practitioners may encounter team-level and organisational-level barriers to self-organisation. On a team-level, these barriers include lack of individual commitment and leadership as well as failure to learn, while pressure to work on multiple projects in parallel, organisational control and organisational insistence on specialists feature account for the organisational-level barriers. These barriers can be overcome by organising cross-training to create generalists, collocating teams in the same room, building trust and commitment and assigning people to one project at a time (Moe et al. 2009).

Ultimately, it seems that a balance is needed between the need for an agile environment and the realities of a large corporate (Vinekar et al. 2006). I-5 sums up why there is still a need for a project manager in agile environments in large corporates:

> ...pure agile from its original definition, particularly the scrum, cannot really work in agile environments, and this is the reason why there is disciplined agile development which is much more suited for a corporate environment.

They see the role of a project manager as someone who ensures that the team:

> 'sticks to some of the culture that exists in project management.' [I-5; male; IT architect]

Serving as a coach and facilitator

If command and control is not appropriate in an agile environment, then what are the alternatives? The implementation team articulated the need for a project manager to act more like a coach and facilitator. I-7 stated that in an agile environment, a project manager must be a people's person and relationship driven. It is not about trying to build friendships, but rather about motivating people to work together (I-7). This is in line with research that shows that project managers need to actively target the development of trust through activities that will build it (Sauer & Reich 2009).

This type of involvement starts with the project manager being more present:

> 'Project managers should be involved. Our team has seen some who are not, where they throw things over the wall and instruct developers or analysts to do their work, and return after the allocated time to report on the progress. The project managers must be involved daily to know what is going on.' [M-3; male; head of PMO]

Closer involvement could pose a challenge however. Sauer and Reich (2009) state that the complexity involved in contemporary IS projects implies that project managers may not be sufficiently knowledgeable in all the relevant aspects of the project. On top of this, project managers typically have a heavy workload and may not have the time to be closely involved.

Project managers must act as facilitators and must acquire facilitation skills (I-1; I-8). Facilitation skills would assist project managers in their mediation role when, for example, they need to negotiate overtime work with both the people who have to conduct the work and the sponsors who have to pay them (I-8). This is in line with the notion that project managers must increasingly take ownership of business goals and identify with the business issues instead of merely accepting that business goals are owned by a sponsor (Sauer & Reich 2009). They have to alter their behaviour to that of a facilitator, someone who does not direct but coordinates individuals in a team (Nerur et al. 2005). Contrary to what most organisations believe, project success does not depend only on aspects such as project schedules, budgets and deliverables. Knowledge sharing and cooperation through facilitation play an important role in project knowledge management, which in turn has a positive bearing on project success (Srikantaiah et al. 2010).

In addition to being a skilled facilitator, I-3 saw the PM role as a humble and serving one, able to work collaboratively with the team and stakeholders to get the job done. I-8 illustrated this type of leadership style by referring to examples of leaders such as Clem Sunter, the Dalai Lama and Nelson Mandela, and referring to them as the kind of individuals who had the characteristics required of a leader of an agile project. Kniberg and Skarin (2010) state that agile teams require coaching rather than management. This is supported by Goodpasture (2015), who agrees that coaching skills are important for project managers.

Not all management participants agreed. M-4 argued to the contrary, pointing out that in an agile environment, the role of servant to the team should be fulfilled by the scrum master and not the project manager. Whether serving or not, I-8 believed that project managers should in any case instil energy and stimulate interest in people, all the while keeping their eye on the project plan to ensure that scope is delivered within the planned timelines and in accordance with the relevant quality assurance processes.

Not everyone was convinced that project managers need to change their behaviour in an agile environment. M-1 argued that the traditional project manager role in the waterfall environment also required coaching and facilitation skills. M-1 believed that the same PM style could work in both waterfall and agile environments. I-4 tended to agree, but stressed that 'one could probably more easily get away with certain styles in waterfall that would not do so well in agile'.

Perhaps the reason for the apparent conflict in expectations from project managers is that 'project managers apply traditional methods on projects for which they are not suited because they must align their efforts with broader organisational expectations' (Sheffield et al. 2013:469). It may also be the case that agile software development drives agility in PM (Stettina & Horz 2015) and that with time, adjustments will be made.

Managerial implications and recommendations

From the findings above, the following recommendations are made:

- Be cognisant of the level of agile maturity in the organisation to gauge the balance between traditional PM and APM needs. This can be achieved by using one of the available agile maturity frameworks to assess the current level of agile maturity and by putting in place improvement initiatives.
- Facilitate open conversations between project managers and their stakeholders to create understanding of what is expected from the project manager role. This can be achieved through facilitated workshops as well as informal discussions initiated by management.
- Train project managers in the art of coaching and facilitation to improve their ability to lead agile teams. Numerous coaching and facilitation courses are available through professional services providers and could be formally incorporated into career development and training programmes.

Conclusion

Knowledge is created through the creation of software during IS implementation projects; however, IS project implementation success is low (Bailin 1997; Savolainen et al. 2012; Shongwe 2015). In an attempt to address the disappointing track-record of successful IS implementation projects, organisations are moving towards agile project implementation methodologies, where reduced formality and increased individual autonomy and self-organising teams are advocated. This shift encroaches on the territory of the traditional project manager role and raises questions about how project managers should adapt in order to remain relevant.

This case study provided insights into the desired behaviours of an agile project manager by exploring the different needs of the management and implementation teams. It would appear that project managers are stuck between a rock and hard place when it comes to fulfilling management and implementation teams' expectations. On the one hand, they are required to fulfil the traditional PM role: both the management and implementation teams require project managers to adhere to classic PM governance functions such as project delivery, risk management, reporting and budgeting. On the other hand, when it comes to the management of the implementation team, the management team preferred a more traditional command and control style project manager. The implementation teams, however, favoured a more agile approach where they expect a project manager to earn their trust, refrain from micromanagement, allow the team to self-organise and act as coach and facilitator.

The conclusion drawn from these findings is that, for project managers to remain relevant in the move towards a more agile IS implementation environment, they must become aware of the different expectations of their various stakeholders and adapt their behaviour accordingly. They need to engage openly with their stakeholders to understand their needs, acquire new skills required in the agile environment such as coaching and facilitation, and strike a balance between employing traditional and APM skills depending on the agile maturity of the organisation.

Limitations and recommendations for future research

This case study was limited to one IS department of a large South African insurance company. Future research should consider expanding the sample to include the views of more stakeholders in both the management and implementation teams and across various industries. It may also be beneficial to specifically obtain the views of project managers on how they see their role in an agile environment. Of the 13 research participants, 8 were from the implementation team and 5 from business. A more equal participant distribution would help ensure that the findings are not potentially distorted. To help address the issue of agile maturity, future research could develop an agility transition framework to help guide and monitor the move from traditional to agile.

Acknowledgements

Competing interests

The authors declare that they have no financial or personal relationship(s) that may have inappropriately influenced them in writing this article.

Authors' contributions

S.N. conducted the research as part of his MBA research project and co-wrote this article. N.T. was his research supervisor and co-wrote this article.

References

Adler, P.S. & Shenhar, A., 1990, 'Adapting your technological base: The organizational challenge', *Sloan Management Review* 32(1), 25–37.

Arikpo, I.I. & Osofisan, A.O., 2010, 'Migrating from traditional software development processes to agile software development: The role of organizational culture', *CIS Journal* 14(2), 17–27.

Augustine, S., Payne, B., Sencindiver, F. & Woodcock, S., 2005, 'Agile project management: Steering from the edges', *Communications of the ACM* 48(12), 85–89. https://doi.org/10.1145/1101779.1101781

Bailin, S., 1997, 'Software development as knowledge creation', *International Journal of Applied Software Technology* 3, 75–89.

Barkema, H., Baum, J. & Mannix, E., 2002, 'Management challenges in a new time', *Academy of Management Journal* 45(5), 916–930. https://doi.org/10.2307/3069322

Barriball, K. & While, A., 1994, 'Collecting data using a semi-structured interview: A discussion paper', *Journal of Advanced Nursing* 19(2), 328–335. https://doi.org/10.1111/j.1365-2648.1994.tb01088.x

Barros, M.O., Werner, C.M.L. & Travassos, G.H., 2004, 'Supporting risks in software project management', *Journal of Systems and Software* 70(2), 21–35. https://doi.org/10.1016/S0164-1212(02)00155-3

Baskerville, R., Ramesh, B., Levine, L., Pries-Heje, J. & Slaughter, S., 2003, 'Is "Internet-speed" software development different?', *IEEE Software* 20(6), 70–77. https://doi.org/10.1109/MS.2003.1241369

Charette, R.N., 2005, 'Why software fails', *IEEE Spectrum* 42(9), 42–49. https://doi.org/10.1109/MSPEC.2005.1502528

Charmaz, K., 2014, *Constructing grounded theory*, Sage, Thousand Oaks, CA.

Chin, G., 2004, *Agile project management: How to succeed in the face of changing project requirements*, AMACOM Division of American Management Association, New York, NY.

Cho, J.Y. & Lee, E.H., 2014, 'Reducing confusion about grounded theory and qualitative content analysis: Similarities and differences', *The Qualitative Report* 19(64), 1–20.

Cockburn, A. & Highsmith, J., 2001, 'Agile software development, the people factor', *Computer* 34(11), 131–133. https://doi.org/10.1109/2.963450

Cohn, M., 2004, *User stories applied: For agile software development*, Pearson Education: Addison-Wesley Professional, Boston, MA.

Conforto, E.C. & Amaral, D.C., 2016, 'Agile project management and stage-gate model – A hybrid framework for technology-based companies', *Journal of Engineering and Technology Management* 40, 1–14. https://doi.org/10.1016/j.jengtecman.2016.02.003

Cooke, J.L., 2014, *Agile productivity unleashed: Proven approaches for achieving real productivity gains in any organization*, 2nd edn., IT Governance Publishing, Cambridge.

Cooper, L.P., 2003, 'A research agenda to reduce risk in new product development through knowledge management: A practitioner perspective', *Journal of Engineering and Technology Management* 20(2), 117–140. https://doi.org/10.1016/S0923-4748(03)00007-9

Corbin, J.M. & Strauss, A., 1990, 'Grounded theory research: Procedures, canons and evaluative criteria', *Qualitative Sociology* 13(1), 3–21. https://doi.org/10.1007/BF00988593

Darke, P., Shanks, G. & Broadbent, M., 1998, 'Successfully completing case study research: Combining rigour, relevance and pragmatism', *Information Systems Journal* 8(4), 273–289. https://doi.org/10.1046/j.1365-2575.1998.00040.x

Dybå, T. & Dingsøyr, T., 2008, 'Empirical studies of agile software development: A systematic review', *Information and Software Technology* 50(9–10), 833–859. https://doi.org/10.1016/j.infsof.2008.01.006

Fowler, M. & Highsmith, J., 2001, 'The agile manifesto', *Software Development* 9(8), 28–35.

Goodpasture, J.C., 2015, *Project management the agile way: Making it work in the enterprise*, 2nd edn., J. Ross Publishing, Fort Lauderdale, FL.

Highsmith, J., 2003, 'Agile project management: Principles and tools', *Cutter Consortium* 4, 1–37.

Hoda, R. & Murugesan, L.K., 2016, 'Multi-level agile project management challenges: A self-organizing team perspective', *Journal of Systems and Software* 117, 245–257. https://doi.org/10.1016/j.jss.2016.02.049

Hoda, R., Noble, J. & Marshall, S., 2008, 'Agile project management', *New Zealand computer science research student conference* 6, 218–221.

Hong, W., Thong, J.Y.L., Chasalow, L.C. & Dhillon, G., 2011, 'User acceptance of agile information systems: A model and empirical test', *Journal of Management Information Systems* 28(1), 235–272. https://doi.org/10.2753/MIS0742-1222280108

Hsieh, H.F. & Shannon, S.E., 2005, 'Three approaches to qualitative content analysis', *Qualitative Health Research* 15(9), 1277–1288. https://doi.org/10.1177/1049732305276687

Karleskey, M., & Voord, M.V., 2008, 'Agile project management (or, Burning Your Gantt Charts)', *Embedded Systems Conference Boston*, Boston, MA, October 26-30, 2008, n.p.

Kniberg, H. & Skarin, M., 2010, *Kanban and Scrum-making the most of both*, C4Media, New York, NY.

Lalsing, V., Kishnah, S. & Pudaruth, S., 2012, 'People factors in agile software development and project management', *International Journal of Software Engineering & Applications* 3(1), 117. https://doi.org/10.5121/ijsea.2012.3109

Lee, S. & Yong, H.S., 2010, 'Distributed agile: Project management in a global environment', *Empirical Software Engineering* 15(2), 204–217. https://doi.org/10.1007/s10664-009-9119-7

Lindvall, M., Muthig, D., Dagnino, A., Wallin, C., Stupperich, M., Kiefer, D., 2004, 'Agile software development in large organizations', *Computer* 37(12), 26–34. https://doi.org/10.1109/MC.2004.231

Merriam, S.B. & Tisdell, E.J., 2015, *Qualitative research: A guide to design and implementation*, John Wiley & Sons, Hoboken, NJ.

Mitchell, R. & Boyle, B., 2010, 'Knowledge creation measurement methods', *Journal of Knowledge Management* 14(1), 67–82. https://doi.org/10.1108/13673271011015570

Moe, N.B., Dingsøyr, T. & Dybå, T., 2009, 'Overcoming barriers to self-management in software teams', *IEEE Software* 26(6), 20–26. https://doi.org/10.1109/MS.2009.182

Nagel, R.N. & Dove, R., 1991, *21st century manufacturing enterprise strategy: An industry-led view*, Diane Publishing, Collingdale, PA.

Neef, D., 2005, 'Managing corporate risk through better knowledge management', *The Learning Organization* 12(2), 112–124. https://doi.org/10.1108/09696470510583502

Nerur, S., Mahapatra, R. & Mangalaraj, G., 2005, 'Challenges of migrating to agile methodologies', *Communications of the ACM* 48(5), 72–78. https://doi.org/10.1145/1060710.1060712

Patel, C. & Ramachandran, M., 2009, 'Agile maturity model (AMM): A software process improvement framework for agile software development practices', *International Journal of Software Engineering* 2(1), 3–28.

Persson, J.S., Mathiassen, L. & Aaen, I., 2012, 'Agile distributed software development: Enacting control through media and context', *Information Systems Journal* 22(6), 411–433. https://doi.org/10.1111/j.1365-2575.2011.00390.x

Rao, K.N., Naidu, G.K. & Chakka, P., 2011, 'A study of the agile software development methods, applicability and implications in industry', *International Journal of Software Engineering and Its Applications* 5(2), 35–45.

Sauer, C. & Reich, B.H., 2009, 'Rethinking IT project management: Evidence of a new mindset and its implications', *International Journal of Project Management* 27, 182–193. https://doi.org/10.1016/j.ijproman.2008.08.003

Savolainen, P., Ahonen, J.J. & Richardson, I., 2012, 'Software development project success and failure from the supplier's perspective: A systematic literature review', *International Journal of Project Management* 30(4), 458–469. https://doi.org/10.1016/j.ijproman.2011.07.002

Schiel, J., 2010, *Enterprise-scale agile software development*, CRC Press, Boca Raton, FL.

Schwaber, K., 2004, *Agile project management with Scrum*, Microsoft Press, Redmond, WA.

Sheffield, J. & Lemétayer J., 2013, 'Factors associated with the software development agility of successful projects', *International Journal of Project Management* 31, 459–472. https://doi.org/10.1016/j.ijproman.2012.09.011

Shongwe, M.M., 2015, 'Knowledge-creation in student software-development teams', *South African Journal of Information Management* 17(1), 1–8. https://doi.org/10.4102/sajim.v17i1.613

Sidky, A., Arthur, J. & Bohner, S., 2007, 'A disciplined approach to adopting agile practices: The agile adoption framework', *Innovations in Systems and Software Engineering : A NASA Journal* 3(3), 203–216. https://doi.org/10.1007/s11334-007-0026-z

Srikantaiah, T.K., Koenig, M.E. & Al-Hawamdeh, S., 2010, *Convergence of project management and knowledge management*, Scarecrow Press, Lanham, MD.

Stavru, S., 2014, 'A critical examination of recent industrial surveys on agile method usage', *Journal of Systems and Software* 94, 87–97. https://doi.org/10.1016/j.jss.2014.03.041

Stettina, C.J. & Hörz J., 2015, 'Agile portfolio management: An empirical perspective on the practice in use', *International Journal of Project Management* 33, 140–152. https://doi.org/10.1016/j.ijproman.2014.03.008

Stoica, M., Mircea, M. & Ghilic-Micu, B., 2013, 'Software development: Agile vs. traditional', *Informatica Economica* 17(4), 64. https://doi.org/10.12948/issn14531305/17.4.2013.06

Terlizzi, M.A., De Souza Meirelles, F. & De Moraes, H.R.O.C., 2016, 'Barriers to the use of an IT project management methodology in a large financial institution', *International Journal of Project Management* 34(3), 467–479. https://doi.org/10.1016/j.ijproman.2015.12.005

The Standish Group International, 2015, *Chaos Manifesto*, viewed 10 November 2016, from https://www.infoq.com/articles/standish-chaos-2015

Vinekar, V., Slinkman, C.W. & Nerur, S., 2006, 'Can agile and traditional systems development approaches coexist? An ambidextrous view', *Information Systems Management* 23(3), 31–42. https://doi.org/10.1201/1078.10580530/46108.23.3.20060601/93705.4

Wilmot, A., 2005, 'Designing sampling strategies for qualitative social research: With particular reference to the Office for National Statistics' Qualitative Respondent Register', *Survey Methodology Bulletin-Office For National Statistics* 56, 53.

Yeo, K.Y., 2002, 'Critical failure factors in information system projects', *International Journal of Project Management* 20, 241–246. https://doi.org/10.1016/S0263-7863(01)00075-8

Zainal, Z., 2007, 'Case study as a research method', *Jurnal Kemanusiaan* 9, 1–6.

The role of information management in project management success: Narratives from entrepreneurs operating within the South African construction industry

Author:
Willie T. Chinyamurindi[1]

Affiliation:
[1]Department of Business Management, University of Fort Hare, South Africa

Corresponding author:
Willie Chinyamurindi,
chinyaz@gmail.com

Background: The South African construction industry is noted to be one of the most popular industries heavily dependent on projects. Calls exist for research that ascertains not just how entrepreneurs act as project managers but also the evaluation of project success and the role information management plays in all this.

Objectives: The aim of this study was to understand the views and experiences of entrepreneurs in how: (1) project management success is conceptualised, and (2) the role that information management played to this within a South African construction industry space.

Method: The study adopts a qualitative research approach using semi-structured interviews to generate narratives and themes around how: (1) project management success is conceptualised, and (2) the role that information management played to this. A sample of 15 entrepreneurs working within the construction industry was used for this study.

Results: Based on the analysis of the narratives of the 15 entrepreneurs, project success was conceptualised mainly along three themes. Firstly, project success was about keeping the customer happy. Secondly, project success in the construction industry meant meeting the set targets, especially those of a financial nature. Finally, project success was about channelling internal synergies to realise external gains. Further, the 15 entrepreneurs espoused one main sub-theme around the role of information management to this conceptualisation of project success. This posits the role of information management to be a currency in effective decision-making.

Conclusion: The study concluded by focusing on the implications and recommendations based on the identified themes.

Introduction

To entrepreneurs and managers, projects potentially play an important role in either the success or failure of their business ventures. Some (e.g. Jansson & Ljung 2013) have even argued for project activity as key in changing organisations. Thus, it becomes imperative not only to study projects as units of analysis but also to manage them, including stakeholder behaviour (Eskerod & Huemann 2013), with the ultimate aim of project success and quests for sustainability (Jansson & Ljung 2013). Further, calls exist for research that seeks to understand the link between project management and entrepreneurship as not only related concepts but also the complexity that characterise both (Hjorth, Holt & Steyaert 2015). Given the existence of such complexity in the two processes (Sergi 2012), there is a need to understand such as a basis for suggesting interventions. However, the journey towards this is somewhat cumbersome. For instance, issues around managing project stakeholder expectations (Baroudi & Rapp 2014), resource challenges (Chang et al. 2010, 2012), capability issues around projects (Crawford, Langston & Barjrachary 2012) and a consensus as to what ensures project success (Shenhar & Dvir 2001) create empirical and practitioner dilemmas.

The management of projects is also argued to be similar and related to the practice of entrepreneurship, united by the performance action in the two disciplines (Lindgren & Packendorff 2003). The active agent of this performative action is the entrepreneur who can also be argued to be a project leader in his or her own right (Flyvbjerg, Landman & Schram 2012). The success of the entrepreneur in projects is influenced by the competition in the environment, and hence, the emphasis on information and its management is essential not just in innovation (Rossi, Vrontis & Thrassou 2012; Jiang, Tao & Santoro 2010) but also performance (De Faria & Mendonca 2011).

As a result of all these, information management is argued to be a potential anchor for an organisation and its business activities (Sequeiraa et al. 2015). Hence, the need to pay attention to those factors that influence project success and also the success of entrepreneurial ventures in which projects can exist (Rossi, Vrontis & Thrassou 2014). Further, the role of agents, such as those managing such entrepreneurial ventures, deserves attention. These agents can be argued to be relevant knowledge assets with the potential of affecting performance through their enactment of decisions (Del Giudice 2011).

This study locates itself within the view that information management, especially in small businesses, is a matter of concern, given the ramifications on both objective and subjective measures of project success (Soto-Acosta, Colomo-Palacious & Popa 2014). Further, given that information management is argued to potentially play a major role in supporting innovation (Dougherty & Dunne 2011), there is a need for a contextual understanding of project management and tenets such as project success (Carvalho, Fleury & Lopes 2013).

Further, there is an acknowledgement from the literature that the success of an entrepreneurial venture (even through its projects) consists of quests for novelty and consistent practices (Blomquist, Hallgren, Nilsson & Soderholm 2010; Drouin, Muller & Sankaran 2013). Key to the success of all these is the value of information management as part of an innovation ecosystem (Adner & Kapeer 2010) that relies on the management of knowledge (Soto-Acosta et al. 2014). Thus, a general research question is proposed: What is the role of information management within project management success from the lens of a sample of entrepreneurs operating within the South African construction industry?

The structure followed in this article is first to put this research into context. Secondly, the theoretical framework underlying this study is presented, leading to the justification of the research question. Thirdly, this is followed by the research design and methodology section. Finally, the results, discussion and a conclusion are presented.

Putting this research into context

One of the significant observations within the South African context is the growth of small, medium and micro enterprises (SMMEs) deemed to be a major driver of the economy (Chimucheka 2014). This realisation of the role of SMMEs has even led to the formation of a new government ministry dedicated to small business development. One of the primary goals of this ministry is to encourage the growth of small businesses, which subsequently has ramifications on the sustained livelihoods of communities. However, small business owners in their entrepreneurial efforts appear to face myriad challenges that impact not just their growth but also their survival (Chimucheka 2014). A key challenge concerns the management of projects that these entrepreneurs are engaged in within their business entities. The idea here is for quests for projects that are sustainable and hence, calls exist for empirical studies that investigate how this can be done (Gareis, Huemann & Martinuzzi 2013; Silvius & Schipper 2014). Further, the role of information management in achieving project success remains unclear. A process not made easy due to tools such as the Internet often results in information overload amongst decision-makers (Harris et al. 2015; Prytherch 2016). These challenges set the stage for calls in empirical work that explores not just the management of information management (Ajibade 2016; Waldman 2016) but also how this links within project management and specifically project success (Ghasabeh & Chabok 2009).

Theoretical background

Although some possible theories exist to explain the idea of project success, this research adopts a multi-theory perspective in understanding the phenomena under study, rather than focusing on any one theory. Key to this are: (1) stakeholder theory (Freeman 1984), (2) resource-based views (RBV) (Wernerfelt 1984), and (3) the human capital theory (Connor & Becker 1975).

Firstly, stakeholder theory can be an underlying theoretical lens to explain quests for project success. For instance, one important stakeholder and recipient of the end-product can be thought of as the customer. Thus, there is need to strive for customer satisfaction through products and services supplied to meet 'expectations' (Kruger, Ramphal & Maritz 2013). In this quest, project success can be conceptualised as meeting the goal set for the entrepreneur by the client who is a customer with needs (Gareis et al. 2013). To this end, information becomes the currency that allows for this to happen (Erasmus, Strydom & Rudansky-Kloppers 2013). There is thus need for quality information that is not only relevant but also on time as a basis for project success (Kruger et al. 2013). Therefore, value, as proposed by Freeman (1984), is in the perspective of the stakeholder and meeting any expectations they may have.

Conversely, another theoretical lens considered from the economics and strategic management disciplines is the RBV of the firm (Grant & Jordan 2015). In essence, what makes a business entity successful also depends on its competitive advantage, uniqueness and ability (Wernerfelt 1984). Thus, an organisation's strategic possessions have the potential to determine project success. Information management within such a context has been found to be a potential determinant of success and the enactment of strategic decisions (Chinyamurindi 2016a). Further, the traditional barometers of project success such as cost, time and scope can be integrated with the internal resources to create value (Ali & Kamaruzzaman 2010). Related to the RBV is the idea of dynamic capabilities that positions how an organisation organises and manages resources and processes to attain a goal (Wernerfelt 1984). Information management within such a process is crucial as there are quests for information that are not only grounded and supported by internal structures but also channelled resources towards success (Grant & Jordan 2015).

Finally, given that the scope of this work is within the entrepreneurship field, the human capital theory is considered. Within this, the entrepreneur is argued to have knowledge and competencies that can affect their venture's effectiveness (Connor & Becker 1975), thus positioning these entrepreneurial pursuits to be crucial for the success of activities and projects (Mueller, Volery & Von Siemens 2012). Therefore, the success of projects can be argued to agentic and dependent on the entrepreneur with aspects such as their experience, knowledge, capability and drive being deemed fundamental to project success (Golini, Kalchschmidt & Landoni 2015). Information management here is also considered to be essential as the entrepreneur is viewed to be an innovator who relies on and manages information to introduce new processes or products (Deakins & Freel 2009).

Determinants of project success and role of information management

There appears to be no agreed measure of project success in general. Emuzei and Smallwood (2011) cite the challenge of quality as affecting the construction industry and hence, benchmarks of success should be based on improving quality. Patrick (2004) attributes project success to be consistent with the delivery of an end-product at the right time, costed properly and with emphasis on quality. Conversely, Ali and Kamaruzzaman (2010) narrow it to four issues as vital to project success: scope, cost, time and quality. Further, Ncwadi and Dangalazana (2006) advise that the success of the South African construction industry is dependent on addressing issues of productivity and quality problems that are significant challenges to the sector. Those engaged in such projects should meet the needs of the client (diverse as they may be) and their specifications (Battikha 2002; Yang et al. 2011).

Others take a different approach to measuring project success and concentrate more on the stakeholder. For instance, various scholars (e.g. Richard et al. 2009; Waddock & Graves 1997) found success to be a situation when a stakeholder is satisfied. Information management within such a setting is viewed to be vital in not only organisational effectiveness but also meeting stakeholder needs (Santos & Brito 2012). An essential aspect of information management here is information and communication technology systems (Prajogo & Olhager 2012) as they can serve an information storage role and also one of analysis and evaluation (Uwizeyemungu & Raymond 2009).

This study is located within the South African construction industry. Internationally, the construction industry is characterised by accelerated growth because of demand for housing as a basic necessity in life, especially in developing countries (Lepatner 2007). In South Africa, the construction industry is one of the fastest growing industries (Mofokeng 2012) although characterised by skilled workers (Human 2006). Notably, the construction industry is heavily dependent on projects as a modality of work (Mofokeng 2012).

In the construction industry, information management can be argued to be crucial, given three main reasons. Firstly, construction projects by nature are dependent on information because of the need for compliance, not just to stakeholder requirements but also to legislative frameworks (Emuzei & Mhlwa 2015). This potentially places cadence on how issues around project success are arrived at and also how information (and the management of it) can be a useful currency. Secondly, the construction industry is competitively intense both locally and internationally (Emuzei & Mhlwa 2015). Within such a context, there is a constant need to benchmark local performance to international standards as a way to solve challenges (Emuzei & Smallwood 2011) and be competitive (Oakland & Marosszeky 2005). Studies that investigate how project success happens (including the role of information management) in such competitively intense industries provide a useful springboard to constantly improve not just the financial performance but also sustainability issues in such industries.

Within the Information Systems (IS) and management disciplines, the construction industry has been the subject of empirical attention. Kelleger (2007) investigated the issues of information security within the construction industry using a sample of contractors. Another stream of work (e.g. Azzar & Karam 2003; Ozumba & Shakantu 2013) within the South African construction industry is around the adoption of information and communication technologies. This research differs from the identified studies within the IS and information management disciplines by seeking to understand how project management success is conceptualised, including the role of information management in arriving at this. This appears to be an empirical gap that has not yet been filled within the South African construction industry.

Research methodology

The study lends to the interpretivist paradigm of thinking (Creswell & Clark 2011), with the aim of understanding the experiences of entrepreneurs (as individual actors) in their practice within the construction industry. Within this, the qualitative approach is adopted to collect information about the individual experience and deduce how these individuals infer meaning based on this experience (Thanh & Thanh 2015). In essence, interpretivism as a philosophy and the qualitative approach were used as they provided deeper insights into the issues under investigation (Creswell & Clark 2011). This is also an argument made (e.g. Konstantinou & Müller 2016) for the need to use more interpretivist approaches both in the disciplines of project management and entrepreneurship, moving away from the dominant positivist and quantitative inclination usually adopted.

Data collection

Given the proposed aims of this study, semi-structured interviews were used as a data collection tool. Such interviews allowed for the opportunity to follow a predetermined structure from which all participants had the opportunity to answer the same questions (Deschambault 2011). The duration of these interviews ranged from 45 to 60 min and were all conducted on the entrepreneurs' premises by appointment over an 8-month period. Ethical clearance was also applied for with the participating institution where the researcher was based. A total of 15 entrepreneurs all operating in the construction industry were interviewed (see Table 1). A purposive sampling approach was adopted (Ritchie et al. 2013) in which the researcher made a deliberate attempt to select participants based on set criteria (Yin 2014). According to Patton (1991), within purposive sampling, a researcher can use the snowball technique. In this study, the researcher relied on existing relationships that may exist between small businesses:

- operating within the Buffalo City Metropolitan Municipality
- operating for a period of 1–5 years since inception
- operating within the construction industry.

Data analysis

All interviews were recorded, and permission was sought from the participating entrepreneurs. As a standard rule, all entrepreneurs were informed that no identifying information was to be made available to them or their firms, hence the use of pseudonyms. Recordings were then transcribed verbatim within 24 h of the interviews being conducted. A qualitative analysis software, QSR International NVivo 9, was used for the purpose of data analysis and data management. Further, a means of data analysis adopted in previous studies was used (e.g. Chinyamurindi 2012, 2016a, 2016b) based on the three levels of meaning-making.

TABLE 1: Participant characteristics.

Entrepreneur (n = 15)	Details of company
Sipho†,‡	Project management firm that does costing for construction projects.
Gift†,‡	Construction company with a special focus on equipment procurement.
Zola†,‡	Construction company with an emphasis on engineering consulting in the Eastern Cape Province of South Africa.
Mary†,§	Compliance and legal advice company.
Sivuyile†,§	Construction and renovation company with leading government departments.
Tshepo†,‡	Construction company with a special focus on equipment procurement.
Nwabisa†,§	Project management firm that does costing for construction projects.
Anele†,‡	Construction engineering company.
Thabs†,§	Construction and infrastructure services company.
Thulani†,‡	Construction engineering company.
Zikhona†,§	Civil and construction services company.
Kwanele†,‡	Project management firm that does costing for construction projects.
Jeremy†,‡	Construction engineering company.
Vuyo†,§	Construction company specialising in social housing projects.
Babalwa†,§	Independent construction consultant and owner of a building evaluation company.

†, Pseudonym; ‡, Male participant; §, Female participant.

Level 1 was helpful in developing a good understanding of the experiences (positive and negative) of entrepreneurs in the projects they engaged in. Further, the role of information management in such experiences was also analysed within this level through analysing each entrepreneur's story. To achieve this, transcripts were read and reread with the research, constantly referring to audio recordings as an information source. This process allowed for the identification of 'markers' in the stories (McCormack 2000:221) and answered questions about each interview, such as 'What kind of story is this?' (Thornhill, Clare & May 2004:188).

Level 2 was achieved through classifying responses from participants into meaningful categories (Nachmias & Nachmias 1996); the categories thus offered a basis to learn more not only about each story but also about the responses as a collective. The final stage consisted of the process of analysing the content extrapolated and generating a narrative through personal accounts, anecdotes and themes (McCormack 2000). The quotes had to be consistent across all the generated stories as prescribed by the literature (Rhodes 2000). Table 2 presents a summary of this data analysis process.

To ensure data credibility and integrity, some steps were taken as suggested from the literature (e.g. Rubin & Rubin 2012). Firstly, a pilot study was conducted on a sample of three entrepreneurs (non-participating). The pilot study offered an opportunity for the researchers to familiarise themselves with nuances around conducting the research in preparation for the main study. Further, during the period of conducting the interviews, the researcher ensured that all interviews were not only recorded but also transcribed within 24 h of data collection. After this, participants were emailed copies of their interviews to verify whether they were a true account of what was stated during the interview. Finally, comprehensive notes as diary entries were also taken as part of the data collection process (Nicholl 2010).

Based on the narratives of the 15 entrepreneurs and the data analysis conducted, the following three main themes emerged:

- Project success as a quest for capitalising on internal and external pursuits.
- Information management role was centred on improving the decision-making capability of small businesses, and the projects entered into.

TABLE 2: Data analysis: Levels of meaning-making.

Level of meaning-making	Description
1	Each interview is written as a brief vignette. After that, each vignette is then developed into a longer narrative about each participant.
2	Narrative themes are conveyed by participants and their experience of career development. After that, preliminary themes are then compared across participants.
3	An analysis of the themes from cross-case comparison begins and illustrating quotes and stories are used.

Source: McCormack, C., 2000, 'From interview transcript to interpretative story: Part 1. Viewing the transcript through multiple lenses', *Field Methods* 12(4): 282–297. https://doi.org/10.1177/1525822X0001200402

- To achieve this information management role of decision-making (as in finding 2), the small business owners rely on a range of tools and techniques.

Each of these three main themes is presented next, including the codes leading to the themes, illustrating quotes and participant narratives.

Findings

Theme 1: Project success as a quest for capitalising on internal and external pursuits

Project success as per the framing of the participants was conceptualised, seeking a balance between internal and external pursuits. Mainly, internal efforts revolved around the channelling of internal synergies to realise external gains. For instance, this included making sure that processes within the small business run, so these can be realised in outputs such as firm performance. The external pursuits revolved around seeking to keep customers not only happy but also satisfied. Thus, project success in the construction industry as framed by participants of this study was driven by meeting set targets, especially those of a financial nature. Table 3 comprises quotes illustrating this first identified theme.

Linked to the quotes in Table 3 is the story shared by Babalwa (pseudonym) to support the findings as expressed in theme one. Babalwa had worked in the construction space for over 15 years with different reputable local and international firms. She stated:

> 'You see I now own my brand, but for 15 years I slaved for some local and international companies. One thing I have always enjoyed after a successful project, the sweet smell of success. Getting that call from a customer to thank my team and me. There is nothing so satisfying in our industry like that. Now in my practice, I still live by the mantra that the customer is king. Keep them happy, and you will smell success all the time in your projects.' [Babalwa, female, 34 years]

Another interesting participant story was from Mary (pseudonym) who ran a company that assisted players within the construction industry to adhere to compliance issues. About the findings expressed in Theme 1 of this research, the emphasis for Mary was meeting the set financial goals; Mary has set manuals on legal and compliance issues within the construction industry. In her interview, Mary shared:

> 'When I do my training and consultation. I always insist my clientele be aware that the law is meant to be there for a reason. Ultimately, I notice people view legal issues as stopping them from making money, but the reality [is] money made within the remit of the law is good. So one of the measures for success especially on construction projects revolves around making money make sense.' [Mary, female, 33 years]

Finally, a story supporting the first theme found in this research illustrates the quest for internal synergies for external gain as a basis for project success. Tshepo (pseudonym) described internal synergies as a form of 'skeleton' whose aim is not only to 'keep the body upright but also firm'. Tshepo, therefore, places cadence to getting the internal issues right first and the rest will follow after that (even external success). The second finding of this research centres on reporting the role of information management within project management and how this realises success.

Theme 2: Information management role was centred on improving the decision-making capability of the small business, and the projects entered into

The entrepreneurs participating in this research attributed information management to playing a role in assisting in the making of decisions for not only the project but also the business success. In arriving at this, the entrepreneurs participating in this study cited examples of how this happened. For instance, the management of information was deemed key when faced with issues around making decisions to complex problems that may be presented by an existing new client. The case of Zola seems to illustrate this:

> 'Within our industry how we manage information has a bearing on not just the decisions you make but also issues around success. Clients come to me requesting me to do costing for their construction projects. I must know the regulated costs as dictated by law. All this information must be kept not only safe but also within convenience so decisions can be made when clients come and see you.' [Zola, male, 45 years]

TABLE 3: Project success as a quest for capitalising on internal and external pursuits.

Sub-theme	Main codes generated during analysis	Illustrating quotes
1: Projects' success – Keeping customers happy	• Keeping clients satisfied • Follow-up on clients' needs • Linking needs of the client before and after • Training on managing client-management issues	'The construction industry is really about deliverables, one key person to have in mind all the time is the customer'. Vuyo 'When I started my company, I realised I need to take the time to understand my customers; they determine my success in the end'. Kwanele 'Project success can never be separated from our clientele's needs. If you can deliver at such a level, realise the benefits'. Zikhona
2: Projects' success – Meeting financial targets	• Financial controls • Fiscal discipline • Budget monitoring	'This for me is a difficult thing; I must stay within the budget all the time, but sometimes it's not always easy'. Jeremy 'I just can't blow money on none essentials. Any wasteful expenditure will reflect negatively not just on me but also the team'. Thabs 'You know they say more money more problems. I choose to rethink all this, more money yes please, else I must stay within the budget. That's the target, a difficult moving target sometimes'. Nwabisa
3: Projects' success – Channelling internal synergies to realise external gains	• Investment on machines and resources • Effective human resource management • Making sure internal processes are working • Information gathering and sharing	'I am doing well because I think I can put the right people in my company to do the right things outside. My best workers for the toughest job. The issue is knowing what these guys can do and then place them outside based on their abilities'. Zola 'We realised we needed new digging equipment and decided to invest in this. In the end, what we have internally gives us money. There is no price one can put on the lack of investment especially on machinery in our industry'. Gift

Another utility function of information management in assisting decision-making was to aid the filling in of tender documents and applying for bids. All participants in this study cited being on the lookout for ways to improving their business function through applying for bids. Further, given laws such as Broad-Based Black Economic Empowerment (BBBEE), the participating entrepreneurs cited benefiting from this corrective instrument of law, given the history of the country. One participant, Jeremy, cited his experiences of applying for bids and submitting tender documents and the value of information management in this.

> 'Every Friday we check The Daily Dispatch newspaper to make decisions on the advertised bids and tenders we can or cannot apply for. I guess as I tell my team all the time we need an effective and efficient digital archiving system that allows us to access files that improve our chances of getting tenders or bids.' [Jeremy, male, 52 years]

Figure 1 comprises quotes illustrating the second identified theme.

Participants in the study also cited the value of tools and techniques that help them in improving their information management role (as identified in finding 2), and these form the next and final finding of this study.

Theme 3: Reliance on tools and techniques to assist information management role for project success

The final theme of this study reports on the range of tools and techniques that assists the entrepreneurs in the construction management for project success. Figure 2 reports on the most popular project information management software used by the entrepreneurs in a year cycle (2016). It would appear that the usage of tools and techniques, including project information management software, is justified for one main reason and as found in the themes: to use information management as a currency for effective decision-making.

Ethical consideration

Ethical clearance was applied for with the participating institution where the researcher was based.

Discussion

The aim of this study was to qualitatively explore the role of information management in the project management success, based on the narratives of a sample of entrepreneurs operating within the South African construction industry. Based on the narratives of the 15 entrepreneurs interviewed in this study, the following three main themes emerged:

- Project success as a quest for capitalising on internal and external pursuits.
- Information management role was centred on improving the decision-making capability of the small business, and the projects entered into.
- To achieve this information management role of decision-making (as in finding 2), the small business owners rely on a range of tools and techniques.

With regards to the extant literature, this study through its findings heightens the focus and attention of the value of information management within entrepreneurial projects (Turner & Müller 2003). Further, the study places focus as previous studies have done on the entrepreneur as an agent, in how small businesses can perform for project success (Achman 2011). One way this agentic power happens (as illustrated in this study) is through the decisions made by the entrepreneur (Eskerod & Huemann 2013). Uniquely, the way this happens as illustrated in this study is through the management of information. Such efforts by entrepreneurs in this context are linked to not only the financial performance but also the sustainability of the entrepreneurial venture (Silvius & Schipper 2014). In this study, as also found in previous studies, keeping customers happy while also seeking to perform better in a competitive environment is fundamental for project success (Baroudi & Rapp 2014). In essence, through the first finding, what happens within the

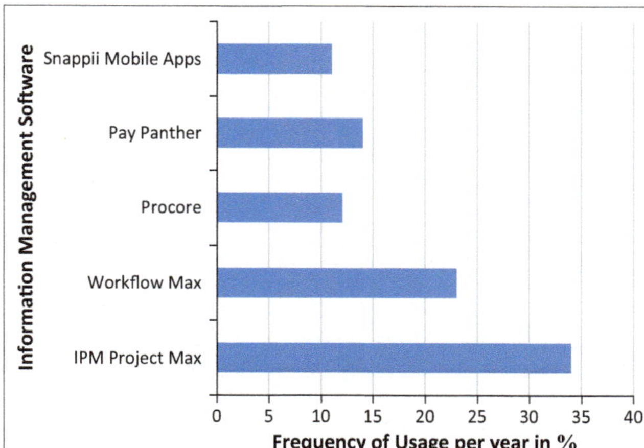

FIGURE 2: Project information management tools, techniques and software used.

Main codes generated during analysis	Illustrating quotes
Basis for planning • Used for costing meetings • Information as a currency • Information decides next move • Information to decide what not to do → Better decision-making	'We work frantically to make sure we have information, not just any information but reliable information. We are as a brand the information we have.'Sipho 'Clients know us for the decisions we make, and these are based on good, sound and financially tested scenarios.'Anele 'Without information management software like Procore, our document audit trail would be a mess. I don't care how expensive the software is. We needed to make good decisions. In the end, this gives us success.'Zola

FIGURE 1: Role of information management in project success.

small business can be a useful precursor to performance outcomes (Crawford et al. 2012).

The study also positions the disciplines of project management and entrepreneurship to be related. In this work, entrepreneurship activities could be framed as projects that position entrepreneurs to be project managers in their own right (Flyvbjerg et al. 2012). Information management can be thought to be a capability that allows the effective functioning of entrepreneurs as project managers. All these, as illustrated in this study, happen in a context driven by hypercompetition (Jiang et al. 2010). Finally, the study gives value to information management as a key anchor to an organisation (Sequeiraa et al. 2015). Notably, information management in project management, especially project management success, is a useful portal to have when making strategic decisions. This study has thus answered calls for empirical work that investigates not just project success but also the success of entrepreneurial ventures in which projects can exist (Rossi et al. 2014). The setting for all these was the construction industry using a sample of entrepreneurs in this industry. The study has contributions that have ramifications for theory, practice and policy. Firstly, calls have been made for more studies that adopt a qualitative focus, especially within the disciplines of project management and entrepreneurship (e.g. Konstantinou & Müller 2016; Thanh & Thanh 2015). This study contributes to the theoretical body of knowledge by not only illustrating the value of the qualitative paradigm but also showing the value of information management within entrepreneurial projects within the construction industry. Secondly, the study and its findings have implications for how practitioners (in this case, entrepreneurs) work within their fields. Practitioners about to enter the construction space, given its popularity in South Africa, can draw a lesson on how to thrive in such a competitive yet lucrative industry. Much can then be done to assist entrepreneurs to improve on how they manage information for the purpose of decision-making. This study heightens focus on improving internal organisational capabilities as they also assist in the use of information for decision-making. A starting premise can be through a personal commitment by the entrepreneurial owners of small businesses to realise that although they may be small, their expansion and growth can be dependent on improving such issues as internal synergies and how information is managed. Finally, policy-makers working in the space of entrepreneurship development can benefit from the findings of this work. Policy-makers cannot only have a deeper understanding of issues that affect entrepreneurs (given their contribution to the economy) but also infuse interventions to assist entrepreneurs.

Limitations

Some limitations exist within this work. Firstly, the study and its findings are in no way generalisable to the entire population of entrepreneurs operating within the construction space in South Africa. Related to this, the sample size used is only of 15 participants and thus, caution should be taken when interpreting the findings. Notably, this work sought to just explore a phenomenon (the conceptualisation of project success in the construction industry and the role of information management). Secondly, even amongst the entrepreneurs used for this study, although all operate in the construction industry, their roles and scope of operation are different. Hence, the diverse viewpoints shared can be a limitation, and an appeal is made to view the findings cautiously. Despite these limitations, the study helped understand the potential linkages that exist between the disciplines of entrepreneurship and project management. In essence, the role of information management in these two disciplines has been argued for as crucial in the making of strategic decisions.

Future research can use a larger sample base that consists of those entrepreneurs who work within the same scope of activity within the construction industry. A triangulation approach can help improve the veracity of this research through using both the quantitative and qualitative research approaches. Because of the way this study was framed, project success appeared to the area of interest. However, future research can investigate experiences of entrepreneurs who may have failed in their projects and draw lessons learnt from this experience. Further, it would be interesting to ascertain the role and approaches adopted even though the projects may have failed. The experiences of project success and failure could be a basis for an interesting comparison. Finally, research could improve this work by comparing the issues addressed between the construction industry and any other industry. Such a comparative approach can be useful to gauge similarities and differences with the view to better understand issues around information management within projects. Further, the study could also benefit from future research in other countries or regions. Again, this can be a useful basis for comparison.

Conclusion

The management of information within entrepreneurial projects has been argued to be an important capability that can determine the success of small business. In achieving this, there is need to continue building on internal and external aspects to the small business as support buffers not just for project success but also for the success of the small business. Within the construction industry as illustrated in this study, this can be possible. However, emphasis should be on making sure that there is a commitment to solving the issues before the entrepreneur.

Acknowledgements

Competing interests

The author declares that he has no financial or personal relationship(s) that may have inappropriately influenced him in writing this article.

References

Achman, R., 2011, 'Stakeholder's perspectives on sustainable project management', Delft: Unpublished master's thesis, Delft University of Technology.

Adner, R. & Kapoor, R., 2010, 'Value creation in innovation ecosystems: How the structure of technological interdependence affects firm performance in new technology generations', *Strategic Management Journal* 31(3), 306–333. https://doi.org/10.1002/smj.821

Ajibade, P., 2016, 'Validating information sensing in a South African University as an impetus to improved information management practice and performances', *Journal of Social Sciences* 48(3), 225–238.

Ali, A.S. & Kamaruzzaman, S.N., 2010, 'Cost performance for building construction projects in Klang Valley', *Journal of Building Performance* 1(1), 113–116.

Azzar, A. & Karam, A.H., 2003, 'A comparative study: With insight into the use of IT in local architectural practices', in R. Amor (ed.), *Proceeding CIB-W78 International Conference on Information Technology for Construction*, University of Auckland, Auckland, New Zealand, April 23–25, pp. 8–14.

Baroudi, B. & Rapp, R.R., 2014, 'Stakeholder management in disaster restoration projects', *International Journal of Disaster Resilience in the Built Environment* 5(2), 182–193. https://doi.org/10.1108/IJDRBE-07-2012-0021

Battikha, M.G., 2002, 'Quality management practice in highway construction', *International Journal of Quality & Reliability Management* 20(5), 7–9.

Blomquist, T., Hällgren, M., Nilsson, A. & Söderholm, A., 2010, 'Project-as-practice: In search of project management research that matters', *Project Management Journal* 41, 5–16. https://doi.org/10.1002/pmj.20141

Carvalho, M.M., Fleury, A. & Lopes, A.P., 2013, 'An overview of the literature on technology road mapping (TRM): Contributions and trends', *Technological Forecast and Social Change* 80, 1418–1437. https://doi.org/10.1016/j.techfore.2012.11.008

Chang, Y., Wilkinson, S., Potangaroa, R. & Seville, E., 2010, 'Resourcing challenges for post-disaster housing reconstruction: A comparative analysis', *Building Research and Information* 38(3), 247–264. https://doi.org/10.1080/09613211003693945

Chang, Y., Wilkinson, S., Seville, E. & Potangaroa, R., 2012, 'Changes in resource need for post-disaster reconstruction: A longitudinal study in China', *Building Research and Information* 40(3), 327–336. https://doi.org/10.1080/09613218.2012.684867

Chimucheka, T., 2014, 'Entrepreneurship education in South Africa', *Mediterranean Journal of Social Sciences* 5(2), 403–416. https://doi.org/10.5901/mjss.2014.v5n2p403

Chinyamurindi, W.T., 2012, 'Stories of career change amongst distance learners in South Africa', *South African Journal of Human Resource Management* 10(2), 1–11.

Chinyamurindi, W.T., 2016a, 'Using narrative analysis to understand factors influencing career choice amongst a sample of distance learning students in South Africa', *South African Journal of Psychology* 46(3), 390–400. https://doi.org/10.1177/0081246315623662

Chinyamurindi, W.T., 2016b, 'A narrative investigation into the meaning and experience of career success: Perspectives from women participants', *South African Journal of Human Resource Management* 14(1), 1–11. https://doi.org/10.4102/sajhrm.v14i1.659

Connor, P.E. & Becker, B.W., 1975, 'Values and the organisation: Suggestions for research', *Academy of Management Journal* 18, 550–561. https://doi.org/10.2307/255684

Crawford, L., Langston, C. & Bajracharya, B., 2012, 'Building capability for disaster resilience', paper presented at the 28th Annual Conference of Association of Researchers in Construction Management (ARCOM), Edinburgh, Scotland, 3–5 September, 2012.

Creswell, J.W. & Clark, V.L., 2011, *Designing and conducting mixed methods research*, 2nd edn., Sage, London.

De Faria, P. & Mendonça, J., 2011, 'Innovation strategy by firms: Do innovative firms grow more?', *International Journal of Entrepreneurship and Small Business* 12(2), 173–184. https://doi.org/10.1504/IJESB.2011.038535

Deakins, D. & Freel, M., 2009, *Entrepreneurship and small firms*, 5th edn., McGraw-Hill, London.

Del Giudice, M., 2011, 'Knowledge management and family business', in M. Del Giudice, M.R. Della Peruta & E.G. Carayannis (eds.), *Knowledge and the family business* (pp. 11–46), Springer, New York.

Deschambault, R., 2011, 'From "analystci nuisance" to interactional resource: Re-viewing small stories within interviews in mixed methods', *Journal of Pragmatics* 43(12), 3080–3090. https://doi.org/10.1016/j.pragma.2011.03.013

Dougherty, D. & Dunne, D.D., 2011, 'Organizing ecologies of complex innovation', *Organization Science* 22(5), 1214–1223. https://doi.org/10.1287/orsc.1100.0605

Drouin, N., Müller, R. & Sankaran, S., 2013, *Novel approaches to organizational project management research*, Copenhagen Business School Press, Copenhagen.

Emuzei, F.A. & Mhlwa, C., 2015, 'Managing quality on construction sites in South Africa: An Eastern Cape study', *Journal of Construction Project Management and Innovation* 5(2), 1224–1237.

Emuzei, F.A. & Smallwood, J.J., 2011, 'Construction industry development: A South African perspective', in *Proceedings of the 2011 CIB-W107-Construction in Developing Countries International Conference*, November 1–3, Hanoi, Vietnam, pp. 109–113.

Erasmus, B.J., Strydom, J.W. & Rudansky-Kloppers, S., 2013, *Introduction to business management*, Oxford University Press, Cape Town.

Eskerod, P. & Huemann, M., 2013, 'Sustainable development and project stakeholder management: What standards say', *International Journal of Management Project and Business* 6(1), 36–50. https://doi.org/10.1108/17538371311291017

Flyvbjerg, B., Landman, T. & Schram, S. (eds.), 2012, *Real social science: Applied phronesis*, Cambridge University Press, Cambridge, UK.

Freeman, R.E., 1984, *Strategic management: A stakeholders approach*, Pitman, Boston.

Gareis, R., Huemann, M. & Martinuzzi, A., 2013, *Project management & sustainable development principles*, Project Management Institute, New-town Square, PA.

Ghasabeh, M.S. & Chabok, K.K., 2009, 'Generic project success and project management success criteria and factors: Literature review and survey', *WSEAS Transactions on Business and Economics* 6(8), 456–468.

Golini, R., Kalchschmidt, M. & Landoni, P., 2015, 'Adoption of project management practices: The impact on international development projects of non-governmental organizations', *International Journal of Project Management* 33, 650–663. https://doi.org/10.1016/j.ijproman.2014.09.006

Grant, R.M. & Jordan, J.J., 2015, *Foundations of strategy*, 2nd edn., Wiley Press, United Kingdom.

Harris, K.J., Harris, R.B., Carlson, J.R. & Carlson, D.S., 2015, 'Resource loss from technology overload and its impact on work-family conflict: Can leaders help?', *Computers in Human Behavior* 50, 411–417. https://doi.org/10.1016/j.chb.2015.04.023

Hjorth, D., Holt, R. & Steyaert, C., 2015, 'Entrepreneurship and process studies', *International Small Business Journal* 33(6), 599–611. https://doi.org/10.1177/0266242615583566

Human, D., 2006, 'Implementation of affirmative action and Black Economic Empowerment (BEE) in the construction industry', viewed 4 March 2016, from http://www.icoste.org/ASAQS_Human.pdf

Jansson, T. & Ljung, L., 2013, 'Strategic project archetypes for effective project steering', *Procedia-Social and Behavioral Sciences* 74, 112–122. https://doi.org/10.1016/j.sbspro.2013.03.042

Jiang R.J., Tao, Q.T & Santoro, M.D., 2010, 'Alliance portfolio diversity and firm performance', *Strategic Management Journal* 31, 1136–1144. https://doi.org/10.1002/smj.869

Kelleger, K., 2007, 'Construction equipment theft a "low risk" gamble', *Journal of Commerce*, viewed 23 February 2016, from http://www.journalofcommerce.com/article/id23659

Konstantinou, E. & Müller, R., 2016, 'The role of philosophy in project management', *Project Management Journal* 47(2), 3–5.

Kruger, D., Ramphal, R. & Maritz, M., 2013, *Operations management*, 3rd edn., Oxford University Press, Cape Town, Southern Africa.

Lepatner, B., 2007, *Broken buildings, busted budgets: How to fix America's trillion dollar construction industry*, University of Chicago, New York.

Lindgren, M. & Packendorff, M., 2003, 'A project-based view of entrepreneurship: Towards action-orientation, seriality and collectivity', in C. Steyaert & D. Hjorth (eds.), *New movements in entrepreneurship*, Edward Elgar, Cheltenham, pp. 86–102.

McCormack, C., 2000, 'From interview transcript to interpretative story: Part 1. Viewing the transcript through multiple lenses', *Field Methods* 12(4): 282–297. https://doi.org/10.1177/1525822X0001200402

Mofokeng, T.G., 2012, 'Assessment of the causes of failure among small and medium sized construction companies in the Free State Province', Doctoral dissertation, University of Johannesburg, South Africa.

Mueller, S., Volery, T. & Von Siemens, B., 2012, 'What do entrepreneurs actually do? An observational study of entrepreneurs' everyday behavior in the start-up and growth stages', *Entrepreneurship Theory and Practice* 36(5): 995–1017. https://doi.org/10.1111/j.1540-6520.2012.00538.x

Nachmias, F.C. & Nachmias, D., 1996, *Research methods in the social sciences*, 5th edn, Worth Publishers, New York.

Ncwadi, M.R. & Dangalazana, T., 2006, 'An analysis of the challenges facing emerging contractors in the Nelson Mandela Metropolis', *Africa Insight* 36(3/4), 189–194.

Nicholl, H., 2010, 'Diaries as a method of data collection in research', *Paediatric Nursing* 22(7), 16–20. https://doi.org/10.7748/paed.22.7.16.s25

Oakland, J.J. & Marosszeky, M., 2005, *Total quality in construction supply chain*, 1st edn., Routledge, New York.

Ozumba, A.O.U. & Shakantu, W.M.W., 2013, 'Investigating barriers to ICT adoption in site management: A pilot study in South Africa', in *Proceedings, RICS COBRA 2013 Conference*, New Delhi, India, Royal Institute of Chartered Surveyors, September 11–13, 2013, pp. 7–18.

Patrick, C., 2004, *Construction project planning and scheduling*, 1st edn., Pearson Education, Upper Saddle River, NJ.

Patton, M.Q., 1991, 'Towards utility in reviews of multivocal literatures', *Review of Educational Research* 61(3), 287–292. https://doi.org/10.3102/00346543061003287

Prajogo, D. & Olhager, J., 2012, 'Supply chain integration and performance: The effects of long-term relationships, information technology and sharing, and logistics integration', *International Journal of Production Economics* 135(1), 514–522. https://doi.org/10.1016/j.ijpe.2011.09.001

Prytherch, R., 2016, *Harrod's librarians' glossary and reference book: A directory of over 10,200 terms, organizations, projects and acronyms in the areas of information management, library science, publishing and archive management*, Routledge, New York.

Rhodes, H., 2000, *Mid-life career change to home-based self-employment in a group of women*, Unpublished master's dissertation, Simon Fraser University, British Columbia, Canada.

Richard, P.J., Devinney, T.M., Yip, G.S. & Johnson, G., 2009, 'Measuring organisational performance: Towards methodological best practice', *Journal of Management* 35(3), 718–804. https://doi.org/10.1177/0149206308330560

Ritchie, J., Lewis, J., Nicholls, C.M. & Ormston, R., 2013, *Qualitative research practice: A guide for social science students & researcher*, Sage Publications, Thousand Oaks, CA.

Rossi, M., Vrontis, D. & Thrassou, A., 2012, 'Wine business in a changing competitive environment-strategic and financial choices of Campania wine firms', *International Journal of Business and Globalisation* 8(1), 112–130. https://doi.org/10.1504/IJBG.2012.043975

Rossi, M., Vrontis, D. & Thrassou, A., 2014, 'Agro business in a changing competitive environment-Campania firms' strategic, marketing and financial choices', *World Review of Entrepreneurship, Management and Sustainable Development* 10(2–3), 312–333.

Rubin, H.J. & Rubin, I.S., 2012, *Qualitative interviewing: The art of hearing data*, 3rd edn., Sage, Thousand Oaks, CA.

Santos, J.B. & Brito, L.A.L., 2012, 'Toward a subjective measurement model for firm performance', *BAR, Rio de Janeiro* 9(6), 95–117.

Sequeiraa, F.R., Frantzb, R.Z., Yevseyevac, I., Emmerichd, M.T.M. & Basto-Fernandese, V., 2015, 'An EAI based integration solution for science and research outcomes information management', *Procedia Computer Science* 64, 894–901. https://doi.org/10.1016/j.procs.2015.08.604

Sergi, V., 2012, 'Bounded becoming: Insights from understanding projects in situation', *International Journal of Managing Projects in Business* 5(3), 345–363. https://doi.org/10.1108/17538371211235263

Shenhar, A.J., Dvir, D., Levy, O. & Maltz, A.C., 2001, 'Project success: A multidimensional strategic concept', *Long Range Planning* 34, 699–725. https://doi.org/10.1016/S0024-6301(01)00097-8

Silvius, A.J.G. & Schipper, R., 2014, 'Sustainability in project management: A literature review and impact analyses', *Social Business* 4(1), 63–96. https://doi.org/10.1362/204440814X13948909253866

Soto-Acosta, P., Colomo-Palacios, R. & Popa, S., 2014, 'Web knowledge sharing and its effect on innovation: An empirical investigation in SMEs. Knowledge management', *Research & Practice* 12(1), 103–113. https://doi.org/10.1057/kmrp.2013.31

Thanh, C.N. & Thanh, T.T., 2015, 'The interconnection between interpretivist paradigm and qualitative methods in education', *American Journal of Educational Science* 1(2), 27–27.

Thornhill, H., Clare, L. & May, R., 2004, 'Escape, enlightenment and endurance: Narratives of recovery from psychosis', *Anthropology and Medicine* 11, 181–199. https://doi.org/10.1080/13648470410001678677

Turner, J.R. & Müller, R., 2003, 'On the nature of the project as a temporary organization', *International Journal of Project Management* 21(1), 1–8. https://doi.org/10.1016/S0263-7863(02)00020-0

Uwizeyemungu, S. & Raymond, L., 2009, 'Exploring an alternative method of evaluating the effects of ERP: A multiple case study', *Journal of Information Technology* 24, 251–268. https://doi.org/10.1057/jit.2008.20

Waddock, S.A. & Graves, S.B., 1997, 'Quality of management and quality of stakeholder relations', *Business and Society* 36(3), 250–279. https://doi.org/10.1177/000765039703600303

Waldman, W., 2016, 'The applications of information technology to the human services: Challenges and opportunities', *Human Service Organizations: Management, Leadership and Governance* 40(5), 441–443. https://doi.org/10.1080/23303131.2016.1165049

Wernerfelt, B., 1984, 'A resource-based view of the firm', *Strategic Management Journal* 5(2), 171–180. https://doi.org/10.1002/smj.4250050207

Yang, J., Shen, Q., Ho, M., Drew, D. & Xue, X., 2011, 'Stakeholder management in construction: An empirical study to address research gaps in previous studies', *International Journal of Civil Engineering and Management* 15(4), 337–340. https://doi.org/10.3846/1392-3730.2009.15.337-348

Yin, R.K., 2014, *Case study research design and methods*, 5th edn., Sage Publications, Thousand Oaks, CA.

20

A knowledge sharing framework in the South African public sector

Author:
Peter L. Mkhize[1]

Affiliation:
[1]School of Computing, University of South Africa, South Africa

Correspondence to:
Peter Mkhize

Email:
mkhizpl@unisa.ac.za

Postal address:
PO Box 392, UNISA 0003, Pretoria, South Africa

In the knowledge economy, organisations are shifting their investment focus to intellectual capital in order to sustain a competitive advantage in the global marketplace. Organisational survival is increasingly dependent on the organisation's ability to create and distribute knowledge that contributes to the improvement of performance. The purpose of this article is to evaluate individual knowledge-acquisition and sharing practices in the South African public sector. I applied the techniques of grounded theory analysis to extract themes from data that could provide insight into the knowledge sharing that takes place in the South African public sector. Findings revealed that the informal sharing of knowledge takes place in discussion forums within communities of practice through web-based, socially orientated platforms. These communities of practice are widespread throughout the public sector and are established with the purpose of soliciting expert knowledge from those who have been using open-source software successfully.

Introduction

Innovation and change in an organisation bring about a need to upskill employees in order to keep up with new organisational demands. In the knowledge economy, efficiency and effectiveness are dependent on the organisation's ability to adapt to rapid technological changes. According to Acton and Golden (2003), organisations need to focus on improving their knowledge-acquisition strategy because skills and knowledge become obsolete quickly.

Durst and Wilhelm (2012) assert that knowledge is increasingly becoming a crucial asset for organisations – unlike in the industrial age, where machinery was the most important asset. According to Pacharapha (2012), knowledge resides with individuals in the organisation and becomes an instrument for process improvement whereby processes become more efficient and effective. Knowledge kept in the individual's mind does not contribute to organisational success if it is not shared by other employees within the organisation. In this article, the researcher investigates some of the knowledge sharing practices in the South African public sector.

Problem statement

Existing skills-training mechanisms are either not used optimally or are failing altogether (Statistics South Africa 2010). Pacharapha (2012) suggests that some individuals in the workforce possess knowledge which could be useful in the improvement of service delivery. Skills transfer from the individuals who have such skills to other employees organisation-wide entails a challenge. Individuals' knowledge does not help the public sector because it could be lost if such individuals leave the organisation through death, retirement or resignation.

The diffusion of knowledge through social media is growing fast in South Africa and other African countries (World Wide Worx 2012). In South Africa, many people have widely adopted social media for social interaction. World Wide Worx (2014) reports show that social media and instant messaging usage has grown exponentially in South Africa, mentioning one of the fastest growing mobile applications such as WhatsApp. Its usage is expected to grow to 63% amongst adults within a year from the date of the report. Despite diffusion through social media, which enables instant collaboration at a minimal cost, social media are not used to facilitate knowledge sharing in the workplace. In this study, the researchers investigate the potential application of social media to share knowledge in the workplace with a specific focus on the biggest employer in the country – the public sector.

Knowledge sharing

According to Andreeva and Kianto (2012), organisations in the global knowledge economy depend on the ability to acquire and share knowledge in order to gain a competitive advantage. In an organisation, there could be individuals who possess valuable knowledge, but individual knowledge is not a competitive advantage for the organisation if it is not shared with other relevant stakeholders (Crane 2012). According to Alavi and Leidner (1999), knowledge sharing enables an entire organisation to gain competitive knowledge and improve its productivity.

Knowledge transfer takes place between individuals and teams (Durst & Wilhem 2012). It could be technical knowledge that is important for functional departments (Mueller 2012). It is imperative to note the fact that every bit of knowledge that could improve business performance is critical, whether it resides within individuals' minds or is shared by teams in departments (Schuima 2012).

Organisations that wish to facilitate knowledge sharing between individuals and teams must be cognisant of the type of knowledge involved. Polanyi (1966) distinguishes between two types of knowledge. The first type is tacit knowledge, characterised by difficulty to articulate and codify. Tacit knowledge is usually acquired through apprenticeship and extended time with experts. Moreover, this type of knowledge is key to the development of competitive advantage as competitors would usually struggle to cope (Nonaka, Von Krogh & Voelpel 2006). Conversely, explicit knowledge, Polanyi's second type of knowledge, is easy to codify and to express in an understandable format. According to Nonaka (1994), this type of knowledge can be expressed through traditional learning methods. It will then be useful to discuss knowledge conversion in the following section by discussing the manipulation of tacit and explicit knowledge.

Knowledge conversion

Nonaka (1994) proposed socialisation, externalisation, combination and internalisation (SECI) as modes of knowledge conversion. These modes are important for organisations that intend to extend their competitive advantage by ensuring that tacit knowledge in the minds of a few is shared within the organisation. Knowledge conversion is important to enable knowledge creation, sharing and retention, especially in the economic sectors that are experiencing a brain drain (Kraak 2004). It is then important to heed Jarrar's (2002) warning that intellectual capital is replacing finance, commodities and natural resources in order to keep up with the rapidly evolving global knowledge economy.

It is important to note that knowledge conversion is also critical as an enabler of dissemination of knowledge within the organisation in order to ensure that tacit knowledge, which resides in the minds of individual employees, can be transferred throughout the organisation (Nonaka & Takeuchi 1995). In line with the SECI modes of knowledge conversion, the public sector needs to create an environment that enables interplay between individuals in the organisations, sharing tacit knowledge through mechanisms such as observation and imitation (Lottering & Dick 2012). According to Martin and Martin (2011), sharing tacit knowledge requires a high level of socialisation that could also involve personal experience and close physical proximity while work is being done. It may even imply building and managing emotional relationships.

Nonaka and Takeuchi (1995) also argue that tacit knowledge can be converted into explicit knowledge through iterative social interaction, and explicit knowledge can be transferred to others in the organisation through a social medium. Explicit knowledge is articulative and can be transferred by electronic media. Meetings and traditional workshops can be used to reconfigure and reconceptualise existing knowledge in the combination mode (Chatti 2012). Externalisation enables articulation of tacit knowledge to explicit knowledge through social interaction (Sowe, Stamelos & Angelis 2008) where individuals involved in the creation of knowledge have to spend extensive amounts of time engaging in mutual interaction (Silva *et al.* 2012). Internalisation, however, relates converting explicit knowledge into tacit knowledge (Wang, Yang & Chou 2008). According to Jeon, Kim and Koh (2011), knowledge sharing initiatives should be organised into communities of practice to create a space where individuals with common interests in the subject matter can interact.

Communities of practice

Balcaen and Hirtz (2007) argue that online-based knowledge sharing promotes critical thinking. Employees participating in online communities have the advantage of engaging the subject of interest critically, especially when they are encouraged to learn independently and work interdependently because they bound by a social contract. Kanuka and Garrison (2004) claim that collaborative, yet reflective, learning has a great potential for facilitating critical thinking, which, in turn, would enable a learning organisation to facilitate the transfer and creation of skills and knowledge. Critical thinking is encouraged within communities of practice as major players in the industry would be able to share insight with employees who also aspire to be experts in their field of interest (Balcaen & Hirtz 2007).

Within a community of practice, knowledge is socially constructed by the group of participants, who weigh each contribution in order to add value to the discussion (Salmon 2002). Each participant in the community of practice is free to make a contribution towards a solution to the problem or to a subject of concern amongst members of the community. Contributors to the discussion and debate become engaged in the debate until consensus is reached, and the agreed solution remains tentative until a better solution comes along (Wenger & Snyder 2000). The facilitator has to be there to ensure that the discussions are not diverted towards the wrong direction and to redirect the discussions, if necessary (Levinsen 2006). In order to realise the success of a community of practice, the sponsor of an online community takes into account participants' demographic characteristics such as culture and economic background. This provides insight into participants' inclinations and preferences so that they can customise knowledge sharing in order to achieve success. Knowledge of participants' demographics can help with initiating collaborative engagement where every member of the community can equally contribute.

Collaborative engagement

Zhu, Valke and Schellens (2009) argue that collaborative engagement is shaped and guided by the fundamentals of the social constructivist paradigm. In this paradigm, collaborative engagement enables the co-creation of knowledge by active participants as they explore the concept of interest (Glover, Hardaker & Xu 2004). Collaborative engagement is carried out through social interaction at group level, based on interdependence between members of the group (Doolan 2013). In the collaborative engagement process, it is imperative that collaborators understand the rules of engagement and the expected outcomes of the process (Bogenrieder & Van Baalen 2007).

According to Glover *et al.* (2004), collaborators are convened for a specific goal, which could be planned or unplanned. It is further mentioned that, in the collaboration process, multiple ideas are presented and explored to create a broader mental model of the concept. This is achieved through mutual engagement of the participant in a coordinated effort (Hudson 2003).

The coordinated effort to combine the knowledge and competencies of a group of people enables concept development. This happens on the condition that individuals in a group engage mutually to achieve a specific goal, and everyone is equally responsible for the activities of creating and sharing knowledge (Doolan 2011). All the participants should understand that they are responsible for the creation and dissemination of knowledge to the entire community of practice.

In an attempt to derive a solution, even partly, to the above research problem, I tried to gain insight from the literature into the importance of knowledge sharing. I also looked at models used to facilitate knowledge sharing within the organisation and between organisations. From the literature, I came to understand the role of collaboration in enabling knowledge sharing within communities of practice. In light of the fact that collaboration thrives on socially orientated media, I went on to conduct empirical research in order better to understand the environment in which public sector employees practise knowledge sharing. I also wanted better to understand the application of social media in facilitating knowledge sharing even if it is not formally institutionalised.

Research questions

In order to achieve the aim of this study, I used the following research questions to provide a guidepost for the subsequent research process:

- What are the key issues that have to be considered in the facilitation of knowledge sharing in the South African public sector?
- How is social media used in the public sector's knowledge sharing practice?
- How do these key constructs interrelate in the design of a knowledge sharing mechanism in the South African public sector?

Research methodology and data analysis

I chose a qualitative approach within the social constructivist paradigm so that I could gain in-depth understanding of the knowledge practice in the workplace. This is in line with the aim to co-create or co-develop a model with the research participants that could provide a solution to some aspects of the problem. Due to the scarcity of literature and theories that specifically address online knowledge sharing in the South African context, I applied the method of grounded theory analysis within a case-study design (Glaser & Strauss 1967).

The unit of analysis is service departments that are actively involved in knowledge sharing practices in the public sector. Even though knowledge sharing practices were not formally institutionalised at the time of collecting data, there were pockets of communities of practice that shared ideas informally, using social media platforms such as blogs and group tweets. A theoretical sample was used to ensure that each participant enrolled for this study has the knowledge required to answer research questions. This was achieved with the help of the gatekeeper who works in the public sector. Sampling also involved elements of the snowballing technique as participants identified each other and then referred the researcher to those they knew had the knowledge required to answer the research questions. A combination of theoretical and snowball sampling processes resulted in the enrolment of 11 participants from the Department of Public Administration. These participants are deployed as training agents in various service departments involved in software migration or are people who required specific knowledge training. Some of the interviews had more than one participant per session, which resulted in seven interview transcripts and policy documents that were used for analysis.

The concept of grounded theory and some of its techniques were used as a framework with which to conduct this research. According to Charmaz (2006), the principles of grounded theory are not prescriptive but provide guidelines for the detailed analysis of qualitative data and the generation of theory. In applying grounded theory, I conducted data collection and analysis concurrently because subsequent interview probing is dependent on the analysis results from the previous interview (Strauss & Corbin 1997).

I developed a case-study protocol, including an interview schedule based on the research questions of the study (Remenyi & Williams 1998). Questions in the interview schedule could be refined from one interview to another as I became more theoretically sensitive (McCallin 2003; McGhee, Marland & Atkinson 2007; Strauss & Corbin 1997). I then applied theoretical sampling to find prospective participants who were more likely to give further information or clarity to the questions which might not have been answered by the initial sample (McCallin 2003). All interviews were transcribed by a qualified transcriber and then uploaded into the qualitative data analysis software, ATLAS.ti.

The techniques of grounded theory analysis were applied by conducting open coding to identify codes as they emerged from data. Codes were extracted from each interview transcript, each representing an attached quotation. A bracketing technique was also used to suppress the researcher's preconceived ideas about the researched subject in the coding process (McGhee *et al.* 2007). Secondly, axial coding was performed in order to categorise emergent codes into families of codes in Atlas. Ti. I then formulated contextual relationships between codes using a relationship network. At this stage of the analysis, I conducted subsequent interviews with new categories in mind. This process was repeated until data saturation was reached. The final stage of analysis was selective coding, which enabled me to formulate conceptual relationship networks between code families in order to create a storyline.

In the discussion of the findings below, I present quotations from transcripts as evidence. In line with Creswell (2007), quotations are presented verbatim in order to honour participants' voices. Some of the quotations may contain grammar errors because they are presented as they were uttered by the participant. In addition to quotations that are used as evidence, I present relationship diagrams that represent a network of codes extracted during the open coding stage.

Discussion of findings

In this section, I present results of the grounded theory analysis by providing a code of networks, depicting relationships with a specific theme. The analysis entails direct quotation from the interview transcripts and the discussions. The networks were formed in the axial coding phase of the analysis. Every code in the network was linked to a quotation. The numbers in each code depict the groundedness of the code and the relationships with other codes in the hermeneutic unit.

Social technology infusion in the public sector

According to my observation, collaborative engagement in the public sector takes place in discussion forums which are based on social technology. In line with Rogers (1995), any technology-enabled initiatives should be introduced with technology-infusion concerns in mind.

Participant 1 revealed that most South African (SA) government departments are engulfed by infrastructural deficiencies. Thus, knowledge sharing practices should be designed to be carried out on a technology platform that is compatible and that could optimally exploit available computing resources. Participant 1 asserts that some departments are trying hard to ensure that the technology resources that are available are used to optimal levels.

P1: 'They get a command they will do this, where you sit about 5 minutes for a screen in the Defence Force you will wait for that screen to come down but with the SAPS that's not the situation so that screen not up for your screen for 15 seconds, they say this useless go away and the same with other students outside your infrastructure is a key constraint'.

P6: 'People resist certain technology because it brings in with it a new strange environment that is not even functioning properly. If you want to introduce people into something new entice them with something good, not too different to what they a familiar with'.

Participant 1 also asserted that infusing technology into the knowledge sharing process could be made easy by introducing

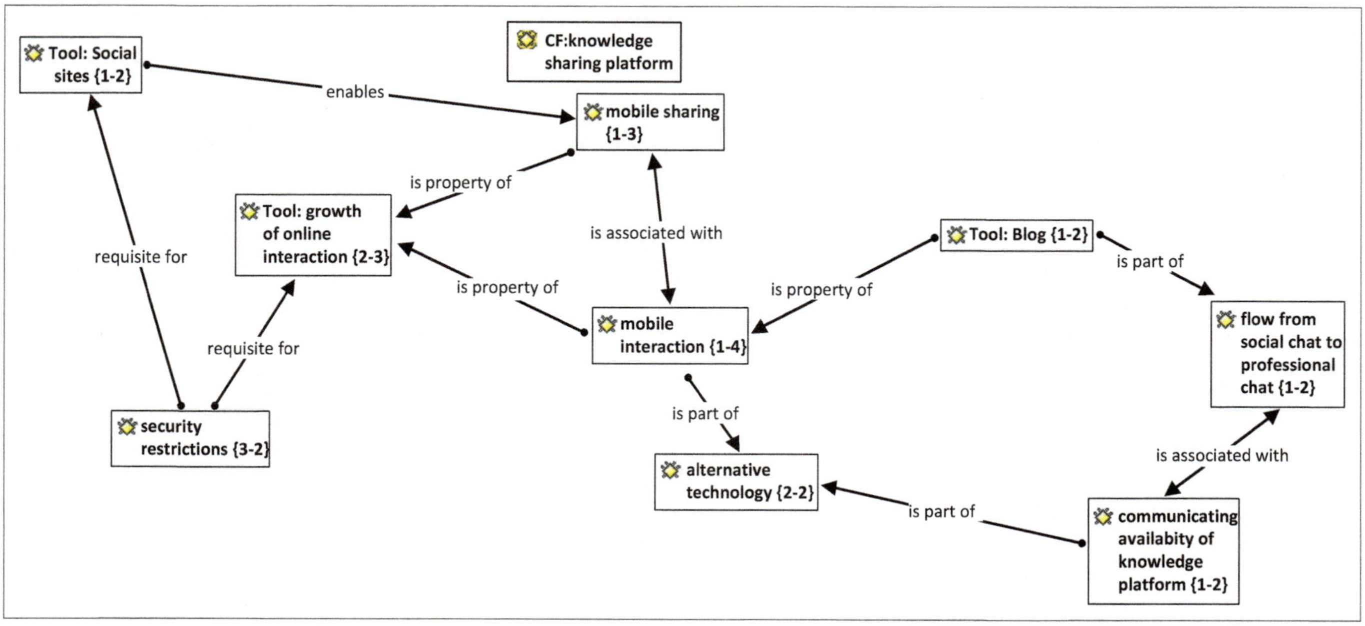

FIGURE 1: Knowledge sharing platform.

it as a social activity. This can be achieved by incorporating social computing concepts during the introduction of technology in the knowledge sharing process. Many social networks such as blogs, Wikis, Facebook and Twitter have gained popularity in many sectors, such as education, and in other private-sector workplaces (World Wide Worx 2012).

Participant 4 argued that social networks should be used as an introductory strategy in the public sector as many employees are already familiar with and using social networks. He also argued that people make meaningful contributions in the social space with respect to social issues. The same principle can be extrapolated to the knowledge sharing environment. Participant 4 also believed that social networks can be used for continuous learning in the workplace where employees can constantly explore new ideas.

> **P4:** 'It's not, you can pinpoint it down as one little tool, it's actually a migration from … networks where 1 person contributes to the content through technology making it available and interactive so that lots of people can contribute to that, people they create their own content and that what Web 2.0 … is, so with this collaboration thing each one of these tools wiki has got certain pros and cons and set application as blog and set applications as social networking so I think what we've seen in the market ... it's got social networking, it's got micro blogging, it's got blogs, it's got Wikis, it's got RSSP's, it's got …, it's got everything, so but on the Internet you could get that is just a blogging tool, it's just wiki tool, ... what's a business problem you want to solve, if you know what a problem is what a problem you want to solve ...'

Social networks are important in facilitating an informal knowledge sharing process. Participant 2 suggested that some artificial intelligence should be built into knowledge sharing platforms such as Wiki and blogs to ensure that the correct content is directed to the appropriate employee. Collaboration in a social space should not be confined to desktop-computer technology but should be extended to mobile technology and other forms of ICT. Therefore, content should be adaptive to different technology platforms such as cellular phones.

> **P1:** 'Adaptation, we need to ... for instance basic one of the ideas being thrown around is M-learning in other words your Mobile Learning, given the fact that the reach of the cell phone is +-90% so if you were to adopt to innovate or use mobile as an alternative or an enhancement to e-learning, that will definitely make a big difference, but trying to get +80% of South Africa to be connected that is more like a dream'.

> **P5:** 'M-learning ... packages that are out there you know about Blackberry and any other phone that is there but firstly the move will be how many people have cell phones in SA for instance, MTN for instance they will say we've got 17.1 million subscribers'.

According to all participants, South Africa is ready to adopt social computing in the workplace. Participants advise that knowledge sharing should be creative. In this process, one should remain aware of the characteristics of the SA workforce such as socio-economic diversity. Such awareness would help in determining the technological platform that can be used for knowledge sharing purposes, and such platform should be accessible to every employee.

Collaborative engagement

Collaboration is gaining popularity in both business and academic institutions where collaborators who share resources or work on the same project can exchange information and ideas in order to co-create solutions to eminent problems and to create knowledge. The sharing of information and ideas could be an interaction between individuals within a community of practice or with individuals from outside of the

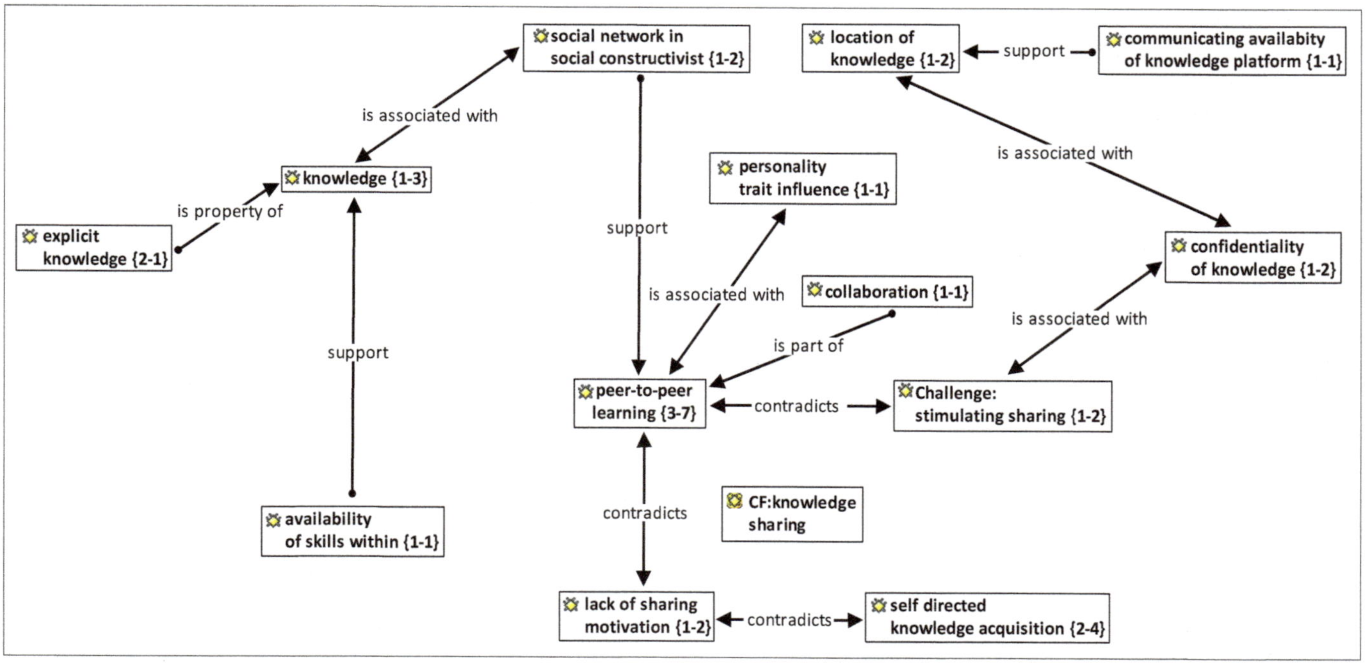

FIGURE 2: Network showing collaborative engagement in the South African public sector.

community (Mkhize, Huisman & Lubbe 2011). Figure 2 shows the network of codes that represent activities involved in the development of collaborative experience in the public sector. Some collaboration is informal and some is well-coordinated, depending on the objectives and resources available to community participants (Allan & Lawless 2005).

Membership of the collaborative forum was by invitation to the qualifying prospective participants, who are expected to make a meaningful contribution to the community. An administrator made a judgement decision about who qualifies to be a participant and then allowed them to join the group that discusses a specific topic regarding a new open-source platform.

> **P4**: 'You might be able to invite external people but then you would qualify them, so in that government-wide collaboration we on the administrator, so I set it up I need to say who's in and who's out and then they would do the same with that'.

The collaboration group sometimes invited subject experts from other collaboration forums by going out of the official government discussion group to find people who may make a major contribution in the current issues of concern. The administrator would even go to the extent of scouting on the social networks to find bloggers who might be experts on a specific subject:

> **P4:** 'Say I was a local developer in SA I would do 1 of 2 things. I would either see if there's existing forums linked in specific groups that are discussing that specific topic, it is possible that those groups won't be focused enough or there might ... but you've got specific needs, what I'll do then is I'll create my own group I'll choose a certain media like I would say I'm going on Facebook or I'm going on this, I would find something that's more like a super cool the kind of personalities that use that, ... I would find something that is suited to my community, having more technical or whatever and then I would start extending that network ... the thinkers in that area and I would extend an invite to that somebody that writing a blog that's ... or start talking to that network and say who are the real experts in open source migration'.

Inviting renowned experts in a certain field allowed the administrator to create a ripple effect by attracting the experts' followers into their discussion forum. Although collaborating groups would need outside experts' contributions to the discussions and debates on issues of concern, it is still important to maintain confidentiality:

> **P4:** 'Think it's just about the confidentiality of the information, say you are in government you typically want to control whoever joins cause you might discuss strategies, communication strategies, things that you want to first vet with different stakeholders before you bring them to the public so in that case you will firstly have the private network'.

As a result, administrators have to be careful in their selection of new members and ensure that confidential information is not openly discussed in the forums. This is to avoid exposure of government's strategies and operational plans.

Participant 5 suggested that a collaborative forum should apply the same model as was applied by early collaborators in government but now with the guidance of an expert to facilitate engagement and debate about topical issues in open-source migration. Through engagement, collaborators would be able to deduce meaning from or come to agreement about new solutions, which could be an extension of existing knowledge. In setting up collaboration, instructional designers can explore the application of technology in facilitating online collaboration. Participant 4 pointed out that Moodle is an effective and efficient collaborative tool for the SITA collaboration group: 'Within Moodle there are some kinds of collaboration or that kind of functionality that you can use and we kinda put them into our project'.

Moodle is an open-source application that can be acquired free of charge. This means easy access and affordability for collaborators. Besides, Moodle incorporates even extended pedagogical features that can be used for the administration and management of the knowledge exchange process.

Instructional designers are facing the task of converting pure collaborative activities into a knowledge transfer mechanism and enabling an environment where knowledge transfer practice can be modelled around the existing collaborative instructional strategy. In doing so, it can ease tensions between management and employees regarding the use of social networks in the office because a formalised collaborative instructional strategy could be institutionalised and then form part of the institutional policy.

Learning by discovery within a community

Some of the participants quoted in the discussion above also mentioned or implied communities of practice (CoP). Figure 3 shows the CoP theme: I shall discuss a concept that seems to be prominent in the transcripts and which is directly related to communities of practice, namely learning by discovery.

Learning by discovery in a community starts with the creation of the community where learners or employees who share common interests converge to discuss critical issues on a specific topic. Participant 4, who administrates the collaboration forum for government collaboration groups, suggested that collaboration should be designed for free social platforms such as Google or any other Web2.0 platform where an instructional designer can create a group that can share text or video files.

The collaborative forum is secured because of the security and confidentiality requirement. Some of the information shared is sensitive in nature, which means that high security measures should take priority over functionality. However, free social networks can be used where security is not a sensitive issue:

> **P4:** 'Start to building that functionality into the tool so whether you in the design of the course or whether you want employees to interact you need to build the social media the social learning at stake as facilitating the process of learning either by using that functionality in the application you use such as Google or just signing up to any free collaboration

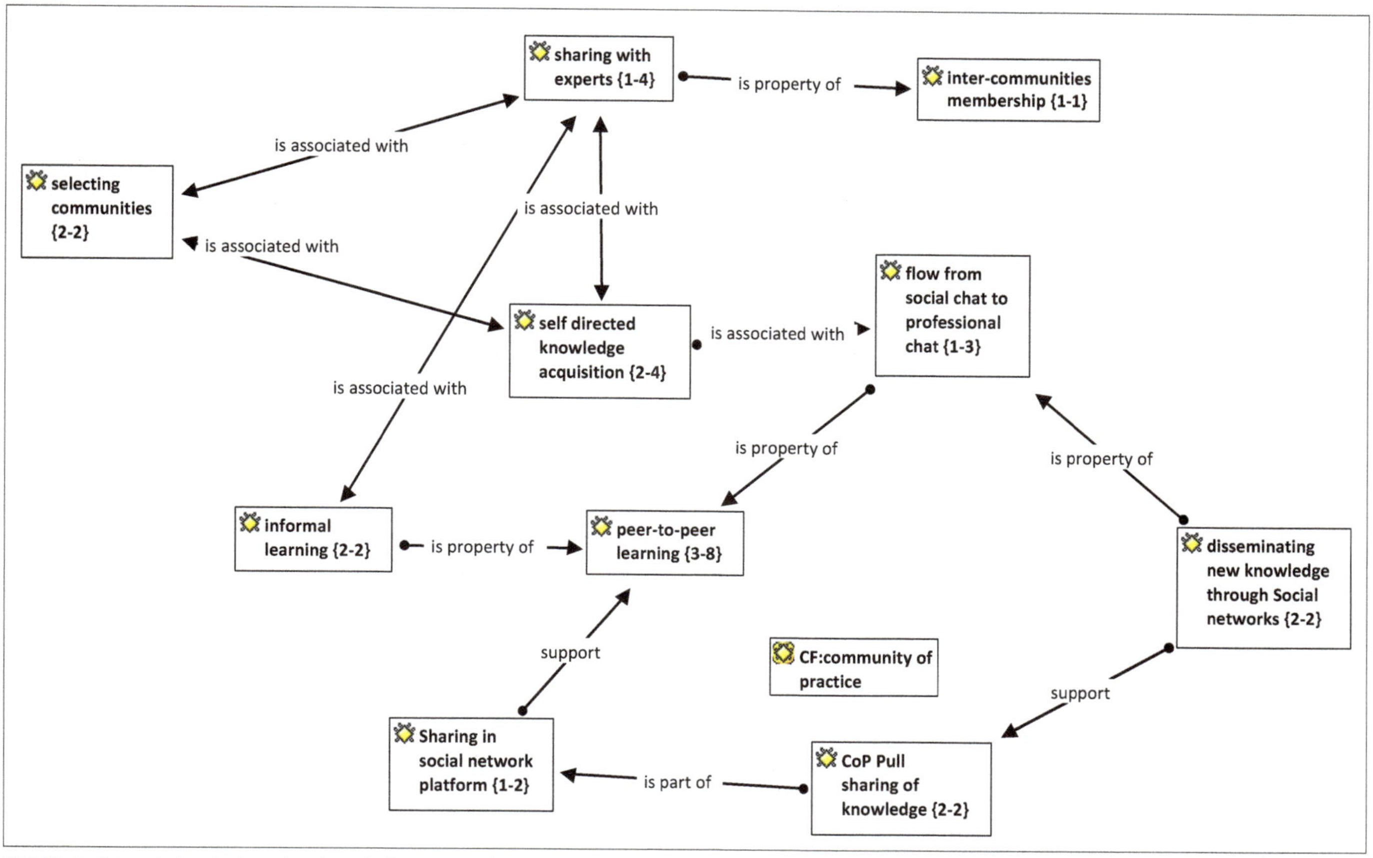

FIGURE 3: Network showing learning through discovery within communities.

tool, create a group then you collaborate so most of these tools they have a model where you can use those functionality for free and those functionalities you can connect with people … which is making sure that if you doing a course for the military then there's specific requirements around security confidentiality, so that's what SITA is doing in this project, we could use social networks or social tools that are on the Internet but because of that requirement we need to have something that can secure on our firewall and the access of control is very strict'.

Once the security requirements have been established in order to create parameters for membership in the collaboration forum, instructional designers have to consider an instructional strategy that is appropriate for the target audience. In line with the collaborative strategy for government's open-source training, a collaborative environment has to be created within a community of practice. Participant 5 thought that social networks represent the most effective platform for collaborative learning within a specialised group, called a community of practice. Interaction within the community can be standardised into specific time intervals, or openness and flexibility:

P5: 'Community of practice would see people who share common interest in a particular field something, they will be able to seat and collaborate, discuss, move forward and look at the development, to me community those are groups … they seat every week or every month or people collaborate through that social platform they are all related and they'll say they also contribute to the management of knowledge and knowledge gathering that can be preserved'.

In these communities, members get to share their experiences and learn from those who have been through the learning curve. That way, members of the community would not have to repeat the same mistakes made by those who have become experts over the years. Less experienced collaborators in the community can learn best practices with regard to a specific trade from more experienced community members without going through trial and error. The sharing of information and knowledge enables all concerned to learn new skills to solve persisting problems:

P4: 'Think the main thing about collaboration in government is the culture is pretty much … so everybody is busy with their own stuff, fighting their own battles and not knowing that another department has maybe kinda a step further in a particular area and they basically got a better solution, so collaboration for us is about creating the tool that can connect these people so that they can form groups, networks of interests and can become aware of other projects, other best practices, other people that have gone through the learning curve, that have got skills'.

A collaborative environment allows for the co-creation of knowledge, based on the collective and agreed interpretation of the studied phenomenon. As members of the community of practice engage one another in a collaborative environment, different forms of expertise interplay into the development of new models that emerge from the convergence of ideas. This is eminent where communities are interlinked in order to engage in issues of common interest, even though communicating individuals might belong to separate communities:

P4: 'Collaboration in terms of the different roles, to ..., and that what's exciting us, getting together to work out a solution for the government we've had architects, we've had business analysts, we've had the now the content developers as where I'm coming from, we've got the technology architects for government and then we've got change managers who are also involved from beginning to end although they are observing what is coming up first more than anything'.

Members of SITA's collaboration group are not restricted to one community of practice: They can join multiple communities of practice. In that way, one can find communities of practice interlinked by dual membership. Those members with dual membership can source some input from peers of the other community where specialised expertise is required to solve a specialised problem – such as that of anti-corruption:

P2: 'More of the discussion forum and semi-informal course that is being run, the course is called anti-corruption, so it's just more of a discussion forum, we calling in experts from time to time to give more information on how to deal with corruption and so on'.

A collaborative environment encourages the exchange of ideas and knowledge amongst learners or employees within a community of practice. This enables learners or employees to learn through discovery. Participants in the knowledge exchange do not have to enrol for a formal classroom course and then expect the lecturer to present learning material to them while they become passive recipients of knowledge. Rather, they actively engage each other on important issues or concepts relating to the current situation, which makes it easier to find direct and relevant solutions.

Proposed framework

Figure 4 shows a proposed framework that could provide conceptual insight into the design and development of a knowledge sharing mechanism in the public sector. It also shows that the knowledge sharing process takes place within the social constructivist paradigm, which means that knowledge is created through social interaction, and everybody involved equally contributes to the creation of knowledge.

The creation and sharing of knowledge in the public sector is facilitated through collaborative engagement that takes place within communities of practice. Subjects of discussion are proposed to the communities, and members of the communities then apply collaborative strategies to openly discuss, analyse and evaluate issues of interest to the community. The process enables learning through discovery as members discover new meanings to current problems. The definition of 'new meaning' is the product of social engagement between the novices and expert employees who openly share knowledge and ideas for the purpose of knowledge development and improving institutional performance.

Knowledge agents in the public sector are already operating within the social constructivist paradigm to allow for social engagement between all parties involved in the knowledge sharing process. They openly debate the extension of their current knowledge as new perspectives emerge from new employees, and both novices and experts learn from one another.

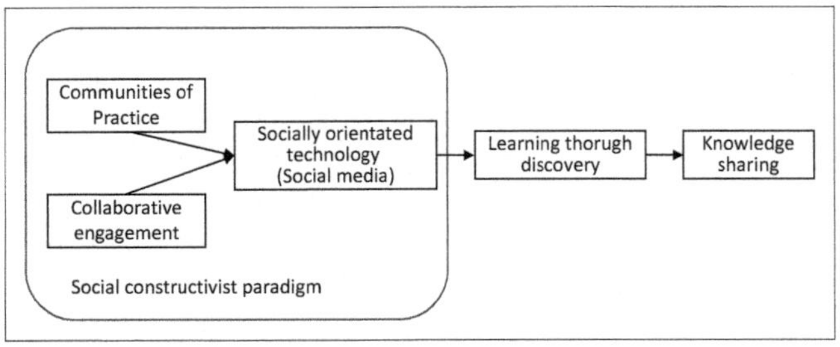

FIGURE 4: Conceptual framework for knowledge transfer in SA public sector.

Contribution of the study

Through this study, I sought to make a theoretical and practical contribution to knowledge sharing practices. In order to eliminate skills challenges, organisations need to create an environment for the instant acquisition of skills. Otherwise, they would miss out on opportunities made possible by the rapidly changing business environment. The rapidity of change in the business environment could be attributed to rapidly changing technology and other factors beyond the control of organisational personnel. However, an organisation such as the public sector can cope with rapid change emanating from both the global and local business environment if personnel could acquire sets of skills required to face changes.

This study also contributes to knowledge practice in the SA public sector by explicating important factors that knowledge agents should take into account when facilitating knowledge sharing initiatives geared towards improved performance (Matlhape & Lessing 2002). Amongst other factors, social media could enable flexible learning, collaborative learning and just-in-time, just-in-context and lifelong learning. Social media could also enhance employees' access to knowledge in already flourishing and easy-to-use technology. This is important for both business practice and academia as the framework above could be applied to provide predictive and explanatory value to the theoretical development of knowledge sharing practices in the South African public sector as the biggest employer in the country. According to Acton and Golden (2003), employees should not dread a knowledge-acquisition initiative but, instead, jubilantly look forward to exciting engagement activities that are made possible by social media.

It is important to note that South Africa and Africa as a whole are said to be engulfed by a digital gap in terms of Internet access and computer literacy (Ziemba, Papaj & Zelazny 2013). However, the social media diffusion in South Africa proves that people do access the Internet and do use computers if they are motivated by social needs, which make a socially orientated platform more attractive as a knowledge sharing platform (Horton & Horton 2003; World Wide Worx 2012; World Wide Worx 2014).

Organisational leaders should start to recognise the impact of social networks, which forms the basis of socially orientated instructional technology as was evident in the London riot of October 2011 where the youth organised themselves, using social media, and brought London to a standstill (Baker 2011; Tonkin, Pfeiffer & Tourte 2012). Socially orientated instructional technology is as powerful in facilitating knowledge sharing in the workplace (World Wide Worx 2014).

Conclusion

This study set out to determine key concepts that have to be considered in the facilitation of a knowledge sharing mechanism in the public sector. The results of the case study revealed that public sector employees are engaging in not-yet institutionalised but effective knowledge sharing initiatives. Amongst the themes that emerged from a grounded theory analysis are the following: collaborative engagement, communities of practice, learning through discovery and the co-creation of meaning. Some of these themes are sub-themes embedded in the themes discussed above.

Despite the existence of comprehensive learning programmes, it is important to formulate guidelines for knowledge sharing that can be transferable to or adapted by different stakeholders in the public sector when knowledge transfer is needed. A limitation to this study is the fact that results cannot be generalised to the entire population because it was a qualitative study. However, the results are transferable to a similar environment (Denzin & Lincoln 2011).

Acknowledgements

Competing interests

The author declares that he has no financial or personal relationships which may have inappropriately influenced him in writing this article.

References

Acton, T. & Golden, W., 2003, 'Training the knowledge worker: A descriptive study of training practices in Irish software companies', *Journal of European Industrial Training* 27(2/3/4), 137–146.

Alavi, M. & Leidner, D.E., 1999, 'Knowledge management systems: Issues, challenges, and benefits', *Communications of Association of Information Systems* 1(7).

Allan, J. & Lawless, N., 2005, 'Learning through online collaboration by SME staff: A scoping investigation into likely team-role stressors', *Education + Training* 47(8/9), 653–664.

Andreeva, T. & Kianto, A., 2012, 'Does knowledge management really matter? Linking knowledge management practices, competitiveness and economic performance', *Journal of Knowledge Management* 16(4), 617–636. http://dx.doi.org/10.1108/13673271211246185

Baker, S.A., 2011, 'The mediated crowd: New social media and new forms of rioting', *Sociological Research Online* 16(4), 21. http://dx.doi.org/10.5153/sro.2553

Balcaen, P. & Hirtz, J., 2007, 'Developing critically thoughtful e-learning communities of practice', *proceedings of the 2nd International Conference on e-Learning*, 27–28 June 2007, University of British Columbia, Canada, p. 11.

Bogenrieder, I. & Van Baalen, P., 2007, 'Contested practice: Multiple inclusion in double-knit organizations', *Journal of Organizational Change Management* 20(4), 579–595. http://dx.doi.org/10.1108/09534810710760090

Charmaz, K., 2006, *Constructing grounded theory: A practical guide through qualitative analysis*, Sage Publications, Thousand Oaks.

Chatti, M.A., 2012, 'Knowledge management: A personal knowledge network perspective', *Journal of Knowledge Management* 16(5), 829–844. http://dx.doi.org/10.1108/13673271211262835

Crane, L., 2012, 'Trust me, I'm an expert: Identity construction and knowledge sharing', *Journal of Knowledge Management* 16(3), 448–460. http://dx.doi.org/10.1108/13673271211238760

Creswell, J.W., 2007, *Qualitative inquiry & research design: Choosing among five approaches*, Sage Publications, Thousand Oaks.

Denzin, N.K. & Lincoln, Y.S., 2011, *The SAGE handbook of qualitative research*, Sage Publications, Thousand Oaks.

Doolan, M.A., 2011, 'Developing a pedagogy: The role of the tutor in enabling student learning through the use of a wiki', *Cutting-edge Technologies in Higher Education* 1, 189–205. http://dx.doi.org/10.1108/S2044-9968(2011)0000001012

Doolan, M.A., 2013, 'A pedagogical framework for collaborative learning in a social blended e-Learning context', *Cutting-edge Technologies in Higher Education* 6, 261–285. http://dx.doi.org/10.1108/S2044-9968(2013)000006G012

Durst, S. & Wilhelm, S., 2012, 'Knowledge management and succession planning in SMEs', *Journal of Knowledge Management* 16(4) 637–646. http://dx.doi.org/10.1108/13673271211246194

Glaser, B.G. & Strauss, A.L., 1967, *The discovery of grounded theory: Strategies for qualitative research*, Aldine de Gruyter, Chicago.

Glover, I., Hardaker, G. & Xu, Z., 2004, 'Collaborative annotation system environment (CASE) for online learning', *Campus-Wide Information Systems* 21(2), 72–80. http://dx.doi.org/10.1108/10650740410529501

Horton, W. & Horton, K., 2003, *E-learning tools and technologies: A consumer's guide for trainers, teachers, educators, and instructional designers*, John Wiley & Sons, Chichester.

Hudson, B., 2003, 'Promoting collaboration in an international online learning community', *Industrial and Commercial Training* 35(3), 88–93. http://dx.doi.org/10.1108/00197850310470294

Jarrar, Y.F., 2002, 'Knowledge management: Learning for organisational experience', *Managerial Auditing Journal* 17(6) 322–328. http://dx.doi.org/10.1108/02686900210434104

Jeon, S., Kim, Y. & Koh, J., 2011, 'Individual, social, and organizational contexts for active knowledge sharing in communities of practice', *Expert Systems with Application* 38, 12423–12431.

Kanuka, H. & Garrison, D.R., 2004, 'Cognitive presence in online learning', *Journal of Computing in Higher Education* 15(2), 21–39. http://dx.doi.org/10.1007/BF02940928

Kraak, A., 2004, *An overview of South African human resources development*, Human Sciences Research Council Press, Cape Town.

Levinsen, K., 2006 'Collaborative on-line teaching: The inevitable path to deep learning and knowledge sharing', *Electronic journal of e-learning* 4(1), 41–48.

Lottering, F. & Dick, A.L., 2012, 'Integrating knowledge seeking into knowledge management models and frameworks', *South African Journal of Information Management* 14(1), 9. http://dx.doi.org/10.4102/sajim.v14i1.515

Martin, E.C. & Martin, N., 2011, 'The role of organisational factors in combating tacit knowledge loss in organisations', *Southern African Business Review* 15(1), 49–69.

Matlhape, M. & Lessing, N., 2002, 'Employees in total quality management', *Acta Commercii* 2, 21–34.

McCallin, A.M., 2003, 'Designing a grounded theory study: Some practicalities', *Nursing in critical care* 8(5), 203–208. http://dx.doi.org/10.1046/j.1362-1017.2003.00033.x

McGhee, G., Marland, G.R. & Atkinson, J., 2007, 'Grounded theory research: Literature reviewing and reflexivity', *Journal of advanced nursing* 60(3), 334–342. http://dx.doi.org/10.1111/j.1365-2648.2007.04436.x

Mkhize, P.L., Huisman, M. & Lubbe, S., 2011, 'Analysis of collaborative learning as prevalent instructional strategy of South African government elearning practices, *proceedings of the 10th European Conference on e-Learning*, University of Brighton, UK, November 10–11, 2011, pp. 492–501.

Mueller, J., 2012, 'Knowledge sharing between project teams and its cultural antecedents', *Journal of Knowledge Management* 16(3), 435–447. http://dx.doi.org/10.1108/13673271211238751

Nonaka, I., 1994, 'A dynamic theory of organizational knowledge creation', *Organizational Science* 5(1), 14–37. http://dx.doi.org/10.1287/orsc.5.1.14

Nonaka, I. & Takeuchi, H., 1995, *The knowledge-creating company: How Japanese companies create the dynamics of innovation*, Oxford University Press, New York.

Nonaka, I., Von Krogh, G. & Voelpel, S., 2006, 'Organizational knowledge creation theory: Evolutionary paths and future advances', *Organization Studies* 27, 1179. http://dx.doi.org/10.1177/0170840606066312

Pacharapha, T., 2012, 'Knowledge acquisition: The roles of perceived value of knowledge content and source', *Journal of Knowledge Management* 16(5), 724–739. http://dx.doi.org/10.1108/13673271211262772

Polanyi, M., 1966, *The tacit dimension*, Routledge and Kegan, London.

Remenyi, D. & Williams, B., 1998, *Doing research in business and management: An introduction to process and method*, Sage Publications, London. http://dx.doi.org/10.4135/9781446280416

Rogers, E.M., 1995, *Diffusion of innovation*, Free Press, New York.

Salmon, G., 2002, *E-tivities: The key to active online learning*, Routledge Falmer, London.

Schuima, G., 2012, 'Managing knowledge for business performance improvement', *Journal of Knowledge Management* 16(4), 515–522. http://dx.doi.org/10.1108/13673271211246103

Silva, L.C.S., Kovaleski, J.L., Gaia, S., De Matos, S.A. & De Francisco, A.C., 2012, 'The challenges faced by Brazil's public universities as a result of knowledge transfer barriers in building the technological innovation center', *African Journal of Business Management* 6(41), 10547–10557. http://dx.doi.org/10.5897/AJBM12.315

Sowe, S.K., Stamelos, I. & Angelis, L., 2008, 'Understanding knowledge sharing activities in free/open source software projects: An empirical study', *Journal of Systems and Software* 81, 431–446. http://dx.doi.org/10.1016/j.jss.2007.03.086

Statistics South Africa, 2010 'Quarterly labour force survey, quarter 1, 2010', Stats SA Library Cataloguing-in-Publication (CIP) Data.

Strauss, A.L. & Corbin, J.M., 1997, *Grounded theory in practice,* Sage Publications, Thousand Oaks.

Tonkin, H., Pfeiffer, H.D. & Tourte, G., 2012, 'Twitter, information sharing and London riots?', *Bulletin of the American Society for Information Science and Technology* 38(2), 49–57. http://dx.doi.org/10.1002/bult.2012.1720380212

Wang, C., Yang, H. & Chou, S.T., 2008, 'Using peer-to-peer technology for knowledge sharing in communities of practices', *Decision Support Systems* 45, 528–540. http://dx.doi.org/10.1016/j.dss.2007.06.012

Wenger, E. & Snyder, W., 2000, 'Communities of practice: The organizational frontier', *Harvard Business Review* 79(1), 139–145.

World Wide Worx, 2012, *Social media breaks barriers in SA,* viewed 25 November 2012, from http://www.worldwideworx.com/socialmedia2012/

World Wide Worx, 2014, *WhatsApp takes SA by storm*, viewed 10 March 2014, from http://www.worldwideworx.com/whatsapp/

Zhu, C., Valke, M. & Schellens, T., 2009, 'A cross-cultural study of online collaborative learning', *Multicultural Education & Technology Journal* 3(1), 33–46. http://dx.doi.org/10.1108/17504970910951138

Ziemba, E., Papaj, T., & Zelazny, R., 2013, 'New perspectives on information society: The maturity of research on a sustainable information society', *Online Journal of Applied Knowledge Management* 1(1), 52–71.

21

Knowledge-creation in student software-development teams

Author:
Mzwandile M. Shongwe[1]

Affiliation:
[1]Department of Information Studies, University of Zululand, South Africa

Correspondence to:
Mzwandile Shongwe

Email:
shongwem@unizulu.ac.za

Postal address:
Private Bag X1001,
Kwadlangezwa 3886,
South Africa

Background: Knowledge-creation is a field of study that has gained popularity in recent times. Knowledge-creation is the creation of new ideas or new innovations. In computing, software-development is regarded as knowledge-creation. This is because software-development involves the creation of a new innovation (software). Knowledge-creation studies in this field tend to focus mainly on knowledge-creation activities in business organisations. They use experienced, professional software-development teams as subjects, largely ignoring novice student development teams. This has denied the field of computing valuable knowledge about how novice teams create knowledge.

Objectives: The study addressed this gap in the literature by investigating knowledge-creation in student software teams.

Method: An ethnographic study was conducted on six student teams developing software in a management-information systems (MIS) course. They were conducting a systems-development project at a university during a term of study. Data were collected over a period of four months through participant observation and interviews.

Results: The results reveal knowledge-creation activities such as problem definition, brainstorming, programming and system documentation. Students use the Internet, books, class notes, class presentations, senior students and professional software developers as sources of information. Mobile phones and BlackBerry devices facilitate knowledge-creation. Challenges to knowledge-creation are the lack of material and financial resources, a lack of technical skills, a lack of time, students staying off-campus and ambivalent team members.

Conclusion: The conclusion drawn from this study is that student teams are capable of creating knowledge (a working system) just like professional teams, but the knowledge-creation process is slightly different.

Introduction

Knowledge-creation is a field of study that has gained popularity in recent times (Mitchell & Boyle 2010). Knowledge-creation is the creation of new ideas or new innovations, for example, a new product, service or process. In computing, software-development is regarded as knowledge-creation (Bailin 1997). Software-development is a process of expressing someone's intensions of how a machine should work (Bailin 1997). Bailin further states that knowledge is generated by building, operating and maintaining the system during the software-development process. This knowledge includes lessons learned during the development of the system, experience gained over time when using the system and broader knowledge acquired over time by the development and customer organisations. Dorairaj, Noble and Malik (2012:1) give a knowledge-management perspective of software-development as '... a series of knowledge-intensive activities that encompasses gathering requirements, analysing problems, designing, coding, testing, and ensuring the software remains up-to-date and bug-free'. Software-development is regarded as knowledge-creation because it is an innovative process which leads to the generation of new ideas and the creation of new software products.

Studies have been conducted in the field of computing to investigate the phenomenon of knowledge-creation. For example, Linden and Cybulski (2009), Wan *et al.* (2010) and Arent and Norbjerg (2000) to name but a few investigated knowledge-creation processes in pattern mining, requirement-elicitation process (REP) and software-process improvement (SPI) respectively. The conclusion of these studies was that all these activities are knowledge-creation activities. The problem with these studies is that they tend to focus mainly on knowledge-creation in business organisations. They also tend to use experienced, professional software-development teams as subjects, largely ignoring public institutions such as higher education institutions and thus ignoring the development teams amongst novice students. This has denied the field of computing valuable knowledge about how novice teams create knowledge. In fact, these novices are future developers, and yet, they are largely ignored by researchers. For example, we do not know what the knowledge-creation activities in software-development teams amongst students entail. What channels of communication facilitate knowledge-creation in student teams? What information sources do students use to create knowledge? And what challenges do student teams face when they create knowledge? A lot has been written about professional, experienced teams. For example, we know what the knowledge-creation activities in professional teams entail (Poh & Erwee 2004). We also know that professional teams use technology and networks of peers (communities of practice) to facilitate knowledge-creation and transfer (Alavi & Leidner 2001; Kimmerle, Cress & Held 2010; Wasko & Faraj 2000; Wenger 1998). We are also aware that rising costs, limited time to complete projects and abandoned projects are some of the challenges concerning knowledge-creation faced by professional development teams (Heeks 2002; Lindvall, Rus & Sinha 2002; Lyytinen & Robey 1999). However, we do not know what is happening in student teams. The study set out to answer these questions in the context of software-development as knowledge-creation.

This article is structured as follows: The following section presents the theoretical foundations on knowledge-creation. That is followed by the methodology and then the results and discussions. Lastly, I present conclusions and recommendations for further research.

Theoretical foundations

This section will briefly highlight the theoretical foundations of knowledge-creation. Firstly, I shall discuss the distinction between data, information and knowledge, and then I shall discuss knowledge-creation.

Data, information and knowledge

The concepts of knowledge, data and information may seem similar, but their meaning may not be uniformly understood. Data is unprocessed information (Hey 2004). It could be bits and numbers with no meaning (Rumizen 2002). Information is data that has been processed for a useful purpose and can be used for decision-making. Chaffey and Wood (2005) describe information as data with value to the understanding of a subject and in a context. Knowledge is '... information possessed in the mind of individuals: it is personal information related to facts, procedures, concepts, interpretations, ideas, observation and judgment' (Alavi & Leidner 2001:109). Knowledge could take several perspectives or forms: a state of mind, an object, a process, a condition of having access to information or a capability (Alavi & Leidner 2001). In software-development, knowledge could be seen from the perspective of either the process or the object. The object is the output or end-product (the software). The process perspective entails the software-development process, for example, generating new ideas, refining them and applying them in the development process. Knowledge could be tacit or explicit (Nonaka & Takeuchi 1995; Polanyi 1962). Tacit knowledge is what the knower knows, knowledge that is derived from experience and that embodies beliefs and values (Nonaka & Takeuchi 1995). It is personal and difficult to formalise, making it difficult to communicate and share with others (Elfving & Funk 2006; Gladstone 2000; Li & Gao 2003). Explicit knowledge is knowledge that has been articulated and, more often than not, captured in the form of text, tables, diagrams and product specifications (Nickols 2000). In software-development, tacit knowledge resides in the developer's mind. It is the hidden knowledge in the form of the experiences of the developer. Explicit knowledge is the end product (the system) and the documentation.

Knowledge-creation

Knowledge-creation is a series of processes and activities that add value to produce an outcome or output such as a product, service or process (Mitchell & Boyle 2010). Holsapple and Singh (2001:84) define knowledge-creation as '... an activity that produces knowledge by discovering it or deriving it from existing knowledge'. It is the coming into existence of new knowledge (Phan & Peridis 2000). It involves the definition of a problem and makes use of complex and discontinuous events to solve the problem (Parent *et al.* 2000; Styhre, Roth & Ingelgard 2002). Knowledge-creation involves the monitoring, production and transfer of knowledge resources within and outside of the organisation (Holsapple & Singh 2001). When defined as a process, knowledge-creation refers to the generation of new ideas that reflect a significant enrichment of existing knowledge. It is defined as an outcome or output when activities and initiatives are undertaken to generate new ideas or objects. It means that new knowledge is diffused, adopted and embedded as new products, services and systems (Mitchell & Boyle 2010). Knowledge-creation takes place at individual, group, organisational and inter-organisational levels (Nonaka & Takeuchi 1995). It is widely agreed that knowledge-creation takes place first at individual level and then amplified at group, organisational and inter-organisational levels (Nonaka & Takeuchi 1995). In fact, it is believed that organisations only offer a space or context in which the knowledge created by individuals is amplified and applied in organisational routines and processes. The organisation could be what Nonaka, Toyama and Konno (1998) refer to as *'ba'* – a shared context where knowledge is created.

Knowledge-creation activities

According to Nonaka and Takeuchi (1995), knowledge is created in five steps: sharing tacit knowledge, creating concepts, justifying concepts, building a prototype and cross-levelling knowledge. At the sharing stage of tacit knowledge, individuals share emotions, feelings and mental models through face-to-face interactions. Creating concepts involves the sharing of both tacit and explicit knowledge. After sharing tacit knowledge, organisational members then articulate the tacit knowledge into explicit knowledge through written concepts. Justifying concepts is a phase whereby created concepts are determined whether they are useful or not in the organisation. The justified concepts are then converted into a tangible or concrete product or model called an archetype. After knowledge has been created, it is levelled across the organisation. This could be inter-organisational or intra-organisational (Nonaka 1994; Nonaka & Takeuchi 1995). This notion is also shared by Wan *et al.* (2010). Examples of knowledge-creation activities in software-development are the following: constructing a software routine, brainstorming, discovering a pattern, solving a problem or achieving a creative insight (Holsapple & Singh 2001).

Knowledge-creation theories

A number of theories are used to study knowledge-creation in organisations. Widely used theories include, amongst others, the organisational learning theory (Argyris & Schon 1978), the learning-organisation (Senge *et al.* 1994) , the theory of organisational knowledge-creation or SECI (Nonaka & Takeuchi 1995), the knowledge-integration theory (Grant 1996) and the communities of practice theory (Wenger 1998). Argyris and Schon's organisational learning theory explains how knowledge is created by the learning of individuals and groups in organisations which facilitate learning at organisational level. Senge's learning-organisation theory defines the principles of a learning organisation. These principles are personal mastery, systems thinking, team learning, mental models and building a shared vision. These principles are believed to facilitate learning in departments and sections of the organisation, which leads to the whole organisation learning and becoming a learning organisation. Nonaka and Takeuchi's theory of organisational knowledge-creation explains how individuals, teams and entire organisations create knowledge by the conversion of tacit and explicit knowledge through four processes: socialisation, externalisation, combination and internalisation. Grant (1996) focuses on knowledge-integration and innovation within a firm. Grant explores the coordinating mechanisms of how individuals in a firm integrate knowledge to foster innovation. Wenger's theory explains how small, informal teams in organisations share and create knowledge from each other through social interactions. Lee and Cole's (2003) community-based model of knowledge-creation explain how knowledge is created by a software community of practice operating outside of formal organisational boundaries.

These theories focus mainly on how knowledge is created in organisations (except Lee and Cole's [2003] model). They explain that knowledge is created, firstly, at individual level and at group level before it becomes organisational knowledge. They also present different scenarios under which knowledge is created. The main limitation of these theories and knowledge-creation literature in general is that the focus is mostly on knowledge-creation by professionals in business organisations. Little has been done to investigate amateur, student teams despite the fact that they are the future innovators. The current study tries to fill this gap in the literature by focusing on students' knowledge-creation activities.

Knowledge-creation in software-development

Software-development is regarded as knowledge-creation (Bailin 1997). It is a knowledge-intensive task, which involves a process of discovery and invention, accumulation, analysis, cognition and integration (Bailin 1997; Dingsoyr 2002; Mitchell & Nicholas 2006). This means that software-development processes (systems analysis, coding, documentation, testing, etc.) are knowledge-creation processes. During these activities, individuals and teams acquire knowledge from different sources; apply their previously acquired knowledge; store acquired knowledge in databases, routines, and procedures and share their knowledge with others to produce a knowledge output (the software product).

A number of studies have been conducted to investigate the knowledge-creation phenomenon in computing. A few examples can suffice. Arent and Norbjerg (2000) investigated software-process improvement (SPI) and concluded that they are knowledge-creation activities. Kess and Haapasalo (2002) investigated knowledge-creation through a software-project review process, and they constructed a tool to improve the software-development process. Klint and Verhoef (2002) investigated how the principles of knowledge-management could be applied in knowledge-creation. Linden and Cybulski (2009) investigated knowledge-creation in pattern mining. This led to the enrichment of the knowledge-creation framework proposed by Wickramasinghe and Lichtenstein. Morner and Von Krogh (2009) explored the conditions under which successful knowledge-creation takes place. They proposed three conditions (perceptibility, systemic memory and modularity) under which the knowledge-creation process could be stabilised. Wan *et al.* (2010) investigated knowledge-creation in requirement-elicitation process (REP) and concluded that it is a knowledge-creation process. Neves *et al.* (2011) conducted a systematic review of knowledge-creation in agile software-development teams and found two knowledge-creation activities, comprehensive software documentation and responding to change as knowledge-creation activities. Spohrer *et al.* (2013) also investigated knowledge-creation activities in peer programming teams working on information-systems development in a large software organisation. They found that knowledge is created by exchanging opinions, solutions, and code, and developers who are observing their peers thus learn from their actions. They found that knowledge is created at individual and team level. If we look at the literature, we can conclude that student teams in software-development are rarely studied. In the list of studies mentioned above, none have used students as subjects, hence the importance of this study.

Methodology

An interpretive, qualitative study was conducted on student software-development teams. Interpretive studies assume that people create their own subjective meanings as they interact with the world around them (Lee 1991; Olikowski & Baroudi 1991). Ethnography was chosen as a research method. Myers (1999) defines ethnography as a study where the researchers immerse themselves in the lives of the people being studied. Ethnographers aim to place the phenomena being studied in the social and cultural context of the people studied. Myers (1999) further states that the ethnographer has to spend a considerable amount of time in the field and to collect data not only through interviews and documents but also through participant observation. In this study, a class of six software-development project teams (24 students) was studied. The groups were supposed to develop an e-commerce interactive website for a client. The researcher joined the class at the beginning of the semester before the project started. He was briefed about the project just like the students and given all necessary documentation. He attended all lectures, presentations and meetings that the teams had. These activities took place in the students' computer laboratory, lecture halls and the library. The aim was to be part of the teams as if the researcher was one of them. Lectures were held once a week for the whole semester. Presentations were held based on need such as when there was a milestone deliverable (e.g. project plan). The teams also had meetings almost daily to discuss and develop the system. During these activities (lectures, presentations and team meetings), the researcher observed and interviewed teams. During observation, detailed notes were taken on how the students developed the system. The researcher observed how, where and what ideas team members shared and the impact of these ideas on the completion of the project. Group interviews were conducted to supplement observation data. They were used to seek further clarification on certain development processes such as the information sources and communication channels used by teams in their projects. The study was conducted for the whole semester, which was four months long. Qualitative content analysis was then used to analyse the responses. Qualitative content analysis is a method for the subjective interpretation of text data through coding and themes or category identification (Hsieh & Shannon 2005). In this study, data were coded and classified into categories. Ethnography has been used before by Suchman (1995) and Myers and Young (1997), amongst others, to study information-systems development.

Results and discussions

This section responds to the research questions posed in the study.

Knowledge-creation activities

This section answers the following question: What knowledge-creation activities do student teams undertake? The results reveal a number of activities which are undertaken at individual and team level.

Individual knowledge-creation activities

The results indicate that individual team members performed a number of activities during the knowledge-creation process. Major individual activities were coding, documentation, preparing slides for presentations, designing the user interface, research and information gathering, sourcing finance and other relevant activities assigned to the individual. One respondent stated: 'I was mainly the website designer, but I also did documentation such as project plan, feasibility study and other activities'. Another reported that '... as an individual, I created forms in the prototype'. Others reported on other minor activities that they did such as writing minutes and arranging future meetings. The importance of individual knowledge activities was emphasised by all group members. One member stated:

> 'The contribution of each member was great. For every task we had to break it down to individual activities. In so doing we shared ideas which enabled us to finish the project quicker'.

These results are consistent with the knowledge-creation literature which highlights the importance of the individual in knowledge-creation, for example Grant (1996). Simon (as cited in Grant 1996:112) shares the same sentiments. Nonaka and Takeuchi (1995) present an excellent account of how individuals create knowledge which is then infused into the whole organisation. In this particular case, individuals used their creative abilities to build the different parts of the system. They used their own existing and newly acquired knowledge to carry out the tasks at hand. These individual activities contributed immensely to the completion of the project. The completed individual tasks would then be taken to the next level of discussion and further refinement. That was at the team level. The team's knowledge-creation activities are discussed in the following section.

Knowledge-creation activities of the team

The tasks given to individuals were then consolidated and adopted at group level. Each individual would bring their tasks to the team for further discussions. The team would reject or adopt the task as team knowledge. Tasks such as coding, preparing documentation and presentations and others were discussed at team level. In fact, all individual tasks were further discussed by the teams before they were accepted to be project knowledge. One such important task that was discussed at team level was problem definition, that is, what the project entailed. At first, students had no idea about what to do. One student lamented: 'I had no idea what I was supposed to do'. These sentiments were echoed by other students who reported that, '... we did not have a clue on what to do'. The teams then converged, discussed the problem and sought assistance from the lecturer and senior students. That was when they understood what they were supposed to do. They reported: 'It was after we met as groups that we shared ideas and came to understand what we had to do'. Morne and von Krogh (2009) also state that, in knowledge-creation, the first step usually lies in a single software problem with which a programmer is confronted. Nonaka and Takeuchi (1995) refer to such a state as intentional creative chaos. According to Nonaka and Takeuchi (1995), 'intentional creative chaos' is a situation whereby management creates a sense of crisis in the organisation by proposing challenging goals. Organisational members respond by defining the problem and finding solutions to the problem. In student teams, the lecturer evokes a crisis by giving students a huge real-life problem, which they have never come across before and which they have to deliver to a real customer within a short space of time. It is after they have met as a team that they properly defined the problem, understood it and planned how to solve it.

Knowledge-creation in teams is also emphasised by a number of knowledge-creation theories. These theories (Hedlund 1994; Nonaka & Takeuchi 1995; Senge *et al.* 1994; Wenger 1998) agree that teams play a crucial part in knowledge-creation. It is at team level where rough ideas are refined and developed into knowledge.

Information sources for knowledge-creation

A number of information sources were used by student teams during the knowledge-creation process. Information sources such as class presentations, the lecturer and lecture notes, text books, the Internet and external sources (senior students and professional software developers) were used.

Class presentations were a good source of information. After a major milestone, for example system analysis, budgeting, prototyping and documentation, the group would present the deliverable to the whole class and lecturer. Other teams and the lecturer would then interrogate the presenting group by asking questions and commenting about the deliverable. Presenters were criticised, praised and advised on how to do the project better. One student stated that '... presentations helped us to know what we did right, where to correct and how to improve the project'. Another one concurred that '... presentations helped us to get clarity as to what is really required from us'. All the groups agreed that the presentations helped them to gain new knowledge about the project in one way or the other. Teams stated that they gained knowledge from the presentations from other teams. They learned communication and presentation skills and to work under pressure. It boosted their morale when they realised that they were making progress. On an individual note, team members indicated that class presentations helped them to gain knowledge from others.

The lecturer also played a crucial role in the knowledge-creation process. Apart from giving them the problem to solve, the lecturer was also involved in helping the teams solve the problem. Apart from teaching, the lecturer played the role of advisor and mentor. At times, classes would be conducted to teach students how to carry out certain activities of the project. Before the start of each major deliverable (e.g. systems analysis), the lecturer would conduct a lecture on the next activity. This helped students understand what was required of them and how to tackle the problem at hand. The lecturer also played a crucial role during the presentations. He would criticise the students' work, offer advice on how the work should be done and give credit to teams that did well. Students would also consult the lecturer for advice whenever they had problems with their projects. This was confirmed by a respondent who stated that '... the lecturer gave us motivation to finish the project'. Another one concurred that '... the lecturer helped by explaining what [*was*] expected'. Another one stated that '... the lecturer made us to attend classes, and provided us with technical skills'. Not all students were happy with the lecturer's role though. Some indicated that the lecturer did not play any role in their knowledge-creation process. They stated: 'The lecturer did not play any role in the successful completion of the project. We struggled while he was present'. Others stated that '... the lecturer had little impact on the project'.

Students also regularly used the Internet for information. The teams indicated that they used the Internet to research how to do the activities of the project, for example, how to budget and how to do systems analysis. They also looked for technical information such as coding. They could surf the Internet to look at how to solve a specific technical problem. One team indicated that they used the Internet to find help on how to set-up the Apache, MySQL, PHP for Windows (WAMP) interface. The w3schools website is said to have provided much support to the teams. They also relied on books, senior students and professionals to complete their projects. Because this was an MIS group, most teams relied on senior students in computer science for technical support such as linking the database to the website and other coding activities. Surprisingly, they also sought help from other competing groups. One group stated that '... we sought help from other groups to do some of the activities'.

This leads to the conclusion that student teams seem to use readily available sources of information for knowledge-creation. These sources are slightly different from sources used by professional teams. Professional teams seem to use mostly in-house databases (experience repositories) containing knowledge from past projects (Basili, Caldiera & Rombach 1994; Spohrer *et al.* 2013). However, the sources that students used were also good enough because they enabled the teams to create new knowledge.

Channels of communication that facilitate knowledge-creation

Different communication channels were used by teams during knowledge-creation. Mobile devices such as mobile phones and BlackBerrys and the Internet were mostly used for information transfer that facilitated knowledge-creation. Teams used these channels of communication to share ideas. They used mostly emails, chat services such as Whats application (WhatsApp), BlackBerry Messenger (BBM), Mxit and social networking sites (Facebook and Twitter). They stated that they used some of these channels at their convenient time and places to look for information and that they shared it faster than other devices. These results are consistent with results found by Kyobe and Shongwe (2011) who concluded that students use devices such as mobile phones and social networks for learning purposes. Juárez-Ramírez and Ocegueda- Miramontes (2013) also found similar results. They concluded that social networks (Facebook in particular) are used widely by students in software-development to solve problems and share knowledge.

Challenges of knowledge-creation

There were a number of challenges facing the teams involved in knowledge-creation. The major challenge was financial resources. Before the start of the project, teams had to identify a client for whom they had to develop a system. The client had to be rurally based. This meant that the teams had to travel to rural areas to find the client and collect information about their business before developing the system. All the teams indicated that they did not have enough money for such an exercise. The average distance they had to travel was 50 km. They did not have enough money for travelling and subsistence. They also lacked financial resources for doing activities such as photocopying and printing documents. One team stated that '... we did not have money to go and interview the client the way we could have liked. We also did not have money for printing our documents'. Another group concurred that '...as a group, we did not have the funds to help us successfully achieve our goal'.

Another challenge that the teams faced was a lack of technical skills. This is not a surprise because these were amateur teams. One team stated that '... we had no skills and experience of web design'. The main technical problem that most teams faced was connecting the database to the website (the WAMP platform).

A lack of material resources was another challenge that the teams faced. The material resources that they lacked were computers, software and a dedicated computer laboratory for their project. Some teams had only one laptop computer to work with. The university's computer laboratory did not have the PHP software, which made it difficult for teams to complete the project. The teams also complained greatly about the ever-crowded school laboratories. One group indicated: 'We encountered the challenge of limited resources that would have helped with the organising, planning, and research about the project'.

Time pressure was another big challenge that student teams faced. Teams stated that there was not enough time to complete the project. They complained that each milestone was to be submitted earlier than they would have liked. They also complained that they had to do courses other than the project. One student lamented: 'I had to juggle between activities of the project and other courses'. Another one concurred: 'The challenge was to balance between the amount of work the project had and studying for other courses'.

Not all students were resident students. Some teams were made up of on-campus and off-campus students. Off-campus students frequently had to travel from off-campus to the campus for group meetings. At times, they had to leave meetings earlier in order for them to travel off-campus. This caused challenges because it delayed the completion of the project. Some group members could not turn up for meetings, which also affected the quality of ideas contributed to the team. One student stated that:

> ... since I am staying off-campus, my difficulty was always travelling to university and going back in the late hours of the day when it is not safe out there.

Other teams complained of lazy team members who did not complete their given activities. Strode and Clark (2007) report similar challenges in their study of student projects. They report that student projects have the following constraints: time and commitment, experience level, scope and complexity, technology and the need to meet the assessment criteria. Issues of time, commitment and technology seemed to be serious challenges to students. Wang (2009) also found that a lack of time was a major challenge in students' software projects. Faculty should look at how this could be addressed. However, these challenges are also faced by professional teams (e.g. time and financial challenges) as reported by Rus and Lindvall (2002).

Successful completion of the project

The teams were then asked to indicate whether they have successfully completed the project. All the teams indicted that they did complete their projects successfully. They indicated that they have successfully built a working e-commerce interactive website. One group stated that, '... although it was hard, we successfully created an e-commerce site that will help our client expand their business'. Another group stated: 'We were able to create a website that is working'. The groups indicted that, although they successfully completed the project, it was a challenging task.

Knowledge gained from the project

All the teams indicated that they had learnt a lot from the project. They indicated that the project had improved their knowledge and experience in software-development ('I have learned how to create a complete website'). Some respondents indicated that they had learnt to work in a team, a skill that is essential in the job market: 'I believe I gained both knowledge and experience when it comes to programming and working in a team'. Others indicated that they had learnt to work under pressure and in a group to achieve a singular goal.

A summary of the research findings is presented in Table 1.

Recommendations and further research

I recommend, therefore, that university departments engaged in such projects should look at the challenges that student teams face because they affect learning. Departments are also encouraged to formally adopt technology devices such as smart phones for teaching because they play an important role in learning. Further research is recommended to investigate the quality of the knowledge that students create and also to investigate the impact that the challenges have on knowledge-creation.

TABLE 1: A summary of research findings.

Research questions	Findings
What knowledge-creation activities take place in student teams?	At the individual level: coding, documentation, preparing slides for presentations, designing the user interface, research and information gathering, sourcing finance. At team level: brainstorming which led to the refinement, consolidation and adoption of individual tasks.
What channels of communication facilitate knowledge-creation in student teams?	Emails, chat services such as Whats Application (WhatsApp), BlackBerry Messenger (BBM), Mxit and social networking sites (Facebook and Twitter).
What information sources do students use to create knowledge?	Class presentations, the lecturer, lecture notes, text books, the Internet and external sources (senior students and professional software developers).
What challenges do student teams face when they create knowledge?	Lack of material and financial resources, lack of technical skills, lack of time, students staying off-campus and ambivalent team members.

Limitations of the study

The major limitation of this study is that it was conducted in only one university and in only one department. This compromises the representativeness of the total population.

Conclusion

The article contributes to the literature by showing how knowledge is created in student software-development teams. The literature on knowledge-creation covers mostly knowledge-creation in professional teams in business organisations. The article presents a different perspective by focusing on knowledge-creation in amateur teams in an education institution. Several conclusions are drawn from the study: (1) Student software-development teams can create knowledge (a working system) just like professional software-development teams; (2) knowledge is created by the whole team, but the knowledge-creation process starts from individual team members; (3) class presentations, lectures, the Internet and senior students and professional developers are major sources of information that students consult to create knowledge; (4) a lack of technical skills, limited time and a lack of resources are major hindrances to knowledge-creation.

Acknowledgements

Competing interests

The author declares that there are no financial and personal relationship(s) that may have inappropriately influenced him when he wrote this article.

References

Alavi, M. & Leidner, D.E., 2001, 'Knowledge management systems: Issues, challenges and benefits', in S. Barnes (ed.), *Knowledge management systems: Theory and practice*, pp. 15–32, Thompson Learning, Oxford.

Arent, J. & Norbjerg, J., 2000, 'Software improvement as organisational knowledge creation: A multiple case analysis', Proceedings of the 33rd International Conference on System Sciences, Hawaii, USA, 4–7 January 2000, p. 105.

Argyris, C. & Schon, D., 1978, *Organisational learning: A theory of action perspective*, Addison-Wesley Publishing Company, Reading.

Bailin, S., 1997, 'Software development as knowledge creation', *International Journal of Applied Software Technology* 3(1), 75–89.

Basili, V.R., Caldiera, G. & Rombach, D.H., 1994, 'The experience factory', *Encyclopedia of Software Engineering* 2, 469–476.

Chaffey, D. & Wood, S., 2005, *Business information management: Improving performance using information systems,* Pearson Education Limited, London.

Dingsoyr, T., 2002, 'Knowledge management in medium-sized software consulting companies', *Empirical Computing* 7(4), 383–386.

Dorairaj, S., Noble, J. & Malik, P., 2012, 'Knowledge management in distributed agile software development', Paper presented at the Agile Conference, Dallas, Texas, United States of America, 13–17 August.

Elfving, S. & Funk, P., 2006, '*Enabling knowledge transfer in product development and production: Methods and techniques from artificial intelligence*', Paper presented at the 1st Nordic Conference on Product Lifecycle Management, Goteborg, Sweden, 25–26 January.

Gladstone, B., 2000, *From know-how to knowledge: The essential guide to understanding and implementing knowledge management*, Industrial Society, London.

Grant, R.M., 1996, 'Toward a knowledge-based theory of the firm', *Strategic Management Journal* 17, 109–122. http://dx.doi.org/10.1002/smj.4250171110

Hedlund, G., 1994, 'A model of knowledge management and the N-Form corporation' *Strategic Management Journal* 15, 73–90. http://dx.doi.org/10.1002/smj.4250151006

Heeks, R., 2002, 'Information systems and developing countries: Failure, success, and local improvisations', *The Information Society* 18(2), 101–112. http://dx.doi.org/10.1080/01972240290075039

Hey, J., 2004, 'The data, information, knowledge, wisdom chain', viewed 16 July 2008, from http://scholar.google.co.za/scholar?q=The+Data,+Information,+Knowledge,+Wisdom+Chain+%2Bhey+2004&hl=en&um=1&ie=UTF-8&oi=scholart

Holsapple, C.W. & Singh, M., 2001, 'The knowledge chain model: Activities for competitiveness', *Expert Systems with Applications* 20(1), 77–98. http://dx.doi.org/10.1016/S0957-4174(00)00050-6

Hsieh, H-F. & Shannon, S.E., 2005, 'Three approaches to qualitative content analysis', *Qualitative Health Research* 15(9), 1277–1288. http://dx.doi.org/10.1177/1049732305276687

Juárez-Ramírez, R. & Ocegueda- Miramontes, R.P-R.V., 2013, 'Supporting the software development process using social media: Experiences with student projects', Proceedings of the Institute of Electrical and Electronics Engineers 37th Annual Computer Software and Applications Conference Workshops, Kyoto, Japan, 22–26 July 2013.

Kess, P. & Haapasalo, H., 2002, 'Knowledge creation through a project review process in software production', *International Journal of Production Economics* 80(1), 49–55. http://dx.doi.org/10.1016/S0925-5273(02)00242-6

Kimmerle, J. Cress, U. & Held, C., 2010, 'The interplay between individual and collective knowledge: Technologies for organisational learning and knowledge building', *Knowledge Management Research & Practice* 8(1), 33–44. http://dx.doi.org/10.1057/kmrp.2009.36

Klint, P. & Verhoef, C., 2002, 'Enabling the creation of knowledge about software assets', *Data & Knowledge Engineering* 41(2/3), 141–158. http://dx.doi.org/10.1016/S0169-023X(02)00038-1

Kyobe, M.E. & Shongwe, M.M., 2011, 'Investigating the extent to which mobile phones reduce knowledge transfer barriers in student project teams', *South African Journal of Information Management*, 13(1).

Lee, A.S., 1991, 'Integrating positivist and interpretive approaches to organisational research', *Organisational Science* 2(4), 242–365. http://dx.doi.org/10.1287/orsc.2.4.342

Lee, G.K. & Cole, R.E., 2003, 'From a firm-based to a community-based model of knowledge creation: The case of the Linux kernel development', *Organisation Science* 14(6), 633–694. http://dx.doi.org/10.1287/orsc.14.6.633.24866

Li, M. & Gao, F., 2003, 'Why Nonaka highlights tacit knowledge: A critical review', *Journal of Knowledge Management* 7(4), 6–14. http://dx.doi.org/10.1108/13673270310492903

Linden, T. & Cybulski, J., 2009, 'Knowledge creation in an application domain: A hermeneutic study in ICKM 2009', Proceedings of the 6th International Conference on Knowledge Management: Managing knowledge for global and collaborative innovations, Hong Kong, China, 3–4 December 2009, pp. 1–13.

Lindvall, M., Rus, I. & Sinha, S., 2002, 'Technology support for knowledge management', in S. Henninger & F. Maurer (eds.), *Advances in learning software organization: Lecture notes in computer science,* pp. 94–113, Springer Verlag, Berlin.

Lyytinen, K. & Robey, D., 1999, 'Learning failure in information systems development', *Information Systems Journal* 9(2), 85–101. http://dx.doi.org/10.1046/j.1365-2575.1999.00051.x

Mitchell, R. & Boyle, B., 2010, 'Knowledge creation measurement methods', *Journal of Knowledge Management* 14(1), 67–82. http://dx.doi.org/10.1108/13673271011015570

Mitchell, R. & Nicholas, S., 2006, 'Knowledge creation in groups: The value of cognitive diversity, transactive memory and open-mindedness norms', *Electronic Journal of Knowledge Management* 4(1), 67–74.

Morner, M. & Von Krogh, G., 2009, 'A note on knowledge creation in open-source software projects: What can we learn from Luhmann's theory of social systems',

Systems Practice and Action Research 22(6), 431–443. http://dx.doi.org/10.1007/s11213-009-9139-7

Myers, M.D., 1999, 'Investigating information systems with ethnographic research', *Communications for the Association of Information Systems* 2(23), 1–20.

Myers, M.D. & Young, L.W., 1997, 'Hidden agendas, power, and managerial assumptions in information systems development: An ethnographic study,' *Information Technology & People* (10)3, 224–240. http://dx.doi.org/10.1108/09593849710178225

Neves, F.T., Correia, A.M.R., Rosa, V.N. & Neto, M., 2011, 'Knowledge creation and sharing in software development teams using Agile methodologies: Key insights affecting their adoption', Proceedings of the 6th Information Systems and Technologies Iberian Conference (CISTI), Chaves, Portugal, 15–18 June 2011, pp. 1–6.

Nickols, F.W., 2000, 'The knowledge in knowledge management', in J.W. Cortada & J.A. Woods (eds.), *The knowledge management yearbook 2000–2001*, pp. 12–21, Butterworth-Heinemann, Boston.

Nonaka, I., 1994, 'A dynamic theory of organisational knowledge creation', *Organisation Science* 5(1), 14–37. http://dx.doi.org/10.1287/orsc.5.1.14

Nonaka, I. & Takeuchi, H., 1995, *The knowledge-creating company*, Oxford University Press, New York.

Nonaka, I., Toyama, R. & Konno, N., 1998, 'SECI, Ba and Leadership: A unified model of dynamic knowledge creation', *Long Range Planning* 33(1), 5–34. http://dx.doi.org/10.1016/S0024-6301(99)00115-6

Olikowski, W.J. & Baroudi, J.J., 1991, 'Studying information technology in organisations: Research approaches and assumptions', *Information Systems research* 2(1), 1–28. http://dx.doi.org/10.1287/isre.2.1.1

Parent, M., Gallupe, R.B., Salisbury, Wm.D. & Handelman, J.M., 2000, 'Knowledge creation in focus groups: Can group technologies help?', *Information & Management* 38(1), 47–58. http://dx.doi.org/10.1016/S0378-7206(00)00053-7

Phan, P.H. & Peridis, T., 2000, Knowledge creation in strategic alliances: Another look at organisational learning', *Asian Pacific Journal of Management* 17(2), 201–222. http://dx.doi.org/10.1023/A:1015857525048

Poh, L-G. & Erwee, R., 2004, Knowledge creation and integration in project teams: A study of international telecommunications companies in Singapore', *Journal of Management & World Business Research* 1(1), 23–44.

Polanyi, M., 1962, 'Tacit knowing: It's bearing on some problems of philosophy', *Reviews of Modern Physics* 34(4), 601–616. http://dx.doi.org/10.1103/RevModPhys.34.601

Rumizen, M.C., 2002, *The complete idiot's guide to knowledge management,* CWL Publishing Enterprise, Madison.

Rus, I. & Lindvall, M., 2002, 'Knowledge management in computing', *Institute of Electrical and Electronic Engineers Software* 19(3), 26–38.

Senge, P.M., Ross, R., Smith, B., Roberts, C. & Kleiner, A., 1994, *The fifth discipline fieldwork: Strategies and tools for building a learning organisation,* Doubleday Inc. Publishers, New York.

Spohrer, K., Kude, T., Schmidt, C.T. & Heinzl, A., 2013, 'Knowledge creation in information systems development teams: The role of pair programming and peer code review,' *Proceedings of the 21st European Conference on Information Systems,* Utrecht, Netherlands, 6–8 June 2013, pp. 1–12.

Strode, D.E. & Clark, J., 2007, 'Methodology in software development capstone projects', *Proceedings of the 20th Annual National Advisory Committee on Computing Qualifications*, Nelson, New Zealand, 8–11 July 2007, pp. 243–251.

Styhre, A., Roth, J. & Ingelgard, A., 2002, 'Care of the other: Knowledge creation through care in professional teams', *Scandinavian Journal of Management* 18(4), 503–520. http://dx.doi.org/10.1016/S0956-5221(01)00022-7

Suchman, L., 1995, 'Making work visible', *Communications of the Association for Computing Machinery* 38(9), 56–64. http://dx.doi.org/10.1145/223248.223263

Wang, A.I., 2009, 'Post-mortem analysis of student game projects in a software architecture course: Successes and challenges in student software architecture game projects,' Paper presented at the International Consumer Electronic Games Innovations Conference, London, England, United Kingdom, 25–28 August.

Wan, J., Zhang, H., Wan, D. & Huang, D., 2010, 'Research on knowledge creation in software requirement development', *Journal of Software Engineering & Applications* 3(5), 487–494. http://dx.doi.org/10.4236/jsea.2010.35055

Wasko, M. & Faraj, S., 2000, 'It is what one does: Why people participate and help others in electronic communities of practice', *The Journal of Strategic Information Systems* 9(2/3), 155–173. http://dx.doi.org/10.1016/S0963-8687(00)00045-7

Wenger, E., 1998, *Communities of practice: Learning, meaning, and identity*, Cambridge University Press, Cambridge. http://dx.doi.org/10.1017/CBO9780511803932

22

Level of data quality from Health Management Information Systems in a resources limited setting and its associated factors, eastern Ethiopia

Authors:
Kidist Teklegiorgis[1]
Kidane Tadesse[2]
Gebremeskel Mirutse[2]
Wondwossen Terefe[2,3]

Affiliations:
[1]Dire Dawa City Administration Health Bureau, Dire Dawa, Ethiopia

[2]Department of Public Health, College of Health Sciences, Mekelle University, Ethiopia

[3]Department of Biostatistics, Tulen University, Ethiopia

Corresponding author:
Kidane Tadesse,
kiducs98@yahoo.com

Background: A Health Information System (HIS) is a system that integrates data collection, processing, reporting, and use of the information necessary for improving health service effectiveness and efficiency through better management at all levels of health services. Despite the credible use of HIS for evidence-based decision-making, countries with the highest burden of ill health and the most in need of accurate and timely data have the weakest HIS in the vast majority of world's poorest countries. Although a Health Management Information System (HMIS) forms a backbone for strong health systems, most developing countries still face a challenge in strengthening routine HIS. The main focus of this study was to assess the current HIS performance and identify factors affecting data quality in a resource-limited setting, such as Ethiopian health facilities.

Methods: A cross-sectional study was conducted by using structured questionnaires in Dire Dawa Administration health facilities. All unit and/or department heads from all government health facilities were selected. The data was analysed using STATA version 11. Frequency and percentages were computed to present the descriptive findings. Association between variables was computed using binary logistic regression.

Results: Over all data quality was found to be 75.3% in unit and/or departments. Trained staff to fill format, decision based on supervisor directives and department heads seek feedback were significantly associated with data quality and their magnitudes were (AOR = 2.253, 95% CI [1.082, 4.692]), (AOR = 2.131, 95% CI [1.073, 4.233]) and (AOR = 2.481, 95% CI [1.262, 4.876]), respectively.

Conclusion: Overall data quality was found to be below the national expectation level. Low data quality was found at health posts compared to health centres and hospitals. There was also a shortage of assigned HIS personnel, separate HIS offices, and assigned budgets for HIS across all units and/or departments.

Introduction

A Health Management Information System (HMIS) is a system that integrates data collection, processing, reporting, and use of the information necessary for improving health service effectiveness and efficiency through better management at all levels of health services. Maintaining a good HMIS is an essential part in strengthening a health system (Chawla, Bansal & Indrayan 1997; World Health Organization Regional Office for the Western Pacific 1986).

In 2007, the World Health Assembly (WHA) passed a resolution on strengthening of Health Information Systems (HISs). The resolution acknowledges that sound information is critical in framing evidence-based health policy and decision-making. It is also fundamental for monitoring programs towards internationally agreed upon health-related development goals. Although a HMIS forms a backbone for strong health systems, most developing countries still face a challenge in strengthening routine HIS (USAID/Ministry of Health 2006; WHO 2008a).

In a good HMIS, data collection should be similar with the data requirements of users (only relevant data) and to the available processing capabilities; also the information generated should be simple to obtain and only the minimum required information must be collected, so that analysis can be done quickly. Feedback to the providers of the health data is an essential component of any reporting system (WHO 2004, 2008b).

The Ethiopian Federal Ministry of Health (FMOH) has emphasised the HMIS as a key component for successful implementation of the Health Sector Development Program (HSDP) strategic plan.

The core health indicators come from routine health service and administrative records through HMIS and Monitoring and Evaluation (M&E) and are complementary processes standardising indicator definitions and data recording and reporting forms; integration of data from different programs into shared channels that improves health system efficiency and effectiveness (GAVI 2002; HMIS Reform Team 2007; TUTAPE 2009).

Research problem

The value of health information is determined by its utilisation in decision-making. Public health decision-making is critically dependent on the timely availability of sound data. Developing countries are reported to have a large amount of unreliable health data, poor human resources, and poor information technology infrastructure, hence effective HISs are needed to improve these problems. In Ethiopia data quality and utilisation of health information remains weak, particularly at primary health care facilities and district levels (Aqil, Lippeveled & Dairiku 2009; MoH 2010; Sahay 2001; WHO 2007). This research aims to answer the question whether or not governmental health facilities currently collect quality data and identify the independent determinant factors associated with the level of data quality.

Literature review

Description and evaluation framework of Health Information System

HISs have been variously described as the 'foundation' for better health. They are composed of inputs, processes, and outputs that are affected by determinants like organisational, technical, and behavioural factors which in turn affect health system performance and consequently lead to better health outcomes (Aqil *et al.* 2009; Lippeveld, Sauerborn & Bodart 2000).

The Health Metrics Network Framework (HMN) has two parts. These are the normative portion (components and standards) and an implementation portion (a roadmap) (WHO 2008a). The Performance of Routine Information System Management (PRISM) framework consists of tools to assess HIS performance and identify technical, behavioural, and organisational factors that affect HIS; aid in designing priority interventions to improve performance; and improve quality and use of health data (MEASURE Evaluation 2010).

Data quality

As originally proposed HIS performance is defined as improved data quality and continuous use of information (USAID/Ministry of Health 2006). Data quality is further described in four dimensions: consistency, completeness, timeliness, and accuracy. Completeness is measured not only as filling in all data elements in the facility report form, but also as the proportion of facilities reporting in an administrative area (province or district). Timeliness is assessed as submission of the reports by an accepted deadline. Accuracy is measured by comparing data between facility records and reports, and between facility reports and administrative area databases, respectively. Consistency is the degree of similarity of patient data on register and patient cards. Timeliness measures whether the health facility reports on the given time schedule to the next level (Lippeveld *et al.* 2000).

Organisational determinants

Governance, planning, availability of resources, training, supervision, finances, information distribution, and promotion of culture of information are organisational factors that can affect HIS performance (Aqil *et al.* 2009). Based on the proximity principle values related to organisational processes that emphasise data quality: use of HIS information, evidence-based decision-making, problem solving, feedback from staff and community, a sense of responsibility, and empowerment and accountability were chosen to measure the culture of information (Ajzen 2005). HMIS is crucial for HIS performance and is measured through availability of HIS vision statements and the establishment and maintenance of HIS support services, such as planning, training, supervision, human resources, logistics, and finance; so by identifying levels of support services, it is possible to prioritise for actions (Odhiambo Otieno 2005a).

Technical determinants

Technical determinant factors are related to the specialised know-how and technology to develop, manage, and improve HIS processes and performance. These factors refer to the development of indicators; designing data collection forms; and preparing procedural manuals, types of information technology and software development for data processing and analysis (Aqil *et al.* 2009). The PRISM framework assumes that if indicators are irrelevant, data collection forms are complex to fill in, and if computer software is not user-friendly, it will affect the confidence level and motivation of HIS implementers. Similarly, when software does not process data properly and in a timely manner the resulting analysis does not provide meaningful conclusions for decision-making, affecting the use of information (Aqil *et al.* 2009).

Behavioural determinants

Behavioural determinants like HIS users' demand, confidence, motivation, and competence to perform HIS tasks, affect HIS processes and performance directly. How an individual feels about the utility or outcomes of a task or his confidence in performing that task, as well as the complexity of the task, all affect the likelihood of that task being performed (Hackman & Oldham 1980).

Previous literatures

Previous studies showed that data quality was poor in different resource-limited settings and different technical, behavioural, and organisational factors have been identified.

In the early twenty-first century increasing evidence showed that routine information systems were not producing the intended results. Studies showed that data quality was poor in different settings like Mozambique and Kenya (Mavimbe, Braa & Bjune 2005; Odhiambo-Otieno 2005b). Similarly, use of information for planning and decision-making was found to be weak in Brazil (Da Silva & Laprega 2005). Many factors contributed to underperforming information systems, such as difficulty in calculating indicators because of poor choices for denominators in the Democratic Republic of Congo (Mapatano & Piripiri 2005). Also observed were errors in HIS reports; inadequacies in computerisation, human, and capital resources; and low management support in Kenya (Odhiambo-Otieno 2005b). In Tanzania, Nsubuga, Eseko and Tadesse (2002) found weaknesses in the areas of standardised case definitions, quality of reporting, analysis, supervision, and feedback.

A study from Uganda showed that there was low information use (24%), which was consistent with the limited observed skills level to interpret (41%) and use information (44%) (Aqil *et al.* 2008). Another study conducted on developments of HMIS in Uganda reported that during the past 5 years, timeliness of monthly reporting of outpatient data from the districts to the central level improved markedly from a national average of 21% in 2000, to 63% in 2002, and to 88% in 2004 (Peter, Miriam & Amos 2005). Limited knowledge of the usefulness of HIS data was found to be a major factor in low data quality and information use in Kenya (Odhiambo-Otieno 2005b).

A study conducted on utilisation of HIS in Jimma Zone by Sultan, Challi and Waju (2011) stated that 8 (26.7%), 57 (31.3%), and 54 (36.0%) units and/or departments of Health Posts, Health Centres, and District Offices, respectively, tried to change data into information, with cumulative (overall utilisation of health information) 32.9% units and/or departments of health facilities used their data/information for decision-making, planning, budget and M&E of their activities. There were also poorly coordinated processes and absence of capacity building activities reported.

Another study conducted in Bahr Dar by Helen T. (2011) on assessment of HMIS implementation reported that there was no incentive for information use or motivation to improve information culture. The same study reported that rules and regulations in the new HMIS were found to be low as 47.5% of the respondents lack confidence to participate and make decisions for HMIS-related activities; 65.7% of respondents lack appropriate technologies to utilise information; and the use of information for decision-making was found to be 45.6%, among them 35.3% used it for future reference and 42.4% used to observe trends, with 42.9% to pass report data to health office.

A report from the assessment done by Gebrekidan, Negus and Hajira (2012) on data quality and information use showed that a limited culture of using information for decision-making in planning and management of implementing programs was observed and only 37% of the facilities exercised discussion and made decisions using findings from routine health information. Similarly there was also inadequate supervision and feedback from senior levels to address the problems of inadequate documentation, late and incomplete reporting, and inaccurate reporting. These findings indicate the extent to which data quality can be adversely affected by limited investment in infrastructure and human resource capacity as well as by the performance of the data aggregation and reporting units of the system. The assessment also identified there was an observed assigned focal person for HMIS at 25 (78%) health facilities with 7 (28%) of the focal persons having information technology training. In addition, regular budget allocation for HMIS running costs were found at 7 (22%) of the health facilities.

A study conducted by Gashaw (2006) on utilisation of HMIS showed that the overall utilisation of HMIS was found to be 22.5% and training, standard data collection methods, data processing, and reporting were the major factors that affect use of information. The HMIS Task Force (2011) reported that although the available information system facilitates the decentralisation process, the information lacks quality and authenticity, and utilising information for decision-making and providing feedback to concerned parties was not yet a common practice.

An assessment was conducted on implementation of the new HMIS by the Ethiopian FMOH and HMN in 2009 on the four pioneer regions focusing on HMIS resources, data quality, information use, motivation of staffs, etc. They found that availability of the HMIS registers, forms, and tools was not up to the expectations and the availability of display charts recommended by the new HMIS and M&E guidelines were found to be less impressive. Similarly there was evidence of compliance with regular performance reviews and use of data for decision making. This assessment also showed that timeliness of reports varied from 67% to 100% for hospitals, from 86% to 100% for health centres, and from 75% to 86% for health posts, whereas completeness of reports ranged from 93% to 96% in hospitals, from 89% to 96% in health centres, and from 83% to 91% in health posts (Woldemariam *et al.* 2010).

Generally, HIS performance is assessed in terms of HIS input, process, and output and this performance is measured by availability of good data quality and continuous use of information. This in turn is affected by technical, behavioural, and organisational factors. The PRISM Conceptual framework presented in Figure 1 is based on the concept that HIS assessment is one of the HIS inputs which assesses its performance and identifies technical, behavioural, and organisational factors that affect data quality and information use which in turn affects the health system of a country. Based on the findings of this assessment HIS strategy will be

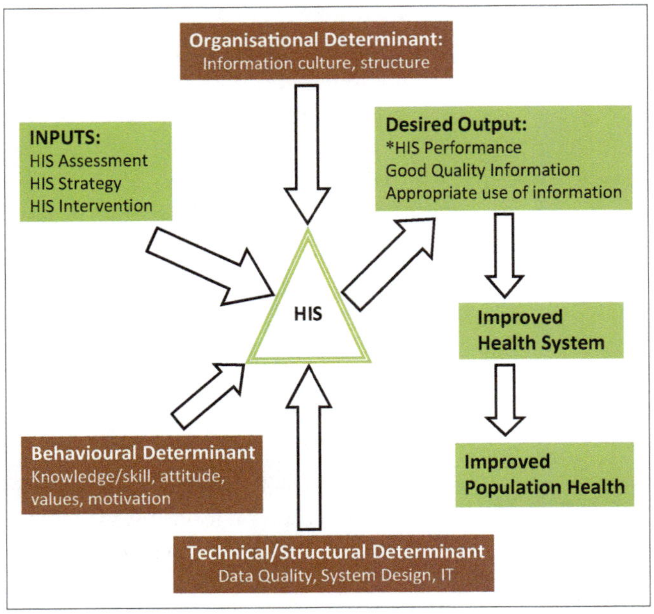

Source: Adopted from MEASURE Evaluation 2008

FIGURE 1: Performance of Routine Information System Management (PRISM) Conceptual Framework.

developed, and according to the strategy, an intervention will be taken.

Research methodology

This study was conducted in Dire Dawa Administration, Ethiopia, health facilities from March 1 to March 31 in 2013. Dire Dawa is one of the two chartered cities in Ethiopia (the other being the capital, Addis Ababa). Dire Dawa lies in the eastern part of Ethiopia which is 501 km away from Addis Ababa. The Dire Dawa Administration has 1 governmental hospital, 16 health centres, and 34 health posts. Except for the regional health bureau, it has no zonal or district health bureau.

Based on the 2007 census conducted by the Central Statistical Agency of Ethiopia (CSA), Dire Dawa has a total population of 342 827, of whom 171 930 were men and 170 897 women; 69.92% of the population are considered urban inhabitants, with an estimated area of 1231.20 km^2.

Research design

The research used a facility-based cross-sectional study design i.e. study participants have been selected at a particular time point to assess the level of information utilisation and data quality and associated factors.

Respondents and sampling

The study population was all unit and/or department heads of hospitals, health centres, and health posts. Because all health facilities in the administration currently implement HMIS, all unit and/or department heads from all health facilities were included in the study. In Dire Dawa Administration, there are a total of 267 unit and/or department heads from all health facilities including health posts.

Data collection procedures, instrument and quality management

A face-to-face interview using a structured questionnaire was used to collect primary data among all unit and/or department heads of the health facilities. The questionnaire was adopted from the PRISM framework assessment tool version 3.1. This tool is useful to collect detailed information on the strengths and weaknesses of HIS in its input, process, and output and identifies factors affecting its performance. It was prepared in English, translated to Amharic and then back to English by another person to ensure consistency. Two health professionals who are members of HIS monitoring team were assigned as supervisors. Six health professionals who had basic HMIS training and had prior experience on data collection were assigned as data collectors. To maintain data quality during the data collection period, the two supervisors and the principal investigators performed the supervision of data collection procedures, checked every completed questionnaire, and gave onsite technical assistance to the data collectors.

Data analysis

The collected data was checked for completeness, and coded, entered, and cleaned using STATA version 11. Analysis of the data was done using the same package. Because all the variables were categorical frequencies, percentages were computed to present the descriptive analysis. Associations between the dependent and independent variables were computed using binary logistic regression. A $p < 0.05$ was considered as cut-off point for statistical significance.

To check whether the fitted model predicted well or not, the ROC curve was analysed and the Hosmer–Lemeshow test used to test overall goodness of fit. Multicollinearity in the variables was checked using Variance Inflation Factor (VIF). Interaction was also checked during the analysis.

Ethical consideration

Institutional ethical clearance was first sought from Mekelle University, College of Health Science. Data was collected after written consent from Dire Dawa regional health bureau. During the interview each participant was informed about the aim of the study. The interviewer discussed the issue of confidentiality and participants were informed that they had full right to refuse or discontinue participating in the research.

Research results

Descriptive analysis

Out of the total 239 respondents 188 (78.7%) were from 16 health centres, 28 (11.7%) were from health posts, and the remaining 23 (9.6%) were from one referral hospital. Of the total departments included on this study 25 (10.4%) were from an adult outpatient department, 12 (5%) were each from emergency, delivery, and antiretroviral therapy departments, 15 (6.3%) were from tuberculosis and leprosy departments,

10 (4.2%) from voluntary counselling and testing departments, and 15 (6.3%) from under 5 outpatient department (OPD) (Table 1).

Health Information System input

The majority of the respondents, 150 (62.7%) reported that there were no assigned HIS personnel and 154 (64.4%) reported there was no separate HIS office in their department. The majority, 195 (81.6%) department heads reported there was no specific budget assigned for HIS. Around 125 (52.3%) of the respondents also revealed there was no legislative, regulatory, and planning framework in their facility (Table 2).

Health Information System process

One hundred ninety-one (79.9%) unit and/or department heads reported that they collect health data on a daily basis.

TABLE 1: Distribution of units and/or departments heads of hospital, health centres and health posts in Dire Dawa Administration health facility, April 2013.

Distribution	Frequency	%
Unit and/or departments		
VCT	10	4.2
Adult OPD	25	10.4
Under 5 OPD	16	6.7
Laboratory	16	6.7
Pharmacy	16	6.7
Family planning	15	6.3
ANC/PMCT	15	6.3
Emergency	12	5.0
Delivery	12	5.0
Environmental	15	6.3
EPI	15	6.3
TBL	15	6.3
ART	12	5.0
Ward/IPD	9	3.8
Statistics unit	8	3.3
Health facility		
Unit and/or departments of health centres	188	78.7
Unit and/or departments of hospital	23	9.6
Units of health post	28	11.7

VCT, voluntary counselling and testing; OPD, outpatient department; ANC, antenatal care; PMCT, prevention of mother to child transmission; EPI, expanded program on immunisation; TBL, tuberculosis and leprosy; IPD, inpatient department.

TABLE 2: Health facility department's HIS inputs in Dire Dawa Administration, April 2013.

HIS input	Frequency			
	Yes		No	
	n	%	*n*	%
Personnel assigned to HIS	89	37.2	150	62.7
Separate unit assigned to HIS	85	35.5	154	64.5
Availability of equipment for HIS	149	62.3	90	37.7
Adequacy of equipment	68	45.6	81	54.4
Specific budget assigned for HIS	44	18.4	195	81.6
Mechanism to facilitate HIS resource	117	49.0	122	51.0
HIS training for staffs	126	52.7	113	47.3
Planning framework to use HIS	114	48.0	125	52.0
Duration of training				
Less than 6 months	28	22.2	-	-
6 months – 1 year	30	23.8	-	-
More than 1 year	68	54.0	-	-

HIS, Health Information System.

The majority, 196 (82.0%) departments also keep patient registration and HIS monthly reports. Among them 137 (57.3%) revealed the records were easily accessible to their staffs. In addition, 164 (68.6%) heads also reported that they received directives in the last 3 months to check data accuracy, to fill formats completely, and to submit the monthly report on time. In this study 185 (77.4%) department heads claimed they submitted HIS reports on time (Table 3).

Health Information System output

Compiling of HIS data and reports containing HIS information was reported by 170 (71.1%) and 162 (67.8%) department heads respectively. Display of key indicators was reported by 145 (60.7%) and quarterly and any other feedback reports were also available in 138 (57.7%) departments. Regarding the use of health information for decision making, 156 (65.3%) reported that they use information to make decisions. Among them 72 (46.2%) use the information for future reference; 66 (42.3%) observe trends of service delivery, and 18 (11.5%) pass reports for other subsidy health offices respectively (Table 4).

Data quality was also determined based on the set criteria and compared by facility type. The analysis revealed that 78.3% of unit and/or departments in the referral hospital were assured data quality, 77% in health centres, and 64% in health posts. On average 75.3% unit and/or departments assured data quality (Figure 2).

Technical determinant characteristics for data quality

Health departments which had a standard set of indicators were 98% more likely to achieve data quality than departments without a standard set of indicators (COR=1.981, 95% CI [1.035, 3.792]). In addition, units and/or departments which had skilled human resource were 3.26 times more likely to achieve data quality than departments without skilled human resource (COR=3.260, 95% CI [1.742, 6.103]). Departments which had well-designed reporting formats

TABLE 3: Health facility department's HIS process in Dire Dawa Administration, April 2013.

HIS process	Frequency			
	Yes		No	
	n	%	*n*	%
Collecting data on daily activities	191	79.9	48	20.1
Keep registration and copies of HIS monthly report	196	82.0	43	18.0
Accessibility of records for staffs	148	62.0	91	38.0
Procedures for distributing and reporting data	178	74.5	61	25.5
Data put at administrative level	205	85.7	34	14.3
Criteria for verification of completeness and consistency	181	75.7	58	24.3
Receive directives in the last 3 month	164	68.6	75	31.4
Timeliness of reported data	185	77.4	54	32.6
Completeness of reported data	196	82.0	43	18.0
Consistency of reported data	188	78.7	51	21.3
Representativeness of data	195	81.9	44	18.1

HIS, Health Information System.

were 2.38 times more likely to achieve data quality than departments without (COR=2.383, 95% CI [1.201, 4.728]). Similarly, departments which had trained staffs able to fill formats were 3.52 times more likely to achieve data quality (COR=3.521, 95% CI [1.799, 6.893]). Departments which had a friendly format for reporting were 2.25 times more likely to achieve data quality than departments without a friendly format, (COR=2.254, 95% CI [1.178, 4.311]). After adjusting with other variables, only trained staffs to fill out formats were found to be statistically significant (AOR=2.253, 95% CI [1.082, 4.692]). Hence, departments who had trained staffs to fill formats were 2.253 times more likely to achieve data quality than those departments without (Table 5).

TABLE 4: Health facility department's HIS output in Dire Dawa Administration, April 2013.

HIS output	Frequency			
	Yes		No	
	n	%	*n*	%
Department compile HIS data	170	71.1	69	28.9
Compile any report containing HIS information	162	67.8	77	32.2
Display key indicators with tables	145	60.7	94	39.3
Presence of catchment area map	163	68.2	76	31.8
Display summary of demographic information	177	74.0	62	26.0
Availability of feedback or other report on HIS data	138	57.7	101	42.3
Use HIS data for decision making	156	65.3	83	34.7
Use HIS data for future reference	72	46.2	-	-
Use HIS data to observe trends	66	42.3	-	-
Use HIS data to pass for subsidy health office	18	11.5	-	-
Present target & performance	147	61.5	92	38.5
Calculation of area coverage	92	38.5	147	61.5
Presence of routine review meeting	146	61.1	93	38.9
Incentive for information use	67	28.1	172	71.9
Policy for information use	87	36.4	152	63.6
Dissemination mechanism of health information	154	64.4	85	35.6

HIS, Health Information System.

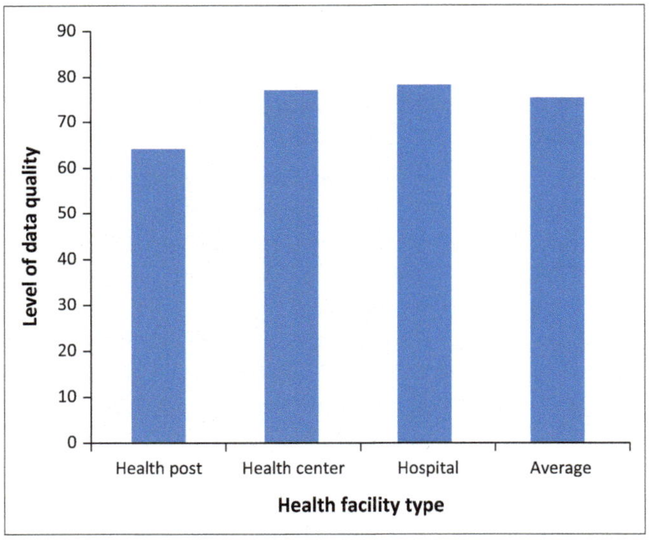

FIGURE 2: Data quality by health facility type in Dire Dawa Administration, April 2013.

Organisational and behavioural determinant characteristics for data quality

Health departments which base their decisions on supervisor directives were 3.26 times more likely to achieve data quality than those departments which did not base their decisions on supervisor directives (COR=3.260, 95% CI [1.742,6.103]). Health departments which had organisational culture were 2.28 times more likely to achieve data quality than departments without (COR=2.282, 95% CI [1.246, 4.178]). Health departments which based their decision on personal liking were 50% less likely to achieve data quality than departments which did not (COR = 0.505, 95% CI [0.267, 0.955]). Whereas departments which based their decisions on evidence and on considering cost were 3.47 and 2.02 times more likely to achieve data quality than departments which did not (COR=3.476, 95% CI [1.775, 6.806]) and (COR=2.020, 95% CI [1.080, 3.777]). Health managers who report on data accuracy regularly were 88% more likely to achieve data quality than those departments in which their managers did not report data accuracy (COR=1.885, 95% CI [1.018, 3.489]). Similarly health managers who seek feedback from supervisors were 3.49 times more likely to achieve data quality than those managers who did not seek feedback, (COR=3.495, 95% CI [1.859, 6.571]); however after adjusting these variables with other variables, only decisions based on supervisor directives and managers seeking feedback were found to be determinant factors for data quality. Hence departments whose decisions were based on supervisor directives were 2.15 times more likely to achieve data quality than those department which did not base their decision on supervisor directives, (AOR=2.131, 95% CI [1.073, 4.233]). Similarly health managers who sought feedback from senior supervisors were 2.54 times more likely to achieve data quality than those managers who did not seek feedback, (AOR=2.481, 95% CI [1.262, 4.876]) (Table 6).

TABLE 5: Associated technical factors for Data quality in all governmental health facilities in Dire Dawa Administration, April 2005 EC.

Determinants	Data quality	COR (1^R)	95% CI	AOR (1^R)	95% CI
Standard set of indicator	Agree	1.981	1.035, 3.792	0.843	0.321, 2.176
	Disagree	-	-	-	-
Well-designed format	Agree	2.383	1.201, 4.729	2.895	0.553, 14.950
	Disagree	-	-	-	-
Trained staff to fill format	Agree	3.521	1.799, 6.893	2.253	1.082, 4.692*
	Disagree	-	-		
Skilled human resource	Agree	3.260	1.742, 6.103	2.325	0.910, 5.931
	Disagree	-	-	-	-
Friendly format for reporting	Agree	2.254	1.178, 4.311	1.477	0.696, 3.113
	Disagree	-	-	-	-

*, $p < 0.05$; 1^R, agree versus disagree ratio; CI, confidence interval; COR, crud odds ratio; AOR, adjusted odds ratio.

TABLE 6: Associated organisational and behavioural determinant characteristics for data quality in all governmental health facilities in Dire Dawa Administration, April 2013.

Determinants	Data quality	COR (1^R)	95% CI	AOR (1^R)	95% CI
Existence of organisational culture	Agree	2.282	1.246, 4.178	1.781	0.943, 3.382
	Disagree	-	-	-	-
Decision based on personal liking	Agree	0.505	0.267, 0.955	0.613	0.320, 1.214
	Disagree	-	-	-	-
Decision based on supervisor directive	Agree	3.260	1.742, 6.103	2.131	1.073, 4.233 *
	Disagree	-	-	-	-
Decision based on evidence/fact	Agree	3.476	1.775, 6.806	2.062	0.831, 5.073
	Disagree	-	-	-	-
Decision based on considering cost	Agree	2.020	1.080, 3.777	1.245	0.601, 2.554
	Disagree	-	-	-	-
Lack of promotion of culture of information	Agree	2.349	1.290, 4.275	1.816	0.951, 3.414
	Disagree	-	-	-	-
Managers seek feedback	Agree	3.495	1.859, 6.571	2.481	1.262, 4.876 *
	Disagree	-	-	-	-
Managers' report on data accuracy	Agree	1.88	1.018, 3.489	1.025	0.413, 1.864
	Disagree	-	-	-	-

*, $p < 0.05$; 1^R, agree versus disagree ratio; CI, confidence interval; COR, crud odds ratio; AOR, adjusted odds ratio.

Discussion of findings

Based on PRISM framework using HIS performance diagnostic tools, this study assessed the current status of HIS performance at health facilities' HIS input, process, and output, and identified possible determinants of technical, organisational, and behavioural factors for HIS data quality.

From the findings of this study 75% of units and/or departments reported that they had trained staffs and skilled human resources who were capable of performing HIS tasks. Only 37% of departments reported there were specifically assigned personnel for HIS activity. Similarly 35% of the facilities have separate HIS offices and 19% have assigned budgets for HIS. These finding were somewhat comparable with a similar study in Bahr-Dar where 45%, 43%, and 21% was reported for availability of HIS personnel, HIS offices, and budgets, respectively (Helen 2011); only 23.8% were reported for trained staff in North Gondar (Gashaw 2006). Regarding availability of HIS equipment, 63% had the necessary equipment. However, availability of coordination mechanisms to facilitate the use of HIS resources and presence of regulatory and planning frameworks to use HIS were found to be below 50%. This may be due to less concern was given to these issues by the majority of the facilities. Considering training on HIS activity, 53% responded for availability of training. It is known that continuous training on HIS activity is important to create awareness and to have trained staff and skilled human resources that are confident and motivated to perform HIS tasks. When compared to a similar study conducted in Jimma, Ethiopia, HIS training was below 50% (Sultan *et al.* 2011).

In order to check the accuracy of the data collected and report at the origin of data source, patient registrations and copies of HIS monthly reports should be kept. According to this study 90% of departments collect health data on daily activity and 82% keep patient registration and HIS monthly reports. These records were also easily accessible to staffs and easily retrieved in 67% of the departments. A similar study done in Jimma, Ethiopia, reported that all health departments collect data on daily activity and 73% keep their registration and monthly reports (Sultan *et al.* 2011). Whereas the study conducted in Bahr Dar, Ethiopia, revealed that only 77% collect data on daily activity. In this study more than 74% of departments had clear procedures for distributing and reporting the collected data, 85% put the data at administrative level and 75% used a set of criteria to verify completeness and consistency of data before reporting. Regarding availability of supervision, 69% of units and/or departments had received supervisor directives to check data accuracy, to fill format completely, and submit monthly reports on time. This was higher when compared with similar studies where availability of supervision was reported below 50% in Bahr-Dar and North Gonder (Helen 2011; Gashaw 2006). This may be because the majority of the health facilities were easily reachable for supervision.

Accurate, consistent, complete, and timely information is essential for public health decision-making and action-taking such as policymaking, planning, programming, and monitoring. In this study, 77.4% of department heads indicated that reports were submitted according to the schedule, which is between the 20th and 22nd of the month for health posts, and the 20th to 24th for health centres and hospitals. Eighty-two per cent of department heads who indicated reports were completely filled before reporting; and 78.7% of these reports were agreed to be consistent. A similar study in North Gonder showed only 50% HMIS reports were submitted timely and 96% of these reports were completely filled (Gashaw 2006). Consistency of reports in this study was slightly higher when compared to the study in Jimma where 62% of respondents claimed consistency of reports (Sultan *et al.* 2011). This increment may be because the majority of units and/or departments had basic HIS training, which in turn had skilled human resources to perform HIS tasks in improving data quality and information use. Another reason could be the availability of good supervision and feedback given by senior supervisors.

About 61% of the units and/or departments reported there were routine meetings for reviewing managerial and administrative matters. This was higher when compared to the assessment report on data quality and information use in selected health facilities (Helen 2011), where only 23.5% of facilities had routine review meetings. In this study, availability of incentives and policies for information use were found to be below 40%. A similar finding was reported on the study conducted in Bahr Dar where only 18.3% and 42.9% respectively were reported for availability of incentives and policies (Helen 2011).

Although the PRISM framework allows for identifying determinant factors for HIS utilisation and data quality, lack of similar studies conducted using this framework did not allow for the comparison of the identified determinant factors between different studies.

Regarding data quality, trained staff to fill format was found to be the predictor for data quality. Among possible organisational and behavioural determinants, decisions based on supervisor directives and managers seeking feedback were found to be determinant factors for data quality.

Conclusion and recommendations

The level of data quality was below the national standard in all health facilities which is below 80%. However hospitals and health centres have better performance compared to health posts. The factors which affect data quality were lack of training, lack of decision based on supervision, and lack of feedback. To improve the data quality at the health facility level managers should supervise and give feedback on time. In addition continuous training should to be provided to health care providers.

Acknowledgements

We are grateful to the research team who dedicated their full time and effort during data collection. We would like to thank the Dire Dawa Administration Health Bureau for cooperation in undertaking this research and also all department heads of hospital, health centres, and health posts for their participation and support in providing the required information for this research.

Competing interests

The authors declare that they have no financial or personal relationships which may have inappropriately influenced them in writing this article.

Authors' contributions

K.T. (Drie Dawa City Administration Health Bureau), K.T. (Mekelle University), G.M. and W.T. conceived and designed the study. K.T. (Drie Dawa City Administration Health Bureau), K.T. (Mekelle University), G.M., W.T. performed the study and analysed the data.

References

Ajzen, I., 2005, 'Laws of human behavior: Symmetry, compatibility, and attitude-behavior correspondence'. In A. Beauducel, B. Biehl, M. Bosniak, W. Conrad, G. Schönberger, & D. Wagener (Eds.), *Multivariate research strategies* (pp. 3-19). Shaker Verlag, Germany.

Aqil, A., Hotchkiss, D., Lippeveld, T., Mukooyo, E. & Asiimwe, S., 2008, *Do the PRISM framework tools produce consistent and valid results? A Uganda study*. Working Paper. National Information Resource Center, Ministry of Health, MEASURE Evaluation, Uganda, 14 March 2008.

Aqil, A., Lippeveled, T. & Dairiku, H., 2009, 'PRISM framework: A paradigm shift for designing, strengthening and evaluating routine health information systems', *Health Policy and Planning* 24(3), 217–228, viewed 08 December 2012, from http://www.qub.ac.uk/cite2write/harvard3l.html

Chawla, R., Bansal, A.K. & Indrayan, A., 1997, 'Informatics technology in health care', *Nati Med* 10(1), 31–50.

Da Silva, A.S. & Laprega, M.R., 2005, 'Critical evaluation of the primary care information system (SIAB) and its implementation in Ribeiero Preto, Sau Paulo, Brazil', *Cadernos de Saude Publica* 21, 1821–1828.

Gashaw, A., 2006, 'Assessment of utilization of Health Information System at district level with particular emphasis to HIV/AIDS program in North Gonder', Master's thesis, Department of Community Health Medical Faculty, Addis Ababa University.

GAVI, 2002, *Monitoring national immunization system using core indicators*, WHO. Geneva.

Gebrekidan, M., Negus, W. & Hajira, M., 2012, 'Data quality and information use: Asystematic review to improve evidence in Ethiopia', *African Health Monitor*, March (14).

Hackman, J.R. & Oldham, G.R., 1980, *Work redesign*, Addison-Wesley, Reading, MA.

Helen, T., 2011, 'Assessment of the Health Management Information System implementation status in public health facilities in Bahir-Dar city', Master's thesis, School of Information Science, Addis Ababa University.

HMIS Reform Team, 2007, *Health management information system/M&E: Information use guidelines and display tools*, Federal Ministry of Health, Addis Abeba.

HMIS Task Force, 2011, *SNNP Regional Government*. MoH. Addis Abeba.

Lippeveld, T., Sauerborn, R. & Bodart, C., 2000, *Design and implementation of health information systems*, WHO, Geneva.

Mapatano, M.A. & Piripiri, L., 2005, 'Some common errors in health information system report (DR Congo)', *Sante´ Publique* 17, 551–558. http://dx.doi.org/10.3917/spub.054.0551

Mavimbe, J.C., Braa, J. & Bjune, G., 2005, 'Assessing immunization data quality from routine reports in Mozambique', *BMC Public Health* 11, 108. http://dx.doi.org/10.1186/1471-2458-5-108

MEASURE Evaluation, 2010, *Performance of Routine Information System Management Framework*, 3.1 edn., USAID, Washington, DC.

MoH, 2010, *Health Facility's Revised Health Management Information System (HMIS) procedural manual*, MoH, Kampala.

Nsubuga, P., Eseko, N. & Tadesse, W., 2002, 'Structure and performance of infectious disease surveillance and response, United Republic of Tanzania, 1998', *Bulletin of the World Health Organization* 80, 196–203.

Odhiambo-Otieno, G.W., 2005a, 'Evaluation criteria for district health management information systems: Lessons from the Ministry of Health, Kenya', *International Journal of Medical Informatics* 74, 31–38. http://dx.doi.org/10.1016/j.ijmedinf.2004.09.003

Odhiambo-Otieno, G.W., 2005b, 'Evaluation of existing district health management information systems: A case study of the district health systems in Kenya', *International Journal of Medical Informatics* 74, 733–744. http://dx.doi.org/10.1016/j.ijmedinf.2005.05.007

Peter, K., Miriam, N. & Amos, N., 2005, 'Development of HMIS in poor countries: Uganda as case study', *Health Policy and Development Journal* 3(1), 48–50.

Sahay, S., 2001, 'Special issues on IT and health care in developing countries', *Electronic Journal of Information Systems in Developing Countries* 5(1), 1-6.

Sultan, A., Challi, J. & Waju, B., 2011, 'Utilization of Health Information System at district level in Jimma zone', *Ethiopian Journal of Health Science* 21, 75–79.

TUTAPE, 2009, *Tullen University supported HMIS Implementation program Training Manual*, TUTAPE, Addis Ababa.

USAID/Ministry of Health, 2006, *Rwanda Health Information System Assessment Report*, RTI International, Rwanda.

WHO, 2004, *Developing Health Management Information System a practical guide for developing countries*, WHO, Geneva.

WHO, 2007, *Assessment of Ethiopian National Health Information System*, WHO, Geneva.

WHO, 2008a, *A Framework and Standards for Country Health Information System Development*, WHO, Geneva.

WHO, 2008b, *Assessing the National Health Information System: An Assessment Tool version, 4*, WHO, Genava.

WHO, 2008c, *Healthmetrics*, viewed 08 December 2012, from http://www.who.int/entity/healthmetrics/hmn

Woldemariam, H., Habtamu, T., Fekadu, N. & Habtamu, A., 2010, 'Implementation of an integrated Health Management Information System and Monitoring and Evaluation (HMIS/M&E) system in Ethiopia: Progress and lessons from pioneering regions', *Quarterly health Bulletin* 3(1), 48–52.

World Health Organization Regional Office for the Western Pacific, 1986, *Workshops on the assessment and development of national Health Information Systems (HIS) and epidemiological surveillance*: WHO, Geneva.

Knowledge creation and transfer amongst post-graduate students

Authors:
Kreeson Naicker[1]
Krishna K. Govender[1,2]
Karunagaran Naidoo[1]

Affiliations:
[1]School of Management, Information Technology & Governance, University of KwaZulu-Natal, South Africa

[2]Regenesys Business School, Johannesburg, South Africa

Correspondence to:
Krishna Govender

Email:
krishnag@regenesys.co.za

Postal address:
4 Pybus Road, Sandton 2146, South Africa

Background: The skill shortages, hyper-competitive economic environments and untapped economies have created a great deal of focus on knowledge. Thus, continuously creating and transferring knowledge is critical for every organisation.

Objectives: This article reports on an exploratory study undertaken to ascertain how knowledge is created and transferred amongst post-graduate (PG) students, using the knowledge (socialisation, externalisation, combination, internalisation [SECI]) spiral model.

Method: After reviewing relevant literature, a personally administered standardised questionnaire was used to collect data from a convenience sample of PG students in the School of Management, IT and Governance at the University of KwaZulu-Natal, South Africa. The data was analysed to determine if it fit the model based on the four modes of knowledge conversion.

Results: Although the School of Management, IT and Governance has mechanisms in place to facilitate knowledge creation and transfer, it nevertheless tends to focus on the four modes of knowledge conversion to varying degrees.

Conclusion: The study confirmed that PG students utilise the 'socialisation' and 'externalisation' modes of knowledge conversion comprehensively; 'internalisation' plays a significant role in their knowledge creation and transfer activities and whilst 'combination' is utilised to a lesser extent, it still plays a role in PG students' knowledge creation and transfer activities. PG students also have 'space' that allows them to bring hunches, thoughts, notions, intuition or tacit knowledge into reality. Trust and dedication are common amongst PG students. With socialisation and externalisation so high, PG students are aware of each other's capabilities and competencies, and trust each other enough to share knowledge.

Introduction

Information on demand is a powerful aspect of the mode in which academic organisations, teams and individuals operate. There is a constant need for academic organisations, teams and individuals to accelerate the communication of information and knowledge to each other and organisations outside the academic sphere (Nelson 2005). An individual is often afraid to share their knowledge and they have a tendency to guard their knowledge and selectively release it. This tendency is often cited as a core problem when working in a team and the cause of poor collaboration between team members (Gilmour 2003). In order to leverage on innovation as one of the most important sources of competitiveness and success, academics need to have access to and mobilise their knowledge resources (Voelpel, Von Pierer & Streb 2006).

Knowledge is generally separated into two types: explicit and tacit knowledge. Hautala (2011:605) explains that 'academic knowledge aims at creating or exploring the new' tacit and explicit elements, which together with theory and practice are used to form knowledge. Tacit knowledge is a personal, contextual and practical entity that is difficult to communicate (Polanyi 1966). For example, balancing a bicycle to ride it requires tacit knowledge that is not easy to explain to someone who has never actually ridden one. Similarly, understanding and conducting a research project as part of an academic field, research group and society also includes tacit knowledge (Hautala 2011:605).

Davenport and Prusak (1998:81) argue that codifying tacit knowledge is difficult, but that 'its substantial value makes it worth the effort'. Notwithstanding some of the challenges cited by the scholars and practitioners referenced above, the decision to focus only on tacit knowledge instead of knowledge in general can be justified by reasons that include, but are not limited to, its substantial volume and value to the organisation (Suppiah & Sandhu 2011). The ability to create, store, disseminate and utilise knowledge and expertise has become a primary way for organisations, teams and individuals to compete (Hayashi 2004). Amassing and synthesising specialised knowledge from multiple sources is a pivotal factor in resolving the technical and operational uncertainties that impede Nonaka and Takeuchi's (1995) knowledge (SECI) spiral theory.

In light of the above, this article focuses on determining which of the four modes of knowledge conversion assist post-graduate (PG) students to access information on demand.

It is widely accepted that there is difficulty in disseminating tacit knowledge, since tacit knowledge is personal and understandable by the possessor (Alavi & Leidner 2001; Nonaka & Takeuchi 1995; Polanyi 1966). Thus, this study also attempts to establish, through an assessment of the knowledge spiral, if extracting tacit knowledge or engaging with explicit knowledge is essential for a paradigm shift when transcending from the old self to the new self.

Literature review

The genesis of the knowledge (SECI) spiral process

Knowledge is sought and shared in a global arena, whether at a corporate or academic level (Hautala 2011). McKenzie and Van Winkelen (2011) argue that:

> sound decisions rely on having the right knowledge in the right place at the right time, to be able to act effectively. 'Right' knowledge may be different for every decision – some decisions require only surface knowledge, some require more investigation and an evidence base, some use tacit expertise, and others creative insight, intuition and judgment. (p. 403)

Rai (2011) believes that despite the subtle differences between the various knowledge definitions, scholars agree that effective and efficient knowledge management is central to organisational performance and success. In order to assess the capacity of an organisational system to generate new knowledge, the first step is to define knowledge and then how to determine if it is 'new' knowledge, as the aforementioned has a justified belief that increases an entity's capacity for effective action (Arling & Chun 2011).

The conversion of tacit knowledge into explicit knowledge helps knowledge to be crystallised and shared by others, which becomes the basis for the creation of new knowledge. The successful conversion of tacit knowledge into explicit knowledge depends on the sequential use of metaphor, analogy and models (Rai 2011). The materialisation of new knowledge always begins with the individual. A resourceful individual may become conscious of a position that has not been developed, which may lead to the growth or advancement of a product, service or theory. An individual's personal knowledge is transformed into organisational knowledge that is valuable to the company. Making personal knowledge available to others is the central activity of the knowledge-creating company. Nonaka and Konno (1998:26) argue that 'it takes place continuously and at all levels of the organisation', in that one's personal knowledge is transformed into organisational knowledge through the interactions between tacit knowledge and explicit knowledge. Within several loops of interaction where community members share their experiences, ideals and ideas, new knowledge – individual as well as collective knowledge – emerges through this process (Renzl 2006). Oguz and Sengün (2011:446) argue that Nonaka and Takeuchi (1995) popularised tacit knowledge in the management literature. Using the example of the bread master, they promote the link between tacit and explicit knowledge. Their work legitimised the tacit-explicit dichotomy by viewing the two as separate spheres of knowledge. Even though they cite and use Polanyi (1966) approvingly, the ontological dimension of knowing remained inconspicuous. In their view, knowledge creation is the result of an interactive spiral between tacit and explicit knowledge. This rendition has been widely accepted in most of the following literature and has created the tendency to see tacit and explicit knowledge as substitutes (e.g. Nonaka & Takeuchi 1998). According to Nonaka and Takeuchi, there are four ways of converting between tacit and explicit knowledge; these are: socialisation (tacit to tacit), externalisation (tacit to explicit), combination (explicit to explicit) and internalisation (explicit to tacit).

Grant (2007) views tacit knowledge as the ability or skill of an individual to do something or to resolve a problem that is based, in part, on one's own experiences and learning, and probably not all of this knowledge can be shared between individuals. Capturing tacit knowledge is seen as the challenge to organisations that want to spread knowledge throughout the organisation or spur greater innovation. It is treated as a reserve deposited deep within the ground that needs to be detected and then pumped out (Mooradian 2005).

The aforementioned development led Nonaka and Takeuchi (1995), the pioneers of the knowledge spiral model, to believe that tacit and explicit are not totally separate but mutually complementary entities; this led them to further develop the notion that tacit and explicit knowledge interact with and interchange into each other in the creative activities of human beings. The interaction between tacit and explicit knowledge is known as knowledge conversion, which consists of four modes. Girard (2006) believes that the four modes of knowledge conversion need to operate in sync. The four modes of knowledge conversion consist of socialisation, externalisation, combination and internalisation, which are shown in Figure 1. It is important to stress that the success of each mode of knowledge conversion will depend on the leadership and culture of the organisation or team. After all, managing knowledge is all about creating a culture that will institutionalise trust and facilitate knowledge creation, transfer and storage (Kermally 2002). Socialisation helps to move knowledge in tacit form between individuals (in this instance post-graduate students), externalisation is the application of tacit insights on an outside entity, combination represents the act of synthesising explicit pieces of knowledge and finally internalisation is the process through which one increases one's knowledge by learning from external events (Desouza & Awazu 2006).

Knowledge (SECI) conversion refers to the four modes of knowledge creation identified by Nonaka and Takeuchi (1995): socialisation that transfers tacit knowledge, externalisation that converts tacit knowledge into explicit knowledge, combination that integrates explicit knowledge and internalisation that embodies new tacit knowledge (Choo & Drummond de Alvarenga Neto 2010). The knowledge conversion (SECI) process (Figure 2) is deemed to be the blueprint for the knowledge spiral model (Figure 2), where the interaction or dialogue between the modes plays an integral role in knowledge creation and transfer.

Arling and Chun (2011) and Perez-Araos *et al.* (2007), after an examination of Alavi and Leidner's (2001) and Nonaka and Takeuchi's (1995) research respectively, explain that socialisation is the process of converting one individual's tacit knowledge to another individual's tacit knowledge through interpersonal interaction. Tacit knowledge to tacit knowledge (socialisation) is a process of sharing experiences in a direct face-to-face approach to create tacit knowledge, often done through shared mental models, technical skills, observation, imitation and practice. Externalisation is the process of converting tacit knowledge to explicit knowledge. Tacit knowledge to explicit knowledge (externalisation) is a knowledge creation process where a part of tacit knowledge is articulated and turned somehow into explicit form, through analogies, concepts, hypothesis, models, reports, and so on. Combination is the process of creating new explicit knowledge by reconfiguring, re-categorising and re-conceptualising existing explicit knowledge. Explicit knowledge to explicit knowledge (combination) is a process of combining different bodies of explicit knowledge and internalisation is the process of converting explicit knowledge to tacit knowledge.

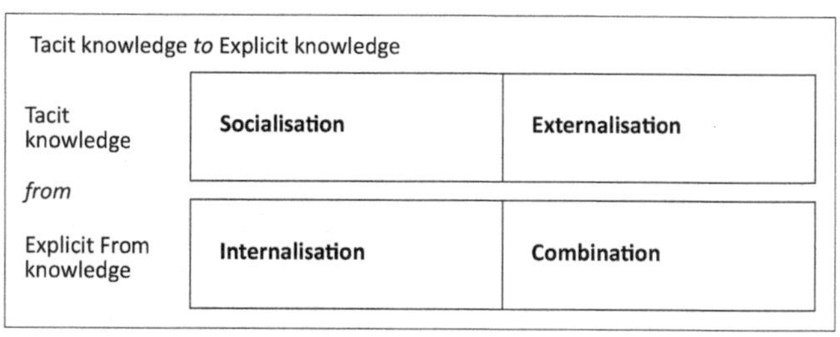

Source: Adapted from Nonaka, I. & Takeuchi, H., 1995, *The knowledge creating company*, Oxford University Press, New York

FIGURE 1: Four modes of knowledge conversion.

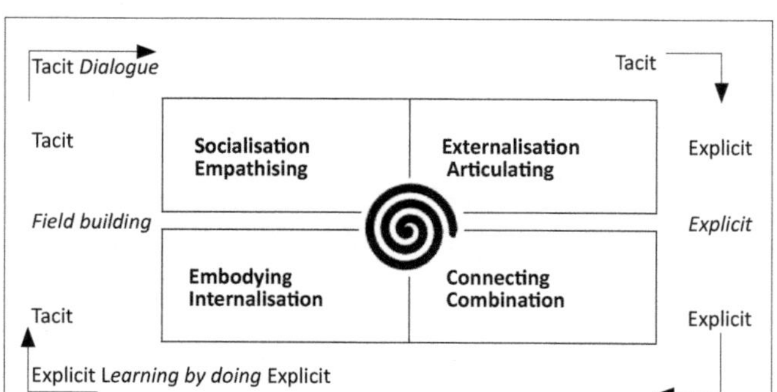

Source: Adapted from Nonaka, I. & Takeuchi, H., 1995, *The knowledge creating company*, Oxford University Press, New York

FIGURE 2: The knowledge spiral.

Explicit knowledge to tacit knowledge (internalisation) is a process of embodying explicit knowledge into tacit knowledge by experiencing knowledge through the explicit source (learning-by-doing approach).

Nonaka and Takeuchi's (1995) knowledge (SECI) spiral model is reliant on the interaction between the micro and macro environments, and changes occur at both the micro and the macro level; an individual (micro) influences and is influenced by the environment (macro) with which they interact (Little, Quintas & Ray 2002).

Against the brief literature review, this study explored knowledge creation and transfer amongst PG students at a research university.

Research methodology

An exploratory research design was employed based on Saunders *et al.*'s (2007:133) affirmation that 'an exploratory study is a valuable means of finding out what is happening; to seek new insights; to ask questions and to assess phenomena in a new light'. Furthermore, Sekaran (2003:119) argues that 'exploratory studies are undertaken to better comprehend the nature of the problem since few studies might have been conducted in that area'.

This study was quantitative in nature, since:

> quantitative methods require the use of standardized measures so that varying perspectives and experiences of people can be fitted into a limited number of predetermined response categories to which numbers are assigned. (Patton 2002:14)

Furthermore:

> the advantage of a quantitative approach is that it's possible to measure the reactions of many people to a limited set of questions, thus facilitating comparison and statistical aggregation of the data. This gives a broad, generalizable set of findings presented succinctly and parsimoniously. (Patton 2002:14)

A questionnaire was used, which comprised a five-point Likert scale that ranged from 1–5 (with 5 = strongly agree and 1 = strongly disagree). The responses were converted to frequencies and percentages, and the results were related to Nonaka and Takeuchi's (1995) knowledge (SECI) spiral model and interpreted accordingly.

As a first step in deciding on the sample, all PG students in the School of Management, Information Technology & Governance, at the University of KwaZulu-Natal constituted the target population. The reason for choosing this group of 'knowledge creators' was a matter of convenience, since a sample from this population would have been easily accessible, since they comprised individuals who were known to the primary researcher. According to McBurney and White (2007) the sampling frame is a population as it is defined for the purposes of selecting subjects for a study; in the context of this study, the *sampling frame* is all accessible post-graduate students in the School of Management, Information

Technology & Governance. The *sample size*, which required making some judgement about the number of participants needed for the study (Devlin 2006), was determined using a non-probability sampling technique, namely convenience sampling. The population of post-graduate students comprises 204 honours students and 132 master's and PhD students. The total number of post graduate students (336) was used in the calculation of the sample size. Using a confidence level of 95% with a confidence interval of 12 results in a sample size of 56 required whilst a confidence level of 95% with a confidence interval of 10 results in a sample size of 75. It was therefore decided to use a sample size within the range of 56 and 75. Approximately 60 students were targeted. The researcher collected 70 completed questionnaires.

Sekaran (2003) explains that for personally administered questionnaires:

> when a survey is confined to a local area, and the organisation is willing and able to assemble groups of employees to respond to the questionnaires at the workplace, a good way to collect data is to personally administer the questionnaires. The main advantage of this is that the researcher or a member of the research team can collect all the completed responses within a short period of time. Any doubts that the respondents might have or any question could be clarified on the spot. (p. 236)

Thus, the questionnaires were personally administered to the PG students.

The reliability of a measure, which indicates the 'extent to which it is without bias (error free) and hence ensures consistent measurement across the various items in the instrument' (Sekaran 2003:203), is reliant on the stability and consistency with which the instrument measures the concept, model or theory. The internal consistency of the measure was maintained as all the sections of the questionnaire focused on measuring if the adaptation of Nonaka and Takeuchi's (1995) knowledge (SECI) spiral model has an influence on the way knowledge is created and transferred by PG students.

Sekaran (2003) proposes that validity is concerned with the authenticity of the cause-and-effect relationships (internal validity), and their generalisability to the external environment (external validity). Although there are several ways of testing validity, this study focused on content validity which is the best test of validity for a questionnaire. Content validity ensures that the measure includes an adequate and representative set of items that tap the concept, theory or model. The questions based on Nonaka and Takeuchi's (1995) knowledge spiral is an adequate and representative set of items that tap into the way knowledge is created and transferred by PG students. The questions are dimensions and elements of Nonaka and Takeuchi's knowledge (SECI) spiral model. For completeness, see the questionnaire in Annexure 1.

Empirical findings

The majority (93%) of respondents were honours students. The remaining 7% were master's students and PhD students. A total of 380 questionnaires were administered.

The Likert scale that was used in the questionnaire had five categories. For the purpose of analysis, all 'strongly agree' and 'agree' responses were collapsed into one category, namely 'agree' because it can be seen from the results that even if 'neutral' is combined with 'disagree' and 'strongly disagree', the results would not be changed.

The use of socialisation

The first mode of the knowledge conversion process, *socialisation*, is determined by seven statements. Table 1 reflects the respondents' agreement or disagreement with each statement.

It is evident from the information in Table 1, that the overwhelming majority of respondents agreed with all seven statements, implying that the 'socialisation' mode was effective in knowledge creation and transfer amongst the PG students.

Use of combination

The third mode of the knowledge conversion process, *combination*, is determined by six statements in the questionnaire.

It is evident from Table 2, that since a two-thirds majority was not achieved for some statements pertaining to 'combination', the 'combination' mode is not predominantly used by the PG students. This confirms that transforming tacit knowledge to explicit knowledge is not a significant activity in the knowledge creation and transfer process.

TABLE 1: Respondents' use of socialisation.

Response	% Who agreed
'I will actively share my experience with others'	82.9
'In my academic team, my teammates and I will share life or work experience with each other'	84.3
'During group discussion, I try to find out others' opinions, thoughts and other information'	94.3
'During discussion, I will bring out some concepts, thoughts or ideas'	92.9
'I often encourage others to express their thoughts'	87.1
'Before group discussion, I will collect necessary information and show it to the group'	68.6
'I like to get to know the people with whom I will work before going into a project together'	75.7

Source: Developed by researchers from the research data

TABLE 2: Respondents' use of combination.

Response	% Who agreed
'During the discussion, I tend to organise ideas and make conclusions to facilitate the discussion'	74.3
'When coming across problems, I tend to use my experience to help solving problems'	84.3
'After every event, I have the habit of organising and making a summary of what happened'	58.6
'During discussion, I will organise everyone's thoughts in my mind'	61.4
'I like to collect new information and make a connection of new and old knowledge to work up new concepts'	77.1
'I like to organise ambiguous concepts into structure'	63.33

Source: Developed by researchers from the research data

The use of internalisation

Five statements (Table 3) served to ascertain information about the respondents' *'internalisation'* of information. From Table 3, it is evident that for the majority (four-fifths) of the statements that comprised 'internalisation,' the sample was in agreement, which implies that this mode is predominantly being used by the PG students in the School of Management, Information Technology & Governance, at the University of KwaZulu-Natal.

The use of externalisation

The second mode of the knowledge conversion process, externalisation, was determined by seven statements.

In order to ascertain whether the mode of 'externalisation' is predominantly used by the PG students, at least a two-thirds majority (66%) agreement (Table 4) with each of the seven statements is required. The study revealed that there was overwhelming agreement for each individual statement. Therefore, the 'externalisation' mode is effective and being frequently used by the PG students. This shows that PG students are able to articulate their tacit knowledge to explicit knowledge effectively, or that there are academic mechanisms in place to help post-graduate students transform their tacit knowledge into explicit knowledge.

Recommendations

More research should be carried out on how knowledge is created and transferred by PG and undergraduate students on a larger scale, since students are the individuals that directly deal with the generation, transfer and storage of knowledge in academic institutes. Both qualitative and quantitative research should be carried out in this area using a larger sample size, at least 1000 students, depending on the student population of the university. Future research in addition should concentrate on the conditions that drive the knowledge spiral process, the five-phase model of the organisational knowledge-creation process (in an academic context) and the factors that affect the knowledge spiral process and the individual modes of knowledge. Moreover, the researcher strongly believes that a study should be done to compare new joiners in corporate university graduate programs, post-graduate students and undergraduate students. A study of the influence of trust, communication, culture, organisational networks, technical infrastructure and other influences such as investment should be carried out, to determine their effects on knowledge creation and transfer in academic institutes. Future studies should also compare knowledge creation, transfer and storage in South African academic institutions with that of other American, European and Asian academic institutions; it should be country specific. This will help to gauge if there are any similarities or differences between academic institutions other than political, social and economic differences. This would also enable future researchers to observe the cultural differences between students or academic institutions.

Future studies on knowledge conversion activities in academic institutes should focus on the years of existence, number of students, faculty, schools and the academic year of the student. Furthermore, future research should determine if students in specific years of study and who have certain access to academic knowledge mechanisms are more adept at creating, transferring and storing knowledge. Finally, as the culture of the university could not be established with a single school or a few disciplines, the author strongly believes that multiple colleges should be surveyed to determine if a knowledge creating and transfer culture exists.

TABLE 3: Use of internalisation.

Response	% Who agreed
'After hearing a new idea or concept, I tend to compare it with my experience to help me comprehend the meaning'	78.6
'I understand others' thoughts better by repeating what they said and asking them "Is this what you mean?"'	78.6
'I will tell others what I think to make sure my understanding is the same as theirs'	84.3
'When I have finished saying something, I will ask the other person if it is necessary to repeat to make sure they understand exactly what I mean'.	60.0
When communicating with others, I will give others time to think about we discussed	77.1

Source: Developed by researchers from the research data

TABLE 4: Respondents' use of externalisation.

Response	% Who agreed
'When others can't understand me, I am usually able to give them examples to help explaining'	95.7
'Most of the time, I can transcribe some of the unorganised thoughts into concrete ideas'	68.6
'I can describe academic or technical terms with conversational language to help communicate in a group'	82.9
'I tend to use analogy when expressing abstract concepts'	84.3
'When I try to express abstract concepts, I tend to explain with examples'	94.3
'I will help others to clearly express what they have in mind by encouraging them to continue what they are saying'	87.1
'When others cannot express themselves clearly, I usually help them clarify their points'	75.7

Source: Developed by researchers from the research data

Conclusion

The aim of this study was to assess how knowledge is created and transferred amongst PG students, using Nonaka and Takeuchi's (1995) knowledge (SECI) spiral model. The study confirmed that PG students utilise the 'socialisation' and 'externalisation' modes of knowledge conversion comprehensively; 'internalisation' plays a significant role in their knowledge creation and transfer activities too, whilst 'combination' is less utilised but still plays a role in their knowledge creation and transfer activities. PG students have space that allows them to bring hunches, thoughts, notions, intuition or tacit knowledge into reality. Trust and dedication are common amongst post-graduate students. With the use of 'socialisation' and 'externalisation' so high, PG students are aware of each others' capabilities and competencies, and trust each other enough to share the knowledge.

As 'socialisation' and 'externalisation' received the majority of the positive responses, the activities associated with these modes will illustrate the trusted source of information and knowledge. Therefore, brainstorming, informal meetings, discussions, dialogues, observation, mentoring, learning groups, as well as meetings, building hypotheses and models, pictures for communication, after-action reviews, workshops, master classes, assignment databases, best practice exchange, diagrams, illustrations, sketches, metaphors and analogies are the trusted sources of information and knowledge for post-graduate students at the School of Management, Information Technology & Governance, at the University of KwaZulu-Natal.

Acknowledgements

Competing interests

There are no financial or non-financial competing interests inherent in the publication of this article, other than the fact that it was extracted from the mini-dissertation of a master's student, whose study was co-supervised by the co-authors.

Authors' contributions

K. Naicker (University of KwaZulu-Natal) is the author of the mini-dissertation from which this article was extracted. However, the article was primarily written by the research supervisor K.K.G. (University of KwaZulu-Natal; Regenesys Business School) and formatted and edited by K. Naidoo (University of KwaZulu-Natal), the co-supervisor.

References

Alavi, M. & Leidner, D.E., 2001, 'Review: Knowledge management and knowledge management systems: Conceptual foundations and research issues', *MIS Quarterly* 25(1), 107–136.

Arling, P.A. & Chun, M.W.S., 2011, 'Facilitating new knowledge creation and obtaining KM maturity', *Journal of Knowledge Management* 15(2), 231–250. http://dx.doi.org/10.1108/13673271111119673

Choo, C.W. & Drummond de Alvarenga Neto, R.C., 2010, 'Beyond the ba: Managing enabling contexts in knowledge organisations', *Journal of Knowledge Management* 14(4), 592–610.

Davenport, T.H. & Prusak, L., 1998, *Working knowledge: How organisations manage what they know*, Harvard Business School Press, Boston.

Desouza, K.C. & Awazu, Y., 2006, 'Knowledge management at SME's: Five peculiarities', *Journal of Knowledge Management* 10(1), 32–43.

Devlin, A.S., 2006, *Research methods: Planning, conducting and presenting research*, Thomson Wadsworth, California.

Gilmour, D., 2003, 'How to fix knowledge management', *Harvard Business Review* 16, 31–38.

Girard, J.P., 2006, 'Where is the knowledge we have lost in managers?', *Journal of Knowledge Management* 10(6), 22–38.

Grant. K.A., 2007, 'Tacit knowledge revisited – We can still learn from Polanyi', *The Electronic Journal of Knowledge Management* 592, 173–180.

Hautala, J., 2011, 'Cognitive proximity in international research groups', *Journal of Knowledge Management* 15(4), 601–624. http://dx.doi.org/10.1108/13673271111151983

Hayashi. A.M., 2004, 'Building better teams', *Sloan Management Review*, Winter, 179–186.

Kermally, S., 2002, *Effective knowledge management*, John Wiley & Sons, Ltd., West Sussex.

Little, S. Quintas, P. & Ray, T., 2002, *Managing knowledge: An essential reader*, Sage Publications Ltd, London.

McBurney, D.H. & White, T.L., 2007, *Research methods*, Thomson Wadsworth, California.

McKenzie, J. & Van Winkelen, C., 2011, 'Developing organizational decision-making capability – A knowledge manager's guide', *Journal of Knowledge Management* 15(3), 403–421.

Mooradian, N., 2005, 'Tacit knowledge: Philosophic roots and role in KM', *Journal of Knowledge Management* 9(6), 104–113.

Nelson, R.R., 2005, 'Economic development from the perspective of evolutionary economic theory', *Oxford Development Studies* 36(1), 9–21.

Nonaka, I. & Konno, N., 1998, 'The concept of "ba": Building a foundation for knowledge creation', *California Management Review* 40, 40–54.

Nonaka, I. & Takeuchi, H., 1995, *The knowledge creating company*, Oxford University Press, New York.

Oguz, F. & Sengün, A.E., 2011. 'Mystery of the unknown: Revisiting tacit knowledge in the organizational literature', *Journal of Knowledge Management* 15(3), 445–461.

Patton, M.Q., 2002, *Qualitative research and evaluation methods*, Sage Publications, Inc., California.

Perez-Araos, A., Barber, K.D., Munive-Hernandez, J.E. & Eldridge, S., 2007, 'Designing a knowledge management tool to support knowledge sharing networks', *Journal of Manufacturing Technology Management* 18(2), 153–168.

Rai, R.K., 2011, 'Knowledge management and organizational culture: A theoretical integrative framework,' *Journal of Knowledge Management* 15(5), 779–801. http://dx.doi.org/10.1108/13673271111174320

Renzl, B., 2006, 'Trust in management knowledge sharing: The mediating effects of fear and knowledge documentation', *Omega* 36(2), 206–230.

Saunders, M.N.K., Saunders, M., Lewis, P. & Thornhill, A., 2011, *Research methods for business*, 5th edn., Pearson, India.

Sekaran, U., 2003, *Research methods for business: A skill building approach*, John Wiley & Sons, Inc., New Jersey.

Suppiah, V. & Sandhu, M.S., 2011, 'Organisational culture's influence on tacit knowledge-sharing behaviour', *Journal of Knowledge Management* 15(3), 462–477. http://dx.doi.org/10.1108/13673271111137439

Voelpel, S.C., Von Pierer, H. & Streb, C.K., 2006, 'Mobilizing organizations for innovation and value creation: An integrated model of the mobile company', *Journal of Knowledge Management* 10(6), 5–21.

Annexure 1 starts on the next page →

Annexure 1

Questionnaire

SECTION A

1. Biographical questions

1.1 Are you a(n)

Honours student	Master's student	PHD student

1.2 Are you

<18 years	18–20 years old	21–23 years old
24–26 years old	**27–29 years old**	**>30 years**

1.3 Are you a

Full-time student	Part-time student

1.4 Are you permanently employed?

Yes	No

1.5 Are you

Male	Female

SECTION B

2. Internalisation

2.1 After hearing a new idea or concept, I tend to compare it with my experience to help me comprehend the meaning.

Strongly agree	Agree	Neutral	Disagree	Strongly disagree

2.2 I understand better by repeating what was said and by asking 'Is that what you mean?'

Strongly agree	Agree	Neutral	Disagree	Strongly disagree

2.3 I will tell others what I think to make sure my understanding is the same as theirs.

Strongly agree	Agree	Neutral	Disagree	Strongly disagree

2.4 When I have finished saying something, I will ask the other person if it is necessary to repeat what I said, to make sure they understand exactly what I mean.

Strongly agree	Agree	Neutral	Disagree	Strongly disagree

2.5 When communicating with others, I will give them time to think about we discussed.

Strongly agree	Agree	Neutral	Disagree	Strongly disagree

2.6 I understand better by repeating what was said and by asking 'Is that what you mean?'

Strongly agree	Agree	Neutral	Disagree	Strongly disagree

3. Externalisation

3.1 When others can't understand me, I am usually able to give examples to help them understand.

Strongly agree	Agree	Neutral	Disagree	Strongly disagree

3.2 Most of the time, I can transcribe some of the unorganised thoughts into concrete ideas.

Strongly agree	Agree	Neutral	Disagree	Strongly disagree

3.3 I can describe academic or technical terms with conversational language to help communication in a group.

Strongly agree	Agree	Neutral	Disagree	Strongly disagree

3.4 I tend to use comparisons when expressing abstract concepts.

Strongly agree	Agree	Neutral	Disagree	Strongly disagree

3.5 When I try to express abstract concepts, I tend to explain using examples.

Strongly agree	Agree	Neutral	Disagree	Strongly disagree

3.6 I will help others to clearly express what they have in mind, by encouraging them to continue what they are saying.

Strongly agree	Agree	Neutral	Disagree	Strongly disagree

3.7 When others cannot express themselves clearly, I usually help them clarify their points.

Strongly agree	Agree	Neutral	Disagree	Strongly disagree

4. Socialisation

4.1 In academic group discussions, I will actively share my experience with others.

Strongly agree	Agree	Neutral	Disagree	Strongly disagree

4.2 In my academic team, my teammates and I will share life or work experiences with each other.

Strongly agree	Agree	Neutral	Disagree	Strongly disagree

Annexure 1 continues on the next page →

4.3 During group discussion, I try to find out others' opinions, thoughts and other information.

Strongly agree	Agree	Neutral	Disagree	Strongly disagree
☐	☐	☐	☐	☐

4.4 During discussions, I will bring out some concepts, thoughts or ideas.

Strongly agree	Agree	Neutral	Disagree	Strongly disagree
☐	☐	☐	☐	☐

4.5 I often encourage others to express their thoughts.

Strongly agree	Agree	Neutral	Disagree	Strongly disagree
☐	☐	☐	☐	☐

4.6 Before group discussions, I will collect necessary information and show it to the group.

Strongly agree	Agree	Neutral	Disagree	Strongly disagree
☐	☐	☐	☐	☐

4.7 I like to get to know the people with whom I will work before going into a project together.

Strongly agree	Agree	Neutral	Disagree	Strongly disagree
☐	☐	☐	☐	☐

5. Combination

5.1 During a discussion, I tend to organise ideas and make conclusions to facilitate the discussion.

Strongly agree	Agree	Neutral	Disagree	Strongly disagree
☐	☐	☐	☐	☐

5.2 When I come across problems, I tend to use my experience to help solve them.

Strongly agree	Agree	Neutral	Disagree	Strongly disagree
☐	☐	☐	☐	☐

5.3 After every event, I have the habit of organising and summarising what happened.

Strongly agree	Agree	Neutral	Disagree	Strongly disagree
☐	☐	☐	☐	☐

5.4 During discussions, I will organise everyone's thoughts in my mind.

Strongly agree	Agree	Neutral	Disagree	Strongly disagree
☐	☐	☐	☐	☐

5.5 I like to collect new information and make a connection between the new and old knowledge to develop new concepts.

Strongly agree	Agree	Neutral	Disagree	Strongly disagree
☐	☐	☐	☐	☐

5.6 I like to organise ambiguous concepts into a structure.

Strongly agree	Agree	Neutral	Disagree	Strongly disagree
☐	☐	☐	☐	☐

Thank you for your participation.

Source: Developed by primary researcher

Permissions

All chapters in this book were first published in SAJIM, by African Online Scientific Information Systems (Pty) Ltd; hereby published with permission under the Creative Commons Attribution License or equivalent. Every chapter published in this book has been scrutinized by our experts. Their significance has been extensively debated. The topics covered herein carry significant findings which will fuel the growth of the discipline. They may even be implemented as practical applications or may be referred to as a beginning point for another development.

The contributors of this book come from diverse backgrounds, making this book a truly international effort. This book will bring forth new frontiers with its revolutionizing research information and detailed analysis of the nascent developments around the world.

We would like to thank all the contributing authors for lending their expertise to make the book truly unique. They have played a crucial role in the development of this book. Without their invaluable contributions this book wouldn't have been possible. They have made vital efforts to compile up to date information on the varied aspects of this subject to make this book a valuable addition to the collection of many professionals and students.

This book was conceptualized with the vision of imparting up-to-date information and advanced data in this field. To ensure the same, a matchless editorial board was set up. Every individual on the board went through rigorous rounds of assessment to prove their worth. After which they invested a large part of their time researching and compiling the most relevant data for our readers.

The editorial board has been involved in producing this book since its inception. They have spent rigorous hours researching and exploring the diverse topics which have resulted in the successful publishing of this book. They have passed on their knowledge of decades through this book. To expedite this challenging task, the publisher supported the team at every step. A small team of assistant editors was also appointed to further simplify the editing procedure and attain best results for the readers.

Apart from the editorial board, the designing team has also invested a significant amount of their time in understanding the subject and creating the most relevant covers. They scrutinized every image to scout for the most suitable representation of the subject and create an appropriate cover for the book.

The publishing team has been an ardent support to the editorial, designing and production team. Their endless efforts to recruit the best for this project, has resulted in the accomplishment of this book. They are a veteran in the field of academics and their pool of knowledge is as vast as their experience in printing. Their expertise and guidance has proved useful at every step. Their uncompromising quality standards have made this book an exceptional effort. Their encouragement from time to time has been an inspiration for everyone.

The publisher and the editorial board hope that this book will prove to be a valuable piece of knowledge for researchers, students, practitioners and scholars across the globe.

List of Contributors

Brett van Niekerk
School of Management, IT and Governance, University of KwaZulu-Natal, South Africa

Madeleine Fombad
Department of Information Science, University of South Africa, South Africa

Joel Chigada
Department of Information Science, University of South Africa, South Africa

Patrick Ngulube
School of Interdisciplinary Research and Postgraduate Studies, University of South Africa, South Africa

Taurayi Mudzana and Manoj Maharaj
School of Management, IT and Governance, University of KwaZulu-Natal, South Africa

Wulystan P. Mtega
Sokoine University of Agriculture, Morogoro, Tanzania

Mpho Ngoepe and Luyanda Dube
Department of Information Sciences, University of South Africa, South Africa

Manthisana Mosese
Centre for Information and Knowledge Management, University of Johannesburg, South Africa

Martie Mearns
Department of Information and Knowledge Management, University of Johannesburg, South Africa

Adeniji K. Adesemowo and Reinhardt A. Botha
School of ICT, Nelson Mandela Metropolitan University, South Africa

Rossouw von Solms
Centre for Research in Information and Cyber Security, Nelson Mandela Metropolitan University, South Africa

Tshilidzi E. Nenzhelele
Department of Business Management, University of South Africa, South Africa

Philip A.E. Serumaga-Zake
School of Business Leadership, University of South Africa, South Africa

Ntabeni J. Jere and Manoj S. Maharaj
School of Management, IT and Governance, University of KwaZulu-Natal, South Africa

Rexwhite T. Enakrire and Dennis N. Ocholla
Department of Information Studies, University of Zululand, South Africa

Margaretha M. Visser
Education and Skills Development Research Programme, Human Sciences Research Council, South Africa

Judith A. Van Biljon
College of Science, Engineering and Technology, School of Computing, University of South Africa, South Africa

Marlien Herselman
College of Science, Engineering and Technology, School of Computing, University of South Africa, South Africa
Council for Scientific and Industrial Research, University of South Africa, South Africa

Nthabiseng N. Mosala- Bryant and Ruth G. Hoskins
Department of Information Studies, University of KwaZulu-Natal, South Africa

Selvarani Moodley and Claudine Storbeck
Centre for Deaf Studies, University of the Witwatersrand, South Africa

Visvanathan Naicker
Department of Business Information and Administration, Cape Peninsula University of Technology, South Africa

Denisha Jairam-Owthar
Graduate School of Business Leadership, University of South Africa, South Africa

Mzwandile M. Shongwe
Department of Information Studies, University of Zululand, South Africa
Department of Information Studies, University of KwaZulu-Natal, South Africa

Boniface Okanga
Department of Business Management, University of Johannesburg,South Africa

Songezo Nkukwana and Nicky H.D. Terblanche
University of Stellenbosch Business School, Stellenbosch University, South Africa

Willie T. Chinyamurindi
Department of Business Management, University of Fort Hare, South Africa

Peter L. Mkhize
School of Computing, University of South Africa, South Africa

Mzwandile M. Shongwe
Department of Information Studies, University of Zululand, South Africa

Kidist Teklegiorgis
Dire Dawa City Administration Health Bureau, Dire Dawa, Ethiopia

Kidane Tadesse and Gebremeskel Mirutse
Department of Public Health, College of Health Sciences, Mekelle University, Ethiopia

Wondwossen Terefe
Department of Public Health, College of Health Sciences, Mekelle University, Ethiopia
Department of Biostatistics, Tulen University, Ethiopia

Kreeson Naicker and Karunagaran Naidoo
School of Management, Information Technology & Governance, University of KwaZulu-Natal, South Africa

Krishna K. Govender
School of Management, Information Technology & Governance, University of KwaZulu-Natal, South Africa
Regenesys Business School, Johannesburg, South Africa

Index